MAKING BETTER INTERNATIONAL LAW:

THE INTERNATIONAL LAW COMMISSION AT 50

Proceedings of the United Nations Colloquium
on Progressive Development and Codification of
International Law

POUR UN MEILLEUR DROIT INTERNATIONAL :

LA COMMISSION DU DROIT INTERNATIONAL À 50 ANS

Actes du Colloque des Nations Unies
sur le développement progressif et la codification
du droit international

UNITED NATIONS · NATIONS UNIES
NEW YORK, 1998

UNITED NATIONS PUBLICATION
Sales No. E/F.98.V.5
ISBN 92-1-033076-5

PUBLICATION DES NATIONS UNIES
Numéro de vente : E/F.98.V.5
ISBN 92-1-033076-5

TABLE OF CONTENTS
TABLE DES MATIÈRES

III

PREFACE

On 21 November 1947, the General Assembly adopted its resolution 174 (II) and the International Law Commission was born. That resolution established the Commission as the Assembly's principal arm in working towards the aim, proclaimed in the Charter of the United Nations, of "encouraging the progressive development of international law and its codification".

During the last 50 years, the International Law Commission has been at the forefront in meeting the challenges facing the international community in the realm of international law. It has succeeded in setting forth basic rules in key areas of international law. Those rules have served in turn as the basis for global treaties governing State activities in many fields. Some of these treaties—such as those regulating diplomatic and consular relations or the law of treaties—have laid the very foundations for international relations as we know them.

The Commission's fiftieth anniversary provided an ideal opportunity to celebrate these achievements. However, it was also an ideal juncture to contemplate the Commission's work in the next century.

The Colloquium on Progressive Development and Codification of International Law brought together a mixed group of policy-makers, practitioners, international law-makers and academics to explore ways of strengthening the Commission and to generate practical proposals that might enable the Commission to contribute still more effectively to the progressive development of international law and its codification.

In recent years, the Commission has been requested by the General Assembly to examine its procedures and review its internal operations with a view to enhancing its efficiency and its productivity. In response, the Commission has taken a number of concrete actions, culminating, in 1996, in the adoption of a lengthy report—reproduced in Part III of the present volume—containing a large number of specific recommendations in that direction. It has also developed more rigorous procedures for identifying new topics for inclusion in its programme of work. In addition, it has displayed a much greater awareness of the many ways in which its work might contribute to the international legal process.

The Colloquium should be seen as part of this ongoing process of review. It is my hope that the many ideas and proposals which it generated will set the tone for new initiatives and so contribute towards realizing an idea which lies at the foundation of the United Nations and which is proclaimed in the preamble of the Charter: the idea of the rule of law in the relations between States.

Kofi Annan
27 March 1998

PRÉFACE

Le 21 novembre 1947, l'Assemblée générale a adopté sa résolution 174 (II) et la Commission du droit international était née. Cette résolution a créé la Commission comme l'instrument principal de l'Assemblée aux fins de la mise en œuvre du but énoncé dans la Charte des Nations Unies « de . . . encourager le développement progressif du droit international et sa codification ».

Au cours des derniers 50 ans, la Commission du droit international a été à l'avant-scène en relevant les défis confrontant la communauté internationale dans le domaine du droit international.

Elle a réussi à établir des règles fondamentales dans des branches clés du droit international. Ces règles ont servi, par la suite, de fondement aux traités globaux régissant les activités des États dans plusieurs domaines. Quelques-uns de ces traités — comme ceux régissant les relations diplomatiques et consulaires ou le droit des traités — ont constitué le fondement même des relations internationales telles que nous les connaissons.

Le cinquantième anniversaire de la Commission offre une occasion idéale de célébrer cette œuvre. En outre, il représente un moment idéal pour une réflexion sur le travail de la Commission au prochain siècle.

Le Colloque sur le devéloppement progressif et la codification du droit international a rassemblé un groupe mixte de dirigeants, praticiens, législateurs internationaux et représentants du monde académique afin d'explorer les moyens de renforcer la Commission et de faire des propositions pratiques qui permettraient à celle-ci de contribuer encore plus effectivement au devéloppement progressif du droit international et à sa codification.

Récemment, l'Assemblée générale a demandé à la Commission d'examiner ses procédures et de reconsidérer ses modes de travail internes en vue d'améliorer son efficacité et sa productivité. En répondant à cette requête, la Commission a entrepris une série d'actions concrètes, culminant, en 1996, en l'adoption d'un long rapport reproduit dans la Partie III du présent volume et contenant un grand nombre de recommandations spécifiques dans ce sens. Elle a aussi mis au point des procédures plus rigoureuses pour identifier des nouveaux sujets à inclure dans son programme de travail. En outre, elle a fait preuve d'une prise de conscience plus nette en ce qui concerne les nombreux moyens par lesquels son travail pourrait contribuer au processus législatif international.

Le Colloque devrait être considéré comme une partie de ce processus continu d'examen. J'espère que les idées et propositions nombreuses qu'il a engendrées marqueront le pas de nouvelles initiatives et, de cette manière, contribueront à la mise en œuvre d'une idée qui constitue le fondement des Nations Unies et dont la proclamation se trouve au Préambule de la Charte : l'idée de la primauté du droit dans les relations entre États.

Kofi Annan
Le 27 mars 1998

FOREWORD

This Colloquium on progressive development and codification of international law was organized by the Secretary-General, pursuant to the General Assembly's request, in order to commemorate the fiftieth anniversary of the establishment of the International Law Commission. It took place on Tuesday and Wednesday, 28 and 29 October 1997, at the United Nations Headquarters in New York.

Participants included representatives of States to the Sixth Committee of the General Assembly, legal advisers of States, current members of the International Law Commission, the representatives of a number of international scientific institutions and some 30 invited experts from the academic and research communities around the world. In order to facilitate a full and frank exchange of views, it was understood that all took part in their personal capacity only and that whatever was said should be understood not to be attributable to any State, organization or institution.

The Colloquium took the form of the successive discussion of six topics pertaining to the core theme of the progressive development and codification of international law.

In order to focus discussion, a number of experts from academic and research institutions were invited to prepare papers on one or other of the topics in the Colloquium's programme setting out their ideas for enhancing the Commission's effectiveness and strengthening the role which it plays in the international law-making process. These papers, which were distributed to all participants in the Colloquium, are reproduced in Part II of the present volume. An analytical summary of the proposals and suggestions contained in these papers, prepared by the Secretariat of the United Nations, was also made available to all participants. It, too, is reproduced here.

At the Colloquium, each panellist was asked to make a presentation setting out his or her key ideas for strengthening the Commission. The floor was then opened for participants to comment or to present their own pertinent ideas and suggestions for how the Commission might be strengthened. An edited version of these presentations and the ensuing discussions appears in Part I of this volume, together with the text of the keynote speech delivered by Judge Stephen Schwebel at the working luncheon which was held in connection with the Colloquium.

In view of their obvious pertinence to the subject matter of the Colloquium and to assist the reader, the Statute of the International Law Commission has been reproduced in Part III of the present volume, as has that section of the Commission's Report on the work of its forty-eighth session which sets out the results of the review which the Commission's Planning Group made of the Commission's programme, procedures and working-methods.

The present volume has been edited and prepared for publication by the staff of the Codification Division of the Office of Legal Affairs of the Secretariat of the United Nations, under the supervision of its Director, Dr Roy S. Lee.

AVANT-PROPOS

Ce Colloque sur le développement progressif et la codification du droit international a été organisé par le Secrétaire général à la suite de la demande de l'Assemblée générale, afin de commémorer le cinquantième anniversaire de l'établissement de la Commission du droit international. Il a eu lieu les mardi et mercredi, 28 et 29 octobre 1997, au Siège des Nations Unies à New York.

Au nombre des participants figuraient des représentants des États à la Sixième Commission de l'Assemblée générale, des conseillers juridiques des États, des membres actuels de la Commission du droit international, des représentants d'un nombre d'institutions scientifiques internationales et à peu près 30 experts invités venant des communautés académiques et de recherche dans le monde. Afin de faciliter un échange des vues complet et franc, il a été entendu que tous les participants y étaient présents en leur capacité personnelle seulement et que tout ce qui a été dit n'était pas censé être attribué à un État ou à une organisation ou institution.

Le Colloque a pris la forme de discussions successives des six sujets relevant du thème central du développement progressif et de la codification du droit international.

Afin d'orienter la discussion, un nombre d'experts des institutions académiques ou de recherche ont été invités à préparer des communications sur un des sujets du programme du Colloque présentant leurs idées pour améliorer l'efficacité de la Commission et pour renforcer le rôle qu'elle joue dans le processus législatif international. Ces communications, qui ont été distribuées à tous les participants au Colloque, sont reproduites dans la Partie II du présent volume.

Un resumé analytique des propositions et suggestions contenues dans ces communications et préparé par le Secrétariat des Nations Unies était aussi disponible à tous les participants. Il est également réproduit ici.

Au cours du Colloque, chaque expert invité a été prié de faire une présentation de ses idées principales pour renforcer la Commission. Par la suite, les débats ont été ouverts aux participants pour faire des commentaires ou pour présenter leurs propres idées et suggestions sur le renforcement de la Commission. Une version revue de ces présentations et des discussions suivantes figure dans la Partie I de ce volume avec le texte d'une déclaration liminaire faite par le juge Stephen Schwebel pendant le déjeuner de travail offert dans le contexte du Colloque.

En vue de leur pertinence évidente pour le sujet même du Colloque et pour aider le lecteur, le Statut de la Commission du droit international ainsi qu'une section du Rapport de la Commission sur le travail de sa quarante-huitième session sont réproduits dans la Partie III du présent volume. La section du Rapport de la Commission concerne les résultats de l'examen par le Groupe de planification de la Commission du programme, des procédures et des méthodes de travail de celle-ci.

Le présent volume a été mis au point et préparé pour la publication par le personnel de la Division de la codification du Bureau des affaires juridiques du Secrétariat des Nations Unies sous la supervision du Directeur de la Division, le docteur Roy S. Lee.

SECRETARIAT OF THE COLLOQUIUM

Mr Hans Corell, Under-Secretary-General for Legal Affairs, Legal Counsel

Dr Roy S. Lee, Director, Codification Division, Office of Legal Affairs

Mr Manuel Rama-Montaldo, Deputy Director, Codification Division, Office of Legal Affairs

Ms Sachiko Kuwabara-Yamamoto, Principal Legal Officer, Codification Division, Office of Legal Affairs

Ms Mahnoush Arsanjani, Senior Legal Officer, Codification Division, Office of Legal Affairs

Mr Mpazi Sinjela, Ms Christiane Bourloyannis-Vrailas, Mr George Korontzis, Mr David Hutchinson, Mr Vladimir Rudnitsky and **Ms Virginia Morris**, Legal Officers, Codification Division, Office of Legal Affairs

Ms Darlene Prescott and **Mr Renan Villacis**, Associate Legal Officers, Codification Division, Office of Legal Affairs

with the editorial assistance of **Ms Barbara Masciangelo**,
Treaties Section, Office of Legal Affairs

SECRÉTARIAT DU COLLOQUE

M. Hans Corell, Secrétaire général adjoint aux affaires juridiques, Conseiller juridique

M. Roy S. Lee, Directeur de la Division de la codification du Bureau des affaires juridiques

M. Manuel Rama-Montaldo, Directeur adjoint de la Division de la codification du Bureau des affaires juridiques

Mme Sachiko Kuwabara-Yamamoto, Juriste principale de la Division de la codification du Bureau des affaires juridiques

Mme Mahnoush Arsanjani, Juriste hors classe de la Division de la codification du Bureau des affaires juridiques

M. Mpazi Sinjela, Mme Christiane Bourloyannis-Vrailas, M. George Korontzis, M. David Hutchinson, M. Vladimir Rudnitsky et **Mme Virginia Morris**, Juristes de la Division de la codification du Bureau des affaires juridiques

Mme Darlene Prescott et **M. Renan Villacis**, Juristes (adjoints de première classe) de la Division de la codification du Bureau des affaires juridiques

avec l'assistance éditoriale de **Mme Barbara Masciangelo** de la Section des traités du Bureau des affaires juridiques

INTRODUCTION

*THE ACHIEVEMENT OF THE INTERNATIONAL LAW COMMISSION**

Article 13 (1) (*a*) of the Charter of the United Nations places upon the General Assembly the obligation to "initiate studies and make recommendations for the purpose of ... encouraging the progressive development of international law and its codification". On 21 November 1947, the General Assembly, in pursuance of its responsibilities under this Article, adopted resolution 174 (II), by which it resolved to establish the International Law Commission.[1] The publication of this collection of essays therefore coincides with the fiftieth anniversary of the Commission's creation.[2] It is accordingly an appropriate time to look back at the work of that body and record its achievement.[3]

The progressive development of international law and its codification have been one of the major aspects in the evolution of international law since the Second World War, one in which the Commission has played a central role. Of the Commission's many accomplishments in this sphere, there are three in particular which are especially worthy of attention and which will be discussed here. First, the Commission has produced over 20 sets of draft articles setting forth basic rules in most of the key areas of international law. Many of these sets of draft articles have, in turn, been transformed into major global treaties within the fields to which they relate. Second, a number of these sets, through the medium of the conventions which have been elaborated on their basis, have assumed a structural or foundational position within the domains to which they relate. Indeed, certain such sets have become fundamental to the very conduct of relations between States. Third, the Commission has succeeded in integrating itself into the process of custom-formation, including, most strikingly of all, the process for the creation of new rules of customary international law. Each of these three major attainments will be reviewed in turn.

---

*Reproduced, without revision, from United Nations, *International Law on the Eve of the Twenty-first Century: Views from the International Law Commission* (1997) (United Nations publication, Sales No. E/F 97.V.4).

[1] This resolution was adopted on the basis of a report (document A/331 and Corr.1) submitted by the Committee on the Progressive Development of International Law and its Codification, which had been established by the General Assembly in the previous year in order to consider the methods by which the General Assembly might most effectively discharge the responsibilities placed on it by Article 13 (1) (*a*) of the Charter.

[2] The first elections to the Commission were conducted in the year following its creation, on 3 November 1948. The Commission opened its first session the year after, on 12 April 1949.

[3] It may be noted that the General Assembly, by its resolution 51/160 of 16 December 1996, has requested the Secretary-General to make appropriate arrangements to commemorate the fiftieth anniversary of the establishment of the International Law Commission through a colloquium on progressive development and codification of international law to be held during the consideration in the Sixth Committee of the report of the Commission on the work of its forty-ninth session (see paragraph 18 of the resolution).

Article 1, paragraph 1, of its Statute provides that "[t]he International Law Commission shall have for its object the promotion of the progressive development of international law and its codification".[4] In pursuance of this objective,[5] the Commission has, to date, produced over 20 sets of draft articles, which set forth rules of international law in many of its key areas. In fact, there are, today, few domains of international law to the development of which it has not contributed in this way.[6] Viewed in these terms, the achievement of the Commission cannot but be recognized as substantial.

The achievement of the Commission is all the greater still in so far as many of the sets of draft articles which it has produced have gone on to serve as the bases of major global conventions which constitute juridical landmarks in the fields to which they relate. That the Commission should play a part in the process of treaty-making was explicitly envisaged by its Statute.[7] The role which was there foreseen for the Commission consisted essentially in preparing draft texts which might serve as the basis of the work of a meeting of States' representatives gathered to elaborate and adopt a convention. While such a role was not without precedent,[8] the structure and organization of the Commission and the procedures and modalities in accordance with which it was to discharge that role were quite novel and without any precise parallel in international practice. It is a singular tribute to the Commission that, without the guidance offered by any directly applicable precedents, it quickly accommodated itself to a role which was basically untried and untested and developed practices which enabled it fully to realize its potential. The following review of the Commission's accomplishments, in terms of the draft articles which it has produced, is eloquent testimony to this fact.[9]

A. In the field of the sources of international law, the Commission has produced three sets of draft articles, two of which have served as the bases of the work of international conferences and have led to the adoption of multilateral conventions on the subjects concerned. In 1966, the Commission adopted a set of 75 draft articles on the law of treaties,[10] which went on to form the basis of

---

[4]The Commission's Statute is annexed to General Assembly resolution 174 (II) of 21 November 1947.

[5]Notwithstanding the general scope of article 1, paragraph 1, articles 16, 17, paragraphs 1 and 2, and 18, paragraphs 2 and 3, of the Statute make it clear that the Commission's task is one which is essentially selective in nature: progressively to develop and to codify international law on those topics in which such an undertaking is deemed to be "necessary", "desirable" or "appropriate". It is, therefore, not the Commission's function to undertake the progressive development and codification of each and every area of international law. Much less does its mission consist in the eventual rendering of that law into some exhaustive written "code". See Report of the International Law Commission on the work of its forty-eighth session, *Official Records of the General Assembly, Fifty-first session, Supplement No. 10* (A/51/10) (hereinafter Report . . . forty-eighth session), p. 206, para. 168.

[6]See the conclusion reached by the Commission in the review which it conducted of the work of its first 25 sessions: *Yearbook of the International Law Commission, 1973*, vol. II, p. 228, document A/9010/Rev.1, para. 156.

[7]See articles 15 and 23, paragraphs 1 (*c*) and (*d*).

[8]For the organization and operation of the Committee of Experts for the Progressive Development of International Law and of the Preparatory Committee for the Codification Conference which were created by the League of Nations, see document A/AC.10/5, pp. 52-70.

[9]For a detailed summary of the operation and activities of the Commission, as well as the texts of the draft articles which it has produced and of the conventions which have been elaborated on the basis of those drafts, see United Nations, *The Work of the International Law Commission*, 5th ed., Sales No. E.95.V.6.

[10]*Yearbook of the International Law Commission, 1966*, vol. II, pp. 177-187, document A/6309/Rev.1.

the Convention on the Law of Treaties, done at Vienna on 23 May 1969.[11] Subsequently, in 1982, the Commission adopted a set of 81 draft articles on the law of treaties between States and international organizations or between international organizations, together with an annex.[12] These served as the basis of the Convention on the Law of Treaties between States and International Organizations or between International Organizations, done at Vienna on 21 March 1986.[13] The third set of draft articles which the Commission has adopted in this domain—the draft articles on most-favoured-nation clauses[14]—were brought to the attention of Member States and interested intergovernmental organizations by the General Assembly in its decision 46/416 of 9 December 1991.

In addition to producing draft articles, the Commission has also provided advice to the General Assembly on three specific matters within the field of the sources of international law: namely, ways and means for making the evidence of customary international law more readily available;[15] extended participation in general multilateral treaties concluded under the auspices of the League of Nations;[16] and reservations to multilateral conventions.[17] As far as this last matter is concerned, the Commission is in the course of addressing it once more, as part of its current programme of work, with the aim of producing a guide to practice.[18]

B.   In the domain of international relations, the Commission has produced a total of five sets of draft articles. Of these, four have gone on to serve as the bases of multilateral conventions:[19] namely, the Convention on Diplomatic Relations, done at Vienna on 18 April 1961;[20] the Convention on Consular Relations, done at Vienna on 24 April 1963;[21] the Convention on Special Missions, adopted by the General Assembly on 8 December 1969;[22] and the Convention on the Representation of States in their Relations with International Organizations of a Universal Character, done at Vienna on 14 March 1975.[23]

---

[11]United Nations, *Treaty Series*, vol. 1155, p. 331.

[12]*Yearbook of the International Law Commission, 1982*, vol. II (Part Two), pp. 17-77.

[13]Document A/CONF.129/15.

[14]*Yearbook of the International Law Commission, 1978*, vol. II (Part Two), pp. 16-73.

[15]*Yearbook of the International Law Commission, 1950*, vol. II, pp. 367-374, document A/1316. That the Commission should conduct a study and make a report on this subject is stipulated in article 24 of the Commission's Statute.

[16]*Yearbook of the International Law Commission, 1963*, vol. II, pp. 217-223, document A/5509.

[17]*Yearbook of the International Law Commission, 1951*, vol. II, pp. 125-131, document A/1858.

[18]For the Commission's proposed plan of work on this topic, see Report of the International Law Commission on the work of its forty-seventh session, *Official Records of the General Assembly, Fiftieth session, Supplement No. 10* (A/50/10) (hereinafter Report . . . forty-seventh session), p. 260, para. 491. The two reports which have so far been submitted by the Special Rapporteur for the topic are to be found in document A/CN.4/470 and Corr.1 and document A/CN.4/477 and Add. 1.

[19]Draft articles on diplomatic intercourse and immunities with commentaries, *Yearbook of the International Law Commission, 1958*, vol. II, pp. 89-105, document A/3859; draft articles on consular relations with commentaries, *Yearbook of the International Law Commission, 1960*, vol. II, pp. 93-128, document A/4843; draft articles on special missions with commentaries, *Yearbook of the International Law Commission, 1967*, vol. II, pp. 347-368, document A/6709/Rev.1 and Rev.1/Corr.1; and draft articles on the representation of States in their relations with international organizations with commentaries and annex, *Yearbook of the International Law Commission, 1971*, vol. II (Part One), pp. 284-338, document A/8410/Rev.1.

[20]United Nations, *Treaty Series*, vol. 500, p. 95.

[21]Ibid., vol. 596, p. 261.

[22]Ibid., vol. 1400, p. 231.

[23]Document A/CONF.67/16.

The fifth set of draft articles produced by the Commission in this field—the draft articles and draft optional protocols one and two on the status of the diplomatic courier and the diplomatic bag not accompanied by diplomatic courier[24]—was brought to the attention of States Members of the United Nations by the General Assembly by means of its decision 50/416 of 11 December 1995.

C.   The sets of draft articles which went on to form the basis of the 1975 Vienna Convention on the Representation of States in their Relations with International Organizations of a Universal Character on the one hand, and the 1986 Vienna Convention on the Law of Treaties between States and International Organizations or between International Organizations on the other,[25] may also be considered a contribution to the field of the law of international organizations.

D.   In the field of jurisdiction and immunities, the Commission has adopted a number of sets of draft articles. In so far as privileges and immunities are concerned, in addition to the five sets of draft articles referred to in section B above,[26] the Commission has also adopted one further set—the draft articles on jurisdictional immunities of States and their property[27]—which the General Assembly, by its resolution 49/61 of 9 December 1994, has decided should be placed before a conference of plenipotentiaries for its consideration. The Commission has also produced one set of draft articles pertaining to the subject of the exercise of jurisdiction.[28] This set went on to serve as the basis of the Convention on the Prevention and Punishment of Crimes against Internationally Protected Persons, including Diplomatic Agents, which was adopted by the General Assembly on 14 December 1973.[29]

E.   In the related field of international criminal law, the Commission has produced three important sets of draft articles: the Principles of International Law Recognized in the Charter of the Nürnberg Tribunal and in the Judgment of the Tribunal;[30] a draft Statute for an International Criminal Court;[31] and the draft Code of Crimes against the Peace and Security of Mankind.[32] As far as the second of these three sets is concerned, the General Assembly has decided, in its resolution 51/207 of 17 December 1996, that a conference of plenipotentiaries should be convened in 1998 to conclude a convention on the subject. The third set—the draft Code of Crimes—is currently the subject of consideration by the General Assembly.[33]

F.   In so far as concerns the position of the individual in international law, the Commission, in addition to its achievements in the field of international criminal law, has adopted two texts: a draft Convention on the Reduction of Future Statelessness and a draft Convention on the Elimination of Future

---

[24] *Yearbook of the International Law Commission, 1989*, vol. II (Part Two), pp. 14-49.

[25] See the text at footnote 12.

[26] See text at footnotes 19-24 above.

[27] *Yearbook of the International Law Commission, 1991*, vol. II (Part Two), pp. 13-62.

[28] Draft articles on the prevention and punishment of crimes against diplomatic agents and other internationally protected persons with commentaries, *Yearbook of the International Law Commission, 1972*, vol. II, pp. 312-323, document A/8710/Rev.1.

[29] United Nations, *Treaty Series*, vol. 1035, p. 167.

[30] *Yearbook of the International Law Commission, 1950*, vol. II, pp. 374-378, document A/1316.

[31] Report of the International Law Commission on the work of its forty-sixth session, *Official Records of the General Assembly, Forty-ninth session, Supplement No. 10* (A/49/10) (hereinafter Report . . . forty-sixth session), pp. 43-146.

[32] Report . . . forty-eighth session, pp. 14-120.

[33] The General Assembly, in paragraph 2 of resolution 51/160 of 16 December 1996, has drawn the attention of States participating in the Preparatory Committee on the Establishment of an International Criminal Court to the relevance of the draft Code to their work.

Statelessness.[34] The former served as the basis of the Convention of the same title which was done at New York on 30 August 1961.[35] It should also be mentioned that the Commission has in its current programme of work the topic of State succession and its impact on the nationality of natural and legal persons.[36]

G. Two sets of draft articles have been adopted by the Commission in the domain of the law of international spaces. One of these went on to serve as the basis of four major multilateral conventions:[37] the Convention on the Territorial Sea and the Contiguous Zone,[38] the Convention on the High Seas,[39] the Convention on Fishing and Conservation of the Living Resources of the High Seas[40] and the Convention on the Continental Shelf,[41] each done at Geneva on 29 April 1958. By its resolution 49/52 of 9 December 1994, the General Assembly determined that another of these sets—the draft articles on the law of the non-navigational uses of international watercourses[42]—should constitute the basis of a framework convention, which is currently being elaborated by its Sixth Committee convening as a Working Group of the Whole.[43]

H. As far as concerns the law and practice of the peaceful settlement of disputes, in addition to a set of Model Rules on Arbitral Procedure,[44] which the General Assembly brought to the attention of Member States by means of its resolution 1262 (XIII) of 14 November 1958, the Commission has adopted specific draft provisions laying down procedures for the resolution of disputes which might arise in the interpretation or application of certain or any of the articles of the drafts which it has produced on a number of the topics which are mentioned in this part.[45]

I. The domain of State succession has been the focus of two sets of draft articles adopted by the Commission,[46] both of which have gone on to serve as

---

[34]*Yearbook of the International Law Commission, 1954*, vol. II, pp. 143-147, document A/2693.

[35]United Nations, *Treaty Series*, vol. 989, p. 175.

[36]For the Commission's proposed plan of work on this topic, see Report . . . forty-eighth session, p. 177, para. 88. For the two reports which the Special Rapporteur for this topic has submitted to date, see document A/CN.4/467 and document A/CN.4/474 and Corr. 1 and 2.

[37]Draft articles concerning the law of the sea, *Yearbook of the International Law Commission, 1956*, vol. II, pp. 256-264, document A/3519.

[38]United Nations, *Treaty Series*, vol. 516, p. 205.

[39]Ibid., vol. 450, p. 11.

[40]Ibid., vol. 559, p. 285.

[41]Ibid., vol. 499, p. 311.

[42]Report . . . forty-sixth session, pp. 197-326.

[43]The Working Group did not complete its work in 1996 and a second session of the Working Group is planned for 1997 (see General Assembly resolution 51/206 of 17 December 1996).

[44]*Yearbook of the International Law Commission, 1958*, vol. II, pp. 83-86, document A/3859.

[45]See draft article 73 of the draft articles concerning the law of the sea (see footnote 37 above); draft article 45 of the draft articles on diplomatic intercourse and immunities (see footnote 19 above); draft article 62 of the draft articles on the law of treaties (see footnote 10 above); draft article 82 of the draft articles on the representation of States in their relations with international organizations (see footnote 19 above); draft article 12 of the draft articles on the prevention and punishment of crimes against diplomatic agents and other internationally protected persons (see footnote 28 above); draft articles 65 and 66 and the draft annex of the draft articles on the law of treaties between States and international organizations or between international organizations (see footnote 12 above); and draft article 33 of the draft articles on the non-navigational uses of international watercourses (see footnote 42 above). Note also draft articles 54 to 60 and draft annexes I and II of the draft articles on State responsibility, as provisionally adopted by the Commission on first reading (see footnote 51 below).

[46]Draft articles on succession of states in respect of treaties and commentaries, *Yearbook of the International Law Commission, 1974*, vol. II (Part One), pp. 174-269, document A/9610/Rev.1, and draft articles on succession of States in respect of State property, archives and debts and commentaries, *Yearbook of the International Law Commission, 1981*, vol. II (Part Two), pp. 20-113.

the bases of multilateral conventions:[47] the Convention on Succession of States in respect of Treaties, done at Vienna on 23 August 1978,[48] and the Convention on Succession of States in respect of State Property, Archives and Debts, done at Vienna on 8 April 1983.[49]

J. The Commission has also adopted one set of draft articles in the field of States' fundamental rights and duties: the draft Declaration on the Rights and Duties of States.[50] By its resolution 375 (IV) of 6 December 1949, the General Assembly commended the draft Declaration to the attention of Member States and of jurists of all nations.

K. The Commission is currently engaged in preparing draft articles on two further subjects, both of which are of fundamental importance to the operation of the international legal system. The first is State responsibility, on which topic the Commission has recently adopted on first reading a set of 60 draft articles and two annexes.[51] The other is liability for injurious consequences arising out of acts not prohibited by international law.[52]

This brief survey makes for an impressive record, attesting to the substantial contribution which the Commission has made to almost all of the major fields of international law.

II

A further measure of the Commission's achievement is the significant effect which its work has had upon the very structure of international law in a number of its constituent fields.

First and foremost, several of the major multilateral conventions which have been concluded on the basis of the Commission's draft articles have become fundamental to the whole conduct of modern international relations.

No instrument has greater claim to that status than the 1961 Vienna Convention on Diplomatic Relations and the 1963 Vienna Convention on Consular Relations. These two conventions have attracted among the highest levels of participation of any treaty in existence, there currently being 178 and 157 States party to them, respectively. In the words of the International Court of Justice, these two instruments are "of cardinal importance for the maintenance of good relations between States in the interdependent world of today".[53] Diplomacy, as the International Court has remarked,[54] is "an instrument essential for effective co-operation in the international community, and for enabling States . . . to achieve mutual understanding and to resolve their differences by peaceful means";[55] while "the unimpeded conduct of consular relations . . . is no less important in the context of present-day international law, in promoting

---

[47]The Commission is also currently working on the topic of State succession and its impact on the nationality of natural and legal persons (see the text at footnote 36 above).

[48]Document A/CONF.80/31.

[49]Document A/CONF.117/14.

[50]*Yearbook of the International Law Commission, 1949*, pp. 287-288, document A/CN.4/13 and Corr.1.

[51]Draft articles on State responsibility, Report . . . forty-eighth session, pp. 125-151.

[52]For an outline of the current state of the Commission's work on this topic, see Report . . . forty-eighth session, pp. 178-182. For the set of draft articles which has been prepared by a working group of the Commission, see ibid., pp. 235-327.

[53]*United States Diplomatic and Consular Staff in Tehran, Judgment, I.C.J. Reports 1980*, p. 3, para. 91. See also ibid., paras. 45 and 92.

[54]*United States Diplomatic and Consular Staff in Tehran, Order of 15 December 1979, I.C.J. Reports 1979*, p. 7.

[55]Ibid., para. 39.

the development of friendly relations among nations".[56] The "imperative obligations" which govern those two institutions the Court has found to be "now codified in the Vienna Conventions of 1961 and 1963".[57]

The 1969 Vienna Convention on the Law of Treaties enjoys a position which is similarly structural to the whole international legal order.[58] As the contents of the almost 1500 volumes of the *Treaty Series* which the United Nations has published to date make clear, treaties play a "fundamental role in . . . international relations" and are of "ever-increasing importance . . . as a source of international law and as a means of developing peaceful cooperation among nations".[59] The 1969 Convention sets forth rules to regulate the use of this basic instrument of international relations. On a large number of occasions, now, the rules which many of its provisions lay down have been declared to possess the status of customary (general) international law by the International Court of Justice,[60] by regional courts and commissions[61]

---

[56]Ibid., para. 40.

[57]Ibid., para. 41. See also *Case concerning United States Diplomatic and Consular Staff in Tehran, Judgment* (see footnote 53 above), para. 45: "[t]he Vienna Conventions [of 1961 and 1963], which codify the law of diplomatic and consular relations, state principles and rules essential for the maintenance of peaceful relations between States and accepted throughout the world by nations of all creeds, cultures and political complexions".

[58]There are currently 81 States Parties to this convention and a further 21 States which are signatories to it.

[59]See the first and second preambular paragraphs of the 1969 Convention. The seventh paragraph of that Convention's preamble further affirms that "the codification and progressive development of the law of treaties achieved in the present Convention will promote the purposes of the United Nations set forth in its Charter, namely, the maintenance of international peace and security, the development of friendly relations and the achievement of co-operation among nations".

[60]The International Court of Justice has cited provisions of the Vienna Convention as laying down rules of general international law in the following cases: *Legal Consequences for States of the Continued Presence of South Africa in Namibia (South West Africa) notwithstanding Security Council Resolution 276 (1970), Advisory Opinion, I.C.J. Reports 1971,* p. 16, para. 94; *Appeal Relating to the Jurisdiction of the ICAO Council, Judgment, I.C.J. Reports 1972,* p. 46, para. 38; *Fisheries Jurisdiction (United Kingdom* v. *Iceland), Jurisdiction of the Court, Judgment, I.C.J. Reports 1973,* p. 3, paras. 24 and 36; *Interpretation of the Agreement of 25 March 1951 between the WHO and Egypt, Advisory Opinion, I.C.J. Reports 1980,* p. 73, para. 47; *Military and Paramilitary Activities in and against Nicaragua (Nicaragua* v. *United States of America), Merits, I.C.J. Reports 1986,* p. 14, para. 178 (note also para. 190); *Frontier Dispute, Judgment, I.C.J. Reports 1986,* p. 554, para. 17; *Border and Transborder Armed Actions (Nicaragua* v. *Honduras), Jurisdiction and Admissibility, Judgment, I.C.J. Reports 1988,* p. 69, para. 35; *Arbitral Award of 31 July 1989, Judgment, I.C.J. Reports 1991,* p. 53, para. 48; *Land, Island and Maritime Frontier Dispute (El Salvador/Honduras: Nicaragua intervening), Judgment of 11 September 1992, I.C.J. Reports 1992,* p. 351, paras. 373, 375 and 380; *Application of the Convention on the Prevention and Punishment of the Crime of Genocide, Provisional Measures, Order of 8 April 1993, I.C.J. Reports 1993,* p. 3, para. 13; *Territorial Dispute (Libyan Arab Jamahiriya/Chad), Judgment, I.C.J. Reports 1994,* p. 6, para. 41; *Maritime Delimitation and Territorial Questions between Qatar and Bahrain, Jurisdiction and Admissibility, Judgment, I.C.J. Reports 1994,* p. 112, para. 23; and *Maritime Delimitation and Territorial Questions between Qatar and Bahrain, Jurisdiction and Admissibility, Judgment, I.C.J. Reports 1995,* p. 6, para. 33.

[61]See, for example, *Golder Case,* European Court of Human Rights, Series A, No. 18, Judgment of 21 February 1975, *International Law Reports,* vol. 57, p. 200, para. 29; *Temeltasch* v. *Switzerland,* European Commission of Human Rights, Application No. 9116/80 of 5 May 1982, Report, *International Law Reports,* vol. 88, p. 619, paras. 68 and 69; *The Effect of Reservations on the Entry into Force of the American Convention,* Inter-American Court of Human Rights, Advisory Opinion No. OC-2/82, 24 September 1982, *International Law Reports,* vol. 67, p. 559, para. 19; *Restrictions to the Death Penalty,* Inter-American Court of Human Rights, Advisory Opinion No. OC-3/83, 8 September 1983, *International Law Reports,* vol. 70, p. 449, para. 48; and *Interpretation of the American Declaration of the Rights and Duties of Man within the Framework of Article 64 of the American Convention on Human Rights,* Inter-American Court of Human Rights, Advisory Opinion No. OC-10/89, 14 July 1989, *International Law Reports,* vol. 96, p. 416, paras. 31-33.

and by various arbitral tribunals,[62] as well as by United Nations treaty-bodies.[63]

Through the medium of the conventions which they have inspired, certain of the sets of draft articles which the Commission has produced have, therefore, played a direct and fundamental role in the regulation of the basic instruments by which international relations are conducted. Equally remarkable is that the conventions in question were concluded and, in the case of the law of treaties, the Commission's draft articles elaborated during a period in which the international community was undergoing a profound societal change as the result of the accession to independence of a great number of new States. By establishing and consolidating rules which are fundamental to the operation of the international system, the instruments in question helped at a crucial time to maintain confidence in international law and to ensure the stability of international society itself.

At the same time as certain of the Commission's draft articles have become fundamental to the very conduct of international relations, certain other sets have played a role which is structural to an entire field or domain of international law, setting forth principles and rules which define the basic lineaments of the law within the area concerned and constituting the framework within which problems are analyzed and legal discourse is carried on.[64] This is certainly so in the case of the draft articles concerning the law of the sea, adopted by the Commission in 1956. The four 1958 Geneva Conventions which were elaborated on the basis of those draft articles laid down a body of rules which, in large part and for a number of years at least, constituted the prevailing law of the sea, as is evidenced by a number of decisions of international courts and tribunals.[65] Although subsequent developments brought about substantial modifications in the structure of that law, the 1958 Conventions continued to embody many of

---

[62]See, for example, *Arbitration between the United Kingdom of Great Britain and Northern Ireland and the French Republic on the Delimitation of the Continental Shelf*, Decision of 30 June 1977, *Reports of International Arbitral Awards*, vol. 18, p. 3, paras. 38, 55 and 61; *The Kingdom of Belgium, The French Republic, The Swiss Confederation, The United Kingdom and The United States of America v. The Federal Republic of Germany*, Decision of 16 May 1980 of the Arbitral Tribunal for the Agreement on German External Debts, *International Law Reports*, vol. 59, p. 495, para. 16; and *Case concerning the difference between New Zealand and France concerning the Interpretation or Application of two Agreements Concluded on 9 July 1986 between the two States and Which Related to the Problems arising from the "Rainbow Warrior" Affair*, Decision of 30 April 1990, *Reports of International Arbitral Awards*, vol. 20, p. 215, paras. 75, 100 and 106.

[63]See especially *General comment on issues relating to reservations made upon ratification or accession to the Covenant or the Optional Protocols thereto, or in relation to declarations under Article 41 of the Covenant*, General Comment Adopted by the Human Rights Committee under Article 40, Paragraph 4, of the International Covenant on Civil and Political Rights, Addendum, General Comment No. 24 (52), document CCPR/C/21/Rev.1/Add.6, footnote 2 and paras. 6, 16 and 17. The United Nations Secretary-General has also remarked that the Convention "is in large measure a codification of international custom". See paragraph 10 of the note verbale to the Permanent Representative of a Member State, reproduced in the *United Nations Juridical Yearbook 1975*, p. 195.

[64]Report . . . forty-eighth session, p. 206, para. 168. As the Commission has remarked, "[t]his marks a clear advance in inter-State relations"; ibid.

[65]The International Court of Justice has treated a number of the provisions of the 1958 Geneva Conventions as enjoying customary status. See *North Sea Continental Shelf (Federal Republic of Germany/Denmark; Federal Republic of Germany/Netherlands), I.C.J. Reports 1969*, p. 4, paras. 19 and 63; *Fisheries Jurisdiction (United Kingdom v. Iceland), Merits, Judgment, I.C.J. Reports 1974*, p. 3, paras. 50 and 67; *Continental Shelf (Tunisia/Libya), I.C.J. Reports 1982*, p. 18, paras. 41-42; and *Land, Island and Maritime Frontier Dispute (El Salvador/ Honduras: Nicaragua intervening)* (see footnote 60 above), para. 383. See also the award of the arbitral tribunal in the *Arbitration between the United Kingdom of Great Britain and Northern Ireland and the French Republic* . . . (see footnote 62 above), paras. 13, 65, 68-70, 75, 84 and 97.

its basic lineaments. They went on, moreover, to serve as models for significant parts of the United Nations Convention on the Law of the Sea, done at Montego Bay on 10 December 1982,[66] in particular the parts of that convention which relate to the regimes of the territorial sea, the contiguous zone, the continental shelf and the high seas.[67] The effects of the 1958 Conventions in defining and setting the structure of the law of the sea are, therefore, still to be felt today.

Some of the sets of draft articles which the Commission has produced might, at first blush, be thought not yet to have fulfilled their potential of assuming a structural role within the domains of international law to which they relate. On closer examination, though, a number in fact turn out also to represent significant achievements.

Cases in point are the two sets of draft articles on the matter of State succession. But few States are currently party to the conventions which were elaborated upon the basis of those drafts: the 1983 Vienna Convention on Succession of States in respect of State Property, Archives and Debts and the 1978 Vienna Convention on Succession of States in respect of Treaties.[68] Nevertheless, there is evidence that the latter convention at least has assumed a significant place within that aspect of the domain of State succession to which it relates. In particular, the 1978 Convention and the Commission's draft articles on which it was based have been regarded as embodying prevailing principles of customary international law in respect of a number of situations involving a succession of States.[69] There are also indications that certain aspects of the 1983 Convention are regarded as possessing the status of customary international law.[70]

Similarly, the significance of the draft articles which the Commission has produced in the field of the law of international organizations is not to be underestimated. It is true that the 1975 Vienna Convention on the Representation

[66]Document A/CONF.62/122 and Corr. 1 to 11. There are currently 113 States which have established their consent to be bound by the 1982 Convention and a further 56 States which are signatories to it. Between States which are party to it, the 1982 Convention supersedes the 1958 Geneva Conventions as the basis of their mutual relations (see article 311, paragraph 1).

[67]Report . . . forty-eighth session, p. 206, footnote 311.

[68] The former has so far attracted but 4 of the 15 instruments of ratification or accession which are needed for it to enter into force, while the latter only achieved that same target-number in 1996.

[69]See, for example, the letter of the United Nations Office of Legal Affairs to the Director of the Legal Division, World Health Organization, reproduced in *United Nations Juridical Yearbook 1972*, p. 195; the letter of the United Nations Office of Legal Affairs to the Secretary of the United Nations Council for Namibia, reproduced in *United Nations Juridical Yearbook 1984*, p. 171 at para. 3 (ii); *Continental Shelf (Tunisia/Libya)* (see footnote 65 above), para. 84; and International Conference on the Former Yugoslavia, Arbitration Commission, Opinion No. 1, *International Law Reports*, vol. 92, p. 162, para. 1 (*e*), and Opinion No. 9, ibid., p. 203, paras. 2 and 4. Note also International Conference on the Former Yugoslavia, Arbitration Commission, Opinion No. 3, ibid., p. 170, para. 2.

It is worthy of note that a Chamber of the International Court of Justice has referred to the Convention, in the same breath as the Vienna Convention on the Law of Treaties 1969, as a "codifying" convention (*une convention "de codification"*), *Frontier Dispute* (see footnote 60 above), para. 17.

A number of statements are to be found by State officials to the effect that certain provisions of the Convention are reflective of customary international law. See, for example, the memorandum of the Legal Adviser of the United States Department of State, reproduced in *Digest of United States Practice in International Law, 1980*, pp. 1026 and 1035 and endnote 43; and the letter of the Republic of Kiribati to the Secretary-General of the United Nations, reproduced in *British Year Book of International Law*, vol. 52 (1981), p. 385.

[70]See the letter of the United Nations Legal Counsel to the Executive Director of the International Cocoa Organization, reproduced in *United Nations Juridical Yearbook 1991*, p. 315. See also International Conference on the Former Yugoslavia, Arbitration Commission, Opinion No. 1 (see the preceding footnote), para. 1 (*e*), and Opinion No. 9 (see the preceding footnote), paras. 2 and 4.

of States in their Relations with International Organizations of a Universal Character is yet to enter into force, more than 20 years after its conclusion.[71] Nevertheless, the fact is that the 1975 Convention is often cited by States and by international organizations in the course of their activities[72] and there has been recognition that a number of its provisions possess the status of customary law or are otherwise reflective of prevailing practice.[73]

A further example is the 1986 Vienna Convention, elaborated on the basis of the set of draft articles that the Commission produced on the law of treaties between States and international organizations or between international organizations, which has attracted but 23 of the 35 ratifications or accessions needed for it to enter into force.[74] Yet there can be little doubt that, like the 1969 Vienna Convention on the Law of Treaties on which it was based, it enjoys a place which is fundamental to the aspect of treaty-law to which it relates. International courts, in particular, have already referred to certain of its provisions as being reflective of prevailing law;[75] and organizations of the United Nations system routinely use the Convention as a guide in the making, interpretation and application of their treaties.

III

A further measure of the International Law Commission's achievement is the important role which it has created for itself in the process of custom-formation.

That the Commission's work and its output would play a role in the custom-forming process itself was not clearly foreseen in its Statute. Yet, as is amply demonstrated by the preceding review of the Commission's accomplishments, the Commission has thoroughly integrated itself into the process of identifying, consolidating, sustaining, adapting and even forming rules of customary, or general, international law. In particular, conventions which have been adopted on the basis of the Commission's draft articles have on many occasions been treated as providing authoritative evidence of the state of customary law, in some cases even before they have entered into force.[76] More dramatically still

---

[71]There are currently only 30 contracting States to this convention, against the 35 which are needed for that purpose. A further seven States are signatories to the Convention.

[72]See the statement of the United Nations Legal Counsel at the 71st meeting of the Committee on Relations with the Host Country, reproduced in *United Nations Juridical Yearbook 1978*, pp. 189-190.

[73]See, for example: para. 10 of the note verbale from the United Nations Secretary-General to the Permanent Representative of a Member State (see footnote 63 above); para. 4 of the memorandum from the United Nations Legal Counsel to the Assistant Chief of Protocol, reproduced in *United Nations Juridical Yearbook 1977*, p. 192; the statement by the United Nations Legal Counsel at the 71st meeting of the Committee on Relations with the Host Country (see the preceding footnote); paras. 4 and 5 of the statement by the United Nations Legal Counsel at the 115th meeting of the Committee on Relations with the Host Country, reproduced in *United Nations Juridical Yearbook 1986*, p. 319; and para. 4 of the memorandum from the United Nations Office of Legal Affairs to the Senior Legal Officer, Office of the Director-General, United Nations Office at Geneva, reproduced in *United Nations Juridical Yearbook 1991*, p. 320.

[74]A further 16 States and ten international organizations are signatories to the Convention.

[75]Both the Court of Justice of the European Communities and its Advocates-General have referred to certain provisions of the Convention as reflective of customary international law. See *French Republic* v. *Commission of the European Communities*, Case C-327/91, *International Law Reports*, vol. 101, p. 31, Opinion of the Advocate-General, para. 12, and Judgment of the Court, para. 25. See also the text at footnote 79 below.

[76]See especially the materials relating to the 1969 Vienna Convention on the Law of Treaties which are cited in footnotes 60 to 63 above, many of which predate the entry into force of that convention.

10

and reflecting yet more directly the achievement of the Commission in this regard, draft articles produced by the Commission have themselves been regarded as evidence of the position at customary law,[77] even, indeed, before their final adoption.[78] So, for example, even before the Commission had concluded its work on its draft articles on the law of treaties between States and international organizations or between international organizations, the International Court of Justice made reference to one of them as representative of customary law.[79] The Commission's work in the field of State responsibility is especially worthy of note in this regard. Even before their first reading was complete, the draft articles which the Commission had adopted to date on that topic were widely invoked as evidence of customary international law. International tribunals in particular have for a number of years now made reference to the Commission's work in addressing issues which have arisen in this field.[80] Indeed, one arbitral award a decade ago characterized Part One of the Commission's draft articles as "the most recent and authoritative statement of current international law in this area".[81]

It may be that, at the point when consideration of a topic within the Commission begins, the relevant customary law may be either unsettled or else at a formative stage of development. Through the work of the Commission, though, new rules of positive customary international law may begin to emerge and gradually take shape. In particular, the analysis which the Commission undertakes of existing State practice and its recommendations as to the form which the law should take might attract a favourable response from States, prompting the further development of practice and of *opinio juris* along the lines

---

[77]See, for example, the decision of the Swiss Federal Tribunal in *M* v. *Federal Department of Justice and Police*, *International Law Reports*, vol. 75, p. 110, which, though it post-dates the adoption of the 1978 Convention on Succession of States in respect of Treaties, refers solely to the Commission's draft articles on which that convention was based.

[78]See, for example, the letter of the United Nations Office of Legal Affairs to the Director of the Legal Division, World Health Organization, *op. cit.* (footnote 69 above).

The Commission's deliberations on a topic have also subsequently been regarded as evidencing the contemporaneous state of the law on the issue under discussion: *North Sea Continental Shelf* (see footnote 65 above), paras. 49-55, 62 and 85; and *Arbitration between the United Kingdom of Great Britain and Northern Ireland and the French Republic* . . . (see footnote 62 above), para. 37.

[79]*Interpretation of the Agreement of 25 March 1951 between the WHO and Egypt* (see footnote 60 above), para. 47.

[80]See, for example, the following awards of the Iran–United States Claims Tribunal: *International Technical Products Corporation and ITP Export Corporation* v. *the Government of the Islamic Republic of Iran et al.*, Award No. 196-302-3 (24 October 1985), *Iran–United States Claims Tribunal Reports*, vol. 9 (1985), p. 206, footnote 35; *Alfred L.W. Short* v. *The Islamic Republic of Iran*, Award No. 312-11135-2 (14 July 1987), ibid., vol. 16 (1987), p. 76, paras. 28 and 33; *Kenneth P. Yeager* v. *The Islamic Republic of Iran*, Award No. 324-10199-1 (2 November 1987), ibid., vol. 17 (1987), p. 92, paras. 33, 42 and 65; *Jack Rankin* v. *The Islamic Republic of Iran*, Award No. 326-10913-2 (3 November 1987), ibid., p. 135, paras. 18, 25 and 30 (c) and (e); and *Phillips Petroleum Company Iran* v. *The Islamic Republic of Iran, The National Iranian Oil Company*, Award No. 425-39-2 (29 June 1989), ibid., vol. 21 (1989), p. 79, footnote 26. See also the following arbitral awards: *Case Concerning the Air Service Agreement of 27 March 1946 between the United States of America and France*, Decision of 9 December 1978, *Reports of International Arbitral Awards*, vol. 18, p. 417, para. 31; *Case concerning the difference between New Zealand and France* . . . (see footnote 62 above), paras. 72, 77, 78, 101 and 105 (and note paras. 113 and 122); *AMCO-Asia Corporation and others* v. *The Republic of Indonesia*, Award on the Merits, 31 May 1990, *International Law Reports*, vol. 89, p. 405, para. 172; and *Libyan Arab Foreign Investment Company* v. *The Republic of Burundi*, Award of 4 March 1991, *International Law Reports*, vol. 96, p. 282, para. 61 (and note paras. 55, 56 and 66).

[81]*Jack Rankin* v. *The Islamic Republic of Iran* (see the preceding footnote), para. 18. Another arbitral award has described the domain as being "in the process of codification by the International Law Commission": *Case concerning the difference between New Zealand and France* . . . (see footnote 62 above), para. 72.

of the Commission's suggestions and leading, in turn, to the reception, at a conference of plenipotentiaries, of the Commission's final draft articles as reflective of the resulting body of practice and opinion as a whole. In this way, the Commission may even play a role in the very formation of rules of customary international law.

So, for example, when the Commission commenced its work on the law of the sea at the beginning of the 1950s, the continental shelf had no positive status in custom, the body of State practice pertaining to that institution having but recently come into existence and being yet incomplete and discordant.[82] Yet, as the International Court of Justice has twice remarked,[83] by the time that the first United Nations Conference on the Law of the Sea came in 1958 to elaborate a convention on the basis of the draft articles which the Commission had prepared concerning the continental shelf, the basic rules governing that institution had come, or at least were coming, to be regarded by States as established and, moreover, as being reflected in the pertinent provisions of the Commission's draft.[84] A broadly similar process of legal development has also been held to have taken place in the law of treaties, in respect of the rules governing reservations.[85]

As the International Court has also affirmed,[86] such a process of legal development may not yet be complete with the elaboration and adoption of a convention based on the Commission's draft articles. Only if and when States subsequently come to accept,[87] or to adapt their practice to,[88] such a convention may new rules of customary law finally come into existence, modelled on those set forth in that instrument.[89] In such a case, once more, it is the work of the Commission which serves, directly or indirectly, as the driving-force behind the crystallization of the new law, acting as a stimulus to, and as a focus for, the development of the *opinio juris* of States and clarifying and co-ordinating their content.

Instrumental in the integration of the Commission into the custom-formation process in all of its aspects has been the Commission's success in creating and sustaining a meaningful dialogue with States. This dialogue, which the Commission carries on through the medium of the Sixth Committee of the

---

[82]*In the matter of an Arbitration between Petroleum Development (Trucial Coast) Ltd. and the Sheikh of Abu Dhabi*, Award of September 1951, *International Law Reports*, vol. 18, p. 144, para. 5 (*e*).

[83]*North Sea Continental Shelf* (see footnote 65 above), para. 63; and *Continental Shelf (Tunisia/Libya)* (see footnote 65 above), paras. 41-42.

[84]In the *North Sea Continental Shelf* cases (see footnote 65 above), the International Court also considered the Commission's consideration of the issue which is the subject of article 6 of the Convention on the Continental Shelf to have contributed to the development of customary law on that point: *loc. cit.*, footnote 78 above.

[85]Thus, at the time that the Commission began its work on the law of treaties, the rules which govern reservations, once widely regarded as well established, had become highly unsettled and uncertain, as a result of a number of recent developments. The work of the Commission acted as a focus for the development of the *opinio juris* of States in this sphere, culminating in the crystallization of a new legal regime with the adoption of the 1969 Vienna Convention on the Law of Treaties, the relevant provisions of which were based on the draft articles which had been adopted by the Commission in 1966. See *Arbitration between the United Kingdom of Great Britain and Northern Ireland and the French Republic . . .* (see footnote 62 above), para. 38.

[86]*North Sea Continental Shelf* (see footnote 65 above), para. 71.

[87]Ibid., para. 73.

[88]Ibid., paras. 74 and 75.

[89]In the *North Sea Continental Shelf* cases (see footnote 65 above), the Court conducted a detailed investigation of whether such a process had taken place in respect of the rules set forth in article 6 of the 1958 Geneva Convention on the Continental Shelf and reached the conclusion that it had not (ibid., para. 81).

12

General Assembly and via the questionnaires which it sends to States individually, together with the requests which it makes of them for comments on its drafts,[90] itself merits inclusion among the Commission's achievements.[91]

IV

The contribution which the Commission has thus made to the progressive development and codification of international law has been variously characterized as "unique and unrivalled", "almost monumental", "distinguished and lasting", "remarkable", of "exceptional importance", "essential", "significant", "appreciable" and "positive". The conduct of international relations has been said to be "unthinkable" without several of the global conventions which have been elaborated upon the basis of the Commission's draft articles. The Commission's contribution to a better understanding of international law has also been acknowledged as remarkable and lasting, and it has been said that its reports and documents constitute an invaluable source of inspiration for all publicists.

Notwithstanding such accolades, the Commission has continued to strive for improvement of its procedures and methods of work in all their aspects. To this end, it has taken a number of actions, culminating, most recently, in the adoption of a substantial report incorporating a large number of specific recommendations for improving its "usefulness and efficiency".[92] It has developed a more rigorous procedure for the better identification of new topics for inclusion in its programme of work.[93] It has displayed, too, an increased sensitivity to the variety of forms which its contribution to the international legal process, in terms of the nature of its final output, might appropriately take, including model rules, declarations, guides to practice, commentaries, advice and so on.[94] The General Assembly, for its part, has also given careful attention to the ways in which it considers the reports of the Commission and has taken steps to improve them, with a view to providing the Commission with more effective guidance.[95]

---

[90]See Report . . . forty-eighth session, p. 208, para. 171, and p. 211, para. 181. For an outline of this dialogue, see *The Work of the International Law Commission, op. cit.* (see footnote 9 above), pp. 21-24.

[91]In recent years, the Commission has striven to enhance this dialogue still further. See, in particular, the recent report of the Commission on its procedures and working methods, which contains a number of specific recommendations to this end, Report . . . forty-eighth session, pp. 197-198, para. 149 (c)-(e), and p. 211, para. 182. Note also p. 210, para. 180, and p. 212, para. 185. The General Assembly has also paid attention to strengthening the dialogue: see text at footnote 95 below and accompanying note.

[92]Report . . . forty-eighth session, pp. 196-230. The General Assembly took note with appreciation of this report in its resolution 51/160 of 16 December 1996, paragraph 9.

[93]For a brief outline of this procedure, see Report . . . forty-eighth session, pp. 205-206, paras. 165-166.

[94]Thus, on the topic of Reservations to treaties, see, for example: Report . . . forty-fifth session, p. 245, para. 430; Report . . . forty-seventh session, pp. 246-247, paras. 435-437 and 439, pp. 256-257, paras. 471-474, and pp. 259-260, paras. 486-488 and 491 (b) and (c); Report . . . forty-eighth session, pp. 185-186, para. 113. Similarly, on the topic of State succession and its impact on the nationality of natural and legal persons, see, for instance: Report . . . forty-fifth session, p. 247, paras. 437 and 439; Report . . . forty-seventh session, pp. 75-76, paras. 169-170, and p. 81, para. 193; and Report . . . forty-eighth session, p. 174, para. 81, and p. 177, para. 88 (b). More generally, see *ibid,* p. 210, para. 178 *in fine.* Compare the earlier approach of the Commission to this issue in *Yearbook of the International Law Commission, 1988,* vol. II (Part Two), p. 110, para. 561.

[95]See, in particular, resolution 41/81 of 3 December 1986, third preambular paragraph and operative paragraph 5 (b); resolution 42/156 of 7 December 1987, fifth preambular paragraph and operative paragraphs 5 (b) and 6; resolution 43/169 of 9 December 1988, operative paragraphs 7 and 8; resolution 44/35 of 4 December 1989, operative paragraph 5; and resolution 50/45 of 11 December 1995, seventh preambular paragraph and operative paragraph 10.

A concerted effort is thus being made to improve the functioning of the Commission so as to enable it to make a still greater contribution to the progressive development and codification of international law.[96] At the foundation of this effort is the conviction, shared both by States and by the Commission, that "there is important continuing value in an orderly process of codification and progressive development"[97] and that the Commission can continue to make an important contribution to that process. There is accordingly every reason to suppose that the International Law Commission will remain, as it has been for the last 50 years, the main organ established by the General Assembly for the codification and progressive development of international law.

---

[96]See, to this effect, General Assembly resolution 50/45 of 11 December 1995, paragraph 9 (a), and Report . . . forty-eighth session, p. 201, para. 154.

[97]Report . . . forty-eighth session, p. 197, para. 148, general conclusion (b). See also p. 206, para. 168, and p. 207, para. 171.

INTRODUCTION

*L'ŒUVRE DE LA COMMISSION DU DROIT INTERNATIONAL**

L'Article 13, paragraphe 1, alinéa *a*, de la Charte des Nations Unies donne mandat à l'Assemblée générale de « provoque[r] des études et fai[re] des recommandations en vue de . . . encourager le développement progressif du droit international et sa codification ». Le 21 novembre 1947, conformément à ce mandat, l'Assemblée générale a adopté la résolution 174 (II) par laquelle elle décidait la création de la Commission du droit international[1]. La publication du présent recueil d'articles coïncide donc avec le cinquantième anniversaire de l'institution de la Commission[2]. Le moment paraît venu de se pencher sur le travail qu'elle a accompli et de faire le bilan de son œuvre[3].

Le développement progressif du droit international et sa codification ont été l'un des aspects les plus marquants de l'évolution du droit international depuis la seconde guerre mondiale et la Commission y a joué un rôle central. Des nombreuses réalisations de la Commission dans ce domaine, il en est trois en particulier qui méritent de retenir spécialement l'attention et qui seront examinées ci-après. En premier lieu, la Commission a préparé plus de vingt projets d'articles qui ont posé des règles fondamentales dans la plupart des secteurs du droit international. Nombreux sont ces projets qui, à leur tour, ont donné naissance à d'importants traités à vocation mondiale dans les matières auxquelles ils se rapportaient. En second lieu, certains de ces projets d'articles ont pris, par l'intermédiaire des conventions auxquelles ils avaient servi de base, une valeur structurante ou fondatrice dans les domaines qu'ils concernaient. Certains d'entre eux sont même devenus fondamentaux, s'agissant de la conduite même des relations entre les États. En troisième lieu, la Commission est parvenue à s'intégrer au processus de formation de la coutume et notamment, ce qui est le plus frappant, au processus aboutissant à la création de règles nouvelles de droit international coutumier. On examinera tour à tour les grandes réalisations de la Commission à ces trois points de vue.

---

*Reproduite, sans révision, de : Nations Unies, *Le droit international à l'aube du XXIᵉ siècle : Réflexions de codificateurs* (1997) [publication des Nations Unies, numéro de vente : E/F 97.V.4.].

[1]Cette résolution a été adoptée sur la base d'un rapport (document A/331 et Corr.1) présenté par la Commission du développement progressif du droit international et sa codification, créée par l'Assemblée générale l'année précédente pour examiner les méthodes selon lesquelles l'Assemblée générale pourrait s'acquitter le plus efficacement possible du mandat que lui confiait la Charte dans son Article 13, paragraphe 1, alinéa *a*.

[2]Les premières élections à la Commission se sont déroulées dans l'année qui a suivi sa création, le 3 novembre 1948. La Commission a ouvert sa première session l'année suivante, le 12 avril 1949.

[3]Dans sa résolution 51/160 du 16 décembre 1996, l'Assemblée générale a prié le Secrétaire général de prendre les dispositions voulues pour marquer le cinquantième anniversaire de la création de la Commission du droit international par la tenue d'un colloque sur le développement progressif et la codification du droit international durant l'examen à la Sixième Commission du rapport de la Commission du droit international sur les travaux de sa quarante-neuvième session (voir le paragraphe 18 du dispositif de la résolution).

I

L'article premier du statut dispose : « La Commission du droit international a pour but de promouvoir le développement progressif du droit international et sa codification »[4]. Conformément à cet objectif[5], la Commission a jusqu'ici préparé plus de vingt projets d'articles qui ont posé des règles de droit international dans nombre de matières essentielles. En fait il n'y a plus aujourd'hui que peu de domaines du droit international au développement desquels elle n'ait pas contribué[6]. Sous cet angle, l'œuvre accomplie par la Commission mérite certainement le qualificatif de considérable.

L'œuvre de la Commission est d'autant plus importante que nombre des projets d'articles préparés par elle ont servi de base aux grandes conventions de portée mondiale qui marquent des étapes juridiques décisives dans les domaines qu'elles concernent. Que la Commission doive jouer un rôle dans le processus normatif est explicitement envisagé dans son statut[7]. Celui-ci lui donnait essentiellement pour rôle de préparer des projets pouvant être utilisés comme base de travail par les représentants d'États réunis pour élaborer et adopter des conventions. Ce rôle n'était pas sans précédent[8], mais aussi bien la structure et l'organisation de la Commission que les procédures et les modalités selon lesquelles elle devait s'acquitter de cette tâche étaient des nouveautés sans équivalent exact dans la pratique internationale. Il est tout à l'honneur de la Commission que, sans pouvoir se guider sur des précédents directement applicables, elle se soit rapidement adaptée à un rôle fondamentalement original et inédit et qu'elle ait mis au point des pratiques lui permettant de réaliser ses potentialités. L'examen de l'action de la Commission, sous l'angle des projets d'articles qu'elle a élaborés, en est l'éloquent témoignage[9].

A. Dans le domaine des sources du droit international, la Commission a préparé trois projets d'articles dont deux ont servi de base aux travaux de conférences internationales et ont permis l'adoption de conventions multilatérales sur les sujets auxquels ils se rapportaient. En 1966, la Commission a adopté un projet de 75 articles sur le droit des traités qui a constitué plus tard la

---

[4]Le statut de la Commission est annexé à la résolution 174 (II) de l'Assemblée générale en date du 21 novembre 1947.

[5]Malgré la portée générale de l'article premier, paragraphe 1, les articles 16, 17, paragraphes 1 et 2, et 18, paragraphes 2 et 3, montrent bien que la tâche de la Commission est essentiellement de nature sélective : il s'agit de développer et de codifier progressivement le droit international dans les matières où une telle entreprise est considérée comme « nécessaire », « souhaitable » ou « appropriée ». Il n'incombe donc pas à la Commission de s'attaquer au développement progressif et à la codification de tous les domaines du droit international. Il lui incombe moins encore de transformer le droit international en une sorte de « code » écrit exhaustif. Voir le Rapport de la Commission du droit international sur les travaux de sa quarante-huitième session, *Documents officiels de l'Assemblée générale, cinquante et unième session, Supplément n° 10* (A/51/10) [ci-après cité sous la forme : Rapport. . . quarante-huitième session], p. 232, par. 168.

[6]Voir la conclusion à laquelle la Commission a abouti lorsqu'elle a examiné les travaux de ses 25 premières sessions : *Annuaire de la Commission du droit international, 1973*, vol. II, p. 232, document A/9010/Rev.1, par. 156.

[7]Voir la conclusion à laquelle la Commission a abouti lorsqu'elle a examiné les travaux de ses 25 premières sessions : *Annuaire de la Commission du droit international, 1973*, vol. II, p. 232, document A/9010/Rev.1, par. 156.

[8]Sur l'organisation et le fonctionnement du Comité de juristes pour le développement progressif du droit international et de la Commission préparatoire à la Conférence de codification, deux organismes créés par la Société des Nations, voir le document A/AC.10/5, p. 54 à 76.

[9]Pour un résumé détaillé du fonctionnement et des activités de la Commission, pour le texte des projets d'articles et des conventions élaborées sur la base de ces projets, voir Nations Unies, *La Commission du droit international et son œuvre*, 4ᵉ éd., n° de vente : F.88.V.1.

base de la Convention sur le droit des traités[10], signée à Vienne le 23 mai 1969[11]. Ultérieurement, en 1982, la Commission a adopté un projet de 81 articles sur le droit des traités entre États et organisations internationales ou entre organisations internationales, accompagné d'une annexe[12]. Ce projet est à l'origine de la Convention sur le droit des traités entre États et organisations internationales ou entre organisations internationales, signée à Vienne le 21 mars 1986[13]. Le troisième projet d'articles que la Commission a adopté dans ce domaine concerne la clause de la nation la plus favorisée[14]; il a été porté à l'attention des États Membres et des organisations intergouvernementales intéressées par l'Assemblée générale dans sa décision 46/416 du 9 décembre 1991.

Indépendamment de l'élaboration de projets d'articles, la Commission a donné des avis à l'Assemblée générale sur trois questions dans le domaine des sources du droit international : les moyens de rendre plus facilement accessible la documentation relative au droit international[15]; l'élargissement de la participation aux traités multilatéraux généraux conclus sous les auspices de la Société des Nations[16]; et les réserves aux conventions multilatérales[17]. La Commission revient sur cette dernière question, dans le cadre de son programme de travail actuel, afin de réaliser un guide de la pratique[18].

B.   Dans le domaine des relations internationales, la Commission a adopté cinq projets d'articles. Quatre d'entre eux ont servi de base à des conventions multilatérales[19], à savoir la Convention sur les relations diplomatiques, conclue à Vienne le 18 avril 1961[20]; la Convention sur les relations consulaires, conclue à Vienne le 24 avril 1963[21]; la Convention sur les missions spéciales, adoptée par l'Assemblée générale le 8 décembre 1969[22]; et la Convention sur la représentation des États dans leurs relations avec les organisations internationales de

[10]*Annuaire de la Commission du droit international, 1966*, vol. II, p. 193 à 203, document A/6309/Rev.1.

[11]Nations Unies, *Recueil des Traités*, vol. 1155, p. 331.

[12]*Annuaire de la Commission du droit international, 1982*, vol. II (deuxième partie), p. 17 à 80.

[13]Document A/CONF.129/15.

[14] *Annuaire de la Commission du droit international, 1978*, vol. II (deuxième partie), p. 19 à 83.

[15]*Yearbook of the International Law Commission, 1950*, vol. II, p. 367 à 374, document A/1316. L'article 24 du statut de la Commission dispose que la Commission doit faire une étude et un rapport en la matière.

[16]*Annuaire de la Commission du droit international, 1963*, vol. II, p. 227 à 234, document A/5509.

[17]*Yearbook of the International Law Commission, 1951*, vol. II, p. 125 à 131, document A/1858.

[18]Pour le plan de travail proposé à cet égard, voir Rapport de la Commission du droit international sur les travaux de sa quarante-septième session, *Documents officiels de l'Assemblée générale, cinquantième session, Supplément n° 10* (A/50/10) [ci-après cité sous la forme : Rapport . . . quarante-septième session], p. 277, par. 491. Les deux rapports présentés jusqu'ici par le Rapporteur spécial chargé de la question figurent dans le document A/CN.4/470 et Corr.1 et le document A/CN.4/477 et Add.1.

[19]Projet d'articles relatifs aux relations et immunités diplomatiques et commentaire, *Annuaire de la Commission du droit international, 1958*, vol. II, p. 89 à 101, document A/3859; projet d'articles relatifs aux relations consulaires et commentaire, *Annuaire de la Commission du droit international, 1961*, vol. II, p. 95 à 133, document A/4843; projet d'articles sur les missions spéciales et commentaire, *Annuaire de la Commission du droit international, 1967*, vol. II, p. 384 à 405, document A/6709/Rev.1 et Rev.1/Corr.1; projet d'articles relatifs à la représentation des États dans leurs relations avec les organisations internationales de caractère universel avec commentaire et annexe, *Annuaire de la Commission du droit international, 1971*, vol. II (première partie), p. 301 à 358, document A/8410/Rev.1.

[20]Nations Unies, *Recueil des Traités*, vol. 500, p. 95.

[21]Ibid., vol. 596, p. 261.

[22]Ibid., vol. 1400, p. 231.

caractère universel, conclue à Vienne le 14 mars 1975[23]. Le cinquième projet préparé par la Commission dans ce domaine — le projet d'articles et les projets de protocoles facultatifs I et II relatifs au statut du courrier diplomatique et de la valise diplomatique non accompagnée par un courrier diplomatique[24] — a été porté à l'attention des États Membres des Nations Unies par l'Assemblée générale dans sa décision 50/416 du 11 décembre 1995.

C. On peut aussi considérer que les projets d'articles qui sont à la base de la Convention de Vienne de 1975 sur la représentation des États dans leurs relations avec les organisations internationales de caractère universel, d'une part, et de la Convention de Vienne de 1986 sur le droit des traités entre États et organisations internationales ou entre organisations internationales, d'autre part[25], constituent un apport au droit des organisations internationales.

D. En ce qui concerne la juridiction et les immunités, la Commission a adopté un certain nombre de projets d'articles. Pour ce qui est des privilèges et immunités, en plus des cinq projets mentionnés plus haut à la section B[26], elle a adopté le projet d'articles sur les immunités juridictionnelles des États et de leurs biens[27] que l'Assemblée générale a décidé, par sa résolution 49/61 du 9 décembre 1994, de soumettre pour examen à une conférence de plénipotentiaires. La Commission a également élaboré un projet d'articles sur la question de l'exercice de la juridiction[28]. Ce projet a servi de base à la Convention sur la prévention et la répression des infractions contre les personnes jouissant d'une protection internationale, y compris les agents diplomatiques, adoptée par l'Assemblée générale le 14 décembre 1973[29].

E. Dans le domaine connexe du droit pénal international, la Commission a élaboré trois importants projets d'articles : les principes de droit international reconnus par le statut du Tribunal de Nuremberg et dans le jugement de ce tribunal[30]; un projet de statut d'une cour criminelle internationale[31]; et un projet de code des crimes contre la paix et la sécurité de l'humanité[32]. S'agissant du projet de statut, l'Assemblée générale a décidé, par sa résolution 51/207 du 17 décembre 1996, qu'une conférence de plénipotentiaires se réunirait en 1998 pour conclure une convention en la matière. Quant au projet de code des crimes, il fait actuellement l'objet d'un examen de la part de l'Assemblée générale[33].

F. En ce qui concerne la place de l'individu en droit international, la Commission a, indépendamment de ses réalisations dans le domaine du droit pénal international, adopté deux textes, à savoir un projet de convention sur la

---

[23]Document A/CONF.67/16.

[24]*Annuaire de la Commission du droit international, 1989*, vol. II (deuxième partie), p. 16 à 54.

[25]Voir *supra* le texte à la note 12.

[26]Voir *supra* le texte aux notes 19 à 24.

[27]*Annuaire de la Commission du droit international, 1991*, vol. II (deuxième partie), p. 13 à 64.

[28]Projet d'articles sur la prévention et la répression des infractions commises contre des agents diplomatiques et d'autres personnes ayant droit à une protection internationale, *Annuaire de la Commission du droit international, 1972*, vol. II, p. 339 à 351, document A/8710/Rev.1.

[29]Nations Unies, *Recueil des Traités*, vol. 1035, p. 167.

[30]*Yearbook of the International Law Commission, 1950*, vol. II, p. 374 à 378, document A/1316.

[31]Rapport de la Commission du droit international sur les travaux de sa quarante-sixième session, *Documents officiels de l'Assemblée générale, quarante-neuvième session, Supplément n° 10*, (A/49/10) [ci-après cité sous la forme : Rapport. . . quarante-sixième session], p. 47 à 160.

[32]Rapport. . . quarante-huitième session, p. 25 à 143.

[33]Au paragraphe 2 de sa résolution 51/160 en date du 16 décembre 1996, l'Assemblée générale a appelé l'attention des États qui participaient au Comité préparatoire pour la création d'une cour criminelle internationale sur l'intérêt que présentait le projet de code pour leurs travaux.

réduction des cas d'apatridie et un projet de convention sur l'élimination de l'apatridie[34]. Le premier a servi de base à la Convention portant le même titre qui a été conclue à New York le 30 août 1961[35]. En outre, la question des conséquences de la succession d'États sur la nationalité des personnes physiques et morales figure au programme de travail actuel de la Commission[36].

G. Deux projets d'articles ont été adoptés par la Commission dans le domaine du droit des espaces internationaux. Le premier a servi de base à quatre grandes conventions multilatérales[37] : la Convention sur la mer territoriale et la zone contiguë[38], la Convention sur la haute mer[39], la Convention sur la pêche et la conservation des ressources biologiques de la haute mer[40] et la Convention sur le plateau continental[41], toutes conventions faites à Genève le 28 avril 1958. Par sa résolution 49/52 du 9 décembre 1994, l'Assemblée générale a décidé que le projet d'articles sur le droit relatif aux utilisations des cours d'eau internationaux à des fins autres que la navigation[42] constituerait la base d'une convention-cadre actuellement élaborée par la Sixième Commission réunie en groupe de travail plénier[43].

H. En ce qui concerne le droit et la pratique du règlement pacifique des différends, la Commission a adopté, outre le Modèle de règles sur la procédure arbitrale[44] — que l'Assemblée générale a porté à l'attention des États Membres dans sa résolution 1262 (XIII) du 14 novembre 1958 — , des projets de dispositions définissant les procédures applicables à la solution des litiges que pourrait soulever l'interprétation ou l'application de certains des projets d'articles élaborés par elle sur quelques-unes des questions mentionnées dans la présente partie[45].

---

[34]*Yearbook of the International Law Commission, 1954,* vol. II, p. 143 à 147, document A/2693.

[35]Nations Unies, *Recueil des Traités,* vol. 989, p. 175.

[36]Pour le plan de travail proposé par la Commission sur cette question, voir Rapport. . . quarante-huitième session, p. 201, par. 88. Pour les deux rapports présentés jusqu'ici par le Rapporteur spécial, voir le document A/CN.4/467 et le document A/3519.

[37]Projet d'articles relatifs au droit de la mer, *Annuaire de la Commission du droit international, 1956,* vol. II, p. 256 à 264, document A/3519.

[38]Nations Unies, *Recueil des Traités,* vol. 516, p. 205.

[39]Ibid., vol. 450, p. 11.

[40]Ibid., vol. 559, p. 285.

[41]Ibid., vol. 499, p. 311.

[42]Rapport . . . quarante-sixième session, p. 217 à 353.

[43]Le groupe de travail n'a pas achevé son examen en 1996 et une deuxième session est prévue en 1997 (voir la résolution 51/206 de l'Assemblée générale en date du 17 décembre 1996).

[44]*Annuaire de la Commission du droit international, 1958,* vol. II, p. 86 à 89, document A/3859.

[45]Voir : projet d'article 73 du projet d'articles relatifs au droit de la mer (voir *supra* note 37); projet d'article 45 du projet d'articles relatifs aux relations et immunités diplomatiques (voir *supra* note 19); projet d'article 62 du projet d'articles sur le droit des traités (voir *supra* note 10); projet d'article 82 du projet d'articles relatifs à la représentation des États dans leurs relations avec les organisations internationales de caractère universel (voir *supra* note 19); projet d'article 12 du projet d'articles sur la prévention et la répression des infractions commises contre des agents diplomatiques et d'autres personnes ayant droit à une protection internationale (voir *supra* note 28); projets d'articles 65 et 66 et projet d'annexe du projet d'articles sur le droit des traités entre États et organisations internationales ou entre organisations internationales (voir *supra* note 12); et projet d'article 33 du projet d'articles sur le droit relatif aux utilisations des cours d'eau internationaux à des fins autres que la navigation (voir *supra* note 42). À noter aussi les projets d'articles 54 à 60 et les projets d'annexes I et II du projet d'articles sur la responsabilité des États, tels qu'ils ont été adoptés provisoirement par la Commission en première lecture (voir *infra* note 51).

I. Dans le domaine de la succession d'États, la Commission a adopté deux projets[46] qui ont servi de base à des conventions multilatérales[47] : la Convention sur la succession d'États en matière de traités, conclue à Vienne le 23 août 1978[48], et la Convention sur la succession d'États en matière de biens, archives et dettes d'État, conclue à Vienne le 8 avril 1983[49].

J. La Commission a également adopté un projet d'articles dans le domaine des droits et devoirs fondamentaux des États : le projet de déclaration sur les droits et les devoirs des États[50]. Par sa résolution 375 (V) du 6 décembre 1949, l'Assemblée générale a recommandé ce texte à l'attention des États Membres et des juristes de toutes les nations.

K. La Commission est actuellement en train d'élaborer des projets d'articles dans deux autres domaines du droit international, tous deux d'une extrême importance pour le fonctionnement de l'ordre juridique international. Le premier projet concerne la responsabilité des États, sujet sur lequel la Commission a récemment adopté en première lecture un ensemble de 60 projets d'articles et deux annexes[51]. L'autre projet porte sur la responsabilité internationale pour les conséquences préjudiciables découlant d'activités qui ne sont pas interdites par le droit international[52].

Ce bref aperçu fait ressortir le remarquable bilan de la Commission et témoigne de l'importance de sa contribution dans presque tous les domaines majeurs du droit international.

II

Un autre aspect de l'œuvre de la Commission mérite d'être relevé, à savoir l'incidence considérable que ses travaux ont eue sur la structure même du droit international dans un certain nombre de ses domaines constitutifs.

Tout d'abord plusieurs des grandes conventions multilatérales qui ont été conclues avec, pour base, les projets d'articles de la Commission sont devenues des éléments fondamentaux dans la conduite des relations internationales contemporaines.

Aucun instrument ne mérite davantage cette qualification que la Convention de Vienne de 1961 sur les relations diplomatiques et la Convention de Vienne de 1963 sur les relations consulaires. Ces deux conventions figurent parmi les traités en vigueur qui ont recueilli la plus large participation — 178 États parties pour la première et 157 pour la seconde. Comme l'a dit la Cour internationale de Justice, ces deux instruments « sont d'une importance capitale pour le maintien de bonnes relations entre États dans le monde interdépendant

---

[46]Projet d'articles sur la succession d'États en matière de traités et commentaire, *Annuaire de la Commission du droit international, 1974*, vol. II (première partie), p. 178 à 280, document A/9610/Rev.1; projet d'articles sur la succession d'États en matière de biens, archives et dettes d'État, *Annuaire de la Commission du droit international, 1981*, vol. II (deuxième partie), p. 19 à 114.

[47]La Commission travaille en ce moment à la question de la succession d'États et nationalité des personnes physiques et morales (voir *supra* le texte à la note 36).

[48]Document A/CONF.80/31.

[49]Document A/CONF.117/14.

[50]*Yearbook of the International Law Commission, 1949*, pp. 287-288, document A/CN.4/13 et Corr.1-3.

[51]Projet d'articles sur la responsabilité des États, Rapport. . . quarante-huitième session, p. 144 à 174.

[52]Pour un aperçu de l'état d'avancement des travaux de la Commission sur cette question, voir Rapport. . . quarante-huitième session, p. 202 à 206. Pour le projet d'articles préparé par un groupe de travail de la Commission, voir ibid., p. 264 à 364.

d'aujourd'hui »[53]. La diplomatie, a fait observer la Cour[54], est « un instrument essentiel de coopération efficace dans la communauté internationale, qui permet aux États . . . de parvenir à la compréhension mutuelle et de résoudre leurs divergences par des moyens pacifiques »[55] et « le déroulement sans entrave des relations consulaires . . . n'est pas moins important dans le contexte du droit international contemporain, en ce qu'il favorise le développement des relations amicales entre les nations »[56]. La Cour a estimé que « les obligations impératives » que ces deux institutions comportent « sont maintenant codifiées dans les conventions de Vienne de 1961 et 1963 »[57].

La Convention de Vienne de 1969 sur le droit des traités touche elle aussi de façon cruciale à l'ordre juridique international[58]. Comme l'atteste le contenu des quelque 1500 volumes du *Recueil des Traités* publiés jusqu'à ce jour par l'Organisation des Nations Unies, les traités jouent un « rôle fondamental dans . . . [les] relations internationales » et ont une « importance de plus en plus grande . . . en tant que source du droit international et en tant que moyen de développer la coopération pacifique entre les nations »[59]. La Convention de 1969 énonce les règles qui doivent régir ces instruments fondamentaux des relations internationales. À maintes reprises, des règles posées dans nombre de dispositions de la Convention ont été considérées comme des normes de droit international (général) coutumier par la Cour internationale de Justice[60], par des tribunaux

[53]*Personnel diplomatique et consulaire des États-Unis à Téhéran, arrêt, C.I.J. Recueil 1980*, par. 91. Voir également ibid., par. 45 et 92.

[54]*Personnel diplomatique et consulaire des États-Unis à Téhéran, mesures conservatoires, ordonnance du 15 décembre 1979, C.I.J. Recueil 1979*, p. 7.

[55]Ibid., par. 39.

[56]Ibid., par. 40.

[57]Ibid., par. 41. Voir aussi *Personnel diplomatique et consulaire des États-Unis à Téhéran, arrêt* (voir *supra* note 53), par. 45 : « Les conventions de Vienne, qui codifient le droit des relations diplomatiques et consulaires, énoncent les principes et règles indispensables au maintien de relations pacifiques entre États et acceptés dans le monde entier par des nations de toutes croyances, cultures et appartenances politiques. »

[58]À l'heure actuelle 81 États sont parties à cette convention et 21 autres États l'ont signée.

[59]Voir les premier et deuxième alinéas du préambule de la Convention de 1969. Le septième alinéa du préambule affirme en outre que « la codification et le développement progressif du droit des traités réalisés dans la présente Convention serviront les buts des Nations Unies énoncés dans la Charte, qui sont de maintenir la paix et la sécurité internationales, de développer entre les nations des relations amicales et de réaliser la coopération internationale. »

[60]La Cour internationale de Justice a estimé que certaines dispositions de la Convention de Vienne énonçaient des règles de droit international général dans les affaires suivantes : *Conséquences juridiques pour les États de la présence continue de l'Afrique du Sud en Namibie (Sud-Ouest africain) nonobstant la résolution 276 (1970) du Conseil de sécurité, avis consultatif, C.I.J. Recueil 1971*, p. 46, par. 94; *Appel concernant la compétence du Conseil de l'OACI, arrêt, C.I.J. Recueil 1972*, p. 67, par. 38; *Compétence en matière de pêcheries (Royaume-Uni c. Islande), compétence de la Cour, arrêt, C.I.J. Recueil 1973*, p. 14 et 18, par. 24 et 36; *Interprétation de l'accord du 25 mars 1951 entre l'OMS et l'Egypte, avis consultatif, C.I.J. Recueil 1980*, p. 94, par. 47; *Activités militaires et paramilitaires au Nicaragua et contre celui-ci (Nicaragua c. États-Unis d'Amérique), fond, arrêt, C.I.J. Recueil 1986*, p. 95, par, 178 (voir aussi p. 100, par. 190); *Différend frontalier, arrêt, C.I.J. Recueil 1986*, p. 563, par. 17; *Actions armées frontalières et transfrontalières (Nicaragua c. Honduras), compétence et recevabilité, arrêt, C.I.J. Recueil 1988*, p. 84, par. 35; *Sentence arbitrale du 31 juillet 1989, arrêt, C.I.J. Recueil 1991*, p. 69, par. 48; *Différend frontalier, terrestre, insulaire et maritime [El Salvador/Honduras; Nicaragua (intervenant)], arrêt, C.I.J. Recueil 1992*, p. 582, 583 et 586, par. 373, 375 et 380; *Application de la Convention pour la prévention et la répression du crime de génocide, mesures conservatoires, ordonnance du 8 avril 1993, C.I.J. Recueil 1993*, p. 3, par. 13; *Différend territorial (Jamahiriya arabe libyenne/Tchad), arrêt, C.I.J. Recueil 1994*, p. 21, par. 41; *Délimitation maritime et questions territoriales entre Qatar et Bahreïn, compétence et recevabilité, arrêt, C.I.J. Recueil 1994*, p. 120, par. 23; *Délimitation maritime et questions territoriales entre Qatar et Bahrein, compétence et recevabilité, arrêt, C.I.J. Recueil 1995*, p. 18, par. 33.

régionaux et des commissions régionales[61], par divers tribunaux arbitraux[62] ainsi que par des organes créés par traité dans le cadre des Nations Unies[63].

Par le truchement des conventions qu'ils ont inspirées, certains des projets d'articles élaborés par la Commission ont donc joué un rôle direct et fondamental dans la mise en place des instruments de base qui régissent les relations internationales. Il est également remarquable que les conventions en question aient été conclues et, dans le cas du droit des traités, que le projet d'articles ait été préparé à un moment où la communauté internationale connaissait une transformation sociétale profonde à la suite de l'accession d'un grand nombre de nouveaux États à l'indépendance. En instituant et en consolidant des règles indispensables au fonctionnement du système international, les instruments en question ont contribué, à un moment crucial, à maintenir la confiance dans le droit international et à assurer la stabilité de la société internationale elle-même.

Si certains des projets d'articles de la Commission sont devenus des éléments fondamentaux dans la conduite même des relations internationales, certains autres ont joué un rôle crucial par rapport à tout un pan du droit international, car ils ont énoncé des principes et des règles qui ont défini la trame du droit dans le domaine en cause et constitué un cadre propice à l'analyse des problèmes et à l'exercice de la pensée juridique[64]. Tel est certainement le cas du projet d'articles relatifs au droit de la mer, adopté par la Commission en 1956. Les quatre conventions de Genève de 1958, élaborées à partir de ce projet d'articles, ont énoncé un corps de règles qui a constitué en grande partie et pendant un certain nombre d'années au moins le droit de la mer en vigueur, comme le montrent maintes décisions émanant de cours et de tribunaux inter-

---

[61]Voir par exemple : affaire *Golder,* Cour européenne des droits de l'homme, *série A,* n° 18, arrêt du 21 février 1975, par. 29; *Temeltasch* c. *Suisse,* Commission européenne des droits de l'homme, requête n° 9116/80 du 5 mai 1982, *Annuaire de la Commission européenne des droits de l'homme,* vol. 31, p. 120, par. 68 et 69; *L'effet des réserves sur l'entrée en vigueur de la Convention américaine,* Cour interaméricaine des droits de l'homme, avis consultatif n° OC-2/82, 24 septembre 1982, *série A,* n° 2, par. 19; *Restrictions à la peine de mort,* Cour interaméricaine des droits de l'homme, avis consultatif n° OC-3/83, 8 septembre 1983, *série A,* n° 3, par. 48; *Interprétation de la déclaration américaine des droits et devoirs de l'homme dans le cadre de l'article 64 de la Convention américaine des droits de l'homme,* Cour interaméricaine des droits de l'homme, avis consultatif n° OC-10/89, 14 juillet 1989, *série A,* n° 9, par. 31 à 33.

[62]Voir par exemple : *Arbitrage entre le Royaume-Uni de Grande-Bretagne et d'Irlande du Nord et la République française sur la délimitation du plateau continental,* décision du 30 juin 1977, *Recueil des sentences arbitrales,* vol. XVIII, par. 38, 55 et 61; *Royaume de Belgique, République française, Confédération suisse, Royaume-Uni et États-Unis d'Amérique* c. *République fédérale d'Allemagne,* décision du Tribunal arbitral pour un accord sur les dettes extérieures allemandes en date du 16 mai 1980, *Revue générale de droit international public,* vol. 84 (1980), p. 1158, par. 16; *Affaire concernant les problèmes nés entre la Nouvelle-Zélande et la France relatifs à l'interprétation ou à l'application de deux accords conclus le 9 juillet 1986, lesquels concernaient les problèmes découlant de l'affaire du «Rainbow Warrior»,* sentence du 30 avril 1990, *Recueil des sentences arbitrales,* vol. XX, p. 215, par. 75, 100 et 106.

[63]Voir en particulier : *Observation générale sur les questions relatives aux réserves émises lors de la ratification du Pacte ou des protocoles additionnels y relatifs, ou lors de l'adhésion à ces instruments, ou au sujet des déclarations faites en vertu de l'article 41 du Pacte, Observation générale adoptée par le Comité des droits de l'homme au titre de l'article 40, paragraphe 4, du Pacte international relatif aux droits civils et politiques, additif, Observation générale n° 24 (52),* document CCPR/C/21/Rev.1/Add.6, note 2 et par. 6, 16 et 17. Le Secrétaire général de l'Organisation des Nations Unies a fait aussi observer que la convention « représente dans une large mesure une codification de la coutume internationale ». Voir le paragraphe 10 de la note verbale adressée au représentant permanent d'un État Membre, reproduite dans *Annuaire juridique des Nations Unies 1975,* p. 203.

[64]Rapport. . . quarante-huitième session, p. 232, par. 168. La Commission note que « c'est là un progrès indiscutable dans les relations entre États », ibid.

22

nationaux[65]. Bien que l'évolution ultérieure ait entraîné des modifications considérables dans la structure de ce droit, les conventions de 1958 ont continué à concrétiser bon nombre de ses éléments. Elles ont en outre servi plus tard de modèles pour certaines parties importantes de la Convention des Nations Unies sur le droit de la mer, signée à Montego Bay le 10 décembre 1982[66], en particulier les passages relatifs aux régimes de la mer territoriale, de la zone contiguë, du plateau continental et de la haute mer[67]. Les conventions de 1958, en définissant et en précisant la structure du droit de la mer, font donc encore aujourd'hui sentir leurs effets.

On pourrait penser au premier abord que certains des projets d'articles mis au point par la Commission ne sont pas encore parvenus, comme ils en avaient la vocation, à jouer un rôle structurant dans les domaines du droit international auxquels ils se rapportaient. À y regarder de plus près, cependant, on constate qu'en fait un certain nombre d'entre eux constituent œuvre considérable.

Tel est le cas pour les deux projets d'articles relatifs à la question de la succession d'États. Quelques États seulement sont parties aux conventions qui ont été élaborées sur la base de ces projets : la Convention de Vienne de 1983 sur la succession d'États en matière de biens, archives et dettes d'État et la Convention de Vienne de 1978 sur la succession d'États en matière de traités[68]. Néanmoins il y a lieu de penser que cette dernière convention au moins occupe une place importante dans le domaine de la succession d'États auquel elle se rattache. En particulier, dans un certain nombre de situations mettant en jeu une succession d'États, on a considéré que la Convention de 1978 et le projet d'articles de la Commission sur lequel elle se fonde consacraient les principes du droit international coutumier en vigueur[69].

---

[65]La Cour internationale de Justice a considéré qu'un certain nombre de dispositions des conventions de Genève de 1958 relevaient du droit coutumier. Voir : *Plateau continental de la mer du Nord (République fédérale d'Allemagne/Danemark; République fédérale d'Allemagne/Pays-Bas), arrêt, C.I.J. Recueil 1969*, p. 22 et 38, par. 19 et 63; *Compétence en matiere de pêcheries (Royaume-Uni c. Islande), fond, arrêt, C.I.J. Recueil 1974*, p. 22 et 29, par. 50 et 67; *Plateau continental (Tunisie/Jamahiriya arabe libyenne), arrêt, C.I.J. Recueil 1982*, p. 45, par. 41 et 42; *Différend frontalier, terrestre, insulaire et maritime [El Salvador/Honduras; Nicaragua (intervenant)]* (voir *supra* note 60), p. 586, par. 383. Voir également la décision du tribunal arbitral dans l'*Arbitrage entre le Royaume-Uni de Grande-Bretagne et d'Irlande du Nord et la République française sur la délimitation du plateau continental* (voir *supra* note 62), par. 13, 65, 68 à 70, 75, 84 et 97.

[66]Document A/CONF.62/122 et Corr.1 à 11. À l'heure actuelle, 113 États ont donné leur consentement à être liés par la Convention de 1982 et 56 autres en sont signataires. Entre les États parties, la Convention de 1982 l'emporte sur les conventions de Genève de 1958 (voir l'article 311, paragraphe 1).

[67]Rapport . . . quarante-huitième session, p. 232, note 311.

[68]La première n'a recueilli que quatre des 15 instruments de ratification ou d'adhésion nécessaires à son entrée en vigueur et la seconde n'est parvenue à ce chiffre qu'en 1996.

[69]Voir par exemple : lettre du Bureau des affaires juridiques de l'Organisation des Nations Unies adressée au chef du Service juridique de l'Organisation mondiale de la santé, reproduite dans *Annuaire juridique des Nations Unies 1972*, p. 204; lettre du Bureau des affaires juridiques de l'Organisation des Nations Unies adressée au Secrétaire du Conseil des Nations Unies pour la Namibie, reproduite dans *Annuaire juridique des Nations Unies 1984*, p. 194, par. 3, ii; *Plateau continental (Tunisie/Jamahiriya arabe libyenne)* [voir *supra* note 65], par. 84; et Conférence internationale sur l'ex-Yougoslavie, Commission d'arbitrage, avis n° 1, *Revue générale de droit international public*, vol. 96 (1992), p. 265, par. 1, *e*, et avis n° 9, *ibid.*, vol. 97 (1993), p. 592, par. 2 et 4. Voir également Conférence internationale sur l'ex-Yougoslavie, Commission d'arbitrage, avis n° 3, *ibid.*, vol. 96 (1992), p. 268, par. 2.

Il est intéressant de noter qu'une chambre de la Cour internationale de Justice a dit que cette convention, tout comme la Convention de Vienne de 1969 sur le droit des traités, était une convention «de codification», *Différend frontalier* (voir *supra* note 60), par. 17.

Aux termes d'un certain nombre de déclarations émanant de fonctionnaires d'État, diverses dispositions de la convention traduiraient le droit international coutumier. Voir, par exemple, le mémorandum du conseiller juridique du Département d'État des États-Unis, reproduit dans *Digest of United States Practice in International Law, 1980*, p. 1026 et 1035 et note 43; la lettre de la République de Kiribati au Secrétaire général de l'Organisation des Nations Unies, reproduite dans *British Year Book of International Law*, vol. 52 (1981), p. 385.

23

Selon diverses indications, certains aspects de la Convention de 1983 sont également considérés comme ayant le statut de droit international coutumier[70].

De même il convient de ne pas sous-estimer l'importance des projets d'articles que la Commission a rédigés dans le domaine du droit des organisations internationales. Certes la Convention de Vienne de 1975 sur la représentation des États dans leurs relations avec les organisations internationales de caractère universel n'est pas encore entrée en vigueur, plus de 20 ans après sa conclusion[71]. Néanmoins le fait est que cette convention est souvent citée par les États et les organisations internationales dans le cours de leur activité[72] et il est admis qu'un certain nombre de ses dispositions ou bien font partie du droit coutumier ou bien reflètent la pratique dominante[73].

Un autre exemple est fourni par la Convention de Vienne de 1986, élaborée sur la base du projet d'articles de la Commission sur le droit des traités entre États et organisations internationales ou entre organisations internationales, qui n'a recueilli que 23 des 35 ratifications ou adhésions qu'exige son entrée en vigueur[74]. Il ne fait cependant guère de doute que, comme la Convention de Vienne de 1969 sur le droit des traités sur laquelle elle se fonde, elle occupe une place fondamentale dans le domaine du droit des traités qu'elle concerne. Les tribunaux internationaux, en particulier, ont déjà mentionné que certaines de ses dispositions traduisaient le droit en vigueur[75] et les organisations du système des Nations Unies utilisent couramment la convention comme un guide pour l'élaboration, l'interprétation et l'application de leurs traités.

III

L'action de la Commission du droit international est remarquable à un autre point de vue : elle s'est taillé une place importante dans le processus de formation de la coutume.

Que les travaux de la Commission et ses réalisations puissent jouer un rôle dans le processus même de formation de la coutume n'était pas clairement prévu

---

[70]Voir la lettre adressée par le conseiller juridique de l'Organisation des Nations Unies au Directeur exécutif de l'Organisation internationale du cacao, reproduite dans *Annuaire juridique des Nations Unies 1991*, p. 315. Voir également Conférence internationale sur l'ex-Yougoslavie, Commission d'arbitrage, avis n° 1 (voir la note précédente), par. 1, *e*, et avis n° 9 (voir la note précédente), par. 2 et 4.

[71]À l'heure actuelle 30 États seulement acceptent d'être liés par la convention alors que 35 acceptations sont nécessaires pour son entrée en vigueur. Sept autres États l'ont signée.

[72]Voir la déclaration faite par le conseiller juridique de l'Organisation des Nations Unies à la 71e séance du Comité des relations avec le pays hôte, reproduite dans *Annuaire juridique des Nations Unies 1978*, p. 237 à 240.

[73]Voir, par exemple : le paragraphe 10 de la note verbale adressée par le Secrétaire général de l'Organisation des Nations Unies au représentant permanent d'un État Membre (voir *supra* note 63); le paragraphe 4 du mémorandum adressé par le conseiller juridique de l'Organisation des Nations Unies au chef adjoint du protocole, reproduit dans *Annuaire juridique des Nations Unies 1977*, p. 208; la déclaration faite par le conseiller juridique de l'Organisation des Nations Unies à la 71e séance du Comité des relations avec le pays hôte (voir la note précédente); les paragraphes 4 et 5 de la déclaration faite par le conseiller juridique à la 115e séance du Comité des relations avec le pays hôte, reproduits dans *Annuaire juridique des Nations Unies 1986*, p. 368; et le paragraphe 4 du mémorandum adressé par le Bureau des affaires juridiques de l'Organisation des Nations Unies au juriste principal, bureau du Directeur général, Office des Nations Unies à Genève, reproduit dans *Annuaire juridique des Nations Unies 1991*, p. 320.

[74]Seize autres États et dix organisations internationales ont signé la Convention.

[75]Tant la Cour de Justice des Communautés européennes que ses avocats généraux ont indiqué que certaines dispositions de la convention reflétaient le droit international coutumier. Voir *République française* c. *Commission des Communautés européennes*, affaire C-327/91, *Recueil de la Jurisprudence de la Cour de Justice*, 1994-8, partie I, conclusions de l'avocat général, p. 3649, par. 12, et arrêt de la Cour, p. 3674, par. 25. Voir aussi *infra* le texte à la note 79.

par le statut. Pourtant, comme l'étude sommaire de l'œuvre de la Commission suffit à le montrer, celle-ci s'est totalement impliquée dans le processus qui consiste à identifier, consolider, maintenir, adapter et même former des règles de droit international coutumier ou général. En particulier on a considéré à maintes reprises que les conventions adoptées sur la base de projets d'articles préparés par la Commission fournissaient une preuve autorisée de l'état du droit coutumier, parfois avant même qu'elles ne soient entrées en vigueur[76]. De façon plus spectaculaire encore et qui illustre bien l'action de la Commission à cet égard, des projets d'articles de la Commission ont été eux-mêmes considérés comme apportant la preuve de la situation prévalant en droit coutumier[77], parfois même avant qu'ils ne soient définitivement adoptés[78]. Ainsi, par exemple, avant même que la Commission ait achevé son travail sur le droit des traités entre États et organisations internationales ou entre organisations internationales, la Cour internationale de Justice a cité l'une des dispositions de ce projet comme représentative du droit coutumier[79]. L'œuvre de la Commission dans le domaine de la responsabilité des États mérite spécialement de retenir l'attention à cet égard. Avant même que la Commission ait achevé la première lecture du projet d'articles relatifs à cette question, les rapports des Rapporteurs spéciaux et les projets d'articles jusque-là adoptés par la Commission étaient déjà fréquemment invoqués à titre de preuves du droit international général. Les tribunaux internationaux en particulier se réfèrent depuis un certain temps aux travaux de la Commission quand ils traitent de problèmes soulevés en la matière[80]. Qui plus est, un tribunal arbitral a jugé, il y a dix ans, que la première partie du projet

---

[76]Voir spécialement les positions relatives à la Convention de Vienne de 1969 sur le droit des traités, cités *supra* notes 60 à 63, et dont beaucoup sont antérieures à l'entrée en vigueur de la convention.

[77]Voir par exemple la décision du Tribunal fédéral suisse dans l'affaire *X* c. *Ministère public de la Confédération, Annuaire suisse de droit international*, vol. 36 (1980), p. 205, qui, bien que postérieure à l'adoption de la Convention de 1978 sur la succession d'États en matière de traités, mentionne uniquement le projet d'articles de la Commission qui a servi de base à la convention.

[78]Voir par exemple la lettre adressée par le Bureau des affaires juridiques de l'Organisation des Nations Unies au chef du Service juridique de l'Organisation mondiale de la santé (voir *supra* note 69).

Les délibérations de la Commission sur un sujet donné ont souvent été considérées plus tard comme traduisant l'état du droit, à l'époque, sur la question considérée : voir *Plateau continental de la mer du Nord* (voir *supra* note 65), par. 49 à 55, 62 et 85; *Arbitrage entre le Royaume-Uni de Grande-Bretagne et d'Irlande du Nord et la République française sur la délimitation du plateau continental* (voir *supra* note 62), par. 37.

[79]*Interprétation de l'accord du 25 mars 1951 entre l'OMS et l'Egypte* (voir *supra* note 60), par. 47.

[80]Voir par exemple les sentences suivantes du Tribunal des différends irano-américains : *International Technical Products Corporation and ITP Export Corporation* v. *the Government of the Islamic Republic of Iran et al.*, sentence nº 196-302-3 (24 octobre 1985), *Iran–United States Claims Tribunal Reports*, vol. 9 (1985), p. 206, note 35; *Alfred L.W. Short* v. *The Islamic Republic of Iran*, sentence nº 312-11135-2 (14 juillet 1987), *ibid.*, vol. 16 (1987), p. 76, par. 28 et 33; *Kenneth P. Yeager* v. *The Islamic Republic of Iran*, sentence nº 324-10199-1 (2 novembre 1987), ibid., vol. 17 (1987), p. 92, par. 33, 42 et 65; *Jack Rankin* v. *The Islamic Republic of Iran*, sentence nº 326-10913-2 (3 novembre 1987), ibid., p. 135, par. 18, 25 et 30, c et e; et *Phillips Petroleun Company Iran* v. *The Islamic Republic of Iran, The National Iranian Oil Company*, sentence nº 425-39-2 (29 juin 1989), ibid., vol. 21 (1989), p. 79, note 26. Voir aussi les sentences arbitrales suivantes : *Affaire concernant l'accord aérien du 27 mars 1946 entre les États-Unis d'Amérique et la France*, sentence du 9 décembre 1978, *Recueil des sentences arbitrales*, vol. XVIII, p. 417, par. 31; *Affaire concernant les problèmes nés entre la Nouvelle-Zélande et la France . . .* (voir *supra* note 62), par. 72, 77, 78, 101 et 105 (et la note relative aux par. 113 et 122); *AMCO-Asia Corporation others* v. *The Republic of Indonesia*, sentence sur le fond, 31 mai 1990, *International Law Reports*, vol. 89, p. 405, par. 172; *Libyan Arab Foreign Investment Company* v. *The Republic of Burundi*, sentence du 4 mars 1991, ibid., vol. 96, p. 282, par. 61 (et note relative aux par. 55, 56 et 66).

d'articles était « l'exposé le plus récent et le plus autorisé du droit international actuel dans ce domaine »[81].

Il se peut qu'au moment où la Commission aborde l'étude d'un sujet le droit coutumier en la matière ou bien ne soit pas fixé ou bien soit à un stade de formation. Grâce au travail de la Commission, des règles nouvelles peuvent commencer à émerger et à prendre progressivement forme dans le droit international coutumier. En particulier l'analyse de la pratique existante des États à laquelle la Commission procède et ses recommandations quant à l'orientation future du droit peuvent déclencher des réactions favorables de la part des États, influencer l'orientation de la pratique et de l'*opinio juris* dans le sens suggéré par la Commission et aboutir finalement à ce que son projet d'articles soit reconnu, lors d'une conférence de plénipotentiaires, comme reflétant la pratique qui s'est dégagée et l'opinion dans son ensemble. De cette manière la Commission peut jouer un rôle éminent dans la formation même des règles du droit international coutumier.

Ainsi, lorsque la Commission a abordé son travail sur le droit de la mer au début des années 1950, le plateau continental n'était pas encore doté d'un statut positif au regard de la coutume, la pratique des États en la matière étant toute récente, encore incomplète et discordante[82]. Pourtant, comme la Cour internationale de Justice l'a noté à deux reprises[83], au moment où la première Conférence des Nations Unies sur le droit de la mer s'est attachée en 1958 à élaborer une convention sur la base du projet d'articles préparé par la Commission sur le plateau continental, les États en étaient venus à considérer que les règles fondamentales de cette institution étaient établies ou sur le point de l'être et qu'elles étaient en outre traduites dans les dispositions pertinentes du projet de la Comission[84]. On a estimé aussi qu'un processus largement similaire de développement juridique avait eu lieu dans le cas du droit des traités, pour ce qui est des règles applicables aux réserves[85].

Comme la Cour l'a également affirmé[86], un tel processus juridique peut ne pas prendre fin avec l'élaboration et l'adoption d'une convention fondée sur le projet d'articles de la Commission. Ce n'est que si les États en viennent ultérieurement à accepter[87] une telle convention ou à y adapter leur pratique[88]

---

[81]*Jack Rankin* v. *The Islamic Republic of Iran* (voir la note précédente), par. 18. Une autre sentence arbitrale a dit que ce domaine était en voie de codification par la Commission du droit intemational : *Affaire concernant les problèmes nés entre la Nouvelle-Zélande et la France...* (voir *supra* note 62), par. 72.

[82]In the matter of an Arbitration between Petroleum *Development (Trucial Coast) Ltd and the Sheikh of Abu Dhabi*, sentence de septembre 1951, *International Law Reports*, vol. 18, p. 144, par. 5, e.

[83]*Plateau continental de la mer du Nord* (voir *supra* note 65), par. 63; *Plateau continental (Tunisie/Jamahiriya arabe libyenne)* [voir *supra* note 65], par. 41 et 42.

[84]Dans les affaires du *Plateau continental de la mer du Nord* (voir *supra* note 65), la Cour internationale de Justice a estimé que l'examen par la Commission de la question sur laquelle porte l'article 6 de la Convention sur le plateau continental avait contribué au développement du droit coutumier sur ce point : *loc. cit.* (*supra* note 78).

[85]C'est ainsi qu'au moment où la Commission commençait son travail sur le droit des traités les règles applicables aux réserves, longtemps considérées comme bien établies, étaient devenues, à la suite d'une évolution récente, très instables et très incertaines. Les travaux de la Commission ont été au cœur du développement de l'*opinio juris* des États en la matière et ont abouti à la cristallisation d'un nouveau régime juridique avec l'adoption à Vienne en 1969 de la Convention sur le droit des traités dont les dispositions relatives aux réserves se fondaient sur le projet d'articles adopté par la Commission en 1966. Voir *Arbitrage entre le Royaume-Uni de Grande-Bretagne et d'Irlande du Nord et la République française* (voir *supra* note 62), par. 38.

[86]*Plateau continental de la mer du Nord* (voir *supra* note 65), par. 71.

[87]Ibid., par 73.

[88]Ibid., par. 74 et 75.

que de nouvelles règles de droit coutumier peuvent finalement voir le jour, modelées sur celles qu'énonce l'instrument en question[89]. Dans un tel cas, c'est le travail de la Commission qui constitue l'agent, direct ou indirect, de la cristallisation du nouveau droit, en ce qu'il aiguillonne et stimule la formation de l'*opinio juris* des États et en ce qu'il précise et coordonne ses éléments.

Le fait que la Commission ait réussi à susciter et à maintenir un dialogue utile avec les États explique qu'elle soit partie prenante au processus de formation de la coutume sous tous ses aspects. Ce dialogue, que la Commission poursuit par l'intermédiaire de la Sixième Commission de l'Assemblée générale, grâce aux questionnaires qu'elle adresse individuellement à chaque État et grâce aux demandes d'observations sur ses projets[90] qu'elle leur envoie, mérite d'être porté à l'actif de la Commission[91].

IV

La contribution que la Commission a ainsi apportée au développement progressif et à la codification du droit international a été qualifiée de diverses manières : « unique et incomparable », « guère moins que prodigieuse », « distinguée et durable », « remarquable », « d'une importance exceptionnelle », « essentielle », « considérable », « appréciable », « positive ». On a affirmé que, si certaines des conventions de portée mondiale élaborées sur la base de projets d'articles de la Commission n'existaient pas, la conduite des relations internationales serait « inimaginable ». On a reconnu aussi la contribution remarquable et durable de la Commission à une meilleure connaissance du droit international et l'on a dit que ses rapports et documents constituaient une source d'inspiration d'une valeur inappréciable pour l'ensemble de la doctrine.

Compliments mis à part, la Commission a continué à s'efforcer de perfectionner ses procédures et méthodes de travail sous tous leurs aspects. À cette fin, elle a pris un certain nombre de mesures, finissant par adopter récemment un rapport important qui contient beaucoup de recommandations spécifiques visant à améliorer son utilité et son efficacité[92]. Elle a mis au point une procédure plus rigoureuse pour mieux choisir les nouveaux sujets à inscrire à son programme de travail[93]. Elle s'est montrée aussi plus ouverte à la diversité des formes que pourrait prendre son travail final, dans le cadre de son apport au processus juridique international, qu'il s'agisse de modèles de règles, de déclarations, de

---

[89]Dans les affaires du *Plateau continental de la mer du Nord* (voir *supra* note 65), la Cour a procédé à une étude détaillée du point de savoir si un tel processus s'était produit en ce qui concernait les règles énoncées à l'article 6 de la Convention de Genève de 1958 sur le plateau continental et a conclu que tel n'était pas le cas (ibid., par. 81).

[90]Voir Rapport. . . quarante-huitième session, p. 234, par. 171, et p. 237, par. 181. Pour avoir un aperçu de ce dialogue, se reporter à *La Commission du droit international et son œuvre, op. cit.* (voir *supra* note 9), p. 21 à 24.

[91]Ces dernières années, la Commission s'est efforcée d'intensifier encore ce dialogue. Voir en particulier le récent rapport de la Commission sur ses procédures et méthodes de travail qui contient un certain nombre de recommandations spécifiques à cet effet, Rapport. . . quarante-huitième session, p. 223, par. 149, *c* à *e*, et p. 238, par. 182. Noter aussi p. 237, par. 180, et p. 239, par. 185. L'Assemblée générale s'est intéressée également au renforcement du dialogue : voir *infra* le texte à la note 95.

[92]Rapport. . . quarante-huitième session, p. 221 à 260. L'Assemblée générale a pris note avec satisfaction de ce rapport dans sa résolution 51/160 du 16 décembre 1996 (par. 9).

[93]Pour un bref aperçu de cette procédure, voir Rapport. . . quarante-huitième session, p. 231 et 232, par. 165 et 166.

guides de la pratique, de commentaires, d'avis, etc.[94]. L'Assemblée générale pour sa part a prêté une grande attention aux modalités selon lesquelles elle examine le rapport de la Commission et a pris des mesures pour les améliorer en vue de fournir à cette dernière des directives plus efficaces[95].

Un effort concerté est donc fait actuellement en vue d'améliorer le fonctionnement de la Commission pour lui permettre de contribuer davantage encore au développement progressif et à la codification du droit international[96]. Cet effort procède de la conviction, partagée tant par les États que par la Commission, qu'« un processus ordonné de codification et de développement progressif continue de présenter un intérêt important »[97] et que la Commission pourra continuer à jouer un rôle considérable dans ce processus. Il y a donc tout lieu de supposer que la Commission du droit international restera ce qu'elle a été ces 50 dernières années : le principal organe établi par l'Assemblée générale dans le domaine du développement progressif et de la codification du droit international.

---

[94]Ainsi, sur la question des réserves aux traités, voir par exemple : Rapport. . . quarante-cinquième session, p. 245, par. 430; Rapport . . . quarante-septième session, p. 262 à 264, par. 435 à 437 et 439, p. 273, par. 471 à 474, et p. 276 et 277, par. 486 à 488 et par. 491, *b* et *c*; Rapport. . . quarante-huitième session, p. 209 et 210, par. 113. De même sur la question des conséquences de la succession d'États sur la nationalité des personnes physiques et morales, voir par exemple : Rapport . . . quarante-cinquième session, p. 261, par. 437 et 439; Rapport. . . quarante-septième session, p. 82, par. 169 et 170, et p. 87 et 88, par. 193; et Rapport. . . quarante-huitième session, p. 198, par. 81, et p. 201, par. 88, *b*. Plus généralement, voir ibid., p. 236, par. 178 *in fine*. Comparer avec la manière dont la Commission abordait la question par le passé, *Annuaire de la Commission du droit international, 1988*, vol. II (deuxième partie), p. 116, par. 561.

[95]Voir en particulier les résolutions suivantes de l'Assemblée générale : résolution 41/81 du 3 décembre 1986, troisième alinéa du préambule et paragraphe 5, *b,* du dispositif; résolution 42/156 du 7 décembre 1987, cinquième alinéa du préambule et paragraphes *5, b,* et 6 du dispositif; résolution 43/169 du 9 décembre 1988, paragraphes 7 et 8 du dispositif; résolution 44/35 du 4 décembre 1989, paragraphe 5 du dispositif; et résolution 50/45 du 11 décembre 1995, septième alinéa du préambule et paragraphe 10 du dispositif.

[96]Voir en ce sens la résolution 50/45 de l'Assemblée générale en date du 11 décembre 1995, paragraphe 9, *a,* du dispositif, et Rapport. . . quarante-huitième session, p. 226, par. 154.

[97]Rapport. . . quarante-huitième session, p. 222, par. 148, *b*. Voir aussi p. 232, par. 168, et p. 234, par. 171.

OPENING STATEMENT

by Mr Hennadiy Udovenko
President of the General Assembly

I am greatly honoured to have the opportunity to open this Colloquium devoted to the commemoration of the fiftieth anniversary of the establishment of the International Law Commission. It is a shining example of unity among international lawyers, who have gathered here from all regions of the world and who represent its full variety of cultures and legal systems.

The codification and progressive development of international law is hardly a new idea. Since the Middle Ages, individual scholars, academic institutions and Governments have made numerous attempts both to restate existing rules of international law and to formulate new norms to govern the relations between States. Some of the schemes which they have proposed may have been rather utopian in their character, but their role in developing and strengthening international law is undeniable. All have been inspired by the notion that written texts might remove the uncertainties which surround customary rules of international law, fill the gaps which exist in those rules and give more concrete meaning to abstract legal principles.

In 1945, the notion of the progressive development of international law and its codification was incorporated into the text of the Charter of the United Nations. The relevant provisions of the Charter might appear limited in their scope, but no one would now question their potential. Thus, upon the apparently rather slender foundation afforded by Article 13, Paragraph 1 (*a*), of the Charter, the General Assembly has fashioned a variety of highly effective law-making institutions and methods of work. There has also been a proliferation more broadly within the United Nations of bodies and procedures for the elaboration of treaties and other legal instruments, bearing witness to the determination of States to establish and strengthen the rule of law in world affairs. Together, these various institutions and mechanisms have been instrumental in bringing about one of the most important developments in international law during the last half-century: its progressive development and codification through the elaboration of written texts. In this process, no institution has played a greater role than the International Law Commission.

Today, the Commission is one of the Organization's principal arms for discharging its responsibility to promote international law as a fundamental instrument for the maintenance of international peace and security and the enhancement of cooperation among nations.

During the half-century of its existence, the Commission has produced over twenty sets of draft articles, setting forth basic rules in key areas of international law. Many of these sets of draft articles have, in turn, been transformed into major global conventions, establishing rules of international law in such important fields as diplomatic and consular intercourse and immunities, the law of treaties, special missions, relations between States and international organizations, the succession of States, the law of the sea and the non-navigational uses of international watercourses. Indeed, certain of these conventions—such as those dealing with diplomatic and consular privileges and immunities and the law governing the making, application and termination of treaties—may claim the distinction of being fundamental to the conduct of modern international relations: without them, international business would simply not be transacted in the way that it is today. Particularly commendable has been the Commission's work on the Draft Code of Crimes against the Peace and Security of Mankind and the Draft Statute for an International Criminal Court, as well as its ongoing work on the topic of State responsibility.

Of great significance, too, is the contribution which the Commission has made both to the stabilization and to the development of customary international law. Conventions which have been adopted on the basis of the Commission's draft articles have many times been cited by the International Court of Justice as authoritative evidence of the current state of customary law. This has sometimes occurred even before those conventions have entered into force. Moreover, the Commission's work has helped in a number of cases to contribute to the formation of new rules of customary law.

The Commission's achievements over the last fifty years, have been variously described as "unique", "distinguished and lasting" and of "exceptional importance". It is quite natural, then, that the General Assembly should have requested the Secretariat to organize this Colloquium in commemoration of the Commission's fiftieth anniversary.

While giving the Commission all due credit for its achievements, it would be extremely useful if the attention of this Colloquium were to be focused on identifying ways and means by which the Commission might more fully exploit its potential. At this time of reform and renewal within the United Nations, careful attention should be given to improving the functioning of the Commission and increasing its effectiveness. To this end, the General Assembly has in recent years requested the Commission to review its working-procedures and to report the results to the Assembly. It is anticipated that this Colloquium will make a contribution to this review-process by identifying practical steps which may be taken to strengthen the International Law Commission and to enable it to continue to play the central role in the international law-making process.

The work and deliberations of experts in international law has always served as an important source of inspiration to the Commission in its work. Accordingly, I am delighted to welcome you to this Colloquium and to wish you a full and fruitful discussion.

IDEAS AND SUGGESTIONS
for strengthening the International Law Commission and enhancing its capability to contribute to the progressive development and codification of international law

This paper brings together in one place and presents in summary form the ideas and suggestions for strengthening the International Law Commission and enhancing its capability to contribute to the progressive development and codification of international law which are contained in the papers which were specially prepared for the Colloquium by invited experts.

Ideas are presented under headings corresponding to the six topics which were considered by the Colloquium. Where, as is frequently the case, an idea is relevant to more than one of those topics, that idea is reproduced solely under that topic to which its relevance is most direct and immediate.

This paper is intended to reflect only the views of the authors whose papers it summarizes. The ideas which it contains are not to be attributed to any other party.

*

1. An overview of the international law-making process and the role of the International Law Commission

Proposals listed under this topic are directed towards identifying and delimiting the role which the Commission should play within the overall international law-making process

Certain proposals foresee a role for the Commission in helping to guide the international law-making process

The Commission should advise and make recommendations on initiatives which should be taken within the international law-making process as a whole, conducting reviews of international law and relations with a view to identifying areas in which rules might advantageously be elaborated, whether by the Commission itself or by some other international law-making body. In particular:

1   it should, on an ongoing basis, review current trends in international relations in order to identify spheres in which rules might advantageously be elaborated ahead of practice—that is, before any significant body of practice in that sphere has yet had a chance to develop;

2   it should periodically review the doctrine of international law and the work of scientific bodies and institutions which are active in the field with a view to identifying new topics which might be suitable for codification or progressive development;

3   it should periodically review the resolutions of international organizations with a view to identifying emerging customary rules which might in time call for codification;

| 4 | it should examine those domains which have acquired new dimensions during the last few decades—such as the topics of international cooperation, the suppression of terrorism, the international solidarity of peoples, international sanctions and the territorial integrity of States—with a view to examining whether or not the law in those domains is "ripe" for codification or progressive development; |
| 5 | it should, on an ongoing basis, review the existing multilateral treaty system and current and projected multilateral treaty-making initiatives with a view to identifying *lacunae* within that system which need to be filled on a priority basis. |

6   The Commission should provide information and advice which might be of help in coordinating and harmonizing the work of the various agencies which are involved in the international law-making process. In particular, it should establish a standing working group charged with gathering information and material on all current and projected multilateral treaty-making initiatives and drawing the attention of those concerned in such initiatives to related and relevant initiatives which are being undertaken by others, as well as providing them with related advice, with a view to avoiding any needless replication of effort and ensuring that the provisions of the drafts on which they are working, or are to work, are properly harmonized and form an integrated whole.

7   The Commission should establish the substantive basis for the work of all international law-making bodies. Specifically, it should undertake a systematic and comprehensive examination of the basic or guiding principles of international law in *all* its fields, identifying them, refining their meaning and producing commentaries on them, with the aim of producing something along the lines of a Restatement of international law. These principles might have the character either of codification or of progressive development and might relate to new or specialized fields, just as much as to the classic domains of international law. The task of drafting rules which apply these principles to the specific issues which arise in a given field should be left to other, specialist or regional, bodies.

*

Certain proposals envisage a role for the Commission in helping to ensure the greater effectiveness of the output of the international law-making process

8   The Commission should be attributed a function whereby it might be requested to give legal advice on the drafting of legislative instruments, including treaties, which are being drawn up by or within other law-making bodies.

The Commission should undertake work towards ensuring the primacy of international law in international relations. In particular, it should:

9	make a study of the concept, its meaning and its normative corollaries;
10	elaborate draft articles on the enforcement of international law, possibly combining the codification of existing rules in this sphere with its own proposals *de lege ferenda*;
11	set up a standing working group to gather material and to conduct studies on the implementation of, compliance with and effective-

ness of international law in all its fields, as well as to evaluate the impact of that law on the quality of life of individual human beings, with a view to recommending means of improving implementation of and increasing compliance with international law, as well as enhancing its positive impact on individuals' lives.

*

Certain proposals aim to delimit in broad strategic terms the sphere within which the Commission is itself to play a direct role in the process of international law-making

In so far as the elaboration of draft articles or rules are concerned, the Commission should limit its activity to those topics which:

12   raise fundamental questions of international law (whether involving the codification of existing law or the development of rules *de lege ferenda*), avoiding those topics which would require the elaboration of technical norms;

13   are of general application or relevance, avoiding particular specialized branches of international law;

In delimiting the sphere of the Commission's activity, it should be recognized that the Commission is a suitable body to deal with:

14   topics which involve the formulation of rules of private, rather than of public, international law;

15   topics involving the elaboration of technical norms, if and in so far as those topics give rise to serious legal problems which have not been satisfactorily addressed by any other international law-making body;

16   areas of international law in which State practice is not yet extensive or fully developed, it being possible that, by employing its rigorous methodology for identifying State practice and determining its legal implications, the Commission might be able usefully to identify emerging trends in legal opinion and practice which are likely to shape the legal regime which will finally emerge;

17   fields in which States are wary of legal regulation, for the same reason;

18   matters on which State practice has only very recently started to develop and is therefore still sparse, since the Commission might none the less usefully undertake the drafting of rules when the trend of what State practice there is clearly favours a particular solution— as, for example, in respect of the issues of human cloning and genetic manipulation;

19   those fields in which the practice of States is of a so-called "soft" law nature, it being possible for the Commission usefully to identify those aspects of that practice which are of legal value;

20   those fields in which practice is developing through the medium of large numbers of bilateral and plurilateral treaties, such as the law of trade and investments, it being possible for the Commission usefully to identify the general legal trends emerging from those treaties.

Certain proposals envisage the development for the Commission of roles which are related only indirectly to the international law-making process

21   The Organization's decision-making bodies, and perhaps the Secretary-General, should make use of the Commission to obtain legal advice on problems arising out of the Organization's activities or which otherwise involve the interpretation and application of the law of the United Nations.

22   The Commission should act, on the request of interested parties, including private persons and entities, as a certifying authority on points of international law, in the same way that foreign ministries issue certificates on points of international law for use in domestic litigation.

2. Major complexities in contemporary international law-making

Proposals listed under this topic are directed towards identifying means of overcoming or avoiding problems which impair the operation of the international law-making process and limit its effectiveness, specifically that part of the process in which the Commission plays a role and which involves the preparation of texts with a view to their adoption and operation as multilateral conventions

Certain proposals envisage the undertaking of reviews of the international law-making process, or certain aspects of it, with a view to identifying possible improvements

23   The Commission should establish a standing working group to review adherence to, implementation of, compliance with and the effectiveness of global multilateral treaties, with a view to recommending necessary or appropriate adjustments to the multilateral treaty-making process.

24   The Commission should make a study of the economics of plenipotentiary conferences with a view to evaluating their efficiency as mechanisms for the elaboration and adoption of multilateral conventions.

Certain proposals envisage specific improvements to the procedures which are employed for making international law

25   In order to assist developing States which currently encounter difficulties in preparing and submitting responses to the Commission's questionnaires or requests for comments, a task force might be formed, composed of doctoral students and young teachers of international law, who would first participate in a "moot" or "model" session of the Commission addressing the topic which is the subject of the Commission's questionnaire or request and who would then go on to be available to give assistance to such States on request.

26   Technical assistance and financial support should be made available to those States which need them and which wish to take part in negotiations for the adoption of a convention in order that they might participate effectively in those negotiations.

27   Technical assistance should be available to those States which need it and which are considering adhering to conventions which have been elaborated on the basis of the Commission's drafts in order that they might better identify the implications of adherence.

*

One proposal envisages measures which should be taken in relation to the texts of conventions which are the final output of the international law-making process with a view to enhancing their acceptability

28   The texts of conventions elaborated on the basis of the Commission's drafts should embody only those rules on which it is possible to achieve consensus, those rules with regard to which this is not possible being embodied separately in one or more optional protocols.

*

Certain proposals envisage steps which might be taken in respect of texts which have already been adopted with a view to improving their acceptability

29   The General Assembly should conduct a review of the conventions which have been adopted on the basis of the Commission's drafts, assessing their current status, identifying the factors which have contributed to the failure of States to adhere to them and exploring concrete measures to increase participation in them, particularly in the case of those treaties which are yet to enter into force or which exhibit a low level of adherence.

30   The Commission should consider the possibility of suggesting revisions to the law in areas in which it has already produced drafts.

31   The Commission should consider resuming consideration of certain of the sets of drafts articles which it has adopted but which have not yet been transformed into conventions and, if appropriate, should undertake their redrafting with a view to facilitating their eventual adoption as conventions.

* * *

3. Selection of topics for codification and progressive development by the Commission and its working-methods

Proposals appearing under this topic are directed towards either (i) specifically identifying the topics which should (and those topics which should not) be included in the Commission's programme of work or (ii) enhancing the efficiency and efficacy of the Commission by adjusting or reforming its constitution, procedures or methods of work

(i) Topics

Certain proposals are directed to identifying the procedures which should be used to identify topics for inclusion in the Commission's programme of work

32   The third world peace conference of 1999 should suggest topics to the General Assembly for inclusion in the Commission's programme of work.

33   The Commission should make known to international scientific institutions, such as the International Law Association, topics which it intends

35

to consider for possible inclusion in its programme of work, in order that such institutions might set up international committees or working groups to study those topics. The Commission would then be in a position to make use of those studies when it came to consider whether or not to recommend those topics for inclusion in its programme.

34   The Secretariat should prepare a new survey of international law, along the lines of the earlier surveys of 1949 and 1971, in order to assist the Commission in identifying new topics which it might propose to General Assembly for inclusion in its programme of work.

*

Certain proposals suggest criteria which should be employed, or considerations which should be taken into account, in helping to identify, within the broad fields within which the Commission is to operate, those particular topics which should be included in the Commission's programme of work

In assessing the suitability of a topic for inclusion in the Commission's programme of work, the following criteria should be employed:

35   the formulation of legal rules on the topic should meet a pressing need which is experienced by the vast majority of States;

36   the topic should not be one which is politically sensitive or over-charged with political considerations and which is likely to give rise to irreconcilable differences between States or between the members of the Commission (such topics being preferably left to be tackled by bodies which are composed of States' representatives).

In determining whether a topic which is suitable for inclusion in the Commission's programme of work should indeed be inserted in that programme:

37   priority should be given to selecting topics whose better legal regulation would help to advance the central function of international law—the protection of human beings—and would meet the needs of people, rather than simply satisfying the interests of States;

38   priority should be given to topics whose nature is such that the Commission may complete work on them within a single quinquennium, in order that the Commission might be better placed to respond in a prompt and timely fashion to emerging needs of the international community for rapid legal regulation;

39   priority should be given to selecting topics which involve the progressive development of international law, rather than its codification.

*

Certain proposals envisage the inclusion of certain specific topics in the Commission's programme of work

The Commission should undertake the elaboration of draft articles on:

40   the rights and duties of aliens;

41   human rights safeguards in the extradition process;

42   foreign investment;

43   trade and investments;

36

44	the elimination of corruption in international commercial transactions;
45	mass exoduses of people under threat of death;
46	the global commons;
47	human cloning and genetic manipulation.
48	The Commission should conduct a study of the inter-relationships of different bodies of law and the relative weights to be attached to them when those bodies interact with each other or suggest different conclusions to a particular legal problem.

* * *

(ii) Working-methods

Certain proposals envisage steps which should be taken with regard to the Commission's membership

In order to safeguard the general intellectual quality of the membership of the Commission and reduce the pernicious effects which the increasing politicization of elections to the Commission has on the readiness of States to pay due regard to this factor in nominating and electing its members:

| 49 | a certain number of members of the Commission should be appointed by learned societies or scientific institutions, rather than being elected by the General Assembly; |
| 50 | candidates nominated by governments for election by the General Assembly should require clearance by learned societies or scientific institutions, or by some other similar mechanism, before they are eligible for election. |

In order to enhance the composition of the Commission's membership and so contribute to its ability to function in a more effective fashion:

51	each member of the Commission should agree to limit the duration of her or his membership in such a way that there should not be a national of the same State in the Commission for more than two successive full terms, thereby helping to ensure the broadest possible participation over time in the work of the Commission, and so in the international law-making process;
52	steps should be taken to ensure that, at the next round of elections to the Commission, a substantial number of women—11 or 12, say—are elected, as a first step towards ensuring the direct and balanced input into the Commission's work of the values and ideas of the world's women as well as its men;
53	one or more members should be elected to the Commission who possess advanced qualifications in the field of sociology or legal anthropology, in order that there might be an input into the Commission's work which is specifically oriented towards enhancing the acceptability of its output and improving its implementation;
54	a number of specialists in the field of private international law should be elected to the Commission, in order that it might gain a different, useful and highly relevant perspective on many of the topics on its agenda;

55 representatives of international organizations, of the business community, of non-governmental organizations and of other such like bodies should be members of the Commission.

In order to protect the independence of the members of the Commission, particularly their independence from the Governments of the States whose nationality they bear:

56 members of the Commission should be required to take an oath that they will serve in an impartial and independent manner and not seek or receive instructions from any Government;

57 during the consideration of the Commission's report within the Sixth Committee, members of the Commission who hold posts within the Governments of States should not sit as part, or otherwise conduct themselves as members, of those States' delegations;

58 the Commission's reports to the General Assembly, likewise the *Yearbooks of the International Law Commission*, should not attribute interventions in the Commission's debates to named individuals or otherwise so reproduce those debates as to make it possible for States to identify which particular members were supportive of which positions or points of view.

Steps should be taken to address the problem of inadequate attendance by a significant proportion of the Commission's membership. In particular:

59 States should nominate for membership in the Commission, and should vote for, only those individuals who are demonstrably able and willing to attend most of its meetings and to participate actively and meaningfully in its work;

60 members of the Commission should take an oath that their attendance will be full and their participation active;

61 records of attendance at the Commission's meetings should be published;

62 members should be barred from re-election if they have attended less than 50 per cent of the Commission's meetings;

63 members who have attended less than 50 per cent of the Commission's meetings on a given topic should be barred from voting on that topic.

64 Steps should be taken with a view to members of the Commission who are nationals of developing States, and nationals of the States of sub-Saharan Africa in particular, playing a more active and influential role within the Commission, including filling, on a proportionate basis, the roles of Chairman and Special Rapporteur.

*

Certain proposals envisage measures for improving the planning and organization of the Commission's work

65 The Commission should do away completely with its long-term programme of work and, at the beginning of each quinquennium, should set itself a five-year plan which should envisage the completion of work on the topics in that plan by the quinquennium's end.

66   The Commission should so organize its plan of work that it considers
      only two or three topics each year, rather than considering annually all
      of the topics which appear in its current programme of work.

67   The Commission should at the beginning of each session set itself a
      time-table for the work it should complete at that session.

*

*Certain proposals aim to delimit the role of the Special Rapporteur or envisage
steps which should be taken in order that Special Rapporteurs might better
discharge their role*

68   Where it is important that work on a topic be completed quickly, use
      should be made of working groups, working either together with a
      Special Rapporteur or, alternatively, alone and without a Special Rap-
      porteur being appointed at all for that topic.

      Measures should be taken towards ensuring that Special Rapporteurs
      receive a greater degree of guidance from the Commission on the
      direction which their work should take. In particular:

69   in order that Special Rapporteurs might receive advice on the
      approach which they should adopt to a topic or to issues arising in
      connection with it, the Commission should appoint a consultative
      group, made up of certain of its members, to work with each Special
      Rapporteur and to be available for consultation by her or him
      between the Commission's sessions, whether by correspondence,
      via the Internet or at actual meetings;

70   in order to assist them in their work, Special Rapporteurs should,
      when appropriate, initiate inter-sessional consultations or discus-
      sions with members of the Commission, either by correspondence,
      via the Internet or, if necessary, by means of video-conferencing.

71   Special Rapporteurs should serve on a full-time basis in order that they
      might be able to devote a greater part of their time and attention to careful
      discharge of the heavy burdens of their office.

      Special Rapporteurs should receive a greater degree of assistance in
      doing their work. In particular:

72   two Special Rapporteurs should be appointed for each topic, rather
      than one—a measure which might also help to limit the negative
      impact on the Commission's work on a topic of the premature
      departure of a Special Rapporteur;

73   procedures should be developed whereby Special Rapporteurs
      might be able to receive more tangible forms of support from other
      members of the Commission;

74   the staffing of the Codification Division of the Office of Legal
      Affairs of the Secretariat of the United Nations should be increased
      so that it might provide full research assistance to Special Rap-
      porteurs on a regular basis.

75   Steps should be taken by Special Rapporteurs to ensure that the Com-
      mission is in a position to give meaningful consideration to their reports.
      In particular, Special Rapporteurs should ensure that the reports which
      they submit are substantial in nature, containing full commentaries on
      any draft articles which they propose, so that members of the Commis-

sion can know from the outset the direction which work on the topic is to take, as well as the principal issues arising.

*

Certain proposals are directed towards improving the effectiveness of the Commission's debates

Steps should be taken towards ensuring that the Commission's debates are more effectively focused on advancing work on those aspects of each topic which actually need the Commission's attention. In particular:

76   in order to maximize the time which is actually available at the Commission's sessions for undertaking work on more difficult and less tractable matters, Special Rapporteurs should initiate inter-sessional consultations or discussions with members of the Commission on specific issues with a view to advancing work on, and even settling, as many issues as possible in advance of the Commission's formal sessions;

77   members of the Commission should aim to limit their interventions to five minutes at the maximum.

*

Certain proposals relate to the decision-making processes and procedures which the Commission should use

The Commission should ensure that consensus is allocated an appropriate role in its decision making. Specifically:

78   every effort should be made to secure consensus within the Commission on every point or issue—though it should be accepted that there are limits to how far this should be done;

79   consensus should be pursued, but not at all costs, particularly when its pursuit is likely to cause substantial delays or to result in the production of vacuous drafts.

In order to help resolve controversial issues which arise within the Commission:

80   greater use should be made of working groups;

81   the Drafting Committee should not be used, if the issue is one of substance.

82   In order to expedite the Commission's work, points on which agreement has been reached or which have otherwise been settled or resolved should be regarded as closed and discussion of them not be reopened.

* * *

4. The Commission's work and the shaping of international la

Proposals appearing under this topic are directed towards identifying the means, the type of instrument or the form of output which should optimally be used to shape international law on those topics on which the Commission may work

One proposal relates to the procedures which should be employed in order to identify the form of output

83   The Commission should not be overly concerned with the views of States as to the form which its final output on a given topic should take. Rather, it should concern itself with the quality of its output and leave it to States to determine the form which should be given to it.

*

One proposal is directed towards prescribing the forms which the Commission's output should take

84   While multilateral conventions should remain the principal end result of the Commission's work, the Commission should further develop its recent trend towards modulating the nature of its output and should explore the possibilities offered by other options, besides that of draft articles prepared with a view to embodiment in a treaty.

*

Certain proposals suggest specific forms which the Commission's output might take, other than that of draft articles for eventual embodiment in a convention

The forms which the Commission's output might take include:

85   draft framework conventions;

86   model treaties;

87   model rules;

88   model laws for adoption at the national level;

89   declarations of principles;

90   restatements of the law;

91   codes of conduct;

92   guidelines;

93   handbooks to assist States in applying the law.

* * *

5.   Enhancing the Commission's relationship with other law-making bodies and relevant academic and professional institutions

Proposals on this topic are directed towards prescribing the relationships which the Commission should establish, maintain and develop with other entities and persons

Certain proposals are directed to improving States' input into the Commission's work

94   With a view to ensuring that the draft articles which it prepares meet the needs and reflect the interests of individual human beings, the Commission should encourage foreign offices, in preparing their responses to its requests for comments on those draft articles, to take steps to facilitate and encourage input from scientific bodies, universities, professional bodies, interest groups, chambers of commerce, corporations and individual citizens.

95   In order to assist governments in preparing their comments on draft articles prepared by the Commission, international scientific institutions, such as the International Law Association, should organize regional seminars on topics on which the Commission is working.

Certain proposals are directed towards enhancing the guidance which the Sixth Committee gives to the Commission

96 The Sixth Committee should play a more assertive, active and dynamic role in guiding or directing the Commission's work. In particular, it should give prompter, clearer and more specific guidance to the Commission regarding the direction in which its work on a topic should proceed, the format which the output of its work should take and even the broad substance of the legal regime which it is desired that it should elaborate, particularly in fields in which State practice is not extensive or in which the Commission's work will partake heavily of the nature of progressive development.

97 The Sixth Committee should make changes to the way in which it considers the Commission's report so as to enable it to provide the Commission with better guidance. In particular, interventions in the Sixth Committee's debate should be concise and to the point in order to allow as many representatives as possible to participate, particularly representatives of States which have not responded to any request which the Commission may have made for comments on draft articles which it has adopted.

The Commission itself should take concrete steps towards securing better guidance from the Sixth Committee. In particular:

98 the Commission should seek policy guidelines from the Sixth Committee on particular issues that divide the Commission;

99 in order to help prevent the debate within the Sixth Committee from simply replicating the debate within the Commission, the Commission's reports should be made less detailed and should not rehearse in detail the discussions which took place within the Commission.

*

Certain proposals aim at strengthening and developing the Commission's relationships with regional intergovernmental organizations or bodies

100 Regional intergovernmental organizations which are active in the field of international law-making should submit brief written reports on their work, together with relevant documents, for circulation in advance of the Commission's sessions, in order that the Commission might better familiarize itself with the many important developments in international law which are occurring nowadays at the regional level.

101 Joint informal working groups and informal meetings should be organized between the members of the Commission and representatives of those regional intergovernmental organizations which are active in the field of international law-making in order to discuss points of common interest.

*

Certain proposals envisage the development of working relationships between the Commission and organizations or bodies which are not intergovernmental in nature

In order to guide the establishment and conduct of relations with such bodies:

| 102 | the Commission should establish a permanent subsidiary organ in order to provide it with pertinent advice, including recommendations as to the criteria which should be adopted for determining those bodies with which relations should be established; |

| 103 | the Commission should be guided by the objective announced in the Secretary-General's Report *Renewing the United Nations: a Programme for Reform* (document A/51/950) that "all United Nations entities [should] be open to and work closely with civil society organizations that are active in their respective sectors" and that "increased consultation and cooperation between the United Nations and such organizations" should be facilitated; |

| 104 | due attention should be paid in selecting those bodies to the importance of ensuring equitable geographical representation, it being important to exercise care not to reinforce any Western bias in the Commission's work. |

The Commission should develop regular working relationships with:

| 105 | international non-governmental organizations which are active in the international legal field; |

| 106 | international scientific societies which are active in the field of international law, such as the Institut de Droit International and the International Law Association; |

| 107 | international associations of legal practitioners, such as the International Bar Association and LAWASIA; |

| 108 | appropriate governmental and non-governmental organizations, learned societies, research institutes and universities at the *national* level; |

| 109 | national law reform bodies. |

The relationships established with such organizations and bodies should enable them to make an effective input into the Commission's work. In particular:

| 110 | those relationships should be such as to facilitate consultation with those bodies and organizations, as well as, in applicable cases, with their members, and to make it easier for them to provide the Commission with their views on the Commission's work; |

| 111 | the organizations and bodies with which relationships are established should set up permanent committees or working groups in order to enable them better to conduct consultations with the Commission and forward their views to it on a regular basis; |

| 112 | joint informal working groups, comprising representatives of such organizations or bodies and members of the Commission, should be set up to consider particular legal problems arising out of the Commission's work. |

*

Certain proposals are directed towards the Commission securing assistance or obtaining views from individual experts and other informed persons

| 113 | Representatives of international organizations, of the business community, of non-governmental organizations and of other such like bodies should be appointed to serve on the Commission as ad hoc members in |

order to provide it with expert assistance during the discussion of particular topics or subjects.

114   The Commission should employ consultants on a part-time basis—from international financial institutions, businesses, universities and other such like bodies—in order to secure expert assistance on technical matters, as well as to gain an outside perspective on the topics with which it is dealing and even to facilitate negotiations within the Commission on those topics.

115   In order that it might be provided with a representative range of views on particular issues, the Commission should seek detailed opinions from outside academic experts. Once these opinions are received, workshops or discussion groups should be held, attended by the academics concerned, the relevant Special Rapporteur and other members of the Commission, in order to debate and explore those issues.

116   The Commission should convene in places other than Geneva in order to meet with and to consult official and unofficial bodies in the host State, legislators, public officials, members of opposition parties and representatives of the private sector. The expenses of holding such meetings outside Geneva might be met by the State concerned, by other States or by private sources.

117   Conferences or colloquia should be organized, either by the Commission or by institutions and bodies which are active in the field of international law, bringing together experts to consider and discuss topics on which the Commission is working, or particular controversial aspects of those topics, so as to help focus thinking in the international legal community and to provide the Commission with views, ideas, guidance and feedback.

118   "Moot" or "model" sessions of the Commission should be organized at the international level for doctoral students and junior lecturers in international law. These sessions would consider the report of a particular Special Rapporteur in advance of its submission to the Commission and generate ideas for the Commission's consideration when it subsequently examines that report.

119   The Commission should make use of the Internet in order to solicit views on work in progress and to seek information from international and national bodies, groups and individuals.

120   The legal profession should consider how it might profitably contribute to the Commission's work and, particularly, how best to exploit—and to suggest to the Commission that it exploit—the possibilities which are afforded by Article 26 (1) of the Commission's Statute.

*

Certain proposals foresee outside bodies providing the Commission with substantive assistance in the form of research

121   The Commission might usefully "farm out" some of its research work, commissioning research from outside bodies, research institutes, universities and scientific bodies such as the Institut de Droit International and the International Law Association.

In order to oversee and coordinate research which is conducted for the Commission, whether by the Secretariat or by outside bodies or persons:

122	the Commission should have a director of research, on the model of that of the International Law Association;
123	the staffing of the Codification Division of the Office of Legal Affairs of the Secretariat of the United Nations should be increased.
124	The possibilities should be explored of obtaining funding from research councils and other funding bodies for the research which is carried out by or for the Commission, including adjusting the nature or parameters of that research so that, as well as meeting the needs of the Commission, it also meets the research needs of those bodies and accords with their agendas and priorities.

* * *

6. Making international law more relevant and readily available

Proposals on this topic are directed towards increasing awareness of international law and promoting its research

Certain proposals envisage a role for the Commission in promoting a greater awareness of international law in general

125	In order to help make international law more accessible to, and improve understanding of it among, national legal practitioners, the Commission should prepare a guide to international law and its sources.
126	With a view to facilitating the better incorporation of international law into national legal systems and its more effective application within those systems, seminars, led by members of the Commission, should be organized in order increase awareness of international law among judges of national courts and tribunals and lawyers whose practice is principally in the field of domestic law.
127	In order to promote greater awareness of international law among present and potential makers of foreign policy and advisers on foreign affairs, an annual seminar, along the lines of the International Law Seminar, should be organized which would be specifically tailored to that audience and which would be open to political scientists and graduates in international relations, as well as to lawyers.

In order to increase awareness of public international law among members of the general public:

128	the Commission should oversee or assist in the production of a textbook of international law for use in secondary, or high, schools;
129	the Commission should support the educational activities of national and international professional associations, such as the African Society of International Law.

*

Certain proposals envisage steps which might be taken to increase awareness specifically of the Commission and its work

130	The Commission should consider how best to take advantage of the information technology revolution in order to help educate the public and the wider legal profession regarding its work.
131	In order to ensure wider awareness of the Commission and its work among decision makers, a pamphlet or brochure should be produced,

giving an at-a-glance overview of the Commission and its work, past, present and future.

132 To improve awareness of the Commission and its work among law students and students of international relations, "moot" or "model" sessions of the Commission should be organized at the national and international levels.

In order to improve awareness of the Commission's work among those who are involved in the researching and teaching of international law:

133 universities and academic institutions should be encouraged to sponsor programmes as part of which members of the Commission would visit those institutions in order to hold seminars on their work (and *vice versa*);

134 international scientific institutions, such as the International Law Association, should organize seminars at a regional level on topics on which the Commission is currently conducting work;

135 arrangements should be put in place whereby individuals from the university sector might undertake internships with the Commission.

136 Measures should be taken to assist lawyers whose practice is in the field of domestic law to gain a greater awareness of the relevance and value to them of the Commission's work.

*

Certain proposals envisage steps which might be taken to facilitate or encourage research of the Commission and its work

137 A bibliographical library should be created and kept up to date, consisting of a bibliography of writings on the Commission and on the topics on which it has completed work or on which it is currently working.

138 In order to enhance the availability of hard copies of documents relating to the Commission's work, selected research centres and universities should be designated to act as International Law Commission libraries, serving, in addition to existing United Nations depositary libraries, as depositaries for the Commission's documents. These centres and universities should also serve as conduits for the transmission of the Commission's documents to interested persons and bodies in the State or region in which they are located.

139 In order to make it possible more easily to follow the Commission's work, an *International Law Commission Newsletter* should be produced two times per year, once early in the year, outlining the programme of work for the forthcoming session of the Commission, and once later in the year, giving a brief review of the work which was completed at that session. The second of these annual issues might be drafted by someone who is already responsible for writing a survey of the Commission's work for one of the major international law journals or yearbooks.

140 To stimulate interest in the Commission's work among students and young researchers, there should be an International Law Commission Prize, awarded by the Commission for research on or relating to the Commission and its work.

Certain proposals foresee steps which the Commission might take towards enriching the literature of international law

141 The Commission should oversee the establishment on the World Wide Web of a comprehensive data-base of international law.

142 In order to facilitate the teaching of international law in developing States at the university level, the Commission should organize or oversee the production of an inexpensive compilation of international law cases and materials which would make coherent reference to governmental and judicial practice from all legal systems of the world and which would reflect and help to promote a truly global perspective on the subject.

In order to ensure more detailed knowledge of the various practices of States and with a view to promoting the eventual harmonization of those practices, the Commission should encourage:

143 the establishment of international networks of universities, grouping together universities from States whose practices are divergent, which might undertake truly international research, leading to publications, on topics proposed by the Commission;

144 the organization of regional colloquia on those topics, following a standard programme elaborated by the Commission and leading to publications of their proceedings;

145 the publication by States of systematic digests, along the lines of the American Law Institute's *Restatement of the Foreign Relations Law of the United States*, setting forth the rules of international law as those States understand and interpret them. These national digests might in turn ultimately serve as the basis of a truly global restatement of international law, prepared by the Commission itself.

With a view to advancing research and enriching the doctrine of international law:

146 the Commission should prepare a list of subjects in the international legal field which merit further research;

147 each member of the Commission should, on taking office, assume responsibility for completion, by the end of the quinquennium, of a study on a topic assigned to him or her by the Commission's Planning Group as meriting in-depth research. These studies, which would not be attributable to the Commission, would be published in the *United Nations Juridical Yearbook*.

IDÉES ET SUGGESTIONS
visant à renforcer la Commission du droit international
et à accroître sa capacité
de développement progressif et de codification
du droit international

Le présent document rassemble en une forme sommaire les idées et suggestions visant à renforcer la Commission du droit international et à accroître sa capacité de développement progressif et de codification du droit international qui sont incluses dans les communications spécialement préparées pour le Colloque par les experts invités.

Les idées sont regroupées dans ce document sous des rubriques correspondant aux six thèmes du Colloque. Lorsque, comme c'est souvent le cas, une proposition en concerne plusieurs, il a été décidé de la présenter sous une seule rubrique, celle avec laquelle elle est le plus directement en rapport.

Ce document ne reflète que les vues des auteurs des communications qui y sont résumées. Les idées y incluses ne devraient pas être attribuées à aucune autre source.

*

1. Vue d'ensemble de l'élaboration du droit international et du rôle de la Commission du droit international

Les propositions regroupées sous cette rubrique visent à définir et cerner le rôle que la Commission devrait jouer dans le processus d'édification du droit international

Selon certaines propositions, la Commission devrait contribuer à orienter le processus d'édification du droit international

La Commission devrait donner son avis et formuler des recommandations sur les initiatives qui s'inscrivent dans le processus d'édification du droit international, en étudiant le droit international et les relations internationales en vue de cerner les domaines pour lesquels il serait opportun que la Commission elle-même ou un autre organe normatif international élabore une réglementation. En particulier, la Commission devrait :

1   Examiner régulièrement les tendances actuelles des relations internationales afin de repérer les domaines dans lesquels il serait opportun d'élaborer des règles avant que la pratique ne se développe largement;

2   Examiner périodiquement la doctrine et les travaux des organes et institutions spécialisés dans le domaine du droit international afin de délimiter de nouveaux sujets qui pourraient se prêter à un travail de codification ou de développement progressif;

3	Examiner périodiquement les résolutions des organisations internationales afin de repérer les nouvelles règles coutumières qui pourraient, à terme, nécessiter une codification;
4	Étudier les sujets qui ont acquis de l'importance au cours des dernières décennies, tels que la coopération internationale, la lutte contre le terrorisme, la solidarité entre les nations, les sanctions internationales et l'intégrité territoriale des États, en vue de déterminer si le moment est venu de codifier ou d'assurer un développement progressif;
5	Réexaminer régulièrement le système des traités multilatéraux et les initiatives prises ou envisagées dans ce domaine afin d'isoler les lacunes auxquelles il conviendrait de remédier au plus tôt.
6	La Commission devrait fournir les renseignements et formuler les recommandations qui permettraient de mieux coordonner et harmoniser les travaux des divers organismes qui concourent à l'élaboration du droit international. En particulier, la Commission devrait créer un groupe de travail permanent chargé : de recueillir des informations et de rassembler de la documentation sur les travaux actuels ou futurs d'élaboration de traités multilatéraux ou en cours; d'appeler l'attention des responsables sur les autres initiatives connexes ou qui pourraient les intéresser; de leur communiquer les informations voulues pour éviter tout chevauchement et faire que les dispositions sur lesquelles ils travaillent ou travailleront soient harmonisées et cohérentes.
7	La Commission devrait poser les fondements théoriques des travaux des organes normatifs internationaux. En particulier, la Commission devrait entreprendre l'examen complet et systématique des principes directeurs du droit international dans tous les domaines, les expliciter, en préciser la signification et les commenter en vue de redéfinir en quelque sorte le droit international. Ces principes pourraient relever soit de la codification soit du développement progressif et toucher tant à des domaines nouveaux ou spécialisés qu'aux domaines traditionnels du droit international. L'élaboration des règles d'application de ces principes à des situations particulières apparaissant dans certains domaines devrait incomber à d'autres organes, soit spécialisés soit régionaux.

*

Selon certaines propositions, la Commission devrait concourir à rendre plus efficace le travail d'élaboration du droit international

8	La Commission devrait recevoir les compétences nécessaires pour donner son avis sur certaines instruments juridiques tels que les traités élaborés par d'autres organes normatifs.

La Commission devrait s'employer à assurer la primauté du droit international dans les relations internationales. En particulier, elle devrait :

9	Étudier la notion même de droit international, sa signification et ses incidences sur le plan normatif;
10	Élaborer des projets d'articles sur l'application du droit international, en associant éventuellement la codification des règles existant dans ce domaine avec ses propres propositions *de lege ferenda*;
11	Créer un groupe de travail permanent chargé de rassembler de la documentation et d'effectuer des études sur l'application, le respect

et l'efficacité du droit international dans tous les domaines et d'évaluer l'impact du droit sur la qualité de la vie, en vue de recommander les moyens d'améliorer l'application et de renforcer le respect du droit international tout en renforçant ses effets positifs sur la vie quotidienne.

*

Certaines propositions concernent les domaines dans lesquels la Commission devrait participer directement au processus d'édification du droit international

Pour ce qui est de l'élaboration de projets d'articles ou de règles, la Commission devrait se borner aux sujets :

12   Qui soulèvent des questions fondamentales (qu'il s'agisse de codifier les règles existantes ou de développer des règles *de lege ferenda*); la Commission devrait éviter les sujets qui nécessitent l'élaboration de normes techniques;

13   Qui sont de portée générale — la Commission devrait éviter les branches spécialisées du droit international.

En délimitant la sphère de compétences de la Commission, il conviendrait de considérer que celle-ci est l'organe compétent à l'égard :

14   Des sujets qui nécessitent une réglementation de droit international privé;

15   Des sujets qui nécessitent l'élaboration des normes techniques à condition et dans le mesure que ces sujets soulèvent des problèmes juridiques graves qui n'ont pas été resolus de manière satisfaisante par un autre organe normatif international;

16   Des domaines du droit international dans lesquels la pratique des États n'est pas encore très développée — en appliquant des méthodes rigoureuses pour définir la pratique des États et en déterminer les effets juridiques, la Commission pourrait isoler les tendances observables de la doctrine et de la pratique, qui sont l'ébauche du régime juridique auquel on aboutira;

17   Des domaines dans lesquels les États hésitent beaucoup à légiférer, pour les mêmes raisons;

18   Des domaines dans lesquels la pratique des États n'a commencé que très récemment à se développer et reste rudimentaire; il serait utile que la Commission entreprenne d'élaborer des règles lorsque la pratique des États, même peu développée, penche en faveur d'une solution précise — comme dans le cas du clonage ou des manipulations génétiques;

19   Des domaines dans lesquels la pratique des États n'a qu'un caractère directif — la Commission pourrait déterminer les aspects de cette pratique qui ont une valeur juridique;

20   Des domaines dans lesquels la pratique se développe dans le cadre d'un grand nombre de traités bilatéraux et multilatéraux, comme le commerce et l'investissement; la Commission pourrait définir les tendances générales se dégageant de ces traités.

*

Certaines propositions envisagent une expansion du rôle de la Commission dans des directions n'ayant qu'un rapport indirect avec l'élaboration du droit international

21 Les organes de décision de l'Organisation, et peut-être le Secrétaire général, devraient solliciter l'avis de la Commission sur les problèmes de droit que soulèvent les activités de l'Organisation ou qui concernent l'interprétation et l'application des règlements et procédures des organes des Nations Unies.

22 La Commission devrait, à la demande des parties intéressées, y compris des particuliers et des entités privées, se prononcer sur des questions de droit international, de la même manière que les ministères des affaires étrangères rendent des avis sur des points de droit international à l'intention des tribunaux nationaux.

* * *

2. Les grandes difficultés contemporaines de l'élaboration du droit international

Les propositions de cette rubrique visent à recenser les moyens de surmonter ou d'éluder les problèmes qui font obstacle à l'élaboration du droit international et qui en limitent l'efficacité, notamment en ce qui concerne la partie des procédures où la Commission intervient et qui porte sur la préparation de textes appelés à être adoptés et appliqués en tant que conventions multilatérales

Certaines propositions prévoient l'examen de la procédure d'élaboration du droit international, ou de certains de ses aspects, afin de déterminer les améliorations qu'il serait possible d'y apporter

23 La Commission devrait créer un groupe de travail permanent chargé d'analyser l'acceptation, l'application, le respect et l'efficacité des traités multilatéraux, et de recommander les ajustements à apporter à la procédure de conclusion des traités multilatéraux.

24 La Commission devrait entreprendre l'étude des aspects économiques des conférences de plénipotentiaires afin d'en évaluer la rentabilité en tant que mécanisme d'élaboration et d'adoption de conventions multilatérales.

*

Certaines propositions envisagent des améliorations précises des procédures d'élaboration du droit international

25 Afin d'aider les États en développement qui ont actuellement du mal à répondre aux questionnaires ou aux demandes de commentaires de la Commission, il serait envisageable de créer une équipe d'étudiants préparant leur doctorat et de jeunes enseignants de droit international qui participeraient dans un premier temps à une session « fictive » ou « modèle » de la Commission, consacrée, à la matière objet du questionnaire ou de la demande de la Commission, et qui seraient par la suite disponibles pour seconder ces États, à la demande de ceux-ci.

26 Il conviendrait de prévoir une assistance technique et une aide financière à l'intention des États qui en ont besoin et qui souhaitent participer aux négociations en vue d'adopter une convention afin qu'ils puissent participer effectivement à ces négociations.

27   Il conviendrait de prévoir une assistance technique à l'intention des États qui en ont besoin et qui envisagent d'adhérer à des conventions découlant des travaux de la Commission, afin qu'ils puissent avoir une idée plus nette des conséquences de leur adhésion.

*

Une proposition envisage des mesures concernant les textes des conventions qui sont l'aboutissement du travail d'élaboration du droit international et visant à rendre ces textes plus facilement acceptables

28   Les textes des conventions mises au point sur la base de projets de la Commission ne devraient énoncer que les règles susceptibles de faire l'objet d'un consensus, les autres étant énoncées dans un protocole facultatif (ou plusieurs).

*

Certaines propositions portent sur les dispositions qu'il faudrait prendre à l'égard de textes déjà adoptés, pour les rendre plus acceptables

29   L'Assemblée générale devrait procéder à un examen des conventions qui ont été adoptées sur la base de projets de la Commission : elle évaluerait l'état de ces conventions, recenserait les facteurs qui ont fait obstacle à l'adhésion des États et chercherait le moyen d'accroître le nombre de parties, notamment dans le cas des traités qui ne sont pas encore entrés en vigueur ou qui ont peu d'adhérents.

30   La Commission devrait envisager de proposer d'amender le droit des domaines dans lesquels elle a déjà rédigé des projets.

31   La Commission devrait envisager de reprendre l'examen de certaines séries de projets d'articles qu'elle a adoptés mais qui ne sont pas encore devenus des conventions et, le cas échéant, en reprendre la rédaction pour en faciliter l'adoption sous forme de convention.

* * *

3.   Sujets proposés à la Commission à des fins de codification et développement progressif et méthodes de travail de la Commission

Les propositions sous cette rubrique visent : a) à indiquer les sujets précis qui devraient (ou ne devraient pas) être inscrits au programme de travail de la Commission; ou b) à améliorer l'efficacité et l'utilité du travail de la Commission en adaptant ou en modifiant la composition de celle-ci, ses procédures et ses méthodes de travail

i)   *Sujets*
Certaines propositions visent à déterminer les procédures à suivre pour choisir les sujets à inscrire au programme de travail de la Commission

32   La troisième conférence mondiale de la paix de 1999 devrait proposer à l'Assemblée générale des sujets à renvoyer à la Commission.

33   La Commission devrait faire connaître à des institutions scientifiques internationales, telles que l'Association du droit international, les sujets qu'elle a l'intention d'examiner en vue de les inscrire à son programme de travail, de sorte que ces institutions puissent établir des comités internationaux ou des groupes de travail pour étudier ces sujets. La

Commission serait alors en mesure d'utiliser ces études lorsqu'elle détermine l'inclusion ou non de ces sujets à son programme.

34 Le Secrétariat devrait préparer un nouvel aperçu général du droit international, selon le schéma des aperçus généraux précédents de 1949 et 1971, afin d'aider la Commission à déterminer les nouveaux sujets dont elle pourrait proposer à l'Assemblée générale l'inclusion dans son programme de travail.

*

Certaines propositions ont trait aux critères qu'il faudrait appliquer ou aux considérations dont il faudrait tenir compte pour déterminer, dans le vaste contexte des domaines dont s'occupe la Commission, les sujets à inscrire au programme de travail de celle-ci

La décision d'inscrire un sujet au programme de travail de la Commission doit se fonder sur les critères suivants :

35 Il faut qu'il s'agisse d'un sujet sur lequel la grande majorité des États estime qu'il faut légiférer d'urgence;

36 Il conviendrait d'éviter tout sujet délicat du point de vue politique, ou lourd de considérations politiques et susceptibles de causer des divergences de vues irréconciliables entre les États ou entre les membres de la Commission (il est préférable de laisser les sujets de ce genre à des organes composés par des représentants des États).

Pour déterminer si un sujet susceptible d'être inscrit au programme de travail de la Commission doit en fait y figurer, il conviendrait :

37 De considérer d'abord s'il fait l'objet d'une législation dont l'amélioration permettrait de faire progresser le droit international dans sa fonction essentielle — la protection des êtres humains — et de répondre aux besoins des individus plutôt qu'aux seuls intérêts des États;

38 De donner la priorité aux sujets qui, par nature, permettraient à la Commission de mener à bien ses travaux en cinq ans au maximum, de sorte qu'elle soit mieux en mesure de répondre promptement et utilement aux besoins de la communauté internationale quand point la nécessité d'élaborer rapidement un texte législatif;

39 De choisir un sujet se prêtant au développement progressif du droit international plutôt qu'à sa codification.

*

Certaines propositions présentent des sujets précis à inscrire au programme de travail de la Commission

La Commission devrait entreprendre la rédaction de projets d'articles sur les matières suivantes :

40 Les droits et les devoirs des étrangers;

41 Les garanties des droits de l'homme dans les procédures d'extradition;

42 L'investissement étranger;

43 Les échanges commerciaux et les investissements;

44	L'élimination de la corruption dans les transactions commerciales internationales;
45	Les exodes massifs en cas de danger mortel;
46	L'indivis mondial;
47	Le clonage de l'homme et la manipulation génétique.
48	La Commission devrait enteprentre une étude sur les relations réciproques des différents domaines normatifs et les valeurs respectives qui s'y rattachent au niveau de leur « interaction » ou lorsque ces domaines aboutissent à des solutions différentes à un problème juridique particulier.

* * *

ii) *Méthodes de travail*

Certaines propositions concernent la composition de la Commission

Afin de maintenir le niveau intellectuel général de la Commission et d'atténuer les effets pervers qu'a la politisation croissante des élections de ses membres sur l'attention que portent les États à cette considération lorsqu'ils proposent des candidats et procèdent aux élections :

| 49 | Un certain nombre de membres devraient être nommés par des sociétés savantes ou des institutions scientifiques, et non élus par l'Assemblée générale; |
| 50 | Les candidats présentés par les gouvernements à l'Assemblée générale devraient avoir l'agrément de sociétés savantes, d'institutions scientifiques, ou de quelque autre entité analogue, avant de pouvoir se soumettre aux suffrages. |

Afin de renforcer la composition de la Commission et d'en rendre ainsi le fonctionnement plus efficace :

51	Chaque membre devrait accepter de limiter la durée de sa présence à la Commission, de sorte que celle-ci ne compte jamais de ressortissant du même État pendant plus de deux mandats successifs, ce qui assurerait avec le temps la participation la plus large possible aux travaux de la Commission — et par là même à l'élaboration du droit international;
52	Il faudrait prendre des dispositions pour qu'aux prochaines élections de la Commission des femmes soient élues en grand nombre — 11 ou 12 par exemple —, ce qui serait un premier pas sur la voie d'une participation directe et équilibrée des femmes dont les intérêts et les idées influeraient sur les travaux de la Commission au même titre que ceux des hommes;
53	Un au moins des membres élus devrait être éminemment compétent en matière de sociologie ou d'anthropologie du droit, les travaux de la Commission bénéficiant ainsi d'un apport qui servirait directement à en faciliter l'acceptation et à en élargir l'application effective;
54	Un certain nombre de spécialistes du droit international privé devraient être élus à la Commission, qui pourrait ainsi bénéficier de points de vue différents, utiles et tout à fait pertinents sur nombre de sujets inscrits à son programme de travail;

55   Il conviendrait que la Commission comprenne des représentants d'organisations internationales, des milieux d'affaires, des organisations non gouvernementales et d'autres entités similaires.

Afin de protéger l'indépendance des membres de la Commission, notamment leur indépendance à l'égard de gouvernements de leur propre pays :

56   Les membres de la Commission devraient s'engager sous serment à travailler impartialement et en toute indépendance et à ne demander ni ne recevoir d'instructions d'aucun gouvernement;

57   Au cours de l'examen du rapport de la Commission par la Sixième Commission, les membres de la Commission occupant des postes dans le gouvernement des États ne devraient pas faire partie ou se conduire en tant que membres des délégations de ces États;

58   Les rapports de la Commission à l'Assemblée générale ainsi que les *Annuaires de la Commission* ne devraient pas rendre compte des interventions en indiquant nommément leurs auteurs, ni sous une forme qui permettrait aux États de savoir quels membres sont favorables à tel ou tel point de vue ou partagent telle ou telle proposition.

Des mesures devraient être prises pour régler le problème de l'absentéisme d'un certain nombre de membres. Notamment :

59   Les États ne devraient proposer que des candidats qui sont manifestement capables et désireux d'assister à la plupart des réunions de la Commission et de participer utilement à ses travaux, et n'accorder leurs suffrages qu'à ces candidats;

60   Les membres de la Commission devraient s'engager sous serment à assister et à participer pleinement et activement aux réunions de la Commission;

61   Les listes des membres présents aux réunions de la Commission devraient être publiées;

62   Les membres qui assistent à moins de la moitié des réunions de la Commission devraient perdre le droit d'être réélus;

63   Les membres qui assistent à moins de la moitié des réunions consacrées par la Commission à un sujet donné ne devraient pas avoir le droit de se prononcer sur ce sujet.

64   Il conviendrait de prendre des dispositions pour que les membres de la Commission qui sont des ressortissants des États en voie de développement, et des États de l'Afrique subsaharienne en particulier, jouent un rôle plus actif et influent au sein de la Commission y compris l'assomption sur une base proportionelle des fonctions de Président ou de Rapporteur spécial.

*

Certaines propositions envisagent des mesures qui visent à améliorer la planification et l'organisation des travaux de la Commission

65   La Commission devrait écarter complètement son programme de travail à long terme et se fixer, au début de chaque quinquennat, un plan de cinq ans tel que les travaux qui y seraient prévus puissent être achevés à la fin de la période.

66   La Commission devrait organiser ses travaux de façon à n'examiner chaque année que deux ou trois sujets au lieu d'étudier tous les ans tous les sujets inscrits à son programme de travail en cours.

67   Au début de chaque session, la Commission devrait fixer un calendrier lui permettant d'achever le travail qu'elle s'est assigné pour la session.

*

Certaines propositions visent à préciser le rôle du Rapporteur spécial ou envisagent les mesures à prendre pour que les Rapporteurs spéciaux s'acquittent mieux de leur mission

68   Si l'on juge important que les travaux sur un sujet donné soient menés rapidement à leur terme, il faudrait recourir à des groupes de travail qui travailleraient soit avec un Rapporteur spécial soit seuls et sans qu'un Rapporteur spécial soit désigné pour le sujet dont il s'agit.

Il conviendrait de prendre des dispositions pour que les Rapporteurs spéciaux reçoivent de la Commission davantage de conseils sur l'orientation que leur travail doit prendre. En particulier :

69   Pour que les Rapporteurs spéciaux puissent recevoir des conseils sur la manière d'aborder un sujet ou certaines questions qui s'y rattacheraient, la Commission devrait nommer un groupe consultatif composé de plusieurs de ses membres, qui collaborerait avec chacun des Rapporteurs spéciaux, que ceux-ci pourraient consulter dans l'intervalle des sessions de la Commission, soit par correspondance, soit par Internet, soit dans des réunions;

70   Pour être soutenus dans leur travail, les Rapporteurs spéciaux devraient, s'il y a lieu, prendre l'initiative de consulter des membres de la Commission ou de discuter avec eux pendant l'intersession soit par correspondance, soit par Internet, soit, le cas échéant, par vidéoconférence.

71   Les Rapporteurs spéciaux devraient occuper leurs fonctions à temps plein pour être en mesure de consacrer plus de temps et plus d'attention à l'accomplissement de leur lourde tâche.

Les Rapporteurs spéciaux devraient être davantage aidés dans leur travail. En particulier :

72   On devrait désigner non pas un Rapporteur spécial mais deux pour chaque sujet — cela contribuerait aussi à limiter l'effet négatif qu'entraîne pour les travaux de la Commission sur un sujet déterminé le départ prématuré d'un Rapporteur spécial;

73   Il faudrait prévoir des procédures en vertu desquelles les Rapporteurs spéciaux pourraient bénéficier d'un appui plus tangible de la part d'autres membres de la Commission;

74   Il conviendrait d'étoffer le personnel de la Division de la codification du Bureau des affaires juridiques du Secrétariat des Nations Unies de façon qu'il puisse aider de façon régulière les Rapporteurs spéciaux dans leurs recherches.

75   Les Rapporteurs spéciaux devraient prendre des dispositions pour que la Commission soit à même d'étudier leurs rapports avec sérieux. En particulier, les Rapporteurs spéciaux devraient faire en sorte que les

rapports qu'ils soumettent soient substantiels et contiennent des commentaires complets sur tous les projets d'articles qu'ils proposent, de façon que les membres de la Commission puissent connaître d'emblée le sens dans lequel on s'oriente, ainsi que les principales questions qui se posent.

*

Certaines propositions visent à rendre plus efficaces les débats de la Commission

Des mesures devraient être prises pour que les débats de la Commission s'attachent à faire plus efficacement progresser les travaux sur les aspects de chaque sujet qui requièrent effectivement l'attention de la Commission. En particulier :

76   Pour utiliser au mieux le temps que la Commission peut effectivement consacrer à l'examen de problèmes plus difficiles et moins solubles, les Rapporteurs spéciaux devraient dans l'intersession prendre l'initiative de consulter des membres de la Commission sur certaines questions ou d'en discuter avec eux afin de faire avancer les travaux sur autant de points que possible — voire aboutir à des solutions — avant les sessions officielles de la Commission;

77   Les membres de la Commission devraient s'efforcer de limiter la durée de leurs interventions à cinq minutes au maximum.

*

Certaines propositions portent sur les processus et procédures de décision que la Commission devrait utiliser

La Commission devrait veiller à reconnaître au consensus un rôle approprié dans les prises de décisions. Plus précisément :

78   Aucun effort ne devrait être négligé pour que l'on parvienne à un consensus au sein de la Commission sur tous les points ou toutes les questions, étant admis cependant que cette méthode a des limites;

79   Si l'on doit s'efforcer d'arriver à un consensus, il ne s'agit pas d'y parvenir à tout prix, en particulier si la recherche du consensus risque d'entraîner de longs retards ou d'aboutir à la rédaction de projets vides.

Pour mieux résoudre les questions controversées qui se posent à la Commission :

80   Il faudrait recourir davantage aux groupes de travail;

81   Il ne faudrait pas saisir le Comité de rédaction d'une question qui porte sur le fond.

82   Afin d'accélérer les travaux de la Commission, on devrait considérer que les questions sur lesquelles on est parvenu à un accord ou qui ont été réglées ou résolues autrement ne se posent plus et que le débat à leur sujet ne doit pas être rouvert.

4. Les travaux de la Commission et la mise en forme du droit international

Certaines propositions visent à trouver les moyens et à définir le type d'instrument ou de produit qu'il conviendrait d'utiliser pour concourir à la mise en forme du droit international dans les domaines que la Commission est susceptible d'examiner

Une proposition concerne les procédures à suivre pour définir les produits

83   La Commission ne devrait pas trop se soucier des vues des États concernant la forme à donner à ses conclusions sur un sujet donné. Elle devrait plutôt se préoccuper de la qualité de ces conclusions et laisser aux États le soin de décider de la forme qu'il convient de leur donner.

*

Une proposition vise à définir les formes que la Commission devrait donner aux résultats de ses travaux

84   Même si l'élaboration de conventions multilatérales doit demeurer le principal objectif de la Commission, celle-ci devrait, comme elle l'a fait récemment, diversifier ses productions et examiner d'autres options que les projets d'articles qu'elle rédige en vue de les faire figurer dans un texte conventionnel.

*

Certaines propositions visent les formes, autres que les projets d'articles à transformer éventuellement en convention, que pourraient prendre les résultats des travaux de la Commission

Il s'agit notamment :

85   Des projets de convention-cadre;

86   Des traités types;

87   Des règles types;

88   Des lois types devant être adoptées à l'échelon national;

89   Des déclarations de principes;

90   De nouvelles formulations (*restatements*) des règles du droit;

91   Des codes de conduite;

92   Des directives;

93   Des guides d'application à l'intention des États.

* * *

5. Renforcement des liens entre la Commission et les autres organes normatifs et les institutions universitaires et professionnelles compétentes

Les propositions relevant de cette rubrique visent à définir les relations que la Commission devrait nouer, cultiver et renforcer avec d'autres entités ou des particuliers

Certaines propositions visent à améliorer le concours que les États prêtent aux travaux de la Commission

94 Pour que les projets d'articles qu'elle établit répondent aux besoins et tiennent compte des intérêts des individus, la Commission devrait encourager les ministères des affaires étrangères, lorsqu'ils répondent à ses demandes d'observations sur ces projets, à prendre des mesures pour que les organismes scientifiques, les universités, les associations professionnelles, les groupes d'intérêts, les chambres de commerce, les sociétés et les particuliers leur apportent leur contribution.

95 Afin d'assister les gouvernements à formuler leurs observations sur les projets d'articles preparés par la Commission, des institutions scientifiques internationales, telles que l'Association du droit international, devraient organiser des seminaires régionaux sur les sujets qui font l'objet des travaux de la Commission.

*

Certaines propositions visent à améliorer la manière dont la Sixième Commission oriente les travaux de la Commission

96 La Sixième Commission devrait jouer un rôle mieux défini, plus actif et plus dynamique dans l'orientation des travaux de la Commission. Il conviendrait notamment qu'elle donne dans de meilleurs délais à la Commission des directives plus claires et plus précises quant à l'orientation de ses réflexions sur un sujet, à la présentation de ses conclusions, voire aux fondements du régime juridique qu'elle devrait mettre au point, en particulier dans les domaines où l'État n'a qu'une expérience limitée ou ceux dans lesquels les travaux de la Commission relèvent essentiellement du développement progressif.

97 La Sixième Commission devrait réorganiser l'examen du rapport de la Commission, afin de mieux orienter les travaux de celle-ci. Notamment, les interventions à la Sixième Commission devraient être concises et ne pas s'éloigner du sujet abordé afin de permettre à autant de représentants que possible de participer aux débats, en particulier aux représentants des États qui n'ont pas donné suite aux demandes éventuelles de la Commission concernant les articles qu'elle a adoptés.

La Commission elle-même devrait prendre des mesures concrètes pour que la Sixième Commission la conseille de façon plus avisée. Il faudrait notamment :

98 Que la Commission obtienne de la Sixième Commission des directives sur certaines questions sur lesquelles elle est divisée;

99 Afin de faire en sorte que les débats de la Sixième Commission ne répètent pas simplement ceux de la Commission, que les rapports de celle-ci soient moins détaillés et ne donnent pas le détail des délibérations.

*

Certaines propositions visent à renforcer et développer les relations de la Commission avec les organisations ou organismes intergouvernementaux régionaux

100 Les organisations intergouvernementales régionales qui participent activement à l'élaboration du droit international devraient présenter de brefs rapports écrits sur leurs travaux, accompagnés des documents y afférents, aux fins de distribution avant la tenue des sessions de la

Commission, ce qui permettrait à celle-ci de se tenir mieux informée des nombreuses idées et tendances nouvelles qui se font jour en droit international au niveau régional.

101 Il faudrait organiser des groupes de travail informels et des réunions informelles, où les membres de la Commission et des représentants des organisations intergouvernementales régionales participant activement à l'élaboration du droit international se retrouveraient et échangeraient leurs vues sur des questions d'intérêt commun.

*

Certaines propositions envisagent l'établissement de relations de travail entre la Commission et des organisations ou organismes qui ne sont pas de nature intergouvernementale

Afin de dégager des orientations concernant l'établissement et la conduite des relations avec ces organismes et organisations :

102 La Commission devrait créer un organe subsidiaire permanent chargé de lui fournir des avis autorisés, notamment des recommandations concernant les critères devant permettre de déterminer les organismes avec lesquels il convient d'établir des relations;

103 La Commission devrait être guidée par l'objectif enoncé dans le Rapport du Secrétaire générale *Rénover l'Organisation des Nations Unies : un programme de réformes* (document A/51/950) visant à ce que « toutes les entités des Nations Unies soient ouvertes aux organisations de la société civile qui mènent des activités dans leurs secteurs de compétence respectifs » et à ce que « les consultations et la coopération entre l'ONU et lesdites organisations » soient facilitées;

104 Il faudrait tenir dûment compte, en choisissant ces organismes, de la nécessité d'assurer une représentation géographique équitable et veiller à ce que les travaux de la Commission ne suivent pas une orientation par trop occidentale.

La Commission devrait entretenir des relations de travail régulières avec :

105 Les organisations non gouvernementales internationales qui œuvrent dans le domaine du droit international;

106 Les sociétés scientifiques internationales qui s'occupent de droit international, comme l'Institut de droit international et l'Association du droit international;

107 Les associations internationales des praticiens du droit, comme l'Association internationale du barreau et l'Association juridique de l'Asie et du Pacifique;

108 Sur le plan national, les organisations gouvernementales et non gouvernementales concernées, les sociétés savantes, les instituts de recherche et les universités;

109 les organes nationaux de révision des lois.

L'établissement de ces relations devrait permettre à ces organisations et organismes de contribuer activement aux travaux de la Commission. En particulier :

110 Ces relations devraient faciliter la tenue de consultations avec ces organismes et organisations, ainsi que, le cas échéant, avec leurs

membres, ce qui permettrait de recueillir plus facilement l'opinion des intéressés sur les travaux de la Commission;

111 Les organisations et organismes avec lesquels des relations sont établies devraient créer des comités ou groupes de travail permanents pour faciliter la tenue de consultations avec la Commission et leur permettre de faire connaître régulièrement leurs vues à celle-ci;

112 Il faudrait créer des groupes de travail informels mixtes où siégeraient des représentants desdits organismes ou organisations et des membres de la Commission en vue d'examiner les problèmes juridiques particuliers qui apparaissent au fil des travaux de la Commission.

*

Certaines propositions visent à permettre à la Commission de solliciter le concours ou de demander l'opinion d'experts et autres personnes informées

113 Des représentants d'organisations internationales, du monde des affaires ou d'organisations non gouvernementales et autres organismes analogues devraient être appelés à siéger à la Commission en qualité de membres ad hoc pour apporter leur concours lors de l'examen de certains thèmes ou sujets.

114 La Commission devrait engager des consultants à temps partiel appartenant à des institutions financières internationales, à des entreprises, à des universités ou autres organismes analogues, afin de s'assurer le concours d'experts dans des matières techniques, de recueillir des opinions extérieures sur les sujets traités et, le cas échéant, faciliter les négociations en son sein sur ces sujets.

115 Afin de disposer d'une gamme étendue d'opinions sur des questions particulières, la Commission devrait demander des opinions détaillées à des experts universitaires du dehors. Une fois ces opinions reçues, des ateliers ou groupes de discussion devraient être organisés avec les experts concernés, le Rapporteur spécial et les autres membres de la Commission en vue de débattre et d'approfondir ces questions.

116 La Commission devrait pouvoir se réunir ailleurs qu'à Genève afin de rencontrer et consulter dans l'État hôte des représentants des organes officiels ou non officiels, des parlementaires, de hauts fonctionnaires, des membres de l'opposition et des représentants du secteur privé. Le coût de ces réunions organisées en dehors de Genève pourrait être supporté par l'État hôte, par d'autres États ou par des sources privées.

117 Des conférences ou des colloques pourraient être organisés par la Commission ou par des institutions et organes participant activement à l'élaboration du droit international. Les experts ainsi réunis examineraient et débattraient les questions inscrites à l'ordre du jour de la Commission ou des aspects controversés de ces questions, ce qui contribuerait à focaliser sur ces questions l'attention des milieux intéressés et fournirait à la Commission des idées, des opinions, des orientations et une action en retour.

118 Des sessions fictives ou des sessions types de la Commission devraient être organisées au niveau international pour des étudiants qui préparent un doctorat en droit international et pour des chargés de cours; on y

examinerait le rapport de tel Rapporteur spécial avant qu'il ne soit présenté à la Commission, et les idées qui sortiraient de ce débat seraient portées à l'attention de la Commission aux fins de l'examen dudit rapport.

119   La Commission devrait utiliser le réseau Internet pour demander des opinions sur les travaux en cours, ainsi que des informations à des organes nationaux et internationaux, à des groupes et à des particuliers.

120   Les juristes devraient se demander comment ils peuvent contribuer le plus utilement aux travaux de la Commission et, en particulier, comment ils peuvent exploiter au mieux, eux-mêmes ainsi que la Commission, les possibilités qu'offre l'article 26 (1) du Statut de la Commission.

*

Certaines propositions envisagent de faire appel à des entités extérieures dont l'assistance à la Commission prendrait la forme de recherches

121   La Commission pourrait utilement sous-traiter certains de ses travaux de recherche à des entités extérieures, instituts de recherche, universités et organes scientifiques, comme l'Institut de droit international et l'Association du droit international.

Pour assurer la supervision et la coordination des recherches ainsi menées pour la Commission soit par le Secrétariat, soit par des entités ou des personnes de l'extérieur :

122   La Commission devrait avoir un directeur de la recherche, en prenant exemple à cet égard sur l'Association du droit international;

123   Il faudrait augmenter les effectifs de la Division de la codification du Bureau des affaires juridiques du Secrétariat des Nations Unies.

124   Il faudrait explorer la possibilité d'obtenir des fonds de conseils de la recherche et autres organismes de financement pour la recherche effectuée par la Commission ou pour le compte de celle-ci, en veillant à adapter la nature ou les paramètres de cette recherche pour qu'elle réponde aux besoins non seulement de la Commission, mais également de ces organismes, et tienne compte des programmes et priorités desdits organismes.

* * *

6.   Rendre le droit international plus proche et d'un accès plus facile

Les propositions formulées ici visent à mieux faire comprendre l'importance du droit international et à encourager les recherches dans ce domaine

Certaines propositions visent à confier à la Commission la tâche de mieux faire comprendre l'importance du droit international en général

125   La Commission devrait preparer un guide du droit international et de ses sources en vue de rendre le droit international d'un accès plus facile et sa comprehension meilleure parmi les juristes nationaux.

126   En vue de faciliter l'incorporation du droit international dans les systèmes juridiques nationaux et d'en améliorer l'application dans le cadre de ces systèmes, il faudrait organiser, sous la conduite de membres de la Commission, des séminaires de sensibilisation au droit international des magistrats et avocats des cours et tribunaux nationaux qui sont plus familiarisés avec le droit interne.

127 En vue de mieux faire comprendre l'importance du droit international parmi les responsables des affaires étrangères et leurs conseillers, il faudrait organiser, à l'instar du séminaire du droit international, un séminaire annuel particulièrement adapté aux besoins de ce public et également ouvert aux spécialistes des sciences politiques, étudiants en relations internationales et avocats.

En vue de mieux faire comprendre l'importance du droit international par le grand public :

128 La Commission devrait superviser ou assister à la production d'un manuel de droit international destiné aux écoles et aux lycées;

129 La Commission devrait encourager les activités scolaires des associations prefessionelles nationales et internationales telles que la Société africaine de droit international et comparé.

*

Certaines propositions ont trait aux mesures qui pourraient être prises pour mieux faire connaître la Commission et ses travaux

130 La Commission devrait examiner la meilleure façon de tirer parti de la révolution informatique pour mieux faire connaître ses travaux des juristes en général et du grand public.

131 Pour mieux faire connaître la Commission et ses travaux aux décideurs, il faudrait concevoir une brochure donnant un aperçu de la Commission et des activités en cours, des activités passées et de celles qui sont envisagées.

132 Pour familiariser davantage les étudiants en droit et les étudiants en relations internationales avec la Commission et ses travaux, il faudrait organiser des sessions fictives ou des sessions types de la Commission aux niveaux national et international.

Pour faire mieux connaître les travaux de la Commission à ceux qui enseignent le droit international ou qui mènent des recherches dans ce domaine :

133 Il faudrait encourager les universités et instituts d'enseignement supérieur à parrainer des programmes dans le cadre desquels des membres de la Commission organiseraient sur place des séminaires sur leurs travaux (et *vice versa*);

134 Les institutions scientifiques internationales telles que l'Association du droit international devraient organiser des seminaires au niveau régional sur des sujets traités actuellement par la Commission;

135 Il faudrait conclure des accords pour permettre à des universitaires de faire des stages auprès de la Commission.

136 Il faudrait aider concrètement les avocats qui s'occupent de droit interne à mieux saisir en quoi les travaux de la Commission les intéressent et sont importants pour eux.

*

Certaines propositions ont trait aux mesures qui pourraient être prises pour faciliter ou encourager des recherches sur la Commission et sur ses travaux

137 Il faudrait créer et tenir à jour un fichier bibliographique de tous les écrits de la Commission et des sujets sur lesquels elle a travaillé ou qu'elle examine actuellement.

138   Pour faciliter la consultation des documents ayant trait aux travaux de la Commission, on pourrait demander à certains centres de recherche et universités de faire fonction de bibliothèques de la Commission du droit international en tant que dépositaires de la Commission, parallèlement aux bibliothèques dépositaires des Nations Unies qui existent déjà. Ces centres et universités pourraient également se charger de transmettre les documents de la Commission aux particuliers et aux institutions intéressés de l'État ou de la région.

139   Pour permettre de suivre plus facilement les travaux de la Commission, il faudrait publier un Bulletin de la Commission du droit international qui paraîtrait deux fois par an; le premier numéro de l'année esquisserait le programme de travail de la prochaine session de la Commission et le second numéro donnerait un bref aperçu des travaux réalisés pendant cette session. La rédaction de ce second numéro pourrait être confiée à la personne qui est déjà chargée de rédiger un aperçu des travaux de la Commission pour un des annuaires ou une des grandes revues de droit international.

140   Afin de stimuler l'intérêt pour les travaux de la Commission parmi les étudiants et les jeunes chercheurs, il faudrait créer un prix de la Commission du droit international qui récompenserait un travail consacré ou ayant trait à la Commission et à ses travaux.

*

Certaines propositions ont trait aux mesures que la Commission pourrait prendre pour enrichir la littérature dans le domaine du droit international

141   La Commission devrait superviser la création sur le World Wide Web d'une banque de données très complète concernant le droit international.

142   Pour faciliter l'enseignement du droit international aux États en voie de développement au niveau universitaire, la Commission devrait organiser ou superviser la production d'une compilation, d'un prix modique, des affaires de droit international et du matériel se référant à la pratique des gouvernements et des organes judiciaires des tous les systemes juridiques du monde, qui refléterait et promouverait une perspective vraiment globale dans ce domaine.

En vue d'améliorer la connaissance des différentes pratiques des États et de promouvoir en dernière analyse l'harmonisation de ces pratiques, la Commission devrait encourager :

143   La création de réseaux internationaux d'universités constitués d'universités établies dans des pays ayant des pratiques divergentes, qui seraient en mesure de mener à bien une recherche authentiquement internationale donnant lieu à des publications sur des sujets proposés par la Commission;

144   L'organisation de colloques régionaux sur ces sujets, selon un programme standard élaboré par la Commission, dont les actes feraient l'objet de publications;

145   La publication par les États de résumés systématiques, à l'instar de la publication *Restatement of the Foreign Relations Law of the United States* publiée par l'American Law Institute, qui énonceraient les règles de droit international telles que les États les comprennent et les interprètent. Ces résumés nationaux pourraient

à leur tour servir de base à une reformulation du droit international dans une perspective universelle, qui serait élaborée par la Commission elle-même.

En vue de contribuer à l'avancement de la recherche et à l'enrichissement de la doctrine du droit international :

146   La Commission devrait dresser une liste de sujets de droit international, qui devrait donner lieu à une recherche plus poussée;

147   Chaque membre de la Commission devrait s'engager, lors de sa prise de fonctions, à mener à bien, avant la fin du quinquennat, une étude sur un sujet que le Groupe de planification de la Commission lui aurait demandé d'approfondir. Ces études, qui ne seraient pas attribuables à la Commission, seraient publiées dans l'*Annuaire juridique des Nations Unies*.

I

1

AN OVERVIEW OF THE INTERNATIONAL LAW-MAKING PROCESS
AND
THE ROLE OF THE INTERNATIONAL LAW COMMISSION

*

APERÇU DU PROCESSUS NORMATIF INTERNATIONAL
ET
RÔLE DE LA COMMISSION DU DROIT INTERNATIONAL

Introduction par l'Animateur, le professeur Alain Pellet*

Cette première matinée de notre Colloque sera consacrée à une discussion générale du processus normatif international, des difficultés qu'il rencontre et du rôle qu'y joue, ou que pourrait y jouer, ou que devrait y jouer la Commission du droit international.

D'abord je donnerai la parole à Monsieur l'Ambassadeur Owada que chacun connaît ici. Il est à la fois un professeur particulièrement éminent de droit international et du droit des organisations internationales, il a enseigné d'abord à l'Université de Tokyo au Japon et puis comme professeur invité a l'Université de Harvard et il continue à enseigner à Columbia University et à New York University. Chacun sait qu'il est aussi un diplomate chevronné, représentant permanent de son pays, le Japon, auprès des Nations Unies.

Le deuxième intervenant sera un vieil ami très cher, le professeur Georges Abi-Saab, dont tout le monde connaît les publications en droit international, mais je ne peux pas m'empêcher de mentioner son remarquable cours général de droit international public à l'Académie de droit international de La Haye, qui a paru très récemment. Il est en outre un praticien éminent. Il a été conseil devant la Cour internationale de Justice à plusieurs reprises. Il a été deux fois juge ad hoc dans des affaires bien connues et il a été juge au Tribunal pénal international pour l'ex-Yougoslavie et au Tribunal international pour le Rwanda.

La troisième présentation sera faite par le professeur Yuri Kolosov, qui est l'auteur de plus de 200 publications en droit international et auquel ses travaux ont valu il y a deux ans la distinction de mérite scientifique de la Féderation de Russie. En outre, depuis 1987 il est titulaire de la chaire de droit international au fameux Institut d'État de Moscou pour le droit international.

---

*Professeur, Université de Paris-X, Paris (France). Membre de la Commission du droit international, 1989- . Président de la Commission pendant sa quarante-neuvième session.

Presentation by **Mr Hisashi Owada**

The mandate of the International Law Commission, namely, "the promotion of the progressive development of international law and its codification",[1] is as relevant today as it was half a century ago, when the Commission was created. Nevertheless, as a result of the many changes that have taken place in international society during the last 50 years, the Commission is now confronted with many new challenges. In particular, one cannot avoid the impression that an ever-increasing number of important treaties on such matters as the law of the sea, outer space, human rights, the environment and disarmament are prepared by other organs, bodies and mechanisms, rather than by the Commission. In order to determine how the Commission might best meet this and other such challenges, it will be useful to review the Commission's work to date and to analyse both its successes and its failures.

Almost three quarters of a century ago, Professor Brierly wrote that "an international legislature, in the sense of a body having power to enact new international law binding on the States of the world or on their peoples, does not exist".[2] While the international community has certainly come a long way since Professor Brierly made this statement, the fundamental structure of the law-making mechanism which he described remains essentially the same. What is nowadays often termed "international legislation" is intrinsically different from domestic legislation in a democracy, in as much as it does not and cannot create a legal regime which is endowed with legal force *erga omnes*. Rather, it takes the form of a multilateral compact agreed upon by those States which wish to be parties to it and binding upon them by virtue of the principle *pacta sunt servanda*.

Taking this as my point of departure, I shall, first of all, identify three different kinds of international legislation, which are to be distinguished from each other according to the nature of the legislative activities which they involve. This threefold categorization is theoretical in nature and accordingly somewhat artificial, but it is, none the less, an important one to make.

First, there is a category of international legislation that is termed "codification"—"codification" meaning the reduction into writing, in the form of a code, of norms which already exist as unwritten rules of customary international law. In essence, it is a process which involves "the more precise formulation and systematization of rules of international law in fields where there already has been extensive State practice, precedent and doctrine".[3] Since codification in this pure and unadulterated form does not and cannot exist in the real world, I shall not spend any further time in discussing it.

The second category of international legislation consists in the codification and development of the law in areas in which the law has not been satisfactorily clarified or in which it has not yet been sufficiently developed in legal form in the practice of States. This process is normally known as "progressive development" and involves a conceptual extension of the first category of law-making. As I emphasize in my paper, any demarcation between the two categories is not easy to make in practice, but, for the purpose of identifying ideal types, it is one that may usefully be made.

---

[1] See article 1 (1) of the Commission's Statute.
[2] Brierly, J.L., *The Law of Nations* (1928), p. 96.
[3] See article 15 of the Commission's Statute.

The third category of international legislation consists of law-making *de novo*—that is, the making of rules on matters which have not yet been the subject of international legal regulation. The tremendous expansion of human activity into areas which hitherto have been free from the attentions of humankind, such as Antarctica, outer space and the deep seabed and ocean floor, has created a need for regulation at the level of international law. At the same time, the ever-greater interdependence between nations and peoples has created a situation in which issues which have hitherto either been allowed to remain unattended or left to the exclusive domain of national competence have come to be the focus of attention within the international community, thus creating a need for a legal assessment of the situation from the point of view of public policy within the international community as a whole. Prominent examples are issues such as human rights, the environment, genetic technology, racial discrimination, gender equality and the rights of the child.

The distinction which I have drawn between the three different categories of international legislation is important for a proper analysis of the work of the International Law Commission and an assessment of its successes and failures. So, for example, it may readily be observed that the Commission's greatest successes, in terms of the generation of law-making conventions, are mainly to be found in areas which fall within the traditional category of international legislation, that is, my category 1 or, by way of extension, my category 2. In contrast, if one considers the kind of international legislation which is my category 3, the balance sheet is a mixed one—there are some successes, but also some notable failures.

If one examines the Commission's record from the point of view of the fields in which it has conducted its work, it is evident that the Commission has been excluded from preparation of some of the most important law-making conventions of our time, notwithstanding that many of those conventions were drawn up within, or under the aegis of, the United Nations.

The law of the sea is a case in point. The Third United Nations Conference on the Law of the Sea was involved in two major kinds of law-making: on the one hand, codification—that is, international legislation belonging to my first category—coupled with elements of progressive development—that is, international legislation belonging to my category 2—and, on the other hand, law-making *de novo*—that is, international legislation belonging to the third of my three categories. That being so and in view of the nature of the problems that such law-making involved, it was not possible for States to leave the matter in the hands of the International Law Commission. Considerations of a broadly similar nature apply to the conventions which have been elaborated in the fields of social development, disarmament and the environment. The last two of these fields were also areas in which the exercise of making international law required a huge amount of technical knowledge of which the members of the International Law Commission were not possessed.

I shall close my presentation with two brief examples which may be of some assistance in considering the proper role of the International Law Commission within the overall international law-making process.

The first example is that of the International Convention Against the Taking of Hostages of 1979, which was drafted and adopted by the General Assembly without the participation of the International Law Commission. It is remarkable that a broadly similar instrument, the Convention on the Prevention and Punishment of Crimes against Internationally Protected Persons, including

Diplomatic Agents, was prepared by the Commission and adopted by the General Assembly just six years earlier, in 1973. The differences between these two conventions would seem to be negligible, at least in so far as their substance is concerned. Yet quite different procedures were employed for their preparation and elaboration. One might be tempted to conclude that there is a need for greater attention to be paid to coordination between the General Assembly and the International Law Commission.

My second example is that of the Draft Statute for an international criminal court. The question of the drafting of such a statute could be said most appropriately to belong to the domain of the International Law Commission and to the field of the progressive development of international law and its codification, particularly if regard is had to the history of the subject. At the same time, though, the very nature of the issues involved might be thought, rather, to draw the whole issue into the area of international legislation which I have characterized as law-making *de novo*—that is, my category 3. After all, the basic decision to create an international criminal court, with compulsory jurisdiction to try individuals who are nationals of Member States, is an eminently political one. That being so, it is small wonder that the Draft Statute which the Commission prepared has been referred by the General Assembly to the careful scrutiny of a preparatory committee, composed of the representatives of States.

Presentation by Professor Georges Abi-Saab

My presentation will focus on the output of the International Law Commission, specifically, on the manner in which that output interacts with the other elements which, together, contribute to and play a part in the process of making international law.

I would, however, preface my remarks with the following observation. As is well known, the Statute of the Commission draws a distinction between two kinds of law-making: namely, the codification of international law, on the one hand, and its progressive development, on the other. However, codification in the strict sense of the term, meaning the taking of a written "snapshot" of the unwritten law, has proved to be an impossible task. Every time that an organ deals with unwritten law and endeavours to reduce it to writing, it operates on that law in some way and adds something to it or otherwise affects its substance. There is, then, always an element of legislation in the process of codification. That element is, moreover, inescapably political in nature.

The Commission was initially conceived as the principal, if not the sole, mechanism through which the law-making work of the United Nations would be conducted. At the same time, there was, among the members of the academic community, little expectation that the Commission would prove to be very productive. This was true not only of the sceptics, like Julius Stone, but even of the enthusiasts for the Commission, like Hersch Lauterpaucht. As matters turned out, the Commission exceeded all expectations during its first 25 years. This was particularly so in the years between 1958, when the four Geneva Conventions on the Law of the Sea were adopted, and 1969, when the United Nations Conference on the Law of Treaties concluded its work. During this "prodigious decade", culminating with the adoption of the Vienna Convention on the Law of Treaties of 1969, the Commission produced an absolutely magnificent corpus of work.

Nowadays, though, law-making in the United Nations is carried on both through the Commission and through a large number of other specialized committees, organs and bodies. The activities of these bodies are broadly similar, but their output varies, ranging from treaties to normative resolutions.

In the paper which I have prepared for this Colloquium, I have compared these two forms of legislative instrument and have analysed their respective advantages and disadvantages. There is no time to make such an analysis here. However, one salient point which I would emphasize is that, whether one uses one mechanism or the other, the principal advantages of codification are the same: namely, making the law more visible and more readily available, involving new States in the process of reformulating the law, making the law clearer and helping to overcome any reluctance which there might be to accept adjudication. The formal normative character of the instrument which is the output of the legislative process is secondary.

By definition, treaties are relative in their effect: that is, they are binding solely upon those States which are party to them. The principal shortcoming of the treaty as an instrument of codification is that its use almost inevitably results in the creation of two legal regimes: the first, the regime of and under the treaty; the second, the regime of and under general, or customary, international law. This dualism can only be overcome in one of two ways—either by more States becoming party to the treaty or by the treaty breaking out of its framework and becoming general international law. The same argument can be made in respect of normative resolutions, which are not binding by and of themselves, but which, if well prepared and well drafted, may end up being recognized as representative of general international law. This process, at least in so far as it involves treaties, was analysed and explained by the International Court of Justice in its Judgments in the cases concerning the *North Sea Continental Shelf*; but what the Court said there may also be extended to the case of normative resolutions, since such an instrument may, just as well as a treaty, have a declaratory, crystallizing or generative effect in respect of custom.

It is quite appealing to refer to custom in this way so as to overcome the difficulties which surround the codification process. However, it is also a little bit odd. Customary international law, as we were used to think of it, was an "inductive" phenomenon, which grew haphazardly as and when the occasion arose or demanded. It blossomed like wild flowers in the wilderness. It was not something which was planned, planted or cultivated. Now, here we have instruments which we may have spent years negotiating—negotiating, perhaps, every word, every comma—and then, once the document is complete, we call in custom and say to it "please, take this set of norms and put it into the realm of general international law". The process by which it is supposed that general international law may be created is quite clearly not the same as that which we were wont to envisage. In other words, we may continue to talk in terms of "custom", but what we are describing is in fact a very different kind of legal process: one which is, in truth, legislative in nature.

My conclusion is that we should have recourse to presumptions—to legal fictions—in order to enhance the development of international law. There is nothing new in this. It is something that lawyers have always done. It is also what was done at Nürnberg and Tokyo. The two war-crimes tribunals considered that the Regulations respecting the Laws and Customs of War on Land annexed to the fourth Hague Convention, having weathered the heavy storms in international relations between 1907 and 1939, had become part of general international law. If, then, a convention weathers international life for a sufficiently long time, the rules which it lays down should be recognized to have passed into general international law. Admittedly, the Tokyo tribunal advanced this proposition in more cautious terms, couching it as a rebuttable presumption; but the general thrust of its reasoning was the same as that of its sister tribunal at Nürnberg. The international community should work on refining and elaborating such a presumption with a view to promoting the development of international law. It should also develop a presumption along the same lines which would be applicable to normative resolutions of the General Assembly.

Presentation by **Professor Yuri Kolosov**

A number of United Nations bodies are involved in the international law-making process, among them the United Nations Commission for International Trade Law (UNCITRAL), the Human Rights Commission, the Committee on the Peaceful Uses of Outer Space and a range of ad hoc bodies. The specialized agencies of the United Nations, such as the International Labour Organization, the International Civil Aviation Organization, the United Nations Educational, Scientific and Cultural Organization and the International Telecommunication Union, also play a significant role in the international legislative process. Mention should be made in this context, too, of the work of regional international organizations, such as the Organization for Security and Co-operation in Europe, the Council of Europe, the Commonwealth of Independent States, the Organization of American States and the Organization of African Unity.

Most of these treaty-making mechanisms have produced legal instruments which are of a specialized character. The International Law Commission, in contrast, has generally been involved in the elaboration of drafts which are general in nature and which are of more transcendental or wide-ranging significance. Moreover, the Commission is perhaps the only law-making mechanism in existence which successfully combines the tasks of codifying and of progressively developing international law.

Notwithstanding the criticism which has been made of it in recent years, the Commission will, in my opinion, continue, as it has done in the past, to play an active and important role in the international legislative process. I am not alone in thinking so. In 1985 Carl-August Fleischhauer, the then Legal Counsel of the United Nations, remarked that "the highly responsible process of codification and progressive development of international law under UN auspices has a long and bright future".[4] We, the community of international lawyers, can together make this prediction a reality.

My confidence in this regard is founded on the fact that the Commission is uniquely placed to fulfil the important function of surveying the present state of international law and identifying probable trends in its future development.

One such trend which may already be perceived concerns the enforcement of international law.

The idea of the primacy of international law in international relations has fascinated international lawyers for centuries. So, for example, the Russian jurist Fedor Martens—one of the promoters of the first and second world peace conferences of 1899 and 1907—dreamed of "the domination of law in the relations between peoples".[5] This ideal has yet to be achieved. This failure is

---

[4]Fleischhauer, "The United Nations and the Progressive Development and Codification of International Law", *Indian Journal of International Law*, vol. 25 (1985), p. 1 at p. 7.

[5]Martens, F.F., *Sovremennoe Mezhdunarodnoe Pravo Tsivilizovannih Narodov*, vol. 1 (1996), pp. 10-21 (in Russian).

sometimes explained either by reference to the insufficiency of international rules or by reference to the specific nature of the international legal system, in particular, the absence within that system of a proper law-enforcement mechanism. These shortcomings of the international legal order cannot be denied. Nevertheless, one cannot fail to take note of some important recent trends in the field of the implementation of international law. Mention might be made of the recent decisions of the Security Council on sanctions, the creation of a number of monitoring mechanisms in the field of human rights and the recent establishment of two war-crimes tribunals. These developments bear witness to the fact that the international community is slowly but surely moving towards accepting some kind of system of law enforcement. If this trend continues, it may even be possible to achieve the ideal of the acceptance of the primacy of international law. One cannot but agree with the words of the current Legal Counsel, Mr Hans Corell, who, at the 1995 United Nations Congress on Public International Law, affirmed, in his opening statement, the importance of the effective application of the principles and rules of international law as the surest way towards achieving peace and harmony among nations.[6]

Against this background, the Commission might wish to examine the possibility of elaborating draft articles on the issue of law enforcement which combine codification of the existing rules with the formulation of some new proposals. The Sixth Committee might also wish to entrust to the Commission the task of making a study of the meaning of the concept of the primacy of international law in international relations.

While all sorts of treaty-making bodies and mechanisms exist under the aegis of the United Nations and its specialized agencies, many of these are ad hoc in nature and lack permanence. They are also typically involved in responding to problems which have already emerged. In contrast, the preventative function of international law stands in need of much greater attention, especially in respect of such matters as the environment and armed conflict. Social disasters may be prevented through the adoption and elaboration of meaningful international legal rules. This goal, though, can only be achieved through the ongoing conduct of a careful holistic study of trends in international affairs and through the timely elaboration of relevant treaties. The undertaking of such a study is a task for which the International Law Commission is eminently suited. Indeed, the Commission is well qualified to play a coordinating role in the overall international law-making process by helping to initiate and steer efforts for the codification and progressive development of international law by the various organs, bodies and agencies within the United Nations system which are possessed of law-making responsibilities.

The contemporary treaty-making process is fragmented and highly specialized in character. Various organs of the United Nations, likewise the specialized agencies, each have an individual expertise in a very concrete area of international affairs and are involved in the drafting of treaties specifically within their respective spheres of competence. The Commission, on the other hand, should have a much broader vision. It should concentrate on topics which are multisectoral in nature: that is, topics which are of relevance to many, if not most, domains of international relations. Among such topics, one might mention the

---

[6]United Nations, *International Law as a Language for International Relations* (1996), p. 1 at p. 3 (United Nations publication, Sales No. T.96.V.4).

problem of the sources of international law (in the light of the new developments in that domain) and the issue of the subjects or actors of international law.

International law reflects the current state of international relations. International relations have been undergoing incessant change in recent years, giving birth to new problems and to new fields of enterprise which require legal regulation. There are also many areas of international relations which, though they are not new, have acquired fresh dimensions during recent times. The Commission might wish to look into these areas to see whether they are ripe for codification and progressive development. Fields which might merit the Commission's attention in this respect include the law of international cooperation, counter-terrorism, the right to international solidarity of peoples, sanctions and the protection of the territorial integrity of States.

"Soft" law has sometimes been said to be a field into which the Commission should enter. In my opinion, "soft" law is an idea which has no real juridical connotation. At the same time, it certainly is the case that the resolutions of international organizations may evidence the emergence of new customary rules which may, in due time, require codification. It might accordingly be appropriate for the Commission to undertake a survey of the resolutions of international organizations with a view to identifying emerging customary rules of international law. To the same end, the Commission might also usefully undertake periodic surveys of the doctrine of international law and of the work of international academic organizations and scientific institutions.

OPEN-FLOOR DISCUSSION

*

DÉBAT

Dr Nabil Elaraby*   Just as reform is now a major area of concern at the United Nations, so it is important that efforts be made to reform the International Law Commission. An important question which needs to be addressed in this regard is how to identify the topics on which the Commission is to conduct its work.

If one makes even a brief review of developments in the international law-making process during the last 30 years, one cannot but be struck by the proliferation which has occurred in the number of organs, bodies, mechanisms and procedures involved in the preparation, drafting and adoption of multilateral conventions. This process is mirrored in the General Assembly itself where practically all of the Main Committees are now involved in the elaboration of major law-making conventions, notwithstanding the clear recommendation in Annex II to the Rules of Procedure of the General Assembly that "whenever a Committee considers the legal aspects of a question important, the Committee should refer it for legal advice to the Sixth Committee or propose that the question should be considered by a joint Committee of itself and the Sixth Committee".[7] Had any of the conventions which have been prepared by or under

---

*Ambassador. Permanent Representative of the Arab Republic of Egypt to the United Nations. Member of the International Law Commission, 1994- .

[7]Rules of Procedure of the General Assembly, Annex II ("Methods and procedures of the General Assembly for dealing with legal and drafting questions"), Part I ("Recommendations of the General Assembly"), paragraph 1 (*d*): document A/520/Rev.15.

the aegis of the First or Third Committees been referred to the Sixth Committee for its advice, the preparation of the instruments concerned might well have ended up being assigned to the International Law Commission. However, it is very rare indeed for another Committee of the General Assembly to refer a legal matter to the Sixth Committee in the manner envisaged in Annex II to the Rules of Procedure. It is hardly surprising, then, that many major law-making conventions are now prepared and adopted without any involvement at all on the part of the Commission.

As Mr Owada remarks, many of the major law-making conventions which have been adopted in recent years deal with areas in which rules of customary law did not exist when work on those instruments began. However, this was no reason not to refer the preparation of those instruments to the Commission. After all, the Commission's Statute envisages that the drafting of multilateral conventions in such fields should form one of the two main branches of the Commission's work.

There has also been, over the years, a clear tendency to avoid referring to the Commission topics which are technical in nature. It is my belief that many of these topics could have been handled by the Commission or that the Commission could at least have made some form of contribution to elaborating the rules that have been adopted on those subjects. After all, the Commission's Statute makes it possible for the Commission to secure the assistance of outside experts—a facility of which the Commission has certainly availed itself in the past when it has been faced with problems of a scientific or technical nature. It would also assist the Commission's cause in this respect if it were fully to appreciate that it need not necessarily aim at the elaboration of what are, in effect, draft conventions and that its work might equally well take the form of declarations, guidelines and model rules.

Lastly, I would remark that now is an appropriate time for the Commission, together with the Sixth Committee of the General Assembly, to review and identify those areas in which there is an urgent need for the elaboration of legal rules so that the preparation of appropriate instruments might be undertaken as soon as possible.

Professor Bruno Simma* Traditionally, the procedure of international legislation has involved the elaboration of multilateral conventions, which, even if not widely ratified on the part of States, may, nevertheless, become part of customary law through the operation of one or other of the processes which were described by the International Court of Justice in the *North Sea Continental Shelf* cases. This traditional procedure can be distinguished from what might be termed the "new" process of international legislation. The latter process involves the elaboration of so-called "soft" law instruments—instruments which are not legally binding as such, but which have been painstakingly negotiated and very carefully drafted within the General Assembly or some other United Nations body. As Professor Abi-Saab nicely expressed it, these "soft" law instruments may become "hard" law through the operation of a form of rebuttable presumption: that is, they will be assumed to state the law in force except if and in so far as practices may exist which deviate from them and detract from their potential legislative force.

---

*Professor of International Law, Faculty of Law, Ludwig-Maximilians University, Munich, Germany. Member of the International Law Commission, 1997- .

I would like to ask Professor Abi-Saab a question in this regard. Would he give texts which the Commission might elaborate and adopt in a "soft" law format the same or similar chances of passing into general or customary international law as those instruments which are prepared in other United Nations bodies whose membership consists of the representatives of States? A case in point might be the draft articles on nationality of natural persons in relation to the succession of States which the Commission provisionally adopted this year on first reading and which are couched in the form of a declaration for adoption by the General Assembly.[8] Would such a text (in its final form) benefit from a rebuttable "legislative" presumption of the type which he described just as much as, say, the so-called "Friendly Relations" Declaration?[9]

Professor Abi-Saab I think that it would depend on how the text were "vehicled", so to speak. If it were adopted in the form of a resolution of the General Assembly and were approved by a very broad majority, I do not see why it should not create the same kind of legal expectation and be treated in the same way as a treaty for the purposes which I have described.

It may be recalled in this connection that the International Court of Justice, in the *Fisheries Jurisdiction* cases of 1974, considered that resolution VI of the first United Nations Conference on the Law of the Sea on Special Situations relating to Coastal Fisheries,[10] together with certain "near-agreements" which just failed of adoption at the unsuccessful Second United Nations Conference on the Law of the Sea, served as the basis for the crystallization of two institutions of general, or customary, international law: namely, the notion of a 12-mile exclusive fisheries zone and the concept of preferential fisheries rights in waters beyond that zone in favour of coastal States in a situation of special dependence upon their offshore fisheries.[11]

My answer to Professor Simma, then, is that it all depends on the circumstances. Accordingly, we should endeavour to refine the parameters and the conditions of application of the presumption which I have advocated in order that we may more easily determine whether or not it should apply in an individual case and, if it does, with what precise effect.

Professor Oscar Schachter* À propos of Professor Abi-Saab's presentation, mention should also be made of the significant role which power plays in the process of the formation of customary international law. As Charles de Visscher rightly remarked, every international custom is the product of power. Our world is marked by great discrepancies between States in terms of the power that they possess. That being so, the concept of formal equality can be but of very little use in analysing and explaining the development of custom. Rather, it is essential that the discrepancies in power between States be taken into account. In this regard, attention needs to be paid not only to the differences which exist

---

*Professor of International Law, Columbia University, New York, United States of America.

[8]Report of the International Law Commission on the work of its forty-ninth session, *Official Records of the General Assembly, Fifty-second Session, Supplement No. 10* (A/52/10), pp. 14-23.

[9]Declaration on Principles of International Law concerning Friendly Relations and Co-operation among States in accordance with the Charter of the United Nations, annexed to General Assembly resolution 2625 (XXV) of 24 October 1970.

[10]Document A/CONF.13/L.56.

[11]*Fisheries Jurisdiction (United Kingdom v. Iceland), Merits, Judgment, I.C.J. Reports 1974,* p. 3 at paras. 52-58, esp. at para. 52; and *Fisheries Jurisdiction (Federal Republic of Germany v. Iceland), Merits, Judgment, I.C.J. Reports 1974,* p. 175 at paras. 44-50, esp. at para. 44.

between States in terms of their military strength and capability, but also to the variations which exist in their levels of economic, social, cultural and educational development. Our world is a pluralist one. It is also highly unbalanced and unequal; and certainly, in the area of customary law, there is an enormous difference between States in the role that they can effectively play and the contribution that they can make.

Professeur Alain Pellet Je dirais au professeur Schachter que probablement les phénomènes de pouvoir ne se limitent pas à la formation du droit coutumier mais empreignent tout le droit international.

Sr Felipe Paolillo* *(Translated from Spanish)* Assessments of the Commission and its work have varied widely. On the one hand, there are those who laud the Commission and maintain that it has made a major contribution to the progressive development and codification of international law. On the other hand, there are those who are disappointed with the results of the Commission's labours and say that it has ceased to play an important role in the task of progressively developing and codifying international law.

I have great sympathy with both of these evaluations; for, in the final assessment, it is rather a matter of saying whether a glass is half full or half empty. Thus, on the one hand, one can certainly say that the Commission's achievements have been substantial and point out that the texts which it has produced are of an extraordinarily high quality. On the other hand, if one considers that some of the best jurists in the world have met and worked together for between 10 and 12 weeks each year for 50 years and that all that has been produced are 15 conventions, of which only 11 are in force, and that, of these 11, only two or three or, at the most, four are of anything approaching universal reach or character, then, one cannot but feel a certain sense of dissatisfaction.

It is my opinion, though, that the Commission has done what it was able to do and that it would not be realistic to expect it to have done more. For it to have played a greater role, it would have been necessary not only to change the Commission's methods of work and the procedures for selecting its topics, but also to transform the Commission's structure and its very nature, to such an extent that it would no longer have been the same body.

It might be useful to compare the experience of the Commission with what has occurred in the field of the international law of the environment.

Since the United Nations Conference on the Human Environment met in Stockholm 25 years ago, a veritable explosion has taken place in this area of the law. On the basis of its past record, it would have taken the International Law Commission centuries to generate the quantity of treaties, conventions and other instruments which have been concluded on environmental matters since 1972. Indeed, such has been the level of activity in this domain that some commentators have talked of "treaty congestion" and have suggested that priority should be given to monitoring and ensuring the execution of existing instruments, rather than to producing yet further new norms.

In this domain of international law, just as in the fields of human rights and international economic law, conditions have prevailed which are of a kind with which the International Law Commission is just not equipped to cope. Likewise,

---

*Ambassador of Uruguay to the Holy See. Permanent Representative of Uruguay to the United Nations Food and Agriculture Organization.

79

practices and techniques have been employed which the Commission has shown itself unable or unwilling to embrace.

In the first place, work in this area has proceeded not on the basis of some previously agreed programme envisaging the progressive, measured, step-by-step development of a system or corpus of environmental law. Rather, the law has been developed in response to specific problems, as and when they arose and became pressing. Many of these problems demanded an immediate response; and this they received. Thus, a number of treaties of great complexity have been negotiated, have been concluded and have entered into force, all within a very short period of time. Of particular note in this connection are the Vienna Convention for the Protection of the Ozone Layer of 1985, the Montreal Protocol on Substances that Deplete the Ozone Layer of 1987 and the United Nations Framework Convention on Climate Change of 1992. I simply cannot conceive of the Commission being able to respond to this type of pressure so fast and so well—or even at all.

Secondly, the response which has been made to these external pressures has taken a variety of forms. It has consisted not simply of conventions and treaties, but, rather, of a multiplicity of different types of instruments, ranging from conventions and treaties, on the one hand, to declarations, codes of conduct, standards, regulations and model rules, on the other. These kinds of document are usually characterized as "soft law"; but, "soft" as they may be, the impact which they have had on the law in the field of the environment is palpable and substantial. In contrast, the International Law Commission has shown a marked preference for the conventional form. In the 50 years of its existence, it is only in exceptional cases that it has generated other forms of output.

The third characteristic of the legislative process in the environmental field has been its decentralization. A great number and variety of fora have been created or employed in order to transact business in this domain. The result has perhaps been the creation of a body of law which is characterized by contradictions, *lacunae* and a certain measure of disorganization. However, it is, none the less, that: a body of law. It is, moreover, a body of law with which States very largely comply.

The fourth significant feature is the political character of the organs and mechanisms which have been employed to make the law. All of these bodies have been composed of States' representatives. The law in the field of the environment has thus developed under the constant guidance and control of States. In contrast, States have no direct involvement in the work of the International Law Commission.

Lastly, the political character of the law-making machinery which has been employed in the environmental field has ensured that the development of the law in that domain has fully taken into account and appropriately responded to a number of highly important political factors. An example might be the development of the principle of so-called common but differentiated responsibility in order to take account of the special needs and circumstances of developing States. It is difficult to imagine the International Law Commission having responded appropriately, or at all, to many of the political and economic factors which have served to shape the law of the environment.

In sum, the Commission could never have produced anything of the nature or quality of modern environmental law. For it to have done so, fundamental changes would have had to have been made to its composition, its structure and even its very nature.

However, it is not my intention to suggest that the Commission should undergo such a radical transformation. With appropriate adjustments in its working methods and with a more imaginative approach to the identification of topics for inclusion into its programme of work—such as that outlined by Professor Orrego Vicuña—the Commission should be able to continue to play a useful role in the international law-making process, just as it has done over the last 50 years.

Professeur Alain Pellet   Peut-être, comme dit M. Paolillo, que la Commission du droit international ne fait pas son métier, mais j'ai quand même été très frappé d'entendre le Président de la Cour internationale de Justice rappeler que le dernier arrêt de la Cour internationale de Justice, dans l'affaire du *Projet Gabčíkovo-Nagymaros*, est une sorte d'hommage à la Commission dont les projets, y compris les projets qui ne sont pas encore devenus des conventions, sont très largement utilisés par la Cour. Donc c'est du droit positif par excellence.

Sr Felipe Paolillo *(Translated from Spanish)*   I do apologize if I have not been very clear in what I have said. Far from maintaining that the Commission has failed to fulfil its mandate, it was my intention to say that it has discharged its functions very well indeed. My point was a different one: namely, that the Commission should continue to play the same role that it has so successfully played to date—codifying the traditional areas of international law—and that it should not aspire to a role in other legal domains, particularly those in which the law is highly dynamic and is evolving under pressures of a political or economic character. It simply is not equipped or designed for a task of this latter type.

Professeur Alain Pellet   Sur ce dernier point au moins, je suis absolument d'accord avec M. Paolillo. Je crois qu'il faut ne pas demander à la Commission du droit international de faire des choses qu'elle ne peut pas faire. Je fais partie de ceux qui sont convaincus que la codification du droit de l'environnement, par exemple, n'est pas une bonne tâche pour la Commission simplement parce que l'arrière-plan écologique, économique, politique et financier même de ce sujet échappe totalement à la Commission par manque d'équipement concret et d'équipement intellectuel.

Mr Tyge Lehmann*   The Commission has been extraordinarily successful in its job of codifying public international law. Most of that field is now codified— or will be when the Commission completes its work on the last major topic of State responsibility. Once it has completed a second reading of its draft articles on that subject, the Commission will find itself in a difficult situation; for, if it is to survive, it will have to redefine its role and its *raison d'être vis-à-vis* the many other law-making bodies which now exist within the United Nations system. Instead of focusing our attention on improving the dialogue between the Commission and the Sixth Committee, we may need, in consequence, to think in broader terms and consider establishing a dialogue between the Commission and other law-making bodies and mechanisms, be they in the field of human rights, disarmament, the environment or whatever.

---

*Representative of Denmark to the Sixth Committee of the General Assembly of the United Nations.

An interesting example of what I have in mind is to be found in this year's Report of the International Law Commission to the General Assembly. The Commission there remarks that:

> "[it] is aware of the discussion currently taking place in other forums on the subject of reservations to normative multilateral treaties, and particularly treaties concerning human rights, and wishes to contribute to this discussion in the framework of the consideration of the subject of reservations to treaties that has been before it since 1993".[12]

It then proceeds to outline a number of preliminary conclusions on the subject,[13] with a view to clarifying the law and so assisting human rights monitoring bodies in handling reservations to the treaties which they oversee, but also with a view to engaging those bodies in a dialogue on the proper development of the law in this field.

Once it has completed its codification of the fundamental areas of international law, the Commission should assume a more visible role within the United Nations system and act as a kind of legal adviser to other United Nations bodies. It is pertinent to note in this regard that the recent experience of the preparation of the Draft Statute for an international criminal court has demonstrated that the Commission can respond swiftly and effectively to requests which may be made of it for its assistance.

Mr Patrick Lipton-Robinson*   The role which the Commission has played in the international law-making process has been quantitatively small, but qualitatively very important. The Commission's output has represented only a small proportion of the global production of international law, whether that be measured in terms of codification or of progressive development. The challenge for the Commission is whether it can increase its output without sacrificing quality. The Commission is essentially a deliberative body and it typically takes some time—sometimes, I am tempted to say, a long time—to conclude its work on a particular subject. Yet there has been a number of recent instances in which the Commission has acted very quickly. Its preparation of a Draft Statute for an international criminal court is the most prominent example. Another might be its recent work on reservations to treaties—though opinions may differ on whether it has in fact acted too quickly in that particular case.

Whether or not the output of the Commission is increased, a question to which both the Commission and the General Assembly should devote their attention is that of how to increase or enhance the role which developing countries play in the international law-making process. Many developing countries have gained their independence since the end of the 1950s and both they and their nationals have become a major presence within international law-making bodies. However, serious questions can be asked about how far that presence has been translated into true and effective participation in the international law-making process, likewise about whether it has exerted a significant and constructive influence on the international law that has been made.

---

*Deputy Solicitor-General of Jamaica. Member of the International Law Commission, 1992-1996.

[12]Report of the International Law Commission on the work of its forty-ninth session, *Official Records of the General Assembly, Fifty-second Session, Supplement No. 10* (A/52/10), p. 126.
[13]Ibid., pp. 126-127.

Lastly, I wish to express some concern with regard to Professor Abi-Saab's suggestion that certain conventions and other law-making instruments benefit from the operation of a form of rebuttable presumption when it comes to determining their status at customary international law. If the effect of that presumption were to be that the mere passage of time was sufficient to transform an instrument into general international law, without any need for States to react to that instrument in any particular way or to adhere to it or otherwise to express their consent to the norms which it contains, then his proposal would not be one to which I could accede.

Professor Abi-Saab It was certainly not my intention to suggest that it is enough for an instrument to exist for a certain period of time in order for that instrument to become law by the operation of some kind of prescription. At the same time, though, it is certainly the case that we lawyers do not like a void. My experience on the bench bears out the conclusion that, when judges are faced with the possibility of a legal vacuum, they will go to the greatest lengths to avoid that result. They will search for anything out of which they might construct a conclusion. They will hang on to whatever they can find and will even fabricate title for the propositions that they adopt. If they have in front of them an instrument which has been very carefully negotiated and drafted and which has been widely accepted by States, they will hang on to it like a lifeboat in a storm. Whatever theoretical explanations we may concoct to explain their behaviour and to justify their conclusions, this phenomenon remains a fact of legal life.

In my paper, I maintain that this phenomenon should be viewed as a kind of "soft" legislative process. In this process, power plays a crucial role. After all, law rationalizes power and, though it may try to civilize it, it cannot ignore it or do away with it. Thus, if one analyses this legislative process, it is the case, first of all, that the instrument concerned has to be adopted; and the powerful can prevent this from taking place. Then, if the instrument in question is a treaty, it must enter into force. Sometimes, even the most powerful of States cannot prevent this from occurring, as is clear from the example of the United Nations Convention on the Law of the Sea of 1982. Next, because of the "soft" nature of the process in hand, there exists a kind of facility for "contracting out" of the rules that it generates; and, here once more, there is room for the operation of relations of power. It has to be said that it is not yet clear what the conditions are for the exercise of this option of "contracting out". There is, of course, the well known phenomenon of the so-called "persistent objector". This condition, though, I consider to be but transitory in nature. A State cannot stand apart forever from important *jus cogens* rules. Thus, France tried to object to the notion of *jus cogens* itself, but that cause is now lost and it can usefully object to that institution no longer. In the case of part XI of the United Nations Convention on the Law of the Sea, on the other hand, the United States and its partners did succeed in getting the international community to make important changes to the rules which it laid down. This, however, was during a transitional stage in the evolution of the pertinent rules. Once the period of transition is over, a general rule exists and it applies to all States without exception.

Therefore, the presumption which I have proposed is not a simplistic or straightforward one. Moreover, it certainly stands in need of further examination and refinement. Nevertheless, I would suggest that it holds out the promise of a more accurate and satisfying analysis of the situations that I have described than a simple, fictitious and all-inclusive explanation by reference to the custom process.

Professeur Alain Pellet Le professeur Abi-Saab a dit que le droit rationalisait la puissance. Je pense qu'en effet le droit est un formidable instrument finalement de la puissance ou du pouvoir, comme l'a dit tout à l'heure le professeur Schachter. Mais en même temps le droit est un piège pour la puissance, c'est-à-dire que, une fois que la puissance est engagée dans un processus juridique, elle peut difficilement en sortir. Cela me semble quand même plus frappant en ce qui concerne le traité, qui est vraiment un piège à volonté et pas du tout à mon avis l'expression d'une volonté, que pour ce qui est de la coutume où les choses sont un peu plus compliquées.

Sir Franklin Berman* À propos of what has been said by Dr Elaraby and Mr Lehmann, one can only wonder why it is that the International Law Commission is perceived to be the exclusive property of the Sixth Committee of the General Assembly. Why is it that the other Main Committees of the General Assembly have never thought of referring topics to the Commission? Is it simply because they are unaware of the possibility? Is it indeed only in the Sixth Committee that the Commission is really known about, respected and appreciated? How would the Sixth Committee react if one of the other Main Committees were to refer a question to the Commission? How would work on such a matter be coordinated? Questions such as these are increasingly important nowadays, when there is more and more discussion of the Commission undertaking work in areas of the law into which it has not ventured in the past.

Turning to the presentations which we have heard, an important qualification or addition needs to be made to what the panellists have said. It is not solely in the field of "hard" law that the Commission conducts its work. In fact, much of what it does falls within the sphere of "soft" law. A unique feature of the International Law Commission, which distinguishes it from nearly every other lawmaking body in the United Nations system, is that its output does not just consist of a carefully considered and coherent legal draft, but comprises also an accompanying commentary on that draft. These commentaries are of inestimable value, setting forth, as they do, the *ratio legis* for all to see. Moreover, they transcend the fate of the drafts which they explain. Thus, whatever the General Assembly's verdict may be upon the Commission's proposals, the commentaries remain and exert a considerable influence upon the reception of the Commission's ideas into international law, whether by the customary route or otherwise.

Dr Pemmaraju Sreenivasa Rao** Professor Schachter has already referred to the influence which power exerts over the making of international law. In the same vein, Mr Lipton-Robinson has remarked how States of the developing world, although they make up the preponderant majority of the international community, have proved unable effectively to avail themselves for their own benefit of the various bodies and mechanisms which exist for making international law. There are, then, two forces or factors which affect when and for what purpose the international law-making process is initiated. On the one hand, those who wield the greatest power would like to limit the role of international law to a minimum and so will only haltingly and hesitatingly make use of it as an instrument to serve their ends. On the other hand, those who have the most need

---

*Legal Adviser, Foreign and Commonwealth Office, United Kingdom of Great Britain and Northern Ireland.

**Joint Secretary and Legal Adviser, Head, Legal and Treaties Division, Ministry of External Affairs, India. Member of the International Law Commission, 1987- .

84

of the law are not fully alive to the possibilities which it offers and are not adequately equipped to operationalize or to develop this instrument for their own protection. As a result of these two forces, international law remains underdeveloped and the processes for its codification, underutilized.

If the output of the International Law Commission has indeed fallen short of expectations, it is accordingly not proper that the blame for this state of affairs should be laid at the Commission's door.

Professeur Alain Pellet   C'est une vision bien pessimiste du droit !

Mr Raul Goco*   When the Charter of the United Nations was being drafted in San Francisco in 1945, a proposal was made to confer law-making powers on the new world organization. This proposal was roundly defeated. Instead, it was decided to vest the General Assembly with the power to "initiate studies and make recommendations for the purpose of . . . encouraging the progressive development of international law and its codification". Over time, the exercise by the General Assembly of this power has resulted in a veritable proliferation of law-making bodies and mechanisms. Each of these has developed its own infrastructure, each has accrued its own vested interests and each has its own particular field of law-making which it claims as its own exclusive province. The fiftieth anniversary of the foundation of the International Law Commission is an appropriate point to reflect on this state of affairs and to consider whether it is not time to bring some order to this vast international legislative complex. In particular, thought should be given to rationalizing the functions of the many law-making organs and bodies which now exist and to harmonizing their particular functions with those of the Commission. Indeed, there is an urgent need to define precisely the role of the Commission.

Now is also an appropriate time to amend the Commission's Statute. That Statute is now 50 years old and a number of its provisions are certainly in need of revision. The most prominent example is article 26 (3), which stipulates that, in conducting consultations with international and national organizations and in compiling a list of those organizations which are to receive the Commission's documents, the Commission and the Secretary-General of the United Nations "shall comply with resolutions of the General Assembly and other principal organs of the United Nations concerning relations with Franco's Spain and shall exclude from consultations and from the list, organizations which have collaborated with the nazis and the fascists". This provision is now irrelevant and it would be best if it were excised from the Statute.

Turning lastly to a remark which was made by Mr Paolillo, the Commission does indeed maintain direct contact with Governments. It is part of the standard practice of the Commission under its Statute to transmit the drafts which it prepares to States for their comments and observations. The Commission, then, does not work independently of, or in isolation from, Governments, but, rather, functions in close cooperation with them.

Mr Hisashi Owada   In my presentation, I made a distinction between three categories of international legislation. My purpose in so doing was to contribute to a better identification of the precise role which the International Law

---

*Ambassador of the Philippines to Canada. Member of the International Law Commission, 1997- .

Commission should play within the overall international law-making process. While the Commission has done a marvellous job to date in the fields in which it has worked, it is hardly suited for all kinds of legislative work. In particular, it should enter the domain of the third category of international law-making— what I have styled law-making *de novo*—only with the greatest of caution. Here, the factors which operate on the law-making process extend beyond the narrowly legal to the political, economic, social and cultural and the weight of these latter factors is often preponderant over the former. It is unlikely that the Commission will be the organ which is best suited to identifying, evaluating and accommodating considerations such as these. To pretend otherwise is to expect the impossible of the Commission and to do a disservice to the cause which it exists to promote.

Turning to the question of ways in which the work of the Commission may be enhanced, it might be useful, first, for the Commission to revisit certain of the topics whose codification it has already completed. In particular, it could usefully review the conventions which have been concluded on the basis of its drafts and which are now in force in order to see how they are actually being applied in practice by the States which are party to them. It is a negative aspect of the codification process that it risks freezing or stultifying the law which it renders into written form. A review of the kind which I am suggesting might help to identify cases in which the law has thus been frozen and contribute to their eventual elimination.

Secondly, it is important that the Commission should establish closer working relationships with the other Main Committees of the General Assembly, besides the Sixth Committee. I particularly have in mind the Third Committee, whose legislative activities could be rendered much more efficient and effective through the involvement of the International Law Commission.

Lastly, consideration should be given to developing an advisory role for the Commission similar to that which was discharged in the League of Nations by the Advisory Committee of Jurists.

2

MAJOR COMPLEXITIES
ENCOUNTERED IN
CONTEMPORARY INTERNATIONAL LAW-MAKING

*

PRINCIPALES DIFFICULTÉS
RENCONTRÉES AUJOURD'HUI
DANS LE PROCESSUS NORMATIF INTERNATIONAL

Introduction par l'Animateur, **le professeur Alain Pellet***

En ce qui concerne le deuxième sujet qui figure dans le programme de ce Colloque, il s'agit d'essayer d'identifier plus spécifiquement les problèmes auquels se heurte le processus normatif dans le monde contemporain, la manière dont ces difficultés peuvent être surmontées et le rôle que la Commission du droit international peut jouer à cette fin.

Nous commencerons la discussion avec un exposé par le professeur Francisco Orrego Vicuña. Le professeur Orrego Vicuña est un ancien membre du Comité juridique interaméricain. Il est actuellement Président du Conseil chilien pour les relations internationales et de la branche chilienne de l'International Law Association. Il est en outre professeur de droit international à l'Université du Chili et a été professeur invité dans plusieurs universités étrangères, notamment celle de Stanford aux États Unis et celle de Paris-II en France.

Le deuxième intervenant sera M. Peter Tomka. Chacun sait qu'actuellement il est Président de la Sixième Commission de l'Assemblée générale des Nations Unies. Il est aussi Conseiller juridique du Ministère des affaires étrangères de la Slovaquie. Il a été l'agent de la Slovaquie devant la Cour internationale de Justice dans l'affaire du *Projet Gabčíkovo-Nagymaros*, dans lequel j'ai moi-même été conseil et avocat. Il a enseigné à l'Université Charles de Prague jusqu'en 1991 et il a rédigé sa thèse sur la codification du droit international aux Nations Unies, ce qui tombe tout à fait à pic en ce qui concerne le sujet de ce Colloque.

Presentation by **Professor Francisco Orrego Vicuña**

The work of the Commission should be examined within the broader framework of international society and the international legal system. The first question which must be asked in this regard is where international society is going. We are still at a stage where the Grotian order prevails, particularly in so

---

*Professeur, Université de Paris-X, Paris (France). Membre de la Commission du droit international, 1989- . Président de la Commission pendant sa quarante-neuvième session.

far as the role of States is concerned. However, there are interesting developments afoot which are influencing and changing the shape of the more traditional Grotian order. These include: a trend towards greater human freedom, dignity and welfare; an increase in regionalism; a curtailment of the exclusive role of States, together with the emergence of a polycentric, multicultural world society; the perfection of international law, particularly through its better enforcement; and a strengthening in the role of international organizations. A variety of factors lie behind and explain these changes, but foremost among them is probably the current technological revolution.

These changes have had specific implications for the contemporary international legal order. Generally speaking, one may say that the role of State consent is no longer what it was, new elements having affected the definition of its role. Limitations need accordingly to be placed on the role of consensus in the theory of sources of international law in order to enable some accommodation to be made between the need for stability and the demands for change.

The basic characteristics of the current international legal order may be summarized as follows: integration of public and private international law; interlinkage of national and international law; a significant role for non-binding agreements; new approaches to solving the problem of compliance; and a certain congestion of the international legal order.

It is within this broad framework that opportunities for the International Law Commission are to be found, but also its limits.

What role can be foreseen, then, for the International Law Commission?

As international society becomes more integrated, there will, without doubt, be an ever-greater need for the development of some form of constitution. Here, there is a task which the International Law Commission can fulfil. The Commission might undertake the systematic identification of the basic governing principles of international law, refine their meaning and content, prepare an appropriate commentary upon each of them and, as the end result of the process, create some kind of "restatement" of international law. In so doing, the Commission could provide important guidance for the development of the international legal system as a whole. Codification and progressive development of the law in a decentralized society require the identification of guiding principles, not the elaboration of rules which are intended to provide for every eventuality and to solve every problem which might arise. The Commission should concentrate on the task of identifying principles and eschew the comprehensive treatment which it has given in the past to nearly every subject that it has studied. The latter approach has proved to be extremely slow and time-consuming and has involved a degree of needless rigidity in the nature and content of its output.

Were the Commission to undertake such a task, it would become possible to think in terms of involving it more broadly than hitherto in the United Nations legislative process; for it might then deal not only with subjects belonging to the domain of "classical" international law, but also with specialized and technical areas of the law. The Commission's lack of involvement in such fields to date has relegated it to a secondary role in the United Nations system and in the international legal order as a whole.

Turning now to the kind of work which the Commission has been doing, it cannot but be remarked that the Commission has been reluctant to address new issues, largely because the methodologies which it has typically employed have been oriented towards a rigorous identification of the practice and *opiniones juris* of States. However, there is just as great a need to identify those elements of State practice which are indicative of legal trends as there is to determine the precise significance of State practice in fields in which that practice is extensive and broadly concordant. Only by embarking on such forms of inquiry will it be possible for the Commission to respond to the current concerns of the international community. Of course, the Commission would be likely to find itself involved in the study and use of so-called "soft" law materials, as well as in the survey and examination of patterns of regional and bilateral treaty-making. However, the Commission's task would continue to be one of codification, albeit conceived in a broader sense than heretofore—just as it would if it followed my suggestion of embarking on the identification of the guiding principles of the international legal order.

For the Commission to engage in projects of the kinds which I have described would have certain consequences. The most significant of these would be that the Commission should cease to be overly concerned about the reaction of States to its work. It should deal with the topics before it in the way that it thinks best and should leave it to the Sixth Committee of the General Assembly to decide the final form which should be given to its output. Certainly, the Commission should not try to anticipate the wishes and desires of States in this regard, as it has done in the past.

A further suggestion which I wish to make is that the Commission should assume some form of interpretative function within the United Nations system. The field of United Nations law has been greatly influenced by the interpretations which have been given to that law by the Security Council and by other organs of the Organization. There is no reason why the International Law Commission should not be requested to issue legal opinions on at least certain aspects of this body of law. The possibility might even be contemplated of the Secretary-General seeking opinions from the Commission on such matters in the exercise of her or his powers under Article 99 of the Charter of the United Nations.

A further new role which the Commission might discharge would be that of certifying points of international law in the manner that ministries for foreign affairs typically do at the domestic level.

Were the preceding suggestions adopted, the Commission would be better able to anticipate the needs of the international community, by preparing rules in response to "legal emergencies" and by anticipating the needs of international society more broadly, as, for example, by identifying trends in the practice of States, even when that practice is not yet extensive in character. An example might be the issue of human cloning. There is widespread agreement within the international community that cloning should not be permitted in the case of human beings; and, although that practice is not yet extensive, there is already a clear indication of what the law might look like in the near future. This sort of issue could be dealt with perfectly well by the International Law Commission.

In order for the Commission to be able to fulfil the roles which I have proposed for it, there would need to be some change in the manner or nature of its composition. One possibility might be to adopt a system of tiered representation. Scholars and government officials would continue to have a role to play in codification processes of the kind which I have described. However, the new actors within the international community should also have some form of input into the Commission's work. To this end, I would suggest that only some of the Commission's members be elected by the General Assembly. Others should be appointed by scientific institutions and yet others by those non-governmental organizations, including business organizations, that have a particular interest in areas of the law on which the Commission is to conduct work.

There is also a need for the members of the Commission to be more accountable to the community that has elected them. I would make two specific suggestions in this respect. First, members should be barred from reelection if they have attended less than 50 per cent of the Commission's meetings. Secondly, members who have attended less than 50 per cent of the meetings on a particular subject should be barred from voting on that subject.

In conclusion, if the role and composition of the Commission are adapted in the ways which I have suggested, it should be possible for the Commission better to serve the needs of the international community in its late Grotian form.

Presentation by Dr Peter Tomka

I will focus on two aspects of the international law making: first, the fragmentation of law-making and, secondly, the length of the preparatory stage of the codification process.

The codification process is initiated by a decision of the General Assembly of the United Nations. The General Assembly selects a topic and then allocates it to an appropriate body for study. The Commission may be the principal subsidiary organ which has been established in order to assist the General Assembly to discharge its mandate under Article 13 (1) (a) of the Charter of the United Nations to advance the "progressive development of international law and its codification"; but it is far from being the only body which is involved in this kind of activity. While the Commission is, as it were, the standing body for public international law manufacturing within the United Nations, the General Assembly has established a number of other committees which have produced the drafts of many conventions. Usually, these other committees have reported to the Sixth Committee of the General Assembly. However, the Sixth Committee has certainly not maintained any kind of "monopoly" in the supervision of international law-making within the United Nations, Indeed, it never had one. The whole area of the international law of the environment has been developed by the United Nations outside the Sixth Committee, with most of the work being done by the United Nations Environment Programme and the Second Committee (Economic and Financial) of the General Assembly. The work of the United Nations in the field of human rights law-making has been supervised by yet another of the Main Committees of the General Assembly, its Third Committee (Social, Humanitarian and Cultural). The law of disarmament has mostly been developed by the United Nations Conference on Disarmament and by the First Committee (Political and Security) of the General Assembly. The law of outer space is yet another example of an area of international law which has remained outside the Sixth Committee's purview while being developed within the United Nations.

There is, then, a plurality of law-making bodies within the United Nations—and that is without even mentioning the specialized agencies. Law-making within the international community is, therefore, "fragmented", at least as far as fora are concerned.

However, this problem—if, indeed, it is a problem—is moot. The United Nations and its specialized agencies provide fora for law-making activities, but they do not have any power to legislate. The United Nations is not a real lawgiver. Limiting our attention here to the international *lex scriptum*, that law is the product of the international legislative activities of States and it embodies their express consent. States retain the final control over that law and it is up to them to take care to avoid conflicts or disharmony between the different normative instruments which they jointly produce. However, even if there should be some form of contradiction between two or more such instruments, international law, in particular the law of treaties, provides remedies in the form of such principles of interpretation as *lex specialis derogat legi generali* and *lex posterior derogat lex priori* and in the rules contained in article 30 of the 1969 Vienna Convention on the Law of Treaties concerning the application of successive treaties relating to the same subject matter.

I make these remarks since concern has sometimes been expressed about the fragmentation of the law-making process and proposals have been advanced, in response to this concern, to entrust the International Law Commission with some kind of supervisory, or coordinating, function with regard to international law-making as a whole. It is, moreover, difficult to imagine how the Commission could effectively perform such a function and at the same time continue to fulfil its principal task of promoting the progressive development of international law and its codification.

The International Law Commission, by virtue of its composition and its working methods, is unique among the various bodies which are involved in international law-making within the United Nations. This should be kept in mind when the General Assembly is deciding to which organ it should refer a topic for consideration and for the elaboration of a draft.

The Commission is particularly suited to dealing with topics which require a detailed and in-depth study of State practice, the discovery of *lacunae* within that practice and the formulation of rules which might appropriately fill them. The Commission can hardly be replaced in the performance of this task by an ad hoc committee composed of the representatives of States. It is doubtful whether such an ad hoc committee would have been able to prepare more efficiently than the Commission a draft such as that which the Commission prepared on the law of treaties. On the other hand, the Commission, had it been asked to do so, would have been equally capable of preparing certain of the instruments which have been drafted by ad hoc committees. My conclusion is that it is not the importance of a topic, but rather its nature, which should guide the General Assembly in deciding to which body its study should be allocated.

The codification process is, of course, a law-making process; but not all law-making processes are also codification processes. Codification is a law-making process which involves, first of all, the identification and formulation of rules of customary law and the development of new rules. If we do not make the distinction between this process and other types of law-making process, then we may easily end up unjustifiably criticizing the Commission for not performing certain functions which it is hardly suited to discharge.

I will now turn to the criticism, which has sometimes been made of the Commission, that its processes are excessively lengthy and slow. On average, it has taken about 10 years for the Commission to prepare a final draft on a topic, the process involving giving two readings to that draft and soliciting and receiving from States written comments on that draft between its first and second readings.

The set of 73 draft articles which the Commission prepared on the law of the sea were prepared over a seven-year period, between 1949 and 1956. The draft which served as a basis for the 1961 Vienna Convention on Diplomatic Relations took four years for the Commission to prepare, between 1954 and 1958. It took six years, between 1955 and 1961, for to the Commission to prepare its set of 71 draft articles on consular relations.

91

To prepare the draft which was subsequently transformed into the 1969 Vienna Convention on the Law of Treaties took the Commission 17 years, between 1949 and 1966. However, the topic was a difficult one. There were also several other factors which contributed to the length of the preparatory process in this case. The first was that there was a succession of four Special Rapporteurs on the topic. The second was that, for much of this time, the Commission was hard at work on other topics and so had little or no time left to consider the reports on the topic which were submitted by its Special Rapporteurs. Thirdly, the Commission, at a certain stage, changed its approach to the topic and opted for the elaboration of a draft convention rather than an expository code. In truth, the Commission's draft was prepared over five years, between 1962 and 1966, on the basis of just five reports from the Special Rapporteur. This was a quite remarkable achievement, given the importance and vastness of the topic concerned.

The Commission prepared its draft articles on special missions expeditiously. The same can be said of its draft on the topic of the relations between States and international organizations and of its draft articles on the succession of States in respect of treaties, a total of just six reports being needed from its Special Rapporteurs in the latter case.

However, starting in the mid-1970s, something began to go wrong in the work of the Commission. It took much longer for the Commission to prepare its drafts, the draft articles of the law of the non-navigational uses of international watercourses and on jurisdictional immunities of States and their property being cases in point.

Several factors would seem to explain this development. First, the Commission has been overburdened. It has had too many topics on its agenda and there has not been sufficient time for it to consider all of them in an efficient and effective way. Secondly, the increase in the number of members of the Commission which the General Assembly introduced in 1981 has had a negative impact on the speed of the Commission's work. Thirdly, beginning in the mid-1970s, States have been slower to submit to the Commission their written comments on the drafts which it has provisionally adopted on the first reading. Whereas, until then, they had usually taken but a couple of months to reply, it now took them more than a year. Moreover, as the President of the International Law Commission remarked yesterday when introducing the Commission's annual report to the General Assembly, the Commission typically now receives a very low number of responses from States to its requests for comments and observations.[1]

A study of the reports of the Commission reveals that the Commission is able to deal effectively with three topics, or at the most four, during its annual 12-week sessions. If it has more topics on its agenda and makes an effort to consider each one at each session, it takes longer to elaborate its final drafts. Moreover, if a greater number of topics is considered at a session, it results in a piecemeal approach. The Commission submits just a few articles on each topic to the General Assembly, which makes it difficult for the Sixth Committee to consider them in a rational manner and to provide the Commission with useful feedback.

The Commission should, therefore, strive to keep the items on its active agenda down to a manageable number. Otherwise, the Commission risks the criticism that the preparatory process is too lengthy. The Commission's goal

---

[1] See document A/C.6/52/SR.16, para. 3.

should be to organize its work in such a manner that it is able to finalize drafts on two topics during each quinquennium.

Open-floor Discussion

*

Débat

Sr Orlando Rebagliati* *(Translated from Spanish)* In order properly to address the problems which beset the making of international law, we should first undertake the systematic and orderly identification of the principal issues which arise in this regard before proceeding to consider the measures which should be taken for their solution. In my opinion, there are two kinds of issues: on the one hand, material issues and, on the other, substantive issues.

In the papers which have been written for this Colloquium, frequent reference has been made to a number of problems of a material character. Examples are the financial and human resource constraints under which international organizations and States of the developing world currently labour.

I, however, would like to focus on the problems of a substantive nature which surround the law-making process. In so doing, it is necessary to bear in mind the current nature of the international community. As Professor Orrego Vicuña rightly remarked, we are still very much in the era of sovereign nation States. The complexity of the international law-making process has its origins in this characteristic of the modern international legal and political order and in the concomitant absence from that order of any centralized law-making organ or process. For rules of international law to be made, those rules must find a basis in the convergent conduct of States operating through one of the various procedures which constitute the sources of international law.

As our modern societies evolve under the ever greater influence of technological developments and economic forces, it is frequently said that there is a "need" for more extensive regulation of this or that activity at the international level. Of course, in certain cases, this "need" is quite genuine; but, in others, it is not. It would be better if the frequent calls which are made for the creation of new rules of international law or the adoption of new international instruments were subjected to more careful scrutiny and a fuller and more thorough assessment made of whether such rules and instruments are indeed necessary. Frequently, it seems, we find ourselves in a precipitate rush to develop new rules of international law on a subject when it would have been much better first to have undertaken the calm and considered study of the alleged need for those rules.

Much of the problem in this regard stems from the multiplicity of organs and bodies which currently exist for developing international legal instruments and making international law. The complexity to which this legislative decentralization gives rise is probably inevitable at the current stage of international relations; for to rationalize and properly institutionalize the procedures for international law-making would presuppose a radical change in the very structure of the international community. However, this does not mean that nothing at all can be done about the problem.

---

*Legal Adviser, Ministry of Foreign Affairs, International Commerce and Culture, Argentina.

It would be useful, for example, if the International Law Commission, with the assistance of the Secretariat of the United Nations, were to provide the international community with a descriptive overview or panorama of the state of contemporary international law. To some extent, the Commission has already served as a focal point for such an exercise. Thus, in 1949, the Secretariat prepared a survey of international law to assist the Commission in formulating its long-term programme of work.[2] The Secretariat prepared a second such survey in 1971.[3] More recently, in 1996, the Commission itself returned to the question and made an inventory of the work which it has completed to date, situating it within the broader framework of the international legal order as a whole.[4] Although normative congestion is probably an unavoidable feature of the current international legal order, the undertaking of a thorough survey of the current state of international law by the Commission would probably make it possible to reduce the extent of the current "legislative overload" and contribute to the better coordination and more considered management of the overall international law-making effort.

Professor Zdzislaw Galicki* The double function of the International Law Commission, which embraces both the codification and the progressive development of international law, reflects the traditional Grotian order. Over the course of the last 50 years, however, the Commission has lost its quasi-monopoly within these fields.

In response, the Commission should: first, more carefully select the topics on which it is to work; secondly, modify its working methods; thirdly, develop cooperative relationships with other law-making bodies; and, fourthly, achieve a balance in its work between academic attractiveness and practical applicability.

· I would add that the Commission's achievements should not be measured by the number of sets of draft articles which it produces. The progressive development of international law is now carried on using a variety of other forms of instruments and in an assortment of other ways, for instance, through the systematic identification of the basic legal principles in a field.

M. Boubacar Tankoano** Deux obstacles majeurs entravent le processus de formation du droit international. Le premier ordre de difficultés, que l'on pourrait qualifier d'« objectives », tient au fait que, lorsqu'elle examine les sujets dont elle est saisie, la Commission du droit international doit concilier les approches des différents systèmes juridiques du monde. Le deuxième ordre de difficultés, que l'on pourrait qualifier de « subjectives », est lié aux jeux politiques auxquels se livrent les gouvernements et aux comportements qu'ils adoptent sur la scène internationale pour défendre leurs intérêts nationaux. L'opinion de chacun des membres de la Commission entre également en jeu.

---

*Professor of International Law, University of Warsaw, Warsaw, Poland. Member of the International Law Commission, 1997- . Adviser of the delegation of Poland to the Sixth Committee of the General Assembly of the United Nations.
**Représentant du Niger auprès de la Sixième Commission de l'Assemblée générale des Nations Unies.
[2]Document A/CN.4/Rev.1 (reprinted in Lauterpacht, E. (ed.), *International Law, being the Collected Papers of Sir Hersch Lauterpacht*, vol. 1 (1970), p. 445).
[3]*Yearbook of the International Law Commission, 1971*, vol. II (Part Two), pp. 1-99.
[4]Report of the International Law Commission on the work of its forty-eighth session, *Official Records of the General Assembly, Fifty-first Session, Supplement No. 10* (A/51/10), pp. 328-334.

Mr Holger Rotkirch* The questions which I would like to address are how to make the best use of the time and resources of the International Law Commission and how to encourage the provision of meaningful feedback on the Commission's work from the Sixth Committee of the General Assembly.

Inadequate attendance at the Commission's meetings has long been a problem. It is doubtful, though, whether this problem is best addressed by sanctioning non-attendance, in the manner suggested by Professor Orrego Vicuña. Rather, attendance might be made more rewarding. As long as the Commission has but one long session with too many topics on the agenda, it is inevitable that there will continue to be problems with attendance.

My proposal would be that the Commission try having shorter sessions, perhaps two a year. In the course of each year, two or, at most, three topics would be addressed, so that the members of the Commission would be able to work effectively on just one item at a time. The Commission's report to the General Assembly would then cover only a couple of topics. Such a report would be much more user-friendly. It would also be easier for States to comment upon the report, which, in turn, would help to make the debate within the Sixth Committee more focused.

I would also suggest that the Commission's report should be more comprehensive in nature. The Commission can hardly expect much in the way of useful feedback from the Sixth Committee if it forwards to the General Assembly just a few articles on a topic at a time. The work of Václav Mikulka as Special Rapporteur on the topic of nationality in relation to the succession of States provides a good example of a more holistic and user-friendly approach, presenting, first, a general outline of the project, then, a list of general principles and, finally, a complete set of draft articles. Making the Commission's report more easily digestible is all the more important since the report is available to delegations only a few weeks before it falls to be discussed in the Sixth Committee.

An improved system of questionnaires would yield more and better information for the Commission, too. Many States currently encounter difficulties in preparing their responses to the Commission's questionnaires. Too much and too detailed information is sometimes requested, which can make it difficult to see the wood for the trees.

For the Commission to hold split sessions might encourage more intensive intersessional consultations between the members of the Commission. Such consultations would be conducive to increased efficiency and productivity, particularly if modern means of communication, such as e-mail or videoconferencing, were employed. I would add that, were the Commission to split its sessions, the two parts need not necessarily be held in different venues, even if convening in New York would make it easier for Government legal advisers to follow the Commission's work and to prepare for the annual discussion of the Commission's report in the Sixth Committee.

Where it is important that work on a topic be completed quickly, use might be made of working groups, working either together with a Special Rapporteur or, alternatively, alone and without a Special Rapporteur being appointed at all for the topic concerned.

Measures should be taken towards ensuring that Special Rapporteurs receive a greater degree of guidance from the Commission on the direction

---

*Ambassador. Director General for Legal Affairs, Ministry for Foreign Affairs, Finland.

which their work should take. In particular, in order that Special Rapporteurs might receive advice on the approach which they should adopt to a topic or to issues arising in connection with it, the Commission should appoint a consultative group, made up of certain of its members, to work with each Special Rapporteur and to be available for consultation by her or him between the Commission's sessions, whether by correspondence, via e-mail or at actual meetings. The Commission has already taken action along these lines, with good results.[5] I would encourage it to continue its efforts.

Professeur Brigitte Stern* J'évoquerai ici deux points que le professeur Orrego Vicuña a soulevés dans son exposé.

En premier lieu, il a avancé l'idée de donner à la Commission le pouvoir d'interpréter le droit international à la demande des principaux organes des Nations Unies, voire à la demande de parties à des instances devant des tribunaux internes. À mon avis, c'est confondre les rôles différents dévolus à une diversité d'organes internationaux. Le Bureau des affaires juridiques du Secrétariat de l'Organisation des Nations Unies et la Cour internationale de Justice peuvent interpréter le droit international mais la Commission du droit international, composée d'experts indépendants, n'est pas habilitée à le faire.

Pour ce qui est de la composition de la Commission, je ne suis pas partisane d'y accueillir des représentants de la société civile, des milieux d'affaires ou d'organisations non gouvernementales. S'il est vrai qu'elle doit prendre en compte les besoins de la société civile, c'est à la faveur du dialogue et des consultations selon les modalités suggérées par le professeur Chinkin dans le document qu'elle a établi pour ce colloque que la Commission doit le faire. Néanmoins, la suggestion du professeur Orrego Vicuña, selon laquelle certains membres de la Commission pourraient être désignés par des établissements universitaires ou des sociétés savantes, mérite notre attention.

Mme. Cristina Aguiar** Les difficultés rencontrées à l'heure actuelle, dans l'entreprise d'élaboration du droit international, peuvent se résumer comme suit. En premier lieu, on citera les ingérences d'ordre politique. En deuxième lieu, la diversité culturelle fait problème. L'existence de systèmes juridiques nationaux si différents les uns des autres ne facilite pas l'œuvre de codification. En troisième lieu, il y a que les objectifs à assigner à la construction de l'ordre juridique international sont loin d'être clairs. La communauté internationale souhaite-t-elle passer d'un droit international fondé sur la coordination à un droit international uniformisé ?

Professor Václav Mikulka*** I would agree with Professor Orrego Vicuña that the International Law Commission might do more to address the preoccupations of today's international community. However, I am surprised by his

---

*Professeur à l'Université Paris-1 (Panthéon-Sorbonne), Paris (France).

**Ambassadeur. Représentant permanent de la République dominicaine auprès de l'Organisation des Nations Unies.

***Member of the International Law Commission, 1992-. Alternate Representative of the Czech Republic to the Sixth Committee of the General Assembly of the United Nations.

[5]See, in particular: Report of the International Law Commission on the work of its forty-eighth session, *General Assembly Official Records, Fifty-first session, Supplement No. 10* (A/51/10), pp. 214-215 at paras. 192-196; and Report of the International Law Commission on the work of its forty-ninth session, *General Assembly Official Records, Fifty-second session, Supplement No. 10* (A/52/10), p. 154 at paras. 236-237.

suggestion that the Commission should not concern itself too much with the views of States regarding the subjects which it should take up.

The Commission's Statute distinguishes between codification of international law and progressive development of international law, reserving the initiative in the choice of subjects for codification to the Commission and in the choice of subjects for progressive development to the General Assembly—that is, to States. Once the process of codification is complete, it is the responsibility of States to choose new topics for the Commission and the Commission cannot do it in their stead.

Having said this, it should be observed that the new topics which are before the Commission have all been proposed by the Commission itself: nationality in relation to the succession of States, unilateral acts of States, diplomatic protection. No new topic has been added to the Commission's programme of work as the result of a suggestion made by a State which was then approved by the General Assembly.

Dr Peter Tomka I fully share the views expressed by Professor Mikulka. The Commission can only work effectively on a topic when it has been given a mandate by the General Assembly. There was some discussion on this point at the Commission's first session. Some members of the Commission were of the view that the Commission might proceed with the consideration of a topic for the purposes of codification without having first received any direction to that effect from the General Assembly.[6] Although the General Assembly endorsed this view at its fourth session,[7] the subsequent practice of the Commission has been to the effect that a request from the General Assembly should be given priority and that the Commission may undertake work on a topic only once a mandate has been given to it by the General Assembly to do so.

The problem is that: sometimes the Commission is given a mandate to work on a topic; sometimes the suggestion that the Commission should undertake work on that topic even originated with one or more States; the Commission works for a number of years on that topic, perhaps for eight or nine years, and receives eight or nine reports from the Special Rapporteur; the Commission finally adopts on second reading a set of draft articles on the topic and forwards it to the General Assembly; but then, after several years, States decide that the draft should be shelved. In such cases, there is a kind of hypocrisy on the part of States. Having repeatedly invited the Commission to continue work on the topic, they decide, once that work is finished, that they do not want or need any strict regulation in that particular area. A case in point is the work which the Commission undertook on the status of the diplomatic courier and the diplomatic bag not accompanied by diplomatic courier.

States or the Commission itself should decide to stop work on a topic if the prospects for progress are bleak. In 1992, the Commission acted very wisely when it decided not to continue work on the second part of the topic of relations between States and international organizations. In my view, the obvious candidate now for deletion from the Commission's programme of work is the topic of international liability for injurious consequences arising out of acts not

---

[6]For a summary of the discussion, see United Nations, *Repertory of Practice of United Nations Organs*, vol. I (1955), pp. 416-418 at paras. 28-37 (United Nations publication, Sales No. 1955.V.2 (Vol. I)).

[7]Ibid., p. 418 at para. 38.

prohibited by international law, except for that part of the topic which relates to prevention of transboundary damage from hazardous activities.

Professor Orrego Vicuña To respond to the point made by Professor Stern, my suggestion that the Commission might give interpretations of points of United Nations law would not have the result of converting the Commission into some kind of tribunal, nor would it have the effect of supplanting the advisory function of the International Court of Justice. In the daily life of the United Nations, interpretations are constantly being made of the Charter, of the Organization's rules and of its law in general. These interpretations lead to the development of that law. The Office of Legal Affairs of the Secretariat of the United Nations provides some input into this process, of course; but would it not be good to be able to call for guidance on the expert opinion of an independent body like the International Law Commission? After all, to request an advisory opinion from the International Court of Justice may not be a realistic alternative, either because the problem is not of an order which merits such a step or because a reply is needed sooner than it can be provided by the Court.

As far as the question of new actors is concerned, if it is the case that new categories of actor are now participating in the work of the United Nations, why should these new actors not also participate in the development of international law? The identities of the actors which should so be involved might be discussed, but I would certainly maintain that they should include representatives of the business sector. The whole field of diplomatic protection, for example, is intimately related to issues of foreign investment. States are interested, too, of course, but investors certainly have a direct and legitimate interest in how the law will be developed on this subject by the International Law Commission.

Lastly, I should like to respond to Mr Mikulka's remarks regarding the procedure for identifying the topics on which the Commission should work. It is true that, formally speaking, the codification of a topic may be initiated by the Commission and that the progressive development of the law on a subject needs to be initiated by States, through the General Assembly and its Sixth Committee. The reality, however, is different. The Commission often takes the lead by approaching key delegations in the General Assembly with a view to creating a body of opinion which will lead to a request for the Commission to take up a subject. This is precisely what should happen. However, often the Commission does precisely the opposite, thinking of which subject it might suggest to the General Assembly that would command its general support. Such conservatism can and should be avoided, since the broad support of States is hardly a prerequisite to the undertaking of work on the development of international law.

Professeur Alain Pellet En guise de très brève conclusion, je me référerai dans l'ordre aux trois questions soulevées par Mme Aguiar.

Elle a déploré l'ingérence constante de la politique dans les travaux de la Commission du droit international. Pour ma part, je ne m'en plains pas. Le droit est une affaire trop sérieuse pour être laissée aux juristes. Les juristes ne peuvent qu'appliquer le droit qui est lui-même le résultat d'un processus politique. C'est clairement à la sphère politique qu'il appartient de décider ce que doit être le droit. Ce que nous pouvons faire, nous autres juristes, c'est éclairer et informer les hommes politiques et les mettre en garde lorsqu'ils s'engagent dans une voie qui risque de les conduire à une violation du droit ou de les entraîner dans de sérieuses difficultés. C'est là que s'arrête le rôle du juriste et celui-ci ne doit pas aller au-delà. La Commission du droit international est une conseillère des États, auxquels elle ne peut pas se substituer.

Le deuxième point soulevé par Mme Aguiar, et évoqué également par M Tankoano, concerne la diversité des traditions juridiques. À la Commission du droit international ou devant la Cour internationale de Justice, on se trouve confronté à de réels problèmes dus aux différences qui existent entre les diverses traditions juridiques. La Commission présente toutefois cet intérêt qu'elle permet aux représentants de différents systèmes juridiques de travailler ensemble et de dégager des approches communes et elle les y contraint. Dans le processus de formation du droit international, la rencontre de plusieurs cultures juridiques est essentielle car elle force à engager un dialogue. Certes, il se tient parfois à la Commission des débats presque surréalistes, un véritable dialogue de sourds entre représentants de la *common law* et représentants du droit romain. Néanmoins, la Commission constitue, somme toute, un cadre de collaboration fructueuse entre représentants de différentes cultures juridiques. On pourrait même affirmer que c'est l'une des réussites de la Commission.

Quant au troisième point soulevé par Mme Aguiar, c'est-à-dire la question de savoir si nous devrions passer d'un droit fondé sur la coopération à un droit d'intégration, il ne relève pas de la Commission du droit international. La Commission a pour mission la codification et le développement progressif du droit international. Il n'entre pas dans le cadre de son mandat de fomenter une révolution dans le domaine du droit. En tant que membre de la Commission, je suis parfois contrarié par les accusations de timidité excessive qui sont portées contre elle. Il me semble qu'être timide fait partie de son travail. Elle n'a pour tâche ni d'introduire des bouleversements dans le droit ni d'«inventer» de nouvelles tendances. Révolutionner le droit international n'est pas une tâche que l'on confie à un groupe de 34 juristes, si éminents soient-ils. Prétendre le contraire serait à mon sens mettre en danger la Commission et ses travaux. C'est pourquoi je me suis, sur plusieurs points, fermement opposé aux propositions formulées par le précédent Rapporteur spécial sur la responsabilité des États, car il me paraissait qu'il comptait apporter au droit des modifications qui allaient bien au-delà du développement progressif et qui me semblaient être eventuellement du ressort exclusif des États et non de la Commission.

Mr Hans Corell* In considering the position in which the Commission now finds itself, it may be useful to reflect upon the considerable changes in the law-making process which have taken place in recent years at the national level. It used to be the case that many national legal systems contained law commissions which were entrusted with tasks of a global or comprehensive nature in respect. This, however, is no longer the case. There might be certain lessons here for the International Law Commission.

With regard to Dr Tomka's remarks regarding the Sixth Committee's "monopoly"—or otherwise—in the field of international law-making, it is interesting to note what is contained in annex II of the Rules of Procedure of the General Assembly of the United Nations.[8] That annex cites certain provisions of General Assembly resolution 684 (VII) of 6 November 1952. That resolution recommends, *inter alia*, that "whenever any Committee [of the General Assem-

---

*Under-Secretary-General for Legal Affairs. The Legal Counsel.
[8]Document A/520/Rev.15 (United Nations publication, Sales No. E.85.I.13).

bly] contemplates making a recommendation to the General Assembly to refer a matter to the International Law Commission, the Committee may, at some appropriate stage of its consideration, consult the Sixth Committee as to the advisability of such a reference and on its drafting".[9] It is noteworthy that the possibility was contemplated in 1952 that any of the Main Committees of the General Assembly, and not only its Sixth Committee, might refer a matter to the International Law Commission. To the best of my knowledge, however, such a reference has never been made. The same resolution also recommends that "when a Committee considers the legal aspects of a question important, the Committee should refer it for legal advice to the Sixth Committee or propose that the question should be considered by a joint Committee of itself and the Sixth Committee".[10] Again, I do not think that such a reference has ever been made or that such a joint committee has ever been formed.

---

[9]See operative paragraph 1 (*b*) of the resolution.
[10]See operative paragraph 1 (*d*) of the resolution.

3

SELECTION OF TOPICS
FOR CODIFICATION BY THE INTERNATIONAL LAW COMMISSION
AND
ITS WORKING METHODS

*

CHOIX DE SUJETS
POUVANT ÊTRE RETENUS PAR LA COMMISSION AUX FINS
DE LA CODIFICATION ET DU DÉVELOPPEMENT PROGRESSIF
ET
MÉTHODES DE TRAVAIL DE LA COMMISSION

Introduction by the Moderator, **Mr Carlos Calero-Rodrigues***

This, the third item in the Colloquium's programme, in fact consists of two quite separate issues. The first is the question of the selection of the topics on which the Commission is to work. There are, in turn, three separate facets to this question. First, the procedures which should be employed to identify those topics and to insert them into the Commission's programme of work. Should the current system be maintained, in which the General Assembly selects topics on the basis of suggestions from the Commission or Governments? Secondly and more importantly, what criteria should be used to identify topics for inclusion in the Commission's programme of work? The third aspect of the question is, of course, the suggestion of actual, concrete topics.

The second issue which is encompassed by this item in the Colloquium's programme is that of the Commission's methods of work. There has, of late, been a tendency to maintain that the Commission stands in need of revitalization and that its working methods need to be changed. Many suggestions have been made in this regard in the academic literature and I am sure that we will hear more during the course of our discussion. The difficult question, though, is which of them would in truth improve the Commission and enhance its efficiency.

Our first panellist is Mr Christopher Pinto. He is currently the Secretary-General of the Iran–United States Claims Tribunal. He was himself a member of the International Law Commission from 1973 to 1981 and, in 1980, its Chairman. From 1967 to 1980, he was a representative of Sri Lanka to the Sixth Committee of the General Assembly of the United Nations. He is the author of a number of well known articles on international law and international law-making.

---

*Member of the International Law Commission, 1982-1996.

The second member of our panel is Professor Maurice Kamto. He is Professor in the Faculty of Law and in the Institute of International Relations of Cameroon at the University of Yaoundé II, Cameroon. He is also an Associate Professor at the University of Ngaoundéré, the University of Douala and the Catholic University of Central Africa. He is one of the best known of the new generation of African jurists.

The third panellist on this topic is Professor M. K. Nawaz. He has taught at many law schools around the world, particularly in India and the United States. He is currently a research consultant at the National Law School, India University, Bangalore, India. He is the author of many articles on international law and is, at present, a member of the Editorial Board of the *Indian Journal of International Law*.

Presentation by Mr Christopher W. Pinto

There is an intimate relationship between the General Assembly of the United Nations and the International Law Commission. The Commission is, after all, a subsidiary organ of the General Assembly, conceived in order to enable the entire membership of the Organization to participate in a regular and orderly fashion in the progressive development of international law and its codification. In consequence of this filial relationship, the General Assembly is cast in three different roles *vis-à-vis* the Commission. First, it is the principal beneficiary of the Commission's work. Secondly, it is the Commission's principal guide and critic. Thirdly and most significantly, it is the Commission's sole benefactor. This last role carries with it substantial responsibilities, since it implies that the General Assembly will provide the Commission with the resources necessary to enable it to carry out its mandate. When all is said and done, the extent to which the States represented in the General Assembly benefit from the Commission is related directly to what the aggregate of their national priorities has determined should be invested in it.

Chief among the Commission's resources are its members. They should not only be appropriately qualified and representative, in accordance with the terms of the Commission's Statute, but they should also be able and willing to devote "quality time" to the work of the Commission, both during its annual sessions and during the rest of the year, when necessary.

In this connection, there are three suggestions which I would like to make. First, the members of the Commission should be invited to take an oath of office, which would include, in particular, an undertaking to devote such time and attention to the Commission and its work as may be required to enable them to participate fully and meaningfully in its work, which would entail attending its annual sessions in their entirety. Secondly, there should be an understanding among States in the General Assembly that at least 10 appropriately qualified women should be elected to the Commission for the next quinquennium. Thirdly, those who are elected to the Commission should voluntarily limit their membership to two full terms. This last suggestion is not intended to detract in any way from the outstanding contributions to the work of the Commission which have been made by those members who have served for longer periods of time. It is a response, rather, to the need to spread a sense of participation in the work of the Commission throughout the Organization by ensuring a frequent turnover among its members.

In so far as concerns the Commission's methods of work, there are two points which I should like to make. First, there is a need for the members of the

Commission to undertake more work outside the framework of its regular sessions. Secondly, the Commission needs to interact to a much greater extent with the "end user" of its product: the private individual. Such interaction could be effected through systematic and frequent consultation with international and national organizations, official and non-official, as is contemplated by article 26 (1) of the Commission's Statute. In order to accomplish these two objectives as economically as possible—intensified intersessional activity and interaction with private persons, individually and in groups—the Commission and its members should become familiar with the new electronic means of communication and information exchange, particularly the Internet. They should also be equipped by the United Nations with the necessary hardware and software.

Finally, I would like to advance some suggestions which are relevant as much to the Commission's methods of work as to the selection of topics for its study.

The Commission should establish four working groups, each consisting of a chairman and, say, five other members of the Commission. With the assistance of the Secretariat of the United Nations, these working groups would collect and analyse information on the following four areas and report on them each year to the Commission.

The first is the implementation of and compliance with multilateral treaties. Study of this field might eventually generate proposals for ways in which to improve the multilateral treaty-making process.

The second area is work-in-progress in the domain of multilateral treaty-making. Study of developments in this field would help to ensure better coordination between the different organs and bodies which are involved in making international law. In particular, it would promote consistency of approach between different law-making initiatives, help to avoid contradictions between the different instruments which they aim to elaborate and draw attention to important *lacunae* in the fabric of international law.

The third working group would maintain close and frequent contact with universities, international and national scientific institutions and learned societies, practitioners' associations, chambers of commerce, large corporations and those citizens' groups which might make a useful contribution to the work of the Commission.

The fourth working group would undertake what might be called "fundamental studies". Charles de Visscher once observed that the United Nations codification process actually constituted a threat to the development of international law. He even went so far as to declare that "the prospects for codification on the universal plane are nil".[1] This is, of course, a rather extreme point of view. At the same time, though, all of us have at one time or another yearned for the means of bringing States to agree on the kind of pre-legislative consensus that would strengthen the codification process, that would firm up the foundations of public international law and that would make it more widely respected, observed and effective. I see the establishment of a working group on "fundamental studies" as a small step in the search for such a pre-legislative consensus.

The task of this fourth working group would be to explore the reasons for the current weaknesses of international law and its aim would be to extend our understanding of that law in the light, and against the background, of the full

---

[1] *Théories et réalités en droit international public* (1st ed., 1953), p. 181.

political context in which it operates. In fulfilment of this mandate, the working group would investigate the impact on international society of such perennial scourges as cultural and ethnic hatreds, bigoted nationalism and what some have described as the clash of civilizations. It would study the possibilities and the challenges opened up or created by the new expeditious means of global communication. It would investigate such phenomena as democratization and globalization, which now seem poised to return to the hands of private individuals much of the power that has for some three centuries resided with princes and governments. The mandate for the group would go beyond mere studies, however, and would extend to the task of developing ways and means of making international law more effective. In that endeavour, it would need to enlist the aid of such allies of the law as religion and science and to have at its disposal insights from disciplines such as sociology, psychology and anthropology.

The Commission, with its substantial intellectual resources and its culturally representative character, is well equipped to establish a position of leadership in this field—better equipped probably than any other body. If it were to focus its efforts in this way, the Commission might become, in time, a resource on which all treaty-making initiatives would rely for guidance on how to maximize the effectiveness of their work. Indeed, the Commission might contribute to the establishment of an international order that would serve humanity as a whole and, more importantly, the individual human being.

Présentation par le professeur Maurice Kamto

Il y a déjà 10 ans que l'on a pris conscience de la nécessité de réexaminer les méthodes de travail de la Commission du droit international et la question du choix des sujets fournissant matière au développement progressif et à la codification des règles du droit international. Dans les résolutions sur le rapport de la Commission du droit international qu'elle a adoptées chaque année depuis 1986, l'Assemblée générale a souligné à plusieurs reprises que la Commission devait réexaminer la manière dont elle choisissait les sujets qu'elle souhaitait traiter ainsi que les méthodes et procédures qu'elle employait pour mener ses travaux.

Pour ce qui est des sujets, j'évoquerai brièvement le Statut de la Commission et la pratique qu'il a sécrétée avant de formuler quelques suggestions sur le type de sujet que la Commission devrait examiner.

Conformément à l'article 16 et au paragraphe 3 de l'article 18 du Statut, c'est l'Assemblée générale qui prend l'initiative de demander à la Commission de traiter certains sujets, surtout ceux qui emportent le développement progressif du droit international. Toutefois, les paragraphes 1 et 2 de l'article 18 ménagent une certaine latitude à la Commission lorsqu'il s'agit de déterminer les sujets donnant matière à codification.

Il a été dit que la distinction établie dans le Statut de la Commission entre le développement progressif du droit international et sa codification était quelque peu artificielle. Elle n'est pas moins utile à des fins d'analyse. À ce jour, la Commission s'est essentiellement orientée vers des domaines où la pratique des États était déjà étendue, pour ainsi dire, mûrs pour la codification, à l'exclusion de sujets qui auraient supposé le développement progressif du droit au sens strict. C'est peut-être tant mieux qu'il en ait été ainsi. On a fait remarquer à juste titre que la Commission n'a pas tant pour vocation de révolutionner le droit ou de transformer l'ordre juridique international que de proposer des évolutions qui correspondaient à l'état actuel des relations internationales.

À la lumière du Statut de la Commission et de la pratique qui s'en est dégagée, on pourrait donc conclure que seule l'Assemblée générale peut suggérer à la Commission d'entreprendre des travaux qui consisteraient à créer le droit international à proprement parler.

Depuis sa première réunion, en 1949, l'essentiel des sujets dont la Commission a traité ont porté sur ce que l'on pourrait appeler les règles « primaires » du droit international, ne s'intéressant que plus récemment aux règles « secondaires ». D'aucuns en ont conclu qu'elle en avait fini avec l'élaboration de règles primaires. Je ne pense pas que cela soit tout à fait exact. Depuis 1949, la Commission a abandonné en cours de route un grand nombre de sujets inscrits à son programme à long terme initial, en dépit du fait qu'il était toujours et qu'il reste nécessaire d'élaborer des règles de droit international en ces matières. La Commission a tout lieu de revenir sur certains de ces sujets et d'apprécier s'ils sont susceptibles de se prêter à la codification et au développement progressif.

On a beaucoup critiqué la Commission pour son prétendu conservatisme. Qu'elles soient fondées ou non, les critiques sont sans aucun doute excessives car on voit mal comment la Commission aurait pu déborder le cadre des sujets sur lesquels elle a travaillé sans gaspiller son énergie sur des problèmes qu'elle est mal préparée à affronter. Par exemple, elle n'aurait probablement pas été en mesure de présenter un projet de texte satisfaisant à la troisième Conférence des Nations Unies sur le droit de la mer. La partie XI de la Convention adoptée à cette conférence se démarquait radicalement du droit existant et une conférence diplomatique était certainement beaucoup mieux placée pour élaborer cet instrument. On a dit que la Commission pourrait traiter des problèmes de cet ordre si elle faisait appel à des experts. Cependant, en demandant à des experts de participer à ses travaux, elle risque fort de voir les considérations techniques l'emporter sur le débat juridique. Au demeurant, une telle démarche aurait également des incidences budgétaires.

La Commission a donc, à tort ou à raison, limité la portée de ses travaux. Elle a néanmoins accompli une œuvre remarquable, et je crois que nous sommes tous d'accord sur ce point. Je suis fermement d'avis que, même si elle avait à son actif le seul projet de base de la Convention sur le droit des traités de 1969, cela aurait été plus que suffisant pour justifier son existence.

Pour ce qui est des méthodes de travail de la Commission, j'estime qu'étant donné l'importance et le volume des travaux auxquels elle doit s'atteler on aurait tort de réduire la durée de ses sessions annuelles. Si l'Assemblée générale souhaite que la Commission effectue un travail satisfaisant sur les sujets qu'elle a décidé de lui soumettre, elle doit lui donner le temps et les moyens nécessaires. Si, au contraire, elle souhaite accorder moins d'importance aux travaux de la Commission, elle devrait le dire clairement et ne pas émettre des messages contradictoires.

Selon une proposition intéressante mentionnée dans l'étude de la Commission qu'a effectuée en 1981 l'Institut des Nations Unies pour la formation et la recherche (UNITAR)[2], la présidence de la Commission devrait être assurée par roulement afin que les pays en développement, en particulier les pays africains, puissent exercer cette fonction. On dit également que ces régions devraient être

---

[2]El Baradei, M., Franck, T., et Trachtenberg, R., *The International Law Commission: The Need for a New Direction* (1981), UNITAR Policy and Efficacy Studies No. 1, p. 30 (publication des Nations Unies, numéro de vente : E.81.XV.PE/1).

équitablement représentées dans la désignation de Rapporteurs spéciaux. Je suis prêt à appuyer ces propositions mais j'ajouterai que les membres de la Commission originaires de pays en développement doivent s'efforcer de gagner le respect de leurs collègues et d'accéder à ces postes prestigieux par des moyens légitimes.

On demande souvent si les membres de la Commission sont véritablement des experts indépendants ou bien s'ils représentent leur gouvernement. En théorie, la réponse va de soi, mais si l'on songe à ce qui s'est passé durant la guerre froide, lorsque plusieurs membres de la Commission exprimaient la position de leur gouvernement sur des questions délicates, on peut légitimement s'interroger, surtout si l'on considère les débats qui ont eu lieu à la Commission sur certaines dispositions de son projet d'articles sur la responsabilité des États.

Les membres de la Commission qui font partie d'une délégation à la Sixième Commission ne devraient pas siéger avec cette délégation lorsque la Sixième Commission examine le rapport de la Commission. Pour être formels et symboliques, les motifs qui m'incitent à formuler cette proposition n'en sont pas moins légitimes. Après tout, il importe que la Commission tout entière défende les projets qu'elle soumet à l'Assemblée générale et l'on ne devrait pas permettre à ses membres, en changeant de place, de livrer une fois de plus des batailles qu'ils auraient peut-être déjà perdues au sein de la Commission lors de l'élaboration du projet en question.

Dans son rapport à l'Assemblée générale, la Commission devrait rester concise et exposer sa position proprement dite sans ressasser les positions de ses différents membres. On éviterait ainsi plus facilement de rouvrir à la Sixième Commission le débat qui a déjà eu lieu à la Commission.

Presentation by Professor M. K. Nawaz

I shall limit my presentation to the first part of the question that is before us: namely, the selection of the topics on which the Commission is to undertake the preparation of rules of international law.

At first, when the question arose as to which topics the Commission should take up, the answer was that those topics should be identified by reference to "the needs of the international community". This criterion was subsequently refined to the "pressing needs of the international community". Later still, it was added that, for the Commission to take up a topic, that topic should not be merely of theoretical interest. Most recently, it has been suggested that the topic should also be one on which work might be completed within a single quinquennium of the Commission.

These criteria may be useful; but, if the Commission is to enter the twenty-first century doing the work which it was created to do—namely, promoting the progressive development and codification of international law— they are hardly sufficient. What is needed is a vision of international law and where that law is going in the twenty-first century. In formulating this vision, humanism must be our watchword. The international law of the future should be oriented far more towards meeting peoples' needs and less towards satisfying the interests of States.

Professor Pellet remarked in the course of this morning's session that the task of the International Law Commission is to promote the progressive development of international law and its codification, not to stage a legal revolution. This may be so; but it remains the case, none the less, that the Commission's Statute absolutely and positively mandates that the Commission should promote not just the codification of international law, but also its progressive development.

In the past, the progressive development of international law was not accorded the emphasis which it deserved. In the doctrine of international law, the progressive development of international law and its codification have generally been understood as a composite—as inseparable components of a single, aggregate process. In the work of the Committee of Experts of the League of Nations, however, they were not conceived in this way, but were thought to constitute two separate and independent functions. We should return to this way of thinking, for only thus will the task of progressive development be accorded its full and proper importance.

Bearing all this in mind, I have composed a list of topics which the Commission might usefully take up and on which it might usefully undertake the drafting of rules of international law. Each of these topics satisfies the criteria which I have mentioned, being future-oriented, reflecting a humanistic approach and being directed towards the promotion of development. These topics are as follows:

(a) Mass exoduses of people facing an imminent threat of death or starvation;

(b) Citizenship of refugees and displaced persons;

(c) Rights and duties of aliens;

(d) Human rights and extradition;

(e) Treatment of foreign investments;

(f) Elimination of corruption in international commercial transactions; and

(g) Global commons.

In my paper, I have indicated the parameters of these topics and my reasons for suggesting them; but I would like now to say a few words on topics (a) and (f).

As far as topic (a) is concerned, the turbulent events that have engulfed Asia, Africa and Central Europe in recent years have highlighted the need for safeguarding the lives and the conditions of groups of people who, en masse, flee their homes for safety. Existing international law fails to provide answers even to the most elementary questions in this domain, such as the definitions of "refugee" and "displaced person", let alone ensures such hapless people the protection which they so badly need. This topic is likely to acquire even greater prominence in years to come; but, in any event, the time is ripe for the codification and progressive development of international law in the field.

Turning to topic (f), the necessity of eliminating corruption and bribery in international commercial transactions has long been felt by States and by international organizations. Last year, the Organization of American States adopted a convention against corruption,[3] including an article—article VIII—on transnational bribery. The General Assembly itself, by its resolution 51/191 of 16 December 1996, adopted the United Nations Declaration against Corruption and Bribery in International Commercial Transactions. Efforts are under way in the Council of Europe, too, to address the problem. The liberalization of world

---

[3]Inter-American Convention against Corruption, done at Caracas on 29 March 1996 (document E/1996/99.

trade and economic policies in the third world have only added a fresh impetus to the need for satisfactory regulation of the topic at the international level.

Both the Sixth Committee of the General Assembly and the International Law Commission are responsible for the restrictive and limited approach which the Commission has taken to the fulfilment of its mandate, in particular for the importance which the Commission has attached to the essentially conservative task of placing the old wine of customary international law into the new bottles of draft conventions. This conservative orientation on the part of the Commission needs to be changed. Here, the greater responsibility lies with the Sixth Committee, which is, after all, the Commission's parent body. The Sixth Committee should encourage, even direct, the Commission to think in terms of topics whose study might contribute to the progressive development of international law. Those members of the Commission who are national leaders or legal advisers or who serve in the Sixth Committee as States' representatives should be encouraged to take the initiative in this regard.

OPEN-FLOOR DISCUSSION

*

DÉBAT

Mr Carlos Calero-Rodrigues I would like briefly to address one of the suggestions which Mr Kamto made in the course of his presentation. He asked whether members of the Commission should act as the representatives of States in the Sixth Committee. This is a question on which I certainly feel qualified to speak, having been a member of the Commission and having served at the same time as a representative of Brazil in the Sixth Committee. Indeed, the two Brazilians who were members of the Commission before me[4] also represented Brazil in the Sixth Committee. I think it was their experience, as it was mine, that there was a certain advantage in being both a member of the Commission and a representative in the Sixth Committee; for we could bring back to the Commission a direct, first hand impression of the state of thinking in that body—an impression which was more complete and more enlightening than any which could be gained from reading the summary records of its debates or even the full written texts of the delegates' statements. There is, then, some advantage in having at least some members of the Commission sitting in the Sixth Committee. It is vitally important, of course, that the independence of those members, and of the Commission itself, should not be compromised; but, as matters stand, there would not seem to be any risk that they might be. When members of the Commission sit in the Sixth Committee, it is well understood that they are simply representing their Governments and that much of what they say does not accord with their own personal views. More important, though, is that, in the Commission, they remain completely independent and that they speak for themselves as independent experts and not as the representatives of any State. As far as myself and my two Brazilian predecessors in the Commission are concerned, we never received instructions from the Brazilian Govern-

---

[4]Gilberto Amado, who was a member of the Commission from 1949 to 1969, and José Sette-Câmara, who was a member of the Commission from 1970 to 1978.

ment in respect of our activities in the Commission and, if we had, we would never have accepted them.

Professeur Maurice Kamto Comme M. Calero-Rodrigues a indiqué, je pense qu'il est tout à l'avantage de la Commission que certains de ses membres soient également des conseillers juridiques gouvernementaux, car ils sont ainsi à même d'informer directement la Commission des opinions et préférences des États concernant les sujets dont elle est saisie. Néanmoins, dès lors que la Commission a achevé ses travaux sur un sujet et a présenté le fruit de ses efforts aux États, à la Sixième Commission, ses membres doivent défendre à l'unisson ce qu'ils ont accompli ensemble. Il est pour le moins regrettable qu'un membre de la Commission qui a participé à l'élaboration d'un texte critique et torpille celui-ci lorsqu'il siège avec sa délégation à la Sixième Commission.

Mr Aurel Preda* I would like to suggest a topic on which the Commission might usefully undertake the codification and progressive development of rules of international law: the concept of good-neighbourliness.

The General Assembly has adopted a number of resolutions relating to this concept. Among these might be mentioned its resolution 2129 (XX) of 21 December 1965, entitled "Actions on the regional level with a view to improving good neighbourly relations among European States having different social systems", which was proposed by Romania.[5] On 14 December 1977, on the recommendation of the First Committee, the General Assembly adopted its resolution 34/99, in which it affirmed that it was necessary to examine the concept with a view to strengthening and further developing its content, as well as ways and modalities of enhancing its effectiveness. The First Committee examined the topic again during the thirty-sixth and thirty-seventh sessions of the General Assembly. At the thirty-eighth session, the matter was taken up by the Sixth Committee. From the fortieth session onwards, the Sixth Committee conducted its work on the subject within the framework of a subcommittee which was specially established for the purpose. The declared objective was to clarify and formulate the elements of the concept as part of a process of elaboration of a suitable international document on the subject.[6] However, in 1991, despite the progress which had been made towards this goal, the General Assembly decided to drop the item from its agenda and to defer consideration of the question to an unspecified future date.[7]

Since that time, the concept of good-neighbourliness has undergone a process of progressive development in the practice of States. Indeed, it has become one of the cornerstones for better relations between nations. Worthy of especial note in this regard is the Pact of Stability in Europe, which was adopted in Paris on 21 March 1995.[8] This Pact, although it is couched only at the level

---

*Representative of Romania to the Sixth Committee of the General Assembly. Director, Legal and Treaties Division, Ministry of Foreign Affairs, Romania. Professor of International Law, Prince Dimitrie Cantemir University, Bucharest, Romania.

[5]Previously to this resolution, the General Assembly had adopted two other resolutions on the subject: resolution 1236 (XII) of 14 December 1957, entitled "Peaceful and neighbourly relations among States", and resolution 1301 (XIII) of 10 December 1958, entitled "Measures aimed at the implementation and promotion of peaceful and neighbourly relations among States".

[6]See paragraph 4 of General Assembly resolution 38/126 of 19 December 1983.

[7]See paragraph 5 of General Assembly resolution 46/62 of 9 December 1991.

[8]The Pact has been deposited with the Organization for Security and Co-operation in Europe. It has not been circulated as a United Nations document.

of general principles, is founded in its entirety upon the complex concept of good-neighbourliness. Drawing inspiration from this Pact, a number of processes and initiatives have, in the last two years, been launched among the States of south-east Europe and the Balkans with a view to promoting good-neighbourliness within the region.[9] These advances in the definition of the concept are mirrored by developments in other regions and sub-regions, such as the South Atlantic, the Mediterranean and the Black Sea.

In view of these significant developments in State practice, the United Nations should resume its work of clarifying and elaborating the elements of the concept of good-neighbourliness. This time, though, the topic should be referred for codification and progressive development to the International Law Commission, rather than to a body composed of the representatives of States.

I will conclude with a quotation from the message which the Secretary-General of the United Nations, Mr Kofi Annan, delivered on 24 October 1997.[10] In the second paragraph of his message, Mr Annan said:

"The United Nations lives in the heart and mind of every citizen striving to end violence and promote tolerance; advance development and ensure equality; protect human rights and alleviate poverty. The United Nations, at its best, enables the achievement of those highest of human aspirations."

Progressive development and codification of the elements of good-neighbourliness could contribute to the achievement of these highest of human aspirations.

M. Marc Perrin de Brichambaut* À ce Colloque, je me suis souvent senti comme un mauvais élève sermonné par ses professeurs. Les intervenants ont donné de mauvaises notes à ceux d'entre nous qui sommes chargés des services juridiques dans les ministères des affaires étrangères. Quatre critiques nous ont été adressées. Premièrement, nous ne faisons appel ni à la Commission du droit international ni à la Sixième Commission de l'Assemblée générale pour élaborer nombre de nos projets de conventions. Deuxièmement, il est dit que depuis le milieu des années 70 nous portons nettement moins d'intérêt qu'auparavant à la Commission et à ses travaux. Troisièmement, nous répugnons à confier de nouveaux sujets à la Commission car nous préférons qu'elle en prenne l'initiative elle-même. Enfin, nous serions conservateurs. Bref, nous ne mettons pas à profit l'outil puissant qui est à notre disposition.

Pour reprendre la formule du *common law*, je plaide coupable de ces chefs. Je crois toutefois pouvoir invoquer un certain nombre de circonstances atténuantes. En premier lieu, il faudrait envisager la situation selon une large perspective. Le mouvement de consolidation du droit international s'est peut-être ralenti au niveau mondial mais, au niveau régional, il a considérablement

---

*Conseiller juridique, Ministère des affaires étrangères, France.

[9]See, in this connection, General Assembly resolutions 46/62 of 9 December 1991, 48/84B of 16 December 1993 and 50/80B of 12 December 1995.

See also, most recently: the Sofia Declaration on Good-Neighbourly Relations, Stability, Security and Cooperation in the Balkans, adopted at the meeting of the Ministers for Foreign Affairs of the Countries of South-Eastern Europe, held at Sofia on 6 and 7 July 1996 (document A/51/211); and the Thessaloniki Declaration on Good-Neighbourly Relations, Stability, Security and Cooperation in the Balkans, adopted at the meeting of the Ministers for Foreign Affairs of Countries of South-Eastern Europe, held at Thessaloniki on 9 and 10 June 1997 (document A/52/217).

[10]Document SG/SM/6367.

progressé, ce qui prouve que le monde se rapproche de plus en plus d'un ordre juridique mieux structuré et développé. En deuxième lieu, nos sociétés deviennent de plus en plus complexes et cette complexité se reflète dans les relations juridiques. L'instrument de codification n'est plus nécessairement adapté à ces réalités nouvelles.

À la question posée par M. Calero-Rodrigues, de savoir « quels critères il faudrait retenir lorsqu'on envisage d'inscrire un sujet au programme de travail de la Commission », je répondrais simplement : de quoi avons-nous besoin précisément ? À quelles difficultés nous heurtons-nous aujourd'hui ? Et que peut faire la Commission du droit international pour nous aider à résoudre ces problèmes ?

Plusieurs sujets proposés par le professeur Nawaz méritent toute notre attention mais je souhaiterais y ajouter celui des conséquences juridiques de la législation d'un État pour les autres États.

Bien entendu, ce sujet n'est pas entièrement nouveau pour la Commission. Il a déjà été mentionné plusieurs fois. En 1992, un groupe de travail a même commencé à le traiter[11] et, en 1993, M. Rao a établi un excellent plan de travail[12]. Son texte n'a finalement pas été adopté mais il constituerait certainement un bon point de départ pour reprendre l'examen de ce sujet que les conseillers juridiques des États ont très souvent à traiter quotidiennement à l'occasion de leur travail.

Même avec la meilleure volonté du monde, chaque État est constamment tenté de légiférer pour les autres États, leurs entreprises et leurs habitants. En fait, l'application extraterritoriale des lois nationales est désormais presque inévitable dans un grand nombre de domaines, en raison de l'interdépendance croissante entre les États, leurs économies, leurs populations et leur environnement. Bien entendu, l'application des lois nationales aux actes, aux biens et aux relations des personnes vivant dans les autres pays n'est pas nécessairement répréhensible, surtout si l'on songe aux activités condamnables que ces lois visent à éliminer. Néanmoins, cela n'est vrai que si, dans leur intention et leurs moyens, les lois en question respectent la souveraineté des autres États et si ceux qui sont chargés de les prendre, de les appliquer et de les faire exécuter savent faire preuve de retenue et d'esprit de coopération.

On touche ici à un domaine très vaste où la Commission pourrait faire œuvre fort utile. Néanmoins, elle devrait pour cela organiser ses travaux avec davantage de souplesse. Au début, il faudrait explorer le terrain de façon ouverte et non dogmatique. Au demeurant, il ne s'agirait pas d'élaborer des projets d'articles qui puissent servir de base à une convention. Il serait plus approprié d'établir des documents beaucoup moins formels. Dans un premier temps, tout au moins, la Commission pourrait se contenter de nous présenter les divers problèmes que le sujet soulève et de suggérer des solutions diverses, en soulignant évidemment la nécessité pour les États de coopérer entre eux à cette fin. Nous réfléchirions ensuite aux meilleurs moyens de donner suite à ces suggestions.

Mr Lars Magnuson* Much has been said and written about the achievements of the International Law Commission and of how its work has resulted in the conclusion of a number of highly important conventions. At the same time, it

---

*Ambassador, Director-General for Legal and Consular Affairs, Ministry for Foreign Affairs, Sweden.
[11]*Annuaire de la Commission du droit international, 1992*, vol. II (deuxième partie), p. 57, par. 368 à 370.
[12]Document A/CN.4/454.

has been remarked that several of the conventions which have been elaborated upon the basis of its drafts have not been widely signed or ratified by States. Various explanations might be offered for why these instruments have enjoyed such a low level of adherence. In the first place, some of them are quite old and were concluded at a time when there were many fewer States in existence than there are today. States which did not exist when the instruments in question were being elaborated and which did not participate in their negotiation and adoption might be thought to have little reason to adhere to them. In the case of other conventions, the principles which they incorporate may not have corresponded to the needs of the international community even at the time of their conclusion; or else it may be that supervening political developments have made those principles outdated.

However, these remarks are nothing more than speculation; for we do not really know why so many of the conventions which have been concluded on the basis of the Commission's drafts have failed so signally to excite the enthusiasm of the international community. Given this state of ignorance, I wonder whether it would not be a good idea for some body—possibly the Commission itself, possibly some other institution or organ—to undertake an in-depth study of the problem and to identify its root causes. Such a study would be useful to us when we come to choose new topics for inclusion in the Commission's programme of work.

Picking up on a suggestion which was made by Mr Owada during this morning's session, it would also be useful if the Commission were to conduct a detailed examination of how those of "its" conventions which are in force have actually been applied in practice. A pertinent example here is the topic of reservations to treaties, which, of course, is currently the subject of active consideration by the Commission.

If, as Dr Tomka remarked during this morning's session, the identification of the topic is the first step in the codification process, it is also the most important. When considering whether to undertake work on a topic, a number of questions need to be asked. Would the articulation of rules of international law on the topic fulfil an urgent need which is experienced by States? Would it take a long time for work on it to be completed? And what form should the end product take?

I do not have any immediate proposals regarding which new topics the Commission should take up. Some suggestions have been made in the course of this Colloquium and we should study them with an open mind. My feeling, though, is that the Commission should continue to concentrate, as it has done in the past, on topics which are drawn from the classical fields of public international law. It certainly should not venture into fields which are the province of other bodies, such as UNCITRAL or the Hague Conference on Private International Law. It is the interests of States, though, which should be determinative of the actual choice of topic. It is to be hoped that these interests will coincide with those of individual human beings.

Some of those who have spoken at this Colloquium have favoured referring to the Commission topics which are wide-ranging and theoretical in nature. I doubt, though, whether it would be wise for the Commission to undertake work on topics of this kind. After all, grand schemes tend to take a long time to come to fruition. One only has to think of two of the topics on which the Commission is currently working, both of which have occupied its attention for many, many years. It is essential that the Commission complete its consideration of a topic in a prompt and timely fashion. Otherwise, it risks having its work regarded as irrelevant. Recent experience is encouraging in this respect, however. In particular, the history of the Draft Statute for an International Criminal Court and the proposed declaration on nationality of natural persons in relation to the succession of States[13] demonstrate that the Commission can deal quickly and efficiently with subjects whose parameters are clear and well-defined.

Once a topic has been identified for inclusion in the Commission's programme of work, it needs to be asked what form the end product should take. In the case of certain topics, it will certainly be entirely appropriate to aim for the elaboration and adoption of a convention. In the case of other topics, though, a declaration, a set of guidelines or a doctrinal study will be a more fitting objective. It is not every topic that calls for the conclusion of a new convention. Here, once more, the topic of reservations to treaties is an excellent example of how the Commission should proceed.

Dr Pemmaraju Sreenivasa Rao* In order to ensure that all of the States which are Members of the United Nations share a sense of participation in the work of the International Law Commission, Mr Pinto suggests that the members of the Commission should voluntarily limit their membership of that body to two full terms. Following that same line of thought, I suppose that States should also abstain from nominating candidates of their own nationality if one of their nationals has already served on the Commission in recent times.

There is great merit in this suggestion, particularly in our part of the world, where there is certainly a need to encourage the emergence of some new faces. At the same time, it needs to be borne in mind that the Commission is hardly a school where one can go to learn one's craft. The responsibilities which membership of the Commission involves require that those who serve on it come to the Commission fully trained and ready to make a substantial and sustained contribution to its work. It is important, after all, that the high quality of the Commission's membership be maintained. Where there are good candidates competing for election to the Commission, I am sure that the mechanism of the invisible hand will ensure that there is an appropriate rotation of membership among the nationals of the States Members of the Organization.

Turning to the question of new topics, Professor Nawaz has outlined an excellent set of criteria for identifying the topics which should be referred to the Commission. Personally, I would not view humanism as a criterion which is independent of the other criteria which he suggests, but as one which permeates and underlies them all. Whatever the case, I would certainly agree with Professor Nawaz, though, that any progressive development of the law on a topic is incapable of justification if it does not address the needs of individual human beings. The large populations of the world are disenfranchised and are unable to make known their points of view. Poverty, ignorance and other such factors prevent them from articulating, formulating or even identifying their demands. It is here that progressive development and justice may play a central role, transcending State boundaries, as they do.

In considering which topics should be referred to the Commission, it also needs to be borne in mind that the Commission is only one among many

---

*Joint Secretary and Legal Adviser, Head, Legal and Treaties Division, Ministry of External Affairs, India. Member of the International Law Commission, 1987- .
[13]Report of the International Law Commission on the work of its forty-ninth session, *Official Records of the General Assembly, Fifty-second Session, Supplement No. 10* (A/52/10), pp. 14-23.

law-making bodies in the international legal system and that many areas of international law-making are already the province of other bodies. Human rights, for example, is fully taken care of by other mechanisms both within and without the United Nations system. Considerations of time and of resources accordingly suggest that we should economize and not duplicate the work of these bodies by referring the topics which are within their field of operations to the International Law Commission.

At the same time, the way in which the Commission works is quite different from any other institution. Bearing this in mind, it follows that the topics which the Commission should take up are those on which a considerable amount of groundwork has already been done, either by a regional legal body or by or within some other institution, association or forum. It is, after all, where there already exists a body of opinion and practice on a subject that the Commission tends to display its particular virtues and manifest its special strengths. Likewise, when what is needed by way of an end product is some type of formal international legal instrument such as a convention, experience demonstrates that the Commission is a suitable body to undertake its preparation.

Professor M. K. Nawaz The topics which will fall to be dealt with in the years to come will require that the Commission change its methods of work and adopt a collaborative approach. The Commission will no longer be able to work in isolation from other agencies and law-making bodies, but will have to think in terms of organizing joint projects and of putting together joint teams and making joint enquiries.

Turning to some of the actual topics which have been proposed, there is much to be said for the Commission's taking a closer look at the subject of the legal consequences of national legislation. The continuing growth in the power of multinational corporations and the rapid globalization of the world economy are going to pose ever greater problems to national regulators and tempt them to extend the reach of their national laws to events occurring, and assets located, within other jurisdictions. As far as good-neighbourliness is concerned, it has already been dealt with in a thorough manner under the rubric of international cooperation in the Declaration on Principles of International Law concerning Friendly Relations and Co-operation among States in accordance with the Charter of the United Nations, annexed to General Assembly resolution 2625 (XXV) of 24 October 1970.

Professeur Maurice Kamto Je souscris entièrement à la suggestion selon laquelle la Commission devrait étudier le sujet des conséquences juridiques que des lois internes peuvent avoir pour les autres États. Elle rejoint tout à fait mon idée sur le type de sujet sur lequel la Commission peut faire œuvre utile. Cette dernière devrait se concentrer sur les sujets qui permettent de dégager des règles de droit international « primaires » ou « secondaires » et d'éviter les sujets techniques ou « sectoriels » comme le régime juridique de la préservation de la diversité biologique. Légiférer sur cette question serait une entreprise extrêmement technique et politique qui exigerait un type de débat que l'on peut difficilement envisager à la Commission.

Mr Adriaan Bos* On the subject of the items which should be studied by the Commission, I should like to draw attention to a matter which is currently being

---

*Legal Adviser, Ministry of Foreign Affairs, Netherlands.

considered by the Sixth Committee: namely, the draft resolution which one hopes will be adopted at the current session of the General Assembly on the commemoration of the centennial of the first International Peace Conference, which was held at The Hague in 1899. That Conference was the first successful effort at codification in the field of international law. It is, moreover, striking that the subjects which were discussed at that Conference are still very much relevant today: namely, the laws and customs of war, disarmament and the peaceful settlement of international disputes. In the draft resolution which is before the Sixth Committee,[14] the International Law Commission is asked to cooperate in the implementation of the Programme of Action dedicated to the centennial of the Conference and to consider participating in the activities which are envisaged in that Programme.[15] As far as the themes of international humanitarian law and the peaceful settlement of disputes are concerned, the Commission could certainly make a significant contribution to their further development for that purpose.[16]

Professeur Hanna Bokor-Szegö* L'expérience montre que les conventions qui ont été adoptées sur la base des projets de la Commission du droit international et qui ne sont pas encore entrés en vigueur, les projets d'articles adoptés par la Commission qui ne sont pas encore devenus des conventions et même les projets d'articles sur lesquels la Commission n'a pas encore achevé ses travaux peuvent influer considérablement sur la formation du droit international et ont parfois contribué à définir de nouvelles règles coutumières. On retiendra à cet égard le projet d'articles sur la nationalité des personnes physiques en relation avec la succession d'États, qui a été adopté provisoirement par la Commission en première lecture cette année[17], et la Convention de Vienne sur la succession d'États en matière de traités de 1978, qui est finalement entrée en vigueur en novembre dernier. Bien qu'elle ne fût pas encore entrée en vigueur à ce moment-là, la Convention de Vienne de 1978 a grandement contribué à régler les effets sur les traités des successions d'États intervenues ces dernières années en Europe centrale et orientale. Pour prendre un autre exemple, que le juge Schwebel a cité dans le discours liminaire qu'il a prononcé aujourd'hui au déjeuner, la Cour internationale de Justice, dans le jugement qu'elle a rendu en l'affaire *Gabčíkovo-Nagymaros*, a évoqué le projet d'articles de la Commission sur la responsabilité des États, tel qu'il avait été adopté provisoirement en première lecture, pour préciser les conditions qu'un État devait remplir pour pouvoir invoquer l'état de nécessité comme ceux d'exclusion de l'illicéité de son comportement[18].

On aurait tort de penser que la Commission n'a mené à bien ses travaux sur un sujet donné que dans la mesure où elle parvient à mettre au point un produit final, moins si ce produit final devient une convention, ou si cette convention entre en vigueur, encore moins si elle recueille l'adhésion d'un grand nombre d'États.

---

*Professeur de droit international, Université de Budapest, Budapest (Hongrie).
[14]Document A/C.6/52/L.2: draft resolution proposed by the Netherlands and the Russian Federation under agenda item 146 (*b*) entitled "Action to be taken dedicated to the 1999 centennial of the First International Peace Conference and to the closing of the United Nations Decade of International Law".
[15]See paragraph 3 of the draft resolution.
[16]Cf. paragraph 1 of the draft resolution.
[17]*Loc. cit. supra*, note n° 13.
[18]*Projet Gabčíkovo-Nagymaros (Hongrie/Slovaquie), arrêt du 25 septembre 1997*, par. 49 à 58, en particulier par. 52.

Il ne faudrait pas perdre de vue ce constat lorsqu'on examine la question des sujets qu'il conviendrait de renvoyer à la Commission. Il n'est pas dit que l'on a raison de lui soumettre les seuls sujets qui auraient des chances réelles de déboucher à terme sur une convention de nature à recueillir l'adhésion d'un grand nombre d'États.

Mr Christopher W. Pinto   With regard to my suggestion that there be a kind of voluntary rotation of membership in the Commission, it was not my intention that there be such a rotation as an invariable rule. Of course, there are States which believe that their nationals should be members of the Commission for more than two terms. Many of them are right to harbour such a belief. In the case of most States, though, it would be helpful if they were voluntarily to make a gesture towards increasing the general sense of participation in the work of the Commission and to forbear from nominating their nationals to occupy a seat in the Commission for more than two terms.

With regard to the identification of new topics on which the Commission might undertake the progressive development and codification of rules of international law, I personally find it very difficult to make any concrete proposals. If one looks at the suggestions which have been made from time to time, by authors, the representatives of States or the members of the Commission itself, one cannot avoid forming the impression that there has been a distinct tendency for many of the topics which have been proposed quickly to become dated and to lose their relevance. The legal aspects of the new international economic order is a prime example. Rather than the identification of new topics being approached as an abstract exercise, it would be better if new topics were to be referred to the Commission as the result of proposals which are made in response to specific concrete problems and immediately felt needs.

Having said this, I hope that the Commission will give some consideration to my suggestion that it set up a working group on fundamental studies. Why does international law work? More importantly, why is it that it sometimes fails to work? How might it be made more effective? How may information regarding international law be made more readily available? Questions such as these are important to smaller countries and the Commission is certainly well equipped to answer them.

Mr Carlos Calero-Rodrigues   The Commission may make suggestions regarding the subjects which it is to take up, but the final decision rests with the General Assembly and, therefore, with States. Once more, it is only natural that, in the selection of new topics, the predominant consideration should be what accords with the interests of States. However, that certainly should not be the only consideration, there being a number of other factors which should also be taken into account.

Hitherto, interest in the identification of new topics has been fitful and sporadic. From time to time, the Commission has turned its attention to the question and has prepared a list—usually, a very long list—of possible candidates. In 1996, the Commission even compiled a comprehensive scheme of the whole of international law in order to assist itself in identifying new topics which

---

[19]See the Report of the International Law Commission on the work of its forty-eighth session, *Official Records of the General Assembly, Fifty-first Session, Supplement No. 10* (A/51/10), pp. 329-334.

it might take up.[19] The practical results of such periodic exercises tend to be nugatory, however. Moreover, when the Sixth Committee turns its mind to the question, its decision is usually taken on the spur of the moment and without the benefit of any serious examination of whether it is indeed a good idea to refer to the Commission the topic which has been proposed. It might accordingly be a good idea if the Commission were to consider the matter on an ongoing basis, perhaps by setting up a standing working group on the identification of new topics.

As far as the Commission's methods of work are concerned, they should be considered to be entirely the responsibility of the Commission itself. The Sixth Committee may exercise a kind of supervision over the Commission in this regard, but, in the final analysis, only the Commission can truly know which are the best ways in which to conduct its work. Its decisions on the subject should be respected—unless, of course, they are preposterous or are taken without any indication of the reasons behind them.

However, I would like to conclude with one suggestion on this subject, which is based on my own experience as a member of the Commission and which coincides with an observation which was made by Judge Schwebel in the keynote speech which he delivered at today's working luncheon.

In accordance with article 2 (1) of the Commission's Statute, as amended by the General Assembly in 1981, the Commission is a body which consists of 34 members. That number is too large. It is all the more so if one accepts the view of certain commentators that members of the Commission should be in attendance at most of its meetings. Thus, at this Colloquium, Mr Pinto has suggested that members of the Commission should take an oath of office which would include an undertaking to attend each of its annual sessions in their entirety, while Professor Orrego Vicuña has suggested that members of the Commission should be penalized if they do not attend at least 50 per cent of its meetings. On the basis of my experience, if all of the 34 members were in attendance at all of the Commission's meetings, the working environment within the Commission would be even more difficult than it already undoubtedly is.

It may be that the number of the Commission's members should remain 34. After all, the increase in the size of the Commission which took place in 1981 grew out of the quite reasonable demand that nationals of more States should participate in its work. It may be, too, that members of the Commission should be encouraged, or even required, to attend all, or at least most, of its meetings. However, if both of these suggestions were taken up, it might be a good idea to create two different categories of members: a category of 17 "core" members, who would participate in all of the Commission's work, including the preparation and drafting of texts, and a category of 17 "other" members, who would have to be present in order for the Commission to be able to take any decisions. This is probably the only way in which to reconcile a total membership of 34 with any requirement that all of the Commission's members participate in its deliberations.

Generally speaking, though, it is my hope that the Commission will continue to do what it has been doing up until now: that is, to conduct an ongoing review of its methods of work and to make changes to those methods only if and when it is shown that those changes are absolutely necessary.

4

THE COMMISSION'S WORK
AND
THE SHAPING OF INTERNATIONAL LAW

*

L'ŒUVRE DE LA COMMISSION
ET
LA MISE EN FORME DU DROIT INTERNATIONAL

Introduction by the Moderator, Mr Carlos Calero-Rodrigues*

The fourth topic in the programme of this Colloquium concerns the ways in which the work of the International Law Commission may contribute to the shaping of international law. It is the purpose of this Colloquium to identify practical measures for enhancing the capability of the Commission to contribute to the progressive development and codification of international law. That being so, the main objective of our discussion should be to identify the means, the type of instrument or the form of output which should optimally be used by the Commission to shape international law on those subjects on which it may conduct its work.

We have two panellists. The first is Sir Kenneth Keith, a Judge of the New Zealand Court of Appeal. He is also a Judge of the Courts of Appeal of Samoa, the Cook Islands and Niue. From 1986 to 1996, he was a member of the New Zealand Law Commission. For many years, he was a member of the Law Faculty of Victoria University, Wellington, New Zealand. I might also mention that, back in the 1960s, he was for a brief time a legal officer in the Codification Division of the Office of Legal Affairs of the Secretariat of the United Nations.

The second member of our panel is Professor Huang Huikang, Professor of International Law at Wu Han University, China. From 1991 to 1994, he was Assistant Secretary-General of the Asian-African Legal Consultative Committee. He now works in the Department of Treaties and Law of the Foreign Ministry of China.

Presentation by Sir Kenneth Keith

The topic before us is very broad and gives rise to very many issues. I will address just four of them. First, I will make some brief remarks regarding the changing context within which the Commission conducts its work. Secondly, I will give some examples of how the Commission has shaped the law, more specifically the law in action, as opposed to the law as it is found in the books.

---

*Member of the International Law Commission, 1982-1986.

Thirdly, I will consider the forms which the Commission's work should take in order to enhance its impact on the international legal order. Fourthly—and looking forward to the sixth topic in the programme of this Colloquium—I will make some brief suggestions as to how the Commission's work might be made more relevant and its availability improved.

Before I turn to the first of these issues, though, I should remark that I have, in my time, been an international civil servant, a law professor, a member of a national law commission and a judge and, from my current position on the bench, I certainly see many of the issues which are before this Colloquium in a quite different light.

First, then, the changing context—a matter which was also discussed by Professor Orrego Vicuña at this morning's session.

Comparing the discussion at this Colloquium with the debates which I used to hear in this same room 30 years ago when I attended the meetings of the Sixth Committee, it is obvious that the world has changed in amazing and quite revolutionary ways. Today, one encounters books with titles such as *The End of the Nation State*;[1] and wherever one travels in the world one can still watch the same news broadcasts on CNN. There is an ever greater reality to the talk of a borderless world and a global village. In some ways, this revolution which we are living through is exhilarating; but it also has its sinister side. The power which was once in the hands of princes and has more recently been vested in the hands of democratically elected governments is now increasingly to be found in private hands and to be beyond the effective reach of democratic processes.

As a result of technological, ideological and demographical changes, then, we live in a very different world from that of 30 years ago. It is, moreover, a world which needs a critical normative component if it is to function properly or at all. In this connection, it is worthwhile to go back to the Charter of the United Nations and to look at its Article 13. Too often, we quote just the parts of subparagraph (*a*) of paragraph 1 of that Article that are concerned with "the progressive development of international law and its codification" and fail to notice that that same subparagraph also makes reference to "international co-operation in the political field", while subparagraph (*b*) of the same paragraph talks in terms of "co-operation in the economic, social, cultural, educational, and health fields". Read as a whole, then, Article 13 bears witness to a vitally important, but much neglected, fact: that there is to the law an essential political or social or scientific or cultural or economic component. As Professor Pellet pithily remarked at this morning's session, law is too important to be left to the lawyers.

Just as today's world is quite different from the world of 30 years ago, so the processes which are available to us for making law are also nowadays more numerous and exhibit a much greater diversity. During the discussion of the last topic, Mr Perrin de Brichambaut referred to the astonishing growth of regional law-making mechanisms to stand alongside those which have for some time existed at the universal level. There is also a choice between mechanisms of public law-making and private law-making, including law-making by private industry and by private trade associations. There are bodies whose remit is general and those whose mandate, expertise and membership are specialized in

---

[1]Ohmae, K., *The End of the Nation State* (1995).

nature. On top of this diversification of law-making bodies, there is also today a much greater range of law-making instruments in use than was the case three decades back.

Before I turn to these instruments, I should like to say a few words about the law in action. In his keynote speech at today's working luncheon, Judge Schwebel gave a splendid account of the impact of the International Law Commission's work on the work of the International Court of Justice. To complement what he has said, my emphasis will be, rather, upon how the Commission's work has served to shape the decisions of courts at the national level.

In this connection, there are three points which stand out. First, as is clear from a review of the decisions which are to be found in the *International Law Reports*, there is an ever-increasing range of human activity which is governed or regulated by international law, including many matters that not so very long ago were thought to belong entirely to the domestic jurisdiction of States. Even in the distant corner of the world from which I hail, the courts are faced every month or two with a case in which major issues of international law play a central role.

Secondly, the Commission's work has played a structural role in the international legal process. It has strongly influenced the way in which we think about international law and has helped to establish the intellectual framework within which we address, solve and answer international legal problems. Judge Schwebel, in his lunchtime address, gave the example of the relationship between the law of treaties and the law of State responsibility—an issue which also troubled us during the *Rainbow Warrior* arbitration.[2] Another example is the fundamental character of the law of diplomatic and consular immunities, which was underlined by the International Court of Justice in the *Tehran* case.[3]

Thirdly, it does not seem to matter, as far as national courts are concerned, what is the form of the text to which they are referred. In my paper, I review a total of 19 cases before national courts in which texts prepared by the International Law Commission have been invoked and applied. In only five of those 19 cases was that text a binding treaty which was directly applicable to the facts of the case. In all the other cases, the courts made use of and relied upon the text concerned, even though it was not formally binding.

This brings me to the third of the four major issues which I wish to address in my presentation: namely, that we need to look very broadly at the range of legislative techniques that are available to us. We should no longer assume that the binding treaty is the only form of legislative instrument. We should also think in terms of model treaties, model laws, restatements and declarations. I also notice that the report which the Commission has adopted this year mentions that its work on the topic of unilateral acts of States might even take the final form of a doctrinal study.[4]

---

[2] *Case concerning the difference between New Zealand and France concerning the interpretation or application of two Agreements, concluded on 9 July 1986 between the two States and which related to the problems arising from the* Rainbow Warrior *Affair, Award of 30 April 1990, Reports of International Arbitral Awards*, vol. 20, p. 215.

[3] *United States Diplomatic and Consular Staff in Tehran, Provisional Measures, Order of 15 December 1979, I.C.J. Reports 1979*, p. 7, and *United States Diplomatic and Consular Staff in Tehran, Judgment, I.C.J. Reports 1980*, p. 3.

[4] Report of the International Law Commission on the work of its forty-ninth session, *Official Records of the General Assembly, Fifty-second Session, Supplement No. 10* (A/52/10), p. 145 at para. 214.

Fourthly and finally, I come to matters of information. To begin with, there is certainly still a need for straightforward, old-fashioned guides. So far as international texts are concerned, it might be useful to produce a new version of the collection of treaty lists, which was so very useful when it was first published back in 1956. The Commission should also consider returning to the question of identifying ways and means for making the evidence of customary international law more readily available—a subject which it last touched upon way back in 1950.[5] The Secretariat of the United Nations, for its part, should give some thought to whether the *United Nations Juridical Yearbook* is as useful as it could be. More importantly, though, it should give serious consideration to the ways in which the work of the Commission might be made more accessible to the vast number of people who nowadays need to be familiar with it, such as the practising lawyers who week after week appear before me in my court. In this connection, I should mention a report which was recently prepared by the New Zealand Law Commission for the purpose of providing lawyers whose practice is in the domestic field with straightforward information about where to find the raw materials of international law.[6]

The suggestion was made by Mr Owada during this morning's session that research should be conducted into the implementation of treaties—a proposal which was supported this afternoon by Mr Magnuson. Work has been done on this subject at a technical level by the Commonwealth Secretariat. However, I think that the Governments of many States are in need of more substantive assistance in this regard—assistance which would enhance their abilities to give real and substantive effect to international legal texts within their domestic legal orders.

There is also a need for the better distribution of information about judgements on matters of international law. UNCITRAL, for example, periodically disseminates a list of the decisions of national courts in which reference has been made to UNCITRAL documents. It would be of great value, both to practising lawyers and to the Commission itself, if there were a similar publication dealing with national citations of the Commission's work and output.

I shall close on a less concrete note with an appeal for a change in mindset. We often hear references to societal differences and to the diversity of legal cultures. In this connection, I am reminded, being in this city, of Chancellor James Kent. When he lectured at Columbia University last century and wrote his famous commentaries, he commenced what he had to say about American law with a treatment of the law of nations. He did not think that it was possible to understand a national legal system unless it were first placed in its wider context. The ability to take a wider view—to see the world steadily and to see it whole—is very important. My final plea, then, is for the generalist, for people who can take the wide view, even while they focus on the particular task that is before them.

Presentation by Professor Huang Huikang

To my mind, there are three basic questions to be asked in respect of the topic before us. First, what has been the impact of the Commission's work upon the shaping of international law? Secondly, what are the principal factors which

---

[5] *Yearbook of the International Law Commission, 1950*, vol. II, p. 367 at paras. 24-94.
[6] Law Commission, *A New Zealand Guide to International Law and Its Sources*, New Zealand Law Commission Report No. 34 (1996).

have prevented the work of the Commission from having a greater—or a yet greater—effect upon the shaping of international law? Thirdly, what can realistically be done in order to remove or to overcome these obstacles?

In answer to the first of these questions, the role which the Commission has played in determining the shape and content of contemporary international law has been a tremendous one. It has produced 21 sets of draft articles, which have dealt with many of the key areas of international law. On the basis of 12 of these drafts, a total of 15 multilateral conventions have been concluded, all of which are landmarks in the domains to which they relate. The contribution which the Commission has made to shaping international law through its non-conventional forms of output should not be overlooked, either. The Commission's drafts have served to clarify the central legal issues in the areas to which they relate and have been invoked by States and by tribunals, national and international, as evidence of the current state of customary international law. Even unfinished drafts have been used in this way, the most noteworthy example being the Commission's draft articles on State responsibility.

The most remarkable of the Commission's achievements are to found in such central fields of international law as the law of diplomatic and consular relations, the law of treaties and the law of the sea. However, the Commission has also made a substantial contribution to the development of the law in such fields as the law of State succession, international criminal law, the law of State responsibility and the law of international organizations.

In the course of codifying the law, the Commission has, at the same time, made a number of major contributions to advancing the development of international law. So, for example, the Commission, through its work on the law of treaties, succeeded in establishing the status of *jus cogens* as part of the contemporary international legal order.

In sum, the achievement of the International Law Commission is without precedent in the history of international law. I emphasize this fact since the Commission has, in recent years, come in for an undue and excessive amount of criticism.

I shall now turn to the second of my three questions. In order to identify the principal factors which have prevented the Commission's work from having an even greater impact on the shape of international law, I have, in my paper, made a thorough review of the current status of the Commission's output. The conclusion at which I have arrived is that there exists a significant gap between the achievements of the Commission, on the one hand, and the response of the international community to those achievements, on the other. Thus, to begin with, States have failed to transform a number of the drafts which the Commission has prepared into conventions. Moreover, when one looks at those of the Commission's drafts which have served as the bases of conventions, one finds that, while most of the conventions in question were adopted by the vote of an overwhelming majority of the States which participated in their negotiation and conclusion, those same conventions have, in the end, tended to attract the adhesion of only a very limited number of States. Indeed, the average rate of adhesion to the conventions which have been elaborated on the basis of the Commission's drafts is surprisingly low, each State on average having established its consent to be bound by only four of those conventions. There is, furthermore, a significant gap between the number of signatures which have been appended to those conventions and the number of ratifications which they have received. Indeed, there are almost 150 signatures which have yet to be followed by the deposit of an instrument of ratification.[7]

The Commission's work is, therefore, prevented from realizing its full potential by the failure of many States, particularly in the developing world, to adhere to the conventions which have been concluded on the basis of its drafts. Even among the States which do adhere to those conventions, there is a general dilatoriness in proceeding to the final stage of ratification or accession.

What can be done in order to address these difficulties? To help answer this, my third question, I would suggest that the General Assembly conduct a thorough survey of the Commission's output with a view to highlighting the Commission's achievements, determining the current status of its end product, identifying the reasons why so many States, particularly from the developing world, are reluctant to adhere to certain of the conventions which have been elaborated upon the basis of its drafts and, most importantly, devising concrete measures to increase the adhesion of States to those conventions. In undertaking this enquiry and in acting on its results, the General Assembly should have as its principal objective to secure universal adhesion to those of the "Commission's" conventions which are in force, but which have to date attracted only a limited number of adhesions. Its second objective should be to identify measures which would facilitate the entry into force of those of the "Commission's" conventions which have not yet attracted the requisite number of ratifications or accessions. Consideration should be given in this connection to providing technical and legal assistance to States which need it in order to study and evaluate the implications of establishing their consent to be bound by the conventions concerned.

As for those of the Commission's drafts which have not yet been transformed into conventions, the Commission should consider resuming discussion of them and, if need be, revising them in order to facilitate their eventual adoption in binding form.

OPEN-FLOOR DISCUSSION

*

DÉBAT

Mr Carlos Calero-Rodrigues Although the presentations of Sir Kenneth Keith and Professor Huang Huikang are apparently quite different in their approach and in their content, they in fact complement each other quite nicely.

It is Sir Kenneth's belief that the Commission has made a substantial contribution to the shaping of the law. Moreover, he points out that this contribution has not only taken the direct and immediate form of the preparation of draft articles to serve as the bases of multilateral conventions. It has taken a more indirect and less apparent form, through the impact which the Commission's work has had upon laws, legislation and judicial decision-making at the national level. Furthermore, he demonstrates that this impact has existed even in those cases in which the Commission's work has "only" taken the form of a

---

[7]Here, for obvious reasons, I discount the recently adopted Convention on the Law of the Non-Navigational Uses of International Watercourses.

draft, even, moreover, when work on that draft has not yet been completed. He is, accordingly, quite sanguine about the current state of the Commission and is unremittingly optimistic about its future. It is on this premiss that his suggestions for enhancing the Commission's work are made.

In contrast, Professor Huang adopts a more pessimistic starting point. The reason why this is so is that he prefers to measure the Commission's contribution in more formal terms. So, for example, he points out that many of the Commission's drafts remain of little or no effect, even when they have been transformed into conventions; for, as he remarks, many of the conventions which have been concluded upon the basis of the Commission's drafts are either not in force at all or are in force for only a relative handful of States.

Mr S. Rama Rao* While I appreciate Mr Calero-Rodrigues's point, I would not depict the difference between the two presentations in such stark terms. Personally, I thought Professor Huang was quite optimistic about the Commission's achievements and also, by implication, about its future.

Professor Huang remarks that the work of the Commission has not been as popular with States as it might have been in terms of the number of adhesions to the conventions which have been elaborated upon the basis of its drafts. It would be interesting in this connection to analyse the subject matter and content of the conventions which have in fact proved popular and to make a comparison with the content and subject matter of those conventions which have not found favour with States. The results of such a study would be of assistance to the General Assembly in considering the kind of topics that should be referred to the Commission.

Having said this, the contribution which the Commission may make to the shaping of international law is naturally defined and limited by the terms of its Statute and by the position which it enjoys within the overall framework of the Charter of the United Nations. After all, one cannot expect the Commission to discharge a function which it is not meant to perform. So, for example, the Commission is hardly an appropriate body to which to refer topics on which instant advice is required. Similarly, highly political topics which are not susceptible to management in legal or forensic terms are not topics on which the Commission should be asked to work. In short, the character of the topic and the kind of professional expertise needed to deal with it are both important factors to bear in mind in any decision as to whether to refer a topic to the Commission, particularly since those two factors will exert a strong influence over the ultimate acceptability or otherwise of the final output.

Turning lastly to a suggestion which was made during this morning's session by Professor Orrego Vicuña, we should indeed give some consideration to whether the Commission might be capable of serving alongside the International Court of Justice as another body which could give advisory opinions on questions of United Nations law.

Professeur Djamchid Momtaz** Le sujet qui me préoccupe est celui des conventions que l'on pourrait qualifier de « mort-nées ». Peut-être devrais-je aussi attirer l'attention des personnes ici présentes sur le risque de voir ces conventions remplacées par des projets établis par la Commission, ce qui, dans

---

*Representative of India to the Sixth Committee of the General Assembly.
**Professeur de droit international, Université de Téhéran, Téhéran (République islamique d'Iran).

une certaine mesure, reviendrait à substituer des projets «mort-nés» à des conventions «mort-nées».

En 1982, la Commission du droit international a terminé ses travaux sur le projet d'articles sur le droit des traités entre États et organisations internationales ou entre organisations internationales. La même année, l'Assemblée générale a décidé qu'une convention serait conclue sur la base du projet d'articles adopté par la Commission[8]; et, l'année suivante, elle a décidé que le cadre approprié pour les négociations sur une telle convention et son adoption serait une conférence de plénipotentiaires[9]. Afin d'assurer le succès de cette conférence, des consultations officieuses se sont tenues en 1984 et 1985, avec l'encouragement et sous l'égide de l'Assemblée générale, sur les questions de procédure relatives au déroulement de la conférence à venir et, chose plus importante, sur un certain nombre de questions de fond majeures découlant du projet de la Commission[10].

Depuis, tous les projets établis par la Commission ont été d'une façon ou d'une autre réexaminés au sein des comités ou des organes spéciaux créés par l'Assemblée générale. Deux exemples méritent une mention particulière à cet égard : le projet d'articles sur le statut du courrier diplomatique et de la valise diplomatique non accompagnée par un courrier diplomatique, adopté par la Commission en 1989, et le projet d'articles sur les immunités juridictionnelles des États et de leurs biens qu'elle a adopté en 1991.

En ce qui concerne le premier de ces deux textes, des consultations officieuses ont eu lieu en 1990, 1991 et 1992 à la Sixième Commission afin d'aplanir les divergences de vues touchant certains articles du projet[11]. Toutefois, ces efforts se sont révélés infructueux et, à sa cinquantième session, l'Assemblée générale a, dans les faits, enterré le sujet[12].

Il est à craindre que le projet d'articles de la Commission sur les immunités juridictionnelles ne connaisse le même sort. Afin de faciliter la conclusion d'une convention, le projet d'articles de la Commission a été examiné d'abord par un groupe de travail de la Sixième Commission puis lors des consultations officieuses tenues dans le cadre de la Sixième Commission dans le but d'arriver à «réduire» les différences existantes entre les États au sujet de certains aspects du projet de la Commission[13]. À la suite de ces efforts, l'Assemblée générale a finalement pu accepter, en 1994, la recommandation de la Commission de convoquer une conférence diplomatique pour conclure une convention[14]. Toutefois, il est apparu nécessaire d'examiner plus avant certaines questions de

---

[8]Voir la résolution 37/112 de l'Assemblée générale, en date du 16 décembre 1982.

[9]Voir la résolution 38/139 de l'Assemblée générale, en date du 19 décembre 1983.

[10]Voir le paragraphe 6 de la résolution 38/139 de l'Assemblée générale, en date du 19 décembre 1983 et le paragraphe 8 de la résolution 39/86 de l'Assemblée générale, en date du 13 décembre 1984. Voir aussi la résolution 40/76 de l'Assemblée générale, en date du 11 décembre 1985, et ses annexes.

[11]Voir les résolutions de l'Assemblée générale 44/36 du 4 décembre 1989, 45/43 du 28 novembre 1990 et 46/57 du 9 décembre 1991, ainsi que la décision 47/415 de l'Assemblée générale, en date du 25 novembre 1992.

[12]Voir la décision 50/416 de l'Assemblée générale, en date du 11 décembre 1995.

[13]Voir la résolution 46/55 de l'Assemblée générale, en date du 9 décembre 1991, et les décisions de l'Assemblée générale 47/414 du 25 novembre 1992 et 48/413 du 9 décembre 1993. Pour les deux rapports du groupe de travail, voir les documents A/C.6/47/L.10 et A/C.6/48/L.4 et Corr. 2. Pour le rapport sur les consultations informelles, voir le document A/C.6/49/L.2.

[14]Voir le paragraphe 1 de la résolution 49/61 de l'Assemblée générale, en date du 9 décembre 1994.

fond soulevées par le projet de la Commission avant de pouvoir tenir une telle conférence. Par conséquent, il a été décidé de reprendre l'examen des questions de fond à la Sixième Commission, mais pas avant 1997 et la session en cours de l'Assemblée générale[15]. Tout porte à croire que, lors de la session en cours, l'Assemblée générale va, une fois de plus, surseoir à prendre les dispositions nécessaires pour la tenue d'une conférence, et ce jusqu'en 1999, soit huit ans après que la Commission lui ait soumis son projet pour la première fois.

Cela étant, il faudrait réfléchir plus avant à la manière de faire en sorte que les projets de la Commission ne soient « mort-nés ». Il faut d'abord et avant tout accorder une attention particulière aux sujets qui sont renvoyés à la Commission pour codification. Comme cette question a déjà fait l'objet de discussions, je ne m'étendrai pas davantage sur ce sujet.

Deuxièmement, il faudrait repenser la manière dont la Sixième Commission procède pour donner des directives à la Commission et orienter son travail. En particulier, la Sixième Commission doit prendre davantage soin de donner à la Commission des orientations claires et précises sur la façon dont elle souhaiterait que cette dernière mène ses travaux sur tel ou tel sujet. À certaines occasions, la Sixième Commission a manifestement échoué à le faire. Résultat : au bout du compte, la Commission a fait du travail pour rien. Ainsi, la Sixième Commission a examiné à 10 reprises les travaux de la Commission sur le statut du courrier diplomatique et de la valise diplomatique; le sort réservé au projet final de la Commission sur ce sujet montre clairement que l'orientation donnée à cette dernière était loin d'être suffisante.

Ma troisième suggestion concerne l'étape suivant la présentation par la Commission d'un projet d'articles final à l'Assemblée générale. Dans le cas où celle-ci jugerait nécessaire de mener des négociations quelconques sur le fond du projet avant de mettre en branle le processus conventionnel proprement dit, on gagnerait à associer des experts de l'Association du droit international ou de l'Institut de droit international, par exemple, à ces négociations d'une certaine façon. Ceux-ci pourraient ainsi offrir leurs compétences aux États et contribuer à sauver des projets qui autrement se révéleraient moribonds.

Enfin, si ces négociations ne permettent pas d'enclencher le processus formel de conclusion d'un traité, l'Assemblée générale devrait faire tout ce qui est en son pouvoir pour sauver ce qui peut l'être. Elle devrait notamment encourager les efforts visant à négocier et approuver un texte, fondé sur le projet de la Commission, qu'elle pourrait adopter sous forme de résolution ou de déclaration. Bien entendu, une telle issue serait moins souhaitable que la conclusion d'un traité, mais, rédigée avec la précision voulue, cette déclaration pourrait néanmoins s'avérer utile.

Professor Yuri Kolosov* À propos of what Professor Momtaz has just said, I think that one has to exercise a large measure of caution when one describes any of the Commission's "children" as "stillborn". Cases in point are the two conventions of 1978 and 1983 on the subject of State succession. For a long time, both these conventions were generally regarded to number among the Commission's "stillborn children". The USSR did not sign either of these conventions, nor did the USSR or the Russian Federation accede to either of them. Nevertheless, both conventions played an extremely active role in regu-

---

*Professor of International Law, Moscow State Institute of International Relations, Moscow, Russian Federation.
[15]Voir le paragraphe 3 de la même résolution.

lating and solving the problems of State succession which fell to be resolved as a result of the dissolution of the Soviet Union. No one would have predicted that this would occur. Who knows which of the Commission's other supposedly "stillborn children" may prove themselves to be of good service in the future and for whom?

On this same issue, I would add that it is sometimes the case that the failure of States to establish their consent to be bound by a convention is to be explained by reference to the fact that many of those to whom it falls to decide whether to take this step do not have a good understanding of international law and do not appreciate the meaning and effect of the convention which is before them.

Mr Raul Goco* The Commission has, without doubt, made a major contribution to the shaping of international law. I doubt, though, that it could be regarded as the only major player in the field. That could hardly be so, given the multitude of law-making bodies, agencies and organizations which there now are. However, if there were agreement that the Commission should enjoy a preeminent role in the international law-making process, then a way could surely be found to amend its Statute in order to give it such a role.

Mr Shabtai Rosenne** In order better to understand the current situation with regard to the codification of international law, it might be a good idea to review its history.

I would date the modern era of codification back to the Franco-Prussian war of 1871. The shock which that war had upon enlightened pacifists of that time led to unofficial attempts by international non-governmental organizations to organize the codification of certain major aspects of international law, particularly the laws of war, as they were then called. These efforts constituted a kind of preparation for the Hague conferences of 1899 and 1907, which were in a way the first modern codification conferences. These were followed by the little-known London conference of 1908 on the codification of prize law—that is, the law regarding the relations of belligerents to neutrals in the conduct of warfare at sea. The technique which the British Government developed for that conference became a model for the preparation of codification conferences. Most importantly, that technique involved, alongside the technical and scientific legal work, a measure of political input in the form of consultations with Governments.

The codification of international law was taken up by the League of Nations in 1924, employing more or less the techniques which had been developed for the 1908 London conference. In that year, the Assembly of the League decided that there should be created a Committee Experts for the Progressive Codification of International Law. This Committee, which might indeed be regarded as the progenitor of the International Law Commission, consisted of 17 members—half as many as the Commission, it may be noted, whereas the League had a membership less than a third of that of the United Nations. While it was understood that it was not the task of this Committee to draw up a single complete code of international law, the League of Nations rather ambitiously decided to convene a codification conference at The Hague in 1930 with no

---

*Ambassador of the Philippines to Canada. Member of the International Law Commission, 1997- .
**Ambassador. Vice-President of the Institut de Droit International. Member of the International Law Commission, 1962-1971.

fewer than three topics on its agenda: nationality, territorial waters and responsibility of States (in the sense of responsibility of States for injuries to aliens).

The Hague Codification Conference of 1930 was widely regarded as a failure at the time. There were two reasons why it did fail in its immediate objectives. First, the preparatory work consisted of the formulation of what were called "bases of discussion", rather than the preparation of a draft convention. Secondly, during the preparatory stage, there was insufficient consultation with Governments. It should be borne in mind in this connection that the League of Nations did not possess anything along the lines of the Sixth Committee of the General Assembly. The First Committee of the Assembly of the League decided to examine what lessons might be learned from the failure of the Hague Conference. Governments were invited to submit their observations and suggestions on the subject. On the recommendation of its First Committee, the Assembly of the League adopted in 1931 a resolution setting out a new procedure for the progressive codification of international law.[16] This procedure involved the preparation of a draft convention, together with an explanatory statement. It also involved much more systematic consultation with Governments during the preparatory phase. It is that resolution which was picked up in 1947 by the Committee on the Progressive Development of International Law and its Codification—the so-called "Committee of Seventeen"[17]—and which thus forms the basis of the Statute of the International Law Commission.

Much of the talk which one hears nowadays of the Commission being in crisis is exaggeration and stems in large part from faulty diagnosis. Analyses of the Commission's work sometimes focus almost exclusively on the formal question of whether a given convention which has been adopted on the basis of one of the Commission's drafts is or is not in force and so legally binding *qua* treaty. As Professor Kolosov rightly remarks and as Sir Kenneth Keith has shown, this is not the sole criterion by which to judge the Commission's work, nor is it the sole measure of that work's value. Conventions which are not in force and may never be, drafts prepared by the Commission which have not yet been and may never be "converted" into conventions and drafts on which the Commission has not even finished work have all been used by Governments as a legal basis for the political solution of many of their problems.

It is sometimes said that the Commission has too many items on its agenda and that this contributes in large measure to its current difficulties. However, the Commission also had a lot of topics in its work programme during the 1960s, when I was a member. We did not act on all them, but, rather, concentrated on two or three topics at a time. One of these topics would be regarded as a "major" topic and the other as a "minor" topic—the term "minor" not being meant to disparage the topic to which it was applied, but being employed, rather, to indicate that the topic concerned was not thought to require the continuous and intense attention which the "major" topic demanded. When the Special Rapporteur for the "major" topic was away, then the Commission would shift its attention to one of the "minor" topics. Notwithstanding this approach, the

---

[16]Resolution adopted by the Assembly of the League of Nations, 25 September 1931, *League of Nations Official Journal, Special Supplement, No. 92, 1931*, p. 9.

[17]This Committee was established by General Assembly resolution 94 (I) of 11 December 1946 in order "to study . . . [t]he methods by which the General Assembly should encourage the progressive development of international law and its eventual codification" and so "discharge its obligations under" Article 13 (1) (a) of the Charter. For the report of the Committee, see document A/331.

Commission never submitted to the General Assembly for its consideration only two or three isolated draft articles at a time, but always a complete section or part of whatever draft it was working on.

If and in so far as the Commission may be in crisis, then, the problem does not lie so much in the Commission's crowded agenda, but elsewhere. It is my belief that the fault lies squarely with the General Assembly and the rapidity and ease with which it refers matters to the Commission without giving any consideration to the impact which such reference may have on the Commission's agenda and its programme of work.

Professeur Maurice Kamto* Les dispositions du statut de la Commission du droit international sont très claires sur le point de savoir qui a le pouvoir de déterminer les sujets sur lesquels la Commission doit travailler. À cet égard, le statut établit une distinction entre les sujets qui concernent la codification du droit international et ceux qui concernent le développement progressif du droit international. Toutefois, comme nous le savons tous, il est difficile dans la pratique d'établir une distinction entre ce que signifie la codification et ce que l'on entend par développement progressif. Cela étant, j'aurais pensé que, tant du point de vue du droit de la pratique, la Commission devrait pouvoir proposer à l'Assemblée générale tout sujet qui, à son avis, se prête à la codification, même s'il comporte aussi du développement progressif dans une certaine mesure. Il serait difficile pour l'Assemblée générale de considérer que la Commission outrepasserait ainsi ses attributions au motif que le sujet en question relèverait davantage du développement progressif du droit international.

Si cette conclusion est juste, il est peu probable que la Commission se trouve un jour à court de sujets, ou à tout le moins de propositions de sujets, qu'elle pourrait soumettre à l'Assemblée générale pour approbation.

Un autre élément déterminant quant au nombre et au type de sujets pouvant être présentés à la Commission est la diversité des formes que les travaux de la Commission peuvent prendre. Le résultat final des travaux de la Commission sur un sujet donné doit-il être nécessairement un projet d'articles prêt à être adopté comme projet de convention, ou pourrait-il prendre, par exemple, la forme d'un ouvrage de doctrine ou d'un rapport succinct à l'Assemblée générale pour l'éclairer sur certaines questions de droit international ? Si cette dernière hypothèse est envisageable — et le statut de la Commission et la pratique montrent clairement qu'elle l'est —, la Commission peut dès lors s'attaquer à une gamme de sujets beaucoup plus étendue qu'elle ne le pourrait si ses travaux ne pouvaient revêtir que la forme de projets d'articles. Bien entendu, certains sujets se prêtent à la codification au sens classique du terme et, dans ces cas-là, la Commission devrait continuer d'établir des projets d'articles. De plus, l'Assemblée générale pourrait lui demander de soumettre des propositions sur tel ou tel sujet sous une forme précise et bien définie; et, en pareil cas aussi, la Commission pourrait s'estimer obligée de donner à ses travaux la même forme. Toutefois, du moins dans le cas des sujets qu'elle choisit elle-même, loin de se donner pour objectif de dégager un produit final aussi formel, cette dernière pourrait se borner à faire une étude, à préparer un rapport, à élaborer des directives ou à établir toute autre forme de document qui aurait plus de chances d'être adopté comme instrument

---

*Professeur à la faculté de droit et à l'Institut des relations internationales de l'Université de Yaoundé II, Yaoundé (Cameroun). Professeur associé à l'Université de Ngaoundéré, à l'Université de Douala et à l'Université catholique d'Afrique centrale.

non contraignant que comme convention formelle. À l'exemple des projets d'articles, les produits de cette nature seront examinés par la Sixième Commission et, comme M. Perrin de Brichambaut l'a souligné lors du débat sur le sujet précédent, les États pourront alors décider de la forme finale qu'ils veulent donner aux travaux de la Commission. S'ils le jugent bon, ils peuvent même renvoyer le sujet en question à la Commission pour qu'elle en approfondisse l'étude en lui donnant des orientations précises quant à la forme qu'ils souhaiteraient donner au produit final.

Professor James Crawford* Mr Rosenne remarks that, in the past, the Commission endeavoured to focus on relatively few topics at any one of its sessions. To some extent, the Commission has been doing just that in recent years. So, for example, during 1993 and 1994, most of its efforts were focused either on preparing the Draft Statute for an International Criminal Court or on finalizing the draft articles on the law of the non-navigational uses of international watercourses. Work on both of these texts was completed expeditiously during that same period. During the current year, the Commission focused squarely on the topic of nationality in relation to the succession of States, with reservations to treaties being the "minor" topic for the year.

In the next few years, it will be important that the Commission continue to focus its efforts on certain topics, particularly reservations to treaties and State responsibility, with a view to completing work on them. At the same time, there is a case for allowing new Special Rapporteurs some time to "get into" their topics. Roberto Ago was appointed Special Rapporteur for the topic of State responsibility back in 1963, but the great reports that he wrote on the topic actually date from the 1970s. He clearly had a period in which he "worked his way into" the topic; and it may be that a similar process will be required in the case of at least some of the new topics in the Commission's programme of work.

It is certainly the case that the affairs of all organizations which have been in existence for a time need to be examined. The Commission is no exception. In recognition of this fact, the Commission has, over the past few years, given careful attention to its methods of work and its agenda. This review has led to the introduction of a number of significant improvements to the way in which the Commission operates and has brought about tangible gains in its productivity. There is every reason to suppose that further improvements will be made. The Commission has even set itself the ambitious task of completing work on its draft articles on State responsibility by the end of the current quinquennium. If this objective is attained, it will be a major achievement, if only in as much as an item which has so long been on the Commission's agenda will be removed and the way cleared for the consideration of new issues.

Any suggestion, though, that the Commission is in crisis is exaggerated. Certainly, the Commission will never be the principal mechanism for legislative preparation within the United Nations system. It is absurd to think otherwise. So much of what has to be done these days in the field of international law-making falls into Mr Owada's third category of law-making—law-making *de novo*—and that is a type of work which is not the Commission's proper province. Admittedly, the preparation of the Draft Statute for the International Criminal Court was, in a way, an exercise in law-making *de novo*; but there were

---

*Whewell Professor of International Law, Jesus College, Cambridge University, Cambridge, United Kingdom. Member of the International Law Commission, 1992- .

curious factors at play in that case which made it appropriate to refer the matter to the Commission, rather than to any other body, and the case should probably be regarded as an exception. However, what emerges from the review which the Commission undertook last year of its procedures and methods of work[18] is a reaffirmation of the value of the Commission's basic project: namely, the progressive codification of international law and the restatement of its main principles—an exercise which is of enormous value, irrespective of whether particular texts may end up as widely ratified conventions.

Mr Hans Corell* Every other year, I, as Legal Counsel, have to engage in a budget exercise in the course of which I have to defend the programmes of the Office of Legal Affairs of the United Nations. One of the questions which I have to field during that exercise is why there have been no further adhesions to certain of the conventions which have been elaborated upon the basis of the International Law Commission's drafts. It is not so easy on such occasions to explain that widespread ratification is not necessary for a convention to be a success.

Every convention, of course, has its own dynamics. So, for example, it took 11 years for the United Nations Convention on the Law of the Sea of 1982 to receive the 60 ratifications and accessions which were needed for it to enter into force. Today, four years later, more than 120 States have ratified or acceded to the Convention—121 to be precise. The history behind this remarkable development is familiar to us all, so I will say no more about it; but it certainly shows that, when there is political interest in an issue and it moves into the mainstream of current affairs, then things start to happen. I hope that the same interest will be shown in the agreements on the privileges and immunities of the International Seabed Authority and the International Tribunal for the Law of the Sea.

To take another example, there are today, 11 years after it was concluded, only 24 States which have established their consent to be bound by the 1986 Vienna Convention on the Law of Treaties between States and International Organizations or between International Organizations. At one time, the failure of more States to ratify or accede to this Convention might have been understandable. Now, though, the obstacles which once prevented certain States from accepting the Convention would seem to have disappeared. However, the practical question remains whether the topic with which the Convention deals is sufficiently within the mainstream for things to happen.

Unless for some reason conventions such as that of 1986 and the question of their ratification are brought into the mainstream of current affairs, they are unlikely to be high on the political agenda in States' capitals. In these circumstances, much of the responsibility for securing wider participation in these conventions falls upon you, in particular, upon those of you who are the representatives of States to the Sixth Committee of the General Assembly and upon those who are in charge of the legal services within States' Ministries for Foreign Affairs. When there is talk of the failure of States to adhere to the conventions which have been concluded on the basis of the International Law Commission's drafts, it is, in effect, an exhortation to you to revisit the issue and to see whether the obstacles which were once thought to prevent the acceptance of those conventions have now disappeared. In the end, of course,

---

*Under-Secretary-General for Legal Affairs, the Legal Counsel.
[18]Report of the International Law Commission on the work of its forty-eighth session, *Official Records of the General Assembly, Fifty-first Session, Supplement No. 10* (A/51/10), pp. 196-230.

you will have to put the question to the politicians and maybe even bring it before parliament; and the politicians may well ask you what the point is in ratifying or acceding to this or that instrument, particularly if everybody is already using and applying it. The rejoinders to that question are familiar to us all and the responsibility will fall upon you to make them as persuasively as possible.

In closing, I would suggest that the issue of encouraging the wider acceptance of multilateral law-making instruments is one which could usefully be taken up at the regional level: within the Asian-African Legal Consultative Committee, for example, or within the Inter-American Juridical Committee or the European Committee on Legal Co-operation and the Committee of Legal Advisers on Public International Law.

Professor Huang Huikang As Mr Corell's remarks make clear, the work of the International Law Commission must be assessed against the background of the conditions prevailing in international society more generally. Whether the Commission's work on a topic meets with success depends upon many external factors; and one should be careful not to lay the blame upon the Commission when the failure of its work should more properly be attributed to the operation of conditions over which it had little or no control.

I certainly appreciate Sir Kenneth Keith's suggestion that we look more carefully at the broad range of legislative techniques and instruments that are nowadays available to us. However, experience demonstrates that the most effective way in which to shape international law is through the conclusion of multilateral conventions. Non-binding instruments such as restatements and model rules are, of course, not without their importance, but their direct relevance to the shaping of international law is necessarily always going to be limited.

I cannot agree with the general thrust of Mr Goco's intervention. While the role which the Commission plays in the shaping of international law is indeed important, it is, none the less, subsidiary by its very nature. For the foreseeable future, it will be the State which will continue to play the central role in forming and moulding international law.

Lastly, it is at the final stage of the legislative process—that is, the stage at which a convention falls to be ratified—that the greatest obstacles exist to the success of the International Law Commission's work. While improvements in the Commission's working methods may increase the efficiency of the preparatory stages of the international law-making process, the work of the Commission will only be able to realize its full potential, in terms of shaping international law, if States, as the key players in the international legal order, are willing and able to assume a greater responsibility for the proper discharge of their role. For example, the 1969 Vienna Convention on the Law of Treaties is generally recognized to be one of the most important conventions that there are; yet, to date, only 83 States have ratified or acceded to it—the most recent to do so being the People's Republic of China. States which have signed this Convention but which have not yet ratified it, as well as States which agree with what it provides but which have not yet acceded to it, should proceed as soon as possible to establish their consent to be bound by it.

In short, I would agree with Mr Corell that without the political commitment of States and their strong support, the International Law Commission will never realize its full potential.

Sir Kenneth Keith During this morning's session, the suggestion was made both by Mr Owada and Professor Orrego Vicuña that the Commission might usefully be empowered to give advisory opinions on points of international law. However, if one looks back at the work which the Commission completed on the subject of reservations in 1951 and if one thinks of the work which it is doing now on that same subject, then one might be forgiven for thinking that the Commission is already very much in the business of giving advisory opinions. Indeed, it is a central part of the Commission's task to express its views—to give its advice—on the current state of international law and that advice is often cited, relied upon and used both by those participating in international litigation and by the tribunals themselves.

On the question of "stillborn" conventions, I am much more optimistic than Professor Momtaz. To take the specific case which he has mentioned, namely, that of the Commission's draft articles on immunities of States and their property, it is interesting to note that the courts of many States which do not yet have specific legislation on that subject—and some of those that do—have made extensive use of the Commission's drafts in order to assist them in resolving concrete cases which have come before them. Whether or not a conference is ever convened to consider them and whether or not a convention is ever concluded on their basis, the Commission's draft articles are clearly regarded as an extremely valuable resource by practitioners and judges in many countries around the world.

Turning to the question of the place which the Commission should enjoy within the overall international legislative process, I would agree with Professor Crawford that the Commission is ill-suited to enter into the province of law-making *de novo*, as Mr Owada styled it. On the other hand, what we do expect from the Commission is the general view—the "big picture"—that other bodies are just not in a position to adopt or equipped to take.

Both Professor Kolosov and Mr Rosenne have referred to the use which is frequently made of conventions which have been concluded on the basis of the Commission's drafts, notwithstanding that those conventions are not yet technically in force. Mr Rosenne has also mentioned the use which is often made of the Commission's drafts, notwithstanding that they have not yet been transformed into conventional form and even that work on them is not yet complete. In my paper, I mention the extensive use which is often made of the Commission's texts by States in their pleadings before the International Court of Justice—a phenomenon which is not always fully reflected in the Court's final judgements in the cases concerned. It would, I think, be extremely useful if a study were made of the relevant State practice in this regard.

Finally, with regard to the issue of wider adhesion to treaty texts which was raised both by Professor Huang and by Mr Corell, emphasis should be placed on the importance and value of straightforward technical assistance, particularly to smaller States, such as many of those in the Pacific region. It would, for example, do much to facilitate wider ratification of conventions if assistance were given to ministers and civil servants so that they might fully appreciate what is involved in preparing appropriate implementing legislation, such that any adhesion to a convention is real, rather than symbolic, and has a tangible effect within the local legal system.

5

ENHANCING THE COMMISSION'S RELATIONSHIPS
WITH OTHER LAW-MAKING BODIES
AND
RELEVANT ACADEMIC AND PROFESSIONAL INSTITUTIONS

*

COMMENT RESSERRER LES LIENS DE LA COMMISSION
AVEC D'AUTRES ORGANES LÉGIFÉRANTS
AINSI QU'AVEC LES UNIVERSITÉS ET
LES INSTITUTS DE RECHERCHE JURIDIQUE SPÉCIALISÉS

Introduction by the Moderator, **Judge Abdul G. Koroma***

Our principal objective in discussing this, the fifth topic in the Colloquium's programme, will be to identify the relationships which the Commission should establish, maintain and develop with other organizations, institutions, entities and persons: for example, with States, whether singly or gathered together in the Sixth Committee of the General Assembly, with intergovernmental organizations, whether belonging to the United Nations family or falling outside that system, with international non-governmental organizations, with national bodies, whether official or unofficial, and, last but not least, with individual experts.

Our first panellist is Professor Christine Chinkin. She has held a number of academic positions around the world: in Oxford, Singapore, Sydney, New York and Southampton. She is now Professor of International Law at the London School of Economics and Political Science in the University of London. She is the author of numerous publications in the field of international law.

The second member of the panel is Professor Alfred Soons, Professor of International law at the University of Ütrecht. He has worked for the Government of the Netherlands in a number of capacities. Recently, he was appointed the Director of Studies of the International Law Association and it is in this capacity that he participates in this Colloquium.

Presentation by **Professor Christine Chinkin**

In order to determine how the relationships between the International Law Commission and other bodies within the international legal system might best be enhanced, three preliminary questions should first be addressed.

---

*Judge of the International Court of Justice. Member of the International Law Commission, 1982-1993.

134

First, with which other bodies, besides the Sixth Committee of the General Assembly, should the Commission maintain relationships? With institutes, governmental and non-governmental bodies, individuals, international civil society?

Secondly, what impact might such relationships have upon the Commission's working methods and its output? Would the task of coordinating and administering the relationships fall upon the Secretariat of the United Nations or upon the members of the Commission? If the latter, would that burden fall to be discharged during the regular working sessions of the Commission or at meetings which were held outside the framework of those sessions?

Thirdly, why should the Commission enhance its relations with other, external bodies? What benefits would there be for the Commission or for the other bodies concerned?

One possible response to the last of these questions is that, by improving the Commission's awareness of current thought and increasing the information at its disposal, enhanced relations between the Commission and other bodies would increase the transparency of its processes—a development which would conform with current concepts of good governance and administration. If there were broader input into the Commission's work in terms of the working documents, drafts, ideas, views and expertise which were put at its disposal, there might be a concomitant change of style and approach within the Commission, which could become a mouthpiece for the advocacy of new ideas. However, the apparently safe niche which the Commission currently enjoys within the United Nations system might be put at risk by such a development.

Of course, having a diversity of views before it is hardly guaranteed to increase the Commission's efficacy or to improve the quality of its work. Furthermore, expanding the Commission's constituency to embrace international civil society might undermine its legitimacy with its traditional constituency: States. As was remarked yesterday, it is a controversial question whether the Commission should continue to operate as it has for the last 50 years or whether there should be changes in its relationships with States. Personally, I think that change would be a good thing; but I know that there are strong opposing views.

Turning to more concrete and practical suggestions, it is important to note that the Commission's Statute does not envisage its working in a vacuum, but gives it broad authorization to consult with scientific institutions and individual experts. Very little use has been made of this authorization, though, at least on a formal level.

It is noteworthy in this regard that other bodies in the international legal system have taken to seeking a wider spectrum of views on the issues with which they have had to deal, consulting not only non-governmental organizations (NGOs), but also individual academics and researchers. The Commission might follow this lead, targeting areas that need fuller research and even commissioning research from individual experts or institutions.

Consultation, as an integral part of the international law-making process, might also be facilitated by circulating the questionnaires currently sent to States to relevant NGOs as well. The materials which are received in response might be appended as annexes to the Commission's reports, thus ensuring their wider dissemination and preserving maximum transparency.

The question which naturally follows is which NGOs should be involved. There are some NGOs, such as the International Law Association, which share the same purpose as the Commission, but there are others which are more political and activist in nature and which are often at odds with States. I would suggest that whatever measures are taken to enhance the Commission's relationships with other bodies should embrace NGOs of the latter category as well as of the former.

Increased participation on the part of NGOs in the later stages of treaty drafting has now become a common feature of the international scene. The contribution of the NGO Coalition for an International Criminal Court to the work of the Preparatory Committee on the Establishment of an International Criminal Court is but one, albeit quite prominent, example of this phenomenon. States have also accommodated within their own internal processes the demands of NGOs for an increased role in the international law-making process. It is important in this regard that there be some coherence in the direct relations which the Commission enjoys with other bodies and the indirect relationships which it has with them, as those relations are mediated through States.

It should be emphasized that none of this means that NGOs should be equated with States. There is, for example, no need that they be sent questionnaires which are identical in all respects to those which are sent to States.

Another possibility would be to make use of the services of consultants for the consideration of particular issues. The input on specific topics of the views and advice of specialist experts, which is frequently sought by national law commissions, might well enhance the workability of the Commission's final product. These experts could also serve as facilitators, raising difficult and controversial issues and assisting in teasing out appropriate and acceptable approaches. A director of research within the Commission could serve as a focal point for coordinating the work of these consultants. An alternative course of action might be to create a new category of members of the Commission whose membership would be restricted to a single issue. Such a step would also encourage attendance at the sessions of the Commission which are devoted to the issue concerned. The costs involved might be offset by reducing the number of general members of the Commission—that is, the number of persons who are members for all topics and all issues—thus providing greater flexibility in terms of the Commission's personnel.

Increasing the Commission's physical contact with other bodies might be achieved by organizing meetings with their representatives or by giving observer status in the Commission, with a right to intervention, to the representatives of NGOs. The organization of meetings in places other than Geneva might also be considered in cases where those bodies which cannot readily get to that city—mainly bodies from the South. Such a step, it should be added, might also increase interest in the Commission and its work among the peoples and States of the South.

Regular programmes and interaction with academic and research institutions might also be considered, including lectures, seminars and short-term visits by members of the Commission, preferably on a reciprocal basis, as well as the organization of student internships with the Commission. One danger of such programmes would be that they might only succeed in enhancing the Commission's relations with bodies from the North. Moreover, the demands which they would place on the members of the Commission would be substantial, participation in them requiring of the members a yet further sacrifice of their time and energy.

Nevertheless, it should be emphasized that the current isolation of the Commission only diminishes its relevance. The study of the Commission which was made by the United Nations Institute for Training and Research (UNITAR) in 1981 concluded that there should be a constant flow of information, advice and reactions from Member States into the Commission. In 1997, this proposition should be extended to other actors in the international legal order.

Presentation by Professor Alfred Soons

I wish to focus on the relationship between the Commission and one of the several academic and professional institutions that has been mentioned by Professor Chinkin: namely, the International Law Association.

The International Law Association is a private organization with approximately 4500 members worldwide. Its objectives overlap with the mandate of the International Law Commission, in so far as they include "the study, elucidation and advancement of [public] international law".[1]

The Association was founded in 1873 and next year will celebrate its one-hundred-and-twenty-fifth anniversary.[2] In that time, the Association has made many important contributions to the codification and progressive development of international law. In the past 50 years, it has carried out work in many of the fields which have also occupied the Commission's attention. There is no doubt that the Commission has benefited from its work on such subjects as the regime of the continental shelf, an international criminal court, State succession, State immunity and the law of international watercourses.

However, I am not going to dwell on the past, since the purpose of this Colloquium is to look towards the future. Rather, I wish to examine how the Commission's relationship with the International Law Association may be enhanced to the Commission's benefit.

For this purpose, a distinction may be made between three categories of topics:

- Topics which have not, or which have not yet, been the subject of active consideration by the Commission;
- Topics which are currently under active consideration by the Commission; and
- Topics on which the Commission has completed work.

As far as the first of these categories is concerned, it should be recalled that the International Law Association has its own programme of studies. The Association's committees deal with many topics which the Commission, for various reasons, will never consider at all. The topic, for example, might be one which is better suited to study by a private, rather than by a public, body. In this respect, the roles of the Commission and the Association are complementary. The work of the Association's committee on the formation of rules of customary international law is a case in point.

More importantly perhaps, the Association may usefully undertake preparatory work on issues which are later to be the subject of work by the Commission. The results of the Association's studies might even be of assist-

---

[1] See article II of the Association's constitution: International Law Association, *Report of the Sixty-fourth Conference, held at Broadbeach, Queensland, Australia, 20 to 25 August 1990* (1991), p. 56. The Association's standing orders may be found at ibid., p. 60.

[2] For a brief note on the history of the Association, see International Law Association, *Report of the Sixty-seventh Conference, held at Helsinki, Finland, 12 to 17 August 1996* (1996), p. 46.

ance to the Commission or the Sixth Committee of the General Assembly in reaching a decision as to whether or when the Commission should take up the subject concerned. The Association's current committees on extradition and human rights and on the accountability of international organizations might be examples of such a phenomenon. In this type of case, some form of consultation between the Commission and the Association would probably be beneficial.

Turning to the second category of topics—namely, those which are currently under active consideration by the Commission—committees of the International Law Association have worked and continue to work in fields which overlap or even coincide with topics on which the Commission has been or is conducting work. Two current examples are the Association's committees on diplomatic protection of persons and property and on aspects of State succession. In cases such as these, the Association's committees will typically comment and make observations on the Commission's work, particularly on any draft articles which the Commission may have provisionally adopted on first reading. The Association intends to pay greater attention to the Commission's work in the future, not only through the traditional mechanism of its committees, but also through the medium of specially established working groups. Under the auspices of these working groups, seminars might be organized in various regions of the world in order to familiarize those from the region with the Commission's work. These seminars might also assist Governments in preparing their comments on draft articles which the Commission has prepared, it being the case that many Governments currently lack the resources to make such comments. The Association is currently exploring the possibilities for funding these working groups and seminars. Here, again, the Association and the Commission might consider ways in which each might benefit from the other's activities.

The third category of topic—those on which the Commission has completed work—is no less important than the second. As in the case of the preceding category, the Association's committees and working groups may comment and hold seminars on drafts which the Commission has adopted on second reading or which are before the General Assembly of the United Nations or a diplomatic conference.

What I have said, of course, presupposes that the Association and its committees and working groups have something important or useful to contribute to the Commission and its work. Professor Chinkin has just mentioned several reasons why contributions from a non-governmental organization like the Association might be useful to the Commission. I should like to add some others.

The fewest questions probably arise with respect to the first category of topics—those which have not, or which have not yet, been the subject of active consideration by the Commission—since, in such cases, anything which other bodies may produce is likely to be of some use to the Commission. It will be the quality of the work, though, that determines its usefulness and, in this context, quality includes the political acceptability of any concrete proposals which may be made. This factor is of even greater importance in the case of the second category of topic, where the Association is commenting on the Commission's work in progress.

More generally, one might ask what kind of substantive contribution the Association's committees or working groups may make to the work of the Commission. After all, mere repetition of the discussion which has already taken place within the Commission is hardly calculated to contribute much to the Commission's work on a topic. I am confident, though, that the Association's work will not merely duplicate that of the Commission. The membership of an organization like the International Law Association makes it possible for it to put together committees whose composition is varied and creative, comprising individuals who have differing methodological approaches and various substantive interests, who have not only knowledge of the practice but also practical sense, including members from a variety of disciplines, if necessary, and generally being alive to questions of policy, just as much as to technical legal issues. Naturally, to avoid the Association simply replicating the Commission's work requires constant vigilance on the part of the Association. The role of the chairs and rapporteurs of the Association's committees is crucial in this regard. However, even if the comments which emanate from the Association's committees may sometimes contribute very little that is new to the work of the Commission, their labours will still have served at least one useful purpose, by informing a large number of experts from various parts of the world about the Commission and its work.

OPEN-FLOOR DISCUSSION

*

DÉBAT

Mr Shabtai Rosenne* The Institut de Droit International is the oldest of the non-governmental professional organizations devoted to the codification and the progressive development of international law. The Institut was established in 1873 by a small group of prominent international lawyers of the day, ranging, in their geographical origins, from Argentina to Russia.[3] It was established as an "exclusively learned society, without any official nature".[4] Its main purpose, as set out in its statutes, was and remains "to promote the progress of international law".[5]

Particular reference is made in the Institut's statutes to the laws of war, as they used to be known, and to the teaching of international law.[6]

As far as international humanitarian law is concerned, the Institut has, since 1949, devoted its attention to a number of different matters which have been left open by the Geneva Conferences. Its last important resolution on the subject, adopted in 1975, related to the conditions of application of rules, other than

---

*Ambassador. Vice-President of the Institut de Droit International. Member of the International Law Commission, 1962-1971.

[3]For a list of the founders of the Institut, see *Annuaire de l'Institut de Droit International*, vol. 66-II (1996), p. 11. For the origins and the history of the Institut, see the brief bibliography published in the *Annuaire*: ibid., p. 482.

[4]See article 1 (1) of the statutes of the Institut, as adopted in revised form in 1910 and as supplemented in 1913, 1947, 1961, 1971 and 1977: ibid., vol. 61-II (1986), p. 310.

For the new article 22 which was added to the Institut's statutes in 1996, see ibid., vol. 66-II (1996), p. 474.

For the rules of the Institut, see: ibid., vol. 61-II (1986), p. 324; ibid., vol. 65-II (1993), p. 310; and ibid., vol. 66-II (1996), p. 474.

[5]See the *chapeau* of article 1 (2) of the statutes of the Institut: loc. cit. above (preceding note).
[6]See article 1 (2) (*d*) and (*f*) of the statutes of the Institut: loc. cit. above (footnote 2).

humanitarian rules, of armed conflict to hostilities in which United Nations forces may be engaged.[7]

As for the teaching of international law, the Institut, following the early lead of the General Assembly, has adopted two resolutions. The first was adopted at its centennial session, in 1973,[8] and the second at Strasbourg, in August. In this second resolution, it paid some attention to the teaching of private, as well as public, international law and recommended that general courses both in public and in private international law should deal with the interrelationships between these two related branches of the law.

The Institut meets in plenary sessions every other year, normally in the country of which its president is a national. The next meeting is to be held in Berlin, the current president being a professor at Heidelberg. The Institut has a small permanent secretariat and has its seat wherever its Secretary-General lives and works—currently Geneva.

The Institut has never adopted a systematic plan for the codification of international law, public or private. Rather, its work has been based on the suggestions of its individual members, their suggestions being prompted, in turn, by the concerns or events of the day.[9] The Institut has, nevertheless, made a major contribution to the evolution of the law, both in terms of its codification and its development. This was particularly so before the International Law Commission was established. In 1947 the Institut established a Programme Committee. Today, the Institut is engaged in a thorough review of its constituent instrument—its statutes—as well as its rules and methods of work. Its Commission des travaux, moreover, is occupied with an examination of its own functions and of the Institut's scientific future.

Notwithstanding a hesitant approach towards some aspects of the "official" codification of international law, the Institut has, since 1947, followed very closely the work of codification being carried out in different official and unofficial organizations around the world, the International Law Commission included. It has worked, and continues to work, both in the spheres of public and of private international law and sometimes, when a topic relates to both fields, has treated both aspects of the topic, either separately or in a single resolution, as appropriate.

The Institut is a completely independent and autonomous organization, relying for its funds on membership dues and voluntary contributions.[10] Among its members are judges of the International Court of Justice, members of the Permanent Court of Arbitration, judges of the International Tribunal of the Law of the Sea, of the European and inter-American courts of human rights and of the two war-crimes tribunals, panel members of the International Centre for the Settlement of Investment Disputes and persons who are active in the International Chamber of Commerce and similar dispute-settlement bodies, as well as serving and retired diplomats and international civil servants. It also has members from the International Committee of the Red Cross—testimony to the importance which the Institut attaches to the development of international humanitarian law.[11]

---

[7]Ibid., vol. 56 (1975), pp. 540-545.

[8]Ibid., vol. 55 (1973), pp. 800-801.

[9]For the procedure for inclusion of a question in the Institut's programme of work, see article 1 of the rules of the Institut: loc. cit. above (footnote 2).

[10]See article 19 of the statutes of the Institut: loc. cit. above (footnote 2).

[11]For the most recently published list of the Institut's honourary members, members and associates, see ibid., vol. 66-II (1996), p. 483.

As a result of this highly qualified membership, which is also widely diffused geographically and representative of all aspects of the profession, the Institut is well informed of the work of the Sixth Committee and of the various bodies which the Sixth Committee has set up in addition to its two permanent commissions, the International Law Commission and the United Nations Commission on International Trade Law. The Institut is accordingly able to make adjustments to its work programme in the light of what it knows to be happening elsewhere. Indeed, there is very close personal contact with other law-making bodies, especially, though not exclusively, those which have been established within the framework of the United Nations and its specialized agencies.

This brings me to a particular matter which might engage the attention of the Sixth Committee and of the Secretariat of the United Nations and perhaps also of the International Law Commission. As this Colloquium has made apparent, international law-making today is widely diffused in nature and it is not an easy matter to keep track of all that is going on. I am not thinking of bodies which prepare detailed regulations for this or that aspect of international administration, but of fundamental law-making. The Institut has asked its Secretary-General if he could prepare a regular survey of what is going on around the world in this respect; but, listening to what has been said here yesterday and today, I have been asking myself if the task is not too onerous to be performed by a single Secretary-General of a non-governmental organization (who himself has much other work to do). It has occurred to me that the Codification Division might be invited to see whether it might undertake such a task and to produce every summer a survey of what it knows of the activities of the different organizations and organs whose work is relevant to the codification and progressive development of international law. We must not overlook either the work which is being carried out by UNCITRAL, by UNIDROIT, by the Hague Conference and by other bodies which are active in the field of private international law.

I will turn now to the future.

Faced with the enormous contribution which the United Nations has made during the last 50 years to the codification and progressive development of international law, the Institut, like other similar official and unofficial bodies, is asking itself what its function is to be and what mode of work it is to adopt in the next century. There is no easy answer to these questions, though I am sure that events such as this Colloquium will be of the greatest assistance to all those who will have to find those answers.

There is no doubt that one of the issues which needs to be addressed concerns proper interdisciplinary coordination, both with other branches of the social sciences and with other disciplines altogether, especially those dealing with applied technology. International law cannot survive in an ivory tower. At the Institut's recent Strasbourg session, the Commission des travaux decided to put in hand feasibility studies of two topics which are on the international agenda and which, it seems, will sooner or later call for the adoption of an interdisciplinary approach. One is the whole problem of the international legal aspects of cybernetics, including telemedicine. The other is something with which UNESCO is dealing at this very moment: bioethics and genetic engineering. Both these vast and delicate topics raise important issues of private and public law. Each one of them impinges upon complex economic interests. Both involve problems of consumer protection. The topic of bioethics also raises delicate moral and social issues. The feasibility studies which are to be conducted on these topics will look into whether there is, in either of them, anything which the Institut might usefully investigate from the point of view of public or private international law.

The Institut has never had any formal relationship with the International Law Commission and, as far as I know, the Commission, notwithstanding article 26 of its Statute, has never sought any formal relationship with the Institut. The absence of any formal relationship between the two bodies, however, has not prevented them from working successfully side by side; and I am sure that, if the Commission should decide that it would like to establish some closer relationship with the Institut, the Institut would view the idea with great sympathy. What is important, though, as far as the Institut is concerned is that nothing should prejudice the Institut's completely independent and autonomous character.

Judge Abdul Koroma I would like to thank Mr Rosenne for bringing the work of the Institut to the wider attention of the international legal community. Although there is no formal relationship between the International Law Commission and the Institut, he himself is an example of the bridges, or links, which exist between the two bodies. There are many members of the Commission who are also Members or Associates of the Institut. There is, then, a kind of symbiotic relationship between the two bodies. The question remains, though, whether this relationship should be put on a formal footing.

Professeur Yves Daudet* Le renforcement du droit international et du rôle de la Commission du droit international repose sur deux éléments : le premier vise à changer notre façon de penser; le second à rechercher de nouveaux moyens de codifier le droit.

En ce qui concerne le premier de ces éléments, la méthode traditionnelle de codification du droit international consiste à élaborer une convention puis à l'ouvrir à la signature et à la ratification des États. Toute autre méthode n'est qu'un pis-aller. De plus, la Commission a toujours fait preuve d'une grande précaution dans ses travaux car elle souhaitait que le produit final de ses délibérations rencontre l'adhésion générale des États. Après tout, comme le faisait remarquer hier le professeur Pellet, quand on veut avoir une convention, il ne faut pas révolutionner le droit international.

L'âge d'or de la Commission est toutefois terminé et nous devons reconnaître que l'adoption de nouvelles méthodes de travail, et la recherche de nouveaux produits par la Commission, n'est pas pour autant synonyme d'échec. Il faut donc trouver de nouveaux moyens de codifier le droit international — sans pour autant abandonner complètement les méthodes traditionnelles. Certes, en adoptant de nouvelles méthodes de codification, la Commission pourrait entrer en concurrence en quelque sorte avec d'autres organes de formation du droit. C'est là toutefois une conséquence qu'elle doit accepter comme inévitable.

Un nouveau moyen de faire progresser la codification du droit international pourrait consister à revoir notre conception générale du droit international. M. Pinto parlait hier de se tourner vers la recherche pure pour favoriser le respect et l'application du droit international, tandis que le professeur Orrego Vicuña évoquait la possibilité de faire un *restatement* du droit international.

---

*Professeur universitaire de Paris-1 (Panthéon-Sorbonne), Paris (France).

Un tel travail de *restatement* du droit international présenterait deux principaux intérêts. D'une part, il préserverait l'unité du droit international et éviterait que ses principes n'évoluent dans des directions divergentes — ce qui risque fort de se produire à l'heure où une multitude d'organes différents travaillent à la formation du droit. D'autre part, il favoriserait la plus grande diffusion possible du droit international. Après tout, comme le faisait remarquer le professeur Maluwa, les praticiens du droit, notamment les avocats et les juges, devraient mieux connaître le droit international.

Je voudrais ajouter que les rapports que la Commission est susceptible d'entretenir avec les organisations spécialisées et les universités ne devraient pas être en sens unique. Le moment est venu pour la Commission de faire souffler un vent de renouveau sur les universités et leurs méthodes d'enseignement du droit international, ainsi que le suggérait le professeur Stern.

Professor Gerhard Hafner* The question is how to increase the relations between the Commission and various other scientific bodies, such as the Institut de Droit International. We should look to the new technologies to help us to achieve this end: the Internet and other electronic information systems and means of communication.

My dream is that one day the Commission will have its own home page on the Internet, where one will be able to find all of the drafts which it has prepared, together with their companion commentaries, and that the public will be able to search these documents, using key words, and download whatever data they may need. National legal advisers and members of the Commission, too, could then easily research what the Commission has said and done. The recent judgements of the International Court of Justice are now posted on the Internet, of course—a development which has already been of great benefit to many of us. In addition to its usefulness as a research tool, a facility of the sort which I have in mind would also help to safeguard the unity of international law and promote its gradual harmonization—a safeguard which is very much needed nowadays, when we are facing a certain fragmentation in international law.

Of course, it may be very costly to create and maintain the kind of facility which I describe. Accordingly, an optical disc system or something of the sort might be used at the initial stage and a more sophisticated system created later.

Moreover, new technologies, particularly e-mail, could be used to improve working relationships between Special Rapporteurs and the members of the Commission, between the Commission and States and between the Commission and members of the scientific community. The Commission's questionnaire system, which is currently in a parlous state, could be greatly improved through the adoption and application of such technological developments.

Judge Abdul Koroma New technologies could indeed be used to make it easier and quicker for States to respond to the Commission's questionnaires and to its requests for information and comments. However, too much should not be expected of the new technologies. E-mail, which we take for granted in this part of the world, is simply not available in most of the developing countries, nor is access to the Internet. The new technologies, therefore, cannot supplant the written word. Moreover, they do not make it possible to consider the material which they disseminate in a leisurely and reflective manner.

---

*University of Vienna, Austria. Member of the International Law Commission, 1997- .

I should like to take this opportunity to draw the attention of those present to the fact that, starting with its report on the work of its forty-eighth session, the reports of the Commission have been posted on the United Nations home page. The International Court of Justice also has its own Web site, as Professor Hafner reminds us, and its judgements are now readily available on the Internet.

Dr Hicham Hamdan* Many of the matters which we are discussing at this Colloquium have also been the subject of discussion in the Sixth Committee of the General Assembly and in the various fora which are considering the reform of the Organization. The Sixth Committee could certainly benefit from many of the ideas which have been advanced here over the last two days. Those ideas would be of great assistance to the Sixth Committee in considering how best to strengthen the International Law Commission and enhance its capability to fulfil its mandate.

One very important matter has not received sufficient attention in this discussion, though: the participation of Governments in the Commission's work. We should examine the various ways in which Governments might assist in advancing that work and how they might help the Commission to discharge its responsibilities in a more effective manner.

There are two points which I would like to make in this regard. First, as Oscar Schachter has remarked, relations of power predominate in international society, as they do in all societies. None the less, a climate should be created which is conducive to securing a responsive attitude from States to the Commission and its work, particularly on the part of those States which belong to the developing world.

The second point has to do with the role of civil society. I should like to thank Professor Chinkin and Professor Soons, who have addressed the matter of cooperation between the Commission and NGOs. The potential of such organizations should be fully explored and realized. There is a need for Governments to encourage the establishment of national associations and other national fora for the development of international law, consisting of judges, professors, practitioners and diplomats. Such groups could undertake studies on matters on which the Commission is working and so assist States in responding to the Commission's requests for comments and observations on its drafts. They might also participate in efforts to secure a wider appreciation of international law and assist in its wider dissemination.

Dr Hartmut Hillgenberg** Congratulations are due to the International Law Commission for 50 years of successful work—work which has been successful both in terms of its quality and its quantity. The Commission's proposals and its commentaries play a major role in international legal circles and are an important source of information on the current state of international law for national Governments and legislatures.

However, the Commission's achievements to date should not blind us to the necessity of considering how to improve its work. In this regard, Professor Soons has made valuable proposals regarding the necessity of extending the Commission's contacts and improving its coordination with other bodies which are active in the field of international law, such as the International Law Association.

---

*Deputy Permanent Representative of Lebanon to the United Nations.
**Director-General for Legal Affairs, Ministry of Foreign Affairs, Germany.

On the other hand, I have some concern about there being any direct contact between the Commission and NGOs, since I do not think that the Commission should venture into the field of politics. That is the role of States. The role of States may be shrinking, but States are still the only entities which are able to coordinate and balance divergent interests and legitimately represent their countries. It is for States to conduct a dialogue with NGOs. However, this should not preclude the Commission from inviting outside experts, including experts from NGOs, to comment on specific issues.

Judge Abdul Koroma If, as Dr Hillgenberg remarks, national Governments and legislatures find the Commission's work useful, so does the International Court of Justice. The Commission is unique, I think, in providing commentaries on the draft articles which it proposes, as Sir Franklin Berman remarked yesterday.

Mr Sang Hoon Cho* In order to advance work on draft articles which are under consideration in the Commission or in the Sixth Committee, a call has often been made for more active participation on the part of States. Yet the response of the Organization's Member States to the Commission's questionnaires and its requests for comments has been quite disappointing, in spite of the exhortations of the General Assembly and the Secretary-General's encouragement.

The Commission cannot fulfil its task on its own, unaided. The time has come to encourage discussion of international law-making at the national level. A good way in which to secure greater participation by States in the codification process might be the organization in every State of core groups, consisting of government officials, professors and experts in international law, which would prepare comments on the issues which the Commission has under active consideration.

The General Assembly might adopt a resolution calling upon each of the Organization's Member States to establish such a national group in order to promote discussion within each Member State on issues arising out of the Commission's work, including its drafts, and to interact with the Commission on these matters.

While the nature and working methods of these national groups might be the subject of further discussion, they would be of great assistance in enhancing awareness of the importance of international law among the general public. They would also assist in the attainment of our common objective of achieving a constant flow into the Commission of information, advice and reaction from Member States.

Judge Abdul Koroma As Mr Cho reminds us, it is important that States should respond to the questionnaires which are circulated by the Commission. I would agree with him, too, that States' responses to these questionnaires have, to date, been disappointing.

A substitute for the responses of States is for the members of the Commission to collect evidence of what is going on in their respective regions, as far as the positions taken by States are concerned. I recall, for example, that Professor Maluwa has made studies on international rivers in Africa and, while we in the Commission were studying the subject of the law of the non-navigational use of international watercourses, his work was one source on which we were able to draw in order to make up for the absence of information from States. I would

---

*Director-General, Treaties Bureau, Ministry of Foreign Affairs, Republic of Korea.

agree, though, that such expedients are "second best" and that States should be encouraged to respond to the Commission's questionnaires.

Professor Bruno Simma* As far as the relationship between the Commission and NGOs is concerned, a distinction should be made between the Institut de Droit International and the International Law Association, on the one hand, and other NGOs, on the other. The Institut and the Association are effectively sister organizations of the International Law Commission. Cross-fertilization between the Commission and these bodies might be increased by the Institut and Association making their conferences and sessions open to the members of the Commission. A division of labour should also be made among the Commission, the Institut and the Association. For example, the topic of bioethics, which was mentioned by Mr Rosenne, is not a good subject for the Commission to consider. Similarly, the preparation of a restatement of international law, as suggested by Professor Daudet and Professor Orrego Vicuña, should be undertaken by the Institut or by the Association, rather than by the Commission, since the Commission lacks the resources and the infrastructure to discharge such a task. The encyclopedia of public international law, it may be noted, has been produced with some involvement on the part of the Institut. Speaking as a writer of textbooks, I would suggest that major restatements should be left to people like myself or to others in this room.

As far as relations between the Commission and academic societies are concerned, let me give two concrete examples. The German Society of International Law decided in 1995 to deal with one of the topics on the Commission's agenda by discussing countermeasures at its 1997 conference. Nobody in the German Society, Professor Tomuschat and myself included, thought that the Commission would get its act together as quickly as it did on the topic of State responsibility. When we came to discuss countermeasures in 1997, we found that we were actually too late and that the Commission had already completed its first reading of its draft articles on State responsibility, countermeasures included. The second example which I would mention is that of the Association of Austrian Lawyers, which has put the work of the Commission on its regular agenda.

With regard to internships, I would mention that there is one programme already in place, which is organized and funded by New York University, involving a three-month stint in Geneva. I am currently setting up a similar programme at the University of Michigan.

When it comes to the Internet and e-mail, it should be borne in mind that there are "dinosaurs" like myself who are either too lazy or else too afraid to use these new technologies. So I would ask the Secretariat of the United Nations not to stop circulating the Commission's reports and documents in hard copy.

Judge Abdul Koroma As far as concerns cooperation between the Commission, on the one hand, and the International Law Association and Institut de Droit International, on the other, I would certainly agree that there is a need for intensification of that cooperation, for further specialization by each of these bodies and for a division of labour among them.

---

*Faculty of Law, Ludwig-Maximilians University, Munich, Germany. Member of the International Law Commission, 1997- .

Professor John Dugard* I would like to make some comments on the subject of relationships between the Commission and NGOs, particularly in the light of what has been said by Professor Chinkin.

There is no difficulty when it comes to cooperation between the Commission and legal NGOs, such as the International Law Association and the Institut de Droit International, since they work in the same field as the Commission and often have the same members. The same can be said of the International Committee of the Red Cross. At this point, I might mention that the members of the Commission held a very useful joint seminar this year with the legal division of the International Committee of the Red Cross, at which we discussed some of the definitions of those international crimes which might fall within the jurisdiction of a future international criminal court.

We must accept, however, that there will be difficulties when it comes to the Commission working closely with NGOs which are of a more "activist" character. Such organizations are, almost by definition, in opposition to Governments and challenge the positions which Governments take. Amnesty International and Greenpeace are the most prominent examples. How would the Sixth Committee respond if the Commission were to take advice from Greenpeace in the field of environmental matters or from Amnesty International on issues of human rights? Dr Hillgenberg has already drawn attention to this issue. The difficulty is a real one. It must be acknowledged that the views of NGOs of the type which I mention would generally not coincide with the views of States, as represented in the Sixth Committee.

A topical example is afforded by the question of reservations to treaties. A difficult issue which arises in this context concerns the extent to which the human rights monitoring bodies may express themselves on reservations which have been formulated to the treaties which they monitor. We all know that human rights NGOs have views which are strongly supportive of the position of the monitoring bodies. On the other hand, we also know that many States are opposed to the activism of the monitoring bodies in this field. What would be the response of the Sixth Committee, then, if the Commission were to be guided in its work by a human rights NGO?

One must face the fact that the Commission, although it is not an intergovernmental organization, is, nevertheless, elected by an intergovernmental organization, which puts it in an awkward position when it comes to its working with NGOs. I do not pretend to have a solution to this problem. I think it is very important that the Commission should work closely with all NGOs, but we must face the fact that, if it does, the Sixth Committee may not be pleased.

Judge Abdul Koroma I would agree with Professor Dugard's remarks. While cooperation with NGOs is certainly desirable, a cautious approach to the subject should be adopted. Although the Commission is not an intergovernmental body, it has the Sixth Committee as its parent.

Ms Bette Shifman** The Permanent Court of Arbitration, which will celebrate its centenary in 1999, is currently undergoing a process of revitalization. The Court's International Bureau acted as a Registry in six cases during 1996

---

*School of Law, University of the Witwatesrand, Johannesburg, South Africa. Member of the International Law Commission, 1997- .

**Deputy Secretary-General, Permanent Court of Arbitration, The Hague, Netherlands.

and two new cases were added to its workload this year, both relating to disputes between States.

There is much interest at the Court in enhancing cooperation between the Court and the International Law Commission. Such collaboration might include sharing with the Commission the Court's expertise in the field of international dispute resolution, providing input on texts which the Commission is drafting and signalling to the Commission areas in which the Court might be in a position to respond to the dispute-resolution needs of the international community.

In preparation for 1999, the Permanent Court set up a Steering Committee back in 1994. The organization is now almost 100 years old and its constituent documents still date from 1899 and 1907. Although the Court now operates under newly established and modern rules of procedure which vary according to the nature of the dispute which is to be resolved, one important question which was submitted to the Steering Committee was whether the 1899 and 1907 conventions for the pacific settlement of international disputes should be revised or replaced. The Committee did not recommend their revision, nor did it recommend their replacement by a new convention, since it felt such an exercise would be too time-consuming and too difficult, particularly if the target date for completion were to be 1999. There was, however, a strong sentiment within the Committee that revision or replacement of the old conventions by means of a new global convention on the peaceful settlement of disputes might well be advisable in the longer term. This might be a subject on which the Commission might appropriately undertake work, perhaps by preparing the draft of such a convention.

Sir Kenneth Keith* The obligation of the Secretariat of the United Nations under article 26 (2) of the Statute of the International Law Commission to distribute the Commission's documents to at least one national organization which is concerned with questions of international law, likewise its task of circulating documents to the States Members of the United Nations, could be facilitated by use of the Internet.

The Commission has the power, under articles 26 (1) and 16 (e) of its Statute, to consult with non-official organizations, national and international, as well as with scientific institutions and individual experts. This power is vested in the Commission in order that it might be able to secure, weigh up and evaluate a full range of opinions and information on the subjects with which it deals. The Commission should make use of this power.

Governments, when they are preparing their responses to the Commission's requests for comments, are always able—and, I would say, should have a responsibility—to seek assistance and to secure comments and suggestions on the Commission's drafts from national bodies, such as national bar associations, and from individual national experts.

The three obligations and powers in the Commission's Statute to which I have referred should be examined during the preparation of the annual resolution on the report of the Commission and some thought given as to how to give them greater contemporary relevance.

---

*Judge of the New Zealand Court of Appeal and of the Courts of Appeal of Samoa, the Cook Islands and Niue.

The third context in which issues of the relevance and availability of international law may arise is that of legal education. What place does international law currently enjoy in that process? To what extent is it part of the standard curricula of our universities? To what extent do works of international law feature as part of the canon in law schools and other institutions that are in the business of producing lawyers and policy makers?

With regard to the role which the International Law Commission may play in enhancing awareness of international law and ensuring its greater relevance, there are, broadly speaking, four respects in which it may make a greater contribution.

First, it might organize or assist in the organization of seminars, workshops and symposia which are aimed at raising public consciousness and awareness of international law.

Secondly, the Commission may have a role to play in raising critical awareness of international law both among lawyers and among current and future policy makers and decision takers.

Thirdly, it should be borne in mind that professional associations, too, have an important role to play in enhancing awareness of international law. In this connection, I should like to mention that one of the most positive developments that has occurred among the international legal community in Africa has been the establishment in 1989 of the African Society of International and Comparative Law. The Society does a lot to advance the cause of international law, through the publication of an international law newsletter, through the African law students internship programme (taking students from one African country and placing them in an internship programme in another) and through the organization of moot court competitions. These moot competitions represent an area in which the Commission might work hand in hand with the African Society with a view to improving awareness of international law among young lawyers.

My fourth, and last, point concerns the place of international law in universities. Only the smaller African States have made international law a compulsory subject on the law curriculum. The International Law Commission should explore ways in which African universities might be encouraged to make international law a compulsory subject in their curricula.

Présentation par le professeur Brigitte Stern

Je voudrais me placer dans une optique prospective et pratique. L'objet principal de ma présentation est une meilleure information concernant la Commission du droit international et également une meilleure information en général concernant le droit international. J'essaierai de donner quelques recettes auxquelles on peut songer, qui sont extrêmement simples, pas très chères.

D'abord, quelques suggestions concernant la manière d'améliorer l'information relative à la Commission.

Il serait utile qu'il existe une brochure d'une vingtaine de pages, un petit peu à l'image de l'ouvrage *La Commission du droit international et son œuvre*[1], mais beaucoup plus restreint, qui puisse servir à quelqu'un ayant besoin de savoir très vite de ce qu'est la Commission du droit international et ce qu'elle fait.

---

[1] *La Commission du droit international et son œuvre* (4ᵉ éd., 1989), publication des Nations Unies, numéro de vente : F.88.V.1. Voir aussi, en anglais seulement, *The Work of the International Law Commission* (5th. ed.; 1996), United Nations publication, Sales No. E.95.V.6.

Pour qu'il y ait également une espèce de possibilité très rapide de savoir ce qui se passe, on pourrait songer à une lettre d'information sur la Commission avec, par exemple, deux numéros par an, la première édition avant la session, qui indiquerait les sujets de cette session, et l'autre publiée en octobre, indiquant très rapidement ce qui vient d'être fait, les rapports qui ont été adoptés, etc.

De plus, on pourrait songer à des sessions fictives de la Commission afin que les étudiants soient au courant de ce qui se passe. On pourrait imaginer deux approches différentes. L'une de ces approches pourrait être plus académique et concernerait des sessions passées. Dans ces sessions les étudiants seraient amenés à étudier un sujet sur lequel la Commission avait déjà travaillé. Les étudiants pourraient comparer leur travail avec ce que la Commission avait fait et ainsi améliorer leurs connaissances. L'autre approche serait de réunir un groupe de gens déjà assez avancés — des jeunes assistants, des doctorants — dans le même format que la Commission pour leur montrer comment s'élabore le droit international, afin qu'ils perçoivent les rapports de force dans les relations internationales. Si on leur donnait un sujet sur lequel la Commission est en train de travailler, on pourrait transmettre les résultats de leur travail au Président de la Commission. Ainsi, on pourrait profiter du potentiel d'apprentissage des jeunes générations et de leur grand pouvoir d'innovation et de créativité. Un tel regard neuf pourrait être extrêmement intéressant.

On pourrait même imaginer que, l'année suivante, les personnes qui ont participé à ce séminaire constituent une sorte de *task force* au service des pays en voie de développement pour leur permettre de remplir les questionnaires de la Commission. Il y aurait donc une sorte de progression : séminaire académique, séminaire de haut niveau, *task force*. Tout cela pourrait être fait en liaison avec les ministères des affaires étrangères qui pourraient dans certains cas accorder des bourses.

Pour stimuler l'intérêt des jeunes chercheurs sur la Commission, on pourrait songer à créer un prix de la Commission.

Concernant l'information sur le droit international en général, nous devrions engager une liaison constante et étroite entre le monde universitaire et ceux qui conduisent les relations internationales des États. Récemment une telle interaction a été initiée en France à l'initiative du service juridique du Ministère des affaires étrangères par la mise sur pied d'une petite cellule d'information universitaire en contact régulier avec les problèmes concrets auxquels le Ministère est confronté.

Nous pourrions également songer à faire des *restatements* internationaux. Comme c'est une tâche qui va peut-être au-delà des tâches que la Commission pourrait faire, nous pourrions songer à des *restatements* nationaux, à l'image du *restatement* américain. Cela pourrait être très utile parce qu'il y aurait alors plusieurs lectures du droit international, pas seulement la lecture américaine. Également, ces différents *restatements* nationaux, à partir du moment où ils existeraient, seraient une sorte de matériaux dont la société internationale pourrait faire non pas l'unification, mais l'unité, ce qui aboutirait finalement à un *restatement* international.

Nous pouvons également songer à développer des séminaires de sensibilisation au droit international pour les avocats, pour les juges. Il est extrêmement important de développer des réflexes internationaux au niveau de tels professionels dans les États. Cela pourrait être fait en liaison avec les sessions de la Commission.

Finalement, en ce qui concerne l'Internet, j'aimerais répondre à deux réticences manifestées sur le développement de ces nouvelles technologies. Premièrement, en ce qui concerne le commentaire du professeur Simma au cours de la discussion du cinquième sujet dans le programme de ce Colloque, je crois qu'il faut résolument aller dans le sens de ces nouvelles technologies. Pour répondre à une préoccupation du Juge Koroma, je pense que les pays en voie de développement ont une chance unique avec ces nouvelles technologies, qui peuvent paraître chères, mais qui en réalité sont extrêmement peu coûteuses. Il suffit d'un ou deux sites où on pourrait adresser des questions pour que le monde entier soit chez eux. Je suis sûre que c'est beaucoup plus accesible au point de vue financier d'être relié à l'Internet que d'essayer d'obtenir des livres, des brochures, des papiers. Ainsi, les pays en voie de développement pourraient obtenir une très large information à un moindre coût.

OPEN-FLOOR DISCUSSION

*

DÉBAT

Judge Abdul Koroma First, I agree with Professor Stern and Professor Maluwa that the Commission should take steps to promote greater awareness of international law, both among members of the general public and among policy makers and judges in particular. Professor Stern's suggestion that the Commission publish a brochure on what the Commission is and what it does, might be very useful in this regard.

Secondly, steps should be taken to facilitate and to encourage research of the Commission and its work, in particular, by young students.

Finally, the Commission should take steps to improve its literature. In this connection, Professor Stern's proposal, that there should not be but one restatement, but many national restatements, is most interesting.

Professor Choung Il Chee* I should like, first, to refer to Article 38 (1) (d) of the Statute of the International Court of Justice, in so far as it concerns "the teachings of the most highly qualified publicists of the various nations". This is precisely the nature of the Commission's work: that is, it constitutes teachings of the most highly qualified publicists of the various nations of the world. Consequently, what the Commission says and does should never be treated lightly. Indeed, Judge Schwebel described in his keynote address the importance which the International Court of Justice has accorded to the Commission's output in its judgements and advisory opinions.

My second point relates to the observations which were made by Professor Müllerson during the discussion of the preceding topic on the necessity of the Commission's adopting an interdisciplinary approach in its work. While I was attending the United Nations Conference on Straddling Fish Stocks and Highly Migratory Fish Stocks, I listened to an expert from the Food and Agriculture Organization of the United Nations, who was the head of its environmental section, giving evidence about the need for the adoption of a precautionary

---

*Professor of International Law, University of Seoul, Seoul, Republic of Korea.

155

approach in dealing with the conservation of high seas fisheries. Another example may be drawn from the United Nations Convention on the Law of the Sea, which provides for the establishment and operation of a Commission on the Limits of the Continental Shelf, composed of legal and technical experts. Here, the technical experts actually participate directly in the law-making process. This is the current practice. I do not see why the Commission should not also make use of experts when it is preparing draft articles which are to serve as the basis of a treaty.

My third point concerns the remarks which have been made during the course of this Colloquium to the effect that the low rate of adhesion to many of the conventions which have been concluded on the basis of the Commission's drafts may be attributed in some way to the quality of the Commission's work. Such remarks fail to grasp the precise nature of the Commission and its function. The Commission does not make the law; it does not make treaties. According to chapter II of its Statute, the Commission's functions are to undertake preparatory work for the conclusion of treaties, including drafting articles on subjects in regard to which, in the words of article 15, "the law has not yet been sufficiently developed in the practice of States". The Commission does not, then, itself make the law. We should not, therefore, be too disappointed with the Commission when States fail to adhere to conventions which have been adopted on the basis of its drafts. The failure in such cases is that of States.

Judge Abdul Koroma   À propos of the remarks of Professor Chee—and of Professor Müllerson and Mr Rosenne during the discussion of the preceding topic—concerning the adoption of interdisciplinary approaches, I should point out that the Commission does retain consultants, or at least has done so in the past. That this is so has not been spelled out by the Commission in its reports, but Special Rapporteurs who have been in a position to do so have sometimes retained consultants when they have been appointed to work on topics which are technical in nature.

M. Zénon Mukongo Ngay*   Je voudrais vous signaler l'existence d'un problème de diversité linguistique qui vient se greffer sur celui de la diversité des systèmes juridiques. Ce problème doit être étudié en ce qu'il touche en particulier les pays en développement d'Afrique. À titre d'exemple, je mentionnerai les modalités de la Sixième Commission de l'Assemblée générale des Nations Unies, organe aux travaux duquel je participe. De façon générale, les consultations officieuses nous causent de sérieux problèmes. Je parle français, langue qui a été imposée à mon pays; et je suis déçu de voir que cette langue est en train de perdre du terrain notamment au sein d'instances telles que celle-ci. L'anglais règne quasiment sans partage maintenant. Ceux d'entre nous à qui l'usage du français a été imposé, nous nous interrogeons sur l'issue d'une telle évolution, d'autant plus que l'on ne parle pas anglais dans la plupart des pays en développement. Assurément, nous ne sommes pas sur la même longueur d'onde que les représentants du monde développé lorsque nous participons aux travaux d'organes tels que la Commission.

---

*Représentant de la République démocratique du Congo auprès de la Sixième Commission de l'Assemblée générale des Nations Unies. Maître assistant à la faculté de droit de Kinshasa (République démocratique du Congo).

Je voudrais évoquer un autre problème qui préoccupe les pays en développement : celui du manque d'accès aux systèmes informatiques. Il faut apporter aux pays en développement l'aide dont ils ont besoin dans ce domaine, notamment en leur proposant du matériel électronique à prix réduits. Ce serait là une contribution tangible au développement progressif du droit international.

Dans le cadre de nos débats sur le développement progressif du droit international et sa codification, nous devons garder à l'esprit que tout ce qui est fait dans ce domaine doit l'être dans l'intérêt et pour l'ensemble de la communauté internationale, ce qui suppose que l'on tienne compte des différents niveaux de progrès technologique atteints par les États. Lorsqu'une assemblée comme la nôtre se réunit, elle doit veiller à ce que soient pris en considération la situation et les besoins propres des pays en développement pour que tous les pays puissent participer à ses travaux sur un pied d'égalité.

Professor Zdzislaw Galicki* I would like to thank Professor Maluwa for addressing the question of the teaching of international law. I would fully agree with him that the important thing is to ensure a proper place for international law in legal education. Of course, the place which international law enjoys in legal education varies from country to country—in Poland, it is a compulsory subject at all universities, I am glad to say—but no State can ignore it completely. I would also agree with Professor Maluwa that the aim of such education should be to increase awareness of international law among the members of the legal profession, including those who participate in the legislative process and those to whom it falls to ensure the practical application of international law. Special attention to the teaching of international law was given by the late Judge Lachs in his lecture at The Hague Academy.[2] I also stressed the importance of teaching international law in the presentation which I gave two years ago at the United Nations Congress on International Law.[3]

The role of the Commission in supporting the teaching of international law has both a passive and an active aspect.

On the one hand, documents and materials elaborated by or within the Commission are of immense value for teaching purposes. I recall my own experience as a student when I was preparing my master's thesis on treaties and third States. I was deeply fascinated by the richness of the ideas on this subject which were advanced by the Commission's Special Rapporteurs. Later, when teaching my own students, I simply could not imagine not using all of the available materials which had been elaborated by the Commission. In this connection, I would add that I can only wish that those materials be made even more easily available to whoever may be interested in them.

On the other hand, a visible sign of the Commission's direct interest in and concern about the teaching of international law is the International Law Seminar, which is each year organized for young lawyers from all over the world and which is held during the course of the Commission's annual session. These seminars have two particularly beneficial aspects to them. First, they enable the

---

*Professor of International Law, University of Warsaw, Warsaw, Poland. Member of the International Law Commission, 1997-.

[2]Lachs, "Teachings and Teaching of International Law", *Recueil des cours de l'Académie de droit international de La Haye*, vol. 151 (1976-III), p. 163.

[3]Galicki, "Traditional and New Fields for the Development of Research and Education in International Law', in *International Law as a Language for International Relations* (1996), p. 352 (United Nations publication, Sales No. T.96.V.4).

Commission's members to pass on their knowledge to students from the different countries of the world. Secondly, the students have the chance to attend the Commission's open meetings and to acquire some familiarity with its activities. These seminars should be continued. Indeed, they should be developed, so that more students from more countries may participate in them.

Professeur Marina Spinedi* En ce qui concerne le rôle de la Commission du droit international dans l'amélioration de la connaissance du droit international, il y a un point qui n'a pas encore été soulevé depuis le début de ce Colloque et sur lequel je voudrais insister : il s'agit du large écho que les travaux de la Commission, et notamment ses rapports, trouvent dans la doctrine du droit international. Il n'existe pas d'ouvrage de droit international qui ne traite de thèmes déjà abordés par la Commission ou ne fasse référence à ses travaux, même inachevés. Au surplus, dans ses rapports, la Commission réunit et analyse la pratique des États, la jurisprudence internationale et la doctrine du droit international, offrant ainsi un instrument essentiel aux chercheurs en droit international.

Je dois avouer que je ne comprends pas pourquoi, comme cela a été suggéré, la Commission devrait se lancer dans un travail de *restatement* du droit international, car je ne vois pas de différence entre une telle entreprise et l'œuvre que la Commission accomplit à l'heure actuelle dans le domaine de la codification et du développement progressif du droit international. En quoi faire un *restatement* du droit international diffère-t-il de la tâche que remplit aujourd'hui la Commission lorsqu'elle élabore des projets d'articles destinés à être adoptés dans le cadre de conventions ?

Aux termes de son statut, la Commission a notamment pour fonctions d'examiner les moyens susceptibles de rendre plus accessible la documentation relative au droit international coutumier, par exemple les documents établissant la pratique des États et des décisions de juridictions nationales sur des questions de droit international[4]. Lorsqu'elle consacre des travaux aux nombreuses questions dont elle est saisie, la Commission accomplit par la même occasion l'œuvre de diffusion que son statut lui a assignée. Il serait toutefois souhaitable, si elle en avait les moyens financiers, qu'elle assure cette diffusion de façon plus exhaustive et systématique. Après tout, les problèmes d'accès à l'information relative à la pratique et à la jurisprudence des autres États ne sont pas le lot des pays en développement. On s'aperçoit en effet que ce sont toujours les mêmes affaires, celles des États qui ont les moyens de diffuser leur jurisprudence et de défendre leurs positions, qui sont citées.

Un autre problème très important a été évoqué : celui de la diffusion des connaissances en droit international auprès des juges et des praticiens du droit. Je suis d'accord avec tous ceux qui ont dit combien il était important que ces personnes se familiarisent avec le droit international, soit directement, soit indirectement, par le biais de leurs organisations professionnelles. Je citerais à ce propos l'exemple de l'Italie et du droit des communautés européennes. Pendant longtemps, ce domaine du droit est resté pratiquement inconnu des juges et des praticiens du droit mais, grâce aux efforts des universités notamment et des communautés européennes elles-mêmes, ce droit est désormais en passe de faire partie intégrante de la vie publique de notre État, et les juges et les

---

*Professeur du droit des organisations internationales, Université de Florence, Florence (Italie).
[4]Voir article 24 du Statut de la Commission.

The Court has the benefit of the carefully crafted arguments of the parties on difficult and developing areas of law. It is equally true that there is a strong element of selectivity and subjectivity in the way those arguments are presented in an adversarial proceeding. At the same time, the Court establishes its own objective legal conclusions. Yet it is the Commission which is in a particular position to subject these same topics to minute, critical and objective scrutiny from all relevant angles before making its recommendations. Certainly no one could accuse the Commission of operating in a deliberative ivory tower and it is no surprise that its work is so widely cited. It is important to recall that, as part of its standard working method, the Commission factors in the observations of States on its drafts as they evolve.

The precise basis on which the Commission is relied on before the Court is not always easy to define in terms of the sources of law set out in the Court's Statute. What is arresting is how often and fully counsel invoke the drafts and the conventions adopted by the Commission. The Commission could certainly be said to have contributed substantially, directly or indirectly, to the "sources" of international law which the Court is bound to apply in accordance with Article 38. It is difficult to confine its relevance to any one of the four sources, though I have yet to hear anyone suggest that the work of the Commission is a fifth source of its own.

The extent to which counsel before the Court rely on the reports and commentaries produced by the Commission shows no signs of diminishing. Quite the reverse. Take the Court's recent experience in the *Gabčikovo-Nagymaros* case between Hungary and Slovakia, on which Judgment was given one month ago, on 25 September. This case proved to be compendious in terms of the range of legal issues it summoned up: the law of treaties, the law of State responsibility, the law of international watercourses, the law of State succession and environmental law. Reliance by the parties on the Commission's pronouncements was both pervasive and persuasive and was characterized by searching analysis. Just how persuasive is evident from the unusual degree of endorsement given by the Court itself to the Commission's statements, in two areas in particular.

Both parties devoted extensive argument to the question of the existence of a state of necessity which would have permitted Hungary to suspend performance of the treaty project without incurring responsibility. They both took the view that such an analysis should proceed from the criteria put forward by the International Law Commission in article 33 of its draft articles on State responsibility, and also referred to the Commission's commentary. The treatment of the question by the Court is squarely based on draft article 33, to the extent that its provisions are held to reflect customary international law, and its interpretation of that article proceeds from the Commission's commentary. Note the weight which counsel—and indeed the Court itself—attached to what remain only *draft* articles on State responsibility—a treatment which counsel in the case concerning *United States Diplomatic and Consular Staff in Tehran* anticipated.

The Commission was also cited in the *Gabčikovo-Nagymaros* case as authoritative in relation to the existence of certain categories of treaties "attaching to . . . territory" which must be considered to be binding on a successor State. Here counsel invoked the terms of a convention in force drafted by the Commission: article 12 of the Vienna Convention on Succession of States in respect of Treaties of 1978. In finding that this article reflects a rule of customary international law, the Court examined its drafting history and itself cited the Commission's commentary.

The Court also relied on the Convention on the Law of the Non-Navigational Uses of International Watercourses of 1997, another product of the Commission.

Whether the Court's Judgment in the *Gabčikovo-Nagymaros* case can be said to have crystallized these areas of law is for the Commission to grapple with and for posterity to decide.

In sum, the influence of the work of the Commission on the Court, and of the judgements and opinions of the Court on the Commission, is long-standing, continuing and profound.

What of the future of the International Law Commission? Permit me a personal thought. Reading the Commission's conclusions on its programme, procedures and working methods contained in its 1996 Report, I was left with the impression that assumptions were being made about the membership and composition of the Commission. Even allowing for the requirements of equitable and ample geographical distribution, is it really necessary to have as many as 34 members? Having reached the stage when difficulties of logistics and coordination have prompted the proposal that sessions be restricted to 10 weeks, and even split in two in 1998, one is tempted to ask not "is this the answer?", but, rather, "is this the right question?"

Perhaps we have lost sight of the essential differences between the International Law Commission and other bodies, for example, the Sixth Committee of the General Assembly. The task of the Commission is one of painstaking and lengthy research, scholarship and deliberation, followed by refined drafting. Such sustained and onerous work is certainly best entrusted to scholars of proven learning and expertise, who are more likely, by definition, to be in a position to dedicate three months of their working year to the Commission's sessions than others who, however outstanding their achievements in the legal world, may have to juggle the competing demands of governmental and diplomatic commitments while sometimes diluting the level of their participation in the Commission. The government official—acting independently of his or her Government—can bring seasoned experience and a valuable grasp of realities to the Commission. But the absentee Commission member may confine his contribution to diminishing the Commission's overextended size. The balance is a difficult one to strike. But the Commission is essentially not, and should not be allowed to become, an intergovernmental deliberative body with an altogether different *raison d'être*. It is not a subcommittee, or even a preparatory commission, of the Sixth Committee. The Commission is unique and it is far too valuable a force for the development and promotion of international law for us ever to lose sight of its independent, expert character and composition.

As Judge Sir Humphrey Waldock observed in May 1974, when he addressed the Commission on its twenty-fifth anniversary, "If the Commission's work [has] come to have its own measure of authority in its own right, it [is] because of the sheer quality of that work".[4] The maintenance of that high standard has to be the paramount consideration for the future.

---

[4] *Yearbook of the International Law Commission, 1974*, vol. I, p. 70 at para. 27.

II

THE INTERNATIONAL LAW COMMISSION
AND
THE PROCESS OF LAW-FORMATION

by Hisashi Owada*

1. The function of law-making in the international community

Almost three quarters of a century ago, Professor James Brierly wrote that "an international legislature, in the sense of a body having power to enact new international law binding on the States of the world or on their peoples, does not exist."[1] The international community, he stated, has been content to rely for the development of its law on the slow growth of custom.

The international community has come a long way since that time. However, the fundamental structure of the law-making mechanism described by Professor Brierly remains essentially the same. What has come to be known as international legislation covers today almost all the fields of human activity, ranging from the regimes of outer space and of the deep seabed and ocean floor to the rights of the child and gender equality. At the same time, it is also true that what is called international legislation is intrinsically different from domestic legislation in a democracy, in as much as it is not a legal regime endowed with legal force *erga omnes*, but a multilateral compact agreed upon by those States which wish to be parties to it and binding upon them by virtue of the principle *pacta sunt servanda*.

In these circumstances, it becomes important to make an intellectual distinction between different types of international legislation, depending upon the nature of the legal norms which are to be incorporated in the legislation concerned. It is suggested that three different kinds of international legislation may be distinguished from this point of view.

First, there is the category of international legislation that is called "codification". In its pure form and as an ideal type, codification can only mean the putting into written form—a "code"—of what already exists in the form of unwritten, customary law. This is codification in the strict sense of the word. It is clear, however, that codification does not exist in reality in this pure form, since any exercise involving the putting into written form of what exists in unwritten form will inevitably involve an exercise in defining the exact contents of the rules in question and defining their precise parameters. With this in mind, an author of a penetrating analysis of the problem of codification of international law stated that "in practice even a strict codification in this sense may also involve the making of a few minor changes in the law".[2] In this sense, codification is defined as meaning "the more precise formulation and systematization

---

*Permanent Representative of Japan to the United Nations, Adjunct Professor of International Law, Columbia University, and Distinguished Visiting Professor, New York University, New York, United States of America.
[1]Brierly, J.L., *The Law of Nations* (1928), p. 96.
[2]Jennings, "The Progressive Development of International Law and its Codification", *British Year Book of International Law*, vol. 24 (1947), p. 301 at p. 301.

of rules of international law in fields where there already has been extensive State practice, precedent and doctrine".[3]

However, even with this modification, the definition of codification as being essentially an exercise in "the more precise formulation and systematization of normative rules" is too strict and restrictive. Thus, another authority on the subject wrote, on the basis of his personal experience as a member of the International Law Commission, that, "once we approach at close quarters practically any branch of international law, we are driven, amidst some feeling of incredulity, to the conclusion that although there is as a rule a consensus of opinion in broad principle—even this may be an overestimate in some cases— there is no semblance of agreement in relation to specific rules and problems."[4] As Professor Jennings has quite persuasively argued, "it is certain that codification in this very strict sense, however useful it may be in consolidating the already developed rules of a mature system, can have little place in a comparatively undeveloped system like international law".[5]

The foregoing analysis brings us to the second category of international legislation, which consists in codifying and developing the law in areas where the law has not been sufficiently clarified or has not yet been sufficiently developed in the practice of States. However, it is important to bear in mind that the case here is either one of the law being ambiguous and lacking in precision beyond a "consensus of opinion in broad principle" or else one of the law being underdeveloped and admitting of *lacunae*, rather than there being a total absence of any law to regulate the field in question. It is submitted that, in such cases, "progressive development" as a conceptual extension of "codification" plays an important role.

Thus, the Committee of the General Assembly which was assigned with the task of giving effect to Article 13, paragraph 1 (*a*), of the Charter of the United Nations and whose report was adopted by the General Assembly on 11 December 1946 concluded that:

> "For the codification of international law, the Committee recognized that no clear-cut distinction between the formulation of the law as it is and the law as it ought to be could be rigidly maintained in practice. It was pointed out that in any work of codification, the codifier inevitably has to fill in gaps and amend the law in the light of new developments. The Committee by a majority vote, however, agreed that for the purposes of the procedures adopted below, the definition given in paragraph 7 would be applicable."[6]

On this basis, the Committee decided to recommend two alternative procedures: one for progressive development and the other for codification. It is submitted, however, that this distinction in procedure between "progressive development" and "codification", as it was recommended by the Committee and

---

[3] Article 15 of the Statute of the International Law Commission.

[4] Lauterpacht, "Codification and Development of International Law", *American Journal of International Law*, vol. 49 (1955), p. 16 at p. 17.

[5] Loc. cit. above (footnote 2), p. 302.

[6] Document A/AC.10/51, para. 10. Paragraph 7 of the Committee's report subsequently developed into article 15 of the Commission's Statute, which provides as follows:

"In the following articles the expression 'progressive development of international law' is used for convenience as meaning the preparation of draft conventions on subjects which have not yet been regulated by international law or in regard to which the law has not yet been sufficiently developed in the practice of States. Similarly, the expression 'codification of international law' is used for convenience as meaning the more precise formulation and systemization of rules of international law in fields where there already has been extensive State practice, precedent and doctrine."

adopted by the General Assembly, was based on a conceptual misunderstanding, first, as to the relationship between codification and progressive development and, secondly, as to the relationship between progressive development of the law as an extension of codification and international law-making *de novo* in areas where no rules exist, such as was the case with outer space and the deep seabed and ocean floor, as we shall see below. Possibly because of the resulting confusion, the differentiation in procedure was later abandoned by the International Law Commission, which came to the conclusion that the distinction established in its Statute between codification and progressive development was unsuited to practical application.

The third category of international legislation consists in law-making *de novo* for those areas which have not in the past been covered by any rules of international law. The tremendous expansion of human activity into areas which have hitherto been free from them, such as Antarctica, outer space and the deep seabed and ocean floor, has created a need for regulation at the international level. It is also true that a rapid increase in interdependence among nations and peoples has created a situation in which issues which have hitherto been left entirely unattended and which have been left to the exclusive domain of national competence have come to be the focus of the international community's attention, giving rise to a need for a legal assessment from the viewpoint of the public policy of the international community as a whole. Examples in this category would include such issues as human rights, the environment and genetic technology, as well as such problems as racial discrimination, gender equality and the rights of the child. All these issues and problems are appropriate subjects for international legislation, just as they are appropriate subjects for regulation within a domestic legislative framework. However, it is clear that international legislation in these fields has characteristics quite different from international legislation in the field of codification or progressive development, as those terms have been defined above.

Legislation is concerned with the regulation of differing and often conflicting interests in society. Harmonization of those differing and conflicting interests at the community level—national or international—is the function of the legislative process. International legislation is no exception. Indeed, the process of reconciliation is even more difficult in the case of international legislation; for, in many areas, the spectrum of diverging interests is much wider than in the case of national legislation on account of the greater degree of heterogeneity among nations in terms of their social, economic and cultural characteristics. Harmonization of differing interests is consequently a more difficult exercise.

A classic case which is cited by one leading authority is the case of "the bitter cleavage which quickly appeared in the 1930 Hague Conference Committee dealing with the Responsibility of States", which was not caused merely by academic disagreements on points of doctrine. "A glance at the list of States ranging themselves on either side is enough to show that it was a cleavage between potential plaintiff states on the one hand and potential defendant states on the other."[7]

Another, more recent example is to be found in the work of the Third United Nations Conference on the Law of the Sea. In contrast with the 1958 United Nations Conference on the Law of the Sea, which was essentially a codification conference organized principally to incorporate all the rules of the existing

---

[7]Jennings, loc. cit. above (footnote 2), p. 319.

customary international law of the sea into the form of a written code, the Third United Nations Conference on the Law of the Sea was largely a matter of law-making *de novo*. This was all the more clear in view of the fact that the Conference had to deal with the novel problem of the exploration and exploitation of the natural resources of the deep seabed and ocean floor—an issue which could not be addressed on the basis of rules of customary international law, no such rules being in existence. Accordingly, the whole process of negotiation was one of the political adjustment of diverging interests, between those who had the capacity to engage in such activities and those who did not and between those who were expected to gain from such activities and those who were expected to lose.

It is clear that, in such cases as these, the route to success lies, not in modifying the law on the basis of such rules of law as may exist and which are relevant to the issue in hand, nor in developing rules along the lines that are discernible in the practice, whether on the issue itself or on some analogous point, but, rather, in engaging in a political process of negotiation in order to adjust the differing or conflicting interests involved. This is exactly what was done at the Third United Nations Conference on the Law of the Sea.

It is submitted that keeping in mind the distinction between these three different categories of international legislation is useful in considering the problem before us today: namely, the tasks that the International Law Commission has to tackle at this juncture in its history.

2. The tasks of the International Law Commission

Article 13, paragraph 1 (*a*), of the Charter of the United Nations provides that the General Assembly "shall initiate studies and make recommendations for the purpose of . . . promoting international co-operation in the political field and encouraging the progressive development of international law and its codification".

The background of this Charter provision is well known. The movement for achieving the codification and development of international law through general law-making treaties has a long history extending back over two centuries. Efforts to codify the legal norms governing inter-State relations may be said to have originated at the Congress of Vienna, where provisions regarding the regime of international rivers, the abolition of the slave trade and the ranking of diplomatic agents were adopted by the signatory powers of the Treaty of Paris of 1814. Since then, international legal rules have been elaborated at diplomatic conferences on many, many other subjects.

However, a new stage was reached in intergovernmental efforts to promote the codification and development of international law with the creation of the League of Nations. The Committee of Experts for the Progressive Codification of International Law, which was created at the request of the Assembly of the League of Nations in 1924, was mandated "[t]o prepare a provisional list of the subjects of International Law, the regulation of which by international agreement would seem to be most desirable and realizable at the present moment" and "to report to the Council on the questions which are sufficiently ripe" for codification.[8] This was the first attempt in history to codify and develop the whole field of international law on a worldwide basis, as opposed to simply

---

[8]Resolution adopted by the Assembly of the League of Nations, 22 September 1924, League of Nations, *Official Journal, Special Supplement, No. 21*, 1924, p. 10.

regulating individual and specific legal problems. On the basis of the decision of the Assembly of the League of Nations in 1927 to convene a diplomatic conference to codify three of the five topics which the Committee of Experts had concluded to be "sufficiently ripe", a codification conference took place at The Hague in 1930. This conference yielded meagre results, succeeding in adopting an international instrument only on the topic of nationality and failing to adopt any convention at all on the other two topics concerned: namely, territorial waters and State responsibility. Nevertheless, it is important to keep in mind that the International Law Commission is a direct descendant of this movement for the general codification of international law and the scope of the tasks of the Commission, as the successor to the legacy of the League, should be understood in the light of this experience.

The States which met at San Francisco to draft and adopt the Charter of the United Nations were overwhelmingly opposed to conferring fully fledged legislative power on the United Nations or making it into a world legislature with the capacity of enacting binding rules of international law. They rejected proposals to confer on the General Assembly the power to impose certain general conventions on States by some form of majority vote.

Seen against this historical background, it would seem clear that, while there was a difference of opinion on the question of the distinction between the progressive development of international law and its codification, the International Law Commission was never conceived as an expert body with exclusive competence to act as the drafting arm of the General Assembly with competence to enact international legislation. Whatever doctrinal differences may have existed on the distinction between the progressive development of international law and its codification, in the strict sense of that word, it would be fair to say that the task of the International Law Commission has primarily been conceived as one of engaging in the codification of international law in the broad sense of the term, including elements of progressive development, but without extending to the field of law-making in areas where no rules yet exist at the international level.

Thus, it is suggested there is nothing abnormal about the recent tendency according to which important international legislation in such new fields is entrusted to organs of the United Nations other than the International Law Commission or to bodies outside the United Nations, without any involvement on the part of the International Law Commission. This has been the case, for example, with regard to the United Nations Convention on the Law of the Sea of 1982, the Treaty on Principles Governing the Activities of States in the Exploration and Use of Outer Space, including the Moon and Other Celestial Bodies, of 1967, and the Antarctic Treaty of 1959, as well as many multilateral conventions in the field of social development, such as the Convention on the Elimination of All Forms of Discrimination Against Women of 1979, the Convention on the Rights of the Child of 1989 and the International Covenant on Civil and Political Rights and the International Covenant on Economic, Social and Cultural Rights of 1966.

As was stated earlier, international legislation in such fields is, by its very nature, an exercise in the creation of entirely new rules in areas where there previously has been none. Legislative work in this category of cases involves principally the consideration of policy perspectives, rather than the consideration of legal principles. While both that international legislation which is in the nature of progressive development of international law (category II, above) and that international legislation which is in the nature of new law-making (category

III, above) involve the same legislative process of adopting multilateral conventions which have the character of general law-making treaties, it is important to make this distinction between the two cases in considering the question as to where the primary competence for initiating the legislative process should lie.

3. Analysis of the achievements of the International Law Commission

I believe that, today, as we observe the International Law Commission's fiftieth anniversary, the mandate of the Commission, as an organ entrusted with the progressive development and codification of international law, is as valid as it was at the time at which the Commission was first established. Because of the changes that have taken place during the last 50 years, however, the Commission is facing new challenges. In order to meet them, it will be useful to review the results of the past efforts of the Commission and to analyse both its successes and its failures.

(A) Cases in which the Commission has succeeded in producing codification conventions

By far the biggest contribution that the International Law Commission has made to the cause of codification and progressive development has been its success in producing codification conventions in a number of the most important fields of international law, its work having served as the basis for several multilateral conventions which have been adopted under the auspices of the United Nations. These include the following:

A. Geneva Conventions on the Law of the Sea (1958)
  1. Convention on the Territorial Sea and the Contiguous Zone
  2. Convention on the High Seas
  3. Convention on Fishing and Conservation of the Living Resources of the High Seas
  4. Convention on the Continental Shelf
B. Convention on the Reduction of Statelessness (1961)
C. Vienna Convention on Diplomatic Relations (1960)
D. Vienna Convention on Consular Relations (1963)
E. Vienna Convention on the Law of Treaties (1969)
F. Convention on Special Missions (1969)
G. Convention on the Prevention and Punishment of Crimes against Internationally Protected Persons, including Diplomatic Agents (1973)
H. Vienna Convention on the Representation of States in their Relations with International Organizations of a Universal Character (1975)
I. Vienna Convention on Succession of States in respect of Treaties (1978)
J. Vienna Convention on Succession of States in respect of State Property, Archives and Debts (1983)
K. Vienna Convention on the Law of Treaties between States and International Organizations or between International Organizations (1986)
L. Convention on the Law of the Non-Navigational Uses of International Watercourses (1997)

It is true that the work of the International Law Commission in this field has been more successful in the case of certain topics than others. One can discern *grosso modo* the following trends.[9]

(*a*) Conventions which are primarily in the nature of codification, as described in section 1 (category I), and which relate to fields that have traditionally been regarded as part of the basic legal framework of international society have achieved greater success in terms of their acceptance by the international community through ratification (cases A1, A2, C, D and E).

(*b*) Conventions which go beyond the realm of codification and enter heavily into the area of progressive development, as described in section 1 (category II), and which relate to fields which, at the time of drafting, were regarded as of current importance have not always been followed by an impressive record of acceptance by the international community through ratification (cases A3, A4, H, I and J).

(*c*) Conventions which are primarily in the nature of codification (category I), but which are concerned with specific technical issues, have not succeeded in capturing the political imagination and interest of States and have accordingly failed either to attract sufficient ratifications to enter into force or to make the instrument concerned viable (cases B, F, H and K).

(B) Cases in which the Commission has been left out of the legislative process

In contrast with the cases discussed under heading (A), there have been many cases in which important international legislation has been adopted without any involvement whatsoever on the part of the International Law Commission. Some prominent examples include the following:

M. The Antarctic Treaty (1960)

N. Treaty on Principles Governing the Activities of States in the Exploration and Use of Outer Space, including the Moon and Other Celestial Bodies (1967)

O. Convention on International Liability for Damage Caused by Space Objects (1971)

P. United Nations Convention on the Law of the Sea (1982)

Q. International Convention Against the Taking of Hostages (1979)

R. Conventions in the field of disarmament:
 1. Treaty Banning Nuclear Weapon Tests in the Atmosphere, in Outer Space and under Water (1963)
 2. Treaty on the Non-Proliferation of Nuclear Weapons (1968)
 3. Convention on the Prohibition of the Development, Production and Stockpiling of Bacteriological (Biological) and Toxin Weapons and on Their Destruction (1972)
 4. Convention on the Prohibition of the Development, Production, Stockpiling and Use of Chemical Weapons and on Their Destruction (1992)

S. International Covenant on Economic, Social and Cultural Rights (1966)

T. International Covenant on Civil and Political Rights (1966)

U. International Convention on the Elimination of All Forms of Racial Discrimination (1965)

---

[9]The classifications that follow inevitably have about them an element of arbitrariness and are, therefore, provisional and subject to further review.

V. Convention on the Elimination of All Forms of Discrimination Against Women (1979)

W. Convention on the Rights of the Child (1989)

X. United Nations Framework Convention on Climate Change (1992)

Y. Convention on Biological Diversity (1992)

The International Law Commission was totally excluded from participating in the preparatory stages of these important conventions, in spite of the fact that most of them were drawn up within the United Nations itself or at least had some link with the Organization.

With regard to these conventions, however, it is important to realize that they are all—or most of them—international legislation of a law-making type (category III), according to the classification that was described in section 1 of this paper. While there is no intrinsic reason why the International Law Commission should not have a say in the preparatory process of international legislation in this category—concrete ways in which the Commission might offer a useful service with regard to this category of instrument will be suggested below, in section 4—it would seem useful to ponder why the Commission was excluded from the legislative process in these important cases. It is submitted that the following factors are relevant to this state of affairs.

(*a*) Many of these multilateral conventions (cases M, N, P and R1, R2, R3 and R4) are in the realm of law-making *de novo* or, from the policy viewpoint, are *de lege ferenda*. In such cases, it is not just a matter of identifying the public policy of the international community, but of adjusting the public policies of the member States of the international community through political negotiations. The Commission is not viewed as offering an ideal forum for such a policy process.

The law of the sea offers an interesting illustration of this point. In contrast with the Geneva Conventions on the Law of the Sea (cases A1, A2, A3 and A4), the United Nations Convention on the Law of the Sea (case P) was negotiated and drawn up entirely within the United Nations—first, in the Committee on the Peaceful Use of the Sea-Bed and Ocean Floor beyond the Limits of National Jurisdiction and then at the Third United Nations Conference on the Law of the Sea—without any participation or involvement on the part of the International Law Commission. Some have viewed this development with concern. However, it would seem that this concern is misplaced in as much as the legislative processes which were involved in the two cases were so different from each other that a facile analogy between them would not be justified. The international legislation which was effected at the Third United Nations Conference on the Law of the Sea involved two major legislative aspects: the aspect of codification (international legislation in category I), coupled with elements of progressive development (international legislation in category II), in particular in so far as Parts I to IV and VII of the 1982 Convention are concerned, and the aspect of law-making *de novo* (international legislation in category III), in particular in so far as concerns Parts V, VI and XI of the Convention. These two aspects were so integrally intertwined in the creation of a unified regime for the oceans that it would have been unacceptable to States to leave the drafting of the entire Convention in the hands of the International Law Commission; and it would have been impossible to divide the Convention into those parts which involved codification and progressive development, on the one hand, and those parts which were concerned with law-making *de novo*, on the other.

(*b*) Somewhat similar considerations might apply, on the whole, to the conventions in the field of social development (cases S, T, U, V and W). This is a field in which one might well consider involving the International Law Commission, in so far as the subject matter principally concerns the issue of equality before the law. While the ideological underpinnings of the issues involved may have made the discussions on some of the conventions quite political in character, the policy issues involved have chiefly been ones of the public policy of the international community and could have been handled by the Commission from an objective point of view in the exercise of its competence for the progressive development of international law (category II), leaving the injection of political elements requiring political negotiations to the General Assembly or to the relevant diplomatic conference, as the case may be.

(*c*) The conventions in the field of disarmament (cases R1, R2, R3 and R4) and in the field of environment (cases X and Y) have gone through a legislative process which is *sui generis*, involving a huge amount of expert technical knowledge, and may, for that reason, have been judged not to be suited to consideration by the International Law Commission.

(*d*) An interesting case is presented by the example of the International Convention against the Taking of Hostages (Q). This Convention was drafted and adopted by the General Assembly without the participation of the International Law Commission. However, a similar convention—the 1973 Convention on the Prevention and Punishment of Crimes against Internationally Protected Persons, including Diplomatic Agents (case G)—was drafted by the Commission at the request of the General Assembly.[10] If one compares these two conventions, the differences between them are negligible, at least in so far as their substance is concerned. This example seems to indicate the need for greater attention to be paid to coordination between the General Assembly and the International Law Commission.

(C) Cases in which the Commission has prepared a draft, but in which there has not been any follow-up action

There is a third category of cases: namely those in which the International Law Commission has been requested to work on a topic and has prepared a draft in the form of a convention or code, but no action has yet been taken by the General Assembly in respect of that draft. There are eight such cases:

1. Draft Declaration on Rights and Duties of States: the General Assembly decided to postpone consideration of the matter (1951).

2. Principles of International Law Recognized in the Charter of the Nürnberg Tribunal and in the Judgment of the Tribunal: the General Assembly decided to send the formulation to Governments for their comments and requested the Commission to take these comments into account in preparing the draft code of offences against the peace and security of mankind (1950).

3. Draft Convention on the Elimination of Future Statelessness: the United Nations Conference on the Elimination or Reduction of Future Statelessness decided to use another draft as the basis of its work (1959).

4. Model Roles on Arbitration Procedure: the General Assembly decided to bring the draft to the attention of Member States for their consideration and

---

[10]General Assembly resolution 2790 (XXVI) of 3 December 1971.

use, in such cases and to such extent as they consider appropriate, in drawing up treaties of arbitration or *compromis* (1958).

5. Draft Articles on Most-Favoured-Nation Clauses: the General Assembly decided to bring the draft to the attention of Member States and interested intergovernmental organizations for their consideration in such cases and to the extent as they deem appropriate (1991).

6. Draft Articles on the Status of the Diplomatic Courier and the Diplomatic Bag Not Accompanied by Diplomatic Courier: the General Assembly decided to bring the draft to the attention of Member States and to remind them of the possibility that the field and any further developments within it might be the subject of codification at an appropriate time in the future (1995).

7. Draft Articles on Jurisdictional Immunities of States and their Property: the General Assembly decided that an international conference of plenipotentiaries be convened to consider the draft and to conclude a convention on the subject, but postponed determination of the arrangements for the conference until its fifty-second or fifty-third session (1994).

8. Draft Code of Crimes against the Peace and Security of Mankind: the General Assembly decided to invite Governments to submit, before the end of the General Assembly's fifty-third session, comments and observations on the action which might be taken in relation to the draft (1996).

Several of these cases merit comment, as do two others.

(*a*) Many of the draft declarations of principles have been left without further action, presumably because they have been judged to be inappropriate for codification in the form of international legislation (cases 1, 2, 4 and 5).

(*b*) The Commission's Draft Articles on the Law of the Non-Navigational Uses of International Watercourses have served as the basis of an eponymous convention, which was adopted by the General Assembly in May 1997, after serious discussion and negotiations in the Sixth Committee of the General Assembly. The Convention is the first codification convention to be adopted in the last 10 years on the basis of one of the Commission's drafts. In this regard, it should be regarded as a significant step forward, if one places it against the background of the growing criticism of the recent activities of the United Nations in the field of the codification and progressive development of international law.

(*c*) The Draft Statute for an International Criminal Court was prepared at the request of the General Assembly, which asked the Commission to undertake its elaboration as a matter of priority.[11] The Commission adopted the draft Statute in its final form in 1994 and recommended that the General Assembly convene an international conference of plenipotentiaries to study the draft and to conclude a convention on the establishment of an international criminal court. The General Assembly, however, decided in 1994 to establish an ad hoc committee, open to all Member States and States members of the specialized agencies, to review the major substantive and administrative issues arising out of the Commission's Draft Statute and, in the light of that review, to consider arrangements for the convening of an international conference of plenipotentiaries.[12] After receiving the report of this ad hoc committee, the General Assembly decided in 1995 to set up a preparatory committee, open to all States Members of the Organization or members of the specialized agencies or Inter-

---

[11]General Assembly resolution 47/33 of 25 November 1992, especially paras. 4, 5 and 6.

national Atomic Energy Agency, in order to discuss these issues further and to draft texts with a view to preparing a widely acceptable consolidated text of a convention as a next step towards consideration by a conference of plenipotentiaries. Last year, the General Assembly reaffirmed the mandate of this preparatory committee and decided that it was to meet three times in 1997 and once in 1998 in order to complete the drafting of a text for submission to a diplomatic conference of plenipotentiaries. It also decided that such a conference shall be held in 1998 with a view to finalizing and adopting a convention on the subject of the establishment of an international criminal court, but it decided to defer making the necessary arrangements for that conference to its fifty-second session.

It is useful to recall here that the issue of the establishment of an international criminal court has, since the turn of the century, been one of the major topics of interest to the international legal community, both academic and governmental. For this reason, the drafting of a statute for an international criminal court could be said to be a proper function of the International Law Commission, belonging to the field of codification of international law and its progressive development. At the same time, however, the question would seem, in view of the intrinsic nature of the issues involved, to contain many elements that tend to draw the issue as a whole into the area of law-making *de novo* (category III), rather than it being a matter of codification (category I) or progressive development (category II).

Furthermore, while many of the major issues involved in this question are, technically speaking, of a legal character, the basic decision to create such an international criminal court, with compulsory jurisdiction to try the nationals of Member States, is an eminently political one and it is going to require the exercise of political judgement on the part of Member States to determine the concrete ways in which such issues are to be dealt with in each of the Statute's provisions.

Seen in this light, it is little wonder that the draft Statute which the Commission prepared has encountered an array of critical comments and has been referred to the careful scrutiny of a committee which has been established for the purpose by the General Assembly.

4. Suggestions for improving the functioning of the International Law Commission

From what has been said by way of analysis of the past performance of the International Law Commission, I should like to draw some conclusions which might be useful for improving the functioning of the Commission, under its current mandate, as currently constituted and without requiring any drastic change to be made in its structure.

(1) My first suggestion is that it is necessary to draw a clearer demarcation in the Commission's activities in the field of international legislation between codification and development, on the one hand, and law-making *de novo*, on the other. It has been argued above that, while such a demarcation is difficult to make, it is one which should be borne in mind when discussing the possibilities and limitations that are inherent in the Commission's work. A number of the examples which have been cited above would seem to justify the proposition that this distinction is a useful one to make for practical purposes, if not entirely

---

[12]General Assembly resolution 49/50 of 9 December 1994.

for theoretical purposes, in order to uphold the authority and usefulness of the Commission as an institution entrusted with the task of promoting the progressive development of international law and its codification.

The recommendation which I wish to make is that the Commission should be as proactive as possible in the field of international legislation, but essentially within the confines of its primary function: namely, "the promotion of the progressive development of international law and its codification", as stipulated in article 1 of the Commission's Statute. New, untrodden fields of human activity, which require regulation through international law-making *de novo*, had better be left, in the first instance at least, to policy decision at the political level.

(2) The second recommendation which one might make in light of the Commission's past successes and failures is that there should be intensive coordination and cooperation between the General Assembly and the Commission. This is something of a trite observation, no doubt; for it is clear that the Commission, as a subsidiary organ of the General Assembly under Article 22 of the Charter of the United Nations, has to maintain close contacts with the General Assembly and with its Sixth Committee, in particular. Nevertheless, a cursory examination of the Commission's record reveals that there have been instances in which drafts which the Commission has prepared have not conformed with the requirements of the General Assembly and so have had to be abandoned without further action.

The conventions which have been adopted by the General Assembly in the field of social development also deserve mention in this connection. Conventions in this field, it is true, tend to contain considerable elements of political controversy and can be said generally to belong to the realm of law-making *de novo*, rather than to that of pure codification. Nevertheless, the essential points to be guaranteed in these conventions are the principles of human dignity and of equality under the rule of law—although it should be conceded, in fairness, that these basic principles, however uncontestable they may be as principles, immediately give rise to political controversies when one gets into the sphere of their concrete application. Given the basic nature of law-making in this field, there would seem to be little reason why the International Law Commission should be excluded from the process. It would seem to be desirable at least that there be much closer coordination and consultation between the General Assembly's Third Committee and the International Law Commission, which is interested in juridical consistency and legal stability as the cornerstones of the promotion of progressive development and codification of international law.

(3) The third suggestion which I wish to make concerns the Commission's relationship with the Governments of Member States. It might sound almost self-contradictory, on the face of it at least, to say that it is essential for the Commission to uphold its independence as a collegiate body and for its individual members to remain free from Government influence and at the same time to suggest that the Commission maintain close working relationships with the Governments of Member States. Nevertheless, I believe that it is extremely important that the Commission do just this.

The work of the Commission must be guided by a high level of pragmatism, in as much as what the Commission is asked to produce is a product for application in the inter-State relations of the real world. What cannot be applied in practice will not be of much use, however lofty its ideals and however correct its theoretical underpinnings. Sensitivity to the demands and desires of the international community and of the individual members of that community is extremely important, as is a preparedness to engage in the pragmatic accommodation of these demands and desires, as long as no issue of basic principle is involved.

In this connection, it may be observed that the Statute of the International Law Commission, as revised, provides in article 2 that "the Commission shall consist of thirty-four members, who shall be persons of recognized competence in international law",[13] but, at the same time, its prescribes in article 8, as a consideration to be borne in mind in the elections to the Commission, that "in the Commission as a whole the representation of the main forms of civilization and of the principal legal systems of the world should be assured". The quality of the Commission's membership, both individually and collectively, is naturally the key factor in fulfilling the double requirement of upholding the Commission's independence and ensuring its sensitivity to the needs of the international community.

From the same viewpoint, it would be beneficial for the Commission to have amongst its members a proper mixture of persons with practical experience and persons with an academic background.

(4)   The fourth and final point which I wish to make concerns the fact that, in the field of codification *stricto sensu*, there are ever fewer topics in respect of which the Commission may offer its services for producing draft international legislation. In these circumstances, it would seem desirable to ponder new areas in respect of which the Commission might usefully offer its services.

(*a*)   The Commission might revisit the scene of its past efforts at codification and review those conventions which are in force from the viewpoint of how they have actually been applied in practice. Useful examples may be found in the practice relating to the 1969 Vienna Convention on the Law of Treaties and the 1961 Vienna Convention on Diplomatic Relations. This exercise would seem particularly useful, given that any exercise in codification has to confront the problem of how to cope with changes and developments in the law which has been codified. An eminent authority on the subject of codification and progressive development stated, in relation to the codification of existing law, that, "even within that very limited field where there is both agreement and considerable practice, the work of codification cannot discard *a limine* the legislative function of developing and improving the law".[14] This dictum applies with equal force in relation to the codified law once the task of codification has been completed.

(*b*)   The Commission might be assigned the task of working closely with the main Committees of the General Assembly when those organs undertake the preparation of draft conventions, as has been suggested above in respect of the Third Committee. This is, admittedly, a delicate task and one in which the Commission can succeed only if an adequate framework of cooperation is established, based on mutual respect and trust. Nevertheless, it is suggested as an idea which may be worth pursuing, in as much as the current law-making activities of the General Assembly's main Committees would seem to be in need of better coordination and oversight from the point of view of maintaining juridical consistency and legal stability in the international community.

---

[13] The Commission's membership was raised to 34 by the General Assembly in its resolution 36/39 of 18 November 1981.

[14] Lauterpacht, loc. cit. above (footnote 4), p. 29.

(*c*)   A new area of law-making which is appropriate for the International Law Commission would seem to be the law of international organizations and of the United Nations, in particular. For example, the law concerning the privileges and immunities which are to be accorded by the State which hosts an international conference convened under the auspices of the United Nations deserves much more careful attention and scrutiny in the light of the present-day conditions in which such conferences are held and in view of the evident need to establish juridical consistency and legal stability in the relationship between the host State and the United Nations. There would seem to exist many more fertile areas to be explored in this field of law concerning the multifarious activities of the United Nations.

(*d*)   Finally, there is an inevitable temptation to try to use the Commission's talents for the benefit of the United Nations. One possible way of doing this would be to assign to the Commission, on top of its current mandate, the role of an advisory body along the lines of the Commission of Jurists of the League of Nations.[15] It goes without saying that such a role would be without prejudice to the advisory function of the International Court of Justice. Without being too ambitious, however, the Commission could be assigned the role of offering legal opinions within the administrative competence of the General Assembly.

---

[15]For the services which were rendered by the Commission of Jurists which was appointed by the League of Nations in 1920 to consider certain aspects of the dispute concerning the Aaland Islands: League of Nations, *Official Journal, Special Supplement, No. 3*, 1920, pp. 8-9.

LA COMMISSION DU DROIT INTERNATIONAL, LA CODIFICATION ET LE PROCESSUS DE FORMATION DE DROIT INTERNATIONAL

par Georges Abi-Saab*

Le but de cette vue d'ensemble est de situer le rôle de la Commission du droit international dans le processus de formation du droit international. Ainsi, après avoir tracé rapidement le cadre général, en essayant de cerner la notion de codification, d'une part, et en décrivant le système envisagé par la Charte des Nations Unies pour remplir cette tâche, d'autre part, l'analyse se concentre sur le produit final de ce processus. À cet effet les avantages et désavantages des deux instruments principaux utilisés (traité et résolution) sont recensés, avant d'examiner les différentes représentations de leur interaction avec le droit international général.

I. Le cadre général

1. La codification

a) *Quatre acceptions*

La codification est une activité juridique connue en droit interne depuis la haute antiquité (Code d'Hammourabi), mais sa transposition en droit international ne se fait pas sans ambiguïté; ce qui nous permet d'en identifier quatre acceptions différentes dans la littérature (acceptions pas toujours différenciées d'ailleurs) :

1) La codification *stricto sensu* : c'est l'instantané ou la version photographique de la coutume qui n'opère qu'une simple mise en mots de son contenu, sans rien ajouter, soustraire ou modifier; une simple formulation et systématisation par écrit de sa substance normative qui n'affecte en rien ses prescriptions. C'est l'acception anglo-américaine traditionnelle de la codification.

2) La codification *lato sensu* : elle intervient davantage sur la coutume, en fournissant une présentation systématique et écrite des règles, tout en remplissant les lacunes, en éliminant les chevauchements et les contradictions et en les mettant à jour. C'est l'acception civiliste de la codification.

Ces deux définitions sont fonction de la matière première (*input*) de laquelle procède la codification. Les deux suivantes sont fonction du produit final (*output*) auquel elle aboutit.

3) Certains, tel le docteur Liang, premier directeur de la Division de la codification du Bureau des affaires juridiques du Secrétariat des Nations Unies, préconisent une acception très large de la codification qui — tout en englobant le développement progressif — se définit par son produit final, recouvrant,

---

*Professeur de droit international, l'Institut universitaire de hautes études internationales, Genève (Suisse). Professeur honoraire, Faculté de droit, Université du Caire (Egypte).

toujours selon le docteur Liang, tous les traités multilatéraux adoptés dans les conférences internationales depuis l'Acte final du Congrès de Vienne, et qui proclament des principes de droit international obligatoires pour un certain nombre de parties[1]. C'est une acception trop large, car elle dépend presque exclusivement de l'instrument utilisé ou produit pour cerner la nature de l'activité juridique dont il est question. Or, comme nous le savons, le traité multilatéral peut servir aussi bien de traité-loi que de traité-contrat, c'est-à-dire, comme instrument d'échange de prestations.

4)   Enfin, la codification se définit parfois par le contenu (ou la structure intellectuelle) de son produit final qui doit être un code, c'est-à-dire un traitement systématique, en forme de règles générales, de tout un sujet ou d'un pan de droit international, quelle que soit la matière première qui est à sa base : coutume ou traité, ou même un exercice *ex nihilo*. En d'autres termes, ceux du professeur Jennings, le premier tenant de cette acception, la codification est elle-même un moyen de développement progressif du droit international[2].

Si nous observons ce qui se fait en pratique au nom de la codification, en matière de droit des traités ou de droit de la mer, par exemple, nous trouvons que cela procède de la deuxième acception pour aboutir à la quatrième; ce qui signifie que la notion contemporaine de codification est une combinaison de ces deux acceptions.

b)   *L'impossible codification* stricto sensu

En effet, la codification *stricto sensu* est impossible en pratique. Car comment effectuer la « mise en mots » de la coutume sans affecter son contenu ?

La formulation et la rationalisation des règles coutumières nécessite une prise de position par rapport aux ambiguïtés et aux lacunes de ces règles, qui sont nécessairement plus importantes que celles attenantes aux règles écrites. Or ces ambiguïtés et ces lacunes ne sont pas le fruit du hasard, dans la mesure où elles se situent dans un espace juridique recouvert par la pratique internationale. Elles reflètent plutôt une absence de consensus sur les points qu'elles recouvrent, laissant apparaître des trous ou des pénombres dans le tissu coutumier qui se forme pour couvrir un certain espace de relations sociales. Et cela d'autant plus qu'en droit international (contrairement au droit interne, où le processus de codification commence d'habitude avec une surabondance de matériau normatif qu'il faut tailler pour le réduire), si on écarte les espaces d'ambiguïté et de lacunes, il ne nous reste que quelques principes de portée trop générale pour être autosuffisants ou opératoires.

Dans ces conditions, dissiper les ambiguïtés et combler les lacunes, en opérant un choix chaque fois qu'il se présente, ne se réduit pas à une activité ou à des retouches mineures, mais constitue plutôt un apport normatif substantiel. C'est transformer un canevas ajouré ou une dentelle très légère en un tissu épais. Il s'agit donc d'une activité nécessairement législative.

Par ailleurs, même la Commission du droit international des Nations Unies — dont l'article 15 du Statut (dans le sillage du paragraphe 1 de l'Article 13 de la Charte) distingue la « codification du droit international » (définie plutôt dans le sens *stricto sensu*) du « développement progressif du droit international »

---

[1]Voir, par exemple, Liang, « Le développement et la codification du droit international », *Recueil des cours de l'Académie de droit international de La Haye*, vol. 73 (1948-II), p. 411, particulièrement p. 422.

[2]Jennings, « The Progressive Development of International Law and its Codification », *British Year Book of International Law*, vol. 24 (1947), p. 302 et 303.

(recouvrant et allant même au-delà de la codification *lato sensu*)[3] — a constaté très tôt, en fait depuis le début de son travail en vue d'élaborer les Conventions de Genève sur le droit de la mer, l'impossibilité pratique d'opérer cette distinction, et n'a pas essayé de la faire dans les projets d'articles qu'elle prépare depuis lors[4].

2. Le système et le processus de l'Article 13 de la Charte : une évolution prodigieuse

L'Article premier de la Charte énonce comme deuxième but des Nations Unies de :

« Développer entre les nations des relations amicales fondées sur le respect du principe de l'égalité de droits des peuples et de leur droit à disposer d'eux-mêmes, et prendre toutes autres mesures propres à consolider la paix du monde. »

C'est une tâche qui, au-delà du traitement des crises et des conflits (qui est l'apanage du maintien de la paix, premier but de l'Organisation), vise au perfectionnement du système international lui-même, et dont un élément important est de perfectionner les règles du jeu formelles de ce système, que sont les règles du droit international, comme le prévoit expressément le paragraphe 1 de l'Article 13 :

« L'Assemblée générale provoque des études et fait des recommandations en vue de :

a. Développer la coopération internationale dans le domaine politique et encourager le développement progressif du droit international et sa codification. »

Le fait que la codification et le développement progressif du droit international soient associés dans cette disposition au développement de la coopération politique montre clairement que la Charte considère qu'ils s'insèrent dans les efforts destinés à perfectionner le système politique international; tâche dont l'Assemblée générale s'est acquittée en premier lieu par la création en 1947 d'un organe subsidiaire spécialisé, la Commission du droit international.

Étant donné l'expérience malheureuse de la Société des Nations avec la Conférence de La Haye de 1930, les attentes à cet égard étaient très modestes. Ni les critiques de la codification (comme Stone[5]) ni même ses partisans (comme Lauterpacht[6]) ne s'attendaient à un produit substantiel, ou à des résultats rapides. Au mieux ces derniers la considéraient-ils comme un exercice à but éducatif. Mais ces attentes sceptiques ou charitablement modestes ont été trompées et largement dépassées par des résultats spectaculaires, en particulier au cours de

---

[3]L'article 15 du Statut de la Commission stipule :
« Dans les articles qui suivent, l'expression "développement progressif du droit international" est employée, pour la commodité, pour viser les cas où il s'agit de rédiger des conventions sur des sujets qui ne sont pas encore réglés par le droit international ou relativement auxquels le droit n'est pas encore suffisamment développé dans la pratique des Etats. De même l'expression "codification du droit international" est employée, pour la commodité, pour viser les cas où il s'agit de formuler avec plus de précision et de systématiser les règles du droit international dans des domaines dans lesquels il existe déjà une pratique étatique considérable, des précédents et des opinions doctrinales. »

[4]Voir Nations Unies, *La Commission du droit international et son œuvre* (4e éd., 1989), p. 15 à 16, et surtout note 28 (publication des Nations Unies, numéro de vente F.88.V.1).

[5]Stone, « On the Vocation of the International Law Commission », *Columbia Law Review*, vol. 57 (1957), p. 16.

[6]Lauterpacht, « Codification and Development of International Law », *American Journal of International Law*, vol. 49 (1955), p. 17.

ce qu'on peut appeler, avec à peine un peu d'exagération, la « décade prodigieuse » de la codification, celle qui va de la première grande réalisation de la Commission du droit international — les quatre Conventions de Genève sur le droit de la mer de 1958 — jusqu'à l'apogée de son œuvre, la Convention de Vienne sur le droit des traités de 1969.

Il s'agit d'un foisonnement de conventions de codification et de développement progressif qui renouvellent et mettent à jour des pans entiers du droit international parmi les plus sollicités dans la pratique. Et comme il a déjà été mentionné, en s'attaquant à la première de ces réalisations, les articles sur le droit de la mer, la Commission est rapidement arrivée à la conclusion qu'il était pratiquement impossible de distinguer entre codification et développement progressif.

Si la Commission du droit international a été conçue initialement comme l'unique instrument de l'Assemblée générale dans le domaine de la codification et du développement progressif du droit international, la prolifération de ces activités normatives les a projetées au-delà de la Commission. De nombreux sujets, et non les moindres, ont été confiés à des comités spéciaux (c'est-à-dire créés spécialement) tels ceux qui ont préparé la Déclaration relative aux principes de droit international touchant les relations amicales et la coopération entre les États conformément à la Charte des Nations Unies[7] et la Définition de l'agression[8]. Un autre exemple des plus importants est la Convention de 1982 sur le droit de la mer, qui est l'aboutissement des travaux successifs d'un comité spécial (sur le statut des fonds marins au-delà des limites de la juridiction nationale), puis d'un comité préparatoire (de la Conférence), suivis par la troisième Conférence des Nations Unies sur le droit de la mer.

D'autres organes subsidiaires ont été créés pour se charger de la codification et du développement progressif du droit (et même plus) dans des domaines spécifiques et sur une base continue, tels que la Commission des Nations Unies pour le droit commercial international (CNUDCI, plus connue sous son sigle anglais UNCITRAL), ou le sous-comité juridique du Comité sur les utilisations pacifiques de l'espace extra-atmosphérique (longtemps présidé par le juge Lachs), organe qui a créé de toutes pièces une nouvelle branche de droit international. De même, la Conférence des Nations Unies pour le commerce et le développement (CNUCED) a joué un rôle important non seulement dans la codification et le développement progressif, mais même dans l'élaboration d'un nouveau droit économique international applicable dans les rapports Nord/Sud (ce que la doctrine française appelle le droit international du développement). Sans oublier enfin les divers organes qui œuvrent dans le domaine tout récent du droit international de l'environnement.

Nous nous trouvons ainsi en présence d'un mécanisme très complexe, car construit (ou plutôt bricolé) progressivement au gré des besoins ressentis et de la conjoncture, qui fonctionne de manière continue pour répondre aux besoins normatifs de la communauté internationale, en retaillant les pièces existantes pour les utiliser comme pierres de construction (*building blocks*) de nouveaux édifices à l'architecture résolument moderne (ou post-moderne), et en allant au besoin au-delà en fabriquant les pièces manquantes; système ou mécanisme qui s'est révélé très vigoureux et très actif, malgré ses inconséquences et ses lacunes et la lourdeur et la lenteur de son fonctionnement.

---

[7] Annexée à la résolution 2625 (XXV) de l'Assemblée générale en date du 24 octobre 1970.
[8] Annexée à la résolution 3314 (XXIX) de l'Assemblée générale en date du 14 décembre 1974.

Ce processus, sans être exhaustif, n'a pratiquement ignoré aucun sujet ni aucune grande branche du droit international. Et là même où l'activité normative n'a pas, ou pas encore, débouché sur un instrument final, par exemple dans le domaine de la responsabilité des États, elle a profondément influencé la communauté juridique et marqué sa vision du sujet traité.

Il faut cependant relever que l'essor de ce processus de codification et de développement progressif du droit international semble avoir dépassé son apogée et qu'il est entré dans une phase de rendements décroissants, du moins pour ce qui est des sujets classiques du droit international, tout en suscitant un scepticisme grandissant[9].

Il n'empêche que l'acquis de cette activité prolifique est proprement impressionnant, non seulement par la mise à jour et les compléments apportés aux règles, mais surtout par l'avènement, au sein de ce qui était jusqu'alors fondamentalement un système de droit coutumier, d'une multitude d'instruments écrits de forme et de portée juridiques diverses (en particulier des traités de codification et des résolutions normatives de l'Assemblée générale). Ces instruments ont substantiellement changé la topographie du droit international contemporain.

Reste à savoir cependant si ce changement quantitatif en droit international a entraîné ou s'est accompagné également d'un changement qualitatif; en d'autres termes quel est son impact ou son effet réel sur les modes de formation du droit international. Question fondamentale sur laquelle nous reviendrons après un examen comparé de ces instruments.

II. Les instruments et leur interaction avec le droit international général

1. Les instruments

A. *La codification par traité*

a) *Avantages de la codification par traité*

Les avantages de la codification en général, et par traité en particulier, peuvent être résumés comme suit :

1) La codification rend les règles plus claires et plus systématiques; et cela sur le double plan de la preuve de l'existence même des règles et de l'identification de leur contenu. En effet, le droit coutumier, droit non écrit, est induit directement du comportement social, ce qui laisse une très grande marge d'appréciation à l'interprète pour constater l'existence des deux éléments de la coutume par rapport à un comportement qui devient ainsi prescrit et pour établir sa teneur normative exacte.

En fournissant une sorte d'interprétation authentique de ces règles, tout en les transformant en règles écrites, la codification dissipe ces incertitudes, et favorise la perception et l'application uniformes du droit.

2) En rendant les règles plus claires, la codification les rend plus visibles et plus accessibles à de larges couches d'utilisateurs potentiels.

3) En associant les États nouvellement indépendants à la reformulation des règles du droit international et en répondant ainsi à leur grief d'exclusion,

---

[9]Voir, par exemple, Zemanek, « Codification of International Law: Salvation or Dead End? », dans Zanardi, P.L., Migliazza, A., Pocar, F., and Ziccardi, P. (éd.), *Le Droit international à l'heure de sa codification : études en l'honneur de Roberto Ago* (1987), vol. I, p. 581.

la codification rend le produit de ce processus — c'est-à-dire les règles codifiées ou le droit tout court — plus « acceptable » psychologiquement et politiquement à leurs yeux.

4) En éliminant les incertitudes qui entourent l'existence et la teneur des règles, la codification pourrait réduire, du moins partiellement, la réticence des États à recourir aux modes juridictionnels de règlement des différends internationaux.

5) La codification par traité transforme également le fondement du caractère obligatoire des règles; ce que certains considèrent comme un avantage, car le traité a un champ et des mécanismes d'application plus clairs et plus nets que la coutume. Mais il s'agit là d'un argument à double tranchant, comme on le verra plus loin.

Il est intéressant de relever que ces avantages de la codification portent beaucoup plus sur l'amélioration du fonctionnement du système juridique en tant que tel, c'est-à-dire sur le perfectionnement et la dynamisation de ses mécanismes (ou de ses règles secondaires), plutôt que sur le contenu des normes (les règles primaires) prises isolément. En d'autres termes, ce sont plutôt ses effets secondaires sur les modes de formation et éventuellement de mise en œuvre du droit international, qui comptent le plus en dernière analyse[10].

b) *Désavantages de la codification*

Cela ne veut pas dire que la codification en général, et par traité en particulier, n'a que des avantages. Car, comme toute activité humaine, elle comporte des dangers et des risques qui ont fait l'objet de maintes critiques à son égard.

1) La première est que la codification risque d'étrangler le droit et d'arrêter son évolution. Elle remonte au XIXe siècle, à Savigny et à son « école historique » en Allemagne, pour qui le droit est, comme la langue, une émanation sociale directe exprimant l'esprit du peuple (*Volksgeist*), son génie propre et sa conscience juridique, à travers la coutume qui se module directement et de manière continue sur l'évolution sociale. La codification rompt cette symbiose et risque d'arrêter l'évolution du droit et même de l'étrangler en le fixant une fois pour toutes et en l'enchaînant dans une camisole de mots.

C'est un risque qui existe, certes, si la codification est par trop détaillée et rigide. Mais il suffit d'en être conscient pour l'éviter facilement.

En réalité, comme le fait remarquer Sir Cecil Hurst[11], les adeptes de cette théorie pensaient à un modèle alternatif de développement jurisprudentiel du droit, celui de la *common law*. Mais ce modèle est inadapté au droit international. En premier lieu, étant donné la base consensuelle du règlement juridictionnel des différends en droit international, l'activité juridictionnelle est trop restreinte pour subvenir même minimalement aux besoins de développement du droit international. Et même en *common law*, le développement est loin d'être

---

[10]En 1911 déjà, Elihu Root écrivait :

« To codify municipal law is to state in systematic form the results of the law-making process already carried on through its established institutional forms. *To codify international law is primarily to set in motion and promote the law-making process itself* in the community of nations in which the institutional forms appropriate for carrying on of such a process have been so vague, indistinct and irregular that they could hardly be said to exist at all. »

Root, « The Function of Private Codification in International Law », *American Journal of International Law*, vol. 5 (1911), p. 579 (c'est nous qui soulignons).

[11]Hurst, « A Plea for the Codification of International Law on New Lines », *Transactions of the Grotius Society*, vol. 32 (1946), p. 151.

exclusivement jurisprudentiel. À sa base se trouve le fameux livre de Bracton, dont plus de la moitié est reprise du droit romain déguisé en droit naturel. Par ailleurs, son évolution est fréquemment ponctuée par des interventions législatives, et en particulier par la création de nouvelles juridictions (*Admiralty, Equity*, etc.) pour contourner la rigidité des tribunaux de *common law*. Il ne s'agit donc pas d'un produit judiciaire ou jurisprudentiel pur.

2) La deuxième critique de la codification se rapporte à son effet potentiellement destructif des règles, et cela quelle qu'en soit l'issue. Car si le processus n'aboutit pas à un accord, cela signifie qu'il existe un désaccord sur les règles coutumières préexistantes, qui par conséquent met en question leur sens et leur existence continue. Si l'accord n'est que partiel, le même danger guette les règles qui sont laissées de côté. Et même s'il y a un accord global, il risque d'intervenir au prix d'une dilution du contenu normatif des règles codifiées pour satisfaire tout le monde.

Tout cela est vrai, mais pas tout à fait vrai. Car si ce risque existe effectivement, il ne faut pas l'exagérer. Tout dépend du sérieux des préparatifs et de la qualité du travail de codification. Prenons le cas du désaccord, et même son exemple classique, celui de la largeur de trois milles marins de la mer territoriale; on dit souvent qu'on est entré à la Conférence de codification de La Haye de 1930 (convoquée par la Société des Nations) avec un semblant de règle, pour en sortir avec la conviction que la règle n'existait pas ou n'existait plus. Le processus de codification aurait ainsi détruit plutôt que consolidé la règle. Cependant, le désaccord était déjà présent, bien que sous-jacent. La règle était entamée dans son élément subjectif bien avant la Conférence qui n'a fait que révéler cet état de choses; ce qui aurait été fait de toute manière à la première occasion où la règle aurait été mise à l'épreuve s'il n'y avait pas eu de Conférence.

Quant aux dangers d'un accord partiel pour ce qu'il ne recouvre pas, il est très facile de les dissiper par des clauses de sauvegarde du type de la fameuse « clause Martens » que nous trouvons dans tous les instruments du droit des conflits armés depuis la Convention de La Haye de 1899 sur les lois et coutumes de la guerre sur terre[12].

Il en est de même pour le risque de dilution ou d'effritement du contenu normatif des règles codifiées, un danger réel auquel nous devons rester très attentifs. Mais il s'agit là de risques et de dangers inhérents à toute activité humaine qui ne condamnent pas cette activité en tant que telle et qui ne se matérialisent pas chaque fois qu'elle est entreprise, mais seulement si elle est mal conçue, mal préparée ou mal exécutée, et qui commandent par conséquent un certain degré de soin et de vigilance pour la mener à bien.

3) On reproche également à la codification qu'en associant des représentants d'États elle politise ce qui doit rester l'apanage du droit et de la technique juridique et offre aux États la possibilité de remettre en question les règles.

Mais il s'agit là d'une méprise totale sur la nature même de l'activité en cause. En effet, comme nous l'avons vu, une codification *stricto sensu*, qui n'affecterait en rien le droit préexistant tout en lui donnant une forme écrite, est une tâche impossible, de sorte que toute codification comporte une dimension législative. Or, la législation est par essence une fonction politique, qui est

---

[12]« En attendant qu'un code plus complet des lois de la guerre puisse être édicté, les Hautes Parties contractantes jugent opportun de constater que, dans les cas non compris dans les dispositions réglementaires adoptées par Elles, les populations et les belligérants restent sous la sauvegarde et sous l'empire des principes du droit des gens, tels qu'ils résultent des usages établis entre nations civilisées, des lois de l'humanité et des exigences de la conscience publique. »

confiée en droit interne aux parlements qui sont des organes éminemment politiques. Au plan international, ce sont les États qui exercent cette fonction. On ne peut donc pas, en parlant du développement du droit international, les éviter. Si on les contourne à l'étape de la formulation, ils nous rattraperont à celle de l'application des règles, même non codifiées.

Les États sont les acteurs principaux dans ce domaine. La seule manière d'avoir un droit international dynamique est de les associer au processus de son développement. S'il y a des désaccords ou des contestations, ce n'est pas nécessairement une mauvaise chose, car le désaccord peut être le premier pas vers l'accord, reflétant les prises de position initiales dans la recherche d'une reformulation de la règle qui soit acceptable pour tous comme réponse aux nouvelles circonstances.

4) Une quatrième critique adressée à la codification est que, contrairement à la législation interne qui, une fois adoptée, abroge et remplace le droit préexistant, un traité de codification ne supplante pas totalement les règles coutumières qu'il codifie et qui continuent à exister en dehors de la communauté conventionnelle établie par le traité, avec tous les inconvénients d'une dualité de régimes juridiques.

Cela n'est vrai cependant que si l'on juge la codification par référence à la législation interne. Or, elle n'en est qu'un reflet lointain, car il lui manque l'effet immédiat et *erga omnes* de la loi, étant donné l'absence d'un pouvoir législatif centralisé et l'effet relatif des traités. Mais si l'on considère la codification dans sa spécificité internationale, comme un processus à effet « cumulatif » ou « progressif » dans le temps, on peut espérer que, si elle est bien faite, cette dualité disparaîtra avec le temps, soit par l'élargissement progressif de la communauté conventionnelle, soit parce que la coutume en dehors du traité finira par évoluer à son image, comme nous le verrons plus loin.

c) *La codification privée ou scientifique est-elle une alternative réelle ?*

Il est à noter que tous ces désavantages et inconvénients sont attribués à la codification par traité, qu'il est impossible de distinguer du « développement progressif ». Les mêmes critiques proposent en lieu et place une autre variété de codification dite « privée » ou « scientifique », qui permettrait, selon eux, une codification *stricto sensu*. Elle serait entreprise par des personnes de haute stature et compétence, agissant à titre privé et non en tant que représentants d'États, et poursuivant des méthodes scientifiques rigoureuses, en d'autres termes politiquement neutres et scientifiquement objectives. Ces personnes seraient en mesure d'établir l'état du droit comme il est, d'en fournir une transcription fidèle, une sorte d'instantané photographique de la *lex lata*. Ce qui n'empêcherait en rien ces auteurs de faire des propositions d'amélioration *de lege ferenda*, tout en opérant clairement et rigoureusement la distinction entre les deux types de propositions.

En effet, des efforts importants dans ce genre viennent immédiatement à l'esprit, tels celui du Suisse Bluntschli au XIXe siècle ou les projets d'articles préparés dans le cadre de la Harvard Research in International Law, sous la direction de Manley O. Hudson, initialement entrepris en anticipation de la Conférence de La Haye, mais qui ont continué au-delà; sans oublier les travaux de vénérables institutions, tels l'Institut de droit international, l'International Law Association et l'American Law Institute.

Tout en reconnaissant son utilité, il faut cependant relever les limites de ce type de codification. Car, aussi bien faite et importante qu'elle soit, une telle codification n'a formellement que le poids et la valeur d'une œuvre doctrinale; bien que sa pesanteur réelle et sa valeur persuasive dépendent, comme pour toute œuvre scientifique, des preuves qu'elle fournit (*evidence*) pour étayer sa formulation de la règle, et qui sont pour certains de ces projets (tel celui de Harvard) assez exhaustives.

Mais hormis cet étalage de matière première, est-il vraiment possible de faire de la codification *stricto sensu*, même en forme de codification privée ? En premier lieu, il convient de constater que la matière première n'est pas abondante en droit international. Il existe trop de lacunes et la pratique disponible se prête à trop d'interprétations pour qu'il soit possible d'en tirer des formules générales, des propositions normatives, sans opérer beaucoup de choix interprétatifs et d'ajouts de pièces manquantes. Par ailleurs, même avec les meilleures intentions au monde et l'emploi de la méthode la plus scientifique, il subsiste une part de jugement subjectif qui est conditionnée par l'environnement et la vision du monde des auteurs. Ainsi, le *Restatement of the Foreign Relations Law of the United States* de l'American Law Institute est très utile non pas comme une présentation neutre et objective de la *lex lata* internationale, mais de la vision américaine du droit international, vision très influente, certes, mais qui ne se confond pas avec le droit international en tant que tel.

Évidemment, il est possible d'entreprendre ce genre de codification par des équipes multinationales. Mais l'exercice devient immédiatement plus difficile, car le choix entre plusieurs interprétations possibles, pour citer Kelsen, est toujours un choix politique, impliquant un jugement de valeur.

C'est précisément pour cette raison qu'on a recours à ces équipes multinationales, afin de représenter un large éventail de systèmes de valeurs en fonction desquels les choix seront effectués. Mais dès qu'intervient la « qualité représentative », elle introduit avec elle le facteur politique, car elle comporte la reconnaissance des limites du « technique », et par conséquent la nécessité de rechercher des compromis politiques pour les dépasser. On se retrouve donc dans un cadre identique ou presque à celui de la Commission du droit international.

C'est la raison pour laquelle même les sociétés savantes, telles que l'Institut de droit international ou l'International Law Association, qui ont essayé depuis le XIXᵉ siècle de servir tant bien que mal d'oracle, en l'absence d'autres voix ou arènes, à une certaine *opinio juris* scientifique au niveau international, ont perdu beaucoup de leur influence dès lors qu'il est devenu possible, surtout grâce aux Nations Unies, d'entendre cette *opinio juris* directement de la bouche des États, plutôt que d'en recevoir une version au second degré ou de seconde main.

Par ailleurs, la codification « publique » ne débouche pas nécessairement sur un traité de codification, car elle peut emprunter la forme d'une résolution. Mais avant d'examiner cette variante de la codification, il convient de recenser rapidement les mécanismes institutionnels qui se sont établis au sein des Nations Unies en ce domaine.

B. *Les résolutions « normatives »*

Par « résolutions normatives », ou « à vocation normative », nous entendons celles qui se veulent porteuses, c'est-à-dire qui servent de « support » ou de vecteur à des propositions normatives de caractère général.

Les résolutions « normatives » doivent être distinguées de celles qui sont adoptées par un organe dans l'exercice du pouvoir réglementaire dont disposent certaines organisations internationales en vertu de leur traité constitutif, et qui s'apparente sous certains aspects au pouvoir législatif en droit interne, telles l'Organisation internationale du Travail, l'Organisation mondiale de la santé et l'Organisation de l'aviation civile internationale, sans oublier le cas particulier de l'Union européenne. La catégorie qui nous intéresse ici est celle des résolutions qui ne portent pas formellement en elles-mêmes que la valeur d'une « recommandation ».

a) *Avantages et désavantages de la résolution normative*

Quels sont les avantages et les désavantages de l'utilisation des résolutions normatives par rapport aux traités de codification comme moyen de développement du droit international ?

Les résolutions normatives semblent *a priori* avoir l'avantage d'être l'issue d'un processus moins compliqué et plus rapide que celui menant à un traité de codification, avec un résultat largement comparable. En d'autres termes, elles permettent de doter la coutume ou le droit international général d'une transcription écrite perfectionnée et mise à jour, sans passer par la lente procédure de préparation d'une convention de codification (Commission du droit international, conférence, ratification). Deux éléments expliquent cet avantage : l'insertion de ce processus dans le cadre institutionnel de l'Assemblée générale elle-même, ce qui facilite grandement son déroulement; et le fait qu'une telle résolution est adoptée par vote ou par consensus, sans passer par un « consentement à être lié » formel et individuel (dans le sens de la Convention de Vienne sur le droit des traités), qui est toujours lent et pénible à obtenir des États.

Cependant, cet avantage n'est souvent qu'apparent. Car dès qu'il s'agit de traiter d'un sujet important, qui risque de soulever des controverses, et si l'on essaye de préparer un texte soigné et largement détaillé (à haut degré de concrétisation), qui puisse être généralement accepté (à haut degré de consensus) comme l'énoncé du droit dans son domaine, le processus devient beaucoup plus laborieux et long. La Déclaration des principes du droit international touchant aux relations amicales et la coopération entre les États conformément à la Charte des Nations Unies et de la définition de l'agression en sont de bons exemples, chacune ayant requis sept ans de préparation au sein des comités spéciaux respectifs.

De plus, les avantages susmentionnés ont leurs propres inconvénients. En effet, la facilité relative avec laquelle on peut adopter des résolutions comporte la tentation d'aller trop vite de l'avant, de « bâcler » le travail et d'adopter des textes qui ne sont pas tout à fait au point quant à la concrétisation et l'affinage de leur contenu normatif ou à la mobilisation d'un large consensus sur ce contenu (voir l'exemple de la Charte des droits et devoirs économiques des États[13]).

Par ailleurs, l'énoncé de règles par résolution laisse dans l'ombre la question du fondement de leur caractère obligatoire, en d'autres termes de leur source formelle. Car, contrairement au traité, la résolution ne saurait changer ce fondement ou fournir cette source, étant donné qu'elle n'en constitue pas une, du moins formellement.

Ainsi, la résolution ne dissipe pas en elle-même l'équivoque qui pourrait subsister quant à l'existence juridique de la règle avant l'adoption de la résolution ou dans la formulation adoptée. Cependant, il ne s'agit pas là d'une simple codification « privée », car elle a derrière elle le poids de la communauté internationale organisée, du moins des États qui ont voté pour elle.

---

[13]Résolution 3281 (XXIX) de l'Assemblée générale en date du 12 décembre 1974.

Vue sous cet angle, la résolution comme moyen de développement du droit international apparaît comme une espèce hybride entre la codification par traité et la jurisprudence. Du point de vue de la forme, la résolution nous fournit un texte écrit, couvrant un sujet ou un ensemble cohérent de règles de droit international formulées de manière générale — c'est-à-dire abstraite et prospective — exactement comme la codification par traité. Mais quand on vient à la base ou au fondement juridique de ces règles, on doit expliquer leur force obligatoire, de la même manière que pour la jurisprudence, par des facteurs ou des considérations qui dépassent l'instrument ou le support d'expression de la règle en tant que tel, qu'il s'agisse de la coutume ou autre chose.

b) *Circonstances favorisant le recours à la résolution*

Ces forces et faiblesses des résolutions normatives déterminent les facteurs qui favorisent le recours ou le choix de cet instrument dans certaines circonstances.

Le premier de ces facteurs est celui du temps. Si un besoin normatif urgent se fait sentir dans la communauté internationale, elle préférera enregistrer rapidement les grandes lignes de la réponse qu'elle préconise dans une résolution, quitte à en perfectionner la formulation et à en élaborer les détails par la suite, éventuellement dans des instruments plus contraignants. C'est le cas par exemple de la Déclaration des principes juridiques régissant les activités des États en matière d'exploration et d'utilisation de l'espace extra-atmosphérique[14], ou de la Déclaration des principes régissant le fond des mers et des océans, ainsi que leur sous-sol, au-delà des limites de la juridiction nationale[15].

La résolution représente dans un tel cas une première approximation rapide d'une réponse juridique, un premier pas ou une première étape, ainsi qu'une mesure provisoire ou conservatoire (*stop-gap*), jusqu'à ce qu'une réponse normative plus complète et définitive soit prête.

Même sans urgence particulière, la résolution peut jouer le rôle d'un premier pas ou d'une première étape dans la recherche de réponses normatives adéquates. Nous retrouvons ici le processus cumulatif qui caractérise la fonction législative internationale. Mais il est clair que nous parlons dans ces deux cas de l'élaboration d'un nouveau droit beaucoup plus que de la codification d'un droit préexistant, même retouché et mis à jour au cours de l'opération.

Deux autres circonstances, découlant de ce qui précède, peuvent entrer en ligne de compte pour favoriser le choix de la résolution. La première d'entre elles est le fait qu'il existe parfois suffisamment de consensus sur quelques aspects ou certaines lignes générales, mais pas sur tous les points et en tout cas pas sur les détails de caractère opératoire. La formule de la résolution peut enregistrer un tel résultat plus facilement qu'un traité, qu'on préfère être un produit juridique « fini » ou « accompli » quant à son contenu, au sens d'être normativement autosuffisant.

On formule parfois cette même considération d'une autre manière, en disant que la résolution s'impose quand le contenu normatif est par trop général ou trop politique pour être inclus dans un traité. Ce qui n'est pas tout à fait juste. Car ce n'est ni la nature « politique » de l'objet ni la « généralité » des propositions normatives qui les rendent moins aptes à figurer dans un traité. C'est plutôt, d'une part, l'absence — à côté des principes généraux — de règles opératoires qui

---

[14]Résolution 1962 (XVIII) de l'Assemblée générale en date du 13 décembre 1963.
[15]Résolution 2749 (XXV) de l'Assemblée générale en date du 17 décembre 1970.

les spécifient en termes de droits et obligations concrets pour leurs destinataires (mais cela peut arriver également dans un traité). D'autre part, si l'objet est hautement controversé, de sorte qu'il est fort improbable qu'un traité le réglant soit largement accepté et ratifié par les États, la voie de la résolution est préférée. La matière ainsi traitée est « politique » dans le sens de « controversée », mais non par référence à sa nature intrinsèque, car un grand nombre de traités portent sur des questions hautement politiques (traités de paix, d'alliance, de désarmement, etc.).

La seconde circonstance qui favorise le recours à la résolution se présente lorsqu'il s'agit de développer des règles, principes, ou notions figurant déjà dans le traité constitutif d'une organisation, et plus particulièrement dans la Charte des Nations Unies. Car dans ce cas le traité existe déjà, et il ne s'agit que d'élaborer et d'arrêter en commun le sens et les conséquences concrètes de certaines normes qui y figurent, même s'il s'agit également de normes de droit international général. En d'autres termes, il s'agit ici d'interpréter le traité, ce qui ne justifie pas aux yeux des États membres (ou pas suffisamment) le temps et l'effort nécessaires pour la préparation d'un autre traité; alors que s'ils ne figuraient pas dans le traité constitutif, le développement de ces principes et de ces règles aurait bien pu faire l'objet d'un traité.

2. Rapport au droit international général

A. *La coutume comme explication polyvalente*

Le traité, même s'il a pour tâche de codifier et de développer le droit international, n'en reste pas moins un traité à effet relatif limité aux États qui l'ont ratifié. Sur quelle base peut-on concevoir que son contenu puisse s'imposer en tant qu'énoncé du droit international général en dehors de ce cercle limité, c'est-à-dire dans la marge, large ou étroite, entre la communauté convention-nelle et la communauté internationale dans son ensemble ? De même, la réso-lution a beau être « normative », elle ne porte cependant formellement que le statut de résolution de l'Assemblée générale, qui ne nous aide pas beaucoup à expliquer juridiquement comment le contenu de la résolution s'impose à la communauté internationale comme énoncé du droit international général. Pour trouver des réponses à ces interrogations, on a recours à la théorie traditionnelle des sources, pour en sortir la coutume comme une explication polyvalente qui répond à tous les besoins.

Il est vrai qu'avec l'essor du processus de l'Article 13 de la Charte on avait l'impression qu'on allait progressivement codifier l'ensemble du droit interna-tional et que les conventions de codification allaient graduellement remplacer la coutume et la pousser vers le statut d'une source purement historique.

Paradoxalement cependant, c'est ce même mouvement de codification et de développement progressif du droit international qui, après un certain temps, fournira l'occasion de faire à nouveau appel à la coutume et de reposer la question de son rôle en droit international contemporain. Comble de paradoxe, cette occasion se présente en 1969 — c'est-à-dire l'année même qui marque l'apogée du mouvement de codification avec l'adoption de la Convention de Vienne sur le droit des traités — en la forme de l'arrêt de la Cour internationale de Justice dans les affaires du *Plateau continental de la mer du Nord*[16].

---

[16]*Plateau continental de la mer du Nord (République fédérale d'Allemagne/Danemark; République fédérale d'Allemagne/Pays-Bas), arrêt, C.I.J. Recueil 1969*, p. 3.

a) *La coutume et les traités de codification*

Cette affaire avait trait au statut juridique de l'article 6 de la Convention de Genève de 1958 sur le plateau continental, qui prévoit l'utilisation de la méthode de l'équidistance pour délimiter le plateau continental des pays limitrophes ou se faisant face, sous certaines conditions et avec certaines exceptions. La question était de savoir si l'équidistance est une règle de droit international général, s'imposant par conséquent au-delà de la communauté conventionnelle de la Convention de Genève (en l'espèce à la République fédérale d'Allemagne).

La Cour est arrivée à la conclusion qu'elle n'était qu'une simple règle conventionnelle. Mais pour y arriver, elle a dû examiner en détail les modes d'interaction entre les traités de codification et la coutume, ce qui a immédiatement suscité l'attention de la doctrine et a donné lieu à une littérature abondante et riche d'enseignements. La quintessence de ces analyses a été résumée de manière aussi simple que frappante par Eduardo Jiménez de Aréchaga, ancien président de la Cour internationale, dans son cours général de 1978[17], en classant les effets possibles que les traités de codification peuvent produire par rapport à la coutume en trois catégories :

— Un effet déclaratoire d'une coutume déjà existante, simple transcription qui lui apporte une expression écrite, sans ajouter à son contenu normatif ni à son statut de règle de droit. C'est l'effet d'une codification *stricto sensu*.

— Un effet cristallisant une coutume naissante, dont le processus de maturation en tant que règle coutumière est mené à terme à travers l'élaboration, la négociation et l'adoption du traité de codification; de sorte que la norme coutumière et son reflet codifié achèvent leur parcours en même temps, l'un portant l'autre dans sa lancée au point d'aboutissement. En d'autres termes, le processus de codification affecte et accélère la formation de la coutume au-delà de son cadre; le meilleur exemple à cet égard est le rôle qu'a eu la troisième Conférence des Nations Unies sur le droit de la mer dans l'avènement en droit international général de l'institution de la zone économique exclusive (dont on pourrait à la limite soutenir qu'elle est arrivée à maturation avant même la conclusion de la Convention).

— Un effet générateur d'une nouvelle coutume, partant du texte et à son image. La convention propose à la communauté internationale une solution commode à un certain problème; la pratique internationale la suit, de sorte que (à la manière d'une *self-fufilling prophecy*) la règle conventionnelle finit par se doubler d'une règle coutumière. Contrairement à l'effet déclaratoire, où la coutume est à la base du texte (son *input*), la coutume est ici le produit du texte (son *output*).

b) *La coutume et les résolutions normatives*

Pour ce qui est des résolutions normatives, de nombreuses analyses doctrinales se sont efforcées également de saisir et d'expliquer leurs effets juridiques par leur interaction avec la coutume. Examinons trois des plus marquantes.

Une première théorie ou réflexion, très simple, commence par constater que les résolutions ont inversé l'ordre chronologique et l'importance relative des deux éléments de la coutume. Auparavant, on exigeait beaucoup de pratique et on inférait indirectement, de la continuité et de la conséquence de cette

---

[17] « International Law in the Past Third of a Century », *Recueil des cours de l'Académie de droit international de La Haye*, vol. 159 (1978-I), p. 14 à 22.

pratique qu'il existait une conviction juridique. La pratique précédait donc cette conviction, qu'on ne pouvait déceler qu'à travers elle. La pratique était donc antérieure dans le temps et plus abondante en volume que l'*opinio juris*, qui n'était qu'une simple projection psychologique de cette pratique. Avec les résolutions, on arrive à une situation où la conviction juridique nous vient directement et explicitement de la bouche des États, qui nous disent ce qu'ils considèrent comme droit. Et cela se passe parfois avant même que la pratique ne se dessine ou du moins ne se consolide. On est donc devant une *opinio juris* déclarée, qui peut même précéder la pratique; en présence de laquelle, notamment si elle est réitérée, on peut se contenter de peu ou de moins de pratique pour constater ou établir l'existence de la coutume[18].

D'autre part, Madame Bastid a qualifié ces résolutions d'« étape » dans l'évolution du droit, c'est-à-dire une station intermédiaire entre la *lex ferenda* et la *lex lata*, qui suivrait en forme de coutume voire de traité[19].

Enfin, la fameuse résolution de 1963 sur le droit de l'espace[20] a fourni au professeur Bin Cheng l'occasion de formuler sa qualification ingénieuse de ces résolutions comme « coutume instantanée » (*instant custom*)[21].

Si les deux premières théories mettent l'accent sur l'effet « générateur » de ces résolutions par rapport à la coutume, tout en faisant apparaître le rôle plus crucial encore de l'*opinio juris* dans cette forme particulière du processus coutumier, le professeur Bin Cheng se contente exclusivement de cette *opinio juris*, reléguant la pratique au rôle de simple agent révélateur dont on peut se passer si l'*opinio juris* est révélée par d'autres moyens.

Tout en reconnaissant à chacune de ces tentatives d'explication théorique son rôle pionnier et sa part de vérité, il est possible de dire qu'à l'heure actuelle la très grande majorité de la doctrine est d'avis que les résolutions normatives de l'Assemblée générale peuvent susciter les mêmes modes d'interaction avec la coutume que ceux que la Cour a identifiés par rapport aux traités de codification, c'est-à-dire qu'elles peuvent produire les mêmes effets potentiels que ceux-ci, déclaratoires, cristallisants ou générateurs de règles coutumières.

Toutes ces analyses mènent ainsi à la conclusion que paradoxalement le mouvement de codification et de développement progressif du droit international en la forme de traités ou de résolutions — mouvement ayant précisément pour but la transcription de la coutume et son remplacement par une *lex scripta* — a donné un second souffle et un nouveau rôle grandissant à la coutume. C'est également un rôle plus démocratique, car cette nouvelle variété de coutume ne reflète pas seulement la pratique de quelques États puissants, mais les desiderata de la communauté internationale dans son ensemble.

Cette manière de voir, qui met l'accent sur la vigueur, l'actualité et l'importance renouvelées de la coutume, est en passe de devenir la nouvelle orthodoxie quant au rôle de la coutume en droit international contemporain.

---

[18]Voir par exemple, Abi-Saab, « The Development of International Law by the United Nations », *Revue égyptienne de droit international*, vol. 24 (1968), p. 100 et 101; et Dupuy, « Coutume sage et coutume sauvage », dans *La communauté internationale : Mélanges offerts à Charles Rousseau* (1974), p. 84.

[19]Bastid, « Observations sur une "étape" dans le développement progressif et la codification des principes du droit international », dans *Recueil d'études de droit international en hommage à Paul Guggenheim* (1968), p. 132.

[20]Voir *supra*, note n° 20.

[21]« United Nations Resolutions on Outer Space : "Instant" International Customary Law? » *Indian Journal of International Law*, vol. 5 (1965), p. 23.

B. *La « nouvelle coutume » et l'ancienne*

Il est permis cependant de se demander si cette analyse est la plus appropriée, si elle est la plus proche de la réalité des choses et si, en parlant de cette « nouvelle coutume » ou « coutume nouvelle vague », on parle toujours de la même coutume. Pour tenter de répondre à de telles interrogations, il serait nécessaire de comparer cette nouvelle version de la coutume avec l'ancienne, en vue d'isoler le nouveau du permanent; en d'autres termes d'identifier ce qui les réunit et ce qui les sépare.

a) *Les deux fonctions de la coutume traditionnelle*

La coutume ancienne mouture remplissait deux fonctions essentielles dans le système traditionnel du droit international (comme d'ailleurs en droit interne). La première et la plus substantielle, c'était d'apporter des solutions commodes et apparemment équitables aux problèmes qui se posent dans la pratique; et cela par approximations successives, par tâtonnements (*trial and error*). C'est un processus auquel s'applique à la perfection l'image utilisée pour décrire la démarche de la *common law* : « trébucher sur la sagesse » (*stumbling into wisdom*); une sagesse ou une solution sage, qui s'affirme et s'affine, se décante et s'explicite d'un précédent à l'autre. C'est la fonction essentielle de la coutume dans un système qui manque de pouvoir législatif centralisé, en tant que source matérielle du contenu des règles.

Mais dans un système juridique, il ne suffit pas de trouver la bonne proposition normative. Il faut en plus la consacrer, lui conférer une légitimation formelle, la faire passer par l'une des sources formelles. Et la coutume remplissait également cette fonction, mais à titre subsidiaire. Elle assurait ainsi le passage « de la régularité à la règle », selon la belle formule de Jean Combacau[22], du « néant » à l'« être » juridique.

La coutume traditionnelle jouait donc à la fois le rôle de source matérielle qui fournit la substance et de source formelle qui fournit la consécration formelle de la règle, son entrée dans l'univers du droit et son intégration au *corpus juris*.

Le *modus operandi* de la coutume dans l'accomplissement de cette seconde fonction, c'est-à-dire la transformation d'une idée ou d'une solution substantielle en norme obligatoire, ou le passage du précédent au statut de règle générale de droit, reste cependant un processus mystérieux et une des énigmes permanentes du droit international. Et pourtant, c'est la capacité d'opérer ce passage, qui fait de la coutume une des sources formelles du droit international, c'est-à-dire un processus reconnu par le système juridique, qui permet de transformer des intérêts et des valeurs sociales en normes obligatoires. Et c'est précisément cet aspect-là qui est invariablement escamoté dans l'analyse de la coutume.

En effet, la plupart des analyses doctrinales, consciemment ou inconsciemment déplacent l'accent du processus qu'elles n'arrivent pas à capter, vers les conditions qui doivent être remplies par le produit final de ce processus, c'est-à-dire vers les deux éléments de la coutume[23].

---

[22]C'est le titre de son « ouverture » du numéro spécial de la revue *Droits* (nº 3, mars 1986), consacré à la coutume.

[23]C'est l'une des thèses maîtresses du professeur Roberto Ago que de considérer que « le droit en vigueur » peut jaillir directement du corps social, en forme de « droit spontané », sans passer par une « source formelle »; en d'autres termes, de considérer la coutume comme une alternative au droit posé ou positif plutôt qu'une de ses variantes. Voir par exemple son cours, « Science juridique et droit international », *Recueil des cours de l'Académie de droit international de La Haye*, vol. 90 (1956-II), p. 851.

b) Le « processus » de la coutume traditionnelle

Le processus lui-même reste ainsi toujours insaisissable, car il s'agit d'un processus exogène, autonome, d'une dynamique émanant directement du corps social, en dehors de tout cadre préétabli, qui est ni réglementé, ni centralisé, ni canalisé. C'est un processus *stricto sensu* dont le système juridique ne prend acte que du résultat, et non un procédé, qui est, selon la définition de François Gény, une procédure prescrite et réglementée par le système lui-même en vue de produire certains effets[24].

C'est donc un mode spontané ou inconscient de création du droit. Mais cela ne veut pas dire que les actions et les réactions qui constituent les précédents sont des actes inconscients. Au contraire, celles-ci sont presque toujours entreprises en vue de parvenir à une certaine solution à un problème actuel ou de la faire échouer. Ce sont donc des actes volontaires qui visent des résultats voulus. Et la solution qui constitue le précédent représente le point d'équilibre (mais pas nécessairement de rencontre) entre les différentes volontés en présence. Mais ce qui n'est pas, ou pas nécessairement, recherché et voulu, c'est « l'effet normatif secondaire », c'est-à-dire la projection de cette solution au-delà de son cadre ponctuel, son abstraction et sa généralisation, en un mot sa transformation en règle générale de droit.

Enfin, il s'agit d'un processus hétérogène; il n'y a pas d'identité, ni de continuité, ni de prévisibilité quant à ceux qui y participent, ni quant aux modalités de son déroulement, y compris dans l'espace et dans le temps. En d'autres termes, il est ad hoc de tous points de vue, agissant de manière ponctuelle, imprévisible et discontinue, au gré des circonstances. C'est ce qui le rend rebelle à toute approche systématique.

Le produit de ce processus est une règle non écrite, qui doit être décelée rétrospectivement, par induction directe du comportement social, des matériaux constituant les différents précédents, et qui est formulée par celui qui est appelé à l'appliquer, ce qui lui laisse une très grande liberté d'appréciation.

c) Le « processus » de la nouvelle coutume

Si nous nous tournons vers la nouvelle coutume, nous constatons que sur tous ces points la situation est l'exact inverse. En lieu et place d'un processus sauvage, rebelle à tout encadrement, on trouve un procédé qui, loin d'être spontané, est utilisé de manière très consciente, dans un but de production normative prononcé et qui est intégré et centralisé au sein du système des Nations Unies, et par conséquent hautement institutionnalisé, avec des procédures préétablies (bien qu'évolutives) et des mécanismes qui fonctionnent de manière stable et continue.

Son produit final est lui aussi très différent. Ce sont des instruments écrits, qui comportent des règles formulées de manière abstraite, générale et prospective, en fonction des situations à venir. Leur interprétation et leur application sont celles des textes écrits. C'est une démarche essentiellement déductive et qui, bien qu'impliquant nécessairement un certain choix de la part de celui qui les entreprend, lui laisse bien moins de liberté que les règles non écrites. Enfin, la preuve de ces règles est également différente. Car l'accent est mis sur l'acceptation générale de la règle plutôt que sur la pratique générale qui la sous-tend.

Ainsi donc, l'universalisation de la communauté internationale, plutôt que d'accroître à son image l'hétérogénéité du processus coutumier, a conduit

---

[24]Voir Gény, F., *Science et technique en droit privé positif* (1921), tome 3, p. 47 et 48, par. 193.

paradoxalement à sa centralisation et à sa concentration dans le cadre du système des Nations Unies. De fleurs sauvages, les règles coutumières sont devenues des plantes de serre, des perles de culture.

d) *La fonction de la « nouvelle coutume » en droit international contemporain*

Ce changement radical, aussi bien dans le processus que dans son produit final, n'est que le reflet d'un changement parallèle dans la fonction que cette nouvelle coutume est appelée à remplir dans le système. Il ne s'agit plus, même à titre subsidiaire, de servir de source matérielle, de trouver et de développer le contenu de la règle (ce qui est et reste la fonction première et primordiale de la coutume traditionnelle). Ce contenu est déjà préparé avec le plus grand soin et dans les plus petits détails avant que la coutume n'entre en scène.

Par rapport à ces dispositions longuement négociées et minutieusement préparées, la coutume n'est appelée qu'après coup, exclusivement comme source formelle et à titre subsidiaire, pour combler le vide entre l'effet relatif du traité de codification et la portée universelle du droit international général, ou pour couvrir le terrain juridiquement vague entre la résolution normative et la terre ferme de la *lex lata*. La coutume sert ainsi de perche pour opérer le saut juridique au-delà de ce vide ou de ce terrain vague. En d'autres termes, par rapport à ces règles toutes faites, la coutume est appelée à leur conférer une légitimation formelle ou plus exactement la marge de légitimation qui leur manque pour devenir du droit international général.

C. *Un processus original de formation de droit ?*

Comment classifier ou qualifier juridiquement ce nouveau mode de production juridique ? Est-ce toujours de la coutume ?

a) *Un processus cumulatif*

Si par coutume on veut simplement désigner tout le droit non conventionnel, on peut alors considérer cette nouvelle coutume comme incluse dans ce sens très large ou cette définition négative du terme (abstraction faite de la théorie volontariste qui considère la coutume comme un accord tacite). Si, en revanche, on comprend par coutume un processus spécifique de génération ou de création normative, on ne peut ignorer les différences entre la coutume traditionnelle et la nouvelle. Ce sont des voies très différentes, pour arriver, il est vrai, au même résultat qui est la production de règles de droit international général. Mais ici on parle de la coutume en tant que source formelle, c'est-à-dire de mode de production normative et non pas de son produit. Et ce mode, comme on vient de le voir, est fondamentalement différent.

À moins que l'on considère que l'élément distinctif de ce processus soit son caractère « cumulatif », en ce sens qu'il produit son effet de manière « progressive » (*incremental*) et non pas « instantanée ou immédiate » (bien que la nouvelle coutume ait aussi des jalons bien précis dans le temps, comme l'adoption de la convention ou de la résolution). Mais est-ce un élément suffisant pour définir la coutume, c'est-à-dire pour saisir toute son essence et sa spécificité ? Il est permis d'en douter.

b) *Un processus législatif, sans effet législatif*

Si nous regardons la réalité en face, sans lunettes ni œillères techniques, nous voyons que la communauté internationale, confrontée au dilemme de la création du droit international général dans le monde éclaté qui est le nôtre, à la fois très hétérogène et très interdépendant, a développé un procédé original de production normative. En internalisant et en institutionnalisant le processus de création du droit international général, elle s'est forgée une procédure ou un procédé législatif, mais — et c'est un grand mais — sans parvenir à lui adjoindre un effet législatif, en l'absence d'un pouvoir législatif centralisé.

Et c'est précisément là qu'on fait appel à la coutume, pour parfaire ce procédé, remplacer le chaînon manquant et combler le hiatus entre le « procédé » et le « pouvoir », en attribuant un « effet législatif » à ce qui a été conçu comme un « acte législatif », sans pour autant pouvoir atteindre sa finalité par ses propres moyens.

C'est la raison pour laquelle, bien que par son encadrement et son déroulement ce procédé se rapproche beaucoup plus que la coutume traditionnelle de la notion de « source formelle », il ne correspond que de loin au type idéal de la législation.

i) *Les échappatoires*

Etant donné la répartition très inégale et très diffuse du pouvoir dans le monde, réalité reconnue par le droit international (faute de pouvoir l'influencer), ce procédé qui s'est développé au sein des structures onusiennes se voit assorti d'échappatoires. En d'autres termes, ce qu'on voit se dessiner sous nos yeux est un pouvoir législatif avec des possibilités de s'y soustraire, par des mécanismes de *contracting-out*, évoquant vaguement le modèle du pouvoir réglementaire qu'on trouve dans la constitution de certaines organisations internationales; sauf qu'il s'agit ici d'un procédé général, c'est-à-dire qui relève du système juridique international en tant que tel et non pas d'un traité constitutif donné.

Si le procédé lui-même s'est clarifié et a acquis un profil reconnaissable, on ne peut en dire autant pour ce qui est des échappatoires, qui font l'objet actuellement d'une lutte au sein de la communauté internationale ayant trait aux possibilités, aux conditions et aux modalités de s'en prévaloir. D'où l'intérêt renouvelé dans ce qu'on a pu percevoir comme une remontée du volontarisme, ainsi que dans le syndrome de l'« objecteur tenace » (*persistent objector*). C'est une lutte qui se situe au niveau de l'évolution constitutionnelle de la communauté internationale (qui rappelle celle engagée il y a deux décennies autour du *jus cogens*), et dont la partie de bras de fer entre les États-Unis et la grande majorité de la communauté internationale sur le régime juridique de la zone internationale en haute mer n'est que l'épisode le plus récent et le plus spectaculaire.

ii) *Le cas de l'« objecteur tenace »*

À cet égard, la notion d'« objecteur tenace » mérite un petit détour. Beaucoup de cas sont faits de cette vague théorie selon laquelle un État qui ne peut empêcher une règle coutumière de se former peut du moins, par sa résistance continue, s'extraire de son champ d'application. Et cela sur la base d'un seul énoncé de la Cour internationale de Justice dans l'affaire des *Pêcheries*[25], qui a été étirée hors contexte et au-delà de toute proportion; ce qui appelle quelques clarifications.

En premier lieu, on doit distinguer la coutume générale ou universelle de la coutume spéciale. Cette dernière repose toujours sur un fond ultime de consentement et s'accommode bien, par conséquent, d'un phénomène tel que

---

[25] *Affaire des Pêcheries, Arrêt du 18 décembre 1951 : C.I.J. Recueil 1951*, p. 116.

l'« objecteur tenace ». Il n'en va pas de même de la coutume universelle. Nous devons distinguer également le contexte particulier de l'énoncé de la Cour internationale de Justice, qui est celui de la délimitation par un État de ses eaux territoriales; un contexte qui soulève la problématique de l'appropriation territoriale et qui fait par conséquent appel à des institutions juridiques telles que l'acquiescement, l'effectivité, les titres historiques, dont l'effet total est de faire de presque chaque espèce un cas d'espèce, et où le consentement ou son absence joue un rôle crucial.

C'est un contexte quasi patrimonial, très différent de celui de la création du droit international général et des traités-lois à vocation franchement universelle, donc législative, notamment quand ils visent la protection d'intérêts communautaires. Dans ce dernier contexte, l'objecteur tenace ne peut qu'être un phénomène transitoire. Ou bien il réussit à empêcher la règle de se former, ou bien, si la règle s'affirme, celle-ci balaye l'objection de son chemin; une dynamique qui est parfaitement illustrée par le sort de la résistance au *jus cogens* au cours des années 60.

Un autre point mérite encore clarification à propos de l'objecteur tenace. Il s'agit du caractère solidaire ou intégral de l'instrument de codification et de développement progressif, ou plutôt de la réglementation juridique qu'il porte. Car il ne s'agit pas d'un assemblage fortuit de règles qui se sont formées au gré du hasard, mais de l'issue d'un processus long et complexe de formulation détaillée et de négociation, dont le produit final doit être accepté comme un tout, comme un *package deal*.

En réalité, même si on suit l'explication coutumière de sa projection en droit international général, on doit cependant reconnaître que la coutume intervient ici *ex post facto*, après l'élaboration de la réglementation normative intégrée; et l'interaction s'opère avec le contenu de l'instrument adopté comme un tout, et non pas avec ses composantes individuelles; ce que démontre bien certaines études récentes[26].

En d'autres termes, si la réglementation normative portée par l'instrument de codification (traité ou résolution) se maintient et finit par rejoindre le droit international général malgré l'opposition de l'objecteur tenace, elle le fera comme un tout et non en pièces détachées, en fonction des objections (cela ne préjuge en rien l'évolution subséquente de cette réglementation en réponse aux demandes de son environnement).

Pour conclure

Il est évidemment possible de continuer de représenter cette situation en termes de coutume, solution de facilité intellectuelle, qui permet de faire passer ou accepter plus aisément cette manière de créer le droit sans pouvoir législatif formalisé. Mais on doit être conscient que cette représentation comporte une bonne part de fiction.

S'il faut faire appel à la fiction, cependant, mieux vaut le faire non pas pour cacher ou occulter le fossé grandissant entre un nouveau phénomène juridique en pleine évolution et une explication théorique figée, mais pour mieux adapter l'explication théorique à ces nouvelles réalités et la rendre moins réfractaire à

---

[26]Voir : Jennings, « Law-Making and Package Deal|», *Mélanges offerts à Paul Reuter* (1981), p. 341; et Caminos et Molitor, « Progressive Development of International Law and the Package Deal|», *American Journal of International Law*, vol. 79 (1985), p. 871.

leur égard. En d'autres termes, mieux vaut le faire pour faciliter plutôt qu'entraver le fonctionnement et l'efficacité de la nouvelle coutume.

Nous pouvons par exemple admettre (ne serait-ce que *de lege ferenda*) certaines présomptions, telles, à l'instar des Tribunaux militaires de Nürnberg et de Tokyo pour les crimes de guerre[27], la présomption qu'un traité de codification et de développement progressif qui perdure pour un certain laps de temps est censé avoir passé en droit international général. Une telle présomption peut être absolue (irréfragable, Nürnberg), ou simple (Tokyo) sous certaines conditions (qui incluraient *inter alia* celles du *contracting out*). De même, on peut identifier certains indices objectifs qui serviraient comme présomptions plausibles témoignant du passage des résolutions normatives en droit international général.

---

[27] *Judgement of the International Military Tribunal for the Trial of Major War Criminals*, Cmd. 6964 (1946), p. 64; *Judgement of the International Military Tribunal for the Far East for 1948, United Nations War Crimes Commission, Law Report of Trials of War Criminals*, vol. 15 (1949), p. 13. Cf. Baxter, « Multilateral Treaties as Evidence of Customary International Law », *British Year Book of International Law*, vol. 41 (1965/1966), p. 299.

OVERVIEW OF THE INTERNATIONAL LAW-MAKING PROCESS
AND
THE ROLE OF THE INTERNATIONAL LAW COMMISSION

by Yuri M. Kolosov*

Introductory remarks

The international law-making process began thousands of years ago, initially through the formation of customary law. The most ancient written bilateral treaty which is known to us is the treaty which was concluded in 1296 B.C. between the king of Egypt, Ramses II, and the king of Hittia, Khattusilis. Unions of cities and communities in the Greece of the sixth century B.C. were based on treaties—treaties which are, perhaps, the earliest multilateral conventions in the history of international law. It was only in the nineteenth century, though, that the codification of international law began. Indeed, as an integral part of the international law-making process, it only really came into being in the middle of this century, with the establishment of the International Law Commission.

The notion of codification as a means of law-making is, then, a very recent phenomenon, at least as far as international law is concerned. At the same time, law has come to be of ever-increasing importance in the conduct of modern international relations. The General Assembly of the United Nations has accordingly given repeated emphasis to "the importance of furthering the progressive development of international law and its codification as a means of implementing the purposes and principles set forth in the Charter of the United Nations".[1] It has also repeatedly stressed the role which the International Law Commission plays in that process—a role which the Commission has fulfilled to date by preparing over 20 sets of draft articles.[2]

Other United Nations bodies have been involved in the law-making process, too, of course, among them the United Nations Commission for International Trade Law (UNCITRAL), the Human Rights Commission and the Committee on the Peaceful Uses of Outer Space, as well as a number of ad hoc bodies. The specialized agencies—the International Labour Organization, the International Civil Aviation Organization, the United Nations Educational, Scientific and Cultural Organization, the International Telecommunications Union and so on—have also actively contributed to the law-making process. Mention should be made, too, in this connection of the activities of regional

*Professor of International Law, Moscow State Institute of International Relations, Moscow, Russian Federation.
    [1]See, for example, the second preambular paragraph of General Assembly resolution 51/160 of 16 December 1996.
    [2]See Report of the International Law Commission on the work of its forty-eighth session, *Official Records of the General Assembly, Fifty-first Session, Supplement No. 10* (A/51/10), pp. 329-334. See also "Introduction: the Achievement of the International Law Commission", in United Nations, *International Law on the Eve of the Twenty-first Century: Views from the International Law Commission* (1997), pp. 1-8 (United Nations publication, Sales No. E/F 97.V.4).

international organizations, such as the Organization for Security and Co-operation in Europe, the Council of Europe, the Commonwealth of Independent States, the Organization of American States and the Organization of African Unity.

Most of these various treaty-making mechanisms have produced legal instruments of a specialized character. In contrast, the draft conventions which the International Law Commission has elaborated are general in nature, in the vast majority of cases, at least. Moreover, the Commission is, perhaps, the only existing law-making mechanism which successfully combines both the codification and the progressive development of international law.

The International Law Commission is, of course, not really a treaty-making body. Treaty-making competence remains vested with the principal subjects of international law—States—as well as with intergovernmental organizations in so far as they may become parties to the negotiations. Within the United Nations, even the General Assembly has no law-making competence as such. In the words of Article 13, paragraph 1, of the Charter of the United Nations, it can only "initiate studies and make recommendations for the purpose of: (a) promoting international co-operation in the political field and encouraging the progressive development of international law and its codification". The General Assembly has fulfilled this function through its Sixth Committee and through the International Law Commission. Actual treaty-making takes place at international conferences of plenipotentiaries or is undertaken by the General Assembly itself, in which case the Assembly in fact transforms itself into a diplomatic conference. So, when we characterize the International Law Commission as a "treaty-making body", what we really mean is that it is a "draft treaty-making body" or, alternatively, that it is a "law-making body"—though, in the latter case once more, what we really have in mind is that it is involved in a preliminary stage of the law-making process.

The International Law Commission and its work have been much criticized over the course of the last two decades. Claims have been made that the Commission is no longer playing the central role that it once did in the international law-making process.[3] It is said that one of the reasons why this is so is that the Commission has failed to accommodate itself to the momentous changes which have taken place in the community which it serves.[4] It has also been said of late that so-called "soft" law has come to be a no less important part of the international legal process than treaty law.[5] This, in turn, is said to indicate that the treaty-making process itself has diminished somewhat in terms of its role and importance.

Notwithstanding such criticism, the International Law Commission will, in my view, continue, as it has done in the past, to play an important role in the process of international law-making. In 1985 Carl-August Fleischhauer, the then Legal Counsel of the United Nations, remarked that "the highly responsible process of codification and progressive development of international law under UN auspices has a long and bright future".[6] The international legal profession can, together, help make this prediction a reality. The role which the Commis-

---

[3]See, for example, Cede, "New Approaches to Law Making in the UN System", *Austrian Review of International and European Law*, vol. 1 (1996), p. 51 at p. 54.

[4]Ibid., at p. 55.

[5]Ibid., at pp. 52 and 54.

[6]Fleischhauer, "The United Nations and the Progressive Development and Codification of International Law", *Indian Journal of International Law*, vol. 25 (1985), p. 1 at p. 7.

sion has to play is, after all, even more important at this, the intersection of the twentieth and twenty-first centuries; for the Commission is a body which is uniquely placed both to meet the need for an evaluation of the present state of international law and, on the basis of the results of such an evaluation, to identify future trends in the treaty-making process.

The primacy of international law

The idea of the primacy of international law in international relations has been one which has concerned international lawyers for centuries. In 1625, Hugo Grotius wrote about the "sanctity" of agreements between States[7]—a term which, at that time, was understood to mean "inviolability". One of the promoters of the first and the second world peace conferences of 1899 and 1907, the Russian jurist Fedor Martens, dreamed of "the domination of law in the relations between peoples".[8]

The reality of international relations has been less encouraging and has led some modern lawyers to a somewhat pessimistic conclusion:

"Political and governmental actors have often treated international law as subordinate to political, military, strategic, or economic considerations. International lawyers, on the other hand, have sometimes tended to exaggerate the significance of international law and to ascribe to it possibilities that it does not possess. This tendency does not strengthen the position of international law . . ."[9]

The drafters of the Charter of the United Nations did not share this opinion, though, when, in 1945, they declared, in the third preambular paragraph of the Charter, their determination "to establish conditions under which justice and respect for the obligations arising from treaties and other sources of international law can be maintained".

This ideal has yet to be achieved. Sometimes this failure has been explained by making reference to the insufficiency of international rules, as well as by reference to the specific nature of the international legal system, particularly the absence within that system of a law-enforcement mechanism. Although these are undeniable facts, one cannot fail to take note of some important trends in the field of the implementation of international law. Suffice it to mention here the decisions of the Security Council on sanctions, a number of monitoring mechanisms which exist in the field of human rights, the European Court of Human Rights being but one example, and the international criminal tribunals which have recently been established. The international community is, then, moving slowly but surely towards accepting a law-enforcement system in international relations. Perhaps, it will be possible after all to achieve the ideal of the establishment of the primacy of international law. In this connection, one cannot but endorse the words of the current Legal Counsel, Mr Hans Corell, who, at the 1995 United Nations Congress on Public International Law, affirmed, in his opening statement, the importance of the effective application of the principles and rules of international law as the surest way towards achieving peace and harmony among nations.

---

[7]Grotius, H., *O Prave Voini i Mira* (3 vols., 1956), p. 825 (in Russian).
[8]Martens, F.F., *Sovremennoe Mezhdunarodnoe Pravo Tsivilizovannih Narodov*, vol. 1 (1996), pp. 10-21 (in Russian).
[9]Damrosch and Müllerson, "The Role of International Law in the Contemporary World", in Damrosch, L., Danilenko, G.M., and Müllerson, R. (eds.), *Beyond Confrontation: International Law for the Post-Cold War Era* (1995), p. 1 at p. 1.

In the light of these circumstances, the International Law Commission might wish to examine the possibility of elaborating draft articles on the issue of international law enforcement. Such a draft might combine the codification of existing rules with the formulation of some proposals *de lege ferenda*. Of course, the preparation of such a draft should not be approached from a purely idealistic perspective. As Professor Graefrath has remarked, "political and legal considerations are interrelated in the work of the [International Law Commission] and the Sixth Committee"[10] and "the Commission must be convinced, from the beginning to the end of its work on a topic, that it has the political backing of the international community, as expressed in the annual debate of the Sixth Committee".[11] At the same time, though, the adoption of the primacy of international law is in itself a political decision. To assist in that decision, the Sixth Committee might wish to entrust to the International Law Commission the task of preparing a study on the meaning of the concept of the primacy of international law in inter-State relations.

Vertical and horizontal law-making processes

In many areas cooperation between States takes place simultaneously both at the regional and at the universal level. Examples are numerous. Disputes, for instance, may be settled through regional mechanisms—such as the methods which exist within the framework of the Organization for Security and Co-operation in Europe—or by means of universal institutions—such as the International Court of Justice or the Permanent Court of Arbitration. International security, to take another example, relies both upon regional treaties—such as the Treaty on Conventional Armed Forces in Europe12—and, at the same, upon conventions of a universal character—such as the Convention on the Prohibition of the Development, Production, Stockpiling and Use of Chemical Weapons and on Their Destruction.[13]

In such cases, the regional and universal mechanisms concerned have an equal degree of importance. No hierarchy exists between them. Any contradictions which there may be between the treaties concluded at these two levels must simply be avoided. The difference between such treaties may accordingly be characterized as "horizontal" in nature. One can, moreover, hardly speak of international law undergoing any form of "fragmentation".

It is part of the International Law Commission's task to take into account international legal instruments which are adopted at the regional, and even at the bilateral, level. That being so, it would only be sensible to strengthen and reinforce relationships between the Commission and regional bodies which are involved in international law-making.

At the same time, treaty-making takes place both within the various different branches of international law—such as outer space law or maritime law—and within an "all-embracing" or "multisectoral" context—as with the law of treaties or the law regarding the effects of the occurrence of a succession of States. Thus, rules of international responsibility exist in various branches of international law. At the same time, the International Law Commission has approached the task of drafting articles on State responsibility in such a way as

---

[10]Graefrath, "The International Law Commission Tomorrow: Improving Its Organization and Methods of Work", *American Journal of International Law*, vol. 85 (1991), p. 595 at p. 600.

[11]Ibid., p. 601.

[12]Document CD/1064.

[13]Document CD/CW/WP.400/Rev.1.

to make the draft articles which it is preparing applicable within all spheres of international life.

Both of these methods would seem to be indispensable. The difference between them, however, is of a character which might be characterized as "vertical". To put it another way, it would be unrealistic to have different rules governing treaty-making in the fields of, say, air law and humanitarian law.

Various bodies and specialized agencies of the United Nations have expertise in particular concrete spheres. The International Law Commission, on the other hand, must have a much broader vision or remit. Horizontally, the Commission has been successful in drafting articles which are acceptable to States from all regions of the world. Vertically, the Commission should concentrate on "multisectoral" topics, the rules which it drafts being applicable to most, if not all, fields of international relations. Among such topics, one might mention the problem of the sources of international law (in the light of the new developments in that domain) and the issue of the subjects or actors of international law.

Codification and progressive development of international law: Mission accomplished or ceaseless quest?

The International Law Commission has recognized that many of the major topics which have traditionally been identified as being ripe for codification have now been addressed and their consideration completed. The Commission, however, has not accepted the view that the task of codifying international law is accomplished. Rather, it has taken the position that the codification and progressive development of international law are a continuing process; for, even in respect of those areas in which codification treaties have already been adopted, new developments will inevitably arise in practice.[14]

This evaluation is, in my view, thoroughly justified. International law is, in essence, a reflexion of the current state of affairs in international relations and international relations, of course, are always changing, constantly giving birth to new problems and to new fields of enterprise which require legal regulation.

There are, moreover, several areas of international relations which, though they are hardly new, have, none the less, acquired or taken on new dimensions during the last few decades. The International Law Commission might wish to look into them and see whether they are ripe for codification and progressive development. Among these areas, one might mention, in particular, international cooperation, the suppression of terrorism, the right to international solidarity of peoples, international sanctions and the territorial integrity of States.

Continuity or "sporadicity" in the codification and progressive development of international law

International relations have been growing ever more intense during the present century and there is no indication that matters will be any different in the century to come. While the codification of international law is something which takes place in the wake of practice and of the formation of customary law, the progressive development of international law may sometimes be undertaken before there has yet been any actual practice in a field. Exemplary in this respect is the Agreement Governing the Activities of States on the Moon and Other

---

[14]Report of the International Law Commission on the work of its forty-eighth session, loc. cit. above (footnote 2), p. 207 at para. 171.

Celestial Bodies of 1979,[15] article 11 of which sets out the legal principles which are to govern the exploitation of the Moon's natural resources, even though such exploitation has yet to become feasible.

While there are all sorts of treaty-making bodies and diplomatic processes which exist under the aegis of the specialized agencies of the United Nations, many are of an ad hoc nature and lack perpetuity. They are, moreover, usually involved in responding to problems which have already emerged. So, for example, to take the case of unlawful interference with civil aviation, there were over 100 cases of hijacking[16] before the adoption, under the aegis of the International Civil Aviation Organization, of the Convention for the Suppression of Unlawful Seizure of Aircraft of 1970[17] and the Convention for the Suppression of Unlawful Acts Against the Safety of Civil Aviation of 1971.[18] Again, it was only in the wake of the Chernobyl disaster that the International Atomic Energy Agency drafted and organized the adoption in 1986 of two conventions on the subject of nuclear catastrophes: the Convention on Early Notification of a Nuclear Accident[19] and the Convention on Assistance in the Case of a Nuclear Accident or Radiological Emergency.[20]

Against this background, one would probably be justified in saying that the preventative function of international law deserves more attention, especially in such important spheres as the environment and armed conflict. Disasters may be prevented through the adoption and application of meaningful international legal rules only if a careful holistic study of trends in international affairs is undertaken on an ongoing basis and an effort made to elaborate pertinent treaties or legal instruments in a prompt and timely fashion. The International Law Commission is well placed to perform such a function. To this end, the Commission might include in the agenda of one of its future sessions the task of preparing an overview of current trends in inter-State relations. To the same end, the Sixth Committee of the General Assembly might also give some consideration to this subject. In this way, the International Law Commission might play a coordinating role in the overall international law-making process, helping to initiate and steer efforts for the codification and progressive development of international law by the various organs, bodies and agencies within the United Nations system which are possessed of law-making responsibilities.

The third world peace conference of 1999, whatever its format may be, might also make some contribution to predicting the shape and direction which international relations will take in the twenty-first century. The conference, in addition, might suggest topics involving the codification and progressive development of international law which the International Law Commission might wish to consider for possible inclusion in its programme of work.

"Soft" law

Many modern scholars claim that resolutions and declarations of universal and regional international organizations give rise to what they like to term "soft"

---

[15]United Nations, *Treaty Series*, vol. 1363, p. 3.
[16]See document A/7656.
[17]United Nations, *Treaty Series*, vol. 860, p. 105.
[18]Ibid., vol. 974, p. 177.
[19]Ibid., vol. 1439, p. 275.
[20]Ibid., vol. 1457, p. 133.

law.[21] Some go further and, like Franz Cede, claim that "the concept of soft law has introduced a flexible and dynamic element into international law-making".[22]

In my view, however, "soft" law has no real legal connotation. Any legal norm must be expressly agreed upon between the subjects of international law. Only violations of juridical norms, moreover, may give rise to international responsibility,[23] which is, furthermore, the most powerful instrument of law enforcement in international relations. Resolutions of international organizations may be used only as a subsidiary means for the determination of rules of international law, along with the teachings of publicists and judicial decisions.

Nevertheless, it does remain the case that resolutions of international organizations may testify to the emergence of a new rule of customary international law—a rule which may in due course require codification. This leads me to suggest that the International Law Commission might wish to include in its programme of work the task of conducting an overview of the resolutions of international organizations with the aim of identifying emerging new customary rules of international law.

The role of teachings and resolutions of scientific bodies in the codification and progressive development of international law

The International Law Commission's Special Rapporteurs have, in the course of their work, drawn greatly upon the teachings of publicists and the conclusions and recommendations of academic or scientific bodies and institutions. Academic writings are often used by Special Rapporteurs to gain preliminary insights into the questions of international law which they are researching. Various scholars mention, too, the impact which doctrine has had upon the progressive development of international law.[24] So, for example, some scholars and academic bodies suggest in their writings possible topics for the progressive development of international law. Some go further still and suggest the very form which that progressive development should take. Thus, in 1990 a number of scholars from Germany, the United States of America and the former Soviet Union prepared a draft convention on manned space flights, which the International Institute of Space Law agreed to submit to the Legal Sub-Committee of the United Nations Committee on the Peaceful Uses of Outer Space.[25]

Two shortcomings of comprehensive codification conventions which are readily apparent are the failure of some of them to gather a sufficient number of ratifications and accessions—as, for example, with the two Vienna conventions on State succession—and the fact that others have attracted an excessive number of reservations and interpretative declarations—for example, the United Nations

---

[21]See, for example: Charney and Danilenko, "Consent and the Creation of International Law", in Damrosch et al., op. cit. above (footnote 9), p. 23 at pp. 50-51; Malanczuk, P., *Akehurst's Modern Introduction to International Law* (7th. rev. ed.; 1997), pp. 54-55; and Lukashuk, I.I., *Mezhdunarodnoe Pravo: Obschaya Chast* (1996), pp. 102-104 (in Russian).

[22]Loc. cit. above (footnote 3), p. 54.

[23]On the origin of international responsibility, see draft article 1 (3) of the International Law Commission's Draft Articles on State Responsibility, as provisionally adopted by the Commission on first reading: Report of the International Law Commission on the work of its forty-eighth session, loc. cit. above (footnote 2), at p. 125.

[24]Slomanson, W.R., *Fundamental Perspectives on International Law* (2nd. ed., 1995), pp. 21-22.

[25]For the text of this draft and its accompanying commentary, see Böckstiegel, "Draft for a Convention on Manned Space Flight", in *Zeitschrift für Luft- und Weltraumrecht*, vol. 40 (1991), p. 3.

Convention on the Rights of the Child.[26] Yet one cannot help thinking that a careful study of the academic literature might have helped to avoid these problems, in so far as it might have helped to make clear the acceptability or otherwise of the drafts of these instruments to the States of the different regions of the world.

Fleischhauer has expressed the view that:

"[t]here must be a careful choice of the subjects in relation to which international law is to be developed. This requires ascertaining, by whatever preliminary inquiries are appropriate, whether there is likely to be sufficient measure of international agreement on sufficiently important legal points to make it worthwhile to initiate the long, complex and often costly treaty-making process."[27]

One of the tasks which the International Law Commission might undertake is periodically to conduct overviews of the academic literature with the aim of identifying and evaluating new suggestions regarding topics for possible inclusion in the Commission's programme of work. It would, of course, be essential in this connection that the Commission receive adequate and effective support from the Secretariat of the United Nations.

---

[26]General Assembly resolution 44/25 of 20 November 1989, Annex.
[27]Loc. cit. above (footnote 6), at p. 6.

MAJOR COMPLEXITIES ENCOUNTERED IN CONTEMPORARY INTERNATIONAL LAW-MAKING

by Peter Tomka*

I

This Colloquium is dedicated to commemorating the fiftieth anniversary of the establishment of the International Law Commission, which came into being on 21 November 1947, when the General Assembly of the United Nations adopted its resolution 174 (II), to which the Commission's Statute was annexed.

This fiftieth anniversary provides a particularly welcome opportunity to take stock of the development of international law-making since the United Nations and the International Law Commission were established as well as to review the changes which the international legal order has undergone in that time.

A simple comparison of recent manuals or treatises on international law with those which were published shortly after the Second World War leads to one clear conclusion: international law has undergone major changes, both in substance and in form.

As far as the changes in substance are concerned, international law has, first, broadened its scope *ratione materiae* to provide legal regulation for the new activities of mankind or to cope with the challenges which mankind has faced. New branches of international law, previously unknown, have developed since 1945, such as the law of outer space, the law concerning peaceful uses of nuclear energy and the law of environment. Secondly, even the traditional branches of international law have undergone changes in substance as a consequence of societal changes in the international community. Thus, new institutions have emerged within the traditional branches of international law such as the law of the sea, the institutions of the continental shelf and of the exclusive economic zone and the concept of the common heritage of mankind being the most prominent examples.

Turning to the changes in form, it cannot but be remarked that, while custom was the predominant form of international law when the United Nations was created, multilateral conventions have since come to the foreground in a dramatic way. Hundreds upon hundreds of international conventions have issued from the law-making activities of States within intergovernmental organizations, dozens of them the outcome of the implementation by the United Nations of its mandate under the Charter. As the current Secretary-General has recently stressed, the most encompassing manifestation of the strength enjoyed by the United Nations, stemming from its universality of membership and the comprehensive scope of its mandate, is in the normative realm.[1] One has to agree with his evaluation that the United Nations has produced impressive results in

---

*Ambassador. Legal Adviser, Ministry of Foreign Affairs, Slovak Republic.
[1]*Renewing the United Nations: A Programme for Reform*, Report of the Secretary-General, document A/51/950, p. 10 at para. 8.

a great variety of fields, including the progressive development and codification of international law.[2]

I have no intention of underestimating the role of custom as a form of universal, or general, international law, being fully aware of the relative, or *inter partes*, effect of treaties, as reflected in article 34 of the 1969 Convention on the Law of Treaties. None the less, I would like to emphasize that multilateral conventions are nowadays one of the key evidences of general customary international law. Of course, one has to take a cautious and prudent approach and to study all of the relevant circumstances before coming to the conclusion that a particular provision in a convention reflects a customary rule, either because it codifies a pre-existing custom or because it has given rise to a new State practice which has in turn generated a new customary rule. The jurisprudence of the International Court of Justice provides a number of examples. Such a role is played *par excellence* by the conventions codifying and progressively developing international law which have been elaborated on the basis of the drafts which the International Law Commission has produced.

The topic assigned to me in the framework of this Colloquium is major complexities encountered in contemporary international law-making. I am not going to deal with the international law-making process in the United Nations in general, nor with the law-making processes in the specialized agencies. I might mention, though, that these questions have been the subject of a three-year multidimensional project, sponsored by the American Society of International Law, the results of which appeared on the eve of the celebration of the United Nations fiftieth anniversary in 1995 as an excellent two-volume publication, edited by Oscar Schachter and Christopher C. Joyner, under the title *United Nations Legal Order*. A revised, updated and abridged version of this work was published this year in a single volume, edited by Christopher C. Joyner, under the title *The United Nations and International Law*.

As this Colloquium should focus on the International Law Commission, I shall confine my attention to the law-making process in which the International Law Commission participates and is involved.

II

The International Law Commission was established in 1947 by the General Assembly as its principal subsidiary organ for discharging its responsibilities under Article 13, paragraph 1 (*a*), of the Charter of the United Nations, namely, "to initiate studies and make recommendations for the purpose of . . . encouraging the progressive development of international law and its codification". While the Statute of the Commission makes the distinction between "progressive development of international law" and "codification of international law", the draft articles prepared by the Commission have always combined both elements or approaches. Accordingly, and also as matter of convenience, I shall use here the expression "codification process" to characterize that international law-making process in which the International Law Commission is involved.

The codification process can be divided into several stages. Roberto Ago, for instance, distinguishes three fundamental stages in the codification of international law.[3] The first stage consists in the selection of the topic, the

---

[2]Ibid., para. 9.

[3]Ago, "La Codification du droit international et les problèmes de sa réalisation", in *Recueil d'études de droit international en hommage à Paul Guggenheim* (1968), p. 93 at p. 102. It is evident that the term codification is used by Ago to denote both the process itself and its end product.

preparation of reports, the discussion of these reports and the elaboration of drafts. The second stage is represented by the convening of a conference of States with a view to discussing the draft and adopting the text of a convention on its basis. Finally, in the third stage, the task is to secure for the text so adopted the final consent of States: first, the consent of the number of States which is required for the convention's entry into force and, then, of a larger number of States, so that the convention may acquire the authority of a real codification.

A former Director of the Codification Division of the Office of Legal Affairs of the United Nations Secretariat, Professor Movchan, also sees in the codification process three distinct stages.[4] He particularly emphasizes the importance of the selection of a topic, which is sometimes a subject of much debate between Member States in the political organs of the United Nations. This leads him to the conclusion that the selection of a topic for codification represents the first stage of the whole process. It is followed by the second stage, which encompasses the identification and elaboration of the rules concerned and their framing in a written, systematically structured document. This stage accordingly covers both the preparatory work in the Commission, as well as the work of the ensuing diplomatic conference. The third, and last, stage of the codification process consists in the recognition and confirmation of these rules as rules of international law.

A different approach is taken by the Polish academic, Professor Klaf-kowski.[5] He adopts as a criterion for distinguishing between stages the end product of the process. On this basis, he makes a distinction between four stages of the codification process. The first one is represented by the resolutions of the General Assembly, the second by declarations of principles for certain areas of international relations, the third by the elaboration of draft articles or draft conventions and the fourth by the adoption of the texts of conventions, either at a special diplomatic conference or as the annex to a resolution of the General Assembly.

Any such classification is, however, not a matter of principle, but, rather, a way of describing, more or less aptly, the process which objectively exists.

To start the codification process, it is necessary to determine the topic which will be the object of the codification effort. Accordingly, the selection of a topic is a prelude to, or a prerequisite for, the codification process. This process, once started, includes the elaboration of a draft, the consideration and adoption of the draft by States and finally the ratification and the entry into force of the end product.

Accordingly, I shall try to identify some of the difficulties of the codification process in which the International Law Commission is involved and to propose possible answers or remedies to them.

Selection of the topic and its allocation to the appropriate body

To set the codification process in motion, then, the General Assembly needs to select a topic and to allocate it to an appropriate body.

The International Law Commission may be the principal subsidiary body which the General Assembly has established under Article 22 of the Charter in order to assist it in discharging its responsibilities under Article 13, paragraph 1,

---

[4]Movchan, A.P., *Kodifikatsya i Progressivnoye Razvityie Mejdunarodnovo Prava* (1972), p. 117 (in Russian).
[5]Klafkowski, A., *Prawo Miedzynarodowe Publiczne* (6th ed., 1981), p. 55 (in Polish).

but it is far from being the only United Nations organ which is involved in the progressive development and codification of international law. While the Commission is the standing body in the United Nations for public international law "manufacturing",[6] the General Assembly has also established a number of ad hoc committees, which have produced the drafts of many conventions. Typically, these ad hoc committees have reported to the Sixth Committee (Legal) of the General Assembly. However, even the Sixth Committee has not maintained its "monopoly" in supervising the making of international law within the United Nations. In fact, it never had one.

The whole area of international law of the environment has been developed in the United Nations outside the Sixth Committee, with the major participation of the United Nations Environment Programme (UNEP) and the Second Committee (Economic and Financial) of the General Assembly. Similarly, the United Nations law-making effort in the field of human rights has been supervised and under the responsibility of another Main Committee of the General Assembly: its Third Committee (Social, Humanitarian and Cultural). Disarmament law has been mostly developed by the United Nations Conference on Disarmament and the First Committee (Political and Security) of the General Assembly. Outer-space law provides another example of an area of international law that has remained beyond the reach of the Sixth Committee while being developed through the United Nations.

This brief survey leads us to the conclusion that there exists a plurality of law-making bodies in the United Nations, not to mention the United Nations specialized agencies. Law-making in the international community, then, is fragmented, at least as far as fora are concerned. However, I consider this problem,[7] if it exists at all, to be moot.

One has not to forget that, while the United Nations and its specialized agencies provide fora for law-making activities, they do not have the power to legislate. The United Nations is not a real law-giver.[8] Limiting our attention here to the international *lex scriptum*, what transforms a text into law is the consent of States, expressed in the necessary form. International *lex scriptum* is the product of the international legislative activities of States and embodies their express consent. States are the law-makers, not the Organization, which simply represents a useful forum for this form of State activity. States retain the final control and they should take care to avoid contradictions between the different normative acts which they jointly produce. However, even if such a contradiction occurs, international law, in particular the law of treaties, provides a remedy in the form of such principles of interpretation as *lex specialis derogat legi generali* and *lex posterior derogat legi priori* and in the rules contained in Article 30 of the 1969 Vienna Convention on the Law of Treaties concerning the application of successive treaties relating to the same subject matter.

I thought it useful to offer this remark, as concern has sometimes been expressed over the fragmentation of international law-making and the proposal has sometimes been advanced that the International Law Commission be en-

---

[6]The other permanent legal organ involved in law-making in the United Nations is the United Nations Commission on International Trade Law; but I do not consider the law of international trade to be part of public international law.

[7]Report of the International Law Commission on the work of its forty-eighth session, *Official Records of the General Assembly, Fifty-first Session, Supplement No. 10* (A/51/10), p. 207 at para. 170.

[8]The term is used by Joyner, in "The United Nations as International Law-Giver", in Joyner, C.C. (ed.), *The United Nations and International Law* (1997), p. 432.

trusted with a kind of supervisory or coordinating function. It is difficult to imagine how the Commission could effectively perform such a function and at the same time continue to fulfil its principal task of progressively developing and codifying international law.

The International Law Commission, by virtue of its composition and working methods, is unique among the bodies involved in law-making within the United Nations. This should be kept in mind when the General Assembly is deciding to which organ it should refer a topic for consideration and for the elaboration of a draft.

The Commission is particularly suited to dealing with topics which require a detailed, in-depth study of State practice or the use of an inductive approach in order to ascertain the customary rules which are established by State practice, discovering *lacunae* and formulating proposals to fill them. The Commission could hardly be replaced in performing such a task by an ad hoc committee composed of the representatives of States. It is doubtful whether such an ad hoc committee would have been able to prepare more efficiently than the Commission a draft such as that which the Commission prepared on the law of treaties. On the other hand, the Commission could have prepared equally well certain of the drafts which were negotiated directly in ad hoc committees.

In my view, the General Assembly should carefully weigh the "pros" and "cons" of referring a topic to the Commission or to an ad hoc committee. Whereas the Commission should be entrusted with topics which require substantive research or the application of an inductive approach in order to identify rules of customary international law, bodies of the latter type should deal with topics which require political compromises to be reached in formulating legal rules in order to respond to the pressing needs of the international community. The nature of a topic, not its importance, should guide the General Assembly in making its decision on the allocation of topics.

According to the Commission's Statute, the Commission should survey the whole field of international law with a view to selecting topics for codification and, when the Commission considers that the codification of a particular topic is necessary or desirable, it should submit its recommendation. The Commission is entitled to undertake substantive work on the topic, though, only once the General Assembly has taken a decision to that effect, authorizing the Commission to start its work. Moreover, the Commission has to give priority to requests of the General Assembly to deal with any question. While, at the very beginning of Commission's life, there was some discussion whether priority should be given to every request of the General Assembly,[9] practice has meant that this question must now be answered in the affirmative.

Once the General Assembly has decided to request the Commission to undertake a work of codification, the process is set in motion.

The codification process in the International Law Commission

I do not intend to deal in detail with the process of codification in the International Law Commission, since it is well known. Rather, I shall concen-

---

[9]In particular, Georges Scelle, the leader of the so-called "autonomists", held the view that this should not be the case. In his opinion, article 18 of the Commission's Statute, properly interpeted, did not place the Commission entirely and without qualification at the disposal of the General Assembly. See *Yearbook of the International Law Commission, 1949*, p. 12 at para. 34 and p. 14 at para. 47.

trate on some aspects of that process which are sometimes the subject of criticism.

Frequently the process is considered too lengthy or slow. Is this criticism justified?

Usually, it has taken about 10 years for the Commission to prepare a draft, the process involving two readings of that draft and the solicitation of written comments from States between its first and second readings. For example, the set of 73 draft articles which the Commission prepared on the law of the sea was produced over the course of seven years, between 1949 and 1956. The draft which served as the basis of the 1961 Vienna Convention on Diplomatic Relations was prepared in four years, between 1954 and 1958; while it took six years, from 1955 to 1961, for the Commission to prepare its 71 draft articles on consular relations.

To prepare the draft which was subsequently transformed into the 1969 Vienna Convention on the Law of Treaties required a larger and much longer effort from the Commission, the Commission working on the draft for 17 years, between 1949 and 1966. A remark should be made here, however. It is beyond doubt that the topic was a difficult one; but this was not the only reason for the length of the preparatory process. That was the result of at least two or three other factors—factors which may have a more general relevance. The first was the fact that there were four successive Special Rapporteurs assigned to the topic, the first having decided not to run for re-election and the two who followed having resigned after their election to the International Court of Justice. The second was the fact that the Commission was hard at work on a number of other topics during much of the period concerned and consequently had little time left to consider the reports submitted by its Special Rapporteurs on the law of treaties. Thus, while the Commission discussed the first and second reports of the first Special Rapporteur on the topic, Professor Brierly, it did not discuss his third report, as he had since resigned from the Commission. The second Special Rapporteur, Professor Lauterpacht, as he then was, submitted two reports, but the Commission was unable to discuss either of them. When, after Lauterpacht's resignation, the third Special Rapporteur, Sir Gerald Fitzmaurice, was appointed, he prepared his drafts *de novo* and framed them in the form of an expository code. While he submitted five reports, the Commission was able to discuss them only once, in 1959, when it gave particular attention to his first report. The fourth Special Rapporteur, appointed in 1961, was Professor Humphrey Waldock. At this stage, the Commission changed its approach and opted for the elaboration of a draft convention. Between 1962 and 1966, Waldock prepared five reports, on the basis of which the Commission adopted, in two readings, 75 draft articles with commentaries. It was a quite remarkable achievement that the Commission was able, within a single quinquennium, to adopt an entire draft on such an important, complex and vast topic.

The 50-article draft which was to become the 1969 Convention on Special Missions was prepared between 1964 and 1967 on the basis of four reports from the pertinent Special Rapporteur, though some consideration had previously been given to this topic at the Commission's 1959 and 1960 sessions.

With regard to the issue of relations between States and international organizations, the Commission, bearing in mind General Assembly resolution 1289 (XIII) of 5 December 1958, decided at its fourteenth session, in 1962, to put the topic on the agenda of its next session, in 1963, and appointed a Special Rapporteur. His first report was submitted in 1963 and considered by the

Commission that same year. The following year, he submitted a working paper on the scope of the subject and the method for its treatment. This paper served as the basis of the Commission's conclusion that "the question of diplomatic law in its application to relations between States and intergovernmental organizations should receive priority". Since, in 1965 and 1966, priority was given in the Commission's work to the completion of its draft on the law of treaties, the topic did not receive any attention in those years. However, starting with 1967, the topic was at the centre of the Commission's attention and, within a quinquennium, between 1967 and 1971, the Special Rapporteur submitted five reports (his second to his sixth). On the basis of these reports, the Commission elaborated, over two readings, a set of 82 draft articles, completing its work in 1971. The Commission, then, was basically able to prepare the draft within five years, there being also some short discussion of the topic at two sessions in the preceding quinquennium.

In 1976, the Commission started its consideration of the second part of the topic, namely, the status, privileges and immunities of international organizations, of their officials and experts and of other persons engaged in their activities other than the representatives of States. The Commission continued its work on this part of the topic over the course of the following 15 years, between 1977 and 1991, but with some interruptions because of the priority which was given to other, more advanced drafts. During this time, the two successive Special Rapporteurs on the topic submitted a total of eight reports between them. Not a single draft article was adopted by the Commission in these 15 years, though 22 were referred to the Drafting Committee. In 1992, the Commission met in its new composition and without a Special Rapporteur for the topic, the former Special Rapporteur having ceased to be a member of the Commission. The Commission noted that "doubts had . . . arisen as to the advisability of continuing the work undertaken in 1976 on the second part of the topic . . . , a matter which seemed to a large extent covered by existing agreements". The Commission accordingly decided not to pursue the topic any further, unless the General Assembly were to decide otherwise. The General Assembly did not lose any time in endorsing the Commission's conclusion.[10] As one commentator with inside information remarked, "after allowing the project to consume too much of its time and resources, probably more out of deference to the special rapporteur than because of any merit of the topic itself, the Commission finally delivered the *coup de grace* in 1992".[11]

The topic of succession of States in respect of treaties was chiefly studied by the Commission in the period between 1968 and 1974, though the approach to the topic of succession in general was considered briefly in 1962 and in more detail in 1963. Between 1968 and 1974, the Commission received six reports, five from one Special Rapporteur and one—the final one—from his successor. However, it should be pointed out that, because of lack of time, the Commission was unable to consider the topic at all at its 1969 and 1971 sessions and it dealt with the topic only briefly at its 1973 session, at which it appointed a new Special Rapporteur. The draft articles, then were considered at four sessions of the Commission only.

The question of the protection and inviolability of diplomatic agents and other persons entitled to special protection is an example of an efficient response

---

[10]See General Assembly resolution 47/33 of 25 November 1992.

[11]McCaffrey, "Is Codification in Decline?", *Hastings International and Comparative Law Review*, vol. 20 (1997), p. 639 at p. 645.

from the Commission to an urgent matter. The question was raised in the Commission in 1971 and, upon the General Assembly's request of the same year, the Commission prepared the draft convention at a single session in 1972—at which session it also completed the first reading of its draft articles on succession of States in respect of treaties—dispensing with the usual appointment of a Special Rapporteur and completing most of the work in a working group.

The endeavour to codify the law relating to the most-favoured-nation clause might appear to have been less successful. The topic was on the Commission's agenda for 11 years, from 1967, when the Commission appointed the first of its two Special Rapporteurs for the topic, to 1978, when it completed work on its 30-article draft. However, the Commission did not consider the topic at its 1970, 1971, 1972 and 1974 sessions, mostly because of lack of time, nor at its 1977 session, when it was awaiting written comments from States on the draft which it had adopted on first reading in 1976. In fact, the Commission's work on the topic was mostly carried out in four years: in 1973, 1975 and 1976, when it carried out the first reading, and in 1978, when it re-examined the draft on second reading. The Commission recommended to the General Assembly that the draft articles should be recommended to Member States with a view to the conclusion of a convention on the subject. However, though the General Assembly had the item on its agenda in 1978, 1980, 1981, 1983, 1985, 1988 and, finally, 1991, such a recommendation from the General Assembly never materialized. The draft was finally shelved by the General Assembly in its decision 46/416 of 9 December 1991, the draft articles being brought to the attention of Member States and interested intergovernmental organizations for their consideration in such cases and to the extent as they might deem appropriate. One may wonder whether the topic had to be inscribed on the Commission's agenda at all or, at least, whether the 13 years of agonizing in the General Assembly could not have been cut short. Did States really need 13 years to study the topic and to determine their respective positions? It is to be doubted. Something went wrong in the United Nations.

From the appointment of Mohammed Bedjaoui as Special Rapporteur in 1967 to the adoption in 1981 of the final draft of what was later to become the 1983 Vienna Convention on Succession of States in respect of State Property, Archives and Debts, 14 years elapsed. In this time, the Special Rapporteur submitted 13 reports to the Commission, but the Commission was unable to work on the topic at its sessions of 1970, 1971, 1972 and 1974, being occupied with other tasks.

The question of treaties concluded between States and international organizations or between two or more international organizations was on the Commission's work programme between 1970 and 1982. The Special Rapporteur, who was appointed in 1971, submitted 10 reports on the topic altogether between 1972 and 1981.

Consideration of the topic of the status of the diplomatic courier and the diplomatic bag not accompanied by diplomatic courier was initiated by the General Assembly in 1975 and 1976. The item was included in the Commission's agenda in 1977 and, after a preliminary consideration of the different issues involved, a Special Rapporteur for the topic was appointed in 1979. Following his appointment, he submitted, between 1980 and 1988, a total of eight reports. The only year when he did not submit a report and the Commission did not consider the item was 1987, when the Commission was waiting for written comments by States on the draft articles which it had adopted on first reading in 1986. The final text of the Commission's 32 draft articles, together with two short draft protocols, was adopted in 1989. This was a rather lengthy exercise, considering the scope of the topic. The Commission recommended that the General Assembly convene an international conference of plenipotentiaries to study the draft and to conclude a convention on the subject. However, after its consideration in the General Assembly in 1989 and at informal consultations in 1990, 1991 and 1992, the draft was shelved, without ceremony, in 1995 by a simple decision of the General Assembly.

The topic of the jurisdictional immunities of States and their property was included in the programme of work of the Commission in 1978, when the Commission also appointed a Special Rapporteur. Between 1979 and 1986, when the Commission completed the first reading of its draft, the Special Rapporteur submitted eight reports. The process of second reading was due to start in 1988, when the new Special Rapporteur on the topic submitted his first report. Because of a lack of time, though, the Commission did not consider the topic that year. The second reading was undertaken at three sessions, between 1989 and 1991, the Special Rapporteur submitting three further reports and the Commission adopting in 1991 the final text of its 22 draft articles on the subject. The Commission also adopted a recommendation to the General Assembly to convene an international conference of plenipotentiaries to consider the draft and to conclude a convention on the subject. It took 11 years for the Commission to prepare a draft consisting of 22 draft articles. The Commission's recommendation was considered by the General Assembly in 1991, 1992, 1993 and, finally, 1994, when, in its resolution 49/61 of 9 December 1994, the General Assembly decided to accept it. This decision has not led to the convening of any conference yet, though. A decision on this question should be taken either in 1997 or in 1998; but, as one of the former members of the Commission has remarked, "prospects for this project do not seem bright in the light of governments' inability to decide what to do with it".[12]

The law of the non-navigational uses of international watercourses was a topic which was recommended to the Commission by the General Assembly. The Commission subsequently included this topic in its programme of work in 1971. The final draft convention was submitted to the General Assembly over 20 years later, in 1994. The speed of the Commission's work, though, was affected by a number of factors. In particular, the work was rather slow in getting started.

The Commission considered the topic in 1974, when it set up a subcommittee to consider the question. Later at that same session, it appointed the first of the five Special Rapporteurs which were to work on the topic. The Commission did not consider the topic in 1975 at all. In 1976 it received the first report from the Special Rapporteur. In 1977 a new Special Rapporteur was appointed, who made an oral presentation of the topic in 1978 and submitted his first report in 1979, that report being considered by the Commission. In 1980 the Commission considered the Special Rapporteur's second report; but it was not able to consider the topic in the following year, as the Special Rapporteur resigned upon his election to the International Court of Justice. In 1982 the Commission appointed the third Special Rapporteur, who submitted his first report in the following year. So, 12 years after the inclusion of the topic on the Commission's agenda, the Commission was still at the very beginning of its work. The Special

---

[12]McCaffrey, loc. cit. above (preceding footnote), p. 645.

Rapporteur was able to submit his second report in 1984 and then resigned, having been elected, like his predecessor, to the International Court.

In 1985 the Commission appointed the fourth Special Rapporteur, who, at the same session, submitted his first report and then regularly supplied the Commission with further reports—seven altogether—leading to the completion in 1991 of the first reading of the Commission's draft. In 1993 the Commission appointed the fifth and last of its Special Rapporteurs, who submitted two reports, on the basis of which the Commission undertook the second reading of its draft. The final text of 33 draft articles was adopted by the Commission in 1994 and submitted to the General Assembly with a recommendation that a convention on the subject be elaborated by the Assembly or by an international conference.

The draft Code of Crimes against the Peace and Security of Mankind was on the Commission's agenda right from the start. At its first session, in 1949, the Commission appointed a Special Rapporteur and, at its third session, in 1951, it adopted its draft Code of Offences against the Peace and Security of Mankind. The Commission took up the matter again in 1953 and completed its work in 1954. On several occasions, the General Assembly deferred consideration of the item and put it on its agenda only in 1977 upon the request of a number of Member States. The topic was included in the agenda of the Commission again in 1982 and, between 1983 and 1991, on the basis of eight reports from its Special Rapporteur, it adopted on the first reading a set of draft articles. The second reading took place between 1994 and 1996, when the Commission adopted a final, substantially reduced, draft, consisting of 20 articles. Therefore, the Commission worked on the topic for four years in the early 1950s and for 11 years in the 1980s and 1990s.

It took much less time for the Commission to elaborate its Draft Statute for an International Criminal Court. While the issue was briefly considered by the Commission in 1950, work on an actual draft was begun in an ad hoc committee, consisting of 17 Member States, in 1951. A new ad hoc committee, which met in 1953, made a number of changes to the 1951 draft. The General Assembly, however, did not take any substantive action on the draft, postponing consideration of it. Upon the invitation of the General Assembly, the Commission decided in 1992 to set up a working group and, over the course of three sessions, was able to prepare a draft statute, consisting of 60 articles. The Draft Statute was submitted to the General Assembly in 1994, together with a recommendation to convene an international conference to study the draft and to conclude a convention on the establishment of an international criminal court.

This survey reveals that the Commission needed just one session to prepare a draft convention on the prevention and punishment of crimes against diplomatic agents and other internationally protected persons. The longest time was required for the elaboration of several drafts in the 1970s, 1980s and early 1990s, in particular the draft on succession of States in respect of State property, archives and debts, the draft on the law of non-navigational uses of international watercourses and the draft Code of Crimes against the Peace and Security of Mankind.

This survey also shows that, in the 1970s and 1980s, the preparatory work in the Commission slowed down. However, it was not only in the Commission that there was a deceleration in the pace of work. States themselves required longer periods in order to submit their written comments. While, in the 1950s and 1960s, they needed just a couple of months to prepare their written comments on the drafts which the Commission adopted on the first reading, starting in the early 1970s States afforded themselves usually more than a year. Curiously, this longer period did not lead to any substantial increase in the number of responses received from Member States.

Study of the Commission's reports reveals that the Commission is able to deal effectively with a maximum of three topics during its annual 12-week sessions. If it has more topics on its agenda and makes an effort to consider each one during each session, it takes longer to elaborate its final drafts. Inevitably, if more topics are considered at a session, it results in a piecemeal approach, the Commission submitting just a few articles on each topic, which which makes their consideration in the Sixth Committee more difficult.

The Commission should strive "to keep the items on its active agenda down to a manageable number".[13] Otherwise, it risks the criticism that the preparatory process is too lengthy. The Commission's goal should be to organize its work in such a way that it is able to complete final drafts on two topics during each quinquennium.

---

[13]McCaffrey, loc. cit. above (footnote 11), p. 656.

COMPLEXITIES IN CONTEMPORARY INTERNATIONAL LAW-MAKING: CHALLENGES FOR THE INTERNATIONAL LAW COMMISSION

by Francisco Orrego Vicuña*

The fiftieth anniversary of the International Law Commission affords a unique opportunity to consider the Commission's role, its achievements and the challenges which lie ahead for it. Not unlike the recent similar commemoration of the founding of the International Court of Justice, this occasion allows for an in-depth examination of the many problems that any such institution must face as time goes by and international conditions and expectations change. The present contribution deals specifically with the issues which arise from the complexities characterizing contemporary international law-making. It emphasizes ideas that could contribute to furthering the tasks of codification and progressive development of international law.

1. Where is international society going?

Authors of every epoch have been fascinated by the perspectives opened up by current changes affecting international society[1] and by the manner in which those changes influence the development of international law in the period concerned.[2] It has been rightly remarked, however, that there is nothing unusual in a phenomenon that responds to the natural evolution of a society and that is accordingly reflected in the legal order.[3] All societies are permanently accommodating the need for stability with the demands of change. International society is no exception.

Societies evolve, but it is history that is in charge of identifying the major landmarks. The Peace of Westphalia is one such landmark, indicating the emergence of modern inter-State society and the Grotian contribution to the understanding of its nature and the advancement of the role of law in its governance.[4] Hedley Bull has identified the five core features of the Grotian view of international society as follows: the central place of natural law; the universality of international society; the role of individuals and non-State groups in that society; solidarism in the enforcement of rules; and the absence of

---

*Professor of International Law, School of Law, University of Chile, Santiago, Chile.
[1]Allott, P., *Eunomia: New Order for a New World* (1990).
[2]Bos, "Aspects phénoménologiques de la codification du droit international public", in Zanardi, P.L., Migliazza, A., Pocar, F., and Ziccardi, P. (eds.), *Le Droit international à l'heure de sa codification : études en l'honneur de Roberto Ago* (1987), vol. I, p. 141 at p. 141.
[3]Weil, "Le Droit international en quête de son identité", *Recueil des cours de l'Académie de Droit International de La Haye*, vol. 237 (1992-VI), p. 13 at p. 26, with particular reference to Bourquin and Fitzmaurice. See also Dupuy, "La Codification du droit international, a-t-elle encore un intéret à l'aube du troisième millénaire?", in Zanardi et al., op. cit. above (preceding footnote), p. 261 at p. 261.
[4]Bull, H., Kingsbury, B., and Roberts, A. (eds.), *Hugo Grotius and International Relations* (1992).

international institutions.[5] Although international society has changed much in the intervening centuries, those features are still predominant in the structure of world society.

Elements of change have appeared, however, in recent decades; and this has led to the identification of the end of the Cold War as another major historical landmark. As the current century and the cuurent millennium come to a close, major theories have emerged announcing a new era of absence of war among democracies,[6] the obsolescence of conflict[7] and even, arrogantly, that history has come to an end with the undisputed prevalence of liberal-democratic principles.[8] The rise and fall of great powers[9] and the collapse of empires[10] have also occupied much attention in the recent literature. However, such ideas as these have also excited critical responses[11]—responses which do not allow for an outlook devoid of war, conflict, ideologies or empires and which are probably closer to human nature than utopian schemes for a world government or perpetual peace.

If the core features of Grotian society referred to above are revisited in the light of current trends, the major developments and changes that are shaping the world community become apparent. First, irrespective of past doctrinal discussions about natural and positive law, it is a fact that most contemporary developments are inspired by the need to ensure human freedom, dignity and welfare, because these aims are inextricably related to the essence of humanity. Secondly, while international society retains its universal nature, "regionalism" has been noted as one of the key trends of our time,[12] with the corollary that centralized international action may only be possible to the extent that it relies on effective regional cooperation. Thirdly, the role of individuals and non-State actors in the international system has become paramount, significantly curtailing the exclusive role of the State and sometimes threatening its very existence.[13] This element, together with regionalism, has led to the emergence of a polycentric and multicultural international society.[14] Fourthly, solidarism in the enforcement of the law still remains largely true in so far as arrangements for collective security are concerned, but there have been major innovations in respect of the enforcement of other types of arrangements, such as those in the fields of trade and the environment. Fifthly, the past absence or limited role of international institutions has given way to the powerful life of current international organizations,[15] still less evident in the political sphere, but of a signifi-

---

[5]Bull, "The Importance of Grotius in the Study of International Relations", in Bull et al., op. cit. above (preceding footnote), p. 65 at pp. 78-91.

[6]See: Babst, "A Force for Peace", *Industrial Research*, vol. 14 (1972), p. 55; Rummel, "Libertarianism and International Violence", *Journal of Conflict Resolution*, vol. 27 (1983), p. 27; and Russett, "The Politics of an Alternative Security System: Toward a More Democratic and Therefore More Peaceful World", in Weston, B. (ed.), *Alternatives to Nuclear Deterrence* (1989).

[7]Mueller, J., *Retreat from Doomsday: The Obsolescence of Major War* (1989).

[8]Fukuyama, "The End of History?", *The National Interest*, no. 16 (summer 1989), p. 3.

[9]Kennedy, P., *The Rise and Fall of Great Powers* (1987).

[10]Trevor-Roper and Urban, "Aftermaths of Empire: The lessons of Upheavals and Destabilisation", *Encounter* (December 1989), p. 3.

[11]Nye, The Misleading Metaphor of Decline", *Atlantic Monthly* (March 1990), p. 86; and Huntington, "No Exit: The Errors of Endism", *The National Interest* (Fall 1989), p. 3.

[12]Rostow, "The Coming Age of Regionalism: A 'Metaphor' for Our Time?", *Encounter* (June 1990), p. 3.

[13]Societé française pour le droit international, *L'État souverain à l'aube du XXIe siècle: Colloque de Nancy* (1994).

[14]Weiss, "The New International Legal System", in Jasentuliyana, N. (ed.), *Perspectives on International Law* (1995), p. 63-82 at p. 66.

[15]Sohn, "The Role of International Law in the 21st Century", address given at the Vrije Universiteit, Brussels, 23 March 1990, at pp. 5-6.

cantly higher profile in other major areas of international cooperation. It is apparent that, although the Grotian society has not come to an end, it has been profoundly transformed.

All these developments are, in turn, immersed in and fuelled by the so-called fourth technological revolution,[16] as well as by the powerful emergence of leading developing economies, which have introduced new dimensions into international competition.[17]

2. Where is the international legal system going?

The changes occurring in world society have had specific implications for the international legal system and its evolution from a relatively simple mechanism for law-making to the highly complex phenomenon that is evident today. In the model of the traditional Grotian society, international law was essentially based on the will and consent of States.[18] Recognition of the manifestations of international law[19] was basically a question of evidence and stringent standards were required in this regard. Customary law and treaty law had their own methods for recognizing the will of States to create rules of international law. However, even in that simple context there was ample room for uncertainty in terms of reliance on other sources, such as general principles of law, which are bound up with considerations of justice, equity, nature and other "looser" forms of identification.[20]

The theory of the sources of international law has become the subject of increasing discussion as a consequence of the changes which have taken place in the international legal system during the past few decades. The slow pace which used to characterize the transition from practice to *opinio juris* and from customary law to its codification in treaty form has given way to what Eduardo Jiménez de Aréchaga aptly described as the simultaneous interplay of sources: while a customary rule may be emerging, it is simultaneously being codified and progressively developed at major international conferences, in turn reflecting the views expressed through resolutions of international organizations and other such acts.[21] In this new process, the measure of uncertainty is inevitably and significantly increased.

The intricacies of this legal process have been approached from two distinct points of view. In the opinion of certain distinguished authors and institutions, the changes may be many, but the basic concepts remain essentially intact, including the role of consensus.[22] Weil has emphasized the permanent standing of international law and the fact that it remains universal in spite of its multicultural components,[23] while, at the same time, cautioning against any lowering in the standards for the identification of customary law and against trying to substitute the models of domestic society for those that characterize the norma-

---

[16]Rostow, loc. cit. above (footnote 12), p. 3.

[17]Loc. cit.

[18]Schachter, O., *International Law in Theory and Practice* (1991), p. 10.

[19]Bos, "Recognized Manifestations of International Law: A New Theory of 'Sources'", *German Yearbook of International Law*, vol. 20 (1977), p. 1 at p. 9. See further Münch, "La Codification inachevée", in Zanardi et al., op. cit. above (footnote 2), p. 373 at pp. 376-377.

[20]Schachter, op. cit. above (footnote 18), p. 50.

[21]Jiménez de Aréchaga, "International Law in the Past Third of a Century", *Recueil des cours de la l'Académie de droit international de La Haye*, vol. 159 (1978-I), p. 1 at pp. 11-34.

[22]American Law Institute, *Restatement of the Law. The Foreign Relations Law of the United States*, vol. I (1987), at p. 19, as cited and discussed by Weil, loc. cit. above (footnote 3), p. 33. See also Münch, loc. cit. above (footnote 19), pp. 376-379.

[23]Weil, loc. cit. above (footnote 3), pp. 33 and 87-88.

tive structure of the international community.[24] However, in the view of other writers, the question lies precisely in how to overcome the limits imposed by consensus and ensure a law-making procedure that is both timely and expeditious, with particular reference to the role of "soft" law and other mechanisms.[25] Again, it is a question of the accommodation of stability and change.

As explained by Edith Brown Weiss, this accommodation is not altogether an easy one to make, since a society based on the independence and sovereign equality of a limited number of States is confronted today with a large number of participants, which has tended to introduce a new hierarchy that weakens the assumptions of sovereign equality.[26] The leading role of important powers and other active countries in the shaping of international law contrasts sharply with the passive attitude of a large number of countries.[27] Non-governmental organizations and individuals have appeared as significant non-State actors in the making of international law, having a major input, not only in the negotiation of international agreements and their implementation, but also in the development of customary law, by influencing State practice.[28] While this phenomenon may be particularly evident in the fields of international environmental law, human rights and trade relations, it is apparent throughout the spectrum of international law.

As a result of this process of accommodation, public international law and private international law are becoming increasingly integrated, national law and international law have developed significant interlinkages, non-binding agreements are a major feature of current international law and new approaches have emerged with the introduction of intertemporal dimensions and intergenerational equity.[29] The geometric progression that Roberto Ago remarked in the appearance of new and frequently unexpected subjects on the horizon of the international legal order[30] is now an everyday reality, posing new problems and requiring pertinent solutions. What has been called the "congestion in the international legal order", where hundreds of different instruments deal with similar or interrelated subjects, needs to be rationalized, partly in order to avoid an unnecessary proliferation of rules and interpretations and partly in order to reduce the costs involved in negotiations, enforcement and the establishment of different bodies.[31] To this end, the creation of a computerized database of the international legal order has been suggested.[32] Equally important is the need to establish a mechanism to ensure the accountability of those engaged in international negotiations, with particular reference to non-State actors, which, today, are largely unaccountable.[33]

---

[24]Ibid., pp. 161-179 and 203 et seq.

[25]See: Chinkin, "The Challenge of Soft Law: Development and Change in International Law", International and Comparative Law Quarterly, vol. 38 (1989), p. 850; and Palmer, "New Ways to Make International Environmental Law", American Journal of International Law, vol. 86 (1992), p. 259.

[26]Weiss, loc. cit. above (footnote 14), pp. 63-66.

[27]Sohn, "The Shaping of International Law", Georgia Journal of International and Comparative Law, vol. 8 (1978), p. 1 at p. 3.

[28]Weiss, loc. cit. above (footnote 14), pp. 67-69.

[29]Ibid., pp. 69-79.

[30]Ago, "Some New Thoughts on the Codification of International Law", in Bello, E.G., and Ajibola, B.A. (eds.), Essays in Honour of Judge Taslim Olawale Elias, volume I, Contemporary International Law and Human Rights (1992), p. 35 at p. 52.

[31]Weiss, loc. cit. above (footnote 14), pp. 80-81.

[32]Ibid., p. 81.

[33]Ibid., p. 82.

The International Law Commission has identified some significant changes in inter-State relations that affect its own legal work, including the technical and administrative character of many new issues, the tendency to treat some of them on a regional or bilateral basis, the proliferation of bodies with law-making mandates and the work of the United Nations specialized agencies.[34]

It is within this broad framework of continuity and change characterizing international society and the international legal order that the International Law Commission finds both its limits and, at the same time, opportunities for the development of international law. Depending upon which of these elements is favoured, the Commission is praised without reserve[35] or is severely criticized.[36] The important question, though, is how the International Law Commission might contribute to the accommodation between such continuity and change, which are, after all, standing features of the world community. This is the question which I shall examine next.

3. Identifying the basic principles of international law

As international society becomes increasingly integrated, the need to identify the basic principles of international law becomes more apparent. At the current stage of evolution of international society, the possibility of adopting a constitution seems remote, but it is, none the less, a process which must begin at some point. As Allott has written, "[t]he generic principles of a constitution are . . . those operating principles which make possible the social process of society".[37] He goes on to identify as the essential rules those that deal with the principles of integration of the law, transformation, delegation of power, intrinsic limitation of power, the supremacy of law, the supremacy of the social interest and social responsibility.[38] The Charter of the United Nations has, to a limited extent, performed this constitutional function for international society,[39] a task also discharged by the major covenants on human rights, the United Nations Convention on the Law of the Sea and other such important instruments. Writers of international law have contributed significantly to this identification of basic governing principles.[40]

This is a task which, with great benefit for international society, the International Law Commission could undertake. The piecemeal approach that the Commission has followed in respect of the selection and treatment of subjects has been criticized,[41] and this situation could be remedied by the systematic examination of the basic principles indicated. It is not a question of drafting the detailed terms of an instrument resembling a constitution, but, more

---

[34]Report of the International Law Commission on the work of its forty-eighth session, *Official Records of the General Assembly, Fifty-first Session, Supplement No. 10* (A/51/10), pp. 206-207 at para. 169.

[35]Sette-Camara, "The International Law Commission: Discourse on Method", in Zanardi et al., op. cit. above (footnote 2), p. 467.

[36]Allott, op. cit. above (footnote 1), p. 316; and Dhokalia, "Reflections on International Law-Making and its Progressive Development in the Contemporary Era of Transition", in Pathak, R.S., and Dhokalia, R.P. (eds.), *International Law in Transition: Essays in Memory of Judge Nagendra Singh* (1992), p. 203.

[37]Allott, op. cit. above (footnote 1), p. 167.

[38]Ibid., p. 168.

[39]Sohn, loc. cit. above (footnote 27), p. 13.

[40]See, especially: Brownlie, I., *Principles of Public International Law* (4th. ed., 1990); and Jennings, Sir R., and Watts, Sir A., *Oppenheim's International Law* (9th ed., 1992), vol. I.

[41]Dhokalia, loc. cit above (footnote 36), p. 221.

simply, of identifying the principles evidenced in State practice and international legislation, refining their meaning and extent and, above all, producing the necessary commentaries on them. To an extent, such an exercise resembles that undertaken by the American Law Institute in producing the Restatement of the Foreign Relations Law of the United States[42]—an initiative that has been repeatedly suggested for the International Law Commission,[43] with the added advantage that a view more broadly representative of the views of the world community could thus be assured.

The International Law Commission has not been unaware of this perspective. The list of topics originally suggested for the Commission in 1949 comprised the 25 areas of the law where the basic principles are to be found.[44] The extensive survey of international law prepared by the Secretary-General in 1971 dealt in a comprehensive manner with the current state of international law and the possibility of furthering the development of the many subjects which it examined.[45] For a variety of reasons—some related to the Commission's working methods—the challenge was not picked up. It is interesting to note, though, that the Commission has been most successful when dealing precisely with those topics that involve the identification and elaboration of the basic principles of international law, such as the law of treaties, succession, responsibility and criminal law, and has been less so when exploring rather unconnected subjects. Moreover, the fact that the Commission has rightly decided to follow a composite approach to codification and progressive development, rather than drawing an artificial distinction between them, and the fact that it assigns particular importance to the orderly process of discharging this task[46] bring the Commission closer to the systematic function suggested above.

4. Providing guidance to the normative system

Because the normative system of international society is a decentralized one and is likely so to remain, both the codification and the progressive development of the universal rules that govern that system should be undertaken at the level of guiding principles, not aspiring to solve through such principles the many issues encountered in any particular area of the law, but aiming at the provision of a common treatment to such areas. The task of specifically applying the principles to given individual regimes or regions should be entrusted to other bodies.

To discharge these guiding functions in an effective manner, the International Law Commission should probably place less emphasis on the comprehensive treatment of each subject—an approach which makes its work excessively slow and time-consuming—and assign greater importance to the

---

[42]American Law Institute, op. cit. above (footnote 22). For a proposal to undertake a systematic collection of international law, together with a commentary, see Sohn, "Making International Law More User-friendly", in United Nations, *International Law as a Language for International Relations* (1996), p. 411 at p. 415.

[43]Cede, "New Approaches to Law Making in the UN-System", *Austrian Review of International and European Law*, vol. 1 (1996), p. 51 at p. 59; and Dhokalia, loc. cit. above (footnote 36), p. 220.

[44]Secretariat Memorandum on the survey of the whole field of international law, document A/CN. 4/1/Rev. 1. See also Lauterpacht, "Survey of International Law in relation to the Work of Codification of the International Law Commission", in Lauterpacht, E. (ed.), *International Law, being the Collected Papers of Sir Hersch Lauterpacht* (1970), vol. 1, p. 445.

[45]*Yearbook of the International Law Commission, 1971*, vol. II (Part Two), p. 1.

[46]Report of the International Law Commission on the work of its forty-eighth session, loc. cit. above (footnote 34), pp. 201-208 at paras. 157-173.

overall coverage of the principles involved. The very rigidity that a comprehensive treatment sometimes introduces to a subject conspires against its acceptability or its practical implementation. It has been noted, for example, that the use of "soft" law instruments gained momentum shortly after the Vienna Convention had hardened the rules governing treaties.[47]

Following an approach such as this, the Institut de Droit International, for example, has been able to deal, in two years, with the basic principles governing responsibility and liability for environmental damage and the procedures for the effective implementation of international environmental law, with meetings which on average have taken 20 days in all, plus the time devoted by each Rapporteur, and with no research support from a secretariat.[48] The International Law Commission could well complete the examination of two or three subjects *per* year on this basis.

It is also important to bear in mind that international society is gradually developing a legislative function—not one which is to be compared with some sort of world parliament, but one whose decentralized manner corresponds to that society's nature. Sohn has aptly described this function as a "quasi-legislative process", not dissimilar from that found at the origins of the common law period.[49] The United Nations, in particular, has become what Pellet describes as a *"formidable machine à « fabriquer » du droit international"*,[50] with the most active role for the General Assembly, an interpretative law-creating function for the Security Council and a renewed role for the Secretary-General under Article 99 of the Charter.[51] In the development of this function, tasks are entrusted to different bodies within and outside the United Nations system. To the extent that the International Law Commission might be able to respond expeditiously to the requests for legal contributions which may be made of it, it will no doubt be able to reassume the position of influence it once enjoyed. The relationship between the Commission, the Sixth Committee, the General Assembly and other bodies, to which much thought has been devoted,[52] will largely depend on the timeliness of this response.

The ideas set out above would allow for other important developments in the work of the Commission. First, the Commission would not be limited, as it has come to be, to those subjects which are considered to pertain to "classical" international law, as distinct from more specialized or contemporary subjects and issues. Basic principles of law could be drawn up by the Commission in every field, either as a matter of codification or as a matter of progressive development. The Commission's work would then serve to guide the work of other bodies, which might be charged with the specific normative development of the principles elaborated by the Commission. It is interesting to note that, among other, very specialized, subjects, the 1971 Survey clearly indicated the need for the Commission to take up the subject of international environmental law;[53] but this suggestion only came to be considered again in 1995 and, then,

---

[47]Chinkin, loc. cit. above (footnote 25), p. 860.

[48]*Annuaire de l'Institut de Droit International*, vol. 67-I (1997) (forthcoming).

[49]Sohn, loc. cit. above (footnote 27), p. 6.

[50]Pellet, "La Formation du droit international dans le cadre des Nations Unies", *European Journal of International Law*, vol. 6 (1995), p. 401 at p. 403. See also Nagendra Singh, "The UN and the Development of International Law", in Roberts, A., and Kingsbury, B. (eds.), *United Nations, Divided World* (1995), p. 384.

[51]Pellet, loc. cit. above (preceding footnote), p. 406.

[52]Report of the International Law Commission on the work of its forty-eighth session, loc. cit. above (footnote 34), pp. 208-212 at paras. 174-185.

[53]Loc. cit. above (footnote 45), pp. 75-76.

with so many precautionary comments regarding the need for feasibility studies and preparatory work[54] that the Commission now risks coming too late to a field of law which has been in full evolution for the past quarter of a century. The basic principles, however, could still be usefully elaborated by the Commission.

A very important step forward which has recently been taken by the Commission has been the preparation, in connection with its long-term programme of work, of a "General Scheme" which provides for an integrated approach to the main fields of international law.[55] If this is to be translated into comprehensive draft articles for each topic in that scheme or the piecemeal approach of the past, it will hardly result in a timely contribution; but, again, if the basic principles of each area are identified in orderly succession, this could mean a significant improvement in the state of international law.

5. Normative stability and new forms of evidence of State practice

The reluctance of the International Law Commission to address certain pressing new issues, or to do so in an expeditious manner, appears to be connected with a legitimate concern about strict observance of the rigorous methods developed by international law to establish the practice and consent of States. However, the technical legal approach which the Commission has followed has also been criticized and has been contrasted with the need to consider larger issues which are frequently related to questions of legal policy and development.[56]

The Commission, to be sure, has to be rigorous in its methods. This is of course evident in so far as customary international law is concerned, in respect of which, as Weil has remarked, the standards for identification of State practice should not be lowered.[57] However, these stringent standards do not exclude the examination of areas of law in which State practice may not yet be extensive or even concordant, but which, nevertheless, reveal trends that are likely to influence the legal outcome. The task in such cases is not to anticipate, much less to invent, State practice, but, rather, to identify such phenomena as they are being born. This in itself would involve a substantive contribution to the development of international law. International environmental law offers more than a few examples of how State practice is being gradually shaped, notwithstanding that it might not be extensive or concordant at a given point in time.[58] To the extent that the current concerns of the international community are kept in mind, this task will be greatly facilitated, as it identifies and reflects the "common opinion of mankind".[59] The same may be said of areas of the law in which States are wary of regulation, as is the case with a number of important security issues. It is not for the Commission to find State practice or to establish legal outcomes where there is no consensus among the key actors in the field concerned, but this does not mean that emerging trends of opinion should be ignored. The topic of humanitarian intervention, for example, illustrates how the absence of consistent practice has not prevented the emergence of important trends of opinion,

---

[54]Report of the International Law Commission on the work of its forty-seventh session, *Official Records of the General Assembly, Fiftieth Session, Supplement No. 10* (A/50/10), pp. 264-265 at para. 506.

[55]Report of the International Law Commission on the work of its forty-eighth session, loc. cit. above (footnote 34), pp. 328-334.

[56]Dhokalia, loc. cit. above (footnote 36), p. 224.

[57]Loc. cit. above (footnote 24).

[58]Palmer, loc. cit. above (footnote 25).

[59]Sohn, loc. cit. above (footnote 27), p. 24.

there being recognition of the need to take action in cases of uncontrolled violence.

The argument has been made that the role and functions of the International Law Commission have been affected by the exhaustion of topics for codification.[60] Viewed from the perspective of those areas of the law where State practice and customary rules might be considered to be abundant, this argument is essentially true, because the Commission has already codified, or is already in the process of codifying, the major subjects of any legal system, such as the law of contracts, responsibility, succession, criminal law and so on. It should be noted, though, that the fact that codification might have been completed in a given area does not mean that appropriate revisions of the law in that area are ruled out. Furthermore, there is always the possibility of undertaking codification of many other subjects where State practice is not lacking.

There is another way of looking at this question, though. State practice finds expression today through new types of mechanisms which are less structured and much less solemn than those of the past, but which contribute significantly to the identification of the consent and will of States. Among such mechanisms there is, above all, the widespread phenomenon of "soft" law. This is not the place to discuss the issues associated with this approach, but it may simply be noted that its significance as an expression of State practice is increasing with every passing day. Resolutions of international organizations, codes of conduct, statements of principles and a number of other forms are currently intensively used. True enough, not all of this is meant by its authors to be law, but it is also true that not all of it is to be disregarded as not law. This is precisely the kind of useful task which could be undertaken by the International Law Commission, which might identify those aspects which might be considered of legal value within the vast field of "soft" law, as it is developed in given areas and on particular subjects. This has been aptly described as a process of "soft codification",[61] essentially involving the drawing of the element of *opinio juris* from the new forms of evidence of State practice.

Evidence of State practice is also to be found in numerous other, more traditional sources of the law, such as regional and bilateral treaties and instruments. The law governing trade and investments has been largely developed in this manner, an example being the numerous bilateral and regional treaties associated with the protection of foreign investments under the International Centre for Settlement of Investment Disputes. Aside from their binding force on the parties, such treaties may well also be of assistance in identifying general State practice and relevant legal trends. Again, this is a task that might usefully be undertaken by the Commission, through the systematic survey of international agreements in given areas of the law, and which might eventually lead to the preparation of model treaties. It might be added that it would be unthinkable today to discuss a topic like diplomatic protection without relying on such new forms of evidence of State practice.[62]

In the light of the above, codification may be a much broader and more dynamic undertaking than has hitherto been the case, precisely because the

---

[60]See the debate which took place in the Sixth Committee of the General Assembly in 1995 in connection with the Report of the International Law Commission on the work of its forty-seventh session, as discussed by Cede, loc. cit. above (footnote 43), p. 62.

[61]Ibid., p. 59. For a criticism of this approach, see ibid., p. 62.

[62]For the general outline of the subject of diplomatic protection, as it has been proposed for consideration by the International Law Commission, see Report of the International Law Commission on the work of its forty-eighth session, loc. cit. above (footnote 34), pp. 335-338.

sources of international law do not today follow an orderly progression, but find simultaneous expression through various means and procedures.

6. Consent and majority in multilateral treaty-making

Because consent is still the rule for multilateral treaty-making in the Grotian order of the world community, the International Law Commission has had good reason for proposing and undertaking work only on those subjects that are likely to command a great measure of support in the General Assembly, in the Sixth Committee and at diplomatic conferences convened to draw up the relevant conventions.[63] However, this very feature of the treaty-making process has been open to criticism, partly because it is typically long and costly and partly because unanimous consent has come to be regarded by some authors as paralyzing progressive development and allowing only for general, vague provisions based on the approach of the lowest common denominator.[64] It has been suggested in this connection, particularly in respect of international environmental law, that the adoption and amendment of basic treaties should be accomplished by majority vote, there already being important precedents for this,[65] and that new institutions should assume a legislative function in the field and the practice of convening diplomatic conferences be discontinued.[66] New ideas are also being developed in connection with the review and implementation of major treaties so as to avoid the difficulties associated with the rigid operation of consent.

It is suggested that the International Law Commission should not be overly concerned by this issue, since it will be for each organ or conference to which the codification work is addressed to decide which approach is preferable in the light of the nature of the subject and the attitude of Governments towards it. In respect of some matters, the preparation of draft articles might be appropriate, as it has been in the past, while, in the case of other subjects, such treaty form may not be adequate.[67] It is quite common in contemporary practice that the final form of the instrument to be adopted is decided only at the very end of the negotiations, a choice being made for treaty procedures or "soft" law approaches and the required majorities or consent being defined in this context. What is important is that the Commission be satisfied with the substantive content of its proposals. Such flexibility might be still more appropriate if the Commission were to opt for proposing basic rules and principles, rather than necessarily proposing comprehensive drafts, as has been suggested above.[68]

Two other issues should be noted in this connection. The first is that consensus has, to a meaningful extent, come to replace unanimous consent, thus introducing an added degree of flexibility into the negotiation process.[69] Consensus is built as the negotiation progresses and cannot be presumed to exist beforehand, thereby evidencing that States have a cooperative, rather than an obstructive, attitude towards attaining a positive result. The work of the Com-

---

[63]See, generally, United Nations, *Review of the Multilateral Treaty-Making Process*, pp. 268-305 (document ST/LEG/SER.B/21; United Nations publication, Sales No. E/F.83.V.8).

[64]Palmer, loc. cit. above (footnote 25), pp. 270-278.

[65]See, in particular, the Montreal Protocol on Substances that Deplete the Ozone Layer, done at Montreal on 16 September 1987 (United Nations, *Treaty Series*, vol. 1522, p. 29). See the discussion by Palmer, loc. cit. above (footnote 25), pp. 274-276.

[66]Ibid., pp. 278-283.

[67]Cede, loc. cit. above (footnote 43), p. 58.

[68]Loc. cit.

[69]Sohn, loc. cit. above (footnote 27), p. 24.

mission can contribute to the attainment of consensus through the elaboration of the basic principles envisaged.

The second issue relates to the function of interpretation in the development of international law. Major treaties often require interpretation. Interpretation, though, is not exclusively a judicial function, judicial interpretation in any event being restricted to the parties before a court. It has been noted above, for example, that the law of the United Nations has been significantly developed through the interpretative function of the Security Council and that of other bodies. It is suggested that the International Law Commission might be associated with this process through the preparation of legal opinions at the request of United Nations decision-making bodies and that even the Secretary-General might take the initiative in this regard under Article 99 of the Charter. An essential condition for the feasibility of such a mechanism, though, would be the timeliness of the opinions given by the Commission. Another aspect of the same function would be to entrust the Commission with the task of certifying points of international law at the request of interested parties, including private entities, just as national Ministries of Foreign Affairs issue certificates on questions of international law.

7. Anticipating the legal needs of the international community

The idea has been advanced of entrusting the Commission with the task of preparing rules in the event of legal emergencies, as arose in the case of the Chernobyl incident.[70] Again, the Commission would need to be prompt in its response.

The Commission could even anticipate some of the major legal needs of the international community when the trend of State practice is decisively in favour of a particular legal solution. The Commission might do this even though the practice concerned may only be very recent and not very extensive. A case in point is that of human cloning. Days after genetic experiments were successfully completed with a sheep, a strong body of international opinion emerged in favour of prohibiting such manipulations in respect of human beings. Governments announced legislation, church leaders condemned such practices and scientific associations made strong warnings about its dangers. The practice could not yet be said to be extensive. Nevertheless, the trend is clearly there and it is not difficult to anticipate that human cloning will be prohibited under international law, as well as under domestic law. This is the type of issue that the International Law Commission might quickly address in response to the concerns of the world community.

8. Fragmentation of the law and functional coordination

The Commission itself has rightly noted the risk of fragmentation in international law stemming from the intervention of so many agencies in the law-making process—something which is also likely to give rise to a degree of duplication and waste.[71] In so far as the Commission might exercise a certain leadership in the field, these risks will be diminished, but functional coordination is still badly needed to this end. Relations between the Commission and other bodies, both intergovernmental and private, have largely been formal in nature[72]

---

[70]Cede, loc. cit. above (footnote 43), p. 57.

[71]Report of the International Law Commission on the work of its forty-eighth session, loc. cit. above (footnote 34), p. 207 at para. 170.

[72]Dhokalia, loc. cit. above (footnote 36), p. 226.

and no real working relations have yet been developed. If they were, they might result in the organization of informal joint working groups, striving for the common objective of the codification and progressive development of the law. It is conceivable, for example, that there might be joint undertakings with institutions such as the Institut de Droit International and the International Law Association.[73] Following the same line of thought, the coverage of private international law issues should not be ruled out in the way which it apparently has been by the Commission.[74] Input on such issues could be provided by a number of scientific and intergovernmental bodies and work which embraced them would reflect the integrating trends of international law remarked above. The United Nations Office of Legal Affairs might be in a unique position to encourage such developments.

One very significant project that the Commission could undertake on a cooperative basis would be the development of a comprehensive database of international law on the Internet.[75] This might not only consist of a collection of treaties, decisions and other such materials, but it might also serve as a means to develop the basis for a code of international law. Inclusion of material in this database would follow precise guidelines as to its acceptability.

9. Recomposition of the International Law Commission

Most of the new perspectives set out above require two further changes in the Commission. One relates to its working methods—a matter which has been extensively discussed elsewhere[76] and which the Commission itself has begun to address.[77]

The second change relates to the Commission's composition. The fact that no woman has ever been elected to the Commission has been noted by the Commission itself[78]—a situation, incidentally, that contrasts with the very distinguished services that staff members of the Office of Legal Affairs, both men and women, have rendered to the Commission in its work. The problem of the composition of the Commission, though, is also one of representation. The academic community was strongly represented in the Commission in its earlier years, later to be followed by an important representation of diplomats with a legal background, politicians and other Government officials. Although this development has been criticized,[79] it may be seen as a response to some of the main forces shaping international law, though, at the same time, a problem relating to the independence of the Commission's members may arise.

It was noted above that a number of new actors are today contributing to the development of international law, including international organizations, private entities, the business community and non-governmental organizations. It would accordingly seem appropriate that these other sectors also be repre-

---

[73]Cede, loc. cit. above (footnote 43), p. 65.

[74]Report of the International Law Commission on the work of its forty-eighth session, loc. cit. above (footnote 34), p. 201 at para. 156.

[75]See the text at footnote 32, above.

[76]See, for example, Cede, loc. cit. above (footnote 43), pp. 59-60. See also Nawaz, "On Ways and Methods for Improving the Work of the International Law Commission", *Indian Journal of International Law*, vol. 25 (1985), p. 634, with particular reference to El Baradei, M., Franck, T., and Trachtenberg, R., *The International Law Commission: The Need for a New Direction* (1981), p. 5 (United Nations publication, Sales No. E.81.XV.PE/1).

[77]Report of the International Law Commission on the work of its forty-eighth session, loc. cit. above (footnote 34), pp. 196-230.

[78]Ibid., p. 209 at para. 176.

[79]Dhokalia, loc. cit. above (footnote 36), pp. 223-224.

sented in the Commission, either as standing members or as members ad hoc for the discussion of particular subjects. A tiered composition for the Commission might be the best solution.

The question of the Commission's composition is, in turn, related to two further important questions. First, there is the question of serious absenteeism. Members' records of attendance should be published every year and made available at the time of elections to the Commission. Candidates for reelection who have attended less than 50 per cent of the Commission's meetings should be automatically barred. Members who have attended less than 50 per cent of the meetings devoted to the discussion of a given subject should not be allowed to vote on that subject. This is the least that can be required in terms of members' accountability in the discharge of their mandate.

Secondly, there is the question of the increasing politicization of the elections to the Commission—a phenomenon which does not help to ensure a high quality membership. Perhaps not all of the members of the Commission should be elected by the General Assembly. A number might be appointed by learned institutions, such as the International Court of Justice, the Institut de Droit International and the International Law Association. Such an approach might be particularly useful if new actors were to be represented in the work of the Commission. Alternatively, candidates nominated by Governments for election by the General Assembly might be required to obtain some form of clearance from learned institutions or from some other mechanism established for the purpose. It goes without saying that many of these thoughts will meet with strong objections; but it is in the interests of the Commission and of international law to have the best possible expertise available.

10. A new world order that is not so new

However dramatic many of the proposals for a new world order might be, most of the issues posed can find some type of positive response within the framework of current arrangements. Continuity does not mean, and in fact has never meant, a disregard for change. If that happens, it is no longer a question of continuity, but of stagnation.

Contemporary international law-making can accommodate many changes and many are in fact being introduced in practice, while at the same time preserving the stability that is essential to any legal order. There is no need to overturn the structure of international society in order to accommodate the most important changes which are aimed at. The suggestions outlined above evidence that continuity and change are two essential components of the progress of international law and, as such, are not to be regarded as antagonistic, but as supplementary, concepts. This is the challenge that the International Law Commission has to face in the discharge of its functions.

THE INTERNATIONAL LAW COMMISSION: METHODS OF WORK AND SELECTION OF TOPICS

by Christopher W. Pinto*

"L'ambition de faire du droit international l'objet d'une discipline scientifique rigoureusement autonome, la crainte de le contaminer au contact des données de la politique, ont beaucoup contribué à l'abus du raisonnement abstrait au détriment de l'esprit d'observation. Elles ont dangereusement voilé l'action du pouvoir sur les orientations du droit international positif. Mais surtout elles ont fait perdre de vue ce qui est la justification dernière de tout droit, les fins humaines du pouvoir, seules capables, par l'assentiment universel qu'elles commandent, de ramener l'Etat à une conception modératrice de la puissance. Ce n'est pas en ignorant les réalités qui déterminent l'action du pouvoir que l'on fortifie le droit international; c'est en prenant conscience de la place qu'elles y tiennent, des nécessités qui les suscitent comme des valeurs qu'elles mettent en jeu. Une critique indépendante peut seule gagner les esprits à une conception fonctionnelle du pouvoir, véritable garantie de sa conversion au service de l'humanité."[1]

I. Introduction: the bearing of power on the perspectives of international law

The following cautionary words of Charles de Visscher have guided this response to an invitation to discuss the International Law Commission's methods of work and the selection of topics for its work: "We cannot strengthen international law by ignoring the realities that determine the operation of power". Accordingly, this paper attempts, first, to place the Commission in its political and constitutional context as a subsidiary organ of the General Assembly.[2] While the stature of its members may appear at times to confer on it a certain "autonomy", there can be no question but that the Commission is wholly dependent on the General Assembly as regards the scope of its mandate, the focus of its work and the facilities and services at its disposal. This means that the General Assembly's Sixth and Fifth Committees will ultimately determine between them the scope of the Commission's activity and that, in the event that the views of the two Committees do not coincide, those of the Fifth are likely to prevail. To restate the point in its starkest terms, it must be recognized that the positions of the major financial contributors to the Organization will be

---

*Secretary-General, Iran–United States Claims Tribunal. Visiting Professor, World Maritime University, Valletta, Malta.
[1] De Visscher, C., *Théories et Réalités en Droit International Public* (1960), pp. 9-10.
[2] On 21 November 1947, the General Assembly adopted its resolution 174 (II), establishing the International Law Commission and approving its Statute. Since then, the Statute has been amended by four further resolutions of the General Assembly.

determinative and that a majority which may choose to ignore those positions would have to decide whether or not to expend their own—perhaps more scarce—resources in pursuit of a particular legislative goal which may not be realized.

It seems reasonable, if not essential, to begin this brief inquiry by examining important aspects of the "parental" relationship of the General Assembly to the Commission, and only thereafter to discuss, within that framework, the Commission's methods of work and the selection of topics. Several of the most distinguished jurists of our time have addressed these latter two subjects, have provided valuable insights and have made useful proposals for improving the Commission's methods and its output. An attempt will be made later to recall some of them, albeit in a very concise form, with a view to stimulating discussion and also for the reason that the modest prescriptions offered in the present paper are often based on those proposals.

II. Universal participation in treaty-making

In the words of a former Secretary-General of the United Nations:

"The General Assembly is the embodiment of the universality of the United Nations and the cornerstone of representation and participation within the United Nations system, today bringing together 185 Member States on the basis of sovereign equality and democratic principles . . ."[3]

The International Law Commission is the subsidiary organ of the General Assembly which is established to assist in implementing the Assembly's function under Article 13, paragraph 1 (*a*), of the Charter, to:

"initiate studies and make recommendations for the purpose of . . . encouraging the progressing development of international law and its codification . . ."

It is a unique body, elected by the General Assembly as nearly as feasible by reference to "democratic principles"—that is, by a majority of votes cast in the General Assembly on a one-State–one-vote basis—the electors being required to bear in mind, first, that the persons to be elected should individually possess the qualifications required and, secondly, that, in the Commission as a whole, representation of the main forms of civilization and of the principal legal systems of the world should be assured. Implicit in the latter requirement, as in the proviso that no two members of the Commission shall be nationals of the same State, is the policy directive that members of the Commission should be elected on as wide a geographical basis as possible. That policy, initially given effect through a "gentlemen's agreement" on the number of members to be elected from each of the regions recognized by the United Nations, received definitive expression when the General Assembly, taking into account the progressive increase in the membership of the Organization, adopted its resolution 36/39 of 18 November 1981, which expanded the Commission's membership from 25 to 34 and specified the number of persons to be elected from each of those regions.

Thus, while the General Assembly retains its responsibility under the Charter of encouraging the "progressive development of international law and

---

[3]Boutros-Ghali, B., *An Agenda for Democratization* (1996), para. 106.

its codification", the International Law Commission is the mechanism, fashioned by the Assembly, that enables the entire membership of the Organization to participate regularly, and in an orderly manner, in that process.[4] The Commission is charged with the following four main categories of functions, the first three by the express terms of its Statute and the last one by implication: (1) progressive development of international law, or "the preparation of draft conventions on subjects which have not yet been regulated by international law or in regard to which the law has not yet been sufficiently developed in the practice of States", contemplated as being in implementation of proposals from (a) the General Assembly or (b) another principal organ of the United Nations, a Member State, a specialized agency or other intergovernmental body with functions similar to those of the Commission; (2) codification of international law, or "the more precise formulation and systematization of rules of international law in fields where there already has been extensive State practice, precedent and doctrine", contemplated as following upon the selection of topics by the Commission after a "survey of the whole field of international law" and as being on the basis of a priority established in consultation with the General Assembly; (3) reporting to the General Assembly on "ways and means for making the evidence of customary international law more readily available"; and (4) from its functions of "surveying the whole field of international law" and consulting with relevant institutions, international as well as national, may be implied a certain coordinative function, at least to the extent of maintaining an awareness of legally relevant events and trends as a necessary input to the Commission's work and in order to minimize or eliminate duplication of effort in the legal field.

As the parent body, the General Assembly is at once the Commission's main beneficiary, its guide and its sternest critic, as well as its sole benefactor: that is, it is the source of its facilities, of its services and, most importantly, of its financial support. As the senior partner in the relationship, the General Assembly has certain essential, not to say vital, responsibilities toward the Commission, in as much as it must provide its subsidiary organ with the basic sustenance needed for a viable and productive existence. The extent to which the Member States represented in the General Assembly benefit from the Commission is thus related directly to what the aggregate of their national priorities has determined should be invested in the Commission. Before addressing the theme of this paper—namely, the Commission's methods of work and choice of topics—it is necessary to note four of the sustaining elements furnished by the General Assembly, which are intimately connected with that theme.

Electing the members of the Commission

The members of the Commission—the Commission's essence and basic asset—are furnished by the General Assembly: 34 persons whom the Member States have decided are both (a) appropriately qualified (of "recognized competence in international law") and (b) representative ("of the main forms of civilization and of the principal legal systems of the world"). Apart from these

---

[4]That multilateral treaties dealing with the progressive development and codification of international law should be open to universal participation is well settled, at least since the adoption of the Declaration on Universal Participation which was adopted at the 1968-1969 United Nations Conference on the Law of Treaties. Cf. the Charter of Economic Rights and Duties of States, which affirms, in its operative paragraph 10, that "All States . . . have the right to participate fully and effectively in the international decision-making process in the solution of world economic, financial and monetary problems . . .".

criteria, which are statutorily prescribed, two others are of comparable importance from the practical point of view: (c) the members should be "representative" also of a range of professional activities in the field of international law; and (d) the members should be able to devote quality time to the work of the Commission. Criterion (c) seeks to ensure that the qualities of practitioners—such as those who have served as counsel before international tribunals or have had judicial experience or advised Governments—combine with those of other professions, such as teaching and diplomacy, to ensure that the work of the Commission remains responsive to a variety of potential applications. Criterion (d) is vital, because the promise implicit in the election of a member—namely, that he or she will actually contribute the expertise and values of his or her profession or "civilization" to the work of the Commission—would not be fulfilled if an elected member were to fail to attend, or attend regularly, or to collaborate effectively because of competing demands on his or her time and energies. Such failure cannot but have an adverse effect on the quality of the Commission's product and its political and particularly its multicultural foundations, as envisaged by the Statute's drafters, besides possibly contributing to delays and misunderstandings in its work.

The electors' observance of criteria concerning the qualifications of the members of the Commission and their geographically and professionally representative character (criteria (a), (b) and (c)) have given rise to little comment. The Statute's prescriptions in the case of criteria (a) and (b) have been met and, whether by chance or design, the Commission's membership has, over the years, included balanced representation of professional categories: persons with legal counselling, teaching, diplomatic and judicial experience. On the other hand, the electors have not given due consideration to criterion (d): the ability of a member to devote quality time to the work of the Commission. This, in turn, is likely to create the impression that, in the view of the electors, the Commission's work is of a merely symbolic order, even that it is of low priority, and that election to the Commission is more in the nature of an accolade, rather than being a mandate to perform a public function which carries with it substantial responsibilities. Such an impression has often arisen in connection with members from developing countries, which have sent to the Commission persons of the highest intellectual and professional capacities. Occupying national positions of high responsibility, it is well-nigh impossible for them to devote quality time to the Commission, which offers complex and time-consuming intellectual and political challenges of its own. The electors are usually well aware of this factor beforehand, but have found difficulty in taking it duly into account. The aim of a nominating Government both to ensure electoral success and to honour a high official by securing for her or him a place on the Commission evokes an accommodating response from the electors, partly with the objective of maintaining or increasing the prestige and authority of the individual concerned, but inspired equally by an element of reciprocity that is calculated to ensure perpetuation of the practice.

The criticism frequently directed at Governments of developing countries which nominate for election high officials who can have little or no time for the work of the Commission is often tempered by the explanation that such a country can have but few qualified personnel and that there are many demands on their time. It is doubtful that such is the case today, though. Most, if not all, nominating Governments today, rich and poor alike, may choose from a range of suitable candidates; but that choice is often made on political, rather than on functional, grounds. The result of such a political choice is often that a large number of members of the Commission elected on that basis are not present for a large proportion of the time allocated to a session. Such irregular attendance is most prevalent in the case of members from the developing countries. Of course, the Commission's work will continue, and its mandate will be discharged satisfactorily, with the burden being borne in large measure by members from the industrialized countries, in particular, those from the "Big Five", whose regular attendance can be relied upon. However, the developing countries' contribution to the Commission's work is thereby diminished, besides being postponed to the stage of governmental responses to the Commission's requests for comment, to statements in the Sixth Committee and, finally, to positions taken at intergovernmental conferences. Even at those stages of the treaty-making process, other priorities distract, often making developing country participation less than optimally effective and laying the validity and utility of the process as such gravely open to question.

Many questions raised by this line of thought go far beyond those that relate to the election of a member of the Commission and, although of the first importance, fall outside the scope of this paper. However, what should be emphasized here is that the election of a suitable candidate is essentially within the special, if not the sole, competence of the electors: that is, nominating, as well as voting, Member States represented in the Sixth Committee. It is only their forethought concerning the availability of a member of the Commission to serve and their forbearance that could provide a remedy. Perhaps an oath or affirmation concerning regular and impartial service should be made mandatory for each member of the Commission. It could be administered by or on behalf of the President of the General Assembly, as a solemn reminder of the priorities implied in membership of the Commission.

There are four other aspects of membership which, if addressed by the electors, could have a salutary effect on the Commission's work. First, the General Assembly, concerned, as it has been, to elect persons of excellence to the Commission, may have given less thought to selecting women in that category. The concern here is not so much that women should be "represented" on the Commission as that, in its discussion of legal norms, the Commission may be missing a contribution of values, ideas and priorities shared by half the world. It is of the first importance that Governments seek to rectify this gender imbalance by nominating as many women as possible as candidates and by instructing their representatives in the Sixth Committee to observe a "gentlemen's agreement" concerning election of a substantial number of women for the next quinquennium—a possible target might be one third of the Commission's membership. Secondly, with a view to encouraging participation in the Commission's work on as broad a basis as possible over time, members might agree voluntarily to limit their membership to two full terms. It is recognized that there would be no way, short of amendment of the Commission's Statute, of implementing such a practice with respect to the politically more influential countries. Nevertheless, a practice of this kind, generally applied, could enhance the role of the Commission as a mechanism to encourage universal participation in treaty-making. Thirdly, the electors, who receive more or less detailed outlines of the personal histories of the candidates, might consider the value of electing to the Commission one or more candidates with qualifications and experience in such fields as sociology and legal anthropology. The knowledge of members so qualified (or, if there were none, of specialists in those fields engaged by the Commission on an ad hoc basis) could contribute substantially to the acceptability and utility of the Commission's work. Their expertise would be of particular value if, as is suggested below, the Commission were to undertake fundamental studies concerning ways and means of enhancing compliance with, and implementation of, international law.

Finally, it may be recalled that, although article 1 of the Commission's Statute contemplates that the Commission is to concern itself primarily with public international law, "it is not precluded from entering the field of private international law". While the potential of this provision might have diminished with the establishment of the Hague Conference on Private International Law and of the United Nations Commission on International Trade Law, there may be important areas of private international law which are as yet untouched by these institutions and in which the Commission may play a useful and effective role. Election to the Commission of specialists in private international law may lead to the inclusion of topics from that field in the Commission's surveys of "the whole field of international law" pursuant to article 18 of its Statute and the selection of some of them by the Commission for more detailed study. In any event, members so qualified could provide the Commission with useful perspectives on issues connected with the implementation of inter-State obligations at the national level and matters of practical importance which might not always be the focus of the Commission's attention: for example, enforcement of the judgements or awards of international tribunals, the taking of evidence abroad and other forms of judicial assistance.

Responding to the Commission's requests

An aspect of the Commission's methods of work that is of the highest importance consists in its exchanges with States Members of the United Nations. Such exchanges may take various forms and may be carried out at various stages of the consideration of a topic. On the thoroughness, timeliness, depth and candour of Member States' responses to the Commission's requests for information or for observations depend, in large measure, the acceptability and ultimately the effectiveness of the Commission's product. Although one may sympathize with the plight of the harassed Foreign Ministry Legal Adviser called upon to prepare those responses, it must be recognized that failure to respond, or to respond adequately, starves the Commission of information and of judgements that are vital to the success of its work. Receipt by the Commission of responses from only a small number of States—often the more affluent, whose legal services are well staffed—increases the Commission's already heavy responsibility for determining political balance, while putting the quality of its product at risk.

If properly approached, the preparation of a Member State's response to the Commission's request for comments is a complex and time-consuming task, in which the Foreign Ministry Legal Adviser will play a central role. With ever-increasing emphasis being placed on the interests and needs of the individual as the "end-user" of the law, it is open to the Foreign Ministry to recognize that it is only one of the many entities for which the rules on which the Commission is working will have relevance. However, the Foreign Ministry has, by tradition, if not by law, a certain primacy, which makes it well-placed to perform a coordinating function. Before formulating a Government's response to the Commission's request for comments, the Foreign Ministry might be expected to notify not only the Government's technical departments which might be concerned, but also, when appropriate, scientific bodies, universities, learned and professional societies, chambers of commerce, large corporations and citizens' associations or non-governmental organizations.

Comment in the Sixth Committee

Governments also have the opportunity to comment on the Commission's work through their representatives in the Sixth Committee at the regular sessions of the General Assembly during the discussion of the Commission's annual reports. Insightful and constructive observations on all aspects of the Commission's work, including its working methods and choice of topics, declared and debated in the Sixth Committee, are a feature of immense importance to the Commission. Unlike the direct response which is received from, or through, a Foreign Ministry Legal Adviser, there is, here, more opportunity to ascertain and to gather support for a trend, as well as to reflect it in a resolution containing appropriate policy directives to the Commission. Well thought-out and candid statements, which are often delivered by members of the Commission speaking in the Sixth Committee as Government representatives, exercise a powerful influence on the Commission's work. It is important that as many Sixth Committee representatives as possible should speak, but particularly those from countries which have not furnished the Commission with their written views. Equally important, as time for discussion in the Sixth Committee is limited, such statements should be as clear, concise and policy-oriented as possible.

Providing the Commission's resources

For the resources at its disposal, the Commission is entirely dependent on its parent body, the General Assembly. Since the quality of the members of the Commission is assured through criteria established and applied by Member States, and since the Commission's methods of work have been steadily adjusted towards optimum efficiency either by the Commission acting *proprio motu* or in response to the Sixth Committee's suggestions, it seems reasonable to suppose that any remaining inadequacies in terms of the Commission's output must be attributable, at least in part, to an insufficiency in the resources allocated for the Commission's work in pursuance of decisions taken by the General Assembly's Sixth and Fifth Committees. In reaching such decisions, due account will have been taken of the importance and level of priority accorded to the Commission's work by the membership of the Organization and, in particular, of the wishes of the 10 or so principal contributors to the Organization's finances. This is not to say that a determined majority could not outvote the opposition, for example, regarding the allocation of funds for the study of a particular topic or for convening a diplomatic conference to adopt a convention on a topic on which the Commission has completed its work. However, such a failure to take account of the wishes of the minority—and of the most politically influential among the Organization's Member States—could result in a Pyrrhic victory, entailing substantial wastage of time and of the Commission's meagre resources, not to speak of the resources of the participating Governments. Conventions adopted in this way may never enter into force, or may do so only after inordinate delay, and may be of little benefit to the course of international relations. They become monuments to wasted effort and should be sober reminders of the significance, for better or worse, of political power in the designing of the legal order.

The resources available to the Commission are the funds allocated by the General Assembly, first, for meeting expenses connected with holding of the Commission's annual session (currently 10 weeks) from May to July at the Commission's seat at Geneva (currently some $1.8 million) and, secondly, a sum—substantial, but difficult to estimate with any accuracy—expended for the maintenance of some seven members of the staff of the Codification Division of the Office of Legal Affairs, who, although forming the core of the Commission's secretariat, are able to spend no more than an estimated 40 per cent of their time on the work of the Commission. Functions not directly related to topics under consideration by the Commission which are regularly performed by the Codification Division include: the preparation of studies and surveys on general questions of international law, as directed by the Legal Counsel; the preparation and publication of the United Nations Legislative Series; the publication of *Reports of International Arbitral Awards*; the publication of those *Official Records of the General Assembly* which have legal aspects, for example, the summary records of the Sixth Committee's regular sessions and of its sessions convened to adopt treaty texts, such as the Convention on the Prevention and Punishment of Crimes against Internationally Protected Persons, including Diplomatic Agents; preparations for United Nations conferences which are convened to consider texts elaborated by the International Law Commission, such as the Vienna conferences on the law of treaties of 1968-1969 and 1986, and the publication of their official records; preparation of sessions of ad hoc or standing committees of the General Assembly dealing with legal questions, such as the Special Committee on the Charter of the United Nations and on the Strengthening of the Role of the Organization, and publication of their official records; revision from time to time of the *Repertory of Practice of United Nations Organs*; and preparation and publication of the *United Nations Juridical Yearbook*.

Taking into account that some 60 per cent of the time of the Commission's secretariat is regularly spent on activities which are not directly relevant to the Commission's work, the General Assembly has, since 1973, endorsed the Commission's recommendation that the staff of the Codification Division be increased with a view to assisting the Commission to make necessary adjustments in its functioning in response to suggestions from Governments. However, as the policies of the national legislatures of Member States are driven by other priorities, the results of that endorsement have been meagre.

To highlight the striking inconsistency between the General Assembly's repeated decisions endorsing the strengthening of the staff of the Commission's secretariat and its failure for over a quarter of a century to implement such decisions is not to imply any criticism. It is intended merely to emphasize three factors that need to be borne in mind in any realistic discussion of ways and means of improving the Commission's methods of work: (*a*) decisions of the General Assembly concerning allocation of funds for the Commission's work, taken at the international level and as far as possible in accordance with democratic principles, have been negated through the operation of democracy at the national level, through the withholding of parliamentary authority for the release of funds; (*b*) it should remind us that, in practice, for the General Assembly's decision on funding to have the result called for by its text, it must have the legislative approval of the 10 or so principal contributors to the Organization's finances: that is, the work of the Organization, and of the Commission in particular, must have acquired a certain priority among influential members of the parliaments of those States, either as serving some national policy objective or, conceivably, as possessing a degree of moral value and weight that would be recognized by the national electorate; and (*c*), unless and until the work of the Commission is perceived by the national legislatures of those principal contributors as yielding desired benefits, no proposal for improving the Commission's methods of work that would entail an increase in its current budget is likely to succeed: for example, strengthening the Commission secretariat, holding longer sessions or holding two sessions each year.

III. Improving the Commission's methods of work

Early commentators were much concerned with the manner in which the Statute's drafters had distinguished the process of "progressive development of international law" from that of "codification of international law" and with the possible implications of that distinction for the methods which the Commission was to follow in dealing with topics in each of those categories. However, the Commission itself has, over the years, adopted approaches to both of these categories which are broadly similar to each other and which are related both to the practical problems raised by a particular topic and to the contemplated outcome of its work, such as a draft convention, a restatement of the law, model rules or a report. These approaches comprise all or most of the following 10 steps, subsequently to the Commission's decision to deal with a topic: (1) preliminary consideration of the topic and report to the Commission by a group of its members chaired by the prospective Special Rapporteur; (2) appointment by the Commission of a Special Rapporteur and of "members to work with the Rapporteur"—that is, a "consultative group" or "working group"; (3) adoption by the Commission of a "plan of work" for the topic, paying due regard to the desirability of completing a discrete phase of the work, such as a preliminary outline or the first or second reading of draft articles, by the end of its five-year term; (4) the sending of questionnaires to Governments and, where appropriate, other bodies, as well as requests for information and documents; (5) consultation with scientific institutions and individual experts; (6) preparation and drafting of articles by the Commission with the guidance of the Special Rapporteur; (7) invitation to individual Governments and to the Sixth Committee to comment on the Commission's draft; (8) consideration ("reading") of draft articles by the Commission; (9) reconsideration and adjustment of the draft articles in the light of comments received; and (10) the Commission's report to the General Assembly setting forth the result of its consideration of the topic and its recommendation as to the action which should be taken with respect to it. A schematic representation of the Commission at work is to be found in annex I to this paper.

Perceived ills and suggested remedies

Over the years a number of distinguished scholars have made valuable proposals for improving the Commission's methods of work, including its choice of topics for study.[5] The Commission has itself, from time to time,

---

[5]Monographs and studies that have dealt extensively with the work of the Commission include the following: El Baradei, M., Franck, T., and Trachtenberg, R., *The International Law Commission: The Need for a New Direction* (1981), p. 5 (United Nations publication, Sales No. E.81.XV.PE/1); Briggs, H.W., *The International Law Commission* (1965); Dhokalia, R.P., *The Codification of International Law* (1970); Higgins, R., *The Development of International Law through the Political Organs of the United Nations* (1963); Ramcharan, B.G., *The International Law Commission: Its Approach to the Codification and Progressive Development of International Law* (1977); Sinclair, Sir I., *The International Law Commission* (1987); and Thirlway, H.W.A., *International Customary Law and Codification: An Examination of the Continuing Role of Custom in the Present period of Codification of International Law* (1972).

Articles which have provided important contemporary insights include the following: Abi-Saab, "The Development of International Law by the United Nations", *Revue égyptienne de droit international*, vol. 24 (1968), p. 95; Ago, "La Codification du droit international et les problèmes de sa réalisation", in *Recueil d'études de droit international en hommage à Paul Guggenheim* (1968), p. 93; Al-Baharna, "Future Topics for the Codification of International Law Viewed in Historical

undertaken that task *proprio motu* or at the urging of the Sixth Committee. Most critics seem to identify the same ills and, as is not surprising, their thoughts on ways of remedying them so as to improve the Commission's efficiency are also similar.

One major study of the Commission lists the following grounds for concern regarding the Commission's working methods: (1) the Commission is too slow in its work; (2) the output of the Commission is too low, compared with the amount of work to be done; (3) the Commission's methods lack flexibility; (4) the Commission's methods result in waste and inefficiency; (5) the Commission has unnecessarily confined itself to the production of draft conventions, instead of putting out restatements and model rules as well; and (6) the Commission spends too much time on line-by-line discussions of its studies.[6]

The same author then lists various suggestions which have been made from time to time for improving the Commission's working methods and thereby certain aspects of its performance: (1) the Commission should be placed on a full-time basis; (2) the duration of the Commission's sessions should be increased; (3) the Commission should hold two sessions each year; (4) the Commission should meet in plenary session twice each day, instead of once, as it does at present; (5) the Commission should appoint subcommissions and working groups on different topics, which could meet, when necessary, intersessionally; (6) the secretariat of the Commission (the Codification Division of the Office of Legal Affairs) should be strengthened and more tasks assigned to it in the form of preparation of background studies on each topic before the

---

Perspective", in United Nations, *International Law on the Eve of the Twenty-first Century: Views from the International Law Commission* (1997), p. 373 (United Nations publication, Sales No. E/F 97.V.4); Bos, "Aspects phénoménologiques de la codification du droit international public", in Zanardi, P.L., Migliazza, A., Pocar, F., and Ziccardi, P. (eds.), *Le Droit international à l'heure de sa codification : études en l'honneur de Roberto Ago* (1987), vol. I, p. 141; Cede, "New Approaches to Law Making in the UN-System", *Austrian Review of International and European Law*, vol. 1 (1996), p. 51; Cheng, "The International Law Commission", *Current Legal Problems*, vol. 5 (1952), p. 250; Dhokalia, "Reflections on International Law-making and its Progressive Development in the Contemporary Era of Transition", in Pathak, R.S., and Dhokalia, R.P. (eds.), *International Law in Transition: Essays in Memory of Judge Nagendra Singh* (1992), p. 203; Dupuy, "La Codification du droit international, a-t-elle encore un intérêt à l'aube du troisième millénaire?", in Zanardi et al., op. cit. above, p. 261; Graefrath, "The International Law Commission Tomorrow: Improving its Organization and Methods of Work", *American Journal of International Law*, vol. 85 (1991), p. 595; Hurst, "A Plea for the Codification of International Law on New Lines", *Transactions of the Grotius Society*, vol. 32 (1946), p. 151; Jennings, "The Progressive Development of International Law and its Codification", *British Year Book of International Law*, vol. 24 (1947), p. 301; Lauterpacht, "Codification and Development of International Law", *American Journal of International Law*, vol. 49 (1955), p. 16; Lee, "The International Law Commission Re-examined", *American Journal of International Law*, vol. 59 (1965), p. 545; Münch, "La Codification inachevée", in Zanardi et al., op. cit. above, p. 373; Nawaz, "On Ways and Methods for Improving the Work of the International Law Commission", *Indian Journal of International Law*, vol. 25 (1985), p. 634; Pellet, "La Formation du droit international dans le cadre des Nations Unies", *European Journal of International Law*, vol. 6 (1995), p. 401; Rosenne, "The International Law Commission, 1949-1959", *British Year Book of International Law*, vol. 36 (1960), p. 104, and "Relations between Governments and the International Law Commission", *Year Book of World Affairs*, vol. 19 (1965), p. 183; Sette-Camara, "The International Law Commission: Discourse on Method", in Zanardi et al., op. cit. above, p. 467; Stone, "On the Vocation of the International Law Commission", *Columbia Law Review*, vol. 57 (1957), p. 16; Suy, "Développement progressif et codification du droit international: le rôle de l'Assemblée générale revisité", in United Nations, *International Law as a Language for International Relations* (1996), p. 215; Yankov, "Strengthening the Process of Codification and Development of International Law: The Evolving Functions of the International Law Commission and Increasing the Commitments of States", in ibid., p. 230; and Zemanek, "Codification of International Law: Salvation or Dead End?", in Zanardi et al., op. cit. above, p. 581.

[6]Ramcharan, op. cit. above (preceding footnote), pp. 38-39.

Commission; (7) the Commission's methods should be made more flexible; (8) the Commission should prepare, in addition to draft conventions, other types of documents on the topics dealt with by it, such as studies, model rules and draft resolutions for adoption by the General Assembly; (9) the Commission should have shorter sessions, each devoted to one topic; and (10) the Commission should appoint experts from outside the Commission either as Special Rapporteurs or to assist its Special Rapporteurs.[7]

This list may be supplemented by the following: (11) of the two proposed sessions, a summer session of eight weeks should be held in Geneva and a winter session of four weeks in New York, the latter to be devoted to issues of drafting, in preparation for the timely circulation of texts for discussion at the next Geneva session; (12) there should be two Drafting Committees working in parallel on different topics; (13) the Commission's permanent bodies should include committees to deal with planning, research and coordination; (14) a topic might be divided between two Special Rapporteurs with a view to spreading the workload, expediting the work and minimizing the adverse effects of the untimely departure of a Special Rapporteur; (15) the Commission should work in chambers or subcommittees; (16) the Commission could continue on a part-time basis, but Special Rapporteurs should be employed full-time; (17) the Commission's agenda should be condensed, so that not every item would be dealt with each year, and items which are no longer important to Governments should be deleted; (18) Special Rapporteurs should be appointed for all priority topics within the Commission's programme and requested to submit provisional reports within two years which would, by the end of a five-year term, be adopted by the Commission as the foundation of its future work; (19) the Commission should try to complete its work on a topic, or a discrete portion or stage of the work, within the Commission's five-year term; (20) the Commission should hold public hearings and conferences of experts in order to assist in securing greater Member-State participation in its work; (21) the Commission should extend and intensify its collaboration with scientific associations, research bodies and universities; (22) arrangements should be made for the Commission to have access to the necessary scientific and technical expertise.

Of the suggestions listed, some—suggestions numbers 1, 2, 3, 6, 10, 11, 16 and 20—are unlikely to be followed up, since they would manifestly involve increased costs, which, given the prevailing scale of priorities referred to above, the Organization would not be in a position to meet. Among these suggestions is at least one that could be of particular value to efforts to improve the Commission's efficiency, including its rate of productivity: namely, strengthening the staff of the Codification Division. From the Commission's inception, the reliance of its members on "their secretariat" has been substantial and the work of successive generations of the staff of the Codification Division has been of immense value to them. However, a proposal to recruit, say, three experienced middle-grade staff members (P.3 or P.4)—something that would materially expand the research and drafting capacities of the Division—would cost at least an additional $300,000 annually and would be unlikely to survive Fifth Committee scrutiny.

A regular 10-week session of the Commission held at its seat in Geneva is reported to cost some $1.8 million, which includes such expenses as airfares, subsistence and honoraria for the members of the Commission and the New York–based staff of the Codification Division, as well as the costs of simulta-

---

[7]Ibid., pp. 39 and 42-57.

neous interpretation, of the preparation of summary records of plenary meetings, of the translation, revision and printing of documents and of other supporting services. Assuming that there are 50 regular working days available in a 10-week session, we may anticipate that 15 hours per week would be utilized for plenary meetings (three hours on Monday afternoon, plus three hours each morning, Tuesday to Friday, totalling 150 hours over the 10-week session) and 12 hours per week would be reserved for meetings of the Drafting Committee (three hours each afternoon, Tuesday to Friday, totalling 120 hours over the session as a whole). Meetings of the Expanded Bureau, the Planning Group and any working groups could meet on an ad hoc basis outside regular hours, whenever they were available. If all 34 members of the Commission were to participate in plenary meetings (there being available a total of $150 \times 60 = 9000$ minutes), each member would have some 265 minutes in which to express her or his considered opinions: at least 30 minutes on each of the, say, six topics before the Commission and on two procedural or administrative questions. In practice, the amount of time available for the expression of a participant's views would be considerably greater. Given an average attendance during a session of only, say, 25 of the Commission's 34 members, each would have $9000 \div 25 = 360$ minutes, which would allow him or her to speak for a total of 45 minutes on each of the six topics before the Commission and on two procedural or administrative matters. On a similar basis, assuming all members were to participate in the work of the Drafting Committee, as they are entitled to do, each would have at her or his disposal some $7200 \div 25 = 288$ minutes: approximately 35 minutes on each of the six topics before the Committee and on two other subjects.

It is recognized, of course, that such figures are mere approximations. No group of human beings dealing with complex issues, let alone the Commission's eminent members, could be expected to make their contributions according to rigid schedules. Moreover, unforeseen incidents can always upset the best laid plans of work. Nevertheless, these simple calculations suggest that a 10-week session, if intended to provide members with the opportunity for a face-to-face exchange of views, could be sufficient; and, at an overall cost of some $36,000 per meeting day, or $6,000 *per* hour (not counting the salaries of the United Nations personnel involved), it could be difficult to persuade Member States' finance ministries of the need to extend the duration of the Commission's regular sessions or to fund additional meetings annually.

Suggestion number 4 (two plenary sessions each day of a session) and suggestion number 9 (shorter sessions, each devoted to a single topic) do not, for the present, seem feasible. The Commission appears to have adopted and implemented in some form, either *proprio motu* or following proposals by Member States, the practices covered by suggestions numbers 5, 7, 13, 15, 18 and 19.

The commissioning of other treaty-drafting bodies

Suggestion number 22 (arrangements for the Commission to have access to the necessary scientific and technical expertise) would be essential if the Commission were to be called upon to deal with the regulation of scientific and technical activities. This has not been the case—a thought that leads us to consider a matter sometimes discussed: the by now frequent practice of negotiating multilateral agreements without a basic text being first drafted by the Commission. Thus far, the Commission has been given, or has itself chosen to assume, responsibility for study of what have been termed the "major themes" of public international law, while Member States have preferred to deal with the regulation of activities of a technical nature through other negotiating and drafting mechanisms, usually those associated with competent intergovernmental organizations which have ready access through established channels to the necessary expertise. Thus, intergovernmental expert groups convened under the auspices of the International Maritime Organization have successfully launched treaties dealing not only with the regulation of activities associated with maritime transportation as such, but also with the protection and preservation of the marine environment. Similarly, intergovernmental legal/technical negotiating groups meeting under the auspices of the United Nations, the United Nations Environment Programme, the International Atomic Energy Agency and the International Civil Aviation Organization have produced multilateral treaty texts dealing with highly technical subjects that have met with widespread acceptance. The International Labour Organization is a pioneer in the field of drafting and monitoring the observance of regulatory treaties in its field. Conceivably, the Commission could have been asked to draft these treaty texts and, if supplied with adequate scientific and technical advice, would certainly have produced work of comparable quality, although it is doubtful whether it could have done so within comparable time frames. In such instances, the needs and opportunities for regulation became apparent quite naturally and spontaneously within specialist institutions familiar with the issues. To have removed the discussions to a forum like the Commission, which would have required extensive technical briefing, would have been neither economical nor prudent.

It was no disrespect to the Commission either that it was not given the task of elaborating a "basic text" for the Third United Nations Conference on the Law of the Sea, as it was for the first such conference convened in 1958: some of the issues to be negotiated at the Third Conference were of such importance, both politically and technically, that few States were willing to forgo direct participation in the negotiations from the start. The concept of negotiating such issues by delegation was simply not acceptable, so that neither the Commission nor any other body of limited membership could ever have been entrusted with that task.

The law of the sea is perhaps the only field in which Member States have attempted treaty-making both with and without the benefit of an in-depth study by the Commission. The Commission's work on the law of the sea which was begun in 1949 resulted in a series of draft articles being placed before the first Conference in 1958 and eventually in four conventions with a total of more than 100 articles, which entered into force in 1962 (the Convention on the High Seas), 1964 (the Convention on the Continental Shelf), 1965 (the Convention on the Territorial Sea and the Contiguous Zone) and 1966 (the Convention on Fishing and Conservation of the Living Resources of the High Seas). The time to fruition of the work was 11, 13, 14 and 15 years, respectively. Work on the Third Conference might be said to have been begun in 1971, with the representatives of Member States negotiating a "list of subjects and issues" to be dealt with at the proposed conference. The Conference itself began in 1973 and ended in 1982, with the adoption, by near-consensus, of a single convention of some 320 articles and 7 annexes. The Convention entered into force—after some fundamental adjustments had been made to provisions on mining of the deep seabed—in 1994. The time to fruition in this case was thus 23 years. Could this period have been shortened if the Commission had been entrusted with the task of making a "basic proposal"? Could funds and personnel resources have been better utilized by Member Governments and the United Nations if the Commission had prepared a draft? These questions may have to remain unanswered for the time being; but the economics of large conferences might well be a subject worthy of study by the Commission.

Interaction with other institutions

Perhaps the most noteworthy of the suggestions listed above, and one that offers possibilities for virtually cost-free implementation, is suggestion number 21: that the Commission should extend and intensify its collaboration with scientific associations, research bodies and universities. Such a suggestion would hardly appear novel to the Commission, empowered, as it is, by article 26, paragraph 1, of its Statute to:

"consult with any international or national organizations, official or non-official, on any subject entrusted to it if it believes that such a procedure might aid it in the performance of its functions".

When compared with the possibilities offered by this provision, the scope of the Commission's current consultative activities appears narrow and conservative, comprising more or less formal exchanges between the Commission and regional intergovernmental bodies—the Asian-African Legal Consultative Committee, the Inter-American Juridical Committee and the European Committee on Legal Co-operation—aimed merely at keeping each organization informed of the other's initiatives. Although such exchanges might "aid [the Commission] in the performance of its functions", it seems clear that greater benefits could be derived from the Commission's mandate to "consult".

Thus, as to consultation with "international organizations", it might be of mutual advantage to maintain regular relations with such recognized institutions as the Institut de Droit International and the International Law Association, as well as international and regional practitioners' associations, such as LAWASIA and other bar associations, so as to be able to exchange views on work in progress, whether at a preliminary stage or when work is at a more stage of drafting, as, for example, when Governments are consulted. The Commission might find it useful to establish a liaison group as a permanent subsidiary organ to advise the Commission on the establishment and conduct of such relations. Partner institutions themselves might find it useful to establish permanent committees or working groups to interact with the Commission on a continuous basis. Such relations should not imply that either the Commission or any partner institution was being invited to take a position on an issue, but, rather, that the members of these bodies were being kept informed and could contribute observations, if they chose to do so. Acknowledgement of learned opinions thus received could appear in the Commission's annual report.

Regular relationships could also usefully be maintained with national organizations, such as learned societies and universities and even non-governmental organizations (NGOs), selected from time to time on the basis of agreed criteria by the Commission's proposed liaison group. Research work which the Commission might not have the resources to undertake might be "contracted out" to universities. The universities may themselves find intrinsic value in having the opportunity to collaborate with the Commission in this way. On the other hand, Governments, in recognition of that value, may consider granting a contracted university more tangible compensation for such research. The use, if any, which is made of the results of such research would, of course, be for the Commission alone to decide.

Regular and direct consultation with national organizations, as authorized by article 26, paragraph 1, of the Commission's Statute, is not only a resource of which the Commission might avail itself: the provision has wider, and potentially even more important, implications for the progressive development of international law. It represents a channel through which the Commission may maintain direct interaction with the individual, the end-user of the law. It offers at once the means of making the Commission's work and product more widely known to people everywhere and the opportunity to receive responses and comments from concerned citizens—responses and comments which might otherwise be lost in the corridors of officialdom. In the future, as protection of the rights and welfare of the individual is recognized as the chief end and purpose of all legislative effort, both the Commission and Member States should become increasingly aware that "democratic principles" would best be served by allowing and facilitating use of the channel contemplated by article 26, paragraph 1, of the Statute. In this connection, the Commission might wish to consider, if it has not already done so, direct communication with national and international institutions through the Internet, which offers an efficient and inexpensive method of reaching and receiving responses from interested individuals and groups everywhere. The Commission should ensure that a complete set of its reports is available in at least one university library in each country and that all important documents concerning work-in-progress, say from 1990 onwards, are made available through the Internet.

Use of the time and capacities of members

The Commission is, without doubt, the supreme planner of the use of its time and capacities, subject always to the direction and the corrective influences of the General Assembly. At each session, the Planning Group and the Bureau undertake the delicate task of apportioning the available time for work on topics so as to take into account not merely the nature of the topic and the stage reached in its consideration by the Commission, but also the optimal participation of members, in particular the Special Rapporteurs, all of whom have competing demands on their time—an inevitable feature of a part-time Commission composed of eminent persons. It is with the greatest circumspection, therefore, that the following suggestions are offered.

(1) Given that membership of the Commission is a vocation undertaken by way of public service, members may be willing to consider devoting additional time to the Commission's work outside the annual session. Thus, in addition to the preparatory study of drafts and commentaries which a member must find time for while pursuing his or her regular professional activities, Special Rapporteurs may initiate discussion of specific issues by correspondence and attempt thereby to shorten and even to eliminate the need for oral exchanges on those issues during the Commission's session. Such a practice, which appears to have been used successfully in the work of committees of the Institut de Droit International, could well save the Commission precious time, while providing a written record of a member's views at greatly reduced cost. (2) Where there appears to be a clear need for extensive spoken exchanges on a specific issue, consideration might be given to arranging, intersessionally, a video conference of, say, a working group, organized and conducted by the Special Rapporteur in such a way as to optimize its guidance value to him or her. Such a practice should, however, be preceded by an assessment of its financial implications and negotiation with the communications company concerned. (3) Discussion and clarification of points of view through intersessional correspondence or video

conferencing could eventually pave the way for voluntary limitation of spoken interventions to, say, five minutes *per* subject. (4) Taking into account the promotional role contemplated by article 1 of the Commission's Statute and the representational character inherent in membership of the Commission, it may be useful to consider assigning the study of selected topics to each member of the Commission. Upon taking office, members might be invited to suggest appropriate topics of interest to them and the Planning Group could, after a survey of the topics and consultation with members, recommend to the Commission how the topics might be assigned. Study of the topic would be completed within the five-year period of membership and would be published in the *United Nations Juridical Yearbook*. The views expressed would be those of the author and not those of the Commission. In this way, the capacities and representational character of each member of the Commission could be reflected more effectively during her or his term of office and a great many international legal issues would receive informed and incisive scrutiny.

IV. Selection of topics for study by the Commission

An overview of the Commission's work programme since 1949, a list of topics proposed by the Commission's working group in 1992 and the headings of a "General Scheme" of possible topics prepared by a working group in 1996 are set out in annex II to this paper in order to illustrate the results of the Commission's own deliberations on the selection of topics for study. From time to time, analyses have been made of the criteria which the Commission has applied to identify the topics on which it should undertake the progressive development and codification of rules of international law. Commentators have also advanced suggestions regarding the criteria which should be employed for this purpose. These criteria are either articulated in terms of the categories of topics that should be avoided by the Commission—"technical" or "political" topics, for example—or else are framed with a view to identifying the topics which the Commission should take up—topics that are "urgent", for example, or that are "ripe" for study.

The late Paul Reuter suggested three categories of criteria that the Commission would be likely to take into account when deciding whether or not to take up a topic:

"The choice of topics presents difficult problems. It entails not only a technical evaluation of the scope of the subject-matter, but also a practical evaluation of the interest it might have for Governments and a political evaluation of the chances of reaching a wide consensus on the basic issues. Members of the Commission are clearly qualified to make the first of those three evaluations, but they might try to express themselves cautiously on the other two points."[8]

Annex III attempts a rough and ready classification, based on Professor Reuter's observations, of the criteria that have been mentioned from time to time.

The Commission's approach to the selection of topics has varied little in 50 years and it can hardly be denied that that approach is the result of the efforts of some of the century's finest legal minds to deal with the questions involved, against a background of what was politically desirable and economically feasible. Viewed in the light of the constraints within which it has had to operate, the Commission's achievements have been outstanding and it would seem merely

---

[8] *Yearbook of the International Law Commission, 1972*, vol. II, pp. 207-208 at para. 10.

presumptuous for a commentator to advocate a radically different approach or merely to urge that the Commission take up or bring forward consideration of a particular topic or postpone its study of another. Instead, the present paper will propose three areas of activity which, if focused on by the Commission, could, it is believed, lead to enhancement in some measure of the capacity of international law to contribute to an ordered world.

First, the Commission might consider establishing a permanent working group which would review the implementation and effectiveness of multilateral treaties. An annual review would report on adherence (signature, ratification, accession) to such treaties[9] and would disseminate information concerning compliance, including the application of remedies for breach, ranging from collective supervision to dispute settlement. The review would cover all universal multilateral treaties, including those of a technical nature, such as those dealing with the environment, shipping, labour, trade and transport. For coverage of the latter, the Commission would depend on information regularly supplied, in an agreed concise form, by the competent international organizations. The material thus digested and reported could be of practical value to foreign office legal advisers everywhere and could, in time, enable the working group to recommend, when appropriate, any necessary adjustments to the multilateral treaty-making process.

The function of a second working group which the Commission might consider establishing might be described broadly as coordination.[10] This working group would be responsible for gathering current, if not advance, information on all multilateral treaty-making activity, with four main objectives: (1) bringing to light possible duplication of effort; (2) calling attention to interrelated studies or initiatives of relevance to current treaty negotiations; (3) noting any inconsistencies in emerging treaty provisions; and (4) recording *lacunae* which might need to be studied with a view to coverage on a priority basis. In carrying out this function and in connection particularly with this last objective, the working group would need to maintain regular contact with the legal advisers of foreign offices. A report published annually could be of substantial practical benefit to all Government legal services and, indeed, to universities, learned societies and concerned citizens' groups.

The focus of the third suggested working group might be described as fundamental studies. The group would gather material and carry out studies in depth concerning the implementation and effectiveness of all international law, evaluating its impact, or lack thereof, on the quality of life of the individual human being. The group would concern itself with how to deal with the problems associated with the creation and implementation of international law in a world: (1) made increasingly and often shockingly aware of cultural and ethnic differences;

---

[9]Stone emphasizes the need for "[s]ystematic studies on . . . the national official level of observance and non-observance behaviour and the motivation therefor . . . [the need] to extend and deepen the social, economic and political stocktaking of traditional international law . . . to delimit clearly segments undergoing change and breakdown and the forces leading thereto . . . to study official behaviour relating to these segments in the full context of factors operating to produce official attitudes . . . [to study] the functioning of the specialized agencies, carrying the inquiries down to the level of decision-making within the several co-operating member States . . . [and to study] the full historical contexts of selected segments of international law of the recent past, particularly . . . those which seem now [in 1957] to be in collapse despite their former apparent success . . .". Stone, loc. cit. above (footnote 5), pp. 48-49.

[10]A proposal along similar lines is made by Ramcharan, who aptly describes the group's function as being "to foster and safeguard the integrated development of the law": op. cit. above (footnote 5), pp. 14-15.

249

(2) in which rapid, if not instantaneous, communication can be maintained between individuals everywhere, making political and geographical divisions virtually irrelevant; (3) in which all communities must come to terms with the inevitability and relevance of political and economic power; and (4) in which "democratization" proceeds apace at the national level, making the individual human being the direct and immediate beneficiary of domestic law, while certain basic concepts of international law prevent that law from penetrating State boundaries to confer its benefits on the individual.

These suggestions are inspired to some extent by an essay on the Commission by the late Julius Stone. Convinced, as are many others, that worthwhile codification activity cannot be effectively approached except after a vast extension of our understanding of international law in the full context of its contemporary operation, he urged that the Commission be given a broad new mandate:

> "to plan, to supervise, and, in part, to carry out a wide and flexible
> program aimed at extending our knowledge and understanding of the
> operation of international law as a means of social control."[11]

Accordingly, he suggested that the Commission might assume "the role of an International Law Research Center", to which could be channelled material from privately financed national research centres the world over. Complete reconstitution and substitution of the Commission's present functions by a mandate limited to carrying out research would, as noted by Professor Stone, necessitate amendment of the Commission's Statute. The suggestions made here do not, however, contemplate any basic change in the Commission's mandate or direction. They proceed, rather, on the basis that the Commission's Statute as a whole gives it adequate authority to apply its resources to working groups with activities such as those outlined here, which would function in parallel with implementation of the Commission's mandate as presently conceived. While the work of these groups could contribute significantly to what Professor Stone called "our understanding of international law in the full context of its contemporary operation", it would also surely aid the Commission and the Sixth Committee to take informed decisions on the selection of topics for progressive development and codification and on the priority to be assigned to each of them.

---

[11]Stone, loc. cit. above (footnote 5), p. 49.

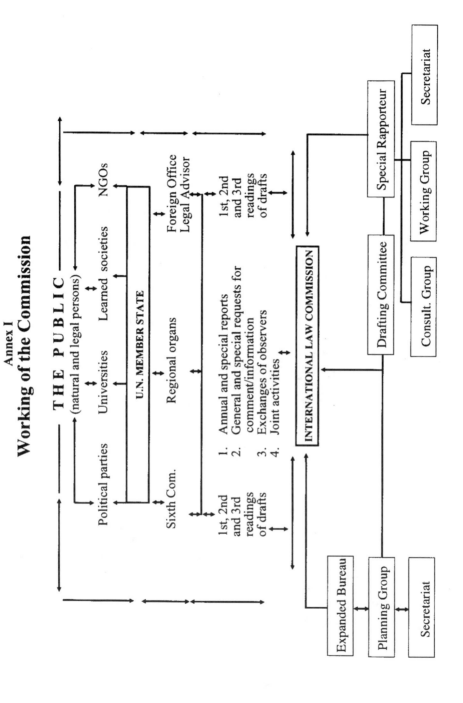

Annex I
Working of the Commission

THE PUBLIC
(natural and legal persons)

Political parties   Universities   Learned societies   NGOs

U.N. MEMBER STATE

Sixth Com.   Regional organs   Foreign Office Legal Advisor

1st, 2nd and 3rd readings of drafts

1. Annual and special reports
2. General and special requests for comment/information
3. Exchanges of observers
4. Joint activities

1st, 2nd and 3rd readings of drafts

INTERNATIONAL LAW COMMISSION

Expanded Bureau

Planning Group

Secretariat

Drafting Committee

Consult. Group

Special Rapporteur

Working Group

Secretariat

251

Annex II

Overview of Commission's Work Programme

1. Recognition of States and Governments. Com./1949/O
2. Succession of States and Governments. Com./1949
    *   Succession in respect of treaties. C(1996)
    *   Succession in matters other than treaties. CN(1983)
    *   Succession in respect of membership of international organizations. (O)
    *   Succession and its impact on the nationality of natural and legal persons. Com./1993/P
3. Jurisdictional immunities of States and their property. Com./1949/RD
4. Jurisdiction with regard to crimes committed outside national territory. Com./1949/O
5. Regime of the high seas. Law of the Sea. Com./1949/4xC (1962-6)
6. Regime of territorial waters. Law of the Sea. (As for no. 5.)
7. Nationality, including statelessness. Com./1949/C(1975)
8. Treatment of aliens. Com./1949/O
9. Right of asylum. Com./1949/O
10. Law of treaties. Com./1949/C(1980)
11. Diplomatic intercourse and immunities. Com./1949/C(1964)
12. Consular intercourse and immunities. Com./1949/C(1967)
13. State responsibility. Com./1949
    *   Origin of international responsibility (RD)
    *   Content, forms and degrees of international responsibility (P)
    *   Implementation of international responsibility and settlement of disputes (P)
14. Arbitral procedure. Com./1949/RD
15. Draft declaration on the rights and duties of States. SA/GA 1947/1949/RD
16. Formulation of the Nürnberg principles. SA/GA 1950/1949/RD
17. Question of international criminal jurisdiction. SA/GA 1950 & 1994/RD
18. Reservations to multilateral conventions. SA/GA 1950/Rep.
19. Question of defining aggression. SA/GA 1950/Rep.
20. Draft code of crimes against the peace and security of mankind. SA/GA 1951 & 1954/RD
21. Relations between States and international organizations. GA 1958
    *   Representation of States in their relations with international organizations of a universal character CN (1975)
    *   Status, privileges and immunities of international organizations (O)
22. Juridical regime of historic waters including historic bays. GA 1959/O

23. Special missions. Com./1959/C(1985)
24. Question of extended participation in general multilateral treaties concluded under the auspices of the League of Nations. SA/GA/1962/Rep.
25. Most-favoured-nation clause. Com./1967/RD
26. Question of treaties concluded between States and international organizations or between international organizations. GA 1969/CN(1986)
27. The law of the non-navigational uses of international watercourses. GA/1970/CN(1997)
28. Question of the protection and inviolability of diplomatic agents and other persons entitled to special protection under international law. SA/GA 1972/C(1977)
29. International liability for injurious consequences arising out of acts not prohibited by international law. Com./1973/RD
    * Prevention of transboundary damage from hazardous activities. (P)
    * International liability. (P)
30. Status of the diplomatic courier and the diplomatic bag not accompanied by diplomatic courier. GA 1976/RD
31. Review of the multilateral treaty-making process. SA/GA 1972/Rep.
32. The law and practice relating to reservations to treaties. Com./1993/P.
33. Diplomatic protection. Com./1993/P
34. Ownership and protection of wrecks beyond the limits of national maritime jurisdiction. Com./1993
35. Unilateral acts of States. Com./1993/P.

KEY

Com.	Selected by the Commission
GA	Referred to the Commission by General Assembly
1949	Item on Commission's 1949 (provisional) list
SA	Special assignment from the General Assembly
RD	Final/first reading report to General Assembly with draft articles/text
Rep.	Final report to General Assembly without draft articles
C (1969)	Convention and year of entry into force
CN (1975)	Convention not yet in force, with year of adoption
O	Not requiring active consideration
P	Remaining on current work programme

Note 1: Topics proposed by the 1992 Working Group

1. The legal conditions of capital investment and agreements pertaining thereto;
2. Ownership and protection of wrecks beyond the limits of national maritime jurisdiction;
3. *Jus cogens*;
4. State succession and its impact on the nationality of natural and legal persons;
5. State succession in respect of membership in international organizations;

6. The law concerning international migrations;
7. The law and practice relating to reservations to treaties;
8. Extraterritorial application of national legislation;
9. The law of (confined) international groundwaters;
10. Global commons; and
11. Rights and duties of the states for the protection of the human environment.

Note 2:   Long-term programme proposed by the 1996 Working Group

The Report of a Working Group appointed by the Commission in 1996 contains a "General Scheme", or non-exhaustive survey of "possible topics", under the following headings:

I	Sources of international law
II	Subjects of international law
III	Succession of States and other legal persons
IV	State jurisdiction / immunity from jurisdiction
V	Law of international organizations
VI	Position of the individual in international law
VII	International criminal law
VIII	Law of international spaces
IX	Law of international relations / responsibility
X	Law of the environment
XI	Law of economic relations
XII	Law of armed conflicts / disarmament
XIII	Settlement of disputes.

The Report concludes with addenda containing outlines on three topics which "in the view of the Commission are appropriate for codification and progressive development":

(*a*) Diplomatic protection

(*b*) Ownership and protection of wrecks beyond the limits of national maritime jurisdiction

(*c*) Unilateral acts of States.

Annex III

Views of Members of the Commission on
Topic-Selection Criteria[12]

Technical criteria

1. The state of international law on the topic.
2. The "ripeness" of the topic for codification.
3. The topic should be of universal application.
4. The topic should have attained the necessary authority to be dealt with objectively.
5. Topics to be avoided include those that are too broad or ill-defined.
6. The Commission should deal only with the "major themes" of international law.
7. The Commission should study "soft law" topics.

Practical criteria

1. The extent to which agreement might be attainable among the members of the Commission.
2. The time likely to be needed to complete work on the topic.
3. The urgency of the topic.
4. The practical importance of the topic to Governments.
5. Avoidance of duplication of the work of other United Nations bodies.
6. Restraint in adding to the work programme, so as to ensure the quality of the Commission's end product.
7. The programme should not encompass too long a term.

Political criteria

1. The importance of the topic.
2. The positions of various States with regard to the topic.
3. Political difficulties which might adversely affect the Commission's work.
4. Bias against the Commission's dealing with "political" or "controversial" subjects.
5. The needs of "international society".
6. Preference for topics that might be settled by international agreement.
7. Bias against the Commission's dealing with a topic that is merely intended to further the political aims of one State alone or of a group of States.
8. The international law of the future should serve the cause of development.

---

[12]Based on material referred to in Ramcharan (op. cit. above (footnote 5), pp. 60-3), and on a categorization suggested by the remarks of the late Paul Reuter (loc. cit. above (footnote 8)).

CHOIX DE SUJETS POUVANT ÊTRE RETENUS PAR LA COMMISSION AUX FINS DE LA CODIFICATION ET DU DÉVELOPPEMENT PROGRESSIF ET MÉTHODES DE TRAVAIL DE LA COMMISSION

par Maurice Kamto*

I. Introduction

Les efforts en vue de la codification de certains aspects du droit international sont relativement anciens. Ils prennent leurs marques avec le congrès de Vienne à la fin des guerres napoléoniennes, en 1815[1]. La création de la Commission du droit international le 21 novembre 1947 par la résolution 174 (II) de l'Assemblée générale fut la consécration d'une pratique qui était sans doute à la recherche d'un cadre permanent. Elle a permis en tout cas de donner suite au paragraphe 1 de l'Article 13 de la Charte des Nations Unies aux termes duquel « l'Assemblée générale provoque des études et fait des recommandations en vue de. . . encourager le développement progressif du droit international et sa codification ».

La codification du droit international, et en particulier le rôle que joue la Commission du droit international en la matière, a déjà fait l'objet de nombreuses et stimulantes réflexions[2]. Les principaux problèmes liés notamment au choix des sujets et aux méthodes de travail de la Commission ont retenu l'attention de la Commission elle-même, et son Rapport sur les travaux de sa quarante-huitième session présente ses analyses ainsi que ses propres conclusions et recommandations à ce sujet[3].

Consentir à réfléchir à nouveau sur ce thème, sans avoir de surcroît aucune expérience d'en dedans du fonctionnement de la Commission, c'est courir inévitablement le risque de ne pas dire mieux que quelques pauvretés. C'est en gardant à l'esprit cet état de fait que l'on se livrera aux quelques développements

---

*Professeur de droit international, Université de Yaoundé II, Yaoundé (Cameroun).

[1] Voir notamment Sette-Camara, « The International Law Commission: Discourse on Method », dans Zanardi, P.L., Migliazza, A., Pocar, F., et Ziccardi, P. (éd.), *Le droit international à l'heure de sa codification : Études en l'honneur de Roberto Ago* (1987), vol. I, p. 468-471.

[2] Il est sans intérêt de rappeler ici l'abondante littérature qui existe dans ce domaine et dont un échantillon significatif sera exploité le long de cette étude. Il suffit d'indiquer que, dès 1948, le Secrétaire général des Nations Unies avait élaboré un mémorandum intitulé « *Examen d'ensemble du droit international en vue des travaux de codification de la Commission du droit international* », document des Nations Unies A/CN.4/1.
Ce qui frappe d'emblée, ce sont les critiques nombreuses et persistantes sur le travail de la Commission. Voir par exemple : Dupuy, « La codification du droit international, a-t-elle encore un intérêt à l'aube du troisième millénaire ? », dans Zanardi *et al., op. cit. supra,* note n° 1, p. 261 et seq.; Zemanek, « Codification of International Law: Salvation or Dead End? », dans ibid., p. 503 et seq.; et McCaffrey, « Is Codification in Decline? », *Hastings International and Comparative Law Review,* vol. 20 (1997), p. 638 et seq.

[3] Voir le Rapport de la Commission du droit international sur les travaux de sa quarante-huitième session, *Documents officiels de l'Assemblée générale, cinquante et unième session, Supplément n° 10* (A/51/10), p. 221 à 258, par. 143 à 244.

qui vont suivre, en les orientant principalement vers l'exploration de quelques pistes délaissées ou insuffisamment explorées.

La nécessité de reconsidérer le choix des sujets pour la codification et le développement progressif du droit international ainsi que les méthodes de travail de la Commission a été ressentie depuis plus d'une décennie déjà. En effet, depuis 1986 toutes les résolutions de l'Assemblée générale sur les rapports de la Commission contiennent un paragraphe où l'Assemblée demande invariablement à la Commission :

« *a*) D'examiner de manière approfondie :

« i) La planification de ses activités pendant la durée du mandat de ses membres, eu égard au fait qu'il est souhaitable de faire avancer le plus possible l'élaboration de projets d'articles sur des sujets spécifiques;

« ii) Ses méthodes de travail sous tous leurs aspects, en ayant à l'esprit la possibilité d'échelonner l'examen de certains sujets;

« *b*) D'indiquer dans son rapport annuel les sujets et questions à propos desquels il serait particulièrement intéressant pour la poursuite de ses travaux que des gouvernements expriment leurs vues soit à la Sixième Commission, soit par écrit[4]. »

Dès le départ donc, l'Assemblée générale a identifié clairement les aspects du travail et du fonctionnement de la Commission qui nécessitent, pour ainsi dire, une évaluation : les méthodes de travail de la Commission et les sujets à inscrire à son programme. Ce sont ces deux points, du moins en certains de leurs aspects, que l'on examinera, avant de dégager quelques conclusions.

II. Choix des sujets

Le choix du sujet est un aspect déterminant du travail de la Commission. En principe, aucun critère autre que le besoin de codification et de développement progressif du droit international ne guide un tel choix. Tout dépend à vrai dire de l'organe qui y procède en vertu du Statut de la Commission. La pratique montre cependant une tendance prononcée vers certains types de sujets, traduisant une préférence qui a d'ailleurs valu à la Commission des critiques sévères.

a) *Le choix possible au regard du Statut de la Commission*

Le Statut de la Commission ne pose aucune limite d'aucune sorte au type de sujets susceptibles d'être examinés par elle. D'entrée de jeu, le paragraphe premier de l'Article 1 indique que la Commission « a pour but de promouvoir le développement progressif du droit international et sa codification ». Et le paragraphe 2 ajoute qu'elle s'occupera prioritairement du droit international public, « sans qu'il lui soit interdit de pénétrer dans le domaine du droit international privé ». Le choix des sujets paraît donc illimité : non seulement le champ opératoire des instances habilitées à proposer des sujets à la Commission s'étend à tout le droit international public, mais elle s'ouvre aussi sur le droit international privé.

---

[4]Résolution 41/81 du 3 décembre 1986; résolution 42/156 du 7 décembre 1987; résolution 43/169 du 9 décembre 1988; résolution 44/35 du 4 décembre 1989; résolution 45/41 du 28 novembre 1990; résolution 46/54 du 9 décembre 1991; résolution 47/33 du 25 novembre 1992; résolution 48/31 du 9 décembre 1993; résolution 49/51 du 9 décembre 1994; résolution 50/45 du 11 décembre 1995; et résolution 51/160 du 16 décembre 1996.

De plus, le pouvoir de choisir les sujets soumis à l'examen de la Commission est un pouvoir partagé. Certes, la primauté revient à l'Assemblée générale : elle « renvoie à la Commission une proposition concernant le développement progressif du droit international » (article 16); et en ce qui concerne la codification, la Commission donne priorité à toute demande émanant d'elle (paragraphe 3 de l'article 18). La Commission dispose quant à elle d'un pouvoir d'initiative : elle « recherche, dans l'ensemble du droit international, les sujets appropriés de codification, en tenant compte des projets existants, qu'ils soient d'origine gouvernementale ou non ». Il résulte du reste de ce paragraphe premier de l'Article 18 qu'en dehors de l'Assemblée générale et de la Commission elle-même les gouvernements peuvent être à l'origine des sujets à codifier. S'y ajoute l'ouverture faite par le paragraphe premier de l'Article 17 qui fait obligation à la Commission d'examiner également « les plans et projets de conventions multilatérales émanant des Membres de l'Organisation des Nations Unies, d'organes principaux des Nations Unies autres que l'Assemblée générale, d'institutions spécialisées ou d'organisations officielles établies par accords inter-gouvernementaux en vue d'encourager le développement progressif du droit international et sa codification que lui transmet à cet effet le Secrétaire général ».

Telles sont autant de voies par lesquelles on peut inscrire des sujets au programme de travail de la Commission. Si elles étaient toutes utilisées en pratique, la Commission serait franchement débordée par l'ampleur de la tâche à accomplir, et la suggestion tendant à la faire fonctionner de façon permanente serait alors largement justifiée[5].

L'affirmation de la compétence de la Commission tant pour la codification que pour le développement progressif du droit international ouvre des perspectives sans borne quant au choix des sujets. En effet, si les sujets pouvant donner lieu à la codification sont relativement plus limités, ceux relevant du développement progressif (distinction envisagée ici de façon purement intellectuelle) embrassent pratiquement tout le champ des relations internationales.

Cependant, non seulement les États ne souhaitent pas toujours une régulation conventionnelle de toutes les activités internationales ou transfrontières, mais encore tous les domaines du droit international ne sont pas susceptibles d'être traités sous la forme de conventions ou ne requièrent pas un tel traitement[6]. C'est pourquoi la pratique est de loin en retrait par rapport à ce qui est possible au regard du Statut de la Commission.

b) *Le choix des sujets à la lumière de la pratique*

Nul ne peut sous-estimer sérieusement l'œuvre accomplie par la Commission après un demi-siècle d'existence. Elle a produit des rapports finaux sur quelque 26 sujets et élaboré pas moins de 20 projets d'articles énonçant des règles fondamentales relatives à nombre de questions cruciales de droit international et servant de base à l'adoption de 15 conventions multilatérales[7]. Mais il

---

[5]Voir El Baradei, M., Franck, T., et Trachtenberg, R., *The International Law Commission: The Need for a New Direction* (1981) UNITAR Policy and Efficacy Studies No. 1 (publication des Nations Unies, numéro de vente : E.81.XV.PE/1), p. 37; ci-après citée Étude de l'UNITAR.

[6]Ibid., p. 55.

[7]Voir Cede « New Approaches to Law Making in the UN-System », *Austrian Review of International and European Law*, vol. 1 (1996), p. 56; et la préface de M. Boutros-Ghali à l'ouvrage collectif publié par la Commission du droit international à l'occasion de son cinquantenaire : Nations Unies, *Le Droit international à l'aube du XXIᵉ siècle : Réflexions de codificateurs* (1997), p. ix (publication des Nations Unies, numéro de vente : E/F 97.V.4).

ajoute l'œuvre non moins considérable des conférences de codification notamment dans des domaines tels que le droit de la mer (Convention de Montego Bay de 1982), les droits de l'homme, le droit de l'espace, etc.

Ensuite, la Commission n'est pas outillée pour traiter convenablement de ces sujets techniques ou par trop scientifiques; de nombreux experts seraient nécessaires pour apprécier chaque règle formulée, bien souvent d'ailleurs sur le plan technique ou scientifique essentiellement. Certes, conformément à son Statut, la Commission peut faire appel à des experts. Mais cette facilité est presque totalement exclue en pratique, non seulement pour les raisons financières qui ne sont pas négligeables, mais aussi parce qu'un appel fréquent à des experts, forcément nombreux au regard de la complexité des sujets envisagés, serait de nature à immerger le travail juridique de la Commission et à compromettre son efficience.

Si la Commission s'est employée dans le passé à la codification du droit de la mer à travers les quatre conventions de Genève de 1958, c'est parce que celles-ci ne s'attaquaient pas au type de problèmes scientifiques et techniques qu'aborde la Convention de Montego Bay de 1982, notamment dans la partie XI. Du reste, la Commission elle-même souligna à propos de ces conventions de 1958 que son projet, dans sa quasi-totalité, n'était qu'une codification du droit international public existant en la matière[25]. Il est certain que la Commission n'aurait réalisé que très difficilement une convention comme celle qui a sanctionné la troisième Conférence des Nations Unies sur le droit de la mer. Certains compromis diplomatiques réalisés au sein de la Conférence sur des questions techniques ou politiques difficiles n'auraient pu être réalisés dans le cadre de la Commission, certaines audaces non plus. Son travail aurait été soit incomplet, soit paralysé.

On peut comprendre l'attrait exercé par les sujets tirés des matières nouvelles ou actuelles telles que l'environnement, les droits humains, les questions économiques, voire le problème des migrations[26]. Mais tous les champs du droit international ne se prêtent pas à la production des normes conventionnelles, et surtout la Commission ne peut tout « codifier ». Ces matières auxquelles certains auteurs et plusieurs membres de la Commission voudraient ouvrir cette dernière sont plus proches de l'expérience des gouvernements et de leurs juristes[27], et l'on gagnerait à les aborder dans les forums intergouvernementaux.

La Commission agit concurremment à d'autres instances de formulation des règles du droit international. Mais elle n'est pas du tout en compétition avec ces instances; elle fait ce que ces dernières ne font pas, ne peuvent pas faire, ou ne pourraient faire que très imparfaitement. Quel autre organisme que la Commission aurait-il pu élaborer la Convention de 1969 sur le droit des traités ? Une conférence diplomatique aurait mis probablement plus de temps encore que la Commission n'en a mis, et sans doute pour un résultat de moins bonne facture. Les derniers sujets que la Commission a inscrit à son ordre du jour (réserves aux traités, actes unilatéraux, protection diplomatique) montrent en tout cas qu'elle concentre ses efforts sur le développement progressif et la codification des règles secondaires, domaine dans lequel il reste beaucoup de travail à faire.

---

[25]Voir Bos, « Aspects phénoménologiques de la codification du droit international public », dans Zanardi *et al.*, *op. cit. supra*, note n° 1, p. 151.

[26]Voir, sur les propositions tendant à faire inscrire le droit des migrations internationales au programme d'activités de la Commission, Nations Unies, document A/CN.4/454, p. 39 à 47; et Al-Baharna, *loc. cit. supra*, note n° 11, p. 382. Voir aussi Dupuy, *loc. cit. supra*, note n° 2, p. 269.

[27]Voir résolution 51/160 de l'Assemblée générale en date du 16 décembre 1996.

Tout en approuvant cette option qui apparaît comme choix de réalisme, d'efficacité mais aussi d'humilité, il convient de souligner que le choix des sujets doit refléter aussi, autant que faire se peut, les préoccupations majeures du monde actuel et répondre à un besoin de droit partagé par la communauté internationale en une matière donnée.

Dans sa résolution 51/160 du 16 décembre 1996, l'Assemblée générale insiste sur l'importance pour la Commission de poursuivre le développement progressif et la codification du droit international comme des moyens de mettre en œuvre l'objet et les principes contenus dans la Charte des Nations Unies ainsi que dans la Déclaration de 1970 relative aux principes du droit international touchant les relations amicales et à la coopération entre les États conformément à la Charte des Nations Unies. Fort de sa compétence et de sa crédibilité, la Commission doit savoir, à cet égard, traduire l'éthique du droit international dans le monde d'aujourd'hui où l'interétatisme et le volontarisme les plus stricts doivent s'accommoder d'une tendance hésitante vers une communauté internationale dont les membres partagent de plus en plus des préoccupations communes et aspirent à un droit protecteur de tous. C'est pourquoi il est souhaitable — et nul ne pourrait lui en faire le reproche — qu'elle garde une ouverture sur des sujets qui, bien que n'étant pas dans le champs de ses thèmes traditionnels précédemment indiqués, posent des problèmes juridiques aigus qui ont du mal à trouver de réponses satisfaisantes dans d'autres cadres de codification et de développement du droit international. Son travail appréciable sur l'utilisation des cours d'eau internationaux à des fins autres que la navigation[28] a montré qu'elle peut le faire de façon fructueuse.

III. Méthodes de travail

Comme le problème du choix des sujets, la question des méthodes de travail de la Commission a été abondamment commentée au sein et en dehors de celle-ci. Plus précisément, des aspects de l'organisation du travail de la Commission tels que le rôle des Rapporteurs spéciaux, la longueur des sessions, les relations de la Commission avec l'Assemblée générale, en l'occurrence sa Sixième Commission, ainsi qu'avec d'autres organismes au sein et en dehors des Nations Unies, la contribution du Secrétariat général de l'Organisation ont été munitieusement examinés par la Commission dans son Rapport de 1996[29] ainsi que par divers auteurs[30].

Indéniablement, les remarques développées à ce sujet ont amené la Commission à améliorer sur divers points ses méthodes de travail, en sorte que la

---

[28]À part quelques conventions régionales, en particulier en Afrique, cette matière importante et très sensible — qui, à en croire certains analystes, pourrait être à l'origine de certains conflits les plus importants du siècle prochain — était régie au plan international uniquement par quelques principes du droit coutumier. Seule l'International Law Association avait fait une tentative de « codification » à travers les fameuses « Règles d'Helsinki » qui guidèrent pendant longtemps la réflexion des juristes en la matière.

Si je pense que la Commission du droit international peut et devrait envisager un sujet particulièrement dans le monde actuel, comme celui des obligations générales des États en matière d'environnement humain par exemple, je vois très mal comment elle aurait pu s'occuper efficacement de l'élaboration de projets d'articles ou de conventions sur la diversité biologique, les changements climatiques, la désertification, etc.

[29]Voir le Rapport de la Commission du droit international sur les travaux de sa quarante-huitième session, *supra*, note n° 3, p. 235 à 258, par. 174 à 244.

[30]Voir notamment : McCaffrey, *loc. cit. supra*, note n° 2, p. 653 à 659; Sette-Camara, *loc. cit. supra*, note n° 1, p. 489 à 502; Graefrath, « The International Law Commission Tomorrow: Improving Its Organization and Methods of Work », *American Journal of International Law*, vol. 85 (1991), p. 595; Étude de l'UNITAR, *supra*, note n° 5; et Nawaz, *loc. cit. supra*, note n° 20, p. 639 à 643.

plupart des commentaires critiques formulés jusqu'à une date récente ont perdu de leur pertinence. De toute évidence en effet, les méthodes de travail de la Commission ont considérablement changé en moins d'une décennie et très nettement dans le sens de leur amélioration[31]. C'est pourquoi une fois rappelés, ces aspects ayant fait l'objet de réformes ou de propositions concrètes de solutions, on s'en tiendra à quelques réflexions sur les aspects qui appellent encore des améliorations.

A. *Aspects ayant fait l'objet des réformes ou de recommandations précises*

Ces aspects se dégagent essentiellement des rapports de la Commission sur les travaux de sa quarante-huitième et de sa quarante-neuvième session. Ils portent sur l'organisation de la session et sa durée, l'organisation interne du travail de la Commission et la conduite des travaux, le programme de travail, la coopération avec d'autres organismes.

1. Organisation de la session et sa durée

Dès 1986, la Commission exprimait le vœu de voir reconsidérée la durée de sa session annuelle dans le sens de son allongement et réitéra depuis lors cette idée dans tous ses rapports. Mais l'Assemblée générale estima chaque fois qu'au regard des exigences du travail de codification et du développement progressif du droit international, de l'ampleur et de la complexité des sujets inscrits à son ordre du jour il était souhaitable que la durée habituelle des sessions de la Commission fût maintenue[32]. Dans son rapport de 1996, la Commission est revenue sur la question sous l'angle d'un découpage de l'unique session annuelle en deux en exposant les avantages d'une telle réorganisation[33]. Il a été admis que la session de 1998 serait ainsi découpée à titre expérimental[34]. Ainsi, compte tenu de la Conférence diplomatique pour l'établissement d'une Cour criminelle internationale prévue de la mi-juin à juillet 1998 et des contraintes financières, il a été décidé que les deux sessions de la Commission en 1998 auraient lieu du 20 avril au 12 juin à Genève, et du 27 juillet au 14 août à New York[35]. De ce réaménagement de l'organisation de la session annuelle de la Commission, l'Assemblée générale en a pris acte dans sa résolution 51/160 du 16 décembre 1996 sur le rapport de la Commission à propos de sa quarante-huitième session. En outre la Commission a indiqué que la session de 10 semaines en 1997 était « une mesure exceptionnelle » décidée pour tenir compte entre autres des difficultés financières des Nations Unies et qu'au regard de son programme quinquennal de travail et de la complexité des sujets en discussion elle devrait tenir une session de 11 semaines en 1998 et une session de 12 semaines en 1999[36].

---

[31]Voir McCaffrey, *loc. cit. supra*, note n° 2, p. 656.

[32]*Annuaire de la Commission du droit international, 1986*, vol. II (deuxième partie), p. 66 et 67, paragraphe 252. Il faut dire qu'en 1986 la durée normale de la session qui était de 12 semaines avait été ramenée à 10 semaines pour des raisons budgétaires, avant d'être ramenée à 12 semaines, à la suite des pressions de la Commission.

[33]Voir paragraphe 6 de la résolution 41/81 de l'Assemblée générale en date du 3 décembre 1986 et toutes les résolutions subséquentes de l'Assemblée générale sur le Rapport de la Commission jusqu'en 1995.

[34]Voir le Rapport de la Commission du droit international sur les travaux de sa quarante-huitième session, *supra*, note n° 3, notamment p. 252 à 254, par. 228 à 233.

[35]Voir le Rapport de la Commission du droit international sur les travaux de sa quarante-neuvième session, *supra*, note n° 19, p. 130 et 131, par. 225 à 227.

[36]Ibid., p. 131, par. 228.

On note à cet égard une certaine souplesse au regard de la résolution 3315 (XXIX) de l'Assemblée générale en date du 14 décembre 1974 qui fixe la durée normale d'une session à 12 semaines. Bien que certains habitués de la Commission paraissent favorables à un racourcissement de la durée de la session à 10 semaines[37], moins d'ailleurs pour des raisons de disponibilité de certains d'entre eux que pour des raisons budgétaires, il paraît raisonnable de maintenir la durée de 12 semaines si la Commission veut faire avancer ses travaux à un rythme acceptable, compte tenu de l'accroissement du nombre de ses membres et des sujets inscrits à son ordre du jour, ainsi que de la complexité des sujets qu'elle a à traiter. Cette durée de 12 semaines paraît d'autant plus raisonnable désormais que l'on tend vers un découpage de la session en deux périodes de durée à peu près égale, comme on l'a rappelé précédemment.

2. Organisation interne du travail et conduite des travaux

La Commission a commencé à introduire des modifications significatives dans ses procédures internes de travail à partir de sa session de 1992 qui suivit le renouvellement de sa composition consécutive à l'élection de 1991 avec l'entrée en son sein d'une bonne moitié de nouveaux membres. De l'avis même de la Commission, l'arrivée massive de ces derniers n'est pas sans rapport avec ces modifications de ses méthodes de travail. Les changements introduits incluaient la création des groupes de travail en vue de surmonter les obstacles à l'avancement des travaux sur certains sujets, la constitution des Comités de rédaction pour différents sujets et le retour au vote lorsque cela s'avère nécessaire pour résoudre certaines difficultés.

La Commission a continué dans cette voie au cours de sa quarante-huitième session répondant ainsi une requête de l'Assemblée générale qui, en 1995, lui a demandé d'évaluer sa procédure de travail en vue de renforcer sa contribution au développement progressif du droit international et à sa codification[38]. Son rapport de 1996 contient à cet égard la liste détaillée des recommandations à introduire dans sa procédure habituelle de travail en vue de son amélioration, ainsi que des analyses de chacune des innovations envisagées. Il en est ainsi notamment :

— Du rôle des Rapporteurs spéciaux dont on souhaite qu'il lui soit demandé de préciser la nature et l'objet de son travail prévu pour la session suivante, que leurs rapports soient disponibles suffisamment à l'avance par rapport à la session au cours de laquelle ils seront débattus, qu'il leur soit demandé de travailler en collaboration avec les membres du Groupe consultatif, qu'il produisent autant que faire se peut des projets de commentaires ou des notes en accompagnement de leurs projets d'articles et que ces projets de commentaires ou de notes soient disponibles bien avant les débats en plénière.

— Du système des débats en plénière de la Commission qui devrait être réformé afin de mieux le structurer et de permettre au Président de la Commission de faire un résumé des débats à la fin des discussions sur la base d'un vote indicatif.

— Du système de travail actuel qui prévoit des Comités de rédaction avec des membres différents pour les différents sujets.

---

[37]Voir, par exemple, McCaffrey, *loc. cit. supra*, note n° 2, p. 637 et p. 655.
[38]Voir résolution 50/45 du 11 décembre 1995.

— Des Groupes de travail, dont on exprime le souhait qu'ils soient utilisés de façon plus intensive, d'autant plus qu'ils ont montré leur efficacité dans la rédaction de certains projets d'articles.

En ce qui concerne la conduite des travaux lors des sessions de la Commission, il a été suggéré, entre autres, que les débats de la Commission sur les projets d'articles à différentes étapes de leur examen — par exemple en plénière et en Comité de rédaction — devraient être conduits de manière à éviter les répétitions et la réouverture des discussions sur les questions déjà examinées. Il a été également suggéré un réajustement du système de rotation régionale de la présidence de la Commission de façon à donner à chaque région géographique l'occasion d'en assumer la présidence au cours du quinquennat[39].

Cette dernière suggestion vise sans doute — même si on ne le dit pas — à donner aux ressortissants des pays du tiers monde (ou en développement), en particulier ceux d'Afrique (subsaharienne notamment), de présider la Commission. Elle rappelle le constat du manque d'influence desdits ressortissants des pays en développement au sein de la Commission établi, par l'étude de l'UNITAR[40]; ce manque d'influence se traduisait alors par le fait qu'aucun Africain subsaharien n'avait jamais été désigné Rapporteur spécial et qu'un seul Asiatique (à l'époque Sompong Sucharitkul) avait été désigné à cette fonction[41]. Certes, la situation n'est plus tout à fait la même aujourd'hui, même si elle n'a pas changé fondamentalement[42]. Tout en partageant le souci d'équité géopolitique qui a sans doute inspiré la suggestion, on ne peut s'empêcher d'exhorter les membres de la Commission ressortissants des pays en développement, et tout particulièrement ceux d'Afrique subsaharienne, à s'imposer davantage au respect intellectuel de leurs collègues afin d'accéder plus nombreux à la fonction de Rapporteur spécial qui est une position privilégiée pour influencer l'élaboration du droit international.

3. Programme de travail de la Commission

Afin de rationaliser davantage son travail, la Commission a estimé nécessaire d'établir désormais un programme de travail pour la durée de son mandat quinquennal, et un programme de travail à long terme. Ces programmes introduisent une prévisibilité dans le travail de la Commission et permettent de faire une meilleure évaluation des progrès accomplis dans l'accomplissement de sa mission. Comme l'indique la Commission, plus particulièrement à propos du

---

[39]Voir le Rapport de la Commission du droit international sur les travaux de sa quarante-neuvième session, *supra*, note n° 19, p. 130, par. 223.

[40]Étude de l'UNITAR, *supra*, note n° 5, p. 30.

[41]Ibid., p. 31. Voir aussi Nawaz, *loc. cit. supra*, note n° 20, p. 637 et 638.

[42]Entre-temps, M. Doudou Thiam, du Sénégal, a été nommé Rapporteur spécial sur le thème du projet des crimes contre la paix et la sécurité de l'humanité, M. Motoo Ogiso, du Japon, a été nommé Rapporteur spécial sur le thème des immunités juridictionnelles des États et de leurs biens, M. Ahmed Mahiou, de l'Algérie, a présidé la Commission en 1996, M. Mohammed Benounna, du Maroc, vient d'être désigné Rapporteur spécial sur la question de la protection diplomatique, et M. P.S. Rao, de l'Inde, Rapporteur spécial sur le thème de la responsabilité internationale pour les conséquences préjudiciables découlant d'activités qui ne sont pas interdites par le droit international, sous le sous-titre « prévention des dommages transfrontières résultant des activités dangereuses ». Mais outre que la situation des membres appartenant à l'Afrique subsaharienne au sein de la Commission évolue très peu en définitive, on doit constater que l'Occident — l'Europe et l'Amérique du Nord — garde la grande prééminence en ce qui concerne la présidence de la Commission et surtout s'agissant des Rapporteurs spéciaux.

programme quinquennal, celui-ci devrait être suffisamment flexible pour permettre certains ajustements qui pourraient s'avérer nécessaires[43].

4. Relations de la Commission avec l'Assemblée générale

Ce point n'apparaît pas dans le Rapport de la Commission sur les travaux de sa quarante-neuvième session, sans doute parce qu'il a été amplement examiné dans son Rapport de 1996[44]. Comme le rappelle la Commission, c'est l'Assemblée générale elle-même qui, à l'alinéa 7 du préambule de sa résolution 50/45 du 11 décembre 1995 sur le rapport de la Commission, insistait sur la nécessité « de renforcer encore les relations entre la Sixième Commission, en sa qualité d'organe de représentants des gouvernements, et la Commission du droit international, en sa qualité d'organe constitué d'experts juridiques indépendants, en vue d'améliorer le dialogue entre l'une et l'autre ». Divers auteurs ont souligné en d'autres occasions cette nécessité[45].

En cette matière, la Commission suggère que son travail pourrait porter aussi bien sur les sujets identifiés par elle-même et approuvés par l'Assemblée générale que sur ceux dégagés ailleurs dans le système des Nations Unies, et soumis de façon spécifique à la Commission par l'Assemblée générale en vertu du Statut de la Commission. S'agissant des commentaires des États sur les travaux en cours de la Commission, celle-ci constate très justement que de nombreux gouvernements, en particulier ceux des pays en développement, ne disposent pas de moyens adéquats ou suffisants pour s'acquitter de cette tâche[46]. Pourtant, l'interaction entre la Commission et les gouvernements reste indispensable dans la mesure où elle conditionne, comme on le verra, le sort des travaux réalisés par la Commission. Quant au rôle de la Sixième Commission de l'Assemblée générale relativement aux projets d'articles finals de la Commission, il est fondamental dans la mesure où précisément la question de savoir si un projet d'article est acceptable, prêt pour l'adoption à un moment donné, est une question essentiellement politique dont la réponse dépend de la Sixième Commission et des États. La Commission estime simplement que, en cas de doutes sérieux sur le caractère acceptable d'un quelconque texte qu'il a produit, il serait utile que cela soit porté d'autorité à sa connaissance par l'Assemblée générale et les gouvernements, et ce suffisamment tôt, au lieu d'attendre le travail final de la Commission pour en faire état[47].

5. Coopération avec d'autres organismes

C'est un aspect non négligeable dans le processus d'accomplissement des missions assignées à la Commission. La Commission doit entretenir avec eux des rapports de collaboration et non pas de méfiance ou de condescendance. On ne saurait à cet égard partager l'opinion du juge Sette-Camara qui, estimant que

---

[43]Voir le Rapport de la Commission du droit international sur les travaux de sa quarante-neuvième session, *supra*, note n° 19, p. 127, par. 220.

[44]Voir le Rapport de la Commission du droit international sur les travaux de sa quarante-huitième session, *supra*, note n° 3, p. 235 à 239, par. 174 à 185.

[45]Voir notamment : Zemanek, « Does Codification Lead to Wider Acceptance? » dans Nations Unies, *op. cit. supra*, note n° 9, p. 228; et Yankov, « Strengthening the Process of Codification and Development of International Law: The Evolving Functions of the International Law Commission and Increasing the Commitments of States », dans *ibid.*, p. 238.

[46]Voir le Rapport de la Commission du droit international sur les travaux de sa quarante-huitième session, *supra*, note n° 3, p. 237 et 238, par. 180 à 182, notamment par. 181.

[47]Ibid., p. 239, par. 185.

les États sont réticents à accepter les projets de texte de caractère académique, (*academic drafts*) écrit : « Why should the International Law Commission devote its energies to competing with the Institute of International Law, the International Law Association, or the Harvard Research[48] ? » Le fait rapporté par l'auteur portant sur le sort réservé par l'Assemblée générale aux « Règles d'Helsinki » de 1966 sur l'« Utilisation des cours d'eau internationaux à des fins autres que la navigation » est incontestable[49]. Mais l'on ne saurait en inférer valablement l'inutilité des organismes concernés ni une supériorité absolue ou de principe de la Commission sur toutes les autres instances de codification et en regard à tous les sujets.

La Commission paraît de toute façon plus ouverte et mieux disposée vis-à-vis des autres organismes, et à cet égard elle se conforme tout simplement aux dispositions pertinentes de son Statut [articles 17, 25 (1) et 26 (1)]. Dans son Rapport de 1996, elle déplore d'ailleurs que les relations avec les Nations Unies et les organismes spécialisés ayant des responsabilités en matière juridique soient négligées et que diverses composantes de l'Organisation mondiale travaillent encore sur ce terrain de façon isolée. De l'avis de la Commission, il serait bien venu de solliciter un échange d'informations avec ces organismes spécialisés sur des questions données. Elle suggère même que l'on pourrait envisager la possibilité d'une étude conjointe entre elle-même et une agence spécialisée dans un domaine donné[50].

Mais ces relations doivent être établies de façon sélective, au cas par cas, sans du reste absorber ou noyer les activités principales de la Commission relatives au développement progressif et à la codification du droit international[51]. Dans cet esprit la Commission a recommandé dans son rapport sur sa quarante-huitième session l'adjonction à la liste des organismes s'occupant du droit international et avec lesquels elle entrerait en relation, notamment le Comité consultatif asiatique-africain, la Société africaine de droit international, la Law Association for Africa and the Pacific et d'autres institutions similaires dans le domaine du droit international public[52].

Les deux dernières sessions de la Commission (1996 et 1997) ont ainsi fait le tour de tous les principaux problèmes généralement considérés comme des objectifs plus ou moins importants à l'efficacité de son travail, et l'Assemblée générale a « [*pris*] *note avec appréciation* des paragraphes 143 à 244 du rapport [de 1997] de la Commission du droit international concernant les procédures et méthodes de travail de la Commission » dans sa résolution 51/160 du 16 décem-

---

[48]*Loc. cit. supra*, note n° 1, p. 500.

[49]L'auteur rappelle en effet qu'après de nombreuses années d'un excellent travail académique visant la codification du droit de l'utilisation des cours d'eau à des fins autres que la navigation, en particulier par l'Université de New York et l'International Rivers Research Project, l'International Law Association adopta, à sa cinquante-deuxième conférence en août 1966, les « Règles d'Helsinki », qui étaient indiscutablement un important travail universitaire, mais contre lequel une large majorité d'États vota un projet de résolution parrainné par la Finlande contenant les points clés desdites « Règles » lors de la vingt-cinquième session de l'Assemblée générale.

[50]Ibid., p. 257, par. 241.

[51]Voir le Rapport de la Commission du droit international sur les travaux de sa quarante-neuvième session, *supra*, note n° 19, p. 132, par. 231.

[52]Ibid., paragraphe 232. Par ailleurs la Commission a reçu au cours de cette session des observations de divers organismes ayant cette vocation : du Comité juridique interaméricain, du Comité européen de coopération juridique, du Comité des conseillers juridiques sur le droit international public et du Comité juridique consultatif africano-asiatique. Ibid., p. 134 et 135, par. 239 à 241.

bre 1996[53]. Quelques aspects non négligeables méritent pourtant quelques remarques.

B. *Quelques interpellations*

Elles portent essentiellement sur deux points dont l'un a trait aux membres de la Commission et l'autre aux relations de celle-ci avec l'Assemblée générale (Sixième Commission) et les États Membres des Nations Unies.

1. Les membres de la Commission : experts indépendants ou représentants des États ?

À première vue, cette question peut paraître déplacée, tant il est vrai que des témoignages autorisés soulignent qu'une ambiance sereine prévaut au sein de la Commission dont les membres feraient suffisamment preuve d'indépendance vis-à-vis de leurs gouvernements respectifs.

Pourtant, il n'est pas douteux que pendant la période de la guerre froide les ressortissants des grandes puissances s'étaient souvent faits l'écho des vues des gouvernements de leurs pays sur les sujets en examen à la Commission. Un auteur remarquait il y a une dizaine d'années à propos de la codification de la coutume sous forme d'un traité qu'elle pouvait être compromise non seulement par une opposition entre intérêts structurellement polarisés, mais aussi du fait de *strong dogmatic or ideological position*[54].

Il n'est pas sûr que cette inclination passée ait aujourd'hui totalement disparue. Car c'est un fait que la Commission « est loin d'être une réunion de juristes coupés du monde et cogitant en commun sur un plan essentiellement technique »[55]. Il y a lieu de douter par exemple que les vues exprimées par certains membres de la Commission sur le projet de code des crimes contre la paix et la sécurité de l'humanité n'aient pas reflété bien souvent les positions officielles des gouvernements de leurs pays, vu la sensibilité politique du sujet et la passion qui a entouré les débats s'y rapportant. On ne peut nier que le droit international reste le reflet des intérêts des puissances[56] et que le processus de son élaboration s'en ressent nécessairement.

L'influence possible des gouvernements sur certains membres de la Commission peut résulter des positions qu'occupent ces derniers dans les structures administratives ou politiques de leurs pays. Sans même insister sur le rôle généralement décisif des gouvernements dans l'élection de leurs ressortissants au sein de la Commission et qui peut conditionner l'attitude de certains membres dans la perspective de leur réélection, il convient de signaler que quelques membres de la Commission exercent des fonctions de jurisconsultes auprès des Ministères des affaires étrangères ou de conseillers juridiques auprès de telles institutions de leurs pays. Dans ces conditions, il n'est pas exclu que les réponses données par certains gouvernements aux questionnaires de la Commission soient rédigées par des membres de la Commission[57].

---

[53]Dans la même résolution, l'Assemblée générale « [e]*ncourage* la Commission du droit international à prendre, concernant ses affaires internes, des décisions qui pourraient contribuer à son efficacité et à sa productivité ».

[54]Zemanek, *loc. cit. supra*, note n° 2, p. 593. Voir aussi Dhokalia, *loc. cit. supra*, note n° 22, notamment p. 220 et 221.

[55]Dupuy, *loc. cit. supra*, note n° 2, p. 267.

[56]Voir, entre autres, Pellet, *loc. cit. supra*, note n° 10, p. 425.

[57]Voir : Cede, *loc. cit. supra*, note n° 7, p. 64; et McCaffrey, *loc. cit. supra*, note n° 2, p. 658.

Ce dédoublement fonctionnel n'a pas nécessairement des implications négatives dans la mesure où il crée une interface qui peut enrichir le travail de la Commission et surtout l'aider à orienter ou à le réorienter grâce à une meilleure connaissance des positions réelles des États. De la sorte, il peut aider la Commission à préparer des textes ayant des meilleures chances d'obtenir l'agrément des États et par la suite d'être adoptés par eux.

Mais il faudrait que par-delà ces apports que constitue l'information de l'en dedans les membres de la Commission se comportent en experts indépendants qu'ils sont dans le champ des compétences de la Commission, en charge des intérêts de la communauté internationale dans son ensemble. Ils sont appelés à un effort de dialectique entre les intérêts nationaux et les préoccupations de la communauté internationale qui, de plus en plus, déterminent la normativité internationale.

2. Les relations de la Commission avec l'Assemblée générale et les États : inconséquence et perplexité

La Commission est, on l'a dit, une création de l'Assemblée générale qui entendait de la sorte se doter d'un instrument pouvant l'aider à s'acquitter le plus efficacement possible du mandat que lui confie la Charte dans son alinéa *a* du paragraphe 1 de l'Article 13, savoir « encourager le développement progressif du droit international et sa codification ». Au demeurant, comme on l'a vu, que ce soit sur la base de l'Article 16 (développement progressif) ou de l'Article 18 (codification) de son Statut, la Commission travaille pour ainsi dire à la demande de l'Assemblée générale, ou avec son aval. Certes la Commission aurait entamé son travail sur des sujets sélectionnés en 1996 et soumis à l'Assemblée générale, sans attendre l'approbation de cette dernière. Mais il s'agit là d'une dérogation, au demeurant fort rare, à la pratique habituelle dans les relations entre la Commission et l'Assemblée générale.

En tout état de cause, le travail de la Commission n'a de sens que s'il se fait en étroite relation avec l'Assemblée générale et avec la pleine collaboration de la Sixième Commission et des gouvernements. On trouve même nécessaire le renforcement du rôle primordial de l'Assemblée générale (Sixième Commission) dans l'orientation et le suivi du travail de la Commission.

Cette collaboration ne peut être efficiente qu'à deux conditions : d'une part, si les gouvernements répondent sérieusement et à temps aux questionnaires que leur adresse la Commission sur le sujet, de façon à permettre à celle-ci d'intégrer le mieux qu'elle puisse leurs préoccupations dans les projets d'articles qui leur seront ensuite soumis pour adoption; d'autre part, si l'on ne transforme pas la Sixième Commission en un cadre où l'on recommence les discussions qui ont eu lieu au sein de la Commission. Pour ce faire, il serait souhaitable que les rapports sur les travaux de la Commission adressés à l'Assemblée générale (Sixième Commission) ne soient pas trop détaillés et ne reproduisent pas, plus ou moins fidèlement, les débats internes de la Commission, car ce sont ces débats avec les clivages qui les accompagnent qui ont tendance à être repris au sein de la Sixième Commission. Certes, comme l'indique le Commission, son rapport

« doit permettre aux membres de la Commission et aux représentants des États au sein de la Sixième Commission, d'une part, de s'assurer que les préoccupations qu'ils ont exprimées lors de la "phase préliminaire" sont effectivement prises en compte et, d'autre part, à l'avenir, de se rendre compte assez précisément de l'état d'avancement des travaux à mesure que ceux-ci progresseront. Il a vocation à être, en quelque sorte, la "boussole" qui permettra au Rapporteur spécial de progresser, sous le contrôle de la Commission, dans la mission difficile qui lui a été confiée. Il devrait également constituer la traîne du guide de la pratique que la Commission s'est donnée pour tâche d'élaborer[58]. »

Mais par souci d'accroître la sérénité des débats au sein de la Sixième Commission, les rapports préparés à l'attention de celle-ci devraient être distincts des comptes rendus élaborés comme de véritables procès-verbaux de réunion. Ceux-ci ne devraient pas être rendus publics jusqu'à l'adoption par l'Assemblée générale ou par les États des résultats des travaux de la Commission sur un sujet donné. Les rapports présentés à l'Assemblée générale (Sixième Commission) et rendus publics devraient donner les vues de la Commission avec référence aux préoccupations exprimées par les États et aux nuances éventuelles exprimées par tels membres sur un sujet, mais sans référence nominative. De la sorte, on peut espérer que les représentants des États à la Sixième Commission ne cherchent pas seulement à reprendre les vues de tels ou tels membres de la Commission, mais se laissent guider par la qualité juridique d'un projet d'articles et la pertinence des arguments avancés pour l'expliquer et l'appuyer.

Il serait également judicieux, comme l'a suggéré un ancien membre de la Commission, que celle-ci ne présente à la Sixième Commission un rapport sur quelques articles seulement tant que la totalité des dispositions d'un chapitre n'est pas prête[59]. Par ailleurs, il serait recommandable que, lors des débats à cette Sixième Commission sur un rapport ou des projets d'articles de la Commission, les membres de celle-ci ne siègent pas au banc de leurs gouvernements, quand bien même ils feraient par ailleurs office de jurisconsultes. Car il convient que la Commission présente son travail aux représentants des États en tant que corps d'experts indépendants œuvrant dans l'intérêt de tous les États et du droit international.

S'agissant enfin du sort réservé aux résultats des travaux de la Commission, l'on doit dire qu'il est assez décevant et laisse d'autant plus perplexe que ce sont les États eux-mêmes, à travers l'Assemblée générale, qui sollicitent l'élaboration de tels projets d'articles par la Commission. Certes, il arrive que celle-ci ne fasse pas, comme elle en a le droit, de recommandation précise à l'Assemblée générale sur la forme dans laquelle le projet de texte qu'elle a élaboré pourrait être adopté[60]. Mais il revient par-dessus tout à l'Assemblée générale de donner une suite diligente aux travaux de la Commission, afin que le travail de cette dernière qui est une œuvre difficile, complexe et de longue haleine ne soit pas peine perdue. Il est frappant et inexplicable que depuis la Convention sur les missions spéciales de 1969, et plus précisément depuis 1985, aucune autre Convention élaborée au sein de la Commission ou à partir de ses travaux ne soit entrée en vigueur jusqu'à 1996[61], alors même que leur élaboration répondait à une demande de traité. La plupart des suggestions faites à ce sujet par Roberto Ago, il y a une trentaine d'années[62], restent alors d'actualité dans la mesure où elles n'ont suscité aucune réaction (positive) au sein des Nations Unies, même

---

[58]Voir le deuxième rapport sur les réserves aux traités de M. Alain Pellet, rapporteur spécial, document A/CN.4/477 (10 mai 1996), p. 23, par. 53.

[59]Voir McCaffrey, *loc. cit. supra*, note n° 2, p. 658.

[60]Cas par exemple du projet de code des crimes contre la paix et la sécurité de l'humanité. Voir le Rapport de la Commission du droit international sur les travaux de sa quarante-huitième session, *supra*, note n° 3, p. 29 et 30, par. 47 et 48.

[61]Quand la Convention de Vienne sur la succession d'États en matière de traités est enfin entrée en vigueur le 6 novembre.

[62]Voir Ago, « La codification du droit international et les problèmes de sa réalisation », dans *Recueil d'études de droit international en hommage à Paul Guggenheim* (1968), p. 93.

si elles ont été accueillies favorablement au sein de la Commission[63]. En tout état de cause l'Assemblée générale devrait exhorter de temps en temps, par le biais de résolution, les États, d'une part, à transformer en projets de conventions, soit dans le cadre de conférences convoquées à cette fin, soit dans le cadre de ses propres sessions, les projets d'articles élaborés par la Commission et, d'autre part, à ratifier ceux des traités ainsi conclus qui ne sont pas encore entrés en vigueur ou qui réunissent un nombre insuffisant de ratifications[64].

IV. Conclusion

La Commission reste l'institution de référence de production du droit international conventionnel[65], et la référence fréquente de la Cour internationale de Justice à ses travaux dans ses arrêts[66] atteste de l'intégrité de son autorité en ce domaine. Elle opère dans une société internationale en procès de changement continu. Les besoins de droit de cette société internationale sont tout aussi changeants et évoluent au gré des défis nouveaux qui interpellent la communauté internationale. Il n'est pas douteux que dans un tel contexte un minimum d'adaptation soit nécessaire afin de permettre à la Commission de s'acquitter le plus efficacement possible de sa mission.

Mais cette adaptation ne saurait être entendue comme une sorte de reniement de ce qui en fait a contribué à bâtir l'autorité de la Commission à la faveur d'une impossible ambition d'être le lieu où se réalise l'ensemble du travail de développement progressif et de codification du droit international. Le choix des sujets pour ce travail doit répondre à des besoins pratiques de droit et ne pas se contenter d'être une pure démarche intellectuelle pouvant déboucher sur un jeu de construction théorique ou d'esthétique juridique. À cet égard, il est de bon ton que la Commission reste ancrée sur le terrain sur lequel elle excelle, à savoir celui de l'affinement des règles du droit international général, laissant aux organismes spécialisés les matières nouvelles, généralement techniques, couvrant des champs sectoriels pour lesquelles ces organismes paraissent mieux outillés.

La Commission ne peut rester la référence en matière de codification et de développement progressif du droit international que si elle continue à avoir une maîtrise suffisante des sujets qu'elle aborde, elle ne peut assumer pleinement sa mission d'instance technique de production des traités pour la communauté internationale que si elle sait proposer, sur un plan général, des socles juridiques à partir desquels peuvent se bâtir des normes sectorielles. Telle est sa double vocation.

Mais elle ne peut y réussir sans un soutien actif des États à travers l'Assemblée générale dont la Sixième Commission doit aider la Commission à réaliser le meilleur texte possible dans des délais raisonnables et non pas s'ériger en adversaire d'un organe qui agit pour son compte et, en principe, dans l'intérêt de la communauté internationale dans son ensemble.

---

[63]Voir Ago, *loc. cit. supra*, note n° 12.

[64]Voir en ce sens Suy, *loc. cit. supra*, note n° 9, p. 222.

[65]Elle nourrit les chercheurs de ses rapports thématiques qui sont d'une qualité exceptionnelle et pourraient contribuer plus méthodiquement à la production de la matière nécessaire à l'enseignement du droit international, comme l'a suggéré M. Lee. Voir Lee, « International Law Reaching Out », dans Macdonald, R.St.J. (éd.), *Essays in Honour of Wang Tieya* (1993), p. 508-509.

[66]Voir l'intervention de M. Jiuyong Shi, représentant M. Stephen Schwebel, président de la Cour, à la quarante-neuvième session de la Commission : le Rapport de la Commission du droit international sur les travaux de sa quarante-neuvième session, *supra*, note n° 19, p. 135, par. 242.

SELECTION OF TOPICS FOR CODIFICATION AND PROGRESSIVE DEVELOPMENT BY THE COMMISSION AND ITS WORKING METHODS

by M. K. Nawaz*

I. Selection of topics

The selection of topics for progressive development and codification is no longer a simple matter. One cannot now select a topic at random, much less instinctively. One needs a method, an approach or some criteria on the basis of which topics for codification and development may be identified.

In the past, whenever the issue of selecting a topic arose, the following tests appear to have been deployed.[1]

- Does the topic serve the needs—better, the current and pressing needs—of the international community?
- Is it of practical, rather than just theoretical, interest?
- Is it specific enough to be tackled in a particular time frame, say, within one of the International Law Commission's quinquennia?

These criteria, useful as they are, cannot be credited with any greater degree of absoluteness than any other inductively derived abstractions. Moreover, it is believed that the progressive development and codification of international law call for a vision of world order:[2] a vision that affords an insight into the purposes and functions of international law in a changing world-society; a vision that recognizes that international law, to be effective, must be adapted to suit the changing circumstances of everyday life; a vision that asks of international law that it serve the needs of peoples without regard to the national frontiers which divide them; a vision that requires that a certain futuristic orientation be imparted to international law. Conceivably, the international law of the future would, as a consequence of the impact of the human rights movement, be far more oriented towards recognizing and meeting peoples' needs, rather than satisfying States' interests. Given this paradigm, topics that had hitherto been considered as falling within the domestic jurisdiction of States might become the subject of regulation by international law. The logical corollary of such an assumption or desideratum is that the task of selecting a topic for progressive development and codification should be guided by humanism, as much as by the "current" or "pressing" needs of the international community or by technical considerations, such as the topic's practicality, specificity or demonstrable interest to States.

---

*Research consultant, National Law School, India University, Bangalore, India.

[1]Documents A/CN.4/1/Rev.1 and A/CN.4/245. The latter of these two documents may also be found in *Yearbook of the International Law Commission, 1971*, vol. II (Part Two), at p. 1.

For a recent reiteration of these tests, see ibid., *1993*, vol. II (Part Two), p. 96 at para. 429.

[2]See Al-Baharna, "Future Topics for the Codification of International Law Viewed in Historical Perspective", in United Nations, *International Law on the Eve of the Twenty-first Century: Views from the International Law Commission* (1997), p. 373 (United Nations Publication, Sales No. E/F.97.V.4).

The need for new thinking and for a new direction in the work of the International Law Commission has been stressed by scholars and by international bodies for some time now.[3] A study carried out by the United Nations Institute for Training and Research (UNITAR)[4] identified two factors as lying behind the Commission's reluctance to take on what it called "important and/or urgent issues of the evolving legal order". First, the Commission itself has never been keen to take up "areas of international law where the elements of progressive development outweighed the elements of codification".[5] Secondly, the Sixth Committee of the General Assembly has been largely responsible for the "conservative orientation of the work of the Commission".[6] Whether or not this diagnosis is correct, it was made at a time when the General Assembly had entrusted the task of elaborating the text of a comprehensive convention on the law of the sea to a plenipotentiary conference, rather than to the International Law Commission. This attitude on the part of the General Assembly is the more surprising as it had earlier entrusted work on that very subject to the Commission. What was the reason for this turn of events? In this connection, the UNITAR Study made the following comment:

"The reluctance of the Third World Nations to entrust their most sensitive and urgent concerns to the International Law Commission stems from the perception that the Commission is wedded in some fundamental way to a relatively static concept of international law."[7]

This is a rather agonizing finding, whether it is true or not. In explanation, one can probably say that third world countries are no more keen than other countries about assigning to the Commission topics which substantially involve the progressive development of international law.

It would seem, though, that there is some misunderstanding of the Commission's functions—a misunderstanding which needs to be removed if the Commission is to play its proper role. It might be recalled that the Commission is a subsidiary organ of the General Assembly, established by a resolution of that body, for the avowed object of promoting the "progressive development of international law and its codification".[8] Both the "letter of the law" and "internal evidence" make it clear that the Commission is not entrusted merely with the "codification of international law", however one interprets that expression.[9] Rather, its task extends to embrace the "progressive development of interna-

---

[3]See, for example, Yankov, "Strengthening the Process of Codification and Development of International Law: The Evolving Functions of the International Law Commission and Increasing the Commitments of States," in United Nations, *International Law as a Language for International Relations* (1996), p. 230, especially at p. 236 (United Nations publication, Sales No. T.96.V.4).

[4]See El Baradei, M., Franck, T., and Trachtenberg, R., *The International Law Commission: the Need for a New Direction* (1981), UNITAR Policy and Efficacy Studies No. 1 (United Nations Publication, Sales No. E.81.XV.PE/1).

[5]Ibid., p. 7.

[6]Ibid., p. 8.

[7]Ibid., p. 13.

[8]See article 1 (1) of the Commission's Statute. This formulation is in conformity with Article 13 of the Charter of the United Nations, which, in paragraph 1 (*a*), stipulates that the General Assembly shall initiate studies for the purpose of "encouraging the progressive development of international law and its codification". That the drafters of the Commission's Statute intended to confer on the Commission the dual functions of "developing" and "codifying" international law is also clear from the Statute's *travaux préparatoires*. See Briggs, H.W., *The International Law Commission* (1965), p. 8.

[9]For an expansive interpretation, see Ago, "Some New Thoughts on the Codification of International Law", in Bello, E.G., and Ajibola, B.A. (eds.), *Essays in Honour of Judge Taslim Olawale Elias, Volume I, Contemporary International Law and Human Rights* (1992), p. 35.

tional law". That this is so is evident from the meanings which are ascribed to these expressions—even if it be for the sake of convenience—by the Statute of the Commission itself. Thus, "codification of international law" is defined in article 15 of the Statute as "the more precise formulation and systematization of rules of international law in fields where there already has been extensive practice, precedent and doctrine", while "progressive development of international law" is said to be "the preparation of draft conventions on subjects which have not yet been regulated by international law or in regard to which the law has not yet been sufficiently developed in the practice of States." The intention of the drafters of the Statute in distinguishing "codification" from "progressive development" is made clearer still in articles 16, 17 and 18.

Accordingly, it may be said that codification was conceived as involving a kind of restatement of the corpus of classical or customary international law, whereas "progressive development" was intended to involve the "enactment" of international law in fields which until then had remained beyond the law's reach or in which international law had not been highly developed.[10]

The intentions of the drafters of the Commission's Statute suffered something of a setback at the hands of the Commission, which preferred to proceed on the basis of a composite idea of "codification and progressive development".[11] In justification of this approach, it has been contended that it is difficult, if not impossible, to draw a distinction in practice between codification of the law and its progressive development.[12] Even if, for the sake of argument, this view were to be accepted, there is no doubt that it has had certain negative consequences. For one thing, it has reduced the potential of the Commission to exercise the full range of its functions under its Statute. For another, it has served to stunt the growth of international law. This state of affairs should be rectified by reorienting the thinking of the members of the Commission, and of the United Nations more generally, towards the progressive development of international law.[13] Such a reorientation would not necessarily involve abandoning the codification of topics which are still of practical interest to the international community. Rather, what is suggested is a balanced approach: one that avoids extremes of one kind or the other.

In the light of the above, I would suggest the following topics for development and codification by the Commission, underlining that the list that follows is not meant to be conclusive or exhaustive, but, rather, simply to be illustrative of the approach which I advocate for the task in hand.

    (*a*)   Mass exoduses of people facing imminent threats of death or starvation;

    (*b*)   Citizenship of refugees and displaced persons;

---

[10]Briggs, op. cit. above (footnote 8), p. 130, referring to Professor Philip Jessup's view that the Commission's task involves "devising the most appropriate procedures for the development of new law to meet the world's needs".

[11]Report of the International Law Commission on the work of its forty-eighth session, *Official Records of the General Assembly, Fifty-first Session, Supplement No. 10* (A/51/10), p. 197 at para. 148 (*a*).

[12]Loc. cit. and ibid., p. 201 at para. 157. See also: Briggs, op. cit. above (footnote 8), pp. 129-141; Rosenne, S., *Practice and Methods of the International Law Commission* (1984), pp. 73-74; and, more recently, Sette-Camara, "The International Law Commission: Discourse on Method", in Zanardi, P.L., Migliazza, A., Pocar, F., and Ziccardi, P. (eds.), *Le Droit international à l'heure de sa codification : études en l'honneur de Roberto Ago* (1987), vol. I, p. 467 at p. 482. Sette-Camara attributes the Commission's success to its adoption of the composite approach, which he characterizes as "flexible and prudent".

[13]Cf. Fleischhauer, "The United Nations and the Progressive Development and Codification of International Law", *Indian Journal of International Law*, vol. 25 (1985), p. 1 at p. 4.

(c)   Rights and duties of aliens;

(d)   Human rights safeguards in the extradition process;

(e)   Treatment of foreign investments;

(f)   Elimination of corruption in international commercial transactions; and

(g)   Global commons.

Some of these topics transcend the classical concerns of the Commission. Some, indeed, are of interest to other United Nations bodies and agencies. However, in view of the opinion which was expressed by the Commission at its forty-eighth session, that it should explore the possibility of joint work with other United Nations bodies,[14] the topics concerned should not be considered out of bounds to the Commission.

A few words may now be said about each of these topics.

(a)   Mass exoduses of people facing imminent threats of death or starvation

The turbulent events that have engulfed Asia, Africa and Central Europe in recent years have highlighted the need for safeguarding the lives and the conditions of groups of people who, *en masse*, flee their homes for safety. Existing international law fails to provide answers even to elementary questions in this domain, such as the definition of "refugee" and "displaced person", let alone ensures such hapless people protection. This topic is likely to acquire even greater prominence in years to come; but, in any event, the time is ripe for the codification and progressive development of international law in the field.

(b)   Citizenship of refugees and displaced persons

The question of the citizenship of refugees and displaced persons has in recent times become a matter of grave concern to the intergovernmental and non-governmental organizations which are interested in humanitarian problems. A central matter for consideration here is how to ameliorate the situation which results from the notion that citizenship is something which falls essentially within States' domestic jurisdiction. How does one balance considerations of a humanitarian nature with the doctrine of domestic jurisdiction? Given the fact that domestic jurisdiction is a relative concept, there need be no shying away from this topic, though.

(c)   Rights and duties of aliens

Classical or traditional international law sought to safeguard the interests of aliens through the principle of "minimum standards of international law". This principle has been rendered somewhat obsolete by the growth of human rights. None the less, the question of the rights of aliens as such remains open and unresolved. It may, therefore, be useful to inquire into the desirability of the codification and development of international law on the topic. To make for a balanced inquiry, it is suggested that the rights of aliens be studied in combination with their duties.

(d)   Human rights safeguards in the extradition process

While extradition is necessary if persons fleeing trial or punishment are to be brought to book, there is a corresponding need for safeguarding the human

---

[14]See the Report of the International Law Commission on the work of its forty-eighth session, op. cit. above (footnote 11), p. 207 at para. 170.

rights of those who may find themselves the subject of such proceedings. The need for determining the circumstances in which acts of terrorism may be considered to fall outside the scope of the so-called "political offence exception" has also become acute. In any event, the relevance of human rights law to the conduct of extradition proceedings is a subject which needs to be examined, along with the issues of terrorism and drug-trafficking.

(e)   Treatment of foreign investments

There now exist numerous bilateral treaties and arrangements for regulating the conduct of a State which is host to foreign investments. Nevertheless, the degree of protection which must be afforded to foreign investments under general international law is a question which remains unanswered. It is, moreover, a question which only gains in importance as trade between countries is liberalized and the world embraces market economics. The conflicts of interest which exist in this connection between developed and developing States only add to the need for regulation of the issue through international law.

(f)   Elimination of corruption in international commercial transactions

The necessity of eliminating corruption and bribery in international commercial transactions has long been felt by States and by international organizations. In March 1996, the Organization of American States adopted a convention against corruption, which includes an article on transnational bribery. The General Assembly itself, by its resolution 51/191 of 16 December 1996, adopted the United Nations Declaration against Corruption and Bribery in International Commercial Transactions. Efforts are currently being made in the Council of Europe, too, to address the problem. The liberalization of world trade and economic policies in the third world have only added a fresh impetus to the need for satisfactory regulation of the topic at the international level.

(g)   Global commons

This topic was the subject of analysis and debate in the Commission at its forty-fourth session. Indeed, it figures as one of the topics in the report which the Commission adopted in 1996 on its long-term programme of work. There is probably little need to demonstrate the importance of developing international law on this topic; but the question might be asked whether the Commission has the right expertise to deal with it. Given the Commission's past practice—it consulted experts in the field in order to help it arrive at a satisfactory definition of the continental shelf—there should be no inherent problem in the Commission's considering this topic.

II.   The Commission's working-methods

The slow pace at which the Commission operates and the delays which have occurred in its work have sometimes been the object of criticism.[15] A number of suggestions have been made for improving the working methods of the Commission. Attention will be focused here on some of the more important ones.

---

[15]It has been pointed out that an average of seven to 10 years has elapsed between the Commission's initial investigation of a topic and its production of a final set of draft articles: El Baradei et al. (eds.), op. cit. above (footnote 4), pp. 33-34. See also Graefrath, "The International Law Commission Tomorrow: Improving Its Organization and Methods of Work", *American Journal of International Law*, vol. 85 (1991), p. 595.

(a) The agenda

For any deliberative body, its agenda is of crucial significance. The tendency of the Commission to consider each year all of the topics which currently figure in its programme has been criticized for holding back work on any single topic.[16] To remedy this situation, the following measures may usefully be deployed.

First of all, the Commission should try to concentrate its attention on just some of the topics on its work programme.[17] The idea that consideration of topics should be staggered has, in the past, run counter to the wishes of Special Rapporteurs.[18] The idea, none the less, met with some approval within the General Assembly, which, at its forty-first session, requested the Commission to bear in mind the possibility of staggering the consideration of some of the topics on its agenda.[19] Although the Commission did not formally decide to stagger consideration of items at its fortieth session, circumstances meant that it had to concentrate discussion only on three topics. This prompted the Brazilian delegate to the Sixth Committee to remark that the *de facto* staggering of items had led to favourable results.[20] To date, however, the Commission has not taken a formal decision on the issue—though it has, from time to time, put off consideration of a particular report, pleading a "lack of time".[21] The idea of staggering appears to me to be worth pursuing.

The UNITAR Study, for its part, suggested that the agenda of the Commission be made "more flexible, timely and business-like".[22] As a first step in this direction, it proposed that the Commission's long-term programme of work be abandoned and that the work of the Commission be planned in five-year blocks, coinciding with the terms of office of the Commission's members. Although such ideas as these are fine in theory, they cannot be applied in practice. The point, none the less, needs to be emphasized that the Commission should at each session fix a schedule for that session within which it should strive to accomplish its work. Such a procedure is to be found in every successful operation nowadays.

(b) Special Rapporteurs

The importance of the Special Rapporteur in the work of the Commission cannot be overemphasized. It is evident that the success of the Commission's work on a subject depends in no small measure upon the efficiency of the Special Rapporteur. The expertise, industry and statesmanship which a Special Rapporteur brings to bear in his reports and presentations have a profound influence on the law-making process. However, the way in which the Commission has allowed the Special Rapporteur to function has served to leave him isolated and bereft of much in the way of guidance in the preparation of his reports. The Commission, in its Report on the work of its forty-eighth session, suggested that

---

[16] According to the UNITAR Study, "working on many topics at one time results in having to consider small bits of each topic at each session": El Baradei et al. (eds.), op. cit. above (footnote 4), p. 25.

[17] Sinclair, I., *The International Law Commission* (1987), p. 43.

[18] Loc. cit.

[19] See General Assembly resolution 41/81 of 3 December 1986.

[20] Document A/C.6/43/SR.38, para. 30.

[21] So, for example, the Commission postponed consideration of the topic of Reservations to Treaties at its forty-eighth session for want of time. See Report of the International Law Commission on the work of its forty-eighth session, op. cit. above (footnote 11), p. 7 at para. 26.

[22] El Baradei et al. (eds.), op. cit. above (footnote 4), p. 24.

a consultative group should be appointed by the Commission in order that the Special Rapporteur might be able to consult the group between sessions on the best possible approach to the topic and on the essential elements of his report. Such a mechanism might be of assistance to Special Rapporteurs, by providing them with input from members of the Commission at a formative stage in their work on a topic and by enhancing the prospects that their reports and draft proposals will prove acceptable to the Commission as a whole. It appears that such a practice obtains in the Institut de Droit International and in the International Law Association; and there is no reason why it should not also be adopted by the Commission.[23]

The draft articles and commentaries which a Special Rapporteur prepares naturally have a great influence on the Commission's work on the topic in hand. In the past, Special Rapporteurs considered it expedient to submit comprehensive reports, covering the whole of a topic or at least a major range of issues. In recent times, though, the trend has developed of Special Rapporteurs submitting only a small number of draft articles to the Commission for its consideration,[24] sometimes even without commentaries.[25] This has resulted in repetitive debates and a loss of valuable time. It is suggested that Special Rapporteurs should present reports which are as substantial as possible, complete with commentaries on the draft articles which they propose, and that they should do this annually, if possible, and biannually, if necessary.

(c) Working groups

Generally, working groups are established by the Commission before a Special Rapporteur is appointed in order to define the scope and direction of work on a topic. However, from time to time, working groups have been appointed to handle a topic as a whole, as occurred in the case of the preparation of the Commission's Draft Articles on the Prevention and Punishment of Crimes against Diplomatic Agents and Other Internationally Protected Persons and its Draft Statute for an International Criminal Court. Given the effectiveness and success of this procedure, it should be considered whether the procedure should be more widely employed of appointing working groups to resolve particular deadlocks within the Commission or to handle topics as a whole where speed is of the essence.

(d) Drafting Committee

If the institution of the Special Rapporteur is important for the codification process, of no less significance is the role and work of the Drafting Committee. A 15-member Drafting Committee is appointed annually by the Commission to assist it in coordinating and consolidating its work on a given topic. The Commission has recognized that this committee plays a vital role in the effective functioning of the Commission.[26] It has recently been said by the Commission

---

[23]Report of the International Law Commission on the work of its forty-eighth session, op. cit. above (footnote 11), pp. 214-215 at paras. 192-196.

[24]Graefrath, loc. cit. above (footnote 15), p. 606. Note also the criticisms advanced by the U.K. and Norway cited by Graefrath: loc. cit., footnote 73.

[25]The importance of commentaries has recently been emphasized by the Commission, it being remarked that "[s]imultaneous work on text and commentary can enhance the acceptability of both": Report of the International Law Commission on the work of its forty-eighth session, op. cit. above (footnote 11), p. 216 at para. 198.

[26]For an account of its functions, see United Nations, *Review of the Multilateral Treaty-making Process* (1985), p. 286 *et seq.* (document ST/LEG/SER.B/21; United Nations publication, Sales No. E/F.83.V.8).

that "[i]n general the Drafting Committee works well".27 However, the manner in which the Drafting Committee functioned in the late 1980s attracted the following critical comment from a past member of the Commission:

"Part of the problem is that the Drafting Committee, in the absence of clear directions from the Commission as a whole, has to operate in some measure as a negotiating body in order to reconcile differences of view that may have emerged as a result of the debate in the Plenary."28

This criticism points to the need for a better definition of the roles and functions of the Plenary and of the Drafting Committee. The Plenary should not prematurely refer draft articles to the Drafting Committee and the Drafting Committee should avoid assuming the role of the Plenary. It may be true that the Drafting Committee does not exist to consider just points of drafting, but that is no reason for transforming its character and its functions. So long as the functions of the Plenary and Drafting Committee are not properly differentiated and so long as the Drafting Committee does not confine itself to its proper role, the Commission is likely to waste its time in protracted debates and negotiations, so delaying its work.

(e) Consensus

The Commission has in recent times been operating on the basis of consensus. In the past, however, it appears that there was frequent recourse to voting. Consensual formulations may well stand a better chance of proving acceptable to the General Assembly and to plenipotentiary conferences; but arriving at consensus is a time-consuming process. The matter becomes all the more grave in the case of politically sensitive topics, as was the case with the Draft Code of Crimes against the Peace and Security of Mankind. It is, therefore, appropriate that the Commission reexamine whether consensus is the right or best procedure in every case. It is suggested that the earlier practice of voting should be resumed, at any rate in dealing with critical issues. In any event, consensus should not be permitted to result in the production of vacuous drafts.29

(f) End product

What form should the end product of the Commission take: a draft convention, an expository code, a guide or a report *simpliciter*? Past practice would seem to indicate that a draft convention has been the Commission's preferred choice by far, although from time to time it has had recourse to other forms of output.30 The Commission has occasionally been criticized for its

---

27Report of the International Law Commission on the work of its forty-eighth session, op. cit. above (footnote 11), p. 221 at para. 217.

28Sinclair, op. cit. above (footnote 17), p. 35.

29See, in this connection, Schachter, "United Nations Law", *American Journal of International Law*, vol. 88 (1994), p. 1. Schachter there remarks that "[t]he prevailing practice of seeking consensus or near unanimity to adopt a convention had led to highly ambiguous or vacuous provisions". See also Schachter, "Recent Trends in International Law Making", *Australian Year Book of International Law*, vol. 12 (1992), p. 1.

30For example: on the topic of Rights and Duties of States, it submitted, in 1949, a draft declaration; on the topic of Offences against the Peace and Security of Mankind, it submitted, in 1951, an expository code; and on the topic of Arbitral Procedure, it submitted, in 1958, a set of model

preference of the draft convention to other possible forms of output. The UNITAR Study suggested that:

"The Commission should explore the possibility of the production of restatements and reports as alternatives to draft articles. On the one hand, reports are suitable to areas where there is little state practice and/or where the circumstances are not ripe for conclusion of convention . . . On the other hand, areas which benefit from the existence of extensive state practice are prime candidates for restatements".[31]

So far as the Commission itself is concerned, its preference for the draft convention seems to be a function of the following considerations:

"Its preciseness, its binding character, the fact that it has gone through the negotiating stage of collective diplomacy at an international conference, the publication and wide dissemination of the conventions, all these are assets that will not be lightly abandoned."[32]

While this evaluation is unexceptionable, it is incorrect to assume that international law can only be developed through the medium of conventions. Depending upon the topic and subject matter, different forms of output may be deployed to this end. It is significant that, in recent years, the Commission has cast the end results of its work in a variety of forms. This trend should be continued and developed.

(g) Role of the Secretariat

It is but to be expected that the Secretariat of the United Nations will have an important role to perform in the progressive development of international law and its codification. Indeed, a division of the Office of Legal Affairs is assigned to codification work. Besides providing professional services at the annual sessions of the Commission, the Codification Division has published general and special studies on the items on the Commission's agenda. In 1971, it also prepared a valuable study surveying the whole field of international law. This survey proved useful to the Commission and to the Sixth Committee in selecting topics for the Commission's long-range programme of work. Regrettably, this practice has not been followed in recent years.[33] Given the usefulness of

rules. More recently, in 1995, the Special Rapporteur on the topic of Reservations to Treaties suggested that the Commission cast its work on that topic in the form of a guide to practice; while, in the case of the topic of State Succession and its Impact on the Nationality of Natural and Legal Persons, the Commission provisionally decided in 1996 to embody its work, so far as the nationality of natural persons is concerned, in the form of a declaration of the General Assembly consisting of articles and commentaries.

[31]El Baradei et al., op. cit. above (footnote 4), p. 27.

[32]*Yearbook of the International Law Commission, 1973*, vol. II, p. 230 at para. 169.

[33]During the Commission's forty-fourth session, a working group was set up to address the question of the Commission's long-term programme of work. This group subsequently suggested the inclusion in that programme of the two topics of the law and practice relating to reservations to treaties and of State succession and its impact on the nationality of natural and legal persons. See *Yearbook of the International Law Commission, 1993*, vol. II (Part Two), pp. 95-97 at paras. 425-443.

More recently, in 1996, the Commission reestablished a working group to assist in selecting topics for future study. This group suggested the following three topics as appropriate for codification and progressive development: diplomatic protection; ownership and protection of wrecks beyond the limits of national maritime jurisdiction and unilateral acts of States. See the Report of the International Law Commission on the work of its forty-eighth session, op. cit. above (footnote 11), p. 230 at para. 249.

Professor Sir Hersch Lauterpacht's original survey of 1949 and of the Secretariat's survey of 1971, the Secretariat should be authorized to prepare a new in-depth study surveying the whole field of international law. This is an assignment which is more suitable and appropriate for the Secretariat to carry out than an outside expert.

III. Relations between the Sixth Committee and the Commission

The General Assembly, which is endowed by Article 13 (1) (*a*) of the Charter of the United Nations with the function of "encouraging the progressive development of international law and its codification", has come to exercise, through the Sixth Committee, a sort of supervision over the work of the International Law Commission. However, this supervisory role has, in the main, been limited to suggesting topics for codification and development and deciding the course of action to be taken with regard to the end product of the Commission's work on a topic. While the Sixth Committee each year reviews the work of the Commission, that review typically results only in the issue of policy guidelines, it being reckoned that the Commission should enjoy a substantial degree of autonomy in its work.[34]

The relationship between the Sixth Committee and the Commission is a matter of great political significance. For the success of the codification process, there must be a clear understanding of the respective roles of the two bodies and a healthy interaction and dialogue between them.[35] At appropriate points, the Commission should seek policy guidelines on issues that divide its members, while the Sixth Committee should exercise its role by giving as objective guidance as possible to the Commission. More importantly, the Sixth Committee should make up its mind in a timely fashion on how it should deal with the end product of the Commission's work. The Sixth Committee's failure to guide the Commission properly in its work on the topic of the Diplomatic Courier and the Diplomatic Bag Not Accompanied by Diplomatic Courier was dismaying. Time, money and effort would have been spared if the Sixth Committee had taken an appropriate decision on the matter at an earlier stage.[36]

The format of the Sixth Committee's annual debate on the work of the Commission has been improved in recent years by the adoption of certain innovatory procedures, but the point should be made that there is still room for improving the way in which the Sixth Committee discharges its role. The Sixth Committee, as the review organ of the parent body, could encourage the Commission to play a more dynamic role than it has hitherto done. There is an element of truth in the criticism that part of the blame for the Commission's recent decline lies with the Sixth Committee for failing to exercise its functions in an appropriate fashion. As was well pointed out by the UNITAR Study, "[t]he Sixth Committee could, if it wanted, entrust the Commission with high priority topics and provide it with the human and material resources necessary for the timely and successful completion of its tasks".[37]

The supervisory or monitoring function of the Sixth Committee leaves much to be desired. As the Commission's effectiveness depends in large part upon the policy guidance which the Sixth Committee gives to it, a more incisive

---

[34]Briggs, op. cit. above (footnote 8), p. 318.
[35]Cede, "New Approaches to Law Making in the UN-System", *Austrian Review of International and European Law*, vol. 1 (1996), p. 51.
[36]Yankov, loc. cit. above (footnote 3).
[37]El Baradei et al., op. cit. above (footnote 4), p. 8.

role on the part of the Committee is called for. However, the Sixth Committee is really nothing more than the Member States of the United Nations acting as a collegiate body. Recognition of that fact brings us, in the final analysis, to the question of the degree of commitment on the part of States themselves to the cause of the codification and progressive development of international law. How does one enhance the commitment of States? It is to be hoped that this Colloquium will prove useful in generating ideas and suggestions to enhance that commitment in a manner which befits the needs of the international community.

THE INTERNATIONAL LAW COMMISSION'S WORK
AND
THE SHAPING OF INTERNATIONAL LAW

by Sir Kenneth Keith*

The impact of the work of the International Law Commission on the shaping of international law is to be seen both in the law in the books and in the law in action. This paper emphasizes the latter. It is also selective in the areas of law which it discusses. Since much legal practice, national as well as international, involves the understanding and application of written law—legislation and treaties—the law of treaties is given a prominent place here. Because of its institutional character, the law of State responsibility is drawn upon and, to stress the law in action, so is international humanitarian law. References to State immunity highlight the relationships between those engaged in the law, be it as legislators, jurists or judges.

The Commission's impact is not confined to the making of international law. Its texts can influence law which is purely national in nature. Its methods can also be relevant to the methods for the development and codification of national law. I begin with comments on these two matters. Then, emphasizing the law in action, I consider the effect in national and international courts of the work of the International Law Commission. I conclude with some related suggestions as to how the Commission's role might be enhanced.

The Commission's impact, actual or potential, on national law-making and on national law

National law-making occurs in a wider political, constitutional and, increasingly, an international context and is effected by a variety of means. There is a danger that one of those means—the making of changes through law-commission processes—may be seen in isolation from that critical wider context. In the international community, Article 13 (1) of the Charter of the United Nations provides an immediate corrective to any such narrowing impulse, by putting the development and codification of law within that wider context:

"The General Assembly shall initiate studies and make recommendations for the purpose of:

"a. promoting international co-operation in the political field and encouraging the progressive development of international law and its codification;

"b. promoting international co-operation in the economic, social, cultural, educational, and health fields, and assisting in the realization of human rights and fundamental freedoms for all without distinction as to race, sex, language, or religion."

---

*Judge of the New Zealand Court of Appeal and of the Courts of Appeal of Samoa, the Cook Islands and Niue.

Sharp lines cannot be drawn between the various matters falling within the General Assembly's responsibility under this provision. The processes for the progressive development and codification of international law, or indeed of national law, will often feed into and draw on these other matters. Such a contextual, or even holistic, approach is emphasized by the Secretary-General's proposals for greater intersectoral and institutional coherence within the United Nations system in his major recent Report, *Renewing the United Nations: A Programme for Reform*.[1] Institutional responses are demanded by the amazing, even revolutionary, ways in which the organization of the world community is changing—changes demonstrated, for instance, by the increasing references in the literature to a "borderless world" and to "the end of the nation State".[2] To adapt the title of an excellent article by the Secretary of the International Law Commission itself, international law-making must itself "reach out".[3] It cannot stand apart.

From somewhat more stable times, I take two examples of the two-way relationship between the development and codification of the law, on the one hand, and the wider political context, on the other. The first appears in the preamble to the Vienna Convention on the Law of Treaties:

"*The States Parties to the present Convention*

"*Considering* the fundamental role of treaties in the history of international relations,

"*Recognizing* the ever-increasing importance of treaties as a source of international law and as a means of developing peaceful cooperation among nations, whatever their constitutional and social systems,

". . .

"*Believing* that the codification and progressive development of the law of treaties achieved in the present Convention will promote the purposes of the United Nations set forth in the Charter, namely, the maintenance of international peace and security, the development of friendly relations and the achievement of cooperation among nations".

My second example is the Commission's work on State responsibility has drawn on much other United Nations activity, for instance the 1970 Declaration of Principles of International Law Concerning Friendly Relations and Cooperation among States in accordance with the Charter of the United Nations and the 1974 Definition of Aggression.[4]

The Convention on the Law of Treaties and its development also illuminate the choices that are constantly being made in law-making processes between different national or international institutions. Which matters are to be seen as having a substantial political content, requiring direct governmental and political control over the law-making process, and which are appropriate for a more

---

[1]Document A/51/950, at paras. 17, 38 and 49, for example.

[2]See, for example: Kennedy, P., *Preparing for the Twenty-first Century* (1993); Reich, R., *The Work of Nations* (1992); Ohmae, K., *The Borderless World* (1990) and *The End of the Nation State* (1995); Strange, S., *The Retreat of the State: the Diffusion of Power in the World Economy* (1996); and Guehenno, J.-M., *The End of the Nation State* (1995) (the original French title of which is *La Fin de la démocratie*).

[3]Lee, "International Law Reaching Out", in Macdonald, R.St.J. (ed.), *Essays in Honour of Wang Tieya* (1993), p. 497.

[4]See, for example, the Secretariat studies relating to State responsibility: *Yearbook of the International Law Commission, 1969*, vol. II, pp. 101 and 114. See also the Secretariat's outstanding study on "Force Majeure" and "fortuitous event", ibid., *1978*, vol. II (Part One), p. 61. The relationship of the Commission's work to the 1970 Declaration is also emphasized in the General Assembly's annual resolutions on the Commission's reports.

independent scientific treatment, involving governmental input rather than control? Which matters should be handled in a specialized forum, rather than in the United Nations?[5] A third choice is between public and private scientific bodies, a matter most interestingly discussed in the United States recently in relation to such bodies as the American Law Institute[6] and over a century ago by Francis Lieber (to refer to a major figure in international humanitarian law).[7] The texts of the private bodies can have no direct formal force. That is also true of the Commission's texts which do not have binding treaty force, either because the appropriate steps to that end have not yet been taken or because no such steps are planned—as, for instance, with the Principles of International Law Recognized in the Charter of the Nürnberg tribunal and in the Judgment of the Tribunal or as with the Model Rules on Arbitral Procedure.[8]

Another choice is that between legislative and judicial law-making. A choice favouring the latter can of course often be made by courts themselves, which may indeed have no option but to make the law in an area of uncertainty. It may also be made by a legislative body or advisory body, which may decide either to use general language or to omit relevant rules, leaving the development of the law in both cases to the courts.

I take as a valuable example some of the choices which were made in the case of the law of treaties, particularly in respect of the law regarding the use of the legislative history, or *travaux préparatoires*, of a treaty in interpreting that treaty's text.

As is well known, the International Law Commission, in its work on the law of treaties, originally intended to prepare an expository code of a general

---

[5]For the complicated relationship in the area of the law of armed conflict between the International Committee of the Red Cross (and related processes) and the United Nations, from 1949 to the present, see the General Reports of Zacklin and Sandoz, in Condorelli, L., La Rosa, A.-M., and Scherrer, S. (eds.), *The United Nations and International Humanitarian Law* (1996), p. 39 and p. 55, respectively.

[6]Schwartz and Scott, "The Political Economy of Private Legislatures", *University of Pennsylvania Law Review*, vol. 143 (1995), p. 595; and Schwarcz, "A Fundamental Inquiry into the Statutory Rule Making Process of Private Legislatures", *Georgia Law Review*, vol. 29 (1995), p. 909. In December 1996 the American Law Institute adopted a new Council Rule on the obligation of members to exercise independent judgment: "To maintain the Institute's reputation for thoughtful, disinterested analysis of legal issues, members are expected to leave client interests at the door . . ."

[7]See the various statements he made about official and private codification efforts, as collected by Elihu Root in his tribute on the occasion of the fiftieth anniversary of the promulgation of General Orders 100 by President Lincoln: Root, "Francis Lieber", *American Journal of International Law*, vol. 7 (1913), p. 453 at pp. 462-66.

[8]See the related suggestion in the 1971 *Survey of International Law* submitted to the Commission by the Secretary-General that a study not in treaty form of the subject of unilateral acts, including definitions of such acts and a statement of their legal effects, together with a succinct commentary, might prove to be of considerable practical value to States. It might provide, or come to provide, a measure of authoritative clarification, irrespective of its formal status: *Yearbook of the International Law Commission, 1971*, vol. II (Part Two), p. 61 at para. 283. In its current work of the matter, the Commission has yet to state its views on the final outcome of its work: Report of the International Law Commission on the work of its forty-ninth ession, *Official Records of the General Assembly, Fifty-second Session, Supplement No. 10* (A/52/10), pp. 145-146 at paras. 214-215. See also Tomuschat, "The UN International Law Commission: Gains and Prospects", *Human Rights Forum*, vol. 5 (1995), p. 89 at p. 102.
The law governing international commercial transactions demonstrates a still wider range of means of regulating international activity. See the excellent discussion by Goode, "Reflections on the Harmonization of Commercial Law", in Cranston, R., and Goode, R. (eds.), *Commercial and Consumer Law: National and International Dimensions* (1993), Ch. 1.
See also Crawford, "Universalism and Regionalism from the Perspective of the Work of the International Law Commission", and Székely, "Non-binding Commitments: a Commentary on the Softening of International Law Evidenced in the Environmental Field", in United Nations, *International Law on the Eve of the Twenty-first Century: Views from the International Law Commission* (1997), pp. 99 and 173, respectively (United Nations publication, UN Sales No. E/F 97.V.4).

character; but in 1961 it decided to prepare draft articles capable of serving as a basis for an international convention. In the following year it gave these two reasons for changing its mind:

> "First, an expository code, however well-formulated, cannot in the nature of things be so effective as a convention for consolidating the law; and the consolidation of the law of treaties is of particular importance at the present time when so many new States have recently become members of the international community. Secondly, the codification of the law of treaties through a multilateral convention would give all the new States the opportunity to participate directly in the formulation of the law if they so wished; and their participation in the work of codification appears to the Commission to be extremely desirable in order that the law of treaties may be placed upon the widest and most secure foundations."[9]

That was one choice made in the course of the law-reform process. Another, more particular one related to the use of legislative history. There had been much discussion about what, if anything, a codifying text should say about the interpretation of treaties, including the use of legislative history.[10] That matter was also increasingly arising within the common law world, where, with the exception of the United States, legislative history, or at least parliamentary history, was said to be irrelevant to determining the meaning of legislation. There was the interesting anomaly, at the same time, that courts were willing, when considering the meaning of legislation implementing treaties, to look at the legislative history of the treaty.[11]

The New Zealand Law Commission addressed this matter in 1990. It took account of extensive national practice in common law countries, legislative changes that had been made or proposed in some of them and the work of the International Law Commission which had culminated in the adoption of articles 31 and 32 of the 1969 Convention on the Law of Treaties. It concluded that, in the light of the developments in New Zealand, where courts had been making careful use of legislative history (while not denying the central binding character of the written text of the law), it was unnecessary for there to be any legislative intervention, either to stop that evolving judicial practice or to codify and

---

[9] *Yearbook of the International Law Commission, 1962*, vol. II, p. 160 at para. 17.

[10] Compare, for example, McDougal, M.S., Lasswell, H.D., and Miller, J.C., *The Interpretation of Agreements and World Public Order: Principles of Content and Procedure* (1967), and Fitzmaurice "*Vae Victis* or Woe to the Negotiators: Your Treaty or Our Interpretation of it?", *American Journal of International Law*, vol. 65 (1971), p. 358, as well as the 1994 reissue of the McDougal book (with an additional introduction and other material).
For the various stages of the development of the Vienna Convention's interpretation provisions, see Rosenne, S., *The Law of Treaties: A Guide to the Legislative History of the Vienna Convention* (1970), pp. 214-219.

[11] See, for example, *Fothergill v. Monarch Airlines Ltd.*, *Appeal Cases* (1981), p. 251 (House of Lords, England and Wales) at pp. 278, 283 and 294-295. The Vienna Convention was also invoked in this case.
There were exceptions to the bar on referring to parliamentary debates. One with a bearing on international law concerned the meaning of the expression "crime of a political character" as a limit on the power of extradition. Justice Stephen, in ruling against the claim of a Swiss citizen, disagreed with what John Stuart Mill had said in a debate in the House of Commons. It was very easy, said the Judge, to give too wide an explanation and his "late friend Mr Mill", he thought, "made a mistake upon the subject, probably because he was not accustomed to use language with that degree of precision which is essential to everyone who has ever had, as I have had on many occasions, to draft Acts of Parliament, which, although they may be easy to understand, people continually try to misunderstand . . ." *Re Castioni, Queen's Bench* (1891-I), p. 148 (Divisional Court, England and Wales) at pp. 167-168.

develop it. The Commission supported that practice and considered that the matter was better left to the courts.[12]

A further step in the story was taken by the courts in London in 1991 and 1992. A taxpayer had challenged a decision taken by the tax authorities. In the course of judicial proceedings, it was discovered that a minister in charge of the relevant legislation had, in the course of parliamentary debates, given an answer regarding the interpretation of the draft statute which was favourable to the taxpayer. A court of seven judges was assembled to hear the case reargued with particular reference to the question whether the courts would, contrary to the rule or practice which had until then prevailed, have regard to parliamentary debates in interpreting the statute. With the Lord Chancellor dissenting, the other six members of the House of Lords decided that the rule excluding reference to parliamentary material as an aid to statutory interpretation should be relaxed. Reference was to be permitted where legislation was ambiguous or obscure or led to absurdity, the material relied upon consisted of one or more statements by a minister or other promoter of the draft legislation (together with such other parliamentary material as was necessary to understand such statements and their effect) and the statements relied upon were clear. In the argument in that case, the successful counsel, as he has generously acknowledged,[13] borrowed extensively from the Report of the New Zealand Law Commission. While referring to the report of the British Law Commission, which opposed the use of parliamentary records, he urged that the New Zealand approach should be preferred. Although the leading judgement does not refer expressly to the Report of the New Zealand Law Commission, the arguments it addresses and the answers it gives are essentially those which are there to be found—with, perhaps, the qualification that the New Zealand practice is not as restrictive as that which the House of Lords stated.[14]

By way of contrast with the steps taken—or not taken—in New Zealand and the United Kingdom, some Australian legislatures, like the Vienna Conference, have enacted legislation expressly authorizing courts to use legislative history for stated purposes. The first such step was taken by the Federal Parliament in 1984:

"15AB (1) Subject to subsection (3), in the interpretation of a provision of an Act, if any material not forming part of the Act is capable of assisting in the ascertainment of the meaning of the provision, consideration may be given to that material:

"(a) to confirm that the meaning of the provision is the ordinary meaning conveyed by the text of the provision taking into account its context in the Act and the purpose or object underlying the Act; or

"(b) to determine the meaning of the provision when:

"(i)   the provision is ambiguous or obscure; or

"(ii) the ordinary meaning conveyed by the text of the provision taking into account its context in the Act and the purpose or object underlying the Act leads to a result that is manifestly absurd or is unreasonable.

---

[12]*A New Interpretation Act: To Avoid "Prolixity" and "Tautology"*, New Zealand Law Commission Report No. 17 (1990), paras. 100-126 and pp. 213-215.

[13]See, for example, Lester, "*Pepper v. Hart* Revisited", *Statute Law Review*, vol. 15 (1994), p. 10, and "English Judges as Law Makers", *Public Law* (1993), p. 269 at p. 275.

[14]*Pepper (Inspector of Taxes)* v. *Hart, Appeal Cases* (1993) p. 593 (House of Lords, England and Wales) at pp. 598-603 and 630-640.

"(2) [*provides a non-exhaustive list of material that might be referred to, including some parliamentary material and treaty texts mentioned in the legislation*]

"(3) In determining whether consideration should be given to any material in accordance with subsection (1), or in considering the weight to be given to any such material, regard shall be had, in addition to any other relevant matters, to:

"(a) the desirability of persons being able to rely on the ordinary meaning conveyed by the text of the provision taking into account its context in the Act and the purpose or object underlying the Act; and

"(b) the need to avoid prolonging legal or other proceedings without compensating advantage."[15]

At critical points, this wording is identical to that of articles 31 and 32 of the Vienna Convention on the Law of Treaties. That is not a coincidence. One, particular, explanation is that the responsible official within the Australian Attorney-General's department had earlier been head of the Australian delegation at the 1968-1969 Vienna Conference, as well as having been the Agent of Australia in the *Nuclear Tests* cases, in which, as discussed below, the Vienna Convention was used extensively by the applicants and by members of the International Court.[16] The broader explanation is that the process of interpreting legal texts in any particular legal system should not be seen as unique. The experiences of others should illuminate and assist, as is made clear by recent lectures given by Justice Antonin Scalia.[17]

Other instances of the uses of international texts in purely national contexts are provided by the adoption in Scotland and New Zealand of the UNCITRAL model law on arbitration for domestic arbitrations as well as for international ones and the adoption in Scotland of the Convention on the International Sale of Goods for domestic sales as well as for international ones.

Gertrude Stein's famous last words "What is the question?" introduce two matters to complete this section of the paper. Those involved in the development and the codification of the law should be helped by the experience of the International Law Commission in formulating—or not—the right questions to be addressed. A prime international instance is provided by the history of the topic of State responsibility and of the related topic of international liability for injurious consequences arising out of acts not prohibited by international law. The 1963 decision to divide the primary and secondary rules of State responsibility (and essentially to put to one side for more than 30 years the particular issue of State responsibility for injuries to foreign nationals) made progress possible, however slow that progress might have been. A somewhat related national example concerns the law governing personal injury. Late last century

---

[15]Acts Interpretation Act 1901 (as enacted in 1984). See also: the New South Wales Interpretation Act 1987, section 34; the Victoria Interpretation of Legislation Act 1984, section 35B; and the Western Australia Interpretation Act 1984, section 19.

[16]Brazil, "Reform of Statutory Interpretation—the Australian Experience of Use of Extrinsic Materials: With a Postscript on Simpler Drafting", *Australian Law Journal*, vol. 62 (1988), p. 503, "Some Reflections on the Vienna Convention on the Law of Treaties", *Federal Law Review*, vol. 6 (1975), p. 223 at pp. 234-239, and "Legislative History and the Sure and True Interpretation of Statutes in General and the Constitution in Particular", *University of Queensland Law Journal*, vol. 4 (1964), p. 1.

[17]Scalia, A., *A Matter of Interpretation: Federal Courts and the Law* (1997). As the subtitle of this work indicates, though, his discussion draws on a rather narrow range of sources.

and early this century, national legislatures decided to divide the right of persons injured at work to be compensated and to be provided with health care from what was seen as the separate matter of the penal and administrative responsibility of their employers under safety laws. It was not possible for the law of civil liability to achieve in an adequate way the purposes of both compensation and deterrence or punishment. Subsequent experience strongly confirms that that was a correct assessment.[18] The liability topic also teaches important general lessons about the creating of obligations to prevent and mitigate danger. Law commissions and like bodies which can stand apart from the detail and responsibilities of particular areas of regulation have perhaps a rare opportunity and ability, with the help of others, to take a broader view of the evolving basic structures and institutions within our legal systems.

Law commissions and similar bodies should also have, and should exercise, the ability to ask and to answer the question prior to the one posed by Gertrude Stein: whether there is even a question to be asked by and of them. Richard Baxter provides an excellent instance in the area of the law of armed conflict in his seminal essay "The Effects of Ill-conceived Codification and Development of International Law".[19]

The shaping of national law to give effect to international law

My immediate concern is, in fact, narrower than this heading suggests, since my emphasis will be on the work of the International Law Commission—although, once more, seen in a wider context. My main examples will be drawn from the jurisprudence of common law countries. In making another necessary selection, I do not mean to diminish the enormously important role of national legislation which gives effect to treaties.[20] I am greatly assisted in my research of the case-law by the indispensable *International Law Reports*. Their more than 100 volumes overwhelmingly confirm the suspicion of the original editors, Arnold McNair and Hersch Lauterpacht, "that there is more international law already in existence and daily accumulating 'than this world dreams of'".[21] Sir Robert Jennings, in his lecture marking the publication of the hundredth volume of the series, calls attention to the Reports' "determinative effect on the shaping

---

[18]See, for example, Dewees, D.N., Duff, D., and Trebilcock, M.J., *Exploring the Domain of Accident Law: Taking the Facts Seriously* (1996). For a very early recognition that the law of civil liability could not achieve both the purposes of compensation and of deterrence and punishment, see Clay, "The Law of Employers' Liability and Insurance against Accidents", Journal of the Society of Comparative Legislation, vol. 2 (1897), p. 1 at pp. 1-2.

[19]*Recueil d'études de droit international en hommage à Paul Guggenheim* (1968), p. 146. Given recent developments concerning the Draft Code of Crimes against the Peace and Security of Mankind and the International Criminal Court, Baxter's views may now require some reassessment. See also the valuable cautionary comments of Fleischhauer, "The United Nations and the Progressive Development and Codification of International Law", *Indian Journal of International Law*, vol. 25 (1985), p. 1 at pp. 5-7.

[20]See, for example: Law Commission, *A New Zealand Guide to International Law and Its Sources*, New Zealand Law Commission Report No. 34 (1996), pp. 14-22; and Crawford, "The International Law Standard in the Statutes of Australia and the United Kingdom", *American Journal of International Law*, vol. 73 (1979), p. 628. I have given relevant papers to: the Commonwealth Law Conference held in Nicosia in 1993 ("Lawyers and the Rule of Law", Conference Papers, 1993); the New Zealand Law Conference held in Dunedin in 1996 ("International Business Law", Conference Papers, vol. 1, p. 170); and the Judicial Colloquium on the Domestic Application of International Human Rights Norms, held in Georgetown, Guyana, in 1996 ("Application of International Human Rights Law in New Zealand", *Texas International Law Journal*, vol. 32 (1997), p. 401).

[21]*Annual Digest of Public International Law Cases, 1925-1926* (1929), p. ix.

and content of substantive international law".[22] He quotes Professor Karl Zemanek for the proposition that domestic courts may play a role in "transforming codification conventions and other unilateral law making treaties into customary law by applying them in non-party States". The current part of this paper provides some evidence that this is indeed so and also supports his broader proposition that the approach to international law in municipal court cases amounts today to a quiet and often unnoticed revolution in the nature and context of international law. This paper as a whole, I trust, might also provide some support for Sir Robert's warning against tendencies to fragmentation within the discipline of international law and within the international legal system.

The most obvious manifestation of the impact of the Commission's work within a national legal system is where a codification treaty becomes part of national law on its ratification or acceptance by the State concerned. That is, however, by no means the whole answer. There are two other potentially important areas of influence: first, where the Commission's text or the final treaty text has not (yet) been completed; and, secondly, where that text has been completed, but is not yet binding. I shall consider the three possibilities in turn.

Questions of foreign State, or sovereign, immunity are now regulated by legislation in several common law countries, including Australia, Canada, the United Kingdom and the United States. In others, such as Ireland and New Zealand, the matter remains governed by general law, which, in the case of both those countries, includes customary international law, either as a consequence of constitutional provision, as in the case of the former country, or under the common law, as in the case of the latter. Decisions of courts in those countries, and likewise in Switzerland, suggest that judges and counsel have varying degrees of knowledge of the material on sovereign immunity which has emanated from the Commission and varying degrees of willingness to make use of it. As Judge Higgins has made plain in her outstanding Hague Lectures, much depends on the culture of the legal profession and especially on its knowledge of, and experience with, international law.[23] There can be no doubt that many lawyers face major educational tasks as they come to grips with the legal consequences of living in an increasingly "borderless" world. This is apparent even in a traditional area such as sovereign immunity.

Recent Irish cases[24] have decided questions of immunity by drawing on Irish, United Kingdom and Privy Council decisions (and one German one), the United States legislation and the European Convention (even though not directly in point). Relevant foreign legislation, however, is accorded very limited significance and there is not one express reference to the work of the International Law Commission—although there is a possible general reference to it in the most recent judgement according immunity to the actions of a British soldier on border patrol in Northern Ireland who had allegedly committed an act of battery against the plaintiff within Ireland.

A New Zealand case provides something of a contrast. It concerned the jurisdiction of a labour court over a dispute between the Governor of Pitcairn

---

[22]"The Judiciary, International and National, and the Development of International Law", *International Law Reports*, vol. 102, p. ix, and *International and Comparative Law Quarterly*, vol. 45 (1996), p. 1.

[23]Higgins, R., *Problems and Process: International Law and How We Use It* (1994), Ch. 12, especially pp. 206-207.

[24]Including *Canada* v. *Employment Appeals Tribunal and Burke*, *International Law Reports*, vol. 95, p. 467, and *McElhinney* v. *Williams*, ibid., vol. 104, p. 691, discussed by Symmons, *Irish Jurist*, vol. 31 (1996), p. 165.

Island (in fact, the United Kingdom High Commissioner in New Zealand) and a staff member employed in New Zealand. One of the two judgements in that case draws on the draft articles which were adopted by the Commission in 1991 and, in particular, on the Commission's draft article 11, relating to contracts of employment. The judge in question exhibits some caution, though, since the draft articles remained—as they still remain—under consideration by the Sixth Committee of the General Assembly. Against that background, he said, it would be premature to conclude that there was or is a settled rule of international law applying to the plaintiff's situation. None the less, the effect of the provision which was most in point was that, since the employee had been recruited to perform functions closely related to the exercise of governmental authority, the matter was covered by sovereign immunity. The conclusion that the judge drew from the description of the duties attached to the plaintiff's position was that her employment was viewed as an integral part of the administration of the office of Governor. It was not an office of a private character. Pursuit of an unjustifiable dismissal claim in the courts of New Zealand would be likely to involve exploring how the office was run and would intrude on the sovereign performance of those responsibilities. The test applied here is very like that in the Commission's draft article 11 and the result is consistent with that reached by courts in the United Kingdom, Ireland, Italy, Germany and the Netherlands, to whose decisions the judge referred. He borrowed a nice image from one of the Irish cases that "once one approaches the Embassy gates one must do so on an amber light".[25] He concluded that the general language of the employment statute was not to be read as overriding that body of law. Accordingly, the plea of immunity succeeded.

In 1989 the Swiss Federal Tribunal decided that former President Marcos of the Philippines and his wife could not invoke Head-of-State immunity in respect of criminal acts committed when he was in office because the Philippine Government had waived his immunity. In so deciding, the Tribunal drew on the Commission's work on State immunity—in that case, the draft articles as they had been provisionally adopted by the Commission on first reading in 1986. The court made use, as well, of the 1961 Convention on Diplomatic Relations and the 1969 Convention on Special Missions, emphasizing that the Head of State should have at least as much protection under the law of sovereign immunity as the various officials protected by those instruments (including, in the case of the latter instrument, the Head of State on a special mission).[26]

To move to the next stage, the Commission-sponsored text is likely to be seen as having greater force once it has had the endorsement of a diplomatic conference, even if it is not yet in force or, though in force, is not binding in respect of the particular issue in hand (among other things because of the position of the States involved). The Vienna Convention on the Law of Treaties is the most notable instance. Long before it was in force, that convention was being invoked by international courts, if not by national courts, as stating the law.[27]

---

[25]*Governor of Pitcairn* v. *Sutton, International Law Reports*, vol. 104, p. 518.

[26]*Marcos and Marcos* v. *Federal Department of Police*, ibid., vol. 102, p. 198 at pp. 202-203. Such uses of the sovereign immunity text perhaps help balance the rather negative view of it which is expressed by McCaffrey: "Is Codification in Decline?", *Hastings International and Comparative Law Review*, vol. 20 (1997), p. 639 at pp. 644-645.

[27]See, for example: *Case concerning claims arising out of decisions of the Mixed Graeco-German Arbitral Tribunal set up under Article 304 in Part X of the Treaty of Versailles, Reports of International Arbitral Awards*, vol. 19, p. 25 at paras. 55-61; and the *Golder Case, International Law Reports*, vol. 57, p. 201 at pp. 213-214, 216-17 and 226. See also the cases before the International Court of Justice which are cited in the "Introduction", in United Nations, op. cit. above (footnote 8), p. 1 at p. 9 footnote 60.

Even after it came into force in 1980, the Convention has frequently been applied in cases in which it has not been formally applicable either because one of the States party to the relevant treaty has not been party to the Convention or because of the non-retroactivity rule contained in its article 4. Nevertheless, as judicial practice, State practice, the Convention's drafting history and much related commentary, as well as article 4 itself, make clear, many, if not all, of the provisions of the Vienna Convention are seen as having customary force—a characterization which is important in those countries, such as many of those in the Commonwealth, in which treaties by themselves cannot bring about a change in the law, since courts may then draw on the rules which the Convention sets forth, even though no legislative action has been taken to incorporate them at the national level. A mundane recent instance is provided by a decision of the Ontario Court of Appeal applying the rule in article 33 (2) of the Convention to decide that only an authenticated text of a treaty can be used in the interpretation of that treaty unless the parties otherwise agree. That rule was applied to the Jay Treaty of 1794, a treaty which came into force between the United States (not a party to the Vienna Convention) and the United Kingdom nearly 200 years before the Vienna Convention's entry into force.[28]

A more significant use of the Convention—by an American court this time—was made by the 9th Circuit Federal Court of Appeals in *Siderman de Blake v. Argentina*.[29] Judge Fletcher there invoked article 53 in ruling that the international law prohibiting torture now has the status of *jus cogens*.[30]

Again, many national courts have, since 1980, used the interpretation rules in the Vienna Convention and its statement of the basic duty to comply with treaties in good faith, one instance being a judgement which was given last month by my court relating to the Human Rights Committee established under the International Covenant on Civil and Political Rights.[31]

The role of national courts is more straightforward when the relevant treaty is in force for the State and is part of the State's national law. Recent volumes of the *International Law Reports* include almost routine applications of the Vienna Convention on Diplomatic Relations, for example. I take three instances. In 1983 and 1984 the Swiss Federal Tribunal rejected an argument by a criminal defendant to the effect that an incident of hostage-taking within the Polish Embassy in Bern was not within the jurisdiction of the Swiss Courts since the Embassy was extraterritorial and the affair was an internal Polish matter. Article 22 (2) of the 1961 Convention was at the centre of the Tribunal's reasoning— though reference was also made to articles 31 and 32. Article 22 (2), the Tribunal held, does not in any way have the effect of separating the premises of a diplomatic mission from the territory of the receiving State. Moreover, the ability of the receiving State's authorities to institute proceedings against and punish those who commit criminal acts in an embassy is an important means by which it may meet its obligations to protect the diplomatic mission.[32]

---

[28]*Regina* v. *Vincent, International Law Reports*, vol. 104, p. 204. Another recent Canadian judgement involving the interpretation of a treaty (the 1951 Geneva Convention relating to the Status of Refugees) makes extensive reference to drafting history and subsequent practice, although without referring to the Vienna Convention to justify so doing: *Canada (Attorney-General)* v. *Ward* (ibid., p. 222).

[29]Ibid., vol. 103, p. 454.

[30]Ibid., at pp. 470-475.

[31]*Wellington District Legal Services Committee* v. *Tangiora* (CA33/97, 10 September 1997).

[32]*Swiss Federal Prosecutor* v. *Kruszyk, International Law Reports*, vol. 102, p. 176.

The immunity provisions of the 1961 Convention provided a principal reason for the grant of a stay by an Australian court in proceedings brought by the Australian Federation of Islamic Councils against a bank in respect of funds which were under the joint control of the Federation and the Ambassador of the Kingdom of Saudi Arabia. The court ruled that article 31, granting the Ambassador immunity from civil jurisdiction except in respect of professional or commercial activity outside his official functions, was applicable. The court went beyond the Convention to the cases to hold that the fact that the claim was only to partial control of the funds made no difference.[33]

In the third case, English courts held that Saudi Arabia was immune from industrial tribunal proceedings brought by a secretary in the Defence Office of its Embassy in London. While State immunity legislation did not confer immunity, the 1961 Convention did. That was so even though the secretary was locally recruited, was a British citizen and was employed in a clerical capacity without diplomatic status and even though her appointment had not been advised to the Foreign and Commonwealth Office as provided for in article 39 of the 1961 Convention. That obligation had nothing to do with Saudi Arabia's immunity.[34]

A critical aspect of national courts' application of treaty language or of national legislation giving effect to treaties is the approach which they adopt to the interpretation of the text. A great English judge with a broad internationalist perspective said in a single sentence all that needs to be said in this regard when interpreting legislation giving the force of law in England to the Convention on the Contract for the International Carriage of Goods by Road:

"I think that the correct approach is to interpret the English text [of the Convention], which after all is likely to be used by many others than British businessmen, in a normal manner, appropriate for the interpretation of an international convention, unconstrained by technical rules of English law, or by English legal precedent, but on broad principles of general acceptation."[35]

If assistance was needed, he said, the equally authoritative French text could be looked to: no threshold test of ambiguity stood in the way of that. As already indicated, British courts, like others, began at about the time of this pronouncement to refer expressly to the interpretation rules of the Vienna Convention.

The shaping of international law in international courts and tribunals

In looking at the relevance which the Commission's work has had for international courts and tribunals, a distinction must, once more, be made between binding treaty texts which are directly in force, on the one hand, and other texts, on the other hand. A spectacular instance of the use of the latter is to be found in the 1981 award of the court of arbitration relating to the border between Dubai and Sharjah.[36] Central to that award was the status of a series of decisions relating to the border which had been given in 1956 and 1957. One question which arose was whether those decisions could be said to have

---

[33] *Federation of Islamic Councils* v. *Westpac, International Law Reports*, vol. 104, p. 405.

[34] *Saudi Arabia* v. *Ahmed*, ibid., p. 629.

[35] *J. Buchanan & Co. Ltd.* v. *Babco (UK) Ltd., Appeal Cases* (1978), p. 141 (House of Lords, England and Wales) at p. 152.

[36] *Dubai-Sharjah Border Arbitration, Award of 19 October 1981, International Law Reports*, vol. 91, p. 543.

constituted arbitral awards. In deciding that they did not have that status, the Tribunal put the Commission's 1958 Model Rules on Arbitral Procedure at the centre of its reasoning. Those rules were, of course, very controversial. Many thought that they went too far in the direction of "judicial" arbitration. According to many States and some scholars,[37] the emphasis should have been on more flexible "diplomatic" arbitration. For their critics, the rules which the Commission prepared filled too many gaps which Governments would have liked to have seen left open. In response to the General Assembly's refusal to act on the Commission's recommendation that a convention be concluded on the basis of the Draft Convention on the subject which it had adopted in 1953, the Commission decided to maintain its text intact and to present it to the General Assembly once more as a set of Model Rules. The result was that in 1958 the General Assembly adopted a resolution which:

> "*Brings* the draft articles on arbitral procedure . . . to the attention of Member States for their consideration and use, in such cases and to such extent that they consider appropriate, in drawing up treaties of arbitration or *compromis*".[38]

To return to the border dispute, the Tribunal recognized the freedom of the parties to choose whether or not to introduce the Commission's Model Rules. They had not in fact adopted any provisions to that effect. Nevertheless, the Commission's text was, for the Tribunal, an authoritative modern expression of the law of arbitral procedure and reference should be made to the principles embodied in that text as indicating the state of customary international law at the period with which the Tribunal was concerned. It was by reference to the Rules that the Tribunal held that the decisions with which it was concerned did not constitute arbitral awards, first, because the maker of those decisions had not given the parties a fair hearing and, secondly, because his failure to give reasons for his decisions was contrary to the modern concept of arbitration.[39]

A recent article on the 1995 phase of the *Nuclear Tests* case has usefully called attention to the often neglected source constituted by the pleadings which are filed in international litigation. As Philippe Sands remarks, citing Professors Guggenheim and Bastid among others, such pleadings have doctrinal and professional value, they assist in the understanding of judicial decisions (notably in the case of orders, which are supported, at best, by limited reasoning) and they provide evidence of international law.[40] An examination of those pleadings again reveals that a significant role is accorded in them to the Commission's drafts, reports and documents. To illustrate this latter point, I shall take matters in which New Zealand has been involved: the *Nuclear Tests* cases of 1973-1974, the *Rainbow Warrior* case of 1989-1990 and the further phase of the *Nuclear Tests* case in 1995.

The Commission's work on treaties, along with the Vienna Convention on the Law of Treaties itself and the work of the diplomatic conference which adopted that convention, were central to the issue which arose in the *Nuclear Tests* cases of 1973-1974 of whether the General Act for the Pacific Settlement of International Disputes was still in force. That issue was pursued in some

---

[37]See, for example: De Visscher, "Reflections on the Present Prospects of International Adjudication", *American Journal of International Law*, vol. 50 (1956), p. 467 at pp. 468-71; and the opinions assembled by Sinclair, Sir I., *The International Law Commission* (1987), pp. 49-50.

[38]General Assembly resolution 1262 (XIII) of 14 November 1958.

[39]Loc. cit. above (footnote 37), at pp. 571-577.

[40]Sands "L'Affaire des essais nucléaires II (Nouvelle-Zélande c. France)", *Revue générale de droit international public*, vol. 101 (1997), p. 447.

depth, both at the interim remedies and jurisdictional phases of those cases; but, because of the way in which the Court handled the jurisdictional phase of the cases in its 1974 Judgments, it did not itself address the substance of the arguments which were made to it on the point. Its earlier 1973 Orders, moreover, are typically brief, saying no more than that there is a *prima facie* showing of jurisdiction.[41] In contrast, the dissenting judges in 1974 gave extensive consideration to the treaty arguments which had been made to the Court; and they, like the applicant States, derived major support from the Convention and the related work of the International Law Commission.[42] New Zealand's written and oral submissions on jurisdiction used the Convention, the Commission's Report of 1966 and the records of the 1968-1969 Vienna Conference in addressing the issue of the basic obligation to comply with treaties, the doctrine of fundamental change of circumstances, the problem of supervening impossibility of performance and the question of desuetude. The argument proceeded on the basis that part V of the Convention, concerning invalidity, termination and suspension of the operation of treaties, was in large part declaratory of customary international law and, to the extent that it was not, it favoured France's contentions. That proposition was based in turn on the history of the Convention and its terms.[43]

In the *Rainbow Warrior* case, treaty issues were again central.[44] Had France acted in breach of the agreements relating to the stay of the two agents on the island of Hao? Central, too, were issues of State responsibility. The written and oral submissions made extensive references to the work of the Commission on that topic. While the parties did not disagree in a significant way about the law as it was stated in the Commission's texts, they did disagree on a related point of principle and on the application of the law to the facts. The difference of principle concerned the balance between those two bodies of law, with New Zealand emphasizing the law of treaties and France the law of State responsibility. That difference in emphasis paralleled events in 1973-1974, when France also asserted broad grounds for avoiding apparently binding treaty obligations—a surprising position, given that in 1969 it cast the lone negative vote against the adoption of the text of the Vienna Convention for the professed reason that certain of its provisions were liable "to jeopardize the stability of treaty law, which was a necessary safeguard of international relations".[45] The Tribunal concluded that, without prejudice to the terms of the agreement between the parties and the applicability of certain important provisions of the Vienna Convention on the Law of Treaties, the existence in this case of certain circumstances precluding wrongfulness, as well as the question of appropriate remedies, should be answered in the context and in the light of the customary law of State responsibility.[46] That somewhat delphic statement (if I may so characterize it) has been the subject of some critical academic

---

[41]*Nuclear Tests (Australia v. France), Interim Protection, Order of 22 June 1973, I.C.J. Reports 1973,* p. 99 at para. 17, and *Nuclear Tests (New Zealand v. France), Interim Protection, Order of 22 June 1973, I.C.J. Reports 1973,* p. 135 at para. 18.

[42]*Nuclear Tests (Australia v. France), Judgment of 20 December 1974, I.C.J. Reports 1974,* p. 253 at pp. 334, 335, 336, 338, 349-50, 357, 377, 381, 383 and 405.

[43]*I.C.J. Pleadings, Nuclear Tests,* vol. II, pp. 182-186 and 270-279.

[44]*Case concerning the difference between New Zealand and France concerning the interpretation or application of two Agreements, concluded on 9 July 1986 between the two States and which related to the problems arising from the* Rainbow Warrior *Affair, Award of 30 April 1990, Reports of International Arbitral Awards,* vol. 20, p. 215.

[45]Document A/CONF.39/11/Add.1, p. 203 at para. 15.

[46]Loc. cit. above (footnote 44), at para. 75.

commentary.[47] There may of course be differences in the application of such broadly stated conclusions—as well as in the application of the relevant rules on the preclusion of wrongfulness. Such differences are apparent if one contrasts the award with the separate opinion.

To come now to 1995, the Commission's work on the liability topic was significant in the presentation of New Zealand's "request for an examination of the situation", to quote from the 1974 *Nuclear Tests* Judgment.[48] Once again the Court's Order, because of its very nature and the circumstances, makes only brief, but important, reference to the substantive law:

"... the present Order is without prejudice to the obligations of States to respect and protect the natural environment, obligations to which both New Zealand and France have in the present instance reaffirmed their commitment".[49]

One way of giving content to that brief statement is to look, as Sands has in great detail, at the argument presented to the Court. New Zealand's argument emphasized the general principle of not causing damage and in particular drew on draft articles 1 and 14 of the Commission's 1995 text on liability. The argument also drew on the related articles 24 and 25 of the Geneva Convention on the High Seas, a text which arose directly out of the Commission's work on the law of the sea. New Zealand was not party to that Convention, but must, nevertheless, have seen those provisions as stating customary international law. The precautionary principle reflected in them was, according to New Zealand, supported in a more concrete way by the duty to make a "risk assessment", as elaborated in other provisions of the 1994 liability text, as well as in the Commission's 1994 Draft Articles on the Law of the Non-Navigational Uses of International Watercourses. The precautionary principle and the requirement of an environmental impact assessment also featured prominently in two of the dissenting opinions.[50]

The greatest use which has been made by an international tribunal of the Commission's work on State responsibility is almost certainly to be seen in the decisions of the Iran–United States Claims Tribunal. So, for example, on the matter of the imputation of the actions of members of revolutionary movements to the new Government, the Tribunal said in a leading case that it had "adopted the criteria set down by the ILC as the most recent and authoritative statement of current international law in this area" and drew freely on the draft articles relating to attribution.[51]

The impact on international law of a treaty which has been elaborated on the basis of the Commission's work and which is binding and in force may perhaps best be exemplified by the case concerning *United States Diplomatic*

---

[47]Marks, "Treaties, State Responsibility and Remedies", *Cambridge Law Journal* (1990), p. 387.

[48]Loc. cit. above (footnote 42), at paras. 60 and 63, respectively.

[49]*Request for an Examination of the Situation in Accordance with Paragraph 63 of the Court's Judgment of 20 December 1974 in the* Nuclear Tests (New Zealand v. France) *Case, I.C.J. Reports 1995,* p. 288 at para. 64.

[50]The 1995 proceedings have been published by the New Zealand Ministry of Foreign Affairs and Trade: *New Zealand at the International Court of Justice, French Nuclear Testing in the Pacific* (1996). For the passages to which reference is made, see pp. 175, 184-185, 290-293 and 344-345.

[51]*Rankin* v. *Islamic Republic of Iran, International Law Reports,* vol. 82, p. 204, referring to *Short* v. *Islamic Republic of Iran,* ibid., p. 148 (where the dissenting member of the Tribunal also used the Commission's text). See also *Yeager* v. *Islamic Republic of Iran,* ibid., p. 179.

and Consular Staff in Tehran before the International Court of Justice.[52] The two Vienna Conventions on Diplomatic Relations and Consular Relations were at the core of United States case and of the 1979 Order and 1980 Judgment of the Court. A third product of the Commission was also relevant there: the 1973 Convention on the Prevention and Punishment of Crimes against Internationally Protected Persons, including Diplomatic Agents. Iran and the United States were parties to all three of these instruments. The Order for interim measures which the Court made at the end of 1979, 16 days after the request was filed and three days after the United States filed its final submissions, gave a central place to the Conventions. There was, said the Court:

" . . . no more fundamental prerequisite for the conduct of relations between States than the inviolability of diplomatic envoys and embassies, so that throughout history nations of all creeds and cultures have observed reciprocal obligations for that purpose; and . . . the obligations thus assumed, notably those for assuring the personal safety of diplomats and their freedom from prosecution, are essential, unqualified, and inherent in their representative character and their diplomatic function;

". . . the institution of diplomacy . . . has withstood the test of centuries and proved to be an instrument essential for effective co-operation in the international community, and for enabling States, irrespective of their differing constitutional and social systems, to achieve mutual understanding and to resolve their differences by peaceful means".[53]

A State which voluntarily enters into diplomatic or consular relations with another:

". . . cannot fail to recognize the imperative obligations inherent therein, now codified in the Vienna Conventions of 1961 and 1963".[54]

The Order, like the Judgment given five months later, refused to water that law down by reference to any wider context in the manner argued for by Iran. The matter before the Court was not to be seen as no more than "a marginal and secondary aspect of an overall problem, one such that it cannot be studied separately, and which involves, *inter alia*, more than 25 years of continual interference by the United States of America in the internal affairs of Iran . . .". That argument and its rejection provide a particular instance of the interrelationship of different bodies of law and their ranking.[55] In this case a court undertook the ranking, as did the Tribunal in the *Rainbow Warrior* case; but it can also be seen as the kind of matter which the International Law Commission may well be better placed to address than others, who may be too closely involved in a particular law-making process. In its 1980 Judgment, the Court emphasized the point by calling attention to the character of the rules of diplomatic law as a

---

[52]One reason for my being so selective is the extensive literature which already exists on the use which the International Court of Justice has made of texts which the International Law Commission has generated. For a helpful brief account, together with the relevant references, see the "Introduction", in United Nations, op. cit. above (footnote 8), at pp. 8-17.

[53]*United States Diplomatic and Consular Staff in Tehran, Provisional Measures, Order of 15 December 1979, I.C.J. Reports 1979*, p. 7 at paras. 38-39.

[54]Ibid., para. 41.

[55]See the Court's discussion of the ill-fated rescue attempt of 24-25 April 1980: *United States Diplomatic and Consular Staff in Tehran, Judgment, I.C.J. Reports 1980*, p. 3 at paras. 93-94. On the fundamental character of the rules, see also the opinions of Judges Lachs and Tarazi: ibid., pp. 48 and 58, respectively.

"self-contained regime": diplomatic relations can be broken off and missions closed (notably, if there are abuses by members of a mission) and an individual diplomat can be declared *persona non grata*.[56]

In its Judgment of May 1980, the Court recalled what it had said in December 1979 about the essential character of the principles and rules of diplomatic and consular relations and their cardinal nature.[57] After mentioning the deplorable frequency with which those principles were being set at nought by individuals or groups, it went on to say:

> "that it considers it to be its duty to draw the attention of the entire international community, of which Iran itself has been a member since time immemorial, to the irreparable harm that may be caused by events of the kind now before the Court. Such events cannot fail to undermine the edifice of law carefully constructed by mankind over a period of centuries, the maintenance of which is vital for the security and well-being of the complex international community of the present day, in which it is more essential than ever that the rules developed to ensure the ordered progress of relations between its members should be constantly and scrupulously respected."[58]

The Court had earlier emphasized the special duty of a receiving State to take all appropriate measures to protect the premises of a mission against any intrusion or damage—the duty which was at the centre of the Swiss case mentioned above. This and its associated obligations, in the Court's view, were not merely contractual obligations, established by the 1961 and 1963 Conventions, but also obligations under general international law.[59]

The United States pleadings in the case once again highlight the value of the work carried out by the Commission preparatory to the conclusion of a treaty. Almost every reference in those pleadings to a provision of the 1961 and 1963 Conventions—and of the 1973 New York Convention—is supported by a reference to background material, most notably the Commission's drafts. The Commission's drafts were also made use of in addressing the subject of attribution in the law of State responsibility.[60]

Some concluding comments and suggestions

We should try, however imperfectly, to see the world steadily and to see it whole, to borrow Matthew Arnold's words. The Secretary-General gives us real help in that endeavour by emphasizing, at the outset of his Report, *Renewing the United Nations*, the critical normative elements of the organized international community and its inclusive vision (while recognizing as well its diversity).[61] The great principles, for instance, in Articles 1 and 2 of the Charter of the United Nations and the more mundane "rules of the road" and their development and application to new problems, such as the growth of "uncivil elements" in a global civil society, are all part of that larger vision.

Those of us engaged in law-development processes must have that vision in mind. We should both draw on and contribute to the experience of those

---

[56]Ibid., paras. 83-89.
[57]Ibid., paras. 45 and 91.
[58]Ibid., para. 92.
[59]Ibid., para. 62.
[60]*I.C.J. Pleadings, United States Diplomatic and Consular Staff in Tehran*, pp. 159-160, 162-171 and 173-79.
[61]Loc. cit. above (footnote 1), at paras. 1-3 and 8-9, for example.

engaged in more practical or technical areas, as well as to the codification and development of private international law. As I have tried to indicate, the experience of national and private bodies in formulating statements of the law is also relevant. A more inclusive approach should aim to break down traditional barriers and recognize the great advantages of more conscious interaction between legislators, jurists and judges.[62]

The Statute of the International Law Commission itself indicates certain possible concrete steps. The Statute and, even more so, the Commission's practice under the Statute emphasize official relationships with the United Nations, Governments and bodies established by Governments, in the initiation of progressive development (articles 16, 17 (1) and 17 (2) (d)), the fixing of priorities (article 18 (3)), the seeking of relevant information (articles 16 (c), 17 (2) (b) and 19 (2)), the seeking of comments (articles 16 (h) and 21 (2)), the consideration of the Commission's drafts and the making of decisions on what is to happen to them (articles 16 (j), 22 and 23) and consultation with other organs and bodies (articles 25 and 26 (4)). However, these relationships need not be exclusively governmental or international:

- Documents are to be distributed if possible to at least one national organization concerned with international law in each Member State of the United Nations and to international organizations concerned with international law questions (article 26 (2)).
- The Commission may consult with any international or national organizations, official or non-official, on any subject entrusted to it, if it believes that such a procedure might aid it in the performance of its functions (article 26 (1)).
- Governments might seek help in responding to a request for information or in preparing comments on drafts, or indeed more generally on the Commission's programme and methods of work.
- The Commission has the power to consult with scientific institutions and individual experts in handling a matter (article 16 (e); see also article 21 (1)).

The Secretary-General gives major emphasis to the growth and strength of civil society in his Report, *Renewing the United Nations*:

"59. Civil society constitutes a major and increasingly important force in international life. In recent years, the United Nations has found that much of its work, particularly at the country level, involves intimately the diverse and dedicated contributions of non-governmental organizations and groups—be it in economics and social development, humanitarian affairs, public health or the promotion of human rights. Similarly, the pronounced growth in the flow of private international economic transactions over the past decade has established the private sector as the major driving force of international economic change. Yet despite those growing manifestations of an ever-more robust global civil society, the United Nations is at present inadequately equipped to engage civil society and make it a true partner in its work.

"60. Accordingly, the Secretary-General is making arrangements for all United Nations entities to be open to and work closely with

---

[62]See, for example, van Caenegem, R.C., *Judges, Legislators and Professors: Chapters in European Legal History* (1987).

civil society organizations that are active in their respective sectors, and to facilitate increased consultation and cooperation between the United Nations and such organizations."

The practice of the International Law Commission stands in rather sharp contrast with such an approach. For instance, the practice under article 26 (4) is limited to formal exchanges with three intergovernmental regional bodies—although some encouragement is to be gained from "the informal exchanges of views" which took place at the Commission's forty-ninth session with representatives of the International Committee of the Red Cross and the International Federation of Red Cross and Red Crescent Societies. The Commission's Statute, new technology and the amazing recent changes in the international community all support much wider relationships with non-governmental bodies and individual experts. The nervousness that arose from difficulties of wider consultation over 30 years ago should no longer hold sway.[63] Many countries now have law reform bodies. Some are on the Internet. Some meet together regionally or at Commonwealth meetings. Those meetings provide another possible opportunity for liaison.

My own recent experience, in small Pacific jurisdictions as well as in New Zealand, suggests two relevant concrete ways in which the Commission and its secretariat might be able to contribute. One is for the Commission to examine once more the question of facilitating access to the physical sources of international law—a matter emphasized in article 24 of the Commission's Statute. Massive changes have occurred since the Commission prepared its initial study on this question and the value of the publications which resulted from that study could usefully be assessed.[64] For instance, does the *United Nations Juridical Yearbook* now serve the purposes that it might? Would not a new version of the *List of Treaty Collections* (1956) be of real value? International law publications increasingly incorporate digests of State practice. What further national actions might be encouraged or taken?

A recent New Zealand Law Commission publication provides one possible model. Against the background of a relative lack of understanding in New Zealand of international law matters, as well as a rapidly globalizing world and the extensive impact of those developments on New Zealand law, the New Zealand Law Commission in 1996 published a *New Zealand Guide to International Law and Its Sources.*[65] This Guide discusses the impact of international law on New Zealand law and the wide range of matters now governed by international law (reflected in a lengthy list of statutes with possible treaty implications), identifies actual sources of the law and provides references to a range of organizations which are concerned with international law matters. The Commission saw the Guide as one means of meeting its statutory responsibility to help make the law of New Zealand as accessible as practicable: that law was not accessible without its international component and context.

The second matter—to be related to the work on the greater acceptance of multilateral treaties and the multilateral law-making process[66]—concerns the methods of implementation of multilateral treaties through national legal sys-

---

[63]See, for example, Briggs, H.W., *The International Law Commission* (1965), pp. 328-329.

[64]For accounts of the action taken under the provision see: Briggs, op. cit. above (preceding footnote), pp. 203-206; and United Nations, *The Work of the International Law Commission* (5th ed., 1996), pp. 27-28 (United Nations publication, Sales No. E.95.V.6).

[65]Op. cit. above (footnote 20).

[66]See United Nations, *Review of the Multilateral Treaty-making Process* (1985) (document ST/LEG/SER.B/21; United Nations publication, Sales No. E/F.83.V.8).

tems. While there are important differences between constitutional systems, many common threads exist. A great deal can be learned by studying different methods of implementation. The Commission and its secretariat could facilitate that process.[67]

To conclude, I return to the governing significance of the "mind-sets" and education of lawyers. The great English commercial lawyer, Lord Mansfield, taught an important, and still pertinent, lesson about these matters in a judgement which he gave over 200 years ago. In the case of *Luke* v. *Lyde*,[68] a shipowner was seeking payment of freight from the defendant, who had shipped fish from the port of St John, Newfoundland, to be carried to Lisbon. After 17 days, and four days out from Lisbon, the ship *Sarah* was taken by a French ship. It was retaken three days later by an English privateer. The cargo owner had the goods back from the recaptors and paid them half of the value of the fish. Was the shipowner entitled to the payment of any freight and, if so, how much? Lord Mansfield:

> " . . . was desirous to have a case made of it, in order to settle the point more deliberately, solemnly, and notoriously; as it was of so extensive a nature; and especially, as the maritime law is not the law of a particular country, but the general law of nations: '*nec erit alia lex Romœ, alia Athenis, alia nunc, alia posthac, sed et apud omnes gentes et omni tempore, una eademque lex obtinebit*'."[69]

The master, he decided, should be paid $^{17}/_{21}$ x $\frac{1}{2}$ of the original agreed freight, the proportions arising directly from the facts. This was not simply a matter of arithmetic. The great judge drew, apparently effortlessly, on an impressive range of authority to support his ruling. He found, he said, by the most ancient laws of the world (the Laws of Rhodes) that the master should have a rateable proportion where he was in no fault. Consolato del Mere ("a Spanish book"), the Laws of Oleron, the Laws of Wisby, a series of scholarly publications and an Ordinance of Louis XIV were also to that effect, as, finally, was a decision of the House of Lords.

As the first English judge to speak the language of the living law (to quote his great biographer C.H.S. Fifoot), he was not agreeing with Cicero that the law was unchanging; but he was saying that we must concentrate on the essence of our times and understand present conditions and future needs. The dictates of common sense should be heard in the language of recorded experience. No source was too vast or too insignificant to explore.[70]

---

[67]The Commonwealth Secretariat has prepared a valuable series of studies on the implementation of certain important multilateral treaties. Those studies are limited in subject-area, though, and are limited in their utility by the dualistic approach to treaty implementation which prevails in much of the Commonwealth. See also footnote 20, above.

[68]*English Reports*, vol. 97, p. 614 (Assizes, England).

[69]The quotation is from Cicero, *De Republica*, 3.22.33. It may be translated as follows: "Nor will it be one law at Rome and a different one at Athens, nor otherwise tomorrow than it is today; but one and the same law will bind all peoples and all ages".

[70]Fifoot, C.H.S., *Lord Mansfield* (1936), pp. 252-287.

THE WORK OF THE INTERNATIONAL LAW COMMISSION AND THE SHAPING OF INTERNATIONAL LAW: IN COMMEMORATION OF THE FIFTIETH ANNIVERSARY OF THE COMMISSION

by Huang Huikang*

It has long been a dream among international lawyers to embody in one or more comprehensive codes all of the rules which are generally applicable in the relations between States. As early as the 1780s, the English philosopher Jeremy Bentham proposed a codification of the whole of international law as an integral part of his scheme for an everlasting peace. In the years preceding the establishment of the United Nations, numerous attempts were made by scholars, learned societies, governments and international organizations to incorporate the rules of international law into some form of written code. As a result of these endeavours, rules were successfully adopted to deal with a number of particular legal problems.[1] Efforts to codify whole sectors or entire domains of international law, however, met with only a very limited degree of success.[2] The foundation of the United Nations and the establishment of the International Law Commission represented a turning point in this regard, ushering in a new era in the progressive development of international law and its codification.

The importance of the codification and progressive development of international law was fully recognized by the States which met at San Francisco. The Charter of the United Nations accordingly proclaims as one of its ends "to establish conditions under which justice and respect for obligations arising from treaties and other sources of international law can be maintained". In pursuance of this objective, Article 13, paragraph 1 (a), of the Charter empowers—indeed, it enjoins—the General Assembly "to initiate studies and make recommendations for the purpose of . . . encouraging the progressive development of international law and its codification".

In 1947, the General Assembly set up a committee to consider how best to discharge its responsibilities under this provision. That committee recommended the establishment of an international law commission, composed of a number of persons of recognized competence in international law, serving in their individual capacities. A draft statute for such a body was subsequently prepared by a subcommittee of the Sixth Committee of the General Assembly; and, on 21 November 1947, the General Assembly adopted its resolution 174 (II), in which it resolved to establish the International Law Commission and approved its Statute. Elections to the Commission were held on 3 November

---

*Professor of International Law, Beijing, Hubei and Human Universities, People's Republic of China.

[1] See documents A/AC.10/5 and A/AC.10/25.

[2] Thus the first attempt of the League of Nations to codify and develop whole sectors of international law on a global basis was also its last. The conference which the League convened for that purpose at The Hague in 1930 succeeded in adopting no more than a single convention and three protocols on the topic of nationality.

1948; and, on 12 April 1949, the Commission opened the first of its annual sessions.

Since that time, many questions have been asked regarding the Commission and its work. To what extent has international law been shaped by the drafts which the Commission has produced? To what extent may the Commission's output be used in order to fill gaps which may exist within international law? What is the current status of the various multilateral conventions which have been concluded on the basis of the Commission's drafts? How do the various States of the world regard those conventions? And so on.

Such questions as these assume a special pertinence on this, the occasion of the Commission's fiftieth anniversary. To assist in answering them, this paper will endeavour to analyse the Commission's achievements to date. In particular, it will review the current status of the conventions which have been elaborated on the basis of the Commission's drafts. It is also hoped to make a modest contribution to the ongoing debate on how to enhance the capability of the Commission to contribute to the progressive development of international law and its codification.

First of all, though, let us briefly review the Commission's record.

Article 1 of the Commission's Statute provides, in its first paragraph, that the "Commission shall have for its object the promotion of the progressive development of international law and its codification". The second paragraph of that article goes on to state that the Commission "shall concern itself primarily with public international law, but [that it] is not precluded from entering the field of private international law". In article 15 of the Statute, the expression "progressive development of international law" is defined, "for convenience", as meaning "the preparation of draft conventions on subjects which have not yet been regulated by international law or in regard to which the law has not yet been sufficiently developed in the practice of States, while the expression "codification of international law" is defined, again "for convenience", as meaning "the more precise formulation and systematization of rules of international law in fields where there already has been extensive State practice, precedent and doctrine".

On the basis of a memorandum which was prepared by the Secretariat of the United Nations,[3] the Commission, at its first session in 1949, drew up a provisional list of 14 topics the codification of which it considered to be necessary or desirable. Together, these 14 topics have constituted the Commission's long-term programme of work. Since then, a further 19 topics have been included in the Commission's programme of work as a result of references by the General Assembly, while one other topic has been added by the Commission itself, in pursuance of article 24 of its Statute. Together with the 14 topics in the 1949 list, these 20 topics have made up the Commission's total programme of work during its first 50 years.

Work on most of the items in this programme has now been completed or else is currently in hand.[4] Since its first session, in 1949, the Commission has

---

[3]Document A/CN.4/1 and Rev.1 (entitled "Survey of international law in relation to the work of codification of the International Law Commission").

[4]For details, see United Nations, *The Work of the International Law Commission* (5th ed., 1996), pp. 9-13. Since the appearance of that publication, the Commission has completed its work on the draft Code of crimes against the Peace and Security of Mankind, adopting, on second reading, a set of draft articles on the topic and forwarding them to the General Assembly with a recommendation that it select the most appropriate form which would ensure the draft Code's widest possible acceptance: Report of the International Law Commission on the work of its forty-eighth session, *Official Records of the General Assembly, Fifty-first Session, Supplement No. 10* (A/51/10), pp. 9-120.

considered a total of 30 topics. In the case of 26 of these topics, the Commission has completed its work and has submitted a report to the General Assembly. The four remaining topics are currently under active consideration by the Commission.

To date, a total of 15 multilateral conventions have been adopted on the basis of sets of draft articles which the Commission has prepared: the Convention on the Territorial Sea and the Contiguous Zone (1958), the Convention on the High Seas (1958), the Convention on Fishing and Conservation of Living Resources of the High Seas (1958), the Convention on the Continental Shelf (1958), the Convention on the Reduction of Statelessness (1961), the Convention on Diplomatic Relations (1961), the Convention on Consular Relations (1963), the Convention on Special Missions (1969), the Convention on the Law of Treaties (1969), the Convention on the Prevention and Punishment of Crimes against International Protected Persons, including Diplomatic Agents (1973), the Convention on the Representation of States in their Relations with International Organizations of a Universal Character (1975), the Convention on Succession of States in respect of Treaties (1978), the Convention on Succession of States in respect of State Property, Archives and Debts (1983), the Convention on the Law of Treaties between States and International Organizations or between International Organizations (1986) and the Convention on the Law of the Non-Navigational Uses of International Watercourses (1997).

A survey of the Commission's work and its output over the last 50 years may be found in annex I, below. Brief though that survey may be, the important role which, in that time, the Commission has played in the codification and progressive development of international law is readily apparent. The Commission's remarkable contribution to the shaping of international law has, of course, principally taken the form of draft articles, the Commission having, to date, produced 21 sets of these, 12 of which have gone on, in turn, to serve as the bases of the 15 landmark conventions listed above. At the same time, though, the Commission has also helped to shape international law through other forms of output which do not bear the character of treaty-drafts, its work in the fields concerned having helped to clarify the current state of the law or to throw light on controversial legal problems. Together, these contributions to the international legal process constitute a record of achievement which is unparalleled in the history of international law.

The most striking examples of the Commission's contribution to the shaping of international law are to be found in the vitally important areas of diplomatic and consular relations, the law of treaties and the law of the sea. When the Commission was established in 1947, the law in each of these domains was predominantly customary in nature, there being few, if any, conventions at the global level in the fields concerned. From its inception, the Commission attached the greatest importance to the codification and progressive development of the law in these domains; and, in each of them, it succeeded in achieving concrete results of the highest quality. A brief account the Commission's achievements in this regard would certainly not be out of place.

Diplomacy is the basic instrument through which States communicate and transact business with each other. Almost every State is today represented in the territories of most of the other States of the world by diplomatic missions and diplomatic agents. The law governing diplomatic relations is accordingly one of the most important branches of international law. However, prior to the conclusion in 1961 of the Vienna Convention on Diplomatic Relations, that law was predominantly one of custom and usage, there being only two multilateral treaties of global import which had been concluded in the field: the 1815 Regulation of Vienna, which codified the classification and order-of-precedence of diplomatic envoys, and the 1818 Protocol of Aix-la-Chapelle, which modified the 1815 Regulation of Vienna.[5] Long before the foundation of the United Nations, developments in diplomatic practice had made a new and more extensive codification of the law necessary; yet it was only with the establishment of the International Law Commission that such an enterprise proved capable of realisation.

At its first session, in 1949, the Commission selected diplomatic intercourse and immunities as one of the 14 topics which it considered ripe for codification. Work on the subject was begun in 1954; and, in 1957, the Commission submitted a set of draft articles with commentaries to the General Assembly and circulated them to States for their comments. In the following year, the Commission revised its draft in the light of the comments which it had received and submitted the draft, as revised, to the General Assembly, together with a proposal that the Assembly recommend it to Member States with a view to the conclusion of a convention. The United Nations Conference on Diplomatic Intercourse and Immunities was subsequently convened in Vienna in 1961 in order to elaborate a convention on the basis of the Commission's draft. After six weeks of work, the Conference adopted, on 14 April 1961, the text of the Convention on Diplomatic Relations, consisting of 53 articles, covering most major aspects of permanent, or "standing", diplomatic relations between States. The Conference also adopted two optional protocols, one concerning acquisition of nationality and the other dealing with the compulsory settlement of disputes. The Convention and the two optional protocols entered into force three years later, on 24 April 1964. As of today, no fewer than 178 States are party to the Convention, giving it an almost universal level of acceptance.

The 1961 Convention on Diplomatic Relations largely codifies the modern law of diplomatic relations. While large parts of that convention were based on existing customs, usages and State practice, certain parts constituted a progressive development of the law, as it existed in 1961. Nevertheless, as the number of parties to the Convention has mounted up, so has it become possible to regard these, latter, parts, like the former, as constituting "best evidence" of general international law. Various contemporary sources accordingly refer to the Convention as representing generally accepted principles of international law.[6] Certainly, the importance of the principles and rules which are embodied in the Convention has been emphasized by the International Court of Justice in the case concerning *United States Diplomatic and Consular Staff in Tehran*. Thus, the Court observed in its Judgment in that case that the obligations of the Iranian Government there in question were "not merely contractual obligations . . . but also obligations under general international law".[7]

In addition to draft articles on diplomatic intercourse and immunities, the Commission has produced four further sets of draft articles on topics in the field of diplomatic law—on special missions, on the protection and inviolability of diplomatic agents and other persons entitled to special protection under international law, on relations between States and international organizations and on the status of the diplomatic courier and the diplomatic bag not accompanied by

[5]Hardy, M., *Modern Diplomatic Law* (1968).
[6]Brownlie, I., *Principles of Public International Law* (4th ed., 1990), p. 347.
[7]*I.C.J. Reports 1980*, p. 3 at para. 62. See also, ibid., at paras. 69 and 90.

diplomatic courier. Multilateral conventions have been adopted on the basis of the first three of these drafts.[8]

The successful codification and development of the law of consular relations is another of the Commission's major achievements.

The law governing consular relations has a long and venerable history. However, prior to the creation of the United Nations and the establishment of the International Law Commission, that law had been slow to evolve and it had signally failed to keep pace with the many developments stemming from the rapid expansion of international commerce and navigation. To fill the resulting gaps in the rules of general international law, States concluded numerous bilateral consular treaties or inserted consular clauses into the commercial agreements which they concluded with each other. As a result of this pattern of treaty-making, the rules which governed the status of consuls and their functions, rights, privileges and immunities gradually began to achieve a degree of uniformity, inviting efforts to codify this branch of international law.[9] However, it was only when the Commission took up the matter in the 1950s that such codification was finally achieved.

Together with diplomatic intercourse and immunities, the Commission included the topic of consular intercourse and immunities in its 1949 list as one of the topics whose codification it considered necessary or desirable. Work on the topic was begun in 1955; and, at its twelfth session, in 1960, the Commission provisionally adopted a set of 65 draft articles, with commentaries, and transmitted them to States for their comments. These draft articles were subsequently revised in the light of observations received and, at the Commission's thirteenth session, in 1961, a final draft, consisting of 71 draft articles with accompanying commentaries, was adopted and submitted to the General Assembly, together with a recommendation that the Assembly convene an international conference of plenipotentiaries to study the draft and to conclude one or more conventions on the subject. Pursuant to General Assembly resolution 1685 (XVI) of 18 December 1961, the United Nations Conference on Consular Relations subsequently met in Vienna, from 4 March to 22 April 1963, and adopted the text of the Convention on Consular Relations, together with an optional protocol concerning acquisition of nationality and an optional protocol on the compulsory settlement of disputes. Together with its two optional protocols, the Convention came into force on nearly four years later, on 19 March 1967. As of today, there are no fewer than 158 States which are party to the Convention.

Most of the provisions of the 1963 Convention represented a codification of the existing rules of customary law. At the same time, though, the Convention contained a significant element of progressive development. So, for example, it brought the status of career consuls nearer to that of diplomatic agents, exempting them, in the same way as diplomats, from taxes and customs duties, while significantly extending the protection and degree of personal inviolability to which they were entitled. Nevertheless, in view of the fact that it has attracted close to 160 instruments of ratification or accession, the 1963 Convention can now generally be regarded as "best evidence" of general international law on

---

[8]While the Commission recommended to the General Assembly that it convene a conference to elaborate a convention on the basis of the fourth of these drafts—the draft articles on status of the diplomatic courier and the diplomatic bag not accompanied by diplomatic courier—the Assembly, in its decision 50/416 of 11 December 1995, limited itself to "bring[ing] the draft articles . . . to the attention of Member States" and "remind[ing them]" of the possibility that this field of international law and any further developments within it may be subject to codification at an appropriate time in the future".

[9]See Lee, L.T., *Consular Law and Practice* (1961).

the subject. Indeed, in its Judgment in the case concerning *United States Diplomatic and Consular Staff in Tehran*, the International Court underlined that the obligations under the Convention which were there in point formed part of general international law and were not just contractual in nature.[10]

The law of treaties is another field in which codification and progressive development of the law has successfully been carried out by the Commission.

The especial importance which the law of treaties enjoys within the international legal system can hardly be exaggerated. Treaties are the basic device by which States transact their business and adjust their mutual relations. Treaties are, moreover, a principal source of international law.[11] However, in spite of the fact that treaties had long formed part of the fabric of international law, the rules of international law which governed them and regulated their creation, application and termination were in no better condition in 1945 than most other rules of customary international law; for, while some of them were clear, a very high proportion were not. Against this background, the work which the Commission has undertaken in the field is particularly worthy of praise. The draft articles and invaluable commentaries which it prepared after more than 15 years of painstaking effort served as the basis of work at the Vienna Conference in 1968 and 1969 and of the Convention on the Law of Treaties which was adopted at that Conference. The 1969 Convention, consisting of 85 articles and an annex, entered into force on 27 January 1980. No fewer than 83 States are now party to it, the State which has most recently established its consent to be bound being the People's Republic of China.[12]

The 1969 Convention—"the treaty on treaties", as it is styled by many jurists—represents a major step forward towards a world in which the rule of law will no longer be just a dream but a reality.[13] The customary rules of treaty-law were largely codified and reformulated in the Convention; but, at the same time, the Convention also contained much that was new and which involved an element of progressive development. However, while the number of parties to the Convention is certainly less than in the case of the 1961 and 1963 conventions on diplomatic and consular relations, it is by no means inferior to those two agreements in terms of its importance and weight. In view of the fact that the Convention was adopted by the vote of the overwhelming majority of the States which attended the Vienna Conference,[14] its provisions are generally regarded as laying down rules of general international law on the matters they address. Thus, in its advisory opinion in the Namibia case, the International Court observed that the rules in the 1969 Convention concerning termination of treaty relationships for material breach might in many respects be considered to represent a codification of existing customary law on the subject.[15] Again, the United States

---

[10]Loc. cit. above (footnote 7).

[11]Article 38 of the Statute of the International Court of Justice accords pride of place in its list of "sources" of international law to "international conventions, whether general or particular, establishing rules expressly recognized by the contesting States".

[12]The less widespread acceptance of this convention is said to be a result, in part, of the inclusion in its text of provisions concerning the compulsory third-party settlement of disputes.

[13]Kearney and Dalton, "The Treaty on Treaties", *American Journal of International Law*, vol. 64 (1970), p. 495 at p. 561.

[14]The vote was 79 in favour to 1 against, with 19 abstentions, the sole negative vote being cast by France: document A/CONF.39/11/Add.1, pp. 206-207 at para. 51.

[15]*Legal Consequences for States of the Continued Presence of South Africa in Namibia (South West Africa) notwithstanding Security Council Resolution 276 (1970), Advisory Opinion, I.C.J. Reports 1971*, p. 16 at para. 94. See also: *Appeal Relating to the Jurisdiction of the ICAO Council, Judgment, I.C.J. Reports 1972*, p. 46 at para. 38; and *Fisheries Jurisdiction (United Kingdom v. Iceland), Jurisdiction of the Court, Judgment, I.C.J. Reports 1973*, p. 3 at paras. 24 and 36.

Department of State declared in 1971 that the Vienna Convention was already "recognized as the authoritative guide to current treaty law and practice", even though the United States was then—and remains today—not party to the Convention.[16]

In addition to the 1969 Convention, two further conventions have been concluded in the field of treaty-law on the basis of the drafts which the Commission has produced: the 1978 Convention on Succession of States in respect of Treaties and the 1986 Convention on the Law of Treaties between States and International Organizations or between International Organizations. The modern law of treaties is, then, largely the product of the International Law Commission's labours.

Let us turn now to the law of the sea, one of the oldest branches of international law and one which, like the law of treaties, was largely customary in nature until it was codified by the Commission in a major undertaking which culminated in the convocation in 1958 of the first United Nations Conference on the Law of the Sea.

Many attempts have been made to codify the rules of customary international law which govern the seas. Most of these, especially in the decades which preceded the foundation of the United Nations, were undertaken by learned societies or institutions, such as the International Law Association, the Institut de Droit International and the Harvard Law School. These efforts yielded reports and sets of resolutions on various topics, such as territorial waters, marine pollution, the seabed and its resources, international waterways, deep sea-bed mining, piracy and port-State jurisdiction. The main value of the work of these bodies, though, lay in their careful collection and analysis of State practice. There was, of course, an "official" attempt by the League of Nations to codify the peace-time rules of the law of the sea. Unfortunately, the Conference which convened for that purpose at The Hague in 1930 did not succeed in adopting a convention on territorial waters, it not being possible to reach agreement on the crucial question of the maximum permissible breadth of the territorial sea. Accordingly, the Conference decided to do no more than refer to States the draft articles on which it did prove possible to reach agreement, in the hope that agreement on the subject as a whole could be reached at some later date.[17]

The law of the sea was the subject of the first completed attempt of the International Law Commission to place a whole sector of international law on a multilateral treaty basis. On the basis of the Commission's work, four conventions, together with an optional protocol, were adopted by the first United Nations Conference on the Law of the Sea, which was held in Geneva in 1958: the Convention on the Territorial Sea and the Contiguous Zone, the Convention on the High Seas, the Convention on the Continental Shelf and the Convention on Fishing and Conservation of Living Resources of the High Seas. The first three of these conventions were based in large measure upon existing customary international law and have accordingly gone on to form the core of the generally accepted rules of the law of the sea relating to maritime zones.[18] All four

---

[16]Henkin, L., Pugh, R.C., Schachter, O., and Smit, H., *International Law: Cases and Materials* (2nd. ed., 1987), p. 387.

[17]Churchill, R.R., and Lowe, A.V., *The Law of the Sea* (1983), pp. 12-14.

[18]Ibid., p. 14. The Convention on Fishing and Conservation of the Living Resources of the High Seas and the Optional Protocol have proved less popular, perhaps partly because they went further than the existing obligations which customary law imposed upon States.

conventions have entered into force and have been ratified or acceded to by a number of States which ranges from 37 to 62.[19]

The Geneva Conventions of 1958 were a considerable achievement, even though they failed to make any stipulation on the basic question of the maximum permissible breadth of the territorial sea—the same question which had defeated the codification efforts of the League of Nations in 1930. Those conventions, of course, have now been overtaken by events, both political and scientific—events which led to the convening of the Third United Nations Conference on the Law of the Sea and the adoption in 1982, after nine years of hard negotiations, of a comprehensive legal code for the oceans in the form of the United Nations Convention on the Law of the Sea.[20] All of the ground which was covered by the four 1958 Conventions is covered by the Convention of 1982. At the same time, though, with the exceptions of those issues which the 1958 Conventions left unresolved and of new issues such as the exclusive economic zone and the deep seabed, many of the provisions of the 1982 Convention repeat, either verbatim or in essence, the provisions of the Geneva Conventions. Articles 4, 5, 8, 9, 12 and 15, for instance, are largely reproductions of provisions which are to be found in the 1958 Convention on the Territorial Sea and the Contiguous Zone. The 1982 Convention may, therefore, be said to have consolidated and reinforced the legal regimes of the territorial sea, the high seas and the continental shelf, as they were laid down in the four Geneva Conventions of 1958.

Even after the entry into force of the 1982 Convention in 1994, the four Geneva Conventions remain an important part of the law of the sea. The Convention of 1982 completely supersedes the Conventions of 1958, of course, as between those States which are parties to both the 1982 Convention and the 1958 Conventions. However, the 1958 Conventions remain fully in force for those States parties to them which are not yet parties to the 1982 Convention. They remain applicable, too, to those States which are parties both to the 1958 and to the 1982 Conventions in so far as their relations with States which are parties to the 1958 Conventions alone are concerned. Moreover, in so far as concerns the provisions of the 1958 Conventions which codify or restate rules of customary law, the rules which they set forth will be binding on all States, whether they are parties to those conventions or not.[21] In this connection, it may be remarked that the International Court of Justice has found itself drawn almost magnetically to the 1958 Conventions when dealing with matters of maritime law.[22]

The work which the Commission carried out in the 1950s on many of the basic aspects of the law of the sea, therefore, retains much of its importance today, notwithstanding the major developments which have since occurred in that field.

In addition to its efforts in the fields of diplomatic and consular law, the law of treaties and the law of the sea, substantial progress has been made by the

---

[19]In view of the convocation of the Third United Nations Conference on the Law of the Sea and the adoption, in 1982, of a new comprehensive code of the law of the sea, the attention of those States which did not participate in the Geneva Conference and which have not signed or ratified the Conventions which it produced has, since 1973, been firmly on the negotiation and acceptance of the new convention, rather than on accepting the instruments which were adopted at the 1958 Conference.

[20]Churchill and Lowe, op. cit. above (footnote 17), pp. 14-16.

[21]The Convention on the High Seas, it may be noted, declares itself in its preamble to be "generally declaratory of established principles of international law".

[22]Harris, D.J., *Cases and Materials on International Law* (4th ed., 1991), p. 351, note 34.

Commission in codifying and progressively developing rules of international law in a number of other key areas of international law. Thus, in addition to the draft articles which have been referred to in the course of the preceding discussion, the Commission has also prepared and submitted to the General Assembly sets of draft articles on the following topics: succession of States in respect of matters other than treaties (submitted in 1981), the law of the non-navigational uses of international watercourses (submitted in 1994), the draft statute of an international criminal court (also submitted in 1994) and the draft code of crimes against the peace and security of mankind (submitted in 1996). Conventions have been adopted on the basis of the first two of these sets of draft articles,[23] while the latter two sets are currently under active consideration by the General Assembly,[24] it being likely that the last set but one will serve as the basis of a convention in the very near future.[25]

In the course of codifying customary law, the Commission has also contributed in a substantial way to the progressive development of the law in the fields concerned. The conventions which have been concluded on the basis of the Commission's drafts afford a number of pertinent examples.

Reference should be made before all else to the introduction into international law of the concept of peremptory norms of general international law (*jus cogens*), representing a major breakthrough in the development of the law of treaties.

A distinction is usually maintained in most domestic legal systems between *jus cogens*—rules and principles of public policy which cannot be derogated from by subjects of the legal system concerned—and *jus dispositivum*—norms which may be discarded, replaced or departed from by legal persons in their private dealings. There have, however, long been divergent views on the question of the existence or otherwise of norms of *jus cogens* in international law. In the 1960s, the majority of jurists from developing States and from Eastern European countries attached great importance to the proposition that a treaty concluded in violation of rule of *jus cogens* should be regarded as void and of no effect. On the other hand, most Western States expressed considerable doubt about the feasibility of introducing the concept of *jus cogens* into international law, considering such a step to be no more than a proposal *de lege ferenda* and

---

[23]Namely, the Convention on Succession of States in respect of State Property, Archives and Debts, done at Vienna on 8 April 1983 (document A/CONF.117/14) and the Convention on the Law of the Non-Navigational Uses of International Watercourses, adopted by the General Assembly on 21 May 1997 (annexed to General Assembly resolution 51/229 of 21 May 1997).

[24]In its resolution 51/160 of 16 December 1996, the General Assembly requested the Secretary-General to invite States to submit comments and observations before the end of the Assembly's fifty-third session regarding the action which might be taken in relation to the draft Code of Crimes. In the same resolution, the Assembly also drew the attention of States participating in the Preparatory Committee for the Establishment of an International Criminal Court to the relevance of the draft Code to their work.

[25]In its resolution 49/53 of 9 December 1994, the General Assembly decided to establish an ad hoc committee to review the major issues arising out of the Commission's draft statute and to consider arrangements for the convening of a plenipotentiary conference. Subsequently, in its resolution 50/46 of 11 December 1995, the General Assembly established the Preparatory Committee for the Establishment of an International Criminal Court and directed it to discuss further the major substantive and administrative issues arising out of the Commission's draft Statute and to proceed to the drafting of texts, with a view to preparing a widely acceptable consolidated text of a convention as a next step towards consideration by a conference of plenipotentiaries. In its resolution 51/207 of 16 December 1996, the General Assembly reaffirmed the Preparatory Committee's mandate and directed it to aim to complete by April 1998 the preparation of a draft consolidated text of a convention for submission to the diplomatic conference which, it decided, is to be held in 1998.

one, moreover, which was vague, indeterminate and undefined. Some of these States emphasized also that, were norms of *jus cogens* to be recognized to form part of the international legal system, their application would have to be made subject to a process of independent, third-party adjudication.[26]

In the course of preparing its draft articles on treaty law, the International Law Commission took a bold step forward and accepted the view of the majority of States and jurists by recognizing the existence of rules of *jus cogens* in the international legal system. The Commission concluded that, "in codifying the law of treaties, it must start from the basis that today there are certain rules from which States are not competent to derogate at all by a treaty arrangement, and which may be changed only by another rule of the same character".[27] "The emergence of rules having the character of *jus cogens*", the Commission considered, "is comparatively recent, while international law is in process of rapid development".[28] The Commission felt "the right course to be to provide in general terms that a treaty is void if it conflicts with a rule of *jus cogens* and to leave the full content of this rule to be worked out in State practice and in the jurisprudence of international tribunals".[29]

With the support of the vast majority of the States attending the Vienna Conference, articles 53, 64 and 66 were successfully incorporated into the text of the 1969 Convention,[30] defining the concept of *jus cogens*, providing that treaties which are or which become contrary to peremptory norms of general international law are or become void and setting up a mechanism for the resolution of disputes regarding the application of such norms.

Progressive development of the law is also strikingly evident in the field of State succession. As a result of the process of decolonization which took place after the Second World War and resulted in the creation of more than 100 new States, State succession became a crucial problem area of international law. The development through the Commission's drafts of the "clear slate" doctrine and the concept of a "newly independent State" were milestones in the evolution of the law in this field[31]—and that notwithstanding that the 1978 Convention on Succession of States in respect of Treaties has only just now entered into force,[32] while the 1983 Convention on Succession of States in respect of State Property, Archives and Debts has yet to do so.[33]

The 1973 Convention on the Prevention and Punishment of Crimes against International Protected Persons, including Diplomatic Agents, is another good example of the Commission's success in advancing the development of international law. The establishment of universal jurisdiction for the kinds of crimes with which this convention deals, the application to these crimes of the principle *aut dedere aut judicare* and their automatic inclusion in existing extradition

---

[26]Sinclair, Sir I., *The Vienna Convention on the Law of Treaties* (2nd ed., 1984), p. 66.

[27]See paragraph 1 of the Commission's Commentary on draft article 50 of its draft articles on the law of treaties: *Yearbook of International Law Commission, 1966*, vol. II, at p. 247.

[28]Ibid., at p. 248 (paragraph 3 of the Commentary).

[29]Loc. cit.

[30]The text of the future article 53 of the Vienna Convention was adopted in the Committee of the Whole by 72 votes to 3, with 18 abstentions: document A/CONF.39/11, p. 472 at para. 16.

[31]See Sette-Camara, "The International Law Commission: Discourse on Method", in Zanardi, P.L., Migliazza, A., Pocar, F., and Ziccardi, P., eds., *Le Droit international à l'heure de sa codification : études en l'honneur de Roberto Ago*, vol. I (1987), p. 467 at pp. 484-485.

[32]The Convention finally entered into force on 6 November 1996 as a result of the deposit on 7 October 1996 of a notification of succession by the former Yugoslav Republic of Macedonia.

[33]The Convention has, to date, attracted but 5 of the 15 ratifications or accessions which are needed for it to enter into force.

treaties and extradition treaties yet to be concluded represented major new developments in the field of international law criminal law.[34]

A further significant achievement of the Commission is that its drafts have frequently been employed by States and by international tribunals as evidence of the current state of international law. Even unfinished drafts have been used in this way, as may be seen from the treatment which the International Court of Justice has accorded the Commission's work on the topic of State responsibility. Thus, in the case concerning *United States Diplomatic and Consular Staff in Tehran*[35] and the case concerning *Military and Paramilitary activities in and against Nicaragua (Merits)*,[36] the Court based itself squarely upon the Commission's conclusions on two basic aspects of the law of State responsibility, using almost identical terms to those employed by the Commission in order to deal with problems of imputability and circumstances precluding wrongfulness. Indeed, the Commission's draft articles on State responsibility appear to have been used by the Court to determine the content of the rules of general international law on those two issues. Yet, at the time of its Judgments in those two cases, the Commission's draft was not yet complete, did not cover more than the first part of the topic and had only been provisionally adopted on first reading.[37]

Some of the Commission's work, of course, has not taken the form of draft articles which are immediately suitable for adoption as conventions. Nevertheless, the contribution of such, other forms of output to the shaping of international law should not be ignored. Because of the Commission's high reputation and the reputations of its individual members, all of its output, conventional or otherwise, has had a long-term effect on the development of international law, partly since it represents one of the ways and means for making the evidence of customary international law more readily available and partly for the reason that it may be thought at the very least to figure among the teachings of the most highly qualified publicists of various nations, within the meaning of Article 38 of the Statute of International Court of Justice, and so to constitute a subsidiary means for the determination of rules of international law.[38] The Draft Declaration on Rights and Duties of States of 1949, the Principles of International Law Recognized in the Charter of the Nürnberg Tribunal and in the Judgment of the Tribunal of 1950, the Commission's report on Reservations to Multilateral Conventions of 1951 and the Model Rules on Arbitral Procedure of 1958, to name but a few, have all had such an effect.[39]

---

[34]The Convention, it may be noted, closely follows, in most major respects, the relevant provisions of the 1970 Hague Convention for the Suppression of Unlawful Seizure of Aircraft and the 1971 Montreal Convention for the Suppression of Unlawful Acts Against the Safety of Civil Aviation.

[35]Loc. cit. above (footnote 7) at paras. 58 *et seq.* and 79 *et seq.*

[36]*I.C.J. Reports 1986*, p. 14 at paras. 115, 116, 277 and 278.

[37]See Ago, "Some New Thoughts on the Codification of International Law", in Bello, E.G., and Ajibola, B.A., eds., *Essays in Honour of Judge Taslim Olawale Elias: Volume I, Contemporary International Law and Human Rights* (1992), p. 35 at pp. 60-61. Indeed, the Commission only completed its first reading of its draft articles on State responsibility in 1996. See the Commission's Report on the work of its forty-eighth session: loc. cit. above (footnote 4), pp. 121-170.

[38]Lauterpacht, "Survey of International Law in Relation to the Work of Codification of the International Law Commission", in Lauterpacht, E., ed., *International Law, being the Collected Papers of H. Lauterpacht, vol. I, The General Works* (1970), p. 445 at p. 465. For a broad historical survey of the role and influence of "teachings" in the development of international law, see Lachs, "Teachings and Teaching of International Law", in *Recueil des cours de l'Académie de droit international de La Haye*, vol. 151 (1976-III), p. 163.

[39]United Nations, op. cit. above (footnote 4), at pp. 26-29, 34-35 and 50-52.

It is patent, then, that the Commission has made a most substantial contribution to the development of international law. However, one should not exaggerate the Commission's role and achievements. The Commission's work and the success of its efforts in any field are contingent upon and subject to many factors, both internal to the Commission and external to it, as will be seen below. Together, these factors serve to define the Commission's potential and to set limits to what it may realistically hope to achieve.

It must be acknowledged that the Commission has encountered strong criticism of late and that its accomplishments have been the subject of negative appraisals both within the General Assembly's Sixth Committee and within academic circles. One frequent criticism which has been levelled against the Commission is that it has confined itself within a kind of ivory tower, limiting itself to the study of the traditional topics of international law and ignoring the current needs of the international community. The consequence, it is said, is that the Commission has been bypassed by other bodies, which have increasingly intruded on its domain. The Commission has also been charged with a number of faults, particularly slowness. Another criticism which is frequently made concerns the Commission's output and its final status in particular, some writers characterizing the situation as one of incomplete codification, while others have even been led to raise the question "Codification of international law: salvation or dead end?"[40]

It would appear that, to a certain extent at least, problems such as these do indeed exist. However, I should like to stress the importance of assessing the Commission's work and achievements in an objective and comprehensive manner and the necessity of taking into account the background conditions in which the Commission has operated. A one-sided approach should be avoided; and, certainly, the Commission's shortcomings should not be overdone, to the point of denying its valuable contribution to international law. Nothing, after all, is perfect; and to place undue emphasis on problems and difficulties is always dangerous and harmful.

First, account should be taken of the fact that the United Nations is neither a super-State, nor a central legislature with law-making power *vis-à-vis* its Member States. Indeed, the States which attended the San Francisco Conference in 1945 were overwhelmingly opposed to conferring on the Organization any power to enact binding rules of international law. They also rejected proposals to confer on the General Assembly the power to impose certain general conventions on States by some form of majority vote.[41] What they entrusted to the General Assembly under Article 13 of the Charter of the United Nations was but a responsibility to encourage—to encourage the progressive development of international law and its codification—and the means which they entrusted to it to pursue this objective were but powers to study and to recommend. Naturally, the functions and powers of the International Law Commission, which was created under this provision of the Charter, may not be greater than those which the General Assembly itself enjoys under that same provision. Indeed, the object of the Commission, according to its Statute, is but to

---

[40]See: Sette-Camara, loc. cit. above (footnote 31), at pp. 489-502; Zemanek, "Codification of International Law: Salvation or Dead End?" in Zanardi et al., op. cit. above (footnote 31), p. 581; and Munch, "La Codification inachevée", ibid., p. 373 at p.383.

[41]*Documents of the United Nations Conference on International Organization, San Francisco, 1945*, vol. III, documents 1 and 2, vol. VIII, document 1151, and vol. IX, documents 203, 416, 507, 536, 571, 792, 795 and 848.

promote—to promote the progressive development of international law and its codification, principally by preparing draft articles on subjects which have not yet been regulated by international law or in regard to which the law has not yet been sufficiently developed in the practice of States and by undertaking the more precise formulation and systematization of rules of international law in fields where there already is extensive State practice, precedent and doctrine. The law-making power within the international community, then, remains vested in sovereign States, which have played, and which will continue to play, a decisive role in creating, establishing or promulgating norms of international law.

As far as the work of the International Law Commission is concerned, the role of States is apparent at every stage of the process. Individually, they create precedents, develop State practice and advocate doctrines, which together represent the basic materials for the codification of international law. They also furnish information at the outset of the Commission's work on a topic and they comment on its drafts. Collectively, they decide upon the initiation of work by the Commission, on the priority which is to be given to that work and on its final outcome. There is no doubt that the Commission has an important role to play in promoting the progressive development of international law and its codification; but this role, however important it may be, is ultimately subsidiary in nature. The leading role in the international law-making process remains that of States, not the Commission's.

International law is essentially created on a consensual basis. Treaty and custom, the two major sources of international law, are both brought into being by the very States which are to be bound by them. Treaties, whether multilateral or bilateral, are, in principle, applicable solely to those States which are party to them.[42] As for custom, it may be binding upon all of the members of the international community, but its formation depends upon the practice and the legal convictions of States. Any State may, therefore, object to the existence and the application to it of a customary rule at the moment of its formation. As the International Court of Justice pointed out in the *Fisheries* case, any State which consistently and explicitly opposes a customary rule *in statu nascendi* and subsequently maintains its opposition is not bound by that rule.[43] The coincidence of law-makers and law-addressees is, then, one of the fundamental features of the international law-making process.

The codification process is, therefore, inevitably diplomatic in its character—a fact which should not be ignored if one is to achieve any objective assessment of the Commission and its work.[44] Although the Commission is technically independent, it works under the political guidance and supervision of the General Assembly. The speed of its work is, therefore, controlled to a great extent by the Member States of the United Nations. Moreover, once a convention is adopted by a diplomatic conference or by the General Assembly, the law-making process enters a new phase—a phase in which States no longer act collectively, but individually. Each individual State is and remains the sole judge of whether or not to ratify a convention. It is the sole judge, too, of the best time to proceed to such ratification. The internal procedures of each State predominate over the international procedures at this stage in the process and one must wait patiently for States, one by one, to establish their consent to be

---

[42]See article 34 of the Vienna Convention on the Law of Treaties.

[43]*Fisheries* case (United Kingdom / Norway), *I.C.J. Reports 1951*, p. 116 at p.131.

[44]Fleischhauer, "The United Nations and Progressive Development and Codification of International Law", *Indian Journal of International Law*, vol. 25 (1985), p. 1 at p. 2.

bound and for the number of contracting States to build up. It is only when a sufficiently large proportion of States have taken this step that the rules which have been so laboriously prepared, elaborated and approved in the earlier stages of the process will assume the formal authority of law. Accordingly, the accusation that codification has proved a slow process should not be levelled against the Commission alone; it is, rather, a more or less inevitable feature of what is, after all, a quite complicated process.

Account should be taken, too, of the fact that participation in the process of the codification and progressive development of international law is, today, not confined to the International Law Commission or even to the United Nations. Any assumption that the Commission should play the central role in the international law-making process is denied by the facts. Indeed, it was never the intention of those who drafted the Commission's Statute to create a monopoly for the Commission in the field of the progressive development and codification of international law. Within the United Nations itself, a Commission on International Trade Law (UNCITRAL), composed of 36 governmental experts, was created in 1966 and has to date produced a number of important draft conventions which have subsequently been adopted at diplomatic conferences: the Convention on the Limitation Period in the International Sale of Goods of 1974, for instance, the United Nations Convention on Contracts for the International Sale of Goods of 1980 and the United Nations Convention on Independent Guarantees and Stand-by Letters of Credit of 1995. The General Assembly has, moreover, never hesitated, when the need has arisen, to entrust the formulation of rules of international law to other bodies, whether standing or ad hoc. Treaties in the field of human rights, for instance, have mostly been prepared within the Commission on Human Rights, while the Committee on Peaceful Uses of Outer Space has been seized with the responsibility of preparing treaties on outer space. Besides the United Nations, many other organizations have also been engaged in the progressive development and codification of international law, each within their particular spheres of interest. So, for example, drafts prepared by the International Committee of the Red Cross served as the basis of the four 1949 Geneva Conventions on international humanitarian law. The International Civil Aviation Organization has produced three conventions on offences committed on board aircraft. And so on. In short, over the course of the last five decades, hundreds of multilateral treaties of a law-making character have been concluded in a variety of fields and most of these have been the products of bodies other than the International Law Commission. There is no shortage of examples in the publication *Multilateral Treaties Deposited with the Secretary-General*.[45] The proliferation of bodies involved in the treaty-making process is a phenomenon which should not be considered in any way abnormal or dysfunctional. There is no way in which the International Law Commission could prepare every draft convention in every area of international law, even if it were a full-time body working around the clock. A certain division of labour and degree of prioritization would appear to be both necessary for and most conducive to the optimum development and codification of international law. This being so, the Commission should not be criticized—or at least be criticized unduly—for the fact that it has worked almost exclusively within the field of public international law.

---

[45]See, for example, *Multilateral Treaties Deposited with the Secretary-General, Status as at 31 December 1996*, document ST/LEG/SER.E/15.

Bearing in mind all of the above, let us now proceed to assess the present state of the end product of the Commission's work, in particular, the status of the multilateral conventions which have been concluded on the basis of the drafts which it has prepared and the attitudes of the various States towards those conventions, and try to identify the major problems confronting the Commission.

The Commission's output over the last five decades has consisted of reports, suggestions, draft declarations, formulations of principles, model rules, draft articles and draft conventions. The Commission has recommended that conventions be concluded on the basis of its drafts in respect of the following 16 topics (the year of recommendation is indicated in parentheses): arbitral procedure (1953); the elimination and reduction of future statelessness (1954);[46] the law of the sea (1956); diplomatic intercourse and immunities (1958); consular relations (1961); the law of treaties (1966); special missions (1967); representation of states in their relations with international organizations (1971); succession of States in respect of treaties (1974); the most-favoured nation clause (1978); succession of States in respect of matters other than treaties (1981); treaties concluded between States and international organizations or between two or more international organizations (1982); the status of the diplomatic courier and the diplomatic bag not accompanied by diplomatic courier (1989); jurisdictional immunities of States and their property (1991); the law of the non-navigational uses of international watercourses (1994); and the draft statute for an international criminal court (1994). The draft articles on 11 of these topics have been successfully transformed into 14 separate conventions—the set of draft articles on the law of the sea having been divided into four separate conventions—while draft articles on two other of these topics are currently under active consideration by the General Assembly. However, the drafts on the remaining three topics have effectively been shelved.[47]

As may be seen in annex II, below, of the 15 conventions which have been concluded so far on the basis of the Commission's drafts,[48] 11 have entered into force. Two conventions—the Convention on Diplomatic Relations of 1961 and the Convention on Consular Relations of 1963—have achieved a nearly universal level of acceptance, as has already been seen. Middle-ranking, as it were, are the 1973 Convention on the Prevention and Punishment of Crimes against Internationally Protected Persons, including Diplomatic Agents, with a total of 95 States parties, and the 1969 Convention on the Law of Treaties, which currently has a total of 83 States parties. The 1969 Convention on Special Missions, the 1961 Convention on the Reduction of Statelessness and the 1978 Convention on Succession of States in respect of Treaties bring up the tail, with 31, 19 and 15 States parties, respectively.

Of the four conventions which are not yet in force, one was concluded only this spring: the 1997 Convention on the Law of the Non-Navigational Uses of International Watercourses. Of the other three, two might be thought to give

---

[46]While the Commission made no specific recommendation in this case that a convention be concluded on the basis of one or other of the two drafts which it prepared, it gave to those drafts the form of draft conventions, having been specifically requested by the Economic and Social Council to prepare the text of one or more draft conventions on the topic concerned.

[47]See United Nations, op. cit. above (footnote 4), part III, *passim*, and footnotes 8 and 25, above.

[48]In addition to the 14 conventions to which reference is made in the previous paragraph, a further convention was elaborated on the basis of the draft articles which the Commission prepared on the topic of the protection and inviolability of diplomatic agents and other persons entitled to special protection under international law.

every appearance of being stillborn:[49] the 1975 Convention on the Representation of States in their Relations with International Organizations of a Universal Character, which, in the 22 years of its existence, has attracted only 30 of the 35 instruments of ratification or accession which are needed for it to enter into force, and the 1983 Convention on Succession of States in respect of State Property, Archives and Debts, which requires 15 instruments of ratification or accession to enter into force, but, to date, has received just 5.

A phenomenon which is worthy of note is that it typically takes longer for a convention to enter into force once it has been adopted than it does for the Commission to consider a topic and to prepare a sets of draft articles on it. The length of the period between the adoption of a convention and its entry into force has been, at its shortest, three to four years, the 1961 Convention on Diplomatic Relations having taken almost exactly three years to enter into force, while the 1963 Convention on Consular Relations took just short of four years. At the longest, on the other hand, a convention may take 15 years or more to enter into force, the 1978 Convention on Succession of States in respect of Treaties having taken more than 18 years to do so, the 1969 Convention on Special Missions more than 15 years and the 1961 Convention on Reduction of Statelessness more than 14 years, while there is one convention—the 1975 Convention on Representation of States in Their Relations with International Organizations of a Universal Character—which has yet to enter into force more than 22 years after it was adopted.

Another interesting phenomenon is that the shorter the time which the Commission spends in completing its consideration of a topic and in preparing draft articles, the quicker the response of States to ratify or to accede to the convention adopted on the basis of that draft and, concomitantly, the sooner its entry into force. Conversely, the longer the gestation of a draft within the Commission, the more slowly have States responded to the convention which has been concluded on the basis of that draft. Examples may be found in annex II, below.

The status of the conventions under review with respect to individual States is indicated below, in annex III. As may there be seen, there is not a single State which has established its consent to be bound by all 15 of the codification conventions in question. Thirteen States, though, have established their consent to be bound by 10 or more conventions out of the 15.[50] The highest records of acceptance have been notched up by two newly independent States—Bosnia and Herzegovina and Croatia—which are each party to 12 conventions. On the other hand, a total of 60 States have established their consent to be bound by two of these conventions or less.[51] Of these 60, no fewer than 11 have failed to take

---

[49]The third convention—the 1986 Convention on the Law of Treaties between States and International Organizations or between International Organizations—has, to date, attracted a total of 24 ratifications and accessions, a further 11 being necessary for it to enter into force.
  [50]Namely, Australia, Bosnia and Herzegovina, Bulgaria, Croatia, the Czech Republic, Denmark, Mexico, the Netherlands, Slovakia, Switzerland, Ukraine, the United Kingdom and Yugoslavia.
  [51]Namely, Afghanistan, Andorra, Angola, Antigua and Barbuda, Bahrain, Bangladesh, Belize, Benin, Botswana, Brazil, Brunei Darussalam, Burundi, Cape Verde, Chad, Comoros, Congo, Cook Islands, Côte d'Ivoire, Djibouti, Equatorial Guinea, Eritrea, Ethiopia, Gambia, Grenada, Guinea, Guinea-Bissau, Guyana, Kyrgyzstan, Lao People's Democratic Republic, Libyan Arab Jamahiriya, Luxembourg, Maldives, Mali, Marshall Islands, Mauritania, Micronesia, Monaco, Mozambique, Myanmar, Namibia, Nauru, Niue, Palau, Papua New Guinea, Qatar, Saint Kitts and Nevis, Saint Lucia, Saint Vincent and the Grenadines, Samoa, San Marino, Sao Tome and Principe, Saudi Arabia, Singapore, Somalia, Sri Lanka, Tuvalu, the United Arab Emirates, Vanuatu, Zambia and Zimbabwe.

any action whatsoever in respect of any of the 15 conventions concerned—either to sign them or to ratify or accede to them.[52] It is worth noting that seven States[53] have established their consent to be bound by but one particular convention—the 1961 Convention on Diplomatic Relations—while a further 31 States[54] have established their consent to be bound by two particular conventions only—the 1961 Convention on Diplomatic Relations and the 1963 Convention on Consular Relations.[55]

It may be the view of some States that certain aspects of international relations are now satisfactorily regulated by the codification conventions which have been adopted on the basis of the Commission's drafts. This may well not be the view of other States, however, particularly those which have only achieved their independence since 1945.[56] They may reasonably consider that much of the existing legal order does not adequately reflect their interests.[57] Change is, accordingly, necessary.

The acceptance by States of the rules which are contained in a given convention depends, to a great extent, upon the relevance of the subject matter of that convention to their fundamental interests. For most developing countries, top priority has been attached to such basic instruments as the 1961 and 1963 Conventions on Diplomatic and Consular Relations and, to a certain extent, the 1969 Convention on the Law of Treaties. On the other hand, it is noticeable that many developed countries have been reluctant to establish their consent to be bound by the 1969 Convention on Special Missions, the 1975 Convention on Representation of States in their Relations with International Organizations of a Universal Character and the 1978 and 1983 Conventions on State Succession—though they have been much readier to adhere to the other conventions which have been concluded on the basis of the Commission's drafts.

The Commission's achievements are certainly remarkable. The response of States to those achievements, on the other hand, can only be characterized as being on the poor side. This imbalance is parallelled by the gap which exists between, on the one hand, the overwhelming support given by States to the adoption of almost all of the conventions which have, to date, been concluded on the basis of the Commission's drafts and, on the other hand, the limited degree to which States have actually been prepared to participate in most of those same conventions. The average rate of acceptance of those conventions is indeed quite low.[58] A gap exists, too, between signatures and ratifications. Putting to one side for the moment the Convention on the Law of the Non-Navigational Uses of International Watercourses, which has only recently been adopted, almost 150 signatures to the conventions which are under discussion have yet to be followed up by ratification on the part of the signatory States concerned.

As a result of this survey of the Commission's output and its current status, the conclusion may be drawn that the value of the work which the Commission

---

[52]These States are identified at the end of annex III, in note 3.

[53]These States are identified at the end of annex III, in note 2.

[54]These States are identified at the end of annex III, in note 1.

[55]It might also be mentioned in this connection that there is one case of a State having established its consent to be bound only by the 1963 Convention on Consular Relations: Vanuatu.

[56]The membership of the international community has more than tripled since the founding of the United Nations. Thus, whereas 51 States signed the Charter of the United Nations in 1945, there are now 185 States which are Members of the Organization.

[57]See Cassese, A., *International Law in a Divided World* (1986), pp. 115-123.

[58]On average, the number of conventions by which each State has established its consent to be bound falls just short of four.

has done to date has not been fully realized and, likewise, that the Commission's potential has not been fully exploited. The principal problems in this regard would appear to be the following: the failure to transform certain of the Commission's drafts into conventions; the insufficient participation of States, particularly from the developing world, in the conventions which have been elaborated on the basis of the Commission's drafts; and excessive delays in the final stages of the treaty-making process, in particular at the adhesion stage.

To overcome these obstacles and to enhance further the Commission's capability to contribute to the progressive development and codification of international law, it is proposed that:

- The General Assembly should conduct a thorough review of the Commission's output, with the purposes of highlighting the Commission's achievements to date, examining the current status of its output, identifying the factors which have contributed to the failure of so many States, particularly from the developing world, to adhere to the conventions which have been adopted on the basis of the Commission's drafts and exploring concrete measures to increase participation in those conventions.

- As a matter of priority, the General Assembly should pay particular attention to identifying measures for encouraging wider participation in those of the Commission's conventions which are yet to enter into force or which, though they are in force, currently exhibit a low level of adherence. The necessity of promoting wider acceptance of the conventions which have been adopted on the basis of the Commission's drafts can hardly be overemphasized, given that, with the exception of two of their number, none of those conventions can be said to have attracted a level of participation which might be characterized as universal. Since almost all of the conventions in question were adopted with the support of an overwhelming majority of States, those States which voted in favour of their adoption or which signed them, but which have yet to proceed to establish their consent to be bound by them, should, as part of the programme of activities of the United Nations Decade of International Law, be encouraged to take this important step, in pursuance of the goal of strengthening the rule of law in the international community.

- The Commission should consider resuming consideration of certain of the sets of drafts articles which it has adopted, but which have not yet been transformed into conventions, and, if appropriate, should undertake their redrafting, with a view to facilitating their eventual adoption as conventions. When it comes to shaping international law, experience shows that the most effective way to achieve definitive results is through the conclusion of multilateral conventions. Non-binding instruments, such as declarations and model rules, are not without their significance, of course, but their law-making effect is limited. In particular, they do not directly give rise to legal obligations for States and they are incapable of having the weight which a treaty enjoys.

- Consideration should also be given to making technical legal assistance and financial support available to States which wish to take part in negotiations for the adoption of codification conventions if and in so far as they might need such aid in order to participate, or participate effectively, in those negotiations. Likewise, consideration should be given to making technical assistance available to those States which need it and which are considering adhering to codification conventions in order that they might better identify the implications of such adherence. There can be no doubt that the States which have gained their independence since 1945 have a strong desire to participate effectively in shaping and changing a body of norms in the creation of which they had no voice. However, many of these States are impeded in doing so by their financial circumstances and their limited human resources. The international law-making process is, after all, a costly one in which to participate. Moreover, many States simply cannot spare the juridical manpower which is needed to take part in it.

- As far as future treaty-making is concerned, care must be exercised, at the very outset, in identifying the topics in respect of which international law is to be developed. In particular, the formulation of legal rules on the topics concerned should meet a pressing need which is experienced by the vast majority of the international community and should comport with the interests of the generality of States. Ill-conceived choices of topic may lead to political deadlock in the course of formulating a draft or else may result in an outcome which is unacceptable to the majority of States.

- In preparing drafts, the desirability of ensuring the widest acceptance of the final end product should always be kept in mind. To that end, an appropriate balance should be maintained between different interest groups and every effort should be made to reach decisions by consensus, both within the Commission and, subsequently, among States. In dealing with controversial issues, the possibility should be borne in mind of incorporating those rules with regard to which it is not possible to achieve any consensus in one or more optional protocols. Such an expedient may not only facilitate the adoption of the convention which is being prepared, but also its entry into force and its wider acceptance by States. The precedents afforded by the 1961 and 1963 Conventions on Diplomatic and Consular Relations are quite instructive in this regard.

Annex I

Illustration of the Commission's Work and Output

No. and Titles of the subject / Source of reference / Period of work / Form of output / Follow-up action by General Assembly

1. Draft Declaration on Rights and Duties of States / referred by GA / 1949 / a draft declaration in the form of 14 articles with commentaries / Comments invited, insufficient replies received, consideration postponed in 1951, no further action since.

2. Ways and Means for Making the Evidence of Customary International Law More Readily Available / Article 24 of the Statute of the ILC / 1949-50 / a report, containing specific suggestions / most suggestions followed by GA, two related conventions adopted by UNESCO in 1958.

3. Formulation of the Nürnberg Principles / referred by GA / 1949-50 / a formulation of the principles of international law recognized in the Charter of the Nürnberg Tribunal and in the Judgment of the Tribunal / sent to States for comments, no further action taken.

4. Question of International Criminal Jurisdiction / referred by GA / 1949-50; resumed 1992-94 / a report in 1950 and a draft statute for an international criminal court in 1994 / currently under consideration by GA.

5. Reservations to Multilateral Conventions / referred by GA / 1951 / a report / recommendations endorsed in part by GA, further action taken by the Commission in respect of the law of treaties.

6. Question of Defining Aggression / referred by GA / 1951 / a report to GA / its conclusions not taken up by GA.

7. Draft Code of Crimes against the Peace and Security of Mankind / referred by GA / 1951-53, resumed 1982-96 / draft articles with commentary / currently being considered by GA.

8. Nationality, including Statelessness / 1949 list / 1950-54 / two draft conventions on the elimination and on the reduction of future statelessness

and a set of suggestions on present statelessness / UN conference, a convention on the reduction of statelessness adopted in 1959.

9   Law of the Sea / 1949 list (as two separate topics: regime of the high sea and regime of territorial waters) / 1949-56 / a final report, containing 73 articles and commentaries / UN conference, four conventions on the law of the sea adopted in 1958.

10 Arbitral Procedure / 1949 list / 1949-58 / model rules on arbitral procedure / brought to attention of States for their consideration and use.

11 Diplomatic Intercourse and Immunities / 1949 list / 1954-58 / draft articles with commentaries / UN conference, a convention and two optional pro-tocols adopted in 1961.

12 Consular Intercourse and Immunities / 1949 list / 1955-61 / draft articles with commentaries / UN conference, a convention and two optional pro-tocols adopted in 1963.

13 Extended Participation in General Multilateral Treaties Concluded under the Auspices of the League of Nations / referred by GA / 1962-63 / a report, containing conclusions / endorsed by GA.

14 Law of Treaties / 1949 list / 1949-66 / draft articles with commentaries / UN conference, a convention adopted in 1969.

15 Special Missions / referred by GA / 1958-67 / draft articles with commen-taries / a convention adopted by GA in 1969.

16 Relations between States and International Organizations / referred by GA / 1962-71 / draft articles with commentaries / UN conference, a convention adopted in 1975.

17 Succession of States in respect of Treaties / 1949 list / 1962-74 / draft articles with commentaries / UN conference, a convention adopted in 1978.

18 Protection and Inviolability of Diplomatic Agents and Other Persons Entitled to Special Protection under International Law / referred by GA / 1972 / draft articles with commentaries / a convention adopted by GA in 1973.

19 Most-Favoured-Nation Clause / referred by GA / 1967-78 / draft articles with commentaries / brought to the attention of States and intergovernmen-tal organizations for their consideration

20 Review of the Multilateral Treaty-Making Process / referred by GA / 1978-79 / observations / considered by GA in course of review of the multilateral treaty-making process.

21 Succession of States in respect of Matters other than Treaties / 1949 list / 1967-81 / draft articles with commentaries / UN conference, a convention adopted in 1983.

22 Treaties Concluded between States and International Organizations and between Two or More International Organizations / referred by GA / 1970-82 / draft articles with commentaries / UN conference, a convention adopted in 1973.

23 Status of the Diplomatic Courier and the Diplomatic Bag not Accompanied by Diplomatic Courier / referred by GA / 1977-89 / draft articles with commentaries / brought to the attention of States with a reminder that the subject may be subject to codification in the future

24 Jurisdictional Immunities of States and Their Property / referred by GA / 1978-91 / draft articles with commentaries / under consideration by GA.

25 Law of the Non-Navigational Uses of International Watercourses / referred by GA / 1971-94 / draft articles with commentaries / a convention adopted by GA in 1997.

26 State Responsibility / 1949 list / 1955-present / not yet completed.

27 International Liability for Injurious Consequences Arising out of Acts not Prohibited by International Law / referred by GA / 1977-present / not yet completed.

28 Law and Practice relating to Reservations to Treaties / referred by GA / 1994-present / not yet completed.

29 State succession and its impact on the nationality of natural and legal persons / referred by GA / 1994-present / not yet completed.

Annex II

Status of Multilateral Conventions Concluded
on the Basis of Draft Articles
Prepared by the Commission

Code no. / Convention / Text / Adopted by / Date when opened for signature / Date of entry into force / Status as of 28 October 1997

1 Convention on the Territorial Sea and the Contiguous Zone / United Nations, *Treaty Series*, vol. 516, p. 205 / UN Conference / 29-04-1958 / 10-09-1965 / Signatories: 42, Parties: 51.

2 Convention on the High Seas / United Nations, *Treaty Series*, vol. 450, p. 11 / UN Conference / 29-04-1958 / 30-09-1962 / Signatories: 47, Parties: 62.

3 Convention on Fishing and Conservation of Living Resources of the High Seas / United Nations, *Treaty Series*, vol. 559, p. 285 / UN Conference / 29-04-1958 / 29-03-1966 / Signatories: 36, Parties: 37.

4 Convention on the Continental Shelf / United Nations, *Treaty Series*, vol. 499, p. 311 / UN Conference / 29-04-1958 / 10-06-1964 /Signatories: 44, Parties: 57.

5 Convention on the Reduction of Statelessness / United Nations, *Treaty Series*, vol. 989, p. 175 / UN Conference/ 30-08-1961 / 13-12-1975 / Signatories: 5, Parties: 19.

6 Convention on Diplomatic Relations / United Nations, *Treaty Series*, vol. 500, p. 95 / UN Conference / 18-04-1961 / 24-04-1964 / Signatories: 61, Parties: 178.

7 Convention on Consular Relations / United Nations, *Treaty Series*, vol. 596, p. 261 / UN Conference / 24-04-1963 / 19-03-1967 / Signatories: 49, Parties: 158.

8 Convention on Special Missions / United Nations, *Treaty Series*, vol. 1400, p. 231 / General Assembly / 16-12-1969 / 21-06-1985 / Signatories: 13, Parties: 31.

9   Convention on the Law of Treaties / United Nations, *Treaty Series*, vol. 1155, p. 331 / UN Conference / 23-05-1969 / 27-01-1980 / Signatories: 47, Parties: 83

10   Convention on the Prevention and Punishment of Crimes Against International Protected Persons, Including Diplomatic Agents / United Nations, *Treaty Series*, vol. 1035, p. 167 / General Assembly / 14-12-1973 / 20-02-1977 / Signatories: 26, Parties: 95.

11   Convention on the Representation of States in Their Relations with International Organizations of a Universal Character / document A/CONF.67/16 / UN Conference / 14-03-1975 / not yet in force, 35 instruments of ratification or accession required / Signatories: 21, Contracting States: 30.

12   Convention on Succession of States in respect of Treaties / document A/CONF.80/31 and Corr. 1 / UN Conference / 23-08-1978 / 06-11-1996 / Signatories: 20, Parties: 15.

13   Convention on Succession of States in respect of State Property, Archives and Debts / document A/CONF.117/14 / UN Conference / 08-04-1983 / Not yet in force, 15 instruments of ratification or accession required / Signatories: 6, Contracting States: 5.

14   Convention on the Law of Treaties Between States and International Organizations and Between International Organizations / document A/CONF.129/15 / UN Conference / 21-03-1986 / Not yet in force, 35 instruments of ratification or accession required / Signatories: 38, Contracting States: 24.

15   Convention on the Law of the Non-Navigational Uses of International Watercourses / General Assembly / document A/RES/51/229, annex / 21-05-1997 / Not yet in force, 35 instruments of ratification, acceptance, approval or accession required / Signatories: 4, Contracting States: 0.

Annex III

Status of Conventions in respect to Particular States
as of 28 October 1997

Coded entries are used in the table as follows:

1-15: Code number of each instrument as used in Annex II.

s   Signature only
R   Ratification
A   Accession
D   Succession

When no entry is made in a column opposite a State's name, that State has neither signed that convention, nor established its consent to be bound by it.

State	1	2	3	4	5	6	7	8	9	10	11	12	13	14	15
Afghanistan	s	s	s	s		A	s								
Albania		A		A		R	A								
Algeria						A	A		A				s		
Angola						A	A					s			
Antigua & Barbuda							D			A					
Argentina	s	s	s	s		R	R	R	R	A	R			s	R
Armenia					A	A	A			A					
Australia	R	R	R	R	A	R	R		A	R				A	
Austria	s	R			A	R	R	A	A	A				R	
Azerbaijan					A										
Bahamas						D	D			A					
Barbados						D	A		R	A	R				
Belarus	R	R		R		R	A	A	A	R	R				
Belgium	A	A	A			R	R		A						
Benin						A	R							s	
Bhutan						A	A			A					
Bolivia	s	s	s	s	A	A	R		s						
Bosnia & Herzeg.	D	D	D	D	A	D	D	D	D	D	D	D	Ts		
Brazil						R	R		s		s	s		s	
Bulgaria	R	R		A		R	A	A	A	R	R			A	

328

State	1	2	3	4	5	6	7	8	9	10	11	12	13	14	15
Burkina Faso		A	A			A	R							s	
Burundi						A			A						
Cambodia	A	A	A	A		A		s							
Cameroon						A	R		A	A	A				
Canada	s	s	s	R	A	R	A		A	R					
Central African R.		A				R	s		A						
Chile				s		R	R	A	R	A	R	s			
China						A	A		A	A					
Colombia	s	s	R	R		R	R		R						
Congo						A	s		R						
Costa Rica	s	R	s	R	A	R	R		R	A					
Côte d'Ivoire						A	s		s			s		s	
Croatia	D	D		D		D	D	D	D	D	D	D	A	A	
Cuba	s	s	s	s		R	R	A			A				
Cyprus		A		A		A	A	R	A	A	A			R	
Czech Republic	D	D		D		D	D	D	D	D	D	s		D	
D.P.R. Korea						A	A	A		A	A				
D.R. Congo						R	R		A	A		s		s	
Denmark	R	R	R	R	A	R	R		R	R				R	
Dominica						D	D				A				
Dominican Rep.	R	R	R	R	s	R	R			A					
Ecuador				s		R	R			A					
Egypt						A	A		A	A		A	s	s	
El Salvador						A	A	s	s	A					
Estonia						A	A	A	A	A	A	A	A	A	
Ethiopia						A			s		R				
Fiji	D	D	D	D		D	A	A							
Finland	R	R	R	R		R	R	s	R	R					
France		s	R	A	s	R	R								
Gabon						A	R			A					
Georgia						A	A		A			A			
Germany		R		s	A	R	R		R	R				R	
Ghana	s	s	s	s		R	R		s	A					
Greece				A		R	A		A	A				R	
Guatemala	s	R		R		R	A	A	R	R	A				
Guyana						A	A		s						
Haiti	R	R	R	R		A	A		A	A					
Holy See	s	s				R	R		R		s	s			
Honduras						A	A		R						
Hungary	R	R				R	A		A	R	R			A	
Iceland	s	s	s			A	A			R					
India						A	A			A					
Indonesia		R	s	s		A	A	A							

329

State	1	2	3	4	5	6	7	8	9	10	11	12	13	14	15
Iran	s	s	s	s		R	R	A	s	A	A				
Iraq						R	A			A		R			
Ireland	s	s		s	A	R	R								
Israel	R	R	s	R	s	R	s	s		A					
Italy	A	A				R	R		R	R				R	
Jamaica	D	D	D	A		A	A	s	R	A	A				
Japan	A	A				R	A		A	A					s
Jordan						A	A		A						
Kazakhstan						A	A		A	A					
Kenya	A	A	A	A		A	A	s							
Kiribati					D	D	D								
Kuwait						A	R		A	A					
Latvia	A	A		A	A	A	A		A	A					
Lebanon		s	s	s		R	R		A						
Lesotho	D	D	D	D		A	A		A						
Liberia	s	s	s	s		R	R		R	A					
Libyan Arab Jam.					A	A									
Liechtenstein						R	R	R	A	A				A	
Lithuania	A					A	A		A						
Luxembourg						R	R	s							s
Madagascar	A	A	A	A		A	A		s			s			
Malawi	A	A	A	A		A	A		A	A				s	
Malaysia	A	A	A	A		A	A		A						
Maldives							A		A						
Malta	D			D		D									
Mauritius	D	D	D	D		D	A		A						
Mexico	A	A	A	A		R	R	A	R	A				R	
Mongolia		A				A	A		A	R	R				
Morocco						A	A		R			A		s	
Nauru						D	A								
Nepal	s	R	A	s		A	A		s	A					
Netherlands	R	R	R	R	R	A	A		A	A				R	
New Zealand	s	s	R	R		R	A		A	A					
Nicaragua						A	A	s		R					
Niger					A	A	R		A	A		s	s		
Nigeria	D	D	D	A		R	A		R		s				
Norway				A	A	R	R		R						
Oman						A	A		A	A					
Pakistan	s	s	s	s		R	A		s	A		s			
Panama	s	s		s		R	R		A	A	R				
Paraguay						A	A	A	A	R		s			
Peru				s		A	R		s	A	s	s	s		
Philippines						R	R	R	R	A					

330

State	1	2	3	4	5	6	7	8	9	10	11	12	13	14	15
Poland		R		R		R	R	A	A	R	R	s			
Portugal	R	R	R	R		A	A			A					
Qatar						A				A					
Rep. of Korea						R	A		R	A				s	
Rep. of Moldova						A	A		A	A				A	
Romania	R	R		A		R	A			R					
Russian Federation	R	R		A		R	A		A	R	R				
Rwanda						A	A	A	A	R	A				
Senegal	A	A	A	A		R	A		A			s		R	
Seychelles						A	A	A		A		A			
Sierra Leone	D	D	D	A		A									
Slovakia	D	D		D		D	D	D	D	D	D	R		D	
Slovenia	D	D				D	D	D	D	D	D	D			
Solomon Islands	D	D	D	D				A							
South Africa	A	A	A	A		R	A								s
Spain	A	A	A	A		A	A		A	A				A	
Sri Lanka	s	s	s	s		R				A					
Sudan						A	A		R	A		s		s	
Suriname						A	A		A						
Swaziland	A	A		A		A									
Sweden				A	A	R	R		R	R				R	
Switzerland	R	R	R	R		R	R	R	A	A				A	
Syrian Arab Rep.						A	A		A	A					s
Tajikistan						A	A		A						
Thailand	R	R		R		R									
The former Yugo. Rep. of Macedonia						D	D				D	D	A		
Togo						A	A		A	A					
Tonga	D	D	s	D		D	A	A							
Trinidad & Tobago	D	D	D	A		A	A		s	A					
Tunisia	s	s	s	s		A	A	R	A	R	A	A			
Turkey						A	A		A	s					
Turkmenistan						A	A		A						
Uganda	A	A	A	A		A									
Ukraine	R	R		R		R	A	A	R	R	A	A			
United Kingdom	R	R	R	R	R	R	R	s	R	R				R	
U.R. of Tanzania						R	A		A		s				
U.S.A.	R	R	R	R		R	R		s	R				s	
Uruguay	s	s	s	s		R	R	A	R	A		s			
Uzbekistan						A	A		A						
Vanuatu						A									
Venezuela	R	R	R	R		R	R								s
Viet Nam						A	A				A				

331

State	1	2	3	4	5	6	7	8	9	10	11	12	13	14	15
Yemen						A	A				A				
Yugoslavia	R	R	R	R		R	R	R	R	R	R	R	s	s	
Zambia						D		s						s	

Notes

Note 1 Twenty-six States have consented to be bound by conventions numbers 6 and 7 only and have taken no action in respect of any other convention: Andorra, Bahrain, Bangladesh, Cape Verde, Djibouti, Equatorial Guinea, Eritrea, Grenada, Guinea, Kyrgyzstan, Lao People's Democratic Republic, Mali, Marshall Islands, Micronesia, Mozambique, Myanmar, Namibia, Papua New Guinea, Saint Lucia, Samoa, Sao Tome and Principe, Saudi Arabia, Somalia, Tuvalu, the United Arab Emirates and Zimbabwe.

Five other States—Angola, Benin, Brazil, Guyana and Luxembourg—have consented to be bound by conventions numbers 6 and 7 only, but have signed one or more other conventions.

Note 2 Five States have consented to be bound by convention number 6 only and have taken no action in respect of any other convention: Botswana, Chad, Guinea-Bissau, Mauritania and San Marino.

Two other States—Côte d'Ivoire and Zambia—have consented to be bound by convention number 6 only, but have signed one or more other conventions.

Note 3 Eleven States have taken no action at all in respect of any of the conventions: Belize, Brunei Darussalam, Comoros, Cook Islands, Gambia, Monaco, Niue, Palau, Saint Kitts and Nevis, Saint Vincent and the Grenadines and Singapore.

ENHANCING THE INTERNATIONAL LAW COMMISSION'S RELATIONSHIPS WITH OTHER LAW-MAKING BODIES AND RELEVANT ACADEMIC AND PROFESSIONAL INSTITUTIONS

by Christine Chinkin*

1. Introduction

In attempting to determine how relationships between the International Law Commission and other bodies within the international legal system might be enhanced, a number of preliminary questions should be borne in mind:

- With which other bodies might it be useful for the Commission to establish relationships? Should the Commission limit its relationships to intergovernmental law-making bodies or should it formally recognize the increasing relevance of non-governmental organizations (NGOs) within the international legal order and develop affiliations accordingly?

- What might be the purpose of any relationships which the Commission might establish with other bodies? Why is it thought desirable to establish or to enhance such relationships? What is it hoped to achieve?

- What form should any such association take? Should there be different levels of interaction with different bodies? Should such relationships be developed at the institutional level, involving the Secretariat of the United Nations in their coordination and management, or should they depend upon networking by the individual members of the Commission?

- Would any changes in the Commission's relationships with other bodies require the amendment of the Commission's Statute, revision of its methods of work or even modification of its very character and functions?

- What would be the resource implications of any changes which might be envisaged? How would any such changes fit in with the Secretary-General's proposals for the financial reform and streamlining of the United Nations?

2. Current relationships between the Commission and other bodies

The Statute of the International Law Commission makes specific provision for communications between the Commission and other international actors. Inevitably, interaction with States is the principal form of interaction which is envisaged.

The Commission's character as a subsidiary organ of the General Assembly is maintained through its submission of an annual report to the General Assembly and through the debates which take place on that report within the Sixth Committee. The relationship between the Commission and the General Assembly is both reactive and proactive. It is reactive in so far as much of the Commission's work is done at the behest of the General Assembly.[1] There is

---

*Professor of International Law, London School of Economics and Political Science, niversity of London, United Kingdom.
[1] Article 16 of the Commission's Statute provides that the General Assembly may refer to the Commission proposals for the progressive development of international law.

also an expectation that its draft texts should as far as possible reflect the debate which takes place within the Sixth Committee.[2] On the other hand, the Commission is proactive in so far as it proposes topics for future codification to the General Assembly and in so far as, in its work, it anticipates governmental acceptance of its views.[3] The Commission's Statute and its practice are built upon the traditional approach to international law-making, which rests upon State consent.[4] The Commission's success has tended to be measured in similar terms: that is, by reference to the level of adherence to the treaty texts that have had their origins in its work.

There are essentially five stages in the work of any advisory law commission: selection of topics; research and collation of materials; consultation; decision-making; and preparation of draft reports and texts. These stages need not necessarily follow each other in strict temporal sequence. They may even take place simultaneously with each other.

The Commission's Statute sets out in some detail the steps which are to be followed by the Commission when it is working on a proposal for the progressive development of international law. It also sets out the steps which it is to take when working on the codification of international law. In both cases, these steps embrace all the five stages which are mentioned above. Since the process is essentially the same both when the Commission is involved in the progressive development of the law and when it is involved in its codification, the Commission has not in practice distinguished between its two functions.[5] After the Commission has completed what it considers to be a satisfactory draft text, the Statute provides for the Secretariat of the United Nations to issue it as a Commission document and to ensure it the "necessary publicity".[6] The Statute does not limit such publication to Governments and its provisions could be interpreted broadly to include bringing the text in question specifically to the attention of academic institutions, intergovernmental bodies and NGOs. In this context, it might be worthwhile actually to make a distinction between the Commission's two legislative functions. Seeking opinions from a broader constituency seems more appropriate when one is involved in developing international law than it does when one is involved in its codification, codification, after all, being an exercise which is principally founded upon the identification and interpretation of an existing body of State practice. At the same time, though, to make any such differentiation between the Commission's legislative functions might backfire and foster a reluctance to embark openly upon the progressive development of the law.

Although it is generally only Governments whose comments are sought, the Commission has on occasions solicited written comments and observations

---

[2]This expectation is only reinforced by the fact that some members of the Commission are also representatives to the Sixth Committee.

[3]See article 18 (1) of the Commission's Statute. Article 18 (2) provides that the Commission shall submit its recommendations for topics for codification to the General Assembly. At an early stage, the Commission established that this did not require prior consent to its selection of topics for codification: Sinclair, Sir I., *The International Law Commission* (1987), pp. 21-32.

[4]A UNITAR Study on the International Law Commission claimed that the Commission had not worked on the progressive development of areas of law of particular concern to the third world: El Baradei, M., Franck, T., and Trachtenberg, R., *The International Law Commission: The Need for a New Direction* (1981) UNITAR Policy and Efficacy Studies No. 1, p. 5 (United Nations publication, Sales No. E.81.XV.PE/1).

[5]For a description of these working methods, see Sinclair, op. cit. above (footnote 3), pp. 32-44.

[6]Articles 16 (g) and 21.

on its drafts from other categories of international actors.[7] Governments them-selves could also be encouraged to canvass a wider range of responses to the Commission's drafts. After all, relationships between the Commission and other bodies might be indirect—that is, mediated through governmental channels—just as much as they might be direct. Admittedly, such mediation carries with it the risk of compromising the independence of the views which are so mediated; but it might at the same time serve to ensure that the Commission's draft will remain acceptable to States, while, at the same time, drawing upon a deeper well of opinion.

The Commission has broad authorization to conduct consultations when preparing draft texts. Thus the Commission's Statute specifically provides that it may consult with scientific institutions and individual experts when working on the progressive development of international law.[8] Furthermore, it may consult with any international or national organization, official or unofficial, on any subject which has been entrusted to it, if it believes that such a procedure might aid it in the performance of its functions.[9]

Consultation is very much a part of the working methods of national law commissions and has a number of potential benefits. It allows for the canvassing of a broader spectrum of opinion and thereby tends to increase the number and diversity of views which are received, considered and taken into account. Consultation may also facilitate the collection of relevant technical, economic, scientific and other expertise.[10] Most importantly, though, it allows for the input of perspectives which are freed from governmental priorities and agendas and, if regularly pursued, enhances transparency and accountability.[11]

The Commission's Statute allows for it to enter into consultation with national, as well as international, bodies. In this connection, it should be borne in mind that there are many valuable lessons of both process and substance that can be learned from national laws. The ever-greater relevance of international law to domestic law also suggests the appropriateness of taking the latter into account at an early stage in the international law-making process.

---

[7]Thus, the opinions of interested United Nations organs, the specialized agencies and other intergovernmental organizations have been sought when the subject matter has made this appropriate, as, for example, in the cases of the preparation of the Commission's draft articles on the representation of States in their relations with international organizations, its draft articles on the prevention and punishment of crimes against diplomatic agents and other internationally protected persons, its draft articles on most-favoured-nation clauses and its draft articles on the law of treaties between States and international organizations or between international organizations. See United Nations, *The Work of the International Law Commission* (5th ed., 1996), pp. 70, 82, 84 and 95 (United Nations publication, Sales No. E.95.V.6).

[8]Article 16 (*e*). The Statute goes on to say that such experts need not be nationals of States which are Members of the United Nations. Although it is not expressly stated, it is, nevertheless, implied in article 21 that scientific or individual experts may also be consulted in the context of a codification exercise.

[9]Article 26 (1) of the Commission's Statute.

[10]Use of technical experts was most successful in the preparatory work for the first Conference on the Law of the Sea: El Baradei et al., op. cit. above (footnote 4), p. 31. The subcommittee of the Commission which was set up in 1974 to consider the topic of international watercourses raised the question whether special arrangements should be made to ensure that the Commission had adequate technical, scientific and economic advice. The United Nations family of agencies dealing with issues of river development and management agreed that they would assist the Commission. United Nations, op. cit. above (footnote 7), p. 113.

[11]Consultation is favoured by national law reform commissions for its contribution to democratic processes. So, it has been remarked, there should be "[w]ide consultation . . . as there is a democratic imperative in such open processes": House of Representatives Standing Committee on Legal and Constitutional Affairs (Australia), *Law Reform: The Challenge Continues* (1994), p. xx.

Notwithstanding the possible benefits of consultation, the contacts which the Commission has had with other institutions and bodies have in practice been quite limited.[12] This is true even in respect of the contacts which it has had with Governments.[13] The low level of governmental response to the Commission's questionnaires and draft texts has even caused the shelving of certain topics.[14] Formal arrangements for observation and reciprocal attendance at meetings have been made with such bodies as the Inter-American Juridical Committee, the Asian-African Legal Consultative Committee, the European Committee on Legal Co-operation and the Arab Commission on International Law.[15] However, exchanges tend to be limited to formal statements, rather than taking the form of a free-flowing dialogue.[16] Routine or regular consultation with other bodies has been extremely limited. The Commission has developed a pattern of working in isolation from the organizations, working parties and committees that have proliferated on the international plane; and the impact which these bodies have had on the international law-making process has not found any reflection whatsoever in the Commission's working methods.

3. Why are the Commission's relationships with other bodies so limited?

The International Law Commission was established in 1947 under Article 13 of the Charter of the United Nations to discharge the General Assembly's responsibilities for the initiation of studies and the making of recommendations "for the purpose of . . . encouraging the progressive development of international law and its codification". Its role is, therefore, to combine providing the General Assembly with detailed research into, and critical analysis of, the current condition of State practice, precedent and doctrine, on the one hand, with proposals for future development and advancement of international law, on the other.[17]

Despite the reformist and forward-looking agenda which is inherent in the concept of progressive development, the Commission is, at the time of its fiftieth anniversary, a predominantly conservative body with little reputation for innovation or for engaging in any radical rethinking of international law. It is an irony of contemporary international law-making that it is in fact the General Assembly itself that is more likely to advance the progressive development of the law through its articulation of aspirational, programmatic resolutions, whereas the work of the Commission may in fact serve to inhibit further evolution of the law. There is a number of factors that reinforce this conserva-

---

[12]United Nations, op. cit. above (footnote 7), p. 24. The Sixth Committee has been criticized for failing to encourage the Commission to have recourse to experts: El Baradei et al., op. cit. above (footnote 4), p. 8.

[13]Graefrath, "The International Law Commission Tomorrow: Improving Its Organization and Methods of Work", *American Journal of International Law*, vol. 85 (1991), p. 595.

[14]As, for example, in the case of the Draft Declaration on Rights and Duties of States. See General Assembly resolution 596 (VI) of 7 December 1951.

[15]This is in accordance with the Commission's Statute, article 26 (4) of which recognizes the desirability of consultation "with intergovernmental organizations whose task is the codification of international law".

[16]Report of the International Law Commission on the work of its forty-eighth session, *Official Records of the General Assembly, Fifty-first Session, Supplement No. 10* (A/51/10), p. 228 at para. 240.

[17]Article 15 of the Commission's Statute defines "progressive development of international law" as "the preparation of draft conventions on subjects which have not yet been regulated by international law or in regard to which the law has not yet been sufficiently developed in the practice of States".

tism. They include the composition of the Commission, its working methods and its relationship with the General Assembly.

The criteria for election to the Commission are that a candidate must be a person of "recognized competence in international law". Moreover, no two members may be nationals of the same State.[18] The requirement of equitable geographical distribution that is applied throughout the United Nations system has been applied to the Commission, too[19]—at times, perhaps, in preference to the selection of the best qualified candidate. Furthermore, candidates nominated by States have tended to be drawn from similar backgrounds, primarily academic or government service. Lastly, one cannot but help observing that, in the Commission's fifty-year history, all of its members have been men.

The part-time nature of the Commission facilitates the fostering of relationships with other bodies in as much as members inevitably spend most of their working lives within other environments, most frequently academia, government or legal practice. Members are likely, in their day-to-day work, to discuss with their colleagues or students issues which are currently before the Commission. They are likely to seek different opinions on those subjects and to participate in relevant seminars and conferences organized by academic and research institutions. If academics, they can introduce the subjects concerned into their curricula and encourage students to prepare research papers on them. However, such exchanges are informal and ad hoc in nature. They also depend upon the willingness of individual members of the Commission to seek and to take advantage of appropriate opportunities.

The Commission has no existence outside its annual meeting, each (northern) summer. This means that any formal development of relationships with other bodies either must take place during that meeting, thereby placing yet further pressures on what is already a very tight schedule, or else must depend upon individual members conducting those relationships at other times of the year and reporting back to the Commission, so placing a full-time commitment upon members, who already must fit the supposedly part-time responsibility of membership of the Commission into their crowded work schedules.

The decision that the Commission should be a part-time body, meeting from 10 to 12 weeks each year, was taken at least in part because of concerns about whether enough well-qualified candidates would in fact be available to fill all of the seats on any full-time body. However, the current working pattern of the Commission itself limits membership to those who can free themselves from their other commitments, public, employment, family or otherwise, for a quarter of each year. Further still, it effectively limits membership to those who are also in a position to do Commission-related work at times outside its annual sessions. Recognition that neither of these things is always possible has fostered tolerance of a relatively high level of absenteeism.

Week after week of consecutive meetings are not necessarily conducive to the most efficient conduct of work, especially when, as is often the case, the reports of Special Rapporteurs are not made available sufficiently in advance of those meetings. In view of the conditions of modern travel and of the new electronic means of communication, there should be a rethink about what would be the most cost-effective and efficient ways for the Commission to conduct its

---

[18]Article 2 (1) and (2) of the Commission's Statute.
[19]Thus, Article 8 of the Commission's Statute provides that "the electors shall bear in mind . . . that in the Commission as a whole representation of the main forms of civilization and of the principal legal systems of the world should be assured".

work. For instance, the Commission might meet more frequently, but for shorter periods, with a limited agenda and specified objectives for each meeting. Between meetings, members might stay in regular contact with each other through the use of electronic means of communication, such as e-mail and teleconferencing.

The process of election to the Commission, the Commission's methods of work and the Commission's relationships with Member States have combined to bring about the formation of a highly homogeneous body, rather than to create a forum for intellectual stimulation and innovation.

Other writers have commented on the change in the Commission's composition from a body made up principally of scholars to one consisting of current and former Government legal advisers, lawyer diplomats and lawyer politicians.[20] On the one hand, this change in the composition of the Commission has enhanced its political assiduity; but it has also led to the "bureaucratization" both of the Commission and of its approach towards international law.[21] The pattern according to which former members of the Commission go on to become Judges of the International Court of Justice raises the question whether the former is perceived as a training ground for the latter. This perception might encourage caution against expressing radical opinions within the Commission and inhibit the sort of provocative debate that would be deemed unsuitable within the judiciary. Whatever the case, this pattern has certainly served to concentrate influence over the development of international law within too few hands, once more to the detriment of innovation.

The parameters of debate within the Commission have, moreover, been limited in so far as discussion has tended to follow the North-South divide that has dominated United Nations law-making to the exclusion of other forces for change within international law.[22] Thus, not only has the Commission failed to be at the forefront in developing legal principles for new areas of international activity, but it has also failed to become engaged in the major theoretical debates about the development of international law. There is no sign in its work, for example, of any awareness of critical legal theory, of feminist approaches to international law or of international economic theory. At the same time, the apparently "safe" course which the Commission has thus steered has not necessarily enhanced its efficacy, if that is measured in terms of its being regarded as the obvious first point of call for the development of international law when speedy and expert work is required[23] or in terms of having its reports widely accepted by Governments and transformed into widely ac-

---

[20]Dhokalia, "Reflections on International Law-making and Its Progressive Development in the Contemporary Era of Transition", in Pathak, R.S., and Dhokalia, R.P. (eds.), *International Law in Transition: Essays in Memory of Judge Nagendra Singh* (1992), p. 203 at p. 223.

[21]"[Bureaucratization] means bureaucratic mentality and spirit in the work which seeks to gain tactical successes for the masters and a control over the development of international law": Dhokalia, loc. cit. above (preceding footnote), at p. 224. For a discussion of the adverse consequences of this phenomenon for the development of the concept of international responsibility, see Allott, "State Responsibility and the Unmaking of International Law", *Harvard International Law Journal*, vol. 29 (1988), p. 1.

[22]There have also been differences of opinion as to whether the Commission should take an activist role in examining topics that are politically sensitive or controversial: El Baradei et al., op. cit. above (footnote 4), p. 11.

[23]There are many examples of cases in which the formulation of treaty principles has not been entrusted to the Commission: for example, on the matters of liability for nuclear accidents and the development of an international legal regime for the prevention and prosecution of hijacking and other terrorist offences.

cepted treaties.[24] In short, the Commission has never satisfactorily resolved the tension, inherent in the concepts of codification and progressive development, between seeking wide acceptance for its texts and making substantial advances in the law.

Since the Commission has neither developed a "winning streak"[25] nor established an unassailable "niche" for itself within the United Nations structure, it might consider changing its character and taking steps to make itself more visible. It could develop into a conduit for new ideas that challenge current understandings of international law and for opening up debate by presenting more radical approaches to existing legal problems. If it were to adopt such an approach, attention to enhancing its relationships with other bodies would then become an especially important issue.

4. Interaction between the Commission and other bodies

There is a number of permanent and ad hoc bodies within the international legal order that undertake legal research and perform law-making tasks. In some instances—for example, UNCITRAL and the Legal Sub-Committee of the Committee on Peaceful Uses of Outer Space—those bodies have specific law-making functions. In others—for example, the specialized agencies, the Human Rights Commission and the United Nations Environment Programme—the mandates of the bodies concerned make them suited to the discharge of a law-making function.

Lack of communication between different parts of this vast law-making system is endemic, causing a needless duplication of work and product and a waste of time and resources. To avoid this situation, exchanges of information and agendas between law-making bodies should be made routine and those bodies should be encouraged to comment on each other's work, even though that would inevitably increase the administrative load upon the secretariats that service them. Moreover, consideration should be given in appropriate cases to those bodies undertaking joint work on matters of common concern.[26] Further-more, it should be borne in mind that the practice of referring matters to ad hoc bodies—for example, the Third United Nations Conference on the Law of the Sea—entails considerable set-up costs and the development *de novo* of substantive and administrative methodologies. Reference of the matters concerned to the Commission might well be a more cost-effective option. The Commission, though, should also look to other international law-making institutions to see whether there are any useful lessons that it can learn from their working methods and techniques.

Perhaps the most controversial question is whether the International Law Commission should develop relationships with NGOs and, if so, at what level that interaction should take place. The focus which there is in the Commission's

---

[24]Until late 1996, no convention elaborated on the basis of a Commission draft had entered into force since June 1985, when the Convention on Special Missions of 1969 entered into force. Cf. Cede ("New Approaches to Law Making in the UN-System", *Austrian Review of International and European Law*, vol. 1 (1996), p. 51 at p. 56), who overlooks the entry into force of this treaty. In November 1996, the Vienna Convention on Succession of States in respect of Treaties of 1978 entered into force, having finally received the necessary 15 instruments of ratification and accession.

[25]The UNITAR Study emphasized the growing isolation of the Commission from areas of international law of any importance, especially to developing States of the South: El Baradei et al., op. cit. above (footnote 4).

[26]Report of the International Law Commission on the work of its forty-eighth session, loc. cit. above (footnote 16), p. 228 at para. 241.

Statute upon the circulation of questionnaires and draft texts to Governments reflects the traditional State-oriented assumptions of international law-making and fails to take into account the ways in which NGOs can, and do, contribute to the law-making process. There are some NGOs with which the International Law Commission has a functional commonality, namely, those bodies which themselves work to produce draft texts and resolutions on particular aspects of public international law, such as the International Law Association and the Institut de Droit International. Liaison with such bodies is enhanced by personal contacts, contributing to what Oscar Schachter has termed the "invisible college" of scholars.[27] While the Commission should certainly keep itself abreast of the work and reports of the Institut and of the committees of the International Law Association, informal relationships are probably sufficient in the case of those bodies, particularly since closer relationships would only be likely to reinforce still further the Commission's conservatism.

Other NGOs have a less analytical and less rigorous approach to international law and pursue an overtly political and activist agenda, often contrary to the express policies of States. Of course, the process of the drafting of treaty texts is oriented towards nation-States, whose acceptance is necessary to bring such instruments into force or to bring about the evolution of the rules which they set forth into rules of customary international law. However, States themselves, especially those in the West, are having to be increasingly responsive to the demands of international civil society, both in so far as the making of international law is concerned and in so far as concerns its implementation. Many States have developed mechanisms for communicating with NGOs and they make use of these mechanisms at intergovernmental conferences, where the goodwill of States generally facilitates the access of NGOs to debates and information. Certain treaty regimes have even provided for forms of NGO participation. The Commission, too, must be alert to the evolving importance of NGOs and to the fact that many States are becoming more amenable to their involvement in law-making.

NGOs contribute to international law-making in a variety of ways. They provide factual information, comment on drafts, draw up alternative texts, lobby Governments, raise consciousness among the general public and even on occasions join the delegations of States. Many law-making bodies have responded to their influence and have drawn upon their expertise and commitment, as, indeed, have a number of States. NGOs were particularly influential in the drafting of the United Nations Convention on the Rights of the Child, for example. The Human Rights Committee has modified its procedures so as to facilitate contact with NGOs, especially in the context of its consideration of States' reports under the International Covenant on Civil and Political Rights. It has used pre-sessional working sessions in order to create opportunities to meet and hold discussions with the representatives of NGOs.

Perhaps the topics with which the Commission deals are unlikely to excite the interest and enthusiasm of NGOs.[28] The areas in which NGOs have partici-

---

[27]Schachter, "The Invisible College of International Lawyers", *Northwestern University Law Review*, vol. 72 (1977), p. 217.

[28]Article 17 (1) of the Commission's Statute appears to exclude NGOs from formally submitting topics to the Commission for its consideration; for the only entities which it mentions as being able to do this are Member States, the principal organs of the United Nations, the specialized agencies and "official bodies established by intergovernmental agreement". However, there is no reason why NGOs should not lobby members of the Commission with their proposals.

pated most actively have been those of human rights, the law of the environment and disarmament—fields in which their perspectives are not infrequently opposed to those of Governments. The Commission's lack of involvement in important areas of international law-making such as these raises the question of its constituency and function. Certainly, its failure to undertake work in these domains has only contributed to its growing irrelevance and the gradual lowering of its profile. Its close relationship with the General Assembly and its focus upon the drafting of treaty texts have meant that its primary concern has been to ensure the acceptability of its output to States and that it has paid little attention to the claims of international civil society. Yet when the Commission has been given a mandate that is less obviously erudite and technical in nature, NGOs have been alert to its draft texts. Illustrative is the formation of an NGO coalition to provide input into governmental responses to the Commission's Draft Statute for an International Criminal Court.[29]

Since NGOs are now increasingly involved at the intergovernmental stages of the law-making process, it might well be thought that they should be consulted at the earlier, preparatory stages of that process, too, for example, when a topic is under consideration by a working group of the Commission. Questionnaires might be circulated to relevant NGOs, identified by reference to the description of their mandates for the purposes of their qualification for consultative status with the Economic and Social Council. A particular advantage of seeking the input of NGOs during the preparation of a treaty is that, if they have been actively involved in its drafting, they are likely to endeavour to persuade States to proceed to its ratification. They are also likely to take steps to monitor its eventual implementation. On the other hand, it should be recognized that there are numerous NGOs, with differing levels of capability, responsibility and commitment, and that, while tapping into their resources might broaden the debate within the Commission and introduce pertinent concerns at an earlier point in the law-making process, there is, at the same time, a risk that involving them in the Commission's work may eventually undermine its legitimacy with Governments. There are, then, considerable advantages in having the first stages of the drafting process undertaken by legal experts working alone and without any intrusion from other entities such as NGOs. However, to allow input from NGOs only at a later stage in the law-making process is apt to create a confrontational environment.

5. Proposals for enhancing the Commission's relationships with other bodies

This final section lists some suggestions for interaction between the Commission and other international bodies. They are not presented in any particular order, nor has their practical or financial feasibility been fully weighed. Many have been previously considered and they are not all mutually compatible.

It would be an easy matter to arrange meetings between members of the Commission and members of other agencies, organizations and individuals which are based in Geneva, likewise, for the members of one body to observe the sessions of the other. The Commission could facilitate matters by setting

---

[29]Members of the NGO Coalition for an International Criminal Court have attended the meetings of the Preparatory Committee on the Establishment of an International Criminal Court as observers, have produced a regular newsletter and have solicited views on the draft texts which the Preparatory Committee has prepared.

aside some parts of its annual session for this purpose. Such arrangements could be coordinated with the annual International Law Seminar.

Contact is less easy with bodies that are located outside Geneva—something which inevitably tends strongly to privilege contact with Western-based bodies. To address this problem, the Commission could meet in different places[30] and take the opportunity to meet with national bodies, both official and unofficial, including legislators, public officials, members of opposition parties and representatives from the private sector. In particular, it should meet in a State of the South,[31] perhaps every other year, so as to counter assertions of dominance by the North. Individual members of the Commission could make visits that fulfilled the same purpose, by undertaking such activities as participating in television or radio programmes or in discussion groups and by addressing professional bodies, universities, community organizations and conferences. Such contacts might encourage Governments to reply to the Commission's questionnaires, raise awareness of the Commission and its work and give members of the Commission a more rounded perspective of national laws and practice. States or private institutions might be prepared to contribute towards meeting the costs of holding such meetings.

The availability of research facilities is crucial to the work of the Commission, but especially to the work of its Special Rapporteurs. Currently, however, the availability of such facilities depends primarily upon the backing of a Government or university at home.[32] Moreover, the Secretariat of the United Nations can offer only limited assistance. This state of affairs is especially problematic for members from the States of the South, which often have only very limited resources at their disposal for this purpose. To address the problem, formal steps could be taken to enhance relationships between the Commission and academic institutions. Currently, these depend primarily upon individual contacts and upon the readiness of researchers to engage with the Commission's drafts through normal academic channels, such as journals and conferences. The level of familiarity with such writings will obviously vary between the Commission's members, but analysis of the Commission's annual reports reveals receptiveness to such forms of input.

A major obstacle to exchange between the Commission and the academic community is the delay which typically occurs in the publication of the Commission's reports. Individual members of the Commission have in some instances published accounts of developments on particular issues,[33] but there is no requirement upon them to do so and their accounts may themselves not always be speedily forthcoming. It is difficult to develop any immediacy in dialogue or debate when one is constrained by a time lag of some years. To improve matters, the Commission might enhance its use of both electronic and traditional media. It could issue brief press releases along the lines of those issued by the International Court of Justice, with the main items in its report presented in bullet-point form. In instances where its work is likely to arouse

---

[30] Article 12 of the Commission's Statute provides that the Commission has "the right to hold meetings at other places after consultation with the Secretary-General".

[31] Suggestions for alternative meeting places have tended to focus upon the idea of holding sessions in New York; but this would essentially only preserve the already North-dominated, bureaucratic character of the Commission's meetings.

[32] Graefrath, loc. cit. above (footnote 13), p. 605.

[33] For example: McCaffrey, "The International Law Commission Adopts Draft Articles on International Watercourses", *American Journal of International Law*, vol. 89 (1995), p. 395; and Crawford, "The ILC Adopts a Statute for an International Criminal Court", ibid., p. 404.

public interest, as with the first draft of the Statute for an International Criminal Court, it could hold a press conference to explain its thinking and its end product. Publication of its reports on the Internet, as well as of issues for discussion, requests for relevant information and details of work in progress, would give the Commission a higher profile, increase the transparency of its processes and encourage communication.

It was once proposed that the International Law Commission might constitute a kind of an international legal research centre.[34] This idea has never been followed up. The Commission could, however, take active steps to stimulate and collate research on particular topics. These topics might be suggested by Special Rapporteurs. For example, the Commission might seek tenders for commissioned research, either by publishing descriptions of what is required in the leading international law journals or by directly approaching persons with particular requests. Such projects might receive research grants from research councils or other funding bodies, especially if the Commission's research needs were made known to these bodies and if these bodies, for their part, were to give some consideration to how their own agendas and priorities might be made to fit with those of the Commission. In this sense at least, one might usefully envisage the "privatization" of the Commission.

The Commission might also follow the example of the International Tribunal for the former Yugoslavia by requesting academic opinions on particular issues. Experience with the Tribunal has shown that academics are willing to prepare and argue—without any fee—detailed written submissions on identified, often quite narrow, subjects. These have provided the Tribunal with a range of opinions and arguments on which it has drawn in its decision-making. The Human Rights Centre has similarly sought opinions on particular issues.[35] If the Commission acted likewise, it could reduce the research pressures on the Secretariat. Submissions could be followed by a workshop or discussion group between those who have responded to the Commission's request, the relevant Special Rapporteur and the members of the Commission in order to explore and develop the ideas that have been raised. The International Tribunal for the former Yugoslavia, it might be added, has also developed a long-term relationship with particular academic departments which it has been able to approach for assistance as and when issues have emerged before it. On the one hand, this has provided some continuity in the assistance that the Tribunal has received. On the other, it has allowed a more detailed understanding of the working methods and needs of the Tribunal to be developed by the departments concerned, facilitating the process of their response.

This proposal leads me to consideration of the use of consultants, from the specialized agencies, from international financial or trade institutions or from academia. Expert consultants, or even part-time commissioners, drawn from a range of disciplines could be engaged for specific topics or issues. These consultants could even include people with legal expertise in particular specialist areas. The expansion of international legal regulation since 1945 has diminished the likelihood of finding people with a thorough and detailed knowledge of international law in all its fields and domains. The strength of the Commission

---

[34]Stone, "On the Vocation of the International Law Commission", *Columbia Law Review*, vol. 17 (1957), p. 49. See also El Baradei et al., op. cit. above (footnote 4), p. 30.

[35]See, for example, Commission on Human Rights Decision 1997/105, 3 April 1997, entitled "Effective implementation of international instruments on human rights, including obligations under international instruments on human rights".

is that it brings together international lawyers with a depth of academic and practical knowledge across the discipline—something that is vital to maintaining the Commission's coherence and integrity. However, members of the Commission might not always be familiar with developments or innovations in certain areas of the law or be aware of how certain principles which they are discussing will impact on the law in particular fields, such as international economic law or the law of the environment. Discourse between generalists and experts could enhance the quality and workability of the Commission's final product. As well as the technical knowledge and outside perspectives they may bring to bear, one should not ignore the role of consultants as facilitators and negotiators who can raise difficult and controversial issues and tease out appropriate solutions.

Engaging people for a single topic might encourage attendance for that issue and reduce the overall level of absenteeism in the Commission. The costs involved might be offset by reducing the size of the "full-time" Commission, which might also have the benefit of enabling it to streamline its working methods. The Commission is, after all, considerably larger than either the International Court of Justice or the largest human rights treaty body; and it is not at all obvious why collective legal drafting should require such a large membership. It has, moreover, proved possible to ensure an equitable geographical distribution of membership within bodies which have many fewer members.

Academic institutions could be requested to sponsor programmes under which members of the Commission would make short-term visits to those institutions in order to give lectures and hold seminars on their work. Research facilities could be made available to them during their visits. Special attempts might be made to arrange such programmes in well-endowed universities in the North for the benefit of members of the Commission who are from States of the South and who do not ready access to library resources in their home State. Moreover, these programmes might be reciprocal, so that members of the institution concerned would, in turn, visit the Commission, participate in its work and lead seminars for its members. A student internship programme might also be introduced. The International Tribunal for the former Yugoslavia has benefited from the work of students and there has been no shortage of well-qualified, highly motivated applicants who have been willing to offer their services for little financial reward.

Many of the preceding ideas would be easier to implement if there were a director of research, similar to the one of the International Law Association, who would oversee and coordinate the overall programme by identifying research projects and supervising research assignments.

The danger with such proposals is that they may only serve to enhance still further relationships with academic institutions and NGOs from the North. After all, prestigious and financially well-endowed academic institutions from the North are those which are most likely to participate in any programmes of the sort that I have described. In this connection, it should be borne in mind that the Commission is already frequently criticized for its preponderance of Western Special Rapporteurs, who bring their legal and cultural assumptions to their work. This note of caution is only reinforced by the experience of the International Tribunal for the former Yugoslavia. Many of the scholars, students and institutions who have given assistance to that body have been Western. It might also be added that such programmes as those which I have described would place yet further demands on the Commission's members outside the framework of its annual meeting. It is likely that many members would not have the time to participate in such activities without making considerable personal sacrifices.

Nevertheless, it can only be observed that the current isolation of the Commission only serves to diminish its relevance. As was said in 1981, ideally "there should be an almost constant flow of information, advice, and reaction from Member States."[36] I would argue that this flow should now be extended to other actors within the international legal order. However, to make such an extension would require a considerable effort on the part of the members of the Commission and of the already over-stretched Secretariat. It also far from clear which other bodies would regard the work of the Commission as sufficiently pertinent to their own work to respond to such overtures.

---

[36]El Baradei et al., op. cit. above (footnote 4), p. 16.

MAKING INTERNATIONAL LAW MORE RELEVANT
AND READILY AVAILABLE

by Tiyanjana Maluwa*

I. Introduction

It is important that international law be made more relevant and readily available. Responsibility for ensuring that this is done lies, broadly speaking, with the General Assembly of the United Nations. This Colloquium is, of course, not the place to analyse the steps which the General Assembly has taken to ensure the increased relevance of international law or to promote its greater availability. Suffice it to mention here that the measures which the General Assembly has taken to these ends may be dated back to 16 December 1963, when it adopted its resolution 1968 (XVIII) regarding technical assistance to promote the teaching, study, dissemination and wider appreciation of international law. The General Assembly's efforts have continued over the last three-and-a-half decades since then and have ranged in scope from the research and promotional programmes of the United Nations Institute for Training and Research (UNITAR) to the activities which have more recently been undertaken within the purview of the United Nations Decade of International Law.

This Colloquium provides an appropriate opportunity for examining the role which the International Law Commission may play in this connection. The question of how international law may be made more relevant and readily available is, of course, a very broad one. It is, moreover, one which has a number of aspects to it. I propose to limit myself to but one of them: how it may best be ensured that international law is taken into account in domestic decision-making processes, be they in the executive, legislative or judicial spheres.

The relevance of international law both to States and to the international community as a whole cannot be overemphasized. International law is created by States to provide the legal framework within which their activities—indeed their very existence—may be regulated. Its relevance to States ought, therefore, to be obvious; yet it is not as widely appreciated or acknowledged as it should be. Part of the explanation for why this is so lies in the lack of awareness which most people have of the very existence of international law. Accordingly, the very first challenge which confronts the community of international lawyers—in the academy, within professional bodies or institutions or in practice—is to ensure that there is better and wider public education in international law.

In examining the ways in which international law may be made more relevant and readily available, I propose to look at three related issues: first, the incorporation of international law into municipal legal systems, especially through constitutional encodement; secondly, the concordance between a State's executive and legislative acts, on the one hand, and its international legal obligations, on the other; and, thirdly, the teaching and dissemination of international law in national institutions and settings.

---

*Professor of International Law, Faculty of Law, University of Cape Town, South Africa.

The first two of these three issues are concerned with ensuring that international law is accorded an integral place in the municipal legal systems and cultures of the various States which make up the international community. Attempts to make international law readily available can hardly have much meaning if there is no clear recognition and acceptance of its status as part of the internal law of States. In addressing this issue, I shall not be concerned with the much-debated question of whether international law is part of the law of the land, much less with theoretical arguments about monism and dualism. Rather, my focus will be on examining the concrete approaches that can be discerned within the actual practice of States. Clearly, the overriding objective in any enterprise which is aimed at making international law more relevant and readily available is to improve the technical competence of those who are involved in that law's practical application as well as to ensure that international law is brought to bear in the decision-making processes of States.

The third of these issues—that of the dissemination and teaching of international law—is relevant to a concern which has been expressed by many commentators over the years: that of how awareness and appreciation of international law among the general public may be enhanced. In a world in which different peoples and communities are pressing for greater recognition of their different identities, but which, at the same time, is growing smaller and turning into an interdependent global village, it is imperative that international law reach all those who live in that world and interact in it. The central issue here is how international law may be made available to ordinary people, and especially to policy makers, and how awareness and knowledge of that law may, in turn, strengthen appreciation of international law's relevance in the world.[1]

The discussion which is to be found in this paper, then, is largely one which is located in an analysis of the actual practice of States. Accordingly, this contribution to the Colloquium does not follow the classical model of an "ideas" paper; for such a paper would invariably focus on an exploration of theoretical paradigms, rather than an assessment of established or actual practical trends. Moreover, only a selection of State practice is examined here; for this paper draws only upon the experience and practice of African States, and of southern African States, in particular. There are two reasons for this selective approach. First, recent developments in southern Africa demonstrate a willingness on the part of some of the States of the region to encode a commitment to international law in their constitutions. Secondly, the emerging constitutional jurisprudence of these countries suggests a readiness on the part of their courts, even in those countries with no explicit constitutional provisions on the subject, to accord international law a heightened role in the process of constitutional interpretation. At the same time, though, I believe that the lessons to be drawn from an examination of the practice of this region hold some relevance for other countries elsewhere, especially those which belong to the so-called third world.

Of course, the proposition that international law is relevant to more than the mere regulation of inter-State relations or of interactions between States and other subjects of international law is one that is accepted by the great majority of commentators. Nevertheless, there continues to be, as noted above, a lack of awareness among most people of the very existence of international law or at least a failure on their part to perceive or to comprehend its relevance. The

---

[1]See, generally, Lee, "International Law Reaching Out", in Macdonald, R.St.J. (ed.), *Essays in Honour of Wang Tieya* (1993), p. 497.

problem was identified by Sir Robert Jennings, a former President of the International Court of Justice, at the beginning of the present decade, when he observed that:

"This lack of awareness about the existence of international law is highly dangerous. In this respect, things are probably worse than they were in the early 1930s. The answer, of course, is education. I must not be tempted to elaborate on [that]. But it is an urgent problem that all of us can do something to alleviate."[2]

Sir Robert's remarks were made shortly after the General Assembly of the United Nations, in its resolution 44/23 of 17 November 1989, had declared the period 1990-1999 the United Nations Decade of International Law. This resolution was itself the result of another declaration which had been adopted at The Hague in June 1989.[3] The Hague Declaration, as it is sometimes called, contained a comprehensive package of proposals which the international community, through the United Nations, was invited to address. Among these was one relating to the need for "public education and better understanding of international law".[4] General Assembly resolution 44/23 accordingly affirmed that one of the main purposes of the Decade should be "to encourage the study, dissemination and wider appreciation of international law". There can be no doubt that this one among the Decade's objectives coincides with at least one of the stated objectives of this Colloquium: to encourage the teaching of international law. I will briefly discuss the first issue to which allusion is made above—the incorporation of international law in African municipal legal systems—before turning to consideration of such other matters.

II. Incorporation of international law in municipal law

The incorporation of international law in municipal law can be general, embracing both customary international law and treaties, or partial, being limited to customary international law or to treaties only.

The incorporation of general international law in national constitutions in post-colonial Africa really begins with the Namibian Constitution of 1990, article 144 of which provides as follows:

"Unless otherwise provided by this Constitution or Act of Parliament, the general rules of public international law and international agreements binding upon Namibia under this Constitution shall form part of the law of Namibia."

The reference to "general rules of public international law" in this provision has been construed to include both customary rules and general principles of law.[5] The Namibian precedent was subsequently adopted in the recent South African and Malawian constitutions. Section 214 of the 1993 interim Constitu-

---

[2]Jennings, "An International Lawyer Takes Stock", *International and Comparative Law Quarterly*, vol. 39 (1990), p. 513 at p. 529.

[3]Documents A/45/430 and Add. 1-3.

[4]The original proposal was made at the Conference of Foreign Ministers of the Movement of Non-Aligned Countries which was held in Nicosia in September 1988. That proposal was subsequently taken up and developed in the declaration which was adopted by the Meeting of the Ministers of Foreign Affairs of the Movement of Non-Aligned Countries to Discuss the Issue of Peace and the Rule of Law in International Affairs which was held at The Hague in June 1989.

[5]Beck, C.H. (ed.), *Grundgesetzkommentar*, vol. 2, (1983), p. 137 *et seq.*; and Bleckmann, A., *Grundgesetz und Volkerrecht* (1975). See also Cassese, "Modern Constitutions and International Law", *Recueil des cours de l'Académie de droit international de La Haye*, vol. 192 (1985-III), p. 331 at pp. 374-376, and the enormous literature cited in endnote 59.

tion of South Africa provided for the incorporation of both customary international law and treaties. The 1996 Constitution of South Africa subsequently confirmed this approach. Section 232 of the 1996 Constitution expressly provides for the incorporation of customary international law, while section 231 (4) incorporates international agreements into national law. Similarly, section 211 of the 1995 Constitution of Malawi declares both customary international law and duly ratified treaties to be part of the law of Malawi. Public international law has, moreover, been accorded a role in the interpretative process under both constitutions: specifically, under sections 39 (1) and 233 of the 1996 South African Constitution and section 11 (2) of the Malawian Constitution. These constitutions are, to borrow a phrase, international law–friendly.[6]

Not all constitutions in Africa are international law-friendly in the sense just described. In fact, altogether, the constitutions of only 20-odd Africa States currently contain provisions which refer to international law. These States may be divided into two categories. To begin with, there are those whose constitutions incorporate international law generally. Here, mention should be made, first and foremost, of the three constitutions of Malawi, Namibia and South Africa, which incorporate both customary international law and treaties as part of municipal law. The 1992 Constitution of Cape Verde can also be said to belong to this category. In fact, it goes beyond a limited reference to treaties and customary international law, also incorporating as part of Cape Verdian law through its article 11 "judicial acts emanating from competent offices of supranational organizations to which Cape Verde belongs" and "rules and principles of international law, validly approved and ratified internationally and nationally, and in force". This provision casts the net quite widely and in fact raises more questions than it answers. What, for example, is meant by "judicial acts emanating from competent offices of supranational organizations"? Is this merely an inelegant reference to, say, the decisions of the International Court of Justice and other international tribunals? How is one to construe the expression "rules and principles . . . validly approved and ratified internationally and nationally"?[7]

The second larger category consists of States which, with the exception of Ethiopia, are all former French colonies. All these States have followed the approach, which is embodied in article 55 of the 1958 French Constitution, of incorporating treaties into national law.[8] Some of the States which belong to this category are: Benin (article 147 of the Constitution of 1990); Burkina Faso

---

[6]Erasmus, "The Namibian Constitution and the Application of International Law", *15 South African Yearbook of International Law*, vol. 15 (1989/90), p. 81 at p. 93.

[7]The full text of article 11 is as follows:

"(1) International Law shall be an integral part of the Cape Verdian judicial system, as long as it is in force in the international legal system.

"(2) International Treaties and Agreements, validly approved and ratified, shall be in force in the Cape Verdian judicial system after their official publication, as long as they are in force in the international legal system.

"(3) Judicial acts emanating from competent offices of supranational organizations to which Cape Verde belongs shall take effect in internal law as soon as they have been established in respective legal conventions.

"(4) Rules and principles of International Law, validly approved and ratified internationally and internally, and in force, shall take precedence over all laws and regulations below the constitutional level."

This English translation of the original Portuguese text may be found in Blaustein, A.P., and Flanz, G.H. (eds.), *Constitutions of the Countries of the World*, vol. IV.

[8]For my survey, I have relied mostly on the texts which are reproduced in Blaustein and Flanz's compilation cited in the preceding footnote. Where necessary, I have checked the English translations found there against the original French texts.

(article 151 of the Constitution of 1991); Central African Republic (article 69 of the Constitution of 1995); Chad (article 106 of the Constitution of 1993); Congo (article 176 of the Constitution of 1992); Côte d'Ivoire (article 56 of the Constitution of 1960); Djibouti (article 37 of the Constitution of 1992); Ethiopia (article 9 of the Constitution of 1994); Guinea (article 79 of the Constitution of 1990); Mali (article 116 of the Constitution of 1992); Mauritania (article 80 of the Constitution of 1991); Niger (article 120 of the Constitution of 1992); and Senegal (article 79 of the Constitution of 1963). The Ethiopian Constitution of 1994 merely declares in article 9 (4) that all international agreements ratified by Ethiopia are an integral part of the laws of the country, without prescribing any hierarchy as between treaties and domestic legislation. By contrast, a 1993 amendment to the Zimbabwean Constitution of 1980 adopts a typical transformation approach by providing that treaties shall not form part of the law of Zimbabwe unless they have been made part of Zimbabwean law by or under an Act of Parliament (article 111B (1)).

Apart from the constitutions of Malawi and Zimbabwe, then, none of the constitutions of the former British colonies ascribes any specific role or status to international law, whether customary or treaty law. As a general observation, therefore, one could say that State practice in anglophone Africa has been one of avoiding the constitutional incorporation of international law altogether. These States have preferred to leave the matter to be determined by the common law approaches developed by the English courts. One lesson to be drawn from this brief survey, though, is that constitution-making in Africa in the post-1990 era seems to indicate that States are becoming more amenable to incorporation not only of human rights but also of international law in general. These commitments must be understood within the specific context of the recent wave of democratization on the continent and the increasing acceptance of the need to entrench respect for human rights globally.

In contrast, as has already been pointed out, a good proportion of the States of francophone Africa have followed France in expressly incorporating treaties into municipal law and according them a superior authority to domestic legislation, subject to the stipulated conditions of ratification or approval, publication and reciprocity. The longest surviving constitutional provision of this nature in francophone Africa is to be found in article 56 of the Constitution of Côte d'Ivoire of 1960.

Ensuring compliance with international law: the role of the judiciary

From the foregoing brief survey, it is clear that the majority of African States are reluctant to incorporate international law directly into their constitutions and thereby make it an integral part of their municipal law. Courts are equally slow to use international law in judicial decision-making. This reluctance seems, in part, to result from the perceived uncertainty of both the existence and interpretation of relevant principles of international law, especially customary international law, in certain contested situations. Of this, Partsch has observed:

> "National judges may prefer to apply a provision of domestic law with which they are familiar instead of making considerable effort to find out whether a rule of customary international law may perhaps be in conflict with this provision."[9]

---

[9]Partsch, "International Law and Municipal Law", in Bernhardt, R. (ed.), *Encyclopedia of Public International Law*, vol. 10 (1991), p. 253.

A number of commentators have also emphasized the relevance of certain political considerations. In particular, it has been argued that account must be taken of the fact that, among newly born States, there exists a certain level of mistrust of legal rules which were created at a time when those States were not yet in a position to participate in the process of the creation of international law. This argument is particularly cogent in respect of customary international law, which is still largely a product of the colonial era. At least this was the attitude of many African and Asian States in the 1960s and early 1970s.[10]

The difficulty here is compounded by the fact that even those constitutions which incorporate international law, or treaties at least, do not contain any clauses enjoining domestic courts to use or have regard to international law as an aid in interpreting and applying the law. Of course, this is not to say that the courts in the countries concerned never take account of international law at all when faced with issues of constitutional or statutory interpretation. One of the principal canons or presumptions of statutory interpretation is that the courts should assume that parliament did not intend to violate international law and that legislation should be interpreted, whenever possible, in such a way as to give it a meaning which is consistent with international law.

In fact, the Malawian Constitution of 1995 and the South African Constitution of 1996 stand out as the only constitutions in Africa with interpretation clauses that specifically call upon the courts to have regard to international law in their decisions. Such a clause is to be found in section 11 (2) of the Malawian Constitution, which provides in part that, in interpreting the provisions of the constitution, a court of law shall "[where] applicable, have regard to current norms of public international law and comparable foreign case law". Section 35 (1) of the South African Interim Constitution contained a similar provision. In a number of cases decided in the period following the adoption of that constitution, South Africa's Constitutional Court has already shown how the judiciary can use international law as an aid in the interpretation and application of domestic legislation and of the constitution itself. So, for example, in *S.* v. *Makwanyane and another*,[11] Chaskalson P. addressed the significance of international law and comparative law relating to the death penalty at some length. The scope of international law, as it was envisioned by Chaskalson P., encompassed not only the "hard" law of customary rules, treaty provisions and judicial decisions, but also the "soft" law contained in resolutions, declarations and guidelines drawn up by appropriate international bodies. In the later case of *Azanian Peoples Organization (AZAPO) and others* v. *President of the Republic of South Africa and others*,[12] the Constitutional Court reiterated its acceptance of international law as a tool of interpretation—although the Constitutional Court there arguably misunderstood and misconstrued the applicable substantive international law.[13] In any case, the role of international law in the interpretative process has now been given constitutional reaffirmation in section 39 (1) of the South African Constitution of 1996. In fact, as one commentator has

---

[10]See, for example: Umozurike, U.O., *International Law and Colonialism in Africa* (1979), *passim*; and Osman, "The Attitude of Newly Independent States Towards International Law: the Need for Progressive Development", *Acta Scandinavica Juris Gentium*, vol. 49 (1979), p. 15.

[11]*Butterworths Constitutional Law Reports* (1995), p. 665 (Constitutional Court).

[12]Ibid. (1996), p. 1015 at pp. 1031-1032 (Constitutional Court).

[13]For one of the most authoritative criticisms of the judgement and the view that Judge Mohammed failed to apply correctly the relevant rules of international law in this case, see Dugard, "Is the Truth and Reconciliation Process Compatible with International Law? An Unanswered Question: *Azapo v. President of the Republic of South Africa*", *South African Journal of Human Rights*, vol. 13 (1997), p. 258.

rightly noted, in one respect section 39 (1) extends the role of international law in the interpretative process even further than was the case under the interim Constitution, since it requires not just "courts", but also other "tribunal(s)" and "forum(s)" to consider international law in interpreting the Bill of Rights.[14]

Section 11 (2) of the Malawian Constitution and sections 39 (1) and 233 of the South African Constitution all strengthen the role of international law in the interpretative process, since they require the courts to apply international law where it is applicable. The new constitutions in Malawi and South Africa provide the courts with an opportunity to develop a constitutional jurisprudence in which international law will play a major part. In fact, whenever courts in these countries employ international law in the context of constitutional and statutory interpretation, they will be following the precedents already established by other courts in the southern African sub-continent. The following examples will suffice.

The question of reliance upon international law was canvassed by the Botswanan Court of Appeal in *Attorney General of Botswana* v. *Unity Dow*.[15] An approach similar to that adopted in this case had already been taken by the same court in an earlier case, *S.* v. *Petrus and another*.[16] The courts in both Zimbabwe and Namibia have also had occasion to examine similar issues and arguments: for example, in the cases of *S.* v. *A Juvenile*[17] and *ex parte Attorney-General, Namibia: in re Corporal Punishment by Organs of State*,[18] respectively.

There have been instructive decisions from outside the southern African region as well. Although the paucity of recorded judicial decisions does not make possible a comprehensive analysis of trends, the general proposition can be advanced that the approach of other courts elsewhere in Africa towards both customary international law and treaty law similarly acknowledges their relevance to the processes of legislative and constitutional interpretation. In the early Moroccan case of *Ecoffard* v. *Cie. Air France*, the court affirmed the "[rule] according to which international law is hierarchically superior to internal law, and prevails over it in case of conflict, particularly in regard to multilateral agreements relating to private law".[19] Similarly, in *Re Draft Ordinance Modifying Law 6/61 Governing Expropriation*, the Supreme Court of Gabon held that, according to article 54 of the Gabonese Constitution of 1961, which was modelled on article 55 of the French Constitution, treaties have priority over any internal law or ordinance.[20] Among more recent examples is the Tanzanian case of *Ephrahim* v. *Pastory and another*.[21] In a much earlier decision, in 1971, the Sierra Leonean Court of Appeal adopted the rule that an incorporated treaty must prevail over other municipal legislation.[22]

The preceding survey is too brief to justify any grand conclusions regarding judicial practice and approaches in all the States of Africa.[23] However, it is

---

[14]Keightley, "Public International Law and the Final Constitution", *South African Journal of Human Rights*, vol. 12 (1996), p. 405 at p. 415.

[15]*Butterworths Constitutional Law Reports* (1994), p. 1 (Botswana).

[16]*Law Reports of the Commonwealth* (1985) p. 699 at p. 714g (Botswana Court of Appeal).

[17]*South African Law Reports* (1990), p. 151 (Zimbabwe Supreme Court).

[18]Ibid. (1991), p. 76 (Namibia Supreme Court).

[19]*International Law Reports*, vol. 39, p. 453 at p. 458.

[20]Ibid., vol. 48, p. 151.

[21]Ibid., vol. 87, p. 106.

[22]*Lansana and others* v. *R.*, ibid., vol. 70, p. 2.

[23]For a more extended discussion of this subject, see my "The Incorporation and Interpretational Role of International Law in Municipal Legal Systems in Africa", *South African Yearbook of International Law*, vol. 22 (1997) (forthcoming).

heartening to note that international law has been invoked by the courts even in those municipal legal systems in which it enjoys no express constitutional affirmation.[24] It can only be hoped that other courts in the new constitutional democracies of Africa will, in time, also accord international law a role in the interpretative process. Although the challenge here falls primarily upon the judiciary, it is a challenge which needs to be taken up by all those involved in the teaching and dissemination of international law, both in the academy and elsewhere. But all this, of course, presupposes that the judiciary itself is familiar with international law. It also assumes that judges, as well as counsel before them, fully appreciate the relevance of international law to legal regulation and the resolution of disputes within the municipal legal sphere. Awareness and appreciation of international law and of its place within the municipal legal system is thus of paramount importance, not only for the general public, but also for the judiciary and the wider legal profession. It is to the question of the dissemination and teaching of international law that I now turn.

III. Dissemination and teaching of international law

(i) The place of international law in legal education

Considerations of space preclude a comprehensive treatment here of the issue of the dissemination and teaching of international law in Africa. Suffice it to note that, following the approach adopted in most universities in the metro-politan colonial countries, on whose traditions and approaches legal education in the new States was modelled, international law was a compulsory subject in the law courses which were taught at most African universities shortly before and after independence. This has not always remained the case. Recent devel-opments in a number of African countries suggest that universities and legal education authorities are no longer prepared to retain international law as a core subject in the law curriculum. It has mostly been relegated to the status of an elective subject, its availability being dependent on the teaching and research interests of faculty members. Thus, while international law continues to be taught as a compulsory subject in some of the smaller universities, for example, in Botswana, Malawi, Swaziland and Zambia, in two of the countries with the best educational resources, Nigeria and South Africa, international law is currently included in law curricula as an optional subject only. The standard law curriculum designed by the National Universities Commission in 1989 con-firmed this position as far as Nigeria is concerned.[25] Similarly, international law has always been taught as an optional subject in South Africa's 20 law schools. One of the explanations for this state of affairs has to do with the recent political history of the country. As Dugard has observed,[26] the apartheid order in South Africa represented a negation of some of the most fundamental principles of international law: self-determination, equality, non-discrimination and so on. Indeed, the very isolation of apartheid South Africa from the international community during the past three decades produced an antipathy towards, and a general cynicism about, international law in South African academic, legal and, most especially, political circles. In the academic environment, this cynicism

---

[24]For example, in Botswana, Tanzania and Zimbabwe. See the cases cited in footnotes 15 to 17 and 21, above.
[25]See Council of Legal Education Circular of 19 April 1989 on criteria for accreditation of law degrees, quoted in Oko, "Legal Education and Training in Nigeria", *African Journal of International and Comparative Law*, vol. 6 (1994), p. 271 at p. 280.
[26]Dugard, J., *International Law: a South African Perspective* (1994), p. 349.

appears to have manifested itself in a lack of real interest in the subject and in a resultant failure to accord it the status of a core subject in South African universities' law curricula.

Although the new South African Constitution incorporates international law into the municipal legal scheme, all South African universities continue to treat it as a marginal, optional subject.[27] In a sense, the apparent marginalization of international law in South Africa, in Nigeria and elsewhere in Africa can be explained using exactly the same terms as were used almost a decade ago by James Crawford in his excellent discussion of teaching and research in international law in Australia. His observations deserve to be quoted *in extenso*:

"The increased range of general law subjects, and the pressure on students to do subjects which are perceived to be particularly useful for professional purposes (especially the commercial law and taxation subjects) has been one factor leading to the offering of smaller elective courses which students can afford to take. Developments in areas of local interest but with international law implications have also led to the offering of subjects in which students do aspects of international law rather than general international law: the proliferation of human rights and humanitarian law courses is the best example of this. It is not normally a prerequisite to the study of these subjects that the students have done the general international law course."[28]

Similar observations have been in relation to the teaching of international law in universities in South Africa as well as in North America.[29] The preference both of academic institutions and of students for the so-called career-oriented subjects is a reflection of the specific priorities of modern society. More than ever before, the usefulness of university education is seen exclusively in terms of the student's preparation for career opportunities. Subjects, such as international law, which are not regarded as immediately relevant for lucrative legal practice are bound to attract less students than the more commercially oriented subjects. This is the economic and social reality within which today's law student has to operate. The challenge that confronts the community of international lawyers, especially those whose careers are already anchored in the teaching profession, is to articulate the usefulness, relevance and practical importance of studying international law. Again, to return to the theme of relevance articulated at the beginning of this discussion: surely the increasing recognition of the importance of human rights and the role of international law in domestic constitutional schemes require that law students be exposed to international law as matter of course.

(ii)   Awareness of international law in the legal profession

Legal practitioners in Africa today are largely products of the universities in which law is taught; and law graduates who have not had the benefit of

---

[27]Apart from a general introductory course on international law, most South African universities also offer a range of electives, drawn from both public and private international law, in such areas as international trade law, international environmental law, international human rights law and international and comparative labour law.

[28]Crawford, "Teaching and Research in International Law in Australia", *Australian Yearbook of International Law*, vol. 10 (1981/83), p. 176 at p. 185.

[29]On South Africa, see Booysen, "International Law as a University Course", *South African Yearbook of International Law*, vol. 21 (1996), p. 147. On the United States, see "Roundtable on the Teaching of International Law", in *American Society of International Law: Proceedings of the 85th Annual Meeting* (1991), pp. 102-123.

studying international law are most unlikely to handle in a competent way issues that require a knowledge of international law. Unfamiliarity with international law and a lack of awareness of the importance attached to that law in other jurisdictions prevent both judges and counsel from making greater use of the occasional opportunities that arise to apply international law in real cases in the courtroom.

An enhanced role for international law in municipal legal systems holds implications for African lawyers, for African law libraries and for legal resources more generally. In one sense, what is called for is a process of reeducation in order to make judges and lawyers who have no previous knowledge of the subject familiar with international law. This is especially important in the context of human rights litigation. Indeed, a recent policy announcement by the South African Minister of Justice, Dullah Omar, points to the need for reeducation of judges and magistrates in the South African judiciary in order to ensure that they are familiar with, and knowledgeable about, the new culture of human rights which underpins the present constitutional order in South Africa.[30] One assumes that this process of judicial reorientation will go beyond human rights issues and embrace the teaching of international law more broadly. Universities can also play a role in this enterprise. Indeed, the present writer has participated in seminars organized by universities and other institutions in South Africa for the purpose of educating judges, magistrates and other civil servants concerned with the administration of justice about the relevance of international law and international human rights law to the new South African constitutional and political order.[31] There can be no doubt that, as the culture of human rights and constitutional rights litigation grows deeper roots in the new constitutional democracies in Africa, the legal profession will have to learn to appreciate the need for greater familiarity and awareness of international law. It can only be hoped that African judges and legal practitioners, already accustomed to the comparative method in commercial and private law, will learn to extend this method to public international law.

IV.   Executive policy, legislative acts and international law

As has been indicated above, the South African Constitution of 1996, following the interim Constitution, commits itself in several places to honouring international law. The interim Constitution contained four provisions with a direct bearing on international law: section 35 (1) enjoined the courts to have regard to public international law in interpreting the fundamental rights enshrined in the Constitution; section 116 (2) empowered the Human Rights Commission to intervene with the national or provincial legislatures where it was of the opinion that any proposed legislation was contrary to human rights

---

[30]See *The Star* (Johannesburg), 12 September 1997. The need for judges in post-apartheid South Africa to appreciate fully the substance and relevance of international law was underlined in the recent case of *S.* v. *December* (*South African Criminal Law Reports* (1995) p. 438 (Appellate Division)), in which the Appellate Division totally failed to consider the relevance of international law to the case at hand. For a critique of the decision, see Dugard, "Abduction: Does the Appellate Division care about International Law?", *South African Journal of Human Rights*, vol. 13 (1996), p. 324.
[31]The Raoul Wallenberg Institute in Sweden has over the last two years co-sponsored workshops with some South African institutions—for example, the Universities of Cape Town, Fort Hare, Pretoria and the Western Cape—aimed at teaching international human rights law to judges, magistrates, police officers and other civil servants drawn from the Department of Justice. Similar workshops and seminars have been organized by both local and international NGOs, such as Lawyers for Human Rights, Legal Resources Centre, Interights and the World Jurists Association.

or other relevant norms of international law; section 227 (2) (*d*) and (*e*) committed the National Defence Force to act only in accordance with rules of international law, both customary and treaty-based; and, as has already been noted, section 231 (4) incorporated rules of customary international law.

These commitments have been reaffirmed in the 1996 Constitution. The provisions in sections 39 (1) (*b*), 231 (4), 232 and 233, dealing with the incorporation and interpretational role of international law, have already been mentioned; but there are other provisions, too, which also relate to international law. Section 198 provides that national security must be pursued in compliance with the law, including international law; while section 199 (5) enjoins the national security services to "[act], teach and require their members to act, in accordance with the Constitution and the law, including customary international law and international agreements binding on the Republic". Similarly, section 200 (1) obligates the national defence force to act in accordance with the principles of international law regulating the use of force. No other constitution in Africa embraces international law so widely. Indeed, the South African approach constitutes a unique exception, rather than the rule, in African constitutional law and practice. Nevertheless, it is an approach that must be recommended to future constitution makers in Africa. The constitutional commitment to honour international law, and not simply to incorporate it as part of municipal law, means that any legislation enacted by parliament and any act performed by the executive have to be assessed for their validity against international law.

It is in the area of foreign policy-making and implementation that the question of concordance between international law and domestic decision-making becomes most pertinent. This is to be expected; for it is in the conduct of foreign affairs that the State is likely, if at all, to find the most relevant use for its international lawyers. In most African countries, international lawyers do not, of course, form part of a single profession.[32] Some are teachers of law at universities or similar institutions. Others work in the public service, as Government legal advisers—usually in the Attorney-General's Department or in the Department of Foreign Affairs—or as career diplomats. A few international lawyers work for non-governmental organizations, especially in special interest or advocacy groups, in the areas of human rights, the environment, and so on. However, it is those who work as legal advisers who stand to make the greatest contribution to enhancing the role of international law in the formulation of State policy, whether external or domestic. This contribution may range from advising Governments on the adoption of a new domestic policy in order to reflect the State's commitments under international law—on arms sales, say, the peaceful settlement of disputes, environmental protection or refugees—to advising them on the need to adhere to treaties or to participate in diplomatic conferences with other States. The most obvious area, though, in which issues arise of compliance of foreign policy with international law is that of human rights. What role should international law, particularly international human rights law, play in the formulation and implementation of foreign policy?

Again, South Africa provides an instructive example. In 1993, before assuming power, Mandela outlined the pillars on which South Africa's foreign policy would rest. Among these was the commitment that "considerations of justice and respect for international law should guide the relations between nations".[33] Shortly after the inauguration of the new Government on 10 May

---

[32]Here I draw on the usage and discussion in Crawford, loc. cit. above (footnote 28).
[33]Mandela, "South African Foreign Policy", *Foreign Affairs*, vol. 73 (1993), p. 87.

1994, the Minister of Foreign Affairs reiterated some of these themes in his first address to the South African Parliament. He declared that South Africa's foreign policy was going to be based on the following guiding principles:

"Firstly, a commitment to human rights, specifically the political, economic, social and environmental circumstances; secondly, a commitment to the promotion of freedom and democracy throughout the world; thirdly, a commitment to the principles of justice and international law in the conduct of relations between nations; fourthly, a commitment to international peace and internationally agreed mechanisms for the resolution of conflict; fifthly, a commitment to the interests of Africa in global affairs; and sixthly, a commitment to expanded regional and international economic co-operation in an interdependent world."[34]

These policy objectives and guidelines have been repeatedly articulated in subsequent parliamentary statements and debates over the last two years. It is clear, at least in official rhetoric, that the promotion of human rights and international law is seen as an integral component of the new foreign policy. Accordingly, the post-apartheid Government has moved fairly quickly to sign all the major human rights treaties.[35] This is a radical departure from the previous regime's policy of refusing to append its signature to these conventions.

There can be no doubt that, domestically, post-apartheid South Africa has laid down a firm foundation for the protection and promotion of all the internationally recognized fundamental human rights. In fact, few would demur to the suggestion that the South African Constitution of 1996 goes much further than any other modern constitution in its protection of these rights. In the realm of foreign relations, the challenge is to ensure that the domestic commitment to human rights and international law also informs all aspects of foreign policy formulation and implementation. Writing soon after the adoption of the interim Constitution of 1993, one commentator in South Africa advanced the basic proposal that parliament should enact legislation which makes assistance to foreign countries conditional upon those countries' protection of human rights. He suggested that, as a starting point, military and economic assistance to other countries should be predicated on the recipient State's compliance with human rights and other relevant norms of international law.[36] None of this has, of course, been taken on board by the post-apartheid Government, nor has any other African country ever adopted such an approach—for the obvious reason that no African country has yet been in the happy position of being a donor of aid to

---

[34]Republic of South Africa, National Assembly, *Hansard's Parliamentary Reports*, 27 May 1994, col. 216.

[35]Among these are: the International Covenant on Civil and Political Rights (United Nations, *Treaty Series*, vol. 999, p. 171); the International Covenant on Economic, Social and Cultural Rights (United Nations, *Treaty Series*, vol. 993, p. 3); the Convention on the Rights of the Child (General Assembly resolution 44/25 of 20 November 1989, annex); the Convention on the Elimination of All Forms of Discrimination Against Women (United Nations, *Treaty Series*, vol. 1249, p. 13); the Convention relating to the Status of Refugees (United Nations, *Treaty Series*, vol. 189, p. 137); the Protocol relating to the Status of Refugees (United Nations, *Treaty Series*, vol. 606, p. 267); the Organization of African Unity Convention Governing the Specific Aspects of Refugee Problems in Africa (United Nations, *Treaty Series*, vol. 1001, p. 45); the Convention Against Torture and Other Cruel, Inhuman or Degrading Treatment or Punishment (United Nations, *Treaty Series*, vol. 1465, p. 85); the International Convention on the Elimination of All Forms of Racial Discrimination (United Nations, *Treaty Series*, vol. 660, p. 195); and the African Charter on Human and Peoples' Rights (OAU Doc. CAB/LEG/67/3/Rev.5).

[36]Klaaren, "Human Rights Legislation for a New South Africa's Foreign Policy", *South African Journal of Human Rights*, vol. 10 (1994), p. 260 at p. 266.

other countries in the manner envisaged by the commentator concerned. Nevertheless, the possibility that South Africa, with its constitutionally entrenched commitment to honour international law and human rights, may one day adopt this legislative route cannot be discounted.

V. New responses to old challenges: the role of the International Law Commission

This discussion has been concerned with identifying strategies for reconfiguring the role of international law, both with regard to its place in national decision-making and in the broader scheme of legal education. It has also been about the search for a better understanding of the present state of international law in Africa.

Commenting on the United Nations Decade of International Law, one writer has made the following observation:

"The encouragement of the progressive development of international law and codification has proved to be the most contentious issue connected with the Decade. Potentially the topic embraces almost any matter including those of a political nature. Accordingly no agreement seems to be obtainable. [It] is in respect of the encouragement of the teaching, study, dissemination and wider appreciation of international law that the Decade has always shown the most likelihood of achieving its purpose. The response to date justifies this confidence."[37]

This observation was made some five years ago. The writer in question cited examples of seminars and symposia organized by certain States—China, Romania and the former Yugoslavia, for instance—as evidence of this positive response. Evidence from Africa does not suggest that any country has taken up this challenge in any serious way. Action is required in four areas here. How can the International Law Commission assist?

First, the organization of seminars, workshops and symposia should be held to raise public consciousness and awareness about international law. After all, international law will only be better served by States when their nationals are able to scrutinize their acts for compliance with international law. Universities should play a leading role in organizing such activities. However, given the parlous financial circumstances of most African universities, it is probable that Government support would be required.

It has been suggested that one means of raising public consciousness might be to introduce international law as a subject on the school curriculum. The production of a United Nations–sponsored textbook for school children has been proposed in this connection.[38] The United Nations University and the International Law Commission could assist in such a project. One example which comes to mind here is the textbook which has been prepared by the New York State Bar's Law, Youth and Citizenship Program for use in secondary schools: *International Law and the Society of Nations: An Introduction to Public International Law in the 1990s*.[39] Obviously, there could not be one single model for all countries. The different cultural and educational approaches and traditions of the various countries of the world would preclude this and would, at the same time, have to be taken into account.

---

[37]Thomas, "A Review of the United Nations Decade of International Law and the African Contribution", *African Society of International and Comparative Law: Proceedings of the 4th Annual Conference* (1992), p. 315 at pp. 320-321.

[38]Lee, loc. cit above (footnote 1), pp. 502-504.

Secondly, it is more critical still that awareness of international law be raised among policy and decision makers in Government. In a thoughtful piece on the subject, Lee has proposed the novel idea of an "international law impact assessment" for all major decisions involving relations with foreign countries:

"It seems fully justified that an impact statement on international law should now be incorporated into the decision-making processes at the national and international level. [Decision] makers might be interested in knowing, for example, what international law is, how decisions at the national level are inextricably interwoven with complex processes in other countries, how the international system interacts with the municipal [systems]."[40]

To bring about greater awareness of international law among this category of actors would require the dissemination of that law through specialist publications and specially tailored seminars. Clearly, there is shared responsibility here between various sections of the international law profession: international lawyers who serve as legal advisers to Ministries of Foreign Affairs, teachers of international law and, where they exist, professional associations. Legal advisers are in a unique position to advise their colleagues in Government decision-making circles on issues of international law. In this way, they can shape and direct the nature of the State's participation in international legal affairs and ensure that there is concordance between the decision-making processes in the domestic arena and the requirements of international law in the international sphere. However, this can only be so if the legal advisers themselves are schooled in international law; and this is not always the case. How can the United Nations and the International Law Commission in particular be of assistance in training international lawyers to take up the challenging responsibilities involved in being a legal adviser? The well established International Law Seminar which is held in conjunction with the sessions of the International Law Commission already represents one way of addressing this need. What may be required, though, is a different kind of seminar, specifically designed for actual and potential makers of foreign policy and advisers on foreign affairs and open to political scientists and graduates in international relations as well as to lawyers.

Thirdly, the role of professional associations needs to be developed. Professional associations in certain countries and jurisdictions already play a significant role in advancing the cause of international law. Very few, for example, would doubt the importance and the usefulness of the formal and informal interactions that go on in the United States between members of the American Society of International Law, the American Branch of the International Law Association and the American Bar Association, on the one hand, and the State Department and Congress, together with its relevant committees, on the other.[41] These professional associations are able in this way to make available expertise and offer ideas to the State Department's Legal Adviser and Government policy makers. Unfortunately, the picture has not always been as rosy on the African continent. To be sure, there have been national associations of international lawyers in some countries, some more active and longer-lasting than others. Among the longest surviving ones are the Egyptian Society of

---

[39]Mentioned in Lee, ibid., p. 503.
[40]Ibid., pp. 501-502.
[41]See, for example, the round-table discussion on "The Role of International Law in U.S. Foreign Policymaking", in *American Society of International Law: Proceedings of the 86th Annual Meeting* (1992), pp. 434-455.

International Law and the South African Society of International Law. Currently, the most active and successful professional association on the continent is the African Society of International and Comparative Law, which was established in 1989 and whose membership comprises a diverse group of (chiefly) public international lawyers drawn from all parts of Africa and beyond. It also publishes a quarterly, the *African Journal of International and Comparative Law*, as well as *Proceedings* of its annual meetings. Unlike the national professional associations, the Society does not seek to exercise any influence over policy-making in individual States. However, this should not stop individual members from getting involved in such policy-making in their individual capacities, if they are invited to do so by particular States. It is also worth noting that the Society has been active in the area of public education and in the dissemination of international law. It does this, in part, through its human rights advocacy and legal aid programmes—now firmly established in Ghana and the Gambia, for example—and its joint sponsorship, with the University of Pretoria's Centre for Human Rights, of an African Law Students Internship Programme and the All Africa Human Rights Moot Competition. The commendable work being undertaken by the Society is almost wholly externally funded and depends upon foreign donors for its continuation.

It is suggested that the International Law Commission could contribute to enhancing public awareness of international law by supporting the educational activities of the Society and other, national professional associations, where they exist.[42] Such support could consist, *inter alia*, in the organization of joint programmes, such as regional seminars and moot competitions, or in sending individual members of the Commission to conferences or activities organized by these associations.

My fourth, and final, point concerns the place of international law in universities. Here it only remains to reiterate the obvious point that today's university students are tomorrow's decision and policy makers. It should also be reiterated that public international law has become too extensive to be covered in its entirety in a single course. The proliferation of specialisms within the broad field of international law must be recognized by universities in Africa and must be catered for in law-school curricula. Students are likely to show greater interest in courses covering the newer branches of international law, such as international environmental law, international human rights law, international business law or international trade law, than in a general international law course dealing with the classical topics—the law of peace and the law of war. Any effort which is aimed at enhancing the relevance of international law and making it more readily available in modern communities must take account of the need to broaden existing university teaching of international law. This broadening of the teaching of international law must embrace international relations and politics students as well, it being the case that currently very few universities in Africa offer international law to such students. Of course, such an initiative will have resource implications, human and financial as well as physical. More critically, it will also require the production of teaching materials. The structural adjustment programmes and declining economic fortunes of States in recent times have not been kind to African universities and research institutions and libraries. A meeting of like-minded international lawyers recognized this prob-

---

[42]To date, the principal donors to the Society have been the Danish International Development Agency, the Swedish International Development Authority and Anglo-American and De Beers Chairman's Fund.

lem, even before the onset of the structural adjustment programmes, at a workshop which was held in Harare, some 15 years ago. That august assembly of African and European scholars resolved "collectively to compile African international law cases and materials for purposes of teaching international law in Africa and elsewhere".[43] This project has never come to fruition. It is, however, the right time to revive the idea and to invite the International Law Commission to consider its possible participation in, and support for, such a project. In doing so, I will borrow from, and conclude with, the pertinent suggestion made by Lee in the paper that I referred to earlier.

In discussing the lamentable state of affairs which has resulted from the increasing cost of textbooks and the need for more international law textbooks, Lee proposed a "publication consisting of coherent reference to governmental and judicial practice produced in an integral manner by a group of distinguished jurists and practitioners from the legal systems of the world".[44] He went on to observe that such a publication would represent an internationally oriented work and that:

> "This kind of publication could serve as a valuable teaching tool for teachers and students worldwide and could also serve as a reference and research source. More importantly, work of this kind could enhance the development of and bring closer to reality a universal international law."[45]

Lee ended with the remark that the International Law Commission was the ideal body to produce this kind of work. For a teacher of international law operating with rather limited library and research facilities in Africa and witnessing daily the enormous financial difficulties that most students face in procuring grossly over-priced law textbooks, I can only endorse this suggestion.

---

[43]See "Concluding and Press Statement" in Ginther, K., and Benedek, W. (eds.), *New Perspectives and Conceptions of International Law: an Afro-European Dialogue* (1983), p. 241 at p. 243.
[44]Loc. cit. above (footnote 1), p. 508.
[45]Loc. cit.

L'INFORMATION RELATIVE AU DROIT INTERNATIONAL EN GÉNÉRAL ET À LA COMMISSION DU DROIT INTERNATIONAL EN PARTICULIER

par Brigitte Stern*

Il y a un peu plus de deux ans, lors du Congrès sur le droit international réuni à l'occasion du cinquantenaire de l'Organisation des Nations Unies, je parlais à propos des opérations de maintien de la paix de l'Organisation de *mid-life crisis*, ce moment parfois difficile où l'on fait le bilan du passé[1]. Mais le regard vers le passé n'est productif que s'il permet aussi, tel Janus, de porter un regard neuf et constructif vers l'avenir.

Nous sommes aujourd'hui réunis à l'occasion du cinquantenaire de l'établissement de la Commission du droit international, qui est très légèrement plus jeune que l'Organisation des Nations Unies, dont elle est un organe subsidiaire, créé en 1947, très exactement le 21 novembre 1947, par la résolution 174 (III) de l'Assemblée générale de l'Organisation. Pour cet anniversaire, la Division de la codification du Bureau des affaires juridiques de l'Organisation a organisé ce rassemblement d'éminentes personnalités venant du monde entier, afin de faire le point sur l'œuvre effectuée, comme sur les tâches encore à venir. Volontairement, a été prévue une participation mixte, c'est-à-dire réunissant à la fois des acteurs impliqués dans le processus d'élaboration du droit international et des acteurs — professeurs et chercheurs — dont le rôle prioritaire est l'étude du système de normes internationales et la diffusion de la connaissance du droit international. Le Colloque s'inscrit dans ce qui a été qualifié de *reflective mood prevalent at the 50th anniversary of the world organization*[2]. Ce bilan se veut sans complaisance, afin d'ouvrir des horizons encore plus fructueux qu'ils ne le furent déjà.

C'est résolument vers l'avenir que les organisateurs de ce Colloque nous ont demandé de regarder, l'idée générale étant de rédiger des contributions *oriented towards the generation of ideas and proposals for revitalizing and enhancing the operation of the International Law Commission and improving its capability to contribute to the progressive development of international law and its codification.*

Cette dernière matinée a pour intitulé « Comment susciter l'intérêt pour le droit international et le rendre plus accessible ». Il nous a été demandé de façon insistante d'avoir non pas une approche théorique de cette question, mais d'adopter une orientation pratique permettant de déboucher sur des suggestions concrètes pouvant améliorer soit le fonctionnement interne de la Commission du droit international, soit ses relations extérieures avec ses multiples partenaires,

---

*Professeur à l'Université Paris I (Panthéon-Sorbonne), Paris (France).

[1]Voir Stern « L'évolution du rôle des Nations Unies dans le maintien de la paix et de la sécurité internationales », dans Nations Unies, *Le droit international comme langage des relations internationales*, p. 58.

[2]Cede, « New Approaches to Law Making in the UN-System », *Austrian Review of International and European Law*, vol. 1 (1996), p. 55 et 56.

conseillers juridiques des gouvernements, parlementaires, politiciens, juges nationaux et internationaux, professeurs, juristes internationalistes, étudiants, et plus généralement citoyens, jeunes ou moins jeunes, concernés par le monde dans lequel ils vivent, qui est de plus en plus globalisé et de plus en plus international.

Dans cette double optique — prospective et concrète — j'ai choisi de concentrer ma réflexion sur l'information relative au droit international en général et à la Commission du droit international en particulier.

Je suis intimement persuadée que la connaissance des choses — et l'information qui est à la base de cette connaissance, ainsi que sa diffusion — est à la base de tout. Ce n'est que si le plus grand nombre prend conscience de l'existence d'un maillage serré — plus serré qu'on ne le croit généralement — de règles internationales, dont de nombreuses ont été formulées ou précisées par la Commission du droit international, que celles-ci ont des chances sérieuses d'être prises en compte. La conscience de l'existence de la règle est le préalable de leur respect, même si ce n'est évidemment pas une condition suffisante. L'objet de cette contribution est de lancer un certain nombre d'idées dont le but est de rendre plus efficace l'information sur la Commission du droit international et la connaissance du droit international, dont elle a pour mission de préciser les contours, que ce soit par la codification ou le développement progressif.

Les idées qui vont être avancées ici sont toutes extrêmement simples, peut-être certains les trouveront-elles même simplistes. J'espère qu'elles pourront néanmoins servir de tremplin ou de stimulant pour le lancement de discussions qui seront productives et innovantes et qui répondront à l'attente de ceux qui ont organisé cette rencontre.

I. L'information relative à la Commission du droit international

Une première idée serait d'élaborer une **Brochure de présentation de la Commission du droit international**. Aujourd'hui, toute personne cherchant des informations sur la Commission doit les glaner à droite et à gauche, dans des articles, ouvrages, thèses, comme évidemment dans les *Annuaires de la Commission du droit international*. À ma connaissance, il n'existe pas de présentation d'ensemble permettant d'un seul coup d'œil d'avoir une vision globale de ce qu'est la Commission, de ce qu'elle a déjà mené à bien et de ce qu'elle est en train de faire. Je joins en annexe un schéma possible pour une telle brochure, qui n'est évidemment qu'un outil de travail et qui est sans aucun doute perfectible, en particulier grâce à l'apport de ceux qui connaissent la Commission de l'intérieur, c'est-à-dire essentiellement ses membres actuels, ou ses anciens membres ou le personnel onusien qui travaille en étroite collaboration avec elle. Ce schéma est en réalité très proche de celui qui a été suivi pour l'ouvrage mentionné, dont le plan pourrait également être retenu.

Cette brochure pourrait être élaborée par une équipe d'étudiants recrutés pour un ou deux mois dans ce but, sous la supervision du Président de la Commission et/ou d'un petit comité composé de membres de la Commission et de personnes du Secrétariat de l'Organisation des Nations Unies travaillant auprès de la Commission, qui accepterait d'encadrer les étudiants et de prendre la responsabilité ultime concernant le contenu de la brochure. Le caractère exhaustif des renseignements fournis, comme leur exactitude, doit en effet être attesté par la Commission elle-même.

Une autre idée serait de lancer une **lettre d'information de la Commission du droit international**. Cette lettre d'information n'aurait pas besoin d'être longue et fréquente, mais devrait permettre un suivi régulier des travaux de la Commission et des activités gravitant autour d'elle. Dans un premier temps, il pourrait être envisagé d'avoir deux lettres d'information par an : l'une, publiée par exemple en février de chaque année, pourrait indiquer le programme de la future session, comme diffuser des informations à l'adresse des étudiants relatives aux bourses de la CDI et au Séminaire de droit international, permettant la participation à la session; l'autre, publiée par exemple en octobre, pourrait donner un compte rendu succinct de la session, un peu à l'image des « communiqués de presse » de la Cour internationale de Justice, qui sortent très peu de temps après le rendu d'un arrêt ou d'un avis de la Cour et qui permettent d'avoir une idée générale des décisions rendues, sans que cela dispense évidemment de la consultation des décisions rendues pour toute étude plus approfondie.

La rédaction de ce compte rendu pourrait être confiée à des auteurs qui suivent les travaux de la Commission pour les grandes revues de droit international : je songe évidemment ici à la chronique des « Travaux de la Commission du droit international » à l'*Annuaire français de droit international*, ou aux comptes rendus de l'*American Journal of International Law*. Bien entendu, la présentation faite dans la lettre d'information serait plus succincte que ne le sont de telles chroniques, afin d'éviter le double emploi avec ce qui existe déjà. Elle devrait se borner à mettre en lumière les points clés d'accord ou de désaccord. En tout état de cause, ce compte rendu des travaux d'une session, outre qu'il aurait l'avantage de suivre de très près la fin de la session, devrait être diffusé dans les différentes langues de l'Organisation des Nations Unies.

La diffusion de cette lettre d'information de la Commission pourrait être faite sur la base de fichiers fournis par les sociétés nationales de droit international. Une solution alternative, qui ferait peser une moins grande charge sur la Commission, pourrait être la diffusion directe de la lettre d'information de la Commission par les sociétés nationales de droit international. Les membres de la Commission pourraient également jouer un rôle clé dans l'élaboration d'un fichier de personnes intéressées dans leurs pays respectifs.

Dans le même ordre d'idées permettant une connaissance plus rapide de la Commission et une démultiplication des recherches effectuées dans le cadre de la Commission, il pourrait être envisagé de mettre à la disposition de ceux qui seraient intéressés des **bibliographies à jour**. En premier lieu pourrait être diffusée une bibliographie sur la Commission du droit international. Le *Printout of a bibliography collected on the basis of an electronic search-string "codification and progressive development of international law"* qui a été adressé aux contributeurs de ce Colloque pourrait être un excellent point de départ. Le personnel de la Bibliothèque de l'Organisation des Nations Unies qui a préparé ce document pourrait se faire aider, si nécessaire, par des étudiants, qui seraient chargés chaque année de faire la mise à jour de cette bibliographie. Il me semble qu'il y aurait là un outil de travail tout à fait appréciable pour tous ceux qui veulent faire des recherches sur la Commission. En second lieu, pourraient également être diffusées et mises à jour les excellentes bibliographies préparées par le Secrétariat, au moment du démarrage de l'étude d'un sujet. L'ensemble ainsi réuni, et surtout constamment mis à jour, constituerait une sorte de bibliothèque de référence de bibliographies sur un certain nombre de sujets fondamentaux du droit international. L'intérêt d'une telle entreprise n'a pas besoin d'être souligné, simplement il faut redire l'importance d'une constante mise à jour, pour qu'une initiative de ce genre remplisse vraiment son rôle.

Afin d'assurer une diffusion de proximité, il pourrait également être envisagé que, en dehors du dépôt des documents de la Commission dans les bibliothèques dépositaires des documents de l'Organisation des Nations Unies, il y ait dans chaque État un ou deux centres de recherche ou institutions particulièrement intéressés par les travaux de la Commission et motivés pour la diffusion de ceux-ci, reconnus comme **Centres dépositaires des documents de la Commission du droit international**. La Commission s'engagerait à adresser dans les meilleurs délais à ces centres agréés les *Annuaires de la Commission* évidemment, mais aussi les rapports sur ses travaux au moment de leur soumission à l'Assemblée générale. En échange, les Centres dépositaires — dont la liste sera fournie dans la brochure de la Commission — s'engageraient à adresser les documents requis par les ressortissants ou institutions de leur État ou d'un groupe d'États préalablement déterminé. Un tel système aurait l'avantage de rapprocher la source d'information de ses utilisateurs. Évidemment, cela exige une stricte sélection des centres de recherche agréés et un véritable engagement de leur part à jouer consciencieusement leur rôle de relais.

Pour ce qui est de la connaissance des travaux de la Commission par les étudiants en droit international, il pourrait être intéressant de mettre sur pied des **sessions fictives (*moot sessions*) de la Commission du droit international** dans le cadre de séminaires organisés à un niveau national et/ou international. Deux approches différentes pourraient être envisagées ici.

La première approche, strictement universitaire et didactique, pourrait consister en un séminaire de haut niveau (DEA en France, *postgraduate* dans les pays anglo-saxons), dont l'objet serait d'examiner un rapport antérieurement étudié par la Commission : deux sessions différentes pourraient être consacrées, l'une à l'examen du rapport, dans une « optique vierge », c'est-à-dire sans recours préalable aux comptes rendus de la session réelle de la Commission, l'autre à une nouvelle approche du rapport à la lumière de la lecture des débats qui ont eu lieu à la Commission. Il pourrait être envisagé qu'un membre de la Commission participe à la seconde session.

Une autre approche, peut-être plus dynamique et interactive, pourrait être à l'origine d'une contribution des jeunes générations étudiantes aux travaux de la Commission. L'idée serait de faire examiner, cette fois en séminaire international de très haut niveau (séminaire réunissant des doctorants qui auraient éventuellement déjà participé antérieurement à un séminaire national et des jeunes enseignants), un rapport de la Commission en cours d'examen avant même la session de la Commission[3], en espérant que des idées originales apparaissent. Un compte rendu des conclusions du séminaire pourrait être adressé au Rapporteur spécial ou au Président de la Commission, et le meilleur étudiant du groupe envoyé pour assister à la session. Bien entendu, il ne convient pas de surestimer l'apport éventuel de tels comptes rendus, mais il me semble qu'une telle formule serait particulièrement stimulante pour les étudiants. Plusieurs formules pourraient être imaginées : on pourrait envisager de recruter des étudiants venant des mêmes pays que les membres de la Commission, pour que le parallélisme soit plus frappant; mais, dans la mesure où la Commission du droit international est composée d'experts indépendants et non de représentants

---

[3]Dès que le rapport est disponible, en espérant que les Rapporteurs spéciaux suivent les exhortations contenues dans le Rapport de la Commission du droit international sur les travaux de sa quarante-huitième session [*Documents officiels de l'Assemblée générale, cinquante et unième session, Supplément nº 10* (A/51/10), p. 223, par. 149, *f*] demandant que ses rapports sont disponibles suffisamment avant la session.

gouvernementaux, un tel choix ne garantirait pas que l'équilibre global soit plus ou moins le même et ne semble donc pas avoir de raison d'être. Par contre, il pourrait être judicieux de prévoir un recrutement de 34 membres, pour que les conditions de travail soient plus ou moins semblables. Il me semble qu'il y aurait là un exercice de premier plan permettant de comprendre comment s'élabore le droit international, de percevoir le rôle des rapports de force et de l'*opinio juris* des différents États dans la naissance ou le maintien des règles internationales, ce qu'aucun exposé, aucun cours magistral ne permettra jamais de transmettre de façon aussi tangible. Il y aurait également là une leçon de réalisme pour les futurs internationalistes, ce qui est aussi une manière de rendre le droit international plus efficace[4].

Les ministères des affaires étrangères pourraient être sollicités pour établir des bourses permettant la réunion d'un tel séminaire de très haut niveau pendant une ou deux semaines. Ces suggestions sont faites, car je suis intimement convaincue à la fois de l'extraordinaire potentiel d'apprentissage des jeunes générations et de leur grand pouvoir d'innovation et de créativité.

Si de tels séminaires s'institutionnalisaient quelque peu, à l'image des concours de procès fictifs tels que les concours Rousseau ou Jessup, on pourrait même imaginer que les participants constituent une sorte de **Task force** au **service des pays en développement** pour la préparation de leurs réponses aux questionnaires de la Commission du droit international. Il a en effet été souligné que de nombreux gouvernements, en particulier des pays en développement n'avaient que des ressources limitées pour faire face au travail nécessité par une réponse aux questionnaires de la Commission[5]. Une première année, les participants à la session fictive du séminaire international de très haut niveau se familiariseraient avec le travail de la Commission, l'année suivante, ils pourraient effectuer une mission auprès d'un pays en développement qui le souhaiterait, afin de l'aider à préparer la session suivante de la Commission. Dans ce même esprit, on songe évidemment également à la possibilité de recruter des **assistants** pour les membres de la Commission, mais une telle idée se heurte certainement aux contraintes budgétaires et n'est donc ici citée que pour mémoire. La plupart des idées avancées jusqu'à présent ont en effet tenu compte des réalités économiques, et n'impliquent de ce fait pas de grands investissements ou de dépenses excessives.

Enfin, pour stimuler l'intérêt des étudiants et des jeunes chercheurs pour les travaux de la Commission, on devrait créer un **Prix de la Commission du droit international**. Ce prix couronnerait un travail de recherche entrepris sur des aspects procéduraux ou formels du travail de la Commission, mais aussi sur des sujets abordés par la Commission, pour lesquels une analyse particulièrement pertinente aurait été effectuée. La remise du prix pourrait se faire durant la session à Genève ou à New York lors de la discussion du rapport de la Commission à la Sixième Commission. Il pourrait consister en la remise de la collection des *Annuaires de la Commission du droit international*, collection fondamentale dans toute bibliothèque de droit international digne de ce nom. Le jury d'attribution du prix serait constitué de quelques membres de la Commission.

---

[4]Alain Pellet souligne, dans un autre ordre d'idées, l'importance d'un certain réalisme, lorsqu'il loue le pragmatisme de l'Assemblée générale à partir des années 60, indiquant qu'il lui semble être une « garantie de l'efficacité normative des résolutions » : « La Formation du droit international dans le cadre des Nations Unies », *Journal européen du droit international*, vol. 6 (1995), p. 411.

[5]Ibid., p. 237, par. 181.

II. L'information sur le droit international

Les problèmes liés à la diffusion de l'information relative au droit international — à son mode d'élaboration comme à son contenu — sont beaucoup plus généraux et donc d'abord plus délicat. Des idées peuvent certes être lancées, mais elles ne dépendent pas de l'action de la Commission du droit international, mais sont bien plutôt tributaires d'initiatives gouvernementales des différents États. Dans la mesure, cependant, où de nombreux directeurs des services juridiques des ministères des affaires étrangères sont présents à ce Colloque de *brain storming*, il n'est pas inutile de tester quelques suggestions tendant à améliorer la connaissance du droit international.

L'université reste bien entendu un vecteur privilégié de diffusion de la connaissance du droit international. Le risque est qu'elle s'enferme quelquefois dans une tour d'ivoire, parfois volontairement par crainte de voir ses belles certitudes ébranlées, parfois bien involontairement par suite d'une difficulté d'accès à l'information sur la réalité des choses. De ce point de vue, une interaction entre le monde universitaire et le Ministère des affaires étrangères devrait être encouragée, voire même privilégiée, dans chaque État. Une telle approche, relativement institutionnalisée, existe dans des pays comme l'Allemagne; le passage d'un monde à l'autre est monnaie courante aux États-Unis et assure de ce fait la symbiose souhaitée; récemment, une telle interaction a été initiée également en France sur l'initiative du service juridique du Ministère des affaires étrangères, par la mise sur pied d'une petite cellule d'universitaires en contact régulier avec les problèmes concrets auxquels est confronté le Ministère, et une telle innovation doit être saluée. La suggestion qui peut être faite ici est donc adressée aux différents États et consiste à **encourager une liaison constante et étroite entre le monde universitaire et ceux qui conduisent les relations internationales du pays**. Mais cette immersion des universitaires dans le monde international réel peut aussi se faire par la collaboration avec les organisations internationales, et bien sûr avec la Commission du droit international, sur une base formelle ou informelle[6].

Pourrait également être encouragée l'élaboration par les différents États de véritables « **Répertoires de la pratique internationale** » (*Digests of international practice*). Certes, il existe des « Répertoires » de la pratique de tel ou tel État, mais aucun n'atteint à la systématisation, comme c'est le cas par exemple du *Restatement of the Law. Third. Foreign Relations Law of the United States*. Il me paraîtrait très utile que les États qui en ont la possibilité matérielle s'attellent à cette tâche, ne serait-ce que pour qu'il y ait, dans le champ international, plusieurs lectures des règles internationales, et pas seulement l'interprétation américaine. Cela permettrait sans doute également à certains États de préciser certaines de leurs positions qui sont floues, et obligerait dans bien des cas à un débat contradictoire. (On sait les affrontements auxquels ont donné lieu certains articles du *Restatement*, comme par exemple ceux qui concernent l'indemnisation en cas de nationalisation.) Bien entendu, cet effort pourrait être fait en parallèle avec un effort identique de la Commission du droit international, qui pourrait effectuer elle aussi une sorte de ***Restatement international***, en s'appuyant éventuellement sur les *Restatements* nationaux, qui aurait évidemment une grande autorité et pourrait avoir un *harmonizing effect*[7].

---

[6]Cf. ce que dit M. Cede dans l'article déjà cité (note n⁰ 2), p. 60 : «With regard to the role of Special Rapporteurs, the Austrian delegation pleaded for providing them with adequate support by academic and research institutions.»

[7]Selon l'expression de M. Cede, qui suggérait lui aussi l'élaboration d'un tel « *Restatement* » ibid., p. 59.

Cette même confrontation des pratiques internationales, qui me semble être un des éléments clés permettant l'émergence d'une règle commune, peut également être effectuée dans le cadre de **réseaux internationaux regroupant des universitaires de plusieurs pays,** représentant des pratiques diversifiées, qui effectueraient des recherches véritablement internationales donnant lieu à des publications. Une telle entreprise a été par exemple menée par un certain nombre de centres de recherche européens — un par État membre de l'Union européenne plus la Suisse — dont le centre de recherche que je dirige, ce qui explique que je puisse faire part de cette expérience. La recherche a été menée pendant plusieurs années sur la question de l'application du droit international en droit interne. Afin d'assurer une cohérence et une efficacité à l'ensemble, les recherches ont été menées sur la base d'un questionnaire lui-même élaboré collectivement. Outre la connaissance de la pratique du droit international des autres pays que le sien — voire du sien — acquis par chaque membre du réseau, la publication qui est issue de ce travail collectif effectué par des auteurs de différentes nationalités participe, me semble-t-il, à la diffusion de la connaissance du droit international tel qu'il est concrètement pratiqué. La Commission du droit international pourrait jouer un rôle d'impulsion pour ce genre d'entreprise, en suggérant des domaines où existent des pratiques variées, qu'il serait intéressant de connaître, pour mieux avancer vers l'harmonisation des pratiques internationales des différents États.

Le même type d'exercice pourrait se faire en utilisant non plus un réseau d'universitaires et de chercheurs travaillant sur une certaine durée, mais une série de **colloques régionaux** réunis plus ou moins en parallèle, sur un même sujet considéré comme important et susceptible d'une étude productive par la Commission du droit international. À titre d'exemple, si la Commission considérait que la mise en œuvre du droit d'asile dans les différentes régions du monde n'est pas uniforme et qu'il conviendrait de connaître exactement les pratiques régionales, afin de parvenir à un développement progressif du droit dans cette matière, la Commission pourrait susciter des colloques sur ce thème dans les différentes régions du monde : Amérique du Nord, Amérique latine, Europe, Asie et Afrique, par exemple. L'utilité de ces colloques régionaux parallèles serait évidemment qu'ils suivraient un schéma similaire, éventuellement élaboré par la Commission. La portée de ces colloques sera d'autant plus grande qu'ils donneront lieu à des publications, qui constitueraient un *corpus* comparatif tout à fait précieux.

On pourrait songer à utiliser cette procédure pour un certain nombre de sujets envisagés par la Commission, soit qu'ils aient été abandonnés, soit qu'ils aient été retenus pour examen par la Commission, les « résultats » des colloques régionaux servant alors de matière première au travail de codification et de développement progressif de la Commission. Cette fois, c'est le monde universitaire qui pourrait féconder le travail de la Commission. Les sujets identifiés récemment par la Commission comme susceptibles d'une étude pourraient parfaitement être retenus pour le lancement de tels colloques : rappelons qu'il s'agit de la protection diplomatique, la propriété et la protection des épaves au-delà des limites de la juridiction maritime des États, les actes unilatéraux des États[8]. Il est très vraisemblable que des convergences significatives apparaîtraient à la lecture croisée des différents colloques régionaux. Outre la suggestion de sujets dignes de ce genre d'étude générale et approfondie par la

---

[8]Voir le Rapport de la Commission du droit international sur les travaux de sa quarante-huitième session, *supra*, note n⁰ 3, addenda 1, 2 et 3, p. 373 à 385.

Commission, le Secrétariat de l'Organisation des Nations Unies pourrait aider les organisateurs de ces colloques régionaux au niveau du rassemblement de la documentation, qui comporterait sans doute une partie générale commune aux différentes régions et une partie spécifique comportant les textes particuliers ayant pu être adoptés dans un cadre régional.

Plus généralement, la Commission du droit international pourrait éventuellement élaborer une **liste de sujets qui lui semblent intéressants à étudier**. Outre les réseaux et les colloques régionaux, les chercheurs individuels pourraient s'en inspirer, dans le cadre d'un article ou d'une thèse : la constante réflexion théorique de la Commission sur les sujets nouveaux susceptibles d'être codifiés ne peut que l'amener à être particulièrement sensibilisée aux domaines nécessitant des recherches théoriques ou pratiques. Même si certains sujets ne se prêtent pas — ou pas encore — à la codification ou au développement progressif, certains des sujets envisagés et non traités par la Commission sont certainement des sujets susceptibles d'une étude théorique stimulante. La Commission pourrait ainsi féconder la recherche universitaire en lui suggérant des pistes de réflexion. Cette liste de sujets éventuels de recherches universitaires pourrait être publiée dans la lettre d'information de la Commission du droit international, dont la création a été suggérée ci-dessus.

De même, pour rendre le droit international plus pertinent, c'est-à-dire pour assurer une meilleure prise en compte des règles internationales dans les prises de décisions, quoi de mieux que d'« immerger » les futurs décideurs dans le droit international afin qu'il devienne pour eux une référence obligée, presque une seconde nature ? De ce point de vue, outre l'éducation des jeunes générations, sur laquelle l'accent a été mis dans la première partie de cette communication, il me semblerait extrêmement souhaitable de développer la connaissance du droit international parmi les juges nationaux, ainsi que les avocats. Il me paraît en effet que l'application du droit international par les tribunaux nationaux est un complément très précieux de l'application du droit international dans la sphère internationale, à travers les mécanismes internationaux. C'est par la prise en compte du droit international par le juge national que le droit international pénètre véritablement dans la vie quotidienne des hommes et des femmes à travers le monde. Or, souvent, les juges nationaux n'ont encore qu'une familiarité trop lointaine avec les règles du droit international, ayant une formation plus nettement orientée vers le droit interne. Il convient de développer chez eux des « réflexes internationaux », une sorte de conscience immédiate de l'importance du droit international dans presque tous les domaines. Bien entendu, les mêmes remarques sont également pertinentes en ce qui concerne les avocats, afin qu'ils soulèvent systématiquement les moyens internationaux existants à l'appui de leurs thèses. Pour ce faire, il est possible d'attendre des initiatives internes, mais il pourrait peut-être être plus efficace de favoriser ce développement souhaitable sur le plan international : cela pourrait se faire soit en encourageant des magistrats et des avocats à participer au Séminaire de droit international, soit, et cela serait sans doute encore plus fructueux, en mettant sur pied des **séminaires de sensibilisation au droit international pour les juges et les avocats**. Ces séminaires pourraient se tenir tous les deux ans à Genève ou à New York. Afin d'éviter de trop grandes généralités, chaque séminaire devrait être centré sur un thème : par exemple, les droits de l'homme, le droit des investissements, le problème des réfugiés, etc. Des membres de la Commission, des membres des services juridiques des ministères des affaires étrangères ou des organisations internationales, comme des universitaires, pourraient participer à l'animation de ces séminaires.

Bien entendu, qui parle aujourd'hui d'information, pense « autoroutes de l'information » et surtout, bien sûr, la plus royale d'entre elles, Internet. Tous les outils indiqués ci-dessus — s'ils doivent à mon avis être impérativement disponibles en support papier — doivent également et tout aussi impérativement être accessible sur le **Serveur web** de la Commission du droit international. On trouve déjà sur Internet, sur le site web de l'Organisation des Nations Unies, le rapport de la Commission à l'Assemblée générale, ce qui est extrêmement positif. Il convient désormais d'étoffer le serveur, en y ajoutant les éléments d'information suggérés antérieurement, car considérés comme importants. La Commission ne doit pas rater la révolution de l'information de cette fin du XXe siècle, qui va donner forme à l'ensemble du réseau d'échanges du XXIe siècle.

En conclusion, je formule simplement le souhait que, même si elles ne prétendent pas révolutionner le monde international, l'une ou l'autre des deux fois sept propositions avancées ici devienne réalité et permette ainsi d'assurer un meilleur fonctionnement de la communauté internationale.

ANNEXE

Organisation des Nations Unies

La Commission du droit international

Date

HISTORIQUE

Antécédents éventuels sous la Société des Nations
Création comme organe subsidiaire
Eventuellement texte de la résolution 174 (III) par laquelle la Commission du droit international a été créée

ATTRIBUTIONS

Une double fonction :
— La codification du droit international
— Le développement progressif du droit international
Le caractère relatif de cette distinction
Liste des sujets initialement retenus :
— Le mémorandum du Secrétariat et ses 25 sujets
— Les 14 sujets retenus par la Commission
Les nouveaux sujets proposés ou envisagés :
— Liste des sujets proposés en 1991
— Liste des sujets retenus en 1993

COMPOSITION

Un double objectif :
— Des spécialistes
— Des représentants des grands systèmes juridiques
Mode d'élection des 34 experts de la Commission

Composition actuelle
Eventuellement, compositions antérieures[9]

FONCTIONNEMENT

Présidence
Bureau
Session(s)
Système des rapporteurs spéciaux
Rôle du Comité de rédaction
Sous-groupes de travail
Groupe de planification
Liaison avec la Sixième Commission de l'Assemblée générale[10]

BILAN DE L'ACTIVITÉ DE LA COMMISSION

Liste des sujets traités, avec mention à chaque fois des points suivants :
— Rapporteur spécial
— Sessions au cours desquelles le texte a été examiné
— Le texte adopté avec les références
— Le devenir du texte : convention, état des ratifications

TRAVAUX EN COURS

Liste des sujets actuellement à l'examen, avec indication des points suivants :
— Rapporteurs spéciaux
— État d'avancement des travaux

SCHÉMA GÉNÉRAL D'ÉTUDE DU DROIT INTERNATIONAL

Il paraît intéressant de mettre à la disposition de tous ce schéma général du droit international élaboré par la Commission pour servir de cadre de référence et de point de repère pour l'ensemble de ses travaux[11]. Ce schéma peut être utile pour situer un certain nombre de problématiques, au cours de diverses recherches.

ACTIVITÉS ANNEXES

Organisation de colloques
Séminaire de droit international
Bourses pour les étudiants
Liens avec les autres organismes s'occupant de codification du droit international
Prix de la Commission du droit international[12]
— Règlement du prix
— Liste des lauréats

---

[9]En notant qu'il n'y a jamais eu de femme membre de la Commission.
[10]Liaison entre un organe composé d'experts indépendants et un organe composé de représentants de gouvernements.
[11]Voir le Rapport de la Commission du droit international sur les travaux de sa quarante-huitième session, *supra*, note n⁰ 3, p. 366 à 372.
[12]S'il est créé conformément aux suggestions faites ici.

PUBLICATIONS

Annuaires de la Commission du droit international

Ouvrage publié à l'occasion du cinquantenaire : Nations Unies, *Le droit international à l'aube du XXIe siècle : Réflexions de codificateurs* (1997)[13]

DOCUMENTATION ET INFORMATIONS GÉNÉRALES

Adresse de la Commission à Genève

Secrétariat

Salle de réunion

Adresse du site web

---

[13]Publication des Nations Unies, numéro de vente : E/F 97.V.4.

III

REPORT OF THE INTERNATIONAL LAW COMMISSION ON THE WORK OF ITS FORTY-EIGHTH SESSION*

Chapter VII

OTHER DECISIONS AND CONCLUSIONS OF THE COMMISSION

A. Programme, procedures and working methods of the Commission and its documentation

141. Having regard to paragraph 9 of General Assembly resolution 50/45 of 11 December 1995,[287] the Commission considered the matter under item 7 of its agenda entitled "Programme, procedures and working methods of the Commission and its documentation" and referred it to the Planning Group of the Enlarged Bureau.

142. The Planning Group held six meetings. It had before it the section of the topical summary of the discussion held in the Sixth Committee of the General Assembly during its fiftieth session, entitled "Other decisions and conclusions of the Commission".[288] Mr Hans Corell, Under-Secretary-General, the Legal Counsel, addressed the Planning Group at its second meeting.

1. PROCEDURES AND WORKING METHODS

143. The Planning Group established an informal working group[289] which discussed all the issues involved. It prepared a draft on the subject which constituted the basis for the report of the Planning Group.

144. At its 2459th to 2461st meetings from 12 to 16 July 1996, the Commission considered and endorsed the Planning Group's report.

PART I

SUMMARY AND PRINCIPAL CONCLUSIONS

The General Assembly's request

145. In 1995, the General Assembly requested the Commission "to examine the procedure of its work for the purpose of further enhancing its contribution to the progressive development and codification of international law and to include its views in its report to the General Assembly at its fifty-first session". It also sought comments from Governments on "the present state of the codification process within the United Nations system".

146. In response to the Assembly's request, Part II of this Report reviews the Commission's procedures and seeks to identify changes which might en-

---

*Official Records of the General Assembly, Fifty-first Session, Supplement No. 10 (A/51/10), pp. 196-230 and 328-334.

[287]See para. 150 below.

[288]Document A/CN.4/472/Add.1, paras. 175-190.

[289]It consisted of Mr J. Crawford (Convenor), Mr D. Bowett, Mr K. Idris, Mr A. Pellet and Mr S. Rao.

hance its usefulness and efficiency. Some of these changes the Commission itself can make; others will require the cooperation of other bodies, especially the Sixth Committee.

147. This Summary sets out the main conclusions and recommendations of the Report.

General conclusions and recommendations

Conclusions

148. To decide what methods will enhance the progressive development and codification of international law requires one to take a view of the present scope for progressive development and codification, after nearly 50 years of work by the Commission. On this question, the Commission reaches the following general conclusions.

(a) The distinction between codification and progressive development is difficult if not impossible to draw in practice; the Commission has proceeded on the basis of a composite idea of codification and progressive development. Distinctions drawn in its Statute between the two processes have proved unworkable and could be eliminated in any review of the Statute (paras. 157-160).

(b) Despite the many changes in international law and organization since 1949, there is important continuing value in an orderly process of codification and progressive development (paras. 168-171).

(c) There are a number of ways in which the Commission's work methods may be made more responsive and efficient, and the relationship with the Sixth Committee structured and enhanced (paras. 172-177).

Recommendations

149. For the reasons given in Part II, the Commission makes the following specific recommendations.

(a) Work should continue, following the procedure established by the Commission in 1992, to identify possible topics of future work to be recommended to the General Assembly (paras. 165-166).

(b) In parallel, the General Assembly—and through it other bodies within the United Nations system—should be encouraged to submit to the Commission possible topics involving codification and progressive development of international law (paras. 166, 178-179).

(c) The Commission should extend its practice of identifying issues on which comment is specifically sought from the Sixth Committee, where possible in advance of the adoption of draft articles on the point (para. 182).

(d) Questionnaires sent to Governments should be "user-friendly"; in particular they should provide clear indications of what is requested and why (para. 182).

(e) The Commission's report should be shorter, more thematic, and should make every attempt to highlight and explain key issues in order to assist in structuring debate on the report in the Sixth Committee (para. 182).

(f) Special Rapporteurs should be asked to specify the nature and scope of work planned for the next session (para. 190). Their reports should be available sufficiently in advance of the session at which they are to be considered (para. 191).

(g)   Special Rapporteurs should be asked to work with a consultative group of members; this system should also be extended to the second reading of State responsibility (paras. 192-196).

(h)   Special Rapporteurs should as far as possible produce draft commentaries or notes to accompany their draft articles, and should revise them in the light of changes made by the Drafting Committee, so that the commentaries are available at the time of the plenary debate (paras. 197-201).

(i)   The system of plenary debates in the Commission should be reformed to provide more structure and to allow for an indicative summary of conclusions by the Chairman at the end of the debate, based if necessary on an indicative vote (paras. 202-211).

(j)   The current system of different membership of the Drafting Committee for different topics should be maintained (para. 215).

(k)   Working groups should be more extensively used, both in an effort to resolve particular disagreements and, in appropriate cases, as an expeditious way of dealing with whole topics; in the latter case, the Working Group will normally act in place of the Drafting Committee (paras. 218-219).

(l)   The Commission should set and report to the General Assembly on its targets at the beginning of, and should review its future work programme at the end of, each quinquennium (para. 222).

(m)   The Commission should revert to the earlier practice of a session of 10 weeks, with the possibility of extension to 12 weeks as required, and especially during the last session of a quinquennium (para. 227).

(n)   The experiment of a split session should be tried in 1998 (paras. 228-233).

(o)   The contribution of the Secretariat to the Commission's work should be maintained and reinforced (paras. 234-235).

(p)   The International Law Seminar should be retained (para. 236).

(q)   Relations with other bodies such as the regional legal bodies should be more encouraged and developed (para. 240).

(r)   The Commission should seek to develop links with other United Nations specialized bodies with law-making responsibilities in their field, and should in particular explore the possibility of exchange of information and even of joint work on selected topics (para. 241).

(s)   Consideration should be given to the consolidation and updating of the Commission's Statute to coincide with the fiftieth anniversary of the Commission in 1999 (paras. 242-244).

PART II

DETAILED ANALYSIS

1.   *Introduction*

150.   By resolution 50/45 of 11 December 1995, the General Assembly, *inter alia*:

"9.   *Requests* the International Law Commission:

(a)   To examine the procedures of its work for the purpose of further enhancing its contribution to the progressive development and codification of international law and to include its views in its report to the General Assembly at its fifty-first session;

(b) To continue to pay special attention to indicating in its annual report for each topic those specific issues, if any, on which expressions of views by Governments, either in the Sixth Committee or in written form, would be of particular interest in providing effective guidance for the Commission in its further work;

10. *Requests* the Secretary-General to invite Governments to comment on the present state of the codification process within the United Nations system and to report thereon to the General Assembly at its fifty-first session . . .".

151. The Commission has kept its work methods under continuous review over the years and has introduced a number of changes.[290] But as the above paragraphs suggest, and as the debate on the Commission's report in the Sixth Committee in 1995 indicated,[291] there is a perceived need for a more comprehensive review of "the present state of the codification process within the United Nations system", and of the future role of the Commission within that process. In accordance with paragraph 9 of General Assembly resolution 50/45, the Commission is asked to examine its own procedures in that regard.

152. This report has been produced by the Commission[292] as part of the continuing consideration within the Commission of its work methods and procedures, and by way of response to the General Assembly's request in paragraph 9 of resolution 50/45. It seeks to identify any changes in the procedures of its work which might enhance the Commission's usefulness and efficiency.[293] As will be seen, some of these changes are within the Commission's power to make; others will require the initiative or cooperation of other bodies, and especially the Sixth Committee itself.

153. Discussion of the Commission's procedures needs to take into account a number of reforms adopted by the Commission in recent years as well as limitations imposed on its work by external factors. Rather than give a general account here, aspects of the Commission's work methods will be referred to in this report when necessary under each heading.

2. *The scope for continuing codification and progressive development*

154. Underlying the Assembly's request in paragraph 9 of General Assembly resolution 50/45 is the aim of "enhancing [the Commission's] contribu-

---

[290]For earlier discussions of work methods, see, for example, the debate recorded in *Yearbook of the International Law Commission, 1958*, vol. II, at pp. 107-110, based on a report by Mr Zourek (A/CN.4/108). During the current (1992-1996) quinquennium, the Commission has sought to streamline its annual report (*Yearbook of the International Law Commission, 1992*, vol. II (Part Two), p. 136), has revised the arrangements for the work of the drafting committee (ibid., pp. 135-136), has processed a major topic (the proposed international criminal court) within three sessions through the use of an ad hoc working group (for the final recommendation see ibid., *1994*, vol. II (Part Two), pp. 26-74) and has introduced a more orderly and comprehensive procedure for consideration of possible new topics.

[291]See the topical summary of the discussion held in the Sixth Committee of the General Assembly during its fiftieth session (document A/CN.4/472/Add.1), pp. 45-49.

[292]An initial draft was produced by a small working group, consisting of Mr Crawford (Convenor), Mr Bowett, Mr Idris, Mr Pellet and Mr Rao, and was revised by that working group to reflect discussion in the Planning Group.

[293]A number of these changes have been introduced in practice in the current quinquennium (see footnote 290 above).

tion to the progressive development and codification of international law". To determine what procedures of work will best achieve that result requires one to take a view as to the present scope for progressive development and codification, after nearly 50 years of work by the Commission.

155. The Commission was established by General Assembly resolution 174 (II) of 21 November 1947,[294] and held its first session, lasting nearly nine weeks, in 1949. There was a substantial body of opinion at the time in favour of a full-time Commission.

156. The object of the Commission is "the promotion of the progressive development of international law and its codification" (article 1 (1) of its Statute); its focus is to be "primarily" public international law, although it is not precluded from entering the field of private international law (article 1 (2) of its Statute). In recent years, the Commission has not so entered, except incidentally and in the course of work on subjects of public international law; moreover, having regard to the work of bodies such as UNCITRAL and the Hague Conference on Private International Law, it may seem unlikely that it will be called on to do so.

(a) *The "distinction" between codification and progressive development*

157. Article 1 of the Statute draws a distinction between "progressive development of international law" and "its codification". That distinction is further developed in article 15, where the idea of "progressive development" is ("for convenience") associated with the preparation of draft conventions, while the idea of codification of international law is associated with "the more precise formulation and systematization of rules of international law in fields where there already has been extensive State practice, precedent and doctrine". As is well known, however, the distinction between codification and progressive development is difficult if not impossible to draw in practice, especially when one descends to the detail which is necessary in order to give more precise effect to a principle.[295] Moreover, it is too simple to suggest that progressive development, as distinct from codification, is particularly associated with the drafting of conventions. Flexibility is necessary in the range of cases and for a range of reasons.

158. Thus the Commission has inevitably proceeded on the basis of a composite idea of "codification and progressive development". In other words, its work has involved the elaboration of multilateral texts on general subjects of concern to all or many States, such texts seeking both to reflect accepted principles of regulation, and to provide such detail, particularity and further development of the ideas as may be required.

(b) *The selection of topics for the Commission's work*

159. A further aspect of the distinction drawn in the Statute between codification and progressive development relates to the selection of topics for work by the Commission. The Statute implies that the initiative for considering

---

[294]The Statute has been amended on six occasions, most recently by General Assembly resolution 36/39 of 18 November 1981, which enlarged the number of members from 18 to 34.

[295]See, for example: Briggs, H.W., *The International Law Commission* (1965), pp. 129-141; Rosenne, S., *Practice and Methods of the International Law Commission* (1984), pp. 73-74; Sinclair, Sir I., *The International Law Commission* (1987), pp. 46-47 and 120-126; and Ago, "*Nouvelles réflexions sur la codification du droit international*", *Revue générale de droit international public*, vol. 92 (1988), p. 539. See also Daudet, Y., *Les conférences des Nations Unies pour la codification du droit international* (1968).

proposals for progressive development will emanate from the General Assembly (article 16) or other bodies (article 17), whereas it is for the Commission itself to select topics for codification which it may recommend to the General Assembly (article 18 (1), (2)).[296] Article 18 (1) provides that:

> "The Commission shall survey the whole field of international law with a view to selecting topics for codification, having in mind existing drafts whether governmental or not."

160.   In practice the procedure for considering most of the subjects which the Commission has taken up has been much the same, whether or not the aspect of progressive development or codification might have been thought to predominate. Since 1970, most of the suggestions for future work have emanated from the Commission, although it was the General Assembly which, for example, reactivated the Code of Crimes against the Peace and Security of Mankind in 1981,[297] and which requested the Commission to study the feasibility of an International Criminal Court.[298] It should be stressed that the Commission has always sought the endorsement of the Assembly before engaging in detailed work on any project.

161.   The survey of "the whole field of international law" for which article 18 (1) of the Statute called was initially carried out on the basis of a Secretariat memorandum, in fact produced by Professor Hersch Lauterpacht, later a member of the Commission.[299] That memorandum reviewed, and the Commission considered, 25 topics, of which the Commission drew up a "provisional list of 14 topics selected for codification".[300] A number of these topics were chosen for initial work.

162.   As at 1996, of the 14 topics which were initially and provisionally selected, 9 have been treated by the Commission, in whole or substantial part.[301]

---

[296]On the other hand, the General Assembly may request the Commission to work on any question of codification, and such requests are to have priority (article 18 (3)).

[297]General Assembly resolution 36/106 of 10 December 1981.

[298]General Assembly resolution 45/41 of 28 November 1990 at para. 3; and General Assembly resolution 46/54 of 9 December 1991.

[299]Document A/CN.4/1/Rev.1; reprinted in Lauterpacht, E. (ed.), *The Collected Papers of Sir Hersch Lauterpacht*, vol. I (1970), p. 445.

[300]*Yearbook of the International Law Commission, 1949*, p. 281.

[301]These topics are as follows (with indications of the eventual outcome of the work):

   (a)   Succession of States and Governments (substantial areas of succession of States have been dealt with by the Commission, leading to the Vienna Conventions of 1978 and 1983; one area, succession with respect to nationality, is newly under consideration. It has never been actively proposed to study succession of Governments, no doubt because, in the light of the virtually uniform practice of continuity of State obligations despite changes of Government there is very little to say);

   (b)   Jurisdictional immunities of States and their property (Draft Articles produced in 1991 but consideration of them deferred by the General Assembly in 1994 for 3-4 years);

   (c)   Regime of the high seas (Geneva Convention on the High Seas of 1958) and Regime of territorial waters (Geneva Convention on the Territorial Sea and the Contiguous Zone of 1958). In fact the Commission also developed draft articles on Fisheries and conservation of the living resources of the high seas and on the Continental shelf (leading to the two further Geneva Conventions of 1958 on these subjects);

   (d)   Nationality, including statelessness (two draft conventions on the elimination / reduction of future Statelessness, leading to the adoption of the Convention on the Reduction of Statelessness of 1961);

   (e)   Law of treaties (Vienna Convention on the Law of Treaties of 1969; Vienna Convention on the Law of Treaties between States and International Organizations or between International Organizations of 1986);

   (f)   Diplomatic intercourse and immunities (Vienna Convention on Diplomatic Relations of 1961);

   (g)   Consular intercourse and immunities (Vienna Convention on Consular Relations of 1963);

   (h)   Arbitral procedure (Model Rules on Arbitral Procedure of 1958).

Of the remaining five, one was taken up without success, was then set aside, but has recently been proposed by the Commission for renewed partial treatment under the heading of Diplomatic protection;[302] one (State responsibility) is still under consideration;[303] and three have never been taken up.[304]

163.   Additional topics were added to the work programme in a number of ways. Especially in the early years of the Commission, a number of matters were specially referred to it by the General Assembly. In total, 16 such requests or recommendations have been made by the General Assembly, but of these no fewer than 7 requests were made in the very early years of the Commission.

164.   From 1971 to 1972, the Commission undertook a further and rather thorough review of its work, based on a series of Secretariat papers.[305] The conclusions reached were modest: work would continue on the main topics then under consideration, and at the request of the General Assembly the topic of non-navigational uses of international watercourses was added.[306]

165.   In 1992, the Commission embarked upon a more rigorous procedure for the selection of topics.[307] A Working Group provisionally identified 12 topics as possible subjects of later work, and individual members of the Commission were asked to write a short synopsis outlining the nature of the topic, the subject matter to be covered, and the extent to which the topic had already been dealt with in treaties or in private codification projects by bodies such as the International Law Association or the Institut de Droit International. These synopses were published,[308] and it was on the basis of the synopses that the Commission recommended in 1993—and the General Assembly agreed—that work should begin on Reservations to treaties and on Succession of States as regards the nationality of natural and legal persons.[309]

166.   The Commission believes this method of selection to be an improvement. Undertaking any new topic involves a measure of uncertainty and requires a degree of judgement: the uncertainty is reduced, and judgement is assisted, if

---

[302]*Viz.* Treatment of aliens. See the reports by Mr H. Garcia Amador: ibid., *1958*, vol. II, pp. 47-73; ibid., *1959*, vol. II, pp. 1-37; ibid., *1960*, vol. II, pp. 41-67; and ibid., *1961*, vol. II, pp. 1-54.

[303]The Commission decided in 1963 to study the general or "secondary" rules of responsibility: ibid., *1963*, vol. II, p. 224. Detailed work did not begin until 1969 and has continued, under successive Special Rapporteurs (Ago, Riphagen, Arangio-Ruiz), until the present session, when it is expected that the first reading of the complete draft articles will be completed.

[304]*Viz.* Recognition of States and Governments; Jurisdiction with regard to crimes committed outside national territory; and Right of Asylum. As to the second of these, the related topic of civil jurisdiction over matters occurring beyond the forum State was not included on the 1949 list—indeed it was hardly recognizable in the longer list from which that list was drawn. See ibid., *1949*, at p. 281.

[305]See: ibid., *1969*, vol. II, pp. 234-235; ibid., *1970*, vol. II, pp. 247-269; and ibid., *1971*, vol. II (Part Two), pp. 1-99. For the Commission's discussion and conclusions, see: ibid., *1971*, vol. II (Part One), pp. 350-351; ibid., *1972*, vol. II, pp. 205-214; and ibid., *1973*, vol. II, pp. 225-231. An earlier review had been carried out in 1962 (ibid., *1962*, vol. II, pp. 84 and 190), when the Commission had declined to add new topics to an already heavy load.

[306]See: ibid., *1973*, vol. II, pp. 230-231; and General Assembly resolution 2780 (XXVI) of 3 December 1971. The second reading of the Draft Articles on the Law of the Non-Navigational Uses of International Watercourses was completed in 1994. See *Yearbook of the International Law Commission, 1994*, vol. II (Part Two), pp. 88-135.

[307]Ibid., *1992*, vol. II (Part Two), p. 54.

[308]Document A/CN.4/454.

[309]*Yearbook of the International Law Commission, 1993*, vol. II (Part Two), pp. 95-97. In 1995, the topic of Diplomatic protection was selected for a feasibility study without prior elaboration through the preparation of a synopsis. See Report of the International Law Commission on the work of its forty-seventh session, *Official Records of the General Assembly, Fiftieth Session, Supplement No. 10* (A/50/10), p. 264. General Assembly resolution A/50/45 of 11 December 1995 noted this "suggestion" in its eighth paragraph and invited Governments to submit comments on it.

the selection is made only after careful consideration on the basis of work which does not commit the Commission either to the topic or to the selection of any particular manner of treatment of it. At the same time, the General Assembly—and, through it, other bodies within the United Nations system—should be encouraged to submit to the Commission possible topics involving codification and progressive development of international law. The Commission's agenda should desirably include both topics referred to it and those generated by it, and approved by the General Assembly, through the procedure described above.

167.   A Working Group on the long-term programme of work, set up by the Commission, established a general scheme of topics of international law which included topics already taken up by the Commission, topics under consideration by the Commission and possible future topics (see Annex II).

(c)   *Codification and progressive development after 50 years*

168.   It was generally accepted after 1945 that international law was in many respects uncertain and undeveloped, and in need both of codification and progressive development. The simple idea that it would be possible, or even desirable, to express the whole of international law in a single "code" was soon dismissed.[310] Quite apart from other considerations, the drafting of such a code would have been a Napoleonic task. But the fruits of long-term codification and progressive development can be seen in such areas as, for example, the law of treaties, diplomatic and consular relations, and the law of the sea.[311] The applicable international rules in each of these fields are contained in texts which constitute the basic starting point for any legal consideration which may arise. This marks a clear advance in inter-State relations. It shows the continued value of an orderly process of "codification and progressive development".

169.   On the other hand, there have been many changes in inter-State relations and international institutions in the past 50 years, which potentially affect the work which it may be useful for the Commission to undertake. Relevant changes include:

(i)   The technical and administrative character of many new legal issues;

(ii)   A tendency to treat certain legal questions on a regional basis (for example, some environmental issues) or even on a bilateral basis (for example, investment protection);

(iii)   The proliferation of bodies with special law-making mandates (whether permanent bodies such as UNCITRAL or the Legal Sub-Committee of the Committee on Peaceful Uses of Outer Space or ad hoc bodies such as the Third United Nations Conference on the Law of the Sea) or with primary institutional competence in a given field (the Human Rights Commission, the Human Rights Committee, United Nations Environmental Programme, World Trade Organization, etc.);

(iv)   The work of United Nations specialized agencies in general (International Maritime Organization, International Civil Aviation Organization, etc.).

---

[310]See *Yearbook of the International Law Commission, 1973*, vol. II, pp. 227-228 at paras. 152-158.

[311]Although the governing instrument is now the United Nations Convention on the Law of the Sea of 1982, in key respects—especially concerning the territorial sea and the high seas—it incorporates the provisions of the Conventions of 1958.

170.   These factors do not all work in the same direction. The scope for the Commission to work without duplicating the work of other bodies is reduced with the proliferation of agencies with specific responsibility for particular fields of law or practice. On the other hand, there is scope for collaboration with such agencies in developing areas of international law which are of general as well as of specialized interest. The tendency to treat particular problems bilaterally may be a response to perceived deficiencies in the general law, deficiencies which ought none the less to be addressed. There is, overall, a risk of fragmentation in international law and practice, which the Commission, with its general mandate and vocation, can help to counteract.

171.   Thus, while it is true that many of the major topics traditionally identified as ripe for codification—for example, the law of the sea, treaties, diplomatic and consular relations—have been completed, the idea that codification is no longer necessary is misplaced. Even in relation to areas now covered by treaty, practice may develop and raise new difficulties requiring further consideration—as, for example, with reservations to treaties. At the international level, codification and progressive development is a continuing process. Moreover, the pace of development of international law is now rapid and the fact is that private bodies which study current problems, such as the International Law Association and the Institut de Droit International, seem to have no difficulty in identifying areas of law requiring, if not codification, then clarification, development and articulation. What the private bodies lack is the ability which the Commission as a body within the United Nations system has to obtain information from and engage in dialogue with Governments. This it can do through the Sixth Committee, through requests to Governments for information and comment, and through the Commission's direct links with regional consultative committees. So long as the process of liaison and dialogue is effective, the need for a body like the Commission is likely to continue.

172.   On the other hand, difficulties have emerged with the Commission's work, even in relation to the *first* generation of projects. For various reasons, some major topics on the Commission's agenda have taken a very long time to complete. These reasons include the importance, size and difficulty of the subjects in question. But none the less this has had the effect of slowing the Commission's progress on other topics on its agenda and of creating doubts as to the desirability of the Commission taking on new work while old work remained incomplete.

173.   In the view of the Commission, a number of changes to its work methods are desirable to cope with the present situation. The remaining sections of this report are devoted to the question of what changes should be made, under the following headings:

(i)   The relations between the Commission and the General Assembly (Sixth Committee) (section 3);

(ii)   The role of the Special Rapporteur (section 4);

(iii) The relations between the Commission, its Drafting Committee and working groups (section 5);

(iv)   The length and structure of sessions (section 6);

(v)   The Commission's relations with other bodies (section 7);

(vi)   Possible revision of the Statute (section 8).

3. The relations between the Commission and the General Assembly (Sixth Committee)

174.   This matter was specifically referred to by the General Assembly in preambular paragraph 7 of its resolution 50/45, which referred to the need . . .

"to enhance further the interaction between the Sixth Committee as a body of government representatives and the International Law Commission as a body of independent legal experts, with a view to improving the dialogue between the two organs".

While succinctly restating the character of the two bodies, this paragraph clearly implies that the dialogue between them could be improved.

175.   Under article 3 of its Statute, members of the Commission are elected by the General Assembly, from candidates nominated by Governments of United Nations Member States. The electors are enjoined to "bear in mind that the persons to be elected to the Commission should individually possess the qualifications required and that in the Commission as a whole representation of the main forms of civilization and of the principal legal systems of the world should be assured" (article 8 of the Statute). The existence of regional groups for the purposes of election is expressly recognized in the Statute as a result of the 1981 amendment (article 9), and this assists in assuring the representativeness of the Commission as a whole. On the other hand, there is a healthy tradition within the Commission, which fully complies with the independent status of its members, that all members participate as individuals and that they are in no sense "representatives".[312]

176.   As to individual qualifications, article 2 (1) requires that members "shall be persons of recognized competence in international law". Members are eligible for re-election without restriction (article 10 of the Statute); there is no age limit. It may be noted that there has never been a woman member of the Commission.

177.   Against this background, the Commission turns to the substantive issues involved in the "interaction between the Sixth Committee as a body of government representatives and the International Law Commission as a body of independent legal experts".

(a) Initiation of work on specified topics

178.   One important way in which new tasks can be generated for the Commission is in response to requests from the General Assembly or other United Nations organs. This is expressly envisaged in articles 16 and 18 (3) of the Statute, but in recent years these provisions have been little used; nor has the debate associated with the "Decade of International Law" seen the development of new ideas for inclusion in the Commission's agenda by the Sixth Committee. As the Commission demonstrated in its work on the subject of protection and inviolability of diplomatic agents and other persons entitled to special protection under international law[313] and, more recently, on the Draft Statute for an International Criminal Court,[314] it is capable of responding promptly to such requests. Its response may involve the provision of commentary or advice, or

---

[312]The Statute itself is silent on the subject.

[313]This request came from the Security Council *via* the General Assembly. See document A/9407 and General Assembly resolution 3166 (XXVIII) of 14 December 1973. See also *Yearbook of the International Law Commission, 1972*, vol. II, p. 312.

[314]See General Assembly resolution 45/41 of 28 November 1990 (para. 3).

(as in the two cases mentioned) the preparation of draft articles in a form appropriate for adoption at a diplomatic conference.

179.   In the view of the Commission, the Commission's workload should desirably include both topics generated within the Commission and approved by the General Assembly, and topics generated elsewhere within the United Nations system and specifically referred to the Commission by the General Assembly under the Statute. Such requests may avoid duplication and encourage coordination in the international law-making effort. Of course, topics referred should be appropriate to the Commission as "a body of independent legal experts" in the field of general international law.

(b)   Review and commentary on work in progress

180.   Discussion and feedback on the Commission's work by States takes a variety of forms. Especially in the early stages of work on a topic, States are asked to provide information about their practice and legislation, and to respond to a questionnaire. Representatives of Member States within the Sixth Committee provide oral comments on the Commission's annual report, and the discussion of the report in the Sixth Committee is now helpfully subdivided so as to focus on the various components of the report. In addition, States are asked to provide formal written comments in response to particular requests made by the Commission in its report and on the draft articles as adopted on first reading on any topic.

181.   There is, however, considerable variation in the extent to which Governments provide information and comment on the Commission's reports and drafts. Governments may be content to allow work on a topic to develop, or being generally able to accept the lines of work may feel no need to comment. Others may wish to change the direction of particular work and may therefore be more vocal. Many Governments, especially those of developing countries, have very limited resources to devote to the task. None the less the fact remains that in many cases requests by the Commission for comments, or even for information, go unanswered.[315] Interaction between the Commission and Governments is vital to the Commission's role, and there is scope for improvement on both sides.

---

[315]The numbers of written responses by Government to Commission's questionnaires on some recent topics have been as follows:

State responsibility:	15	(Yearbook of the International Law Commission, 1980, vol. II (Part One), p. 153;
		(ibid., 1981, vol. II (Part One), p. 71)
Watercourses:	21	(document A/CN.4/447 and Add.1-3)
Draft code of crimes:	13	(Yearbook of the International Law Commission, 1985, vol. II (Part One), p. 84;
		(ibid., 1987, vol. II (Part One), p. 11;
		(ibid., 1990, vol. II (Part One), p. 23)
Immunity of States:	28	(ibid., 1988, vol. II (Part One), p. 45)
Diplomatic bag:	30	(ibid., p. 121;
		(ibid., 1989, vol. II (Part One), p. 75)
Treaty reservations:	13	(as at 5 June 1996).

182. For its part the Commission believes that it should strive to extend its practice of identifying issues on which comment is specifically sought, if possible in advance of the adoption of draft articles on the point. These issues should be of a more general, "strategic" character rather than relate to issues of drafting technique. The Commission should strive to ensure that the report and any questionnaires sent to Governments are more "user-friendly" and that they provide clear indications of what is requested and why. In particular, the Commission's report should be shorter, more thematic, and should make every attempt to highlight and explain key issues. The role of the General Rapporteur in the preparation of the report should be enhanced.[316] The Commission should return to those issues in the new quinquennium.

(c) *The Sixth Committee's role in dealing with final drafts of the Commission*

183. The task of the Commission in relation to a given topic is completed when it presents a completed set of draft articles on that topic to the Sixth Committee. The purpose of the Commission is—it is believed—fully performed if the draft articles and accompanying commentary articulate the relevant principles in a manner generally suitable for adoption by States. On the other hand, whether a particular set of draft articles is acceptable or appropriate for adoption at a given time is essentially a matter of policy for the Sixth Committee and for Member States.

184. The response to a set of draft articles or other work of the Commission can take a variety of forms. In transmitting its work the Commission will itself make an initial recommendation on the point,[317] but the choice of means is a matter for the Sixth Committee. In the case of a text which is not recommended for adoption as a convention, a less extended procedure of noting or incorporation in a General Assembly resolution may be all that is required. In the case of draft articles which could form the basis for a convention, the Sixth Committee can merely note the outcome, can deal with it in a preliminary way through a working group or convene a preparatory conference for a similar purpose, can convene a diplomatic conference forthwith, or (as with the Draft Articles on the Law of the Non-navigational Uses of International Watercourses, currently under consideration) can elect to deal with the draft articles itself. Article 23 (2) of the Statute also contemplates that the Assembly "may refer drafts back to the Commission for reconsideration or redrafting". This possibility might be more effectively used.

185. The Commission would simply note that if there are serious doubts about the acceptability of *any* text on a given subject, it would be helpful if these were made known authoritatively by the General Assembly and Governments at an earlier stage, rather than being postponed or the difficulties shelved until after the Commission has completed its work and presented it to the Sixth Committee.

4. *The role of the Special Rapporteur*

(a) *Appointment*

186. Central to the working of the Commission has been the role of the Special Rapporteur. In fact, the Statute only expressly envisages such an appointment in the case of projects for progressive development (article 16

---

[316]See document A/CN.4/L.473, p. 7.
[317]Article 23 of the Statute.

(a)).[318] But from the very first, the practice of the Commission has been to appoint a Special Rapporteur very early in the consideration of a project and to do so without regard to whether the project might be classified as one of codification or progressive development.[319]

187. In practice, rapporteurships tend to be distributed among members from different regions. This system, provided that it is applied with some flexibility, has many advantages, in particular in that it helps to ensure that different approaches and different legal cultures are brought to bear in the formulation of reports and proposals.

188. It should be stressed that difficulties which have been experienced in the Commission's work have largely been due not to the appointment of a Special Rapporteur for a topic but to the fact that Special Rapporteurs have tended, or even been expected, to operate in isolation from the Commission, with little guidance during the preparation of reports on the direction of future work. It is to this essential point, as the Commission identifies it, that the following paragraphs are largely directed.

(b)   *Elaboration of reports*

189. It is through the preparation of (usually annual) reports that Special Rapporteurs mark out and develop their topic, explain the state of the law and make proposals for draft articles. A number of issues arise with respect to the preparation of reports.

(i)   *Need for prior approval by the Commission of the nature and scope of work planned for the next session*

190. Present practice in the Commission is not uniform. Some Rapporteurs disclose in fair detail the kind of report they have in mind to present to the next session; others do not. On balance, and whilst conceding the need for Rapporteurs to enjoy a certain independence, disclosure ought to be the rule. It is essential that future reports should meet the needs of the Commission as a whole. Disclosure gives the possibility of feedback, both on matters of general direction and on particular points of substance. By contrast a report which treats an issue which the Commission regards as peripheral, or which fails to treat an issue which the Commission regards as central, will mean in effect that a session has been wasted.

(ii)   *Availability of reports before the beginning of the session*

191. Here again present practice is not uniform. Some reports are circulated in advance of the session, some are not. Delays in translation and circulation due to financial constraints on the United Nations or to its rules for documentation are, of course, beyond the control of a Special Rapporteur.[320] But it is highly desirable that all reports should be available to Commission

---

[318]Article 16 of the Statute qualifies this requirement with the words "in general", but the Rapporteur is clearly considered as central to the process laid down (for example, in subparagraphs (*d*), (*f*) and (*i*)).

[319]See, for example, *Yearbook of the International Law Commission, 1949*, at p. 281 (initial appointment of Rapporteurs for the topics law of treaties, arbitral procedure and regime of the high seas). The Commission at the same time sought data from Governments under article 19 (2) of the Statute, which is formally applicable only to codification projects: ibid.

[320]It may be noted that the deadline for responses to questionnaires, available the previous September, is often set very late—for example, in March or April of the following year—making it difficult for Special Rapporteurs to take the responses fully into account in their reports of that year.

members some weeks before the commencement of the session, to enable study and reflection. This would be even more the case with a shorter session.

(c)   *Need for a standing consultative group*

192.   Article 16 (*d*) of the Statute envisages that "where the General Assembly refers to the Commission a proposal for the progressive development of international law", the Commission may "appoint some of its members to work with the Rapporteur on the preparation of drafts pending receipt of replies" to the questionnaire circulated to Governments. This may imply that, furnished with replies, the Special Rapporteur is thereafter to work independently. But in most cases the practice has been for the Special Rapporteur to work largely in isolation in preparing reports. In other words, in the period between sessions a Special Rapporteur has no formal contact with other members of the Commission.

193.   Other bodies, such as the International Law Association and the Institut de Droit International, work differently. Various members are chosen to act as a consultative group so that, between sessions, the Rapporteur may consult over the best and most acceptable approach to be taken, and over the essential elements to the next report. Through questionnaires, the circulation of reports or exceptionally the holding of interim meetings, the group's advice is available. Although the report remains that of the Rapporteur, it is likely that the input obtained will ensure that it is acceptable to the membership of the committee and by extension to the membership of the body as a whole.

194.   The Commission notes that this method has been fruitfully employed in relation to the recent topic of State succession with respect to nationality. It believes that the method should be generally adopted, especially in so far as new projects are concerned, and especially in relation to the early work, including the strategic planning, on a subject. The consultative group should be appointed by the Commission itself and should be broadly representative.[321]

195.   No doubt care should be taken not to over-formalize matters, and it should be stressed that the report will remain the responsibility of the Special Rapporteur, rather than of the group as a whole. It is not the function of the group to approve the Special Rapporteur's report, but to provide input on its general direction and on any particular issues the Special Rapporteur wishes to raise. Whether the group is appointed for the duration of the quinquennium, or for some shorter period, can be determined on a case-by-case basis, in consultation with the Special Rapporteur.

196.   Although these changes can be implemented without any amendment to the Statute, the Commission also recommends that in any revision of the Statute the principle of such a group should be recognized. Unlike the present Statute (see para. 186 above), this should be done without any distinction being drawn between codification and progressive development.

(d)   *Preparation of commentaries to draft articles*

197.   There is a distinction between a report which analyses the area of law and practice under study, and a focused commentary on draft articles. The preparation of the former is, of course, a key task of a Special Rapporteur, but

---

[321] It could also be adopted in the second reading of State responsibility, which it is very desirable should be completed within the forthcoming quinquennium.

so too is the latter. At present, it is not unusual for draft articles to be referred to the Drafting Committee without commentaries having been prepared contrary to the earlier practice of the Commission. Indeed, draft articles are sometimes presented for final consideration by the Commission without commentaries, and the commentaries are only adopted, with little time for consideration, in the last stages of a session.

198.   It can be argued that, since the draft articles are likely to be changed substantially in the Drafting Committee, the provision of commentaries by a Special Rapporteur in advance is premature. On the other hand, the Drafting Committee is in a much better position if it has available to it at the same time both draft articles and commentaries (or at least an outline of what the commentaries will contain). The commentaries help to explain the purpose of the draft articles and to clarify their scope and effect. It often happens that disagreement over some aspect of a draft can be resolved by the provision of additional commentary, or by the transfer of some provision from text to commentary or vice versa. The provision of articles alone precludes such flexibility, and may give the inclusion of some element in the text more importance than it deserves. Simultaneous work on text and commentary can enhance the acceptability of both. It may help avoid the undesirable practice of inserting examples in the text of an article—as is presently the case with draft article 19 (3) of Part One of State Responsibility. It will also form a valuable part of the *travaux préparatoires* of any treaty provision which may be adopted on the basis of the proposed text.

199.   It should be stressed that commentaries in their final form are intended primarily as explanations of the text as finally adopted. Although an account of the evolution of that text is appropriate, the main function of a commentary is to explain the text itself, with appropriate references to key decisions, doctrine and State practice, so that the reader can see the extent to which the Commission's text reflects or, as the case may be, develops or extends the law. Generally speaking, it is not the function of such commentaries to reflect disagreements on the text as adopted on second reading; this can be done in plenary at the time of final adoption of the text and appropriately reflected in the report.[322]

200.   Given the pressure of work on it, the Drafting Committee itself cannot be expected to produce revised commentaries. But, as soon as the Drafting Committee has approved a particular article, the commentary to that article should be prepared or, as the case may be, revised by the Special Rapporteur, with the assistance of the Secretariat. It should then be circulated either to members of the Drafting Committee or (as appropriate) to the members of the consultative group for the topic, to enable them to comment individually on it. As the Statute makes clear,[323] draft articles should not be considered finally adopted without the Commission having approved the commentaries before it.

---

[322]The position is rather different at first reading. Article 20 (*c*) (ii) of the Statute (which, however, deals with codification as distinct from progressive development) provides that the commentaries on texts adopted at first reading should indicate "divergencies and disagreements which exist, as well as arguments invoked in favour of one or another solution". But the Statute contains no such indication with respect to final draft articles: see article 22.

[323]Article 16 (*i*) of the Statute provides that "[t]he Rapporteur and the members appointed for that purpose . . . shall prepare a final draft and explanatory report which they shall submit for consideration and adoption by the Commission". To similar effect, see article 22.

(e) *The Special Rapporteur's role within the Drafting Committee*

201.   In practice it is in the Drafting Committee that divergent views on a topic are most clearly expressed and have to be reconciled; it is, equally, here that the independent role of the Special Rapporteur has to be accommodated with the range of views within the Commission. The demands of particular topics, and the approach of particular Special Rapporteurs, will always produce some diversity of practice. But as a general rule the Planning Group suggests that the role of the Special Rapporteur should comprise the following elements:

(i)   To produce clear and complete articles, as far as possible accompanied either by commentaries or by notes which could form the basis for commentaries;

(ii)   To explain, succinctly, the rationale behind the draft articles currently before the Drafting Committee, including any changes that may be indicated;

(iii)   In the final analysis, to accept the view of the Drafting Committee as a whole, even if it is contrary to the views advanced by the Special Rapporteur, and, as necessary, to reflect the view of the Drafting Committee in revised articles and/or commentary. In performing this function, the Special Rapporteur should act as servant of the Commission rather than defender of any personal views *avant la lettre*.

202.   Of course, a Special Rapporteur who disagrees with the eventual views of the Drafting Committee has every right to explain the disagreement in plenary when the report of the Drafting Committee is presented. It is open to the plenary to prefer the views of the Special Rapporteur to those of the Drafting Committee in such a case. Having regard to the size of the Drafting Committee and to its role *vis-à-vis* the plenary, however, there are likely to be few such cases. Moreover, it is better for major disagreements which cannot be resolved in the Drafting Committee to be reported at an earlier stage to the plenary, with the possibility of an indicative vote to settle the matter (see below, paras. 203-205).

5. *The role and relationships of the plenary to the Drafting Committee and Working Groups*

(a) *General debates in plenary*

203.   The primary role of the general debate in plenary is to establish the broad approach of the Commission to a topic. This is essential if the Drafting Committee, or a working group, is to undertake its task with confidence. Such subsidiary organs need to be sure that they are working along lines broadly acceptable to the Commission as a whole.

204.   Plenary debates at present do not serve this purpose very well, and there are two main reasons for this. The first is that the plenary debate tends to be too general, covering the whole of a perhaps lengthy report without distinction between various issues and sometimes descending to particular textual points which would be better dealt with in the Drafting Committee.

205.   A second factor is a tendency to make lengthy speeches, as if the Commission were a lecture audience, to be instructed rather than persuaded. Long speeches are not the ideal form of debate, which becomes diffuse and

ceases to serve its primary purpose of giving guidance to the Commission, its committees and Special Rapporteurs on directions to be taken.

206. In the early days of the Commission speeches were almost invariably short and focused on particular issues which may have given rise to difficulty or disagreement. In the Commission's view this is much the better practice, and the Commission should take steps to reinstate it as the norm.

207. Possible remedies include the following:

(i) First, an attempt should be made to provide a structure for the debate so that the Commission moves from point to point, with observations being restricted to the point under discussion.[324]

(ii) Secondly, members should exercise restraint. The best way to achieve this, in the view of the Planning Group, is by the proper structuring of debate. In addition, an informal "code of conduct" might be adopted favouring shorter interventions: the Chairman could call attention to this from time to time, if required.

(iii) Thirdly, at the conclusion of the debate, the Chairman should attempt a summary of the Commission's broad conclusions on the point, at the same time noting any disagreement that may have been expressed.[325] No doubt this may sometimes be a difficult task, but if carefully performed, and if generally accepted as accurate by members, it will substantially assist the Drafting Committee or working group in their subsequent consideration of the issues. In the consideration of final drafts of articles, the function should be performed by the Chairman of the Drafting Committee, in conjunction with the Special Rapporteur.

208. This leads to consideration of the method of voting. At present, the Commission and its subsidiary bodies attempt to reach consensus and there is no doubt that as a general rule this is right.

209. But there is a difference between the adoption of decisions which are effectively final and the type of conclusions we suggest the Chairman should express in concluding a plenary debate. These would be provisional and tentative; they would be for guidance only, as much would remain to be done before final decisions could be taken. On particular points which may be controversial, there is much to be said for the Chairman testing the acceptability of his conclusions by calling for an indicative vote. Even more so on points of detail, where it is better to resolve the issue, one way or another, and move on. Minority views can of course be reflected in the summary records and in the Commission's report.

210. Analogous situations will arise in subsidiary bodies such as the Drafting Committee. As work progresses, "decisions" need to be taken which are far from final, and it is burdensome and time-consuming to demand a consensus on all such matters. Members not in a majority in relation to an indicative vote would remain free to maintain their views at a later stage. However if there is a major disagreement on a point of principle, it may be

---

[324]This technique was usefully adopted in the discussion of Mr Thiam's Ninth Report on the Code of Crimes: *Yearbook of the International Law Commission, 1991*, vol. I, pp. 5-50.

[325]At present, this task, if performed at all, is performed by the Special Rapporteur. It might be better performed by the Chairman, leaving the Special Rapporteur as the author of the report under discussion to provide clarifications, and counter-arguments in response to comments.

appropriate that this be referred to the plenary for decision by an indicative vote or other means.

211.   When decisions ultimately come to be taken, again every effort should be made to reach a consensus, but if this is not possible in the time available, a vote may have to be taken, perhaps after a "cooling-off period" to allow time for discussion and reflection. Such a vote may be a better indication of the opinion of the Commission than a "false consensus" adopted simply in order to save time.

212.   One minor change which could usefully be introduced is to establish a convention that any congratulatory or honorific statements that may be called for should come from the Chairman alone, speaking on behalf of the whole Commission. The time of the Commission should be spent on the substance of its work.

(b)   *The Drafting Committee*

213.   In 1958, the Commission formally recognized that the Drafting Committee was "a committee to which could be referred not merely pure drafting points, but also points of substance which the full Commission had been unable to resolve, or which seemed likely to give rise to unduly protracted discussion".[326] The need for the Drafting Committee to fulfil that role was accentuated with the further increase in the Commission's membership in 1981, and there can be no doubt that such a role continues to be vital.

214.   This is not to say that the Drafting Committee should be the *only* body to perform that role. It will often be appropriate for issues on which there is an identified disagreement of principle to be referred to a smaller working group for discussion. Even if the point cannot be resolved by that group, the main lines of disagreement can usually be articulated and presented to the plenary in a form which allows a decision to be made, or an indicative vote taken. But in many other cases, issues of a lesser character will arise, or unforeseen points of principle emerge in the course of drafting, and inevitably the Drafting Committee will have the task of seeking to resolve these.

215.   Membership of the Drafting Committee is burdensome: it meets on most days, and sometimes both mornings and afternoons. For this reason the recent practice of having Drafting Committees of largely different composition for different topics is to be welcomed, since it shares the burden between more members.[327]

216.   On any given topic the Drafting Committee will usually consist of between 12 and 14 members (with other members sitting as observers, and only occasionally speaking). This has the advantage that a consensus in the Drafting Committee is likely to attract substantial support in plenary.

217.   Long statements are rare (and are to be discouraged). There is often a genuine debate. Discussion is predominantly in English and French, coinciding with the working language of the text under discussion, but members are free to use other official languages. In general the Drafting Committee works well.

---

[326]See *Yearbook of the International Law Commission, 1958*, vol. II, p. 108.
[327]The practice was introduced in 1992: see ibid., *1992*, vol. II (Part Two), p. 54.

(c) *Working Groups*

218. Working groups have been established by the Commission or by the Planning Group for different purposes and with different mandates. For example, it is usual to establish a working group on a new topic prior to the appointment of a Special Rapporteur, to help define the scope and direction of work. Another kind of group has the function of addressing and if possible resolving particular deadlocks.[328] In addition, working groups have sometimes been formed to handle a topic as a whole, for example, in case of urgency, and will usually be of substantial size. The difference between this kind of working group and the Drafting Committee lies in the fact that, whereas the Drafting Committee works on texts of articles (and ideally on commentaries) prepared by a Special Rapporteur, a working group will begin work at an earlier stage in the process, when ideas are still developing.[329] It may well continue its work over several sessions, with substantial continuity of membership, whereas the composition of the Drafting Committee changes from year to year. Such a working group is thus more closely involved in the formulation of an approach and in the formulation of drafts. A good example is the Working Group which elaborated the Statute for a Permanent International Criminal Court, which began by focusing on some basic propositions on which agreement could be reached, before even attempting to draft any articles.[330] Its role could certainly not have been performed by the Drafting Committee.

219. In such a Working Group there may be no Special Rapporteur, or the Special Rapporteur may have a limited role. In most cases, if the working group has undertaken careful drafting, we see no advantage in having its work redone by the Drafting Committee before submission to plenary. This may duplicate work or even lead to mistakes if the members of the Drafting Committee have not been party to the detailed discussion which underlies a particular text. On occasions the Drafting Committee may have a role in engaging in a final review ("toilette") of a text from the perspective of adequacy and consistency of language. But in such cases the procedure by way of a working group is an alternative, not a mere preliminary, to discussion in the Drafting Committee.

220. Whatever its mandate, a working group is always subordinate to the Plenary, the Planning Group or the other organ which establishes it. It is for the relevant organ to issue the necessary mandate, to lay down the parameters of any study, to review and, if necessary, modify proposals and to make a decision on the product of the work.

6. *Structure of Commission meetings*

221. In the light of this discussion, we turn to issues of the structure of Commission meetings, including the planning of work over a quinquennium, and the length and arrangement of sessions.

---

[328]See, for example, the working group established in 1995 on "Rights and Duties of States for the Protection of the Environment": Report of the International Law Commission on the work of its forty-seventh session, loc. cit. above (footnote 309), pp. 264-265.

[329]In the case of the Working Group on the International Criminal Court, it divided itself into subgroups at one stage for the purpose of drafting.

[330]*Yearbook of the International Law Commission, 1992*, vol. II (Part Two), p. 58.

(a) *Planning of work over a quinquennium*

222.   At the first session of the current quinquennium in 1992, the Commission set targets for the quinquennium, targets which it has met and in one respect exceeded.[331] The Commission expects that a similar exercise will be carried out in 1997, the first year of the next quinquennium. It is also desirable that a review be carried out at the end of the quinquennium of the goals set and of any preparations which should be made to enable the planning of the following quinquennium to be decided on expeditiously at the beginning of its first year.

(b) *Length of sessions*

223.   The Statute does not specify the length of sessions, although it does say that they will normally be held in Geneva (article 12, as amended in 1955). In fact all sessions have been held in Geneva except the 1954 session which was held in Paris, and the 1965 session which was split between Geneva and Monaco. It was no doubt assumed that sessions would be held annually, and this has in fact been the case since 1949. The length of sessions was normally 10 weeks: 12 weeks became the norm following General Assembly resolution 3315 (XXIX) of 14 December 1974. Except for the 1965 session, sessions have always been held in a single continuous period.

224.   In 1986 the normal 12-week session was reduced to 10 weeks for budgetary reasons, but in response to a strongly expressed view of the Commission, the 12-week session was restored in the following year and has been maintained since. The General Assembly has reaffirmed the need for the Commission to sit for the usual period of 12 weeks.[332] The Commission now has almost twice as many members as it did originally. Its proceedings are inevitably lengthier, and this factor must be borne in mind when comparisons are made.

225.   In principle, the Commission should be able to make a judgement on a year-to-year basis as to the likely required length of the following session (namely, 12 weeks or less), having regard to the state of work and to any priorities laid down by the Assembly for the completion of particular topics.

226.   In some years, a session of less than 12 weeks will be sufficient. In others, especially the last year in a quinquennium, nothing less that 12 weeks will suffice to enable complete texts to be finished on first or second reading with the same membership. For various reasons, the Planning Group believes that in 1997 a 10-week session will be sufficient to cope with work in hand.

227.   In the longer term, the length of sessions is related to the question of their organization, and in particular to the possibility of split sessions, to be discussed in the following section. Especially if a split session is adopted, the Commission believes that its work can usually be effectively done in a period of less than 12 weeks a year. It sees good reason for reverting to the older practice

---

[331] For the goals set in 1992, see document A/CN.4/L.473, para. 15. Consistently with those goals the Commission finished the second reading of the watercourses topic in 1994 and of the Draft Code of Crimes in 1996. It completed the first reading of State responsibility in 1996. Through a working group, it made progress on the topic of international liability for injurious consequences of acts not prohibited by international law (specifically in relation to prevention) and began work on two new topics. An additional achievement was the commencement and completion of the Draft Statute for an International Criminal Court, which was not envisaged in the 1992 report.

[332] See, for example, General Assembly resolutions 41/81 of 3 December 1986, 42/156 of 7 December 1987 and, most recently, 50/45 of 11 December 1995 (para. 11).

of a total annual provision of 10 weeks, with the possibility of extension to 12 weeks in particular years as required—and especially in the last year in a quinquennium.

(c) *Possibility of a split session*

228. Article 12 of the Statute (as amended in 1955) provides that the Commission is to sit at the United Nations Office in Geneva, although "after consultation with the Secretary-General" the Commission has "the right to hold meetings at other places". There is thus no statutory restriction on the Commission splitting its annual session into two parts, and for that matter sitting for one part of the session at United Nations Headquarters in New York. In 1991/92 a procedure of split sessions was suggested but set aside for the time being.[333]

229. Those in favour of a single session argue that it is only through a continuous process of work that the necessary careful consideration can be given to proposed draft articles, both in plenary and in the Drafting Committee. At any one session, the Commission is usually working actively on four or five topics, of which two may have priority. In the context of a split shorter session, consideration of topics not given priority at that session may well be perfunctory, leading to episodic progress on those topics and a lack of guidance to the Special Rapporteur. It should be stressed that the task of reaching a genuine consensus on draft articles may be difficult and inevitably takes time. The Commission does not merely endorse proposals of Special Rapporteurs but has to give them careful and critical consideration. With 34 members, coming from different legal, cultural and linguistic backgrounds, this process cannot be rushed. Moreover, there is a problem of "critical mass": it is only by careful collective consideration in plenary, in the Drafting Committee and in working groups that really satisfactory conclusions can be worked out, and the splitting of the session would tend to interrupt and fragment this process. In the view of these members, a continuous session is necessary to assure the best results on priority topics while maintaining progress and direction on other topics.

230. On the other hand, those in favour of a split session argue that it would facilitate reflection and study by members of the Commission, and in particular that it would allow inter-sessional preparation to be carried out in a way that would make the second part of a split session much more productive. For example, reports or proposals debated in plenary at the first part of the session could be dealt with by the Drafting Committee at the second part. Conversely, the Drafting Committee, having completed consideration of particular articles in the first part, the amended articles and accompanying commentary could be got ready for the plenary in the second half, and members will have had the opportunity to read and consider them in advance. A split session would also encourage inter-sessional work of an informal kind, and give time to Special Rapporteurs to reconsider proposals discussed at the first part of a session. It would allow the Drafting Committee or a working group to occupy, for example, a week at the end of the first part of a session or at the beginning of the second half, without requiring members of the Commission who are not members of that committee or group to attend. It opens the prospect of membership to those who for professional or other reasons simply cannot make the commitment to a continuous period of 12 weeks in Geneva. It is more likely that members of the Commission with other commitments (whether as government

---

[333] *Yearbook of the International Law Commission, 1992*, vol. II (Part Two), p. 55.

legal advisers, private sector lawyers or university law professors) may be able to spend a continuous period of 4-5 weeks in session than that they can do so for 12 weeks. Currently, some members of the Commission find it necessary to be away from Geneva for considerable periods. Although conflicting commitments can never be excluded, two shorter sessions are likely to facilitate better and more continuous attendance. In short, it will be more flexible.

231. The choice is affected by financial considerations which are beyond the Commission's control. Tentative calculations suggest that a 10-week session, split evenly between New York and Geneva, would be significantly cheaper than a continuous 12-week session. Even for a session of the same total length, it seems that a split session may not be significantly more expensive, because additional travel costs for members will be largely offset by the reduced cost of sending New York-based Secretariat personnel to Geneva.

232. In the view of the Commission, the experiment of a split session should be tried. For various reasons, including budgetary limits and the fact that 1997 is the first year of a quinquennium, however, it seems best to undertake the experiment in 1998. This will enable the proper planning of a split session—the advantages and disadvantages of which may be assessed in practice.

233. The planning of the distribution of work between the two parts of a split session is essential. Planning will necessarily be done on a year-to-year basis, and some flexibility will be necessary. But it may involve, for example, consideration in the first part of the session of reports of Special Rapporteurs and of draft articles by the Drafting Committee and, in the second part of the session, of consideration in plenary of reports of the Drafting Committee, other groups and the Commission's report itself. It will be necessary for the second part of the session to end not later than the end of July in order to allow the Commission's report to the General Assembly to be produced by early September.

(d)   *The essential contribution of the Secretariat*

234. Article 14 of the Commission's Statute provides simply that the Secretary-General shall "so far as he is able, make available staff and facilities required by the Commission to fulfil its task".

235. In practice, the contribution of the Secretariat is essential. In addition to servicing the Commission and its subsidiary bodies, considerable research is undertaken by the Secretariat, often at short notice. Members of the Secretariat assist the officers of the Commission, providing the agenda, keeping records, preparing drafts of reports to plenary, etc. They assist in the preparation of the commentary to draft articles, although the Commission remains of the view that this is the primary responsibility of the Special Rapporteurs. In working groups, where there may be no Special Rapporteur, this assistance is invaluable. The members of the Secretariat should be encouraged to make an even greater contribution to the Commission's work.

(e)   *The International Law Seminar*

236. The Seminar has been a characteristic part of Commission sessions for many years, and many hundreds of younger professionals have been introduced to the United Nations and to the ILC's work through the seminar. It is hoped that it can be continued despite current financial constraints.

(f) *Publishing the work of the Commission*

237. The Commission's annual report to the Sixth Committee is produced within weeks of the end of the session, and subsequently reprinted in the *Yearbook*, which is the essential record of the Commission's work. The *Yearbook* contains summary records of plenary debates, the full texts of draft articles and commentaries as finally adopted, reports of Special Rapporteurs and other selected documents. Some progress has been made in catching up on the backlog with the *Yearbook*. In addition the United Nations publishes periodically a most useful survey entitled *The Work of the International Law Commission*. This summarizes the Commission's work and reprints draft articles adopted by it or, as the case may be, conventions or other texts concluded on the basis of such draft articles. The fifth edition appeared in 1996.

238. Unofficial accounts of the Commission's work appear in the international law literature. There is, for example, an annual review of the Commission's work published in the *American Journal of International Law* and the *Annuaire français de droit international*. Similar essays in the other languages of the Commission are to be encouraged.

7. *The Commission's relationship with other bodies*
(within and outside the United Nations)

239. The Commission's single most important relationship is its reporting relationship to the General Assembly through the Sixth Committee. But the Commission's Statute envisages that it may have a range of relationships with other bodies:

(a) Under articles 16 (c), 17 (2) (b) and 21 (2), the Commission must circulate questionnaires to or seek comments from the Governments on any project it is considering.

(b) Under article 17, the Commission may consider "proposals and draft multilateral conventions submitted by Members of the United Nations, the principal organs of the United Nations other than the General Assembly, specialized agencies, or official bodies established by intergovernmental agreement to encourage the progressive development of international law and its codification, and transmitted to it for that purpose by the Secretary-General".

(c) Under chapter III of its Statute the Commission has a quite general power to consult with United Nations organs on any subject within their competence, and with any other organizations, intergovernmental or otherwise, national or international, on any subject entrusted to it (see articles 25 (1), 26 (1)).

(d) In a number of cases the Commission has consulted with particular agencies in a systematic way (for example, with FAO, on the issue of fisheries beyond territorial waters). It has also sought advice from experts (for example, on issues of maritime delimitation and drawing of baselines).

240. It is the practice of the Commission to hear reports from delegates from the Asian-African Legal Consultative Committee, the European Committee on Legal Cooperation and the Inter-American Juridical Committee during each session. These are useful, but they tend to be rather formal, complementary exchanges. The Commission welcomes these exchanges but believes that they could be enhanced if a short written report of the work of the organization, with relevant documents, could be circulated in advance. A brief formal exchange of views for the record could be supplemented by a less formal discussion involv-

ing members of the Commission and dealing with selected issues of interest to both bodies. Increased cooperation between these bodies and the Commission's Special Rapporteurs, as relevant, should also be encouraged, as well as cooperation between the Commission's secretariat and the secretariats of these bodies, and exchanges of documentation.

241. A potentially important set of relationships is currently rather neglected. We refer to the work of United Nations and other specialized bodies with legal implications or responsibilities. At least it is appropriate for bodies with specific responsibilities in a given field to be asked to exchange information and to comment on the Commission's work where relevant—but at present the various component parts of the United Nations system operate largely in isolation from each other. Another possibility might be, in effect, a joint study of a particular legal topic conducted by the Commission with the agency responsible in the given field. National law commissions have conducted such joint studies in technical fields such as customs law and insolvency. There is no a priori reason to exclude the possibility at the international level.

8. *Possible revision of the Statute*

242. The Commission's Statute was drafted shortly after the end of the Second World War, and although it has been amended on a number of occasions it has never been the subject of a thorough review and revision. On the whole, the Statute has been flexible enough to allow modifications in practice. For example, the Statute makes more or less adequate provision for such matters as approval of a plan of work for a topic,[334] and the appointment of a group of members to work with the Special Rapporteur.[335] With respect to other matters discussed here (for example, split sessions), it does not preclude appropriate changes being made. Most of the changes discussed in this report can be implemented without any amendment to the Statute.

243. Nevertheless there are aspects of the Statute which warrant review and revision as the Commission approaches its fiftieth year. Some few provisions of the Statute are anachronistic, and could be removed: for example, article 26 (3), which refers to "relations with Franco Spain" and to "organizations which have collaborated with the Nazis and Fascists". The mention in article 26 (4) of intergovernmental organizations whose task is the codification of international law could be broadened beyond the Pan-American Union to include, for example, the Asian-African Legal Consultative Committee, the Hague Conference on Private International Law, and UNIDROIT. At a more substantive level the distinction drawn in articles 1, 15 and elsewhere between codification and progressive development of international law has proved to be unworkable, and the procedure for both should be expressly assimilated. In particular the freedom expressly recognized to the Commission in respect of "codification" to "adopt a plan of work appropriate to each case" (article 19 (1) of its Statute) should be formally extended to all the Commission's work. A number of other substantive issues will need to be considered.

---

[334]Article 16 (*b*), article 17 (2) (*a*), 19 (1) of the Commission's Statute.

[335]Ibid., article 16 (2) (*d*) (although this provision only relates to the period after the questionnaire has been circulated to Governments, and only "pending receipt of replies to this questionnaire"). This provision could be redrafted in more general form, and made applicable to the whole process of consideration of a topic, whether or not involving the appointment of a Special Rapporteur.

244.   The Commission recommends that the Commission may at its next session give thought to the possibility of recommending to the General Assembly a review of the Statute to coincide with the fiftieth anniversary of the Commission in 1999.

2.   LONG-TERM PROGRAMME OF WORK

245.   Having regard to the progress made and work that has been completed during this session, the Commission re-established a Working Group to assist it in selecting topics for future study.

246.   The Commission adopted the report of the Working Group and decided to include it as an annex to its report.[336]

247.   The Commission noted that although, in its almost 50 years of existence, it had taken up and completed numerous topics in various fields of public international law, still much remained to be done. This could be discerned both from the general list of subjects of international law as well as from the various topics raised in the Commission at one time or another as possible topics for codification and progressive development of international law.

248.   In order to provide a global review of the main fields of general public international law, the Commission established a general scheme of topics classified under 13 main fields of public international law (for example, sources, State jurisdiction, international criminal law, international organizations, international spaces, etc.).[337] This list, not meant to be exhaustive, included topics which had already been completed by the Commission, topics taken up but "abandoned" for various reasons, topics presently under consideration and possible future topics.

249.   For the present purpose, three topics had been identified as appropriate for codification and progressive development: diplomatic protection; ownership and protection of wrecks beyond the limits of national maritime jurisdiction; and unilateral acts of States. A tentative outline covering the main legal issues raised under each of the three topics was also attached. Reasons for current interest were given in the notes in each addendum.*

---

*These addenda have not been reproduced here.
[336]See Annex II.
[337]Ibid.

Annex II

Report on the Long-Term Programme of Work

1.   During its almost 50 years of existence, the Commission has undertaken and completed numerous topics belonging to various fields of public international law.[1] However, if one sets work completed either against international law in its generality or even against the list of topics raised at one time or another as possible topics for codification and progressive development of international law by the Commission[2] it is clear that much remains to be done.

2.   The present paper does not purport to offer a complete survey of possible topics (in particular, the suggestions for "possible future topics" reflect proposals at different times by some of its members). Indeed, some topics proposed in the paper have been taken up by other bodies. The report as a whole aims at:

(a)   Classifying some very general fields of public international law governed mainly by rules of customary international law;

(b)   Enumerating, under each of these very general headings, various topics which, at some time or another, have been proposed by the Commission or by individual members as possible topics for the ILC (dates of initial proposal are shown below in square brackets);

(c)   Adding some possible topics on which the Commission does not intend to take a firm position on their feasibility for future work;

(d)   Indicating those which have already been completed in whole or in part; and

(e)   Setting out a very general outline of the main legal problems raised by three of the possible future topics which, in the view of the Commission are appropriate for codification and progressive development. These topics are the following:*

(i)   Diplomatic protection (Addendum 1);
(ii)   Ownership and protection of wrecks beyond the limits of national maritime jurisdiction (Addendum 2);
(iii) Unilateral acts of States (Addendum 3).

These three topics have been indicated in bold-faced letters in the general scheme below.

3.   The general scheme proposed below is an example of a general approach which, in the view of the Commission offers a way of integrating in a global review of the main fields of general public international law some possible topics for future studies. The Commission is fully aware of the fact that some of the topics mentioned fall within the scope of activities of other bodies; they are referred to for the purpose of illustrating the scope of international law.

---

*The Addenda mentioned below are not reproduced here.
[1]See the General Scheme, below, for details.
[2]Ibid.

The Commission has no intention of overlapping with the competence of the institutions concerned.

4. If this approach seems fruitful to the Commission and to the Sixth Committee, it is suggested that further study could be made during the next session of the Commission of topics additional to those suggested in Addenda 1 to 3.

GENERAL SCHEME[3]

I. SOURCES OF INTERNATIONAL LAW

1. *Topics already completed*:
   - (a) Law of treaties:
      - (i) Vienna Convention on the law of treaties, 1969;
      - (ii) Vienna Convention on the law of treaties between States and international organizations or between two or more international organizations, 1986;
      - (iii) Draft articles on most-favoured-nation clauses, 1978.

2. *Topics under consideration by the Commission*:
   Reservations to treaties.

3. *Possible future topics*:
   - (a) Law of treaties:
     Multilateral treaty-making process [1979];
   - (b) Law of unilateral acts [1971]:
      - (i) **Unilateral acts of States**;
      - (ii) Law applicable to resolutions of international organizations;
      - (iii) Control of validity of the resolutions of international organizations;
   - (c) Customary international law:
      - (i) Formation of customary rules;
      - (ii) Legal effects of customary rules;
   - (d) *Jus cogens* (and related concepts) [1992];
   - (e) Non-binding instruments.

II. SUBJECTS OF INTERNATIONAL LAW

1. *Topics taken up but abandoned*:
   - (i) Fundamental rights and duties of States [1949];
   - (ii) "Succession" of Governments [1949];

2. *Possible future topics*:
   - (a) Subjects of international law [1949];

---

[3]This list is for illustrative purposes; neither the formulations nor the content commit the Commission in its future undertakings.

(b) Statehood:
  (i) Position of States in international law [1971];
  (ii) Criteria for recognition [1949];
  (iii) Independence and sovereignty of States [1962];
(c) Government:
  (i) Recognition of Governments [1949];
  (ii) Representative Governments.

III. SUCCESSION OF STATES AND OTHER LEGAL PERSONS

1. *Topics already completed*:

  (a) Vienna Convention on State succession with respect to treaties, 1978;
  (b) Vienna Convention on State succession with respect to State property, archives and debts, 1986.

2. *Topics under consideration by the Commission*:

  Succession of States with respect to nationality.

3. *Possible future topics*:

  (a) Succession of States in respect of membership of, and obligations towards, international organizations;
  (b) "Acquired rights" in relation to State succession;
  (c) Succession of international organizations.

IV. STATE JURISDICTION/IMMUNITY FROM JURISDICTION

1. *Topics already completed*:

  Jurisdictional immunities of States and their property, 1991.

2. *Possible future topics*:

  (a) Immunities from execution;
  (b) Extraterritorial jurisdiction:
    (i) Recognition of acts of foreign States [1949];
    (ii) Jurisdiction over foreign States [1949];
    (iii) Jurisdiction with respect to crimes committed outside national territory [1949];
    (iv) Extraterritorial application of national legislation [1992];
  (c) Territorial jurisdiction:
    Territorial domain of States [1949];
  (d) Jurisdiction relating to public services ("compétences relatives aux services publics").

V. LAW OF INTERNATIONAL ORGANIZATIONS

1. *Topics already completed*:

  Vienna Convention on the representation of States in their relations with international organizations of a universal character, 1975.

2. *Topics taken up but not continued*:

Status, privileges and immunities of international organizations, their officials, experts, etc.

3. *Possible future topics*:
    (a) General principles of law of the international civil service;
    (b) International legal personality of international organizations;
    (c) Jurisdiction of international organizations:
        (i) Implied powers;
        (ii) Personal jurisdiction;
        (iii) Territorial jurisdiction.

VI. POSITION OF THE INDIVIDUAL IN INTERNATIONAL LAW

1. *Topics already completed*:

Convention on the Reduction of Statelessness, 1961.

2. *Possible future topics*:
    (a) International law relating to individuals [1971]:
        The individual in international law;
    (b) Treatment of aliens [1949]:
        (i) Right of asylum [1949];
        (ii) Extradition [1949];
    (c) Law concerning international migrations [1992];
    (d) Human rights and defence of democracy [1962].

VII. INTERNATIONAL CRIMINAL LAW

1. *Topics already completed*:
    (a) Draft statute for an international criminal court, 1994;
    (b) Code of crimes against the peace and security of mankind, 1996.

2. *Possible future topics*:
    (a) The principle *"Aut dedere aut judicare"*;
    (b) International crimes other than those referred to in the Code of Crimes against the peace and security of mankind.

VIII. LAW OF INTERNATIONAL SPACES

1. *Topics already completed*:
    (a) Law of the sea:
        Four Geneva Conventions, 1958.
    (b) Legal regime of international rivers:
        Draft articles on the Law of non-navigational uses of international watercourses, 1994.

2. *Topics taken up and abandoned*:
   Juridical regime of historical waters, 1962.

3. *Possible future topics*:
   (a) Law of the sea:
   Ownership and protection of wrecks beyond the limits of national maritime jurisdiction;
   (b) Legal regime of international rivers and related topics:
   Navigation on international rivers;
   (c) Law of the air [1971];
   (d) Law of space [1962];
   (e) Shared natural resources:
      (i) Global commons [1992];
      (ii) The common heritage of mankind;
      (iii) Transboundary resources;
      (iv) The law of continued international groundwaters;
      (v) Common interest of mankind.

IX. LAW OF INTERNATIONAL RELATIONS/RESPONSIBILITY

1. *Topics already completed*:
   (a) Diplomatic and consular relations:
      (i) Vienna Convention on diplomatic relations, 1961;
      (ii) Vienna Convention on consular relations, 1963;
      (iii) Vienna Convention on special missions, 1969;
      (iv) Convention on the prevention and punishment of crimes against internationally protected persons, including diplomatic agents, 1973;
      (v) Status of the diplomatic courier and the diplomatic bag not accompanied by diplomatic courier, 1989.

2. *Topics under consideration by the Commission*:
   (a) State responsibility;
   (b) International liability for injurious consequences of acts not prohibited by international law.

3. *Possible future topics*:
   (a) International responsibility:
      (i) **Diplomatic protection;**
      (ii) International responsibility of international organizations;
      (iii) Functional protection;
   (b) International representation of international organizations.

146. Pour répondre à la demande de l'Assemblée, la deuxième partie du présent rapport passe en revue les procédures de la Commission et tente de repérer les changements qui pourraient les rendre plus utiles et plus rationnelles. Parmi ces changements, il en est quelques-uns que la Commission peut opérer elle-même; d'autres exigeront la coopération d'autres organes et, en particulier, de la Sixième Commission.

147. On trouvera dans le résumé ci-après les principales conclusions et recommandations formulées dans le rapport.

Conclusions et recommandations générales

Conclusions

148. Pour décider quelles sont les méthodes propres à mieux assurer le développement progressif et la codification du droit international, il faut se faire une idée des possibilités de développement progressif et de codification qui s'offrent aujourd'hui, après la cinquantaine d'années de travaux que la Commission a à son actif. Sur cette question, la Commission est parvenue aux conclusions générales exposées ci-après.

a) La distinction entre codification et développement progressif est difficile, sinon impossible, à établir dans la pratique; la Commission est partie d'une idée composite de codification et de développement progressif. Les distinctions que son Statut établit entre les deux processus se sont révélées impraticables, et elles pourraient être supprimées si le Statut était révisé (par. 157 à 160).

b) Malgré les nombreux changements qui ont jalonné l'évolution du droit international et de l'organisation de la société internationale depuis 1949, un processus ordonné de codification et de développement progressif continue de présenter un intérêt important (par. 168 à 171).

c) Il y a un certain nombre de moyens de rendre les méthodes de travail de la Commission plus souples et plus rationnelles et de structurer et de renforcer ses relations avec la Sixième Commission (par. 172 à 177).

Recommandations

149. Pour les raisons indiquées dans la deuxième partie, la Commission formule les recommandations qui suivent.

a) Il faudrait continuer, suivant la procédure établie par la Commission en 1992, à recenser les sujets pouvant faire l'objet de travaux futurs à recommander à l'Assemblée générale (par. 165 et 166).

b) Parallèlement, l'Assemblée générale et, par son intermédiaire, d'autres organismes des Nations Unies devraient être encouragés à soumettre à la Commission des sujets se prêtant à la codification et au développement progressif du droit international (par. 166, 178 et 179).

c) La Commission devrait étendre la pratique qui consiste à recenser les questions précises sur lesquelles elle souhaite que la Sixième Commission lui fasse part de ses observations, si possible avant l'adoption des projets d'articles y afférents (par. 182).

d) Les questionnaires adressés aux gouvernements devraient être d'utilisation facile; en particulier, ils devraient donner des indications claires au sujet de l'objet et des raisons des demandes qui y sont formulées (par. 182).

e) Le rapport de la Commission devrait être plus bref et plus thématique et tenter par tous les moyens de mettre en relief et d'expliquer les problèmes clefs pour permettre de structurer plus facilement les débats sur le rapport à la Sixième Commission (par. 182).

f) Il devrait être demandé aux Rapporteurs spéciaux de préciser la nature et l'envergure des travaux prévus pour la session suivante (par. 190). Leurs rapports devraient être disponibles suffisamment longtemps avant la session à laquelle ils doivent être examinés (par. 191).

g) Il devrait être demandé aux Rapporteurs spéciaux de travailler avec un groupe de membres qui aurait un rôle consultatif; cette formule devrait aussi être étendue à la seconde lecture du projet sur la responsabilité des États (par. 192 à 196).

h) Les Rapporteurs spéciaux devraient autant que possible accompagner leurs projets d'articles de projets de commentaires ou de notes et les réviser à la lumière des modifications apportées par le Comité de rédaction, afin que les commentaires soient disponibles au moment du débat en plénière (par. 197 à 201).

i) Il faudrait revoir le système des débats en plénière à la Commission pour mieux les structurer et permettre au Président de récapituler à titre indicatif les conclusions qui en découlent, en s'appuyant au besoin sur les résultats d'un vote auquel il serait procédé à titre indicatif (par. 202 à 211).

j) Le système actuel de composition différente du Comité de rédaction selon le sujet étudié devrait être conservé (par. 215).

k) Il faudrait faire plus largement appel à des groupes de travail, tant pour essayer de régler tel ou tel désaccord que pour accélérer, lorsqu'il y a lieu, l'examen d'un sujet tout entier; dans ce dernier cas, le groupe de travail ferait normalement office de Comité de rédaction (par. 218 et 219).

l) La Commission devrait fixer ses objectifs, et faire rapport à ce sujet à l'Assemblée générale, au début de chaque quinquennat et revoir son programme de travail futur à la fin du quinquennat (par. 222).

m) La Commission devrait revenir à l'ancienne pratique d'une session de dix semaines avec la possibilité d'une prolongation de deux semaines en cas de nécessité, tout spécialement pour la dernière session d'un quinquennat (par. 227).

n) Il faudrait tenter en 1998 l'expérience d'une session en deux temps (par. 228 à 233).

o) La contribution du Secrétariat aux travaux de la Commission devrait être préservée et renforcée (par. 234 et 235).

p) Il faudrait conserver le Séminaire de droit international (par. 236).

q) Il faudrait stimuler davantage et développer les relations avec d'autres organismes comme les organismes juridiques régionaux (par. 240).

r) La Commission devrait chercher à nouer des liens avec d'autres organes spécialisés des Nations Unies exerçant des fonctions normatives dans leurs domaines respectifs, et en particulier étudier la possibilité d'échanges d'information et même de travaux conjoints sur certains sujets (par. 241).

s) Il faudrait envisager de refondre et mettre à jour le Statut de la Commission à l'occasion de son cinquantième anniversaire, en 1999 (par. 242 à 244).

ANALYSE DÉTAILLÉE

1. *Introduction*

150. Le 11 décembre 1995, l'Assemblée générale a adopté la résolution 50/45, par laquelle, notamment, elle :

« 9. *Prie* la Commission du droit international :

« *a*) D'examiner ses méthodes de travail afin de contribuer davantage encore au développement progressif et à la codification du droit international et d'inclure ses vues sur la question dans son rapport à l'Assemblée générale à sa cinquante et unième session;

« *b*) De continuer à veiller spécialement à indiquer dans son rapport annuel, pour chaque sujet, les points éventuels sur lesquels il serait particulièrement intéressant que les gouvernements expriment leurs vues, soit à la Sixième Commission, soit par écrit, afin de la guider utilement dans la poursuite de ses travaux;

« 10. *Prie* le Secrétaire général d'inviter les gouvernements à présenter des observations sur le stade atteint par le processus de codification dans le système des Nations Unies et de lui faire rapport sur la question à sa cinquante et unième session. . . »

151. La Commission n'a pas manqué de garder à l'étude, au fil des ans, la question de ses méthodes de travail, auxquelles elle a apporté un certain nombre de changements[290]. Mais comme les paragraphes susmentionnés de la résolution le laissent entendre et comme le débat sur le rapport de la Commission auquel la Sixième Commission a procédé en 1995 le montre[291], il se révèle nécessaire d'entreprendre une analyse plus approfondie du « stade atteint par le processus de codification dans le système des Nations Unies », ainsi que du rôle futur de la Commission dans ce processus. C'est dans cet esprit qu'aux termes du paragraphe 9 de sa résolution 50/45 l'Assemblée générale a invité la Commission à examiner ses méthodes de travail.

152. Le présent rapport a été établi par la Commission[292] dans le cadre de l'examen permanent de ses méthodes de travail et de ses procédures engagé par la Commission et en réponse à la demande formulée par l'Assemblée générale au paragraphe 9 de sa résolution 50/45. Il dresse un inventaire des modifications qui pourraient être apportées aux méthodes de travail de la

---

[290]Pour l'examen dans le passé des méthodes de travail, voir par exemple la discussion dont il est rendu compte dans *Annuaire de la Commission du droit international, 1958*, vol. II, p. 111 à 115, et qui s'est déroulée sur la base d'un rapport établi par M. Zourek (document A/CN.4/108). Au cours du présent quinquennat (1992-1996), la Commission a cherché à restructurer son rapport annuel [*Annuaire de la Commission du droit international, 1992*, vol. II (deuxième partie), p. 57 et 58], a revu les arrangements relatifs aux travaux du Comité de rédaction (ibid., p. 57), a traité en trois sessions un sujet majeur (le projet de statut pour une cour criminelle internationale) en le confiant à un groupe de travail [pour la recommandation finale, voir ibid., *1994*, vol. II (deuxième partie), p. 28 à 79] et a adopté une procédure plus méthodique et exhaustive pour l'examen de nouveaux sujets éventuels.

[291]Voir le résumé thématique des débats tenus à la Sixième Commission de l'Assemblée générale pendant sa cinquantième session (document A/CN.4/472/Add.1), p. 46 à 51.

[292]Un groupe de travail restreint, composé de M. Crawford (Président), M. Bowett, M. Idris, M. Pellet et M. Rao, a établi un avant-projet, qu'il a révisé compte tenu du débat qui s'est déroulé au sein du Groupe de planification.

Commission pour renforcer son utilité et son efficacité[293]. Comme il apparaîtra plus loin, certaines de ces modifications sont du ressort de la Commission; d'autres appellent une initiative ou la coopération d'autres organes, et en particulier la Sixième Commission elle-même.

153. Pour analyser les procédures suivies par la Commission, il faut tenir compte d'un certain nombre de réformes qu'elle a adoptées ces dernières années, ainsi que des limitations imposées par des facteurs externes. Il sera rendu compte ici, non pas des méthodes de travail de la Commission en général, mais de tel ou tel de leurs aspects, selon que de besoin, dans la section correspondante.

2. Les perspectives en matière de codification et de développement progressif du droit international

154. La demande formulée par l'Assemblée générale au paragraphe 9 de sa résolution 50/45 a pour objectif d'amener la Commission à « contribuer davantage encore au développement progressif et à la codification du droit international ». Pour déterminer les méthodes de travail de la Commission qui serviront le mieux cet objectif, il importe de se pencher tout d'abord sur les perspectives actuelles du développement progressif et de la codification du droit international, après près de cinquante ans d'activité.

155. La Commission a été créée par l'Assemblée générale, aux termes de sa résolution 174 (II) en date du 21 novembre 1947[294], et elle a tenu sa première session, qui a duré près de neuf semaines, en 1949. Il existait à l'époque un fort courant en faveur d'une commission à plein temps.

156. La Commission a pour but de « promouvoir le développement progressif du droit international et sa codification » (paragraphe 1 du premier article du Statut); elle doit s'occuper « au premier chef » du droit international public, sans qu'il lui soit interdit de pénétrer dans le domaine du droit international privé (paragraphe 2 du premier article du Statut). Ces dernières années, la Commission n'a pas pénétré dans le domaine du droit international privé, si ce n'est incidemment et à l'occasion de travaux sur des matières de droit international public; de toute manière, compte tenu des travaux d'organes comme la CNUDCI et la Conférence de La Haye de droit international privé, il semble improbable qu'elle soit appelée à le faire.

a) La « distinction » entre codification et développement progressif

157. À l'article premier du Statut, une distinction est établie entre « le développement progressif du droit international » et « sa codification ». Cette distinction est développée ensuite à l'article 15, où l'expression « développement progressif » est (« pour la commodité ») associée à l'élaboration de projets de convention et l'idée de codification du droit international, au cas où il s'agit « de formuler avec plus de précision et de systématiser les règles du droit international dans des domaines dans lesquels il existe déjà une pratique étatique considérable, des précédents et des opinions doctrinales ». Mais il est bien connu que la distinction entre codification et développement progressif est difficile, voire impossible, à établir dans la pratique, notamment lorsque l'on entre dans le détail qui est nécessaire pour donner effet avec plus de précision à

---

[293]Un certain nombre de changements ont été mis en œuvre au cours du présent quinquennat (voir *supra*, note n° 290).
[294]Le Statut de la Commission a été modifié à six reprises, et en dernier par la résolution 36/39 de l'Assemblée générale, en date du 18 novembre 1981, qui a porté le nombre de ses membres de 18 à 34.

un principe[295]. Qui plus est, il est trop simple de prétendre que le développement progressif du droit international, par opposition à la codification, est associé en particulier à l'élaboration de conventions. La souplesse s'impose dans tous les cas et pour bien des raisons.

158. C'est ainsi que la Commission a, inévitablement, procédé à partir d'une idée composite de « codification et développement progressif ». En d'autres termes, ses travaux ont porté sur l'élaboration de textes multilatéraux concernant des sujets généraux qui intéressent tous les États ou nombre d'entre eux et cherchant à la fois à refléter les principes acceptés pour les régir et à préciser, à définir et à développer plus avant les idées selon que de besoin.

b) *Le choix des sujets à inscrire au programme de travail de la Commission*

159. Le choix des sujets à inscrire au programme de travail de la Commission constitue un autre aspect de la distinction établie dans le Statut entre codification et développement progressif du droit international. Il est sous-entendu dans le Statut que l'initiative de l'examen de propositions concernant le développement progressif du droit international émanera de l'Assemblée générale (article 16) ou d'autres organes (article 17), tandis qu'il appartient à la Commission elle-même de choisir les sujets de codification qu'elle peut recommander à l'Assemblée générale (paragraphes 1 et 2 de l'article 18)[296]. Le paragraphe 1 de l'article 18 dispose que :

« La Commission recherche, dans l'ensemble du droit international, les sujets appropriés de codification, en tenant compte des projets existants, qu'ils soient d'origine gouvernementale ou non. »

160. Dans la pratique, la procédure suivie pour l'examen de la plupart des sujets auquel la Commission a procédé a été sensiblement la même, que l'aspect développement progressif ou l'aspect codification ait été réputé prédominer. Depuis 1970, la plupart des propositions concernant les sujets à traiter ont émané de la Commission, même si c'est l'Assemblée générale qui, par exemple, a relancé la question du Code des crimes contre la paix et la sécurité de l'humanité en 1981[297] et qui a invité la Commission à explorer la possibilité de créer un Tribunal pénal international[298]. Il est à souligner que la Commission s'est toujours attachée à obtenir l'approbation de l'Assemblée générale avant de s'engager dans l'étude détaillée d'un sujet.

161. La recherche des sujets « dans l'ensemble du droit international » dont il est question au paragraphe 1 de l'article 18 du Statut a été conduite initialement à partir d'un mémorandum du Secrétariat, en fait un mémorandum établi par le professeur Hersch Lauterpacht, devenu ultérieurement membre de la Commission[299]. Dans ce mémorandum, 25 sujets étaient passés en revue, que

---

[295]Voir par exemple Briggs, H.W., *The International Law Commission* (1965), p. 129 à 141; Rosenne, S., *Practice and Methods of the International Law Commission* (1984), p. 73 et 74; Sinclair, Sir I., *The International Law Commission* (1987), p. 46 et 47 et 120 à 126; et Ago, « Nouvelles réflexions sur la codification du droit international », *Revue générale de droit international public*, vol. 92 (1988), p. 539. Voir également Daudet, Y., *Les conférences des Nations Unies pour la codification du droit international* (1968).

[296]D'un autre côté, l'Assemblée générale peut demander à la Commission de traiter de toute question de codification, et les demandes dans ce sens ont la priorité (art. 18, par. 3).

[297]Résolution 36/106 de l'Assemblée générale, en date du 10 décembre 1981.

[298]Résolution 45/41 de l'Assemblée générale, en date du 28 novembre 1990, paragraphe 3; et résolution 46/54 de l'Assemblée générale, en date du 9 décembre 1991.

[299]Document A/CN.4/1/Rev.1; réédité sous la direction de Lauterpacht, E., dans *The Collected Papers of Sir Hersch Lauterpacht*, vol. I (1970), p. 445.

la Commission a analysés et à partir desquels elle a dressé une « liste provisoire de 14 matières choisies en vue de leur codification »[300]. Un certain nombre de ces matières ont été retenues pour faire l'objet des premiers travaux de la Commission.

162. Sur les 14 sujets retenus au départ et à titre provisoire, la Commission, en 1996, en avait traité, en tout ou en grande partie, neuf[301]. Sur les cinq autres sujets, un a été abordé sans succès, puis abandonné, mais proposé récemment par la Commission pour être traité de nouveau en partie sous l'intitulé « Protection diplomatique »[302]; un (Responsabilité des États) est toujours en cours d'examen[303]; et trois n'ont jamais été abordés[304].

163. D'autres matières ont été ajoutées au programme de travail, selon diverses modalités. En particulier dans les premières années d'existence de la Commission, l'Assemblée générale lui a renvoyé un certain nombre de questions. La Commission a ainsi reçu au total de l'Assemblée générale 16 demandes ou recommandations, dont pas moins de sept à ses tout débuts.

164. De 1971 à 1972, la Commission a procédé à un nouvel examen, assez approfondi, de ses activités, en se fondant sur une série de documents établis par

---

[300]*Annuaire de la Commission du droit international, 1949*, p. 281.

[301]Il s'agit des sujets suivants (avec indication de l'issue éventuelle des travaux) :

a) Succession d'États et de gouvernements (d'importantes matières relevant de la succession d'États ont été examinées par la Commission, et les travaux ont abouti aux Conventions de Vienne de 1978 et 1983; une matière, la succession d'États et la nationalité, est depuis peu en cours d'examen. Il n'a jamais été insisté pour étudier le sujet de la succession de gouvernements, sans doute parce que, compte tenu de la pratique quasiment uniforme qui consacre la continuité des obligations prises par les États en dépit des changements de gouvernement, il y a très peu de choses à dire sur ce point);

b) Immunités juridictionnelles des États et de leurs biens (projet d'articles mis au point en 1991, mais l'Assemblée générale, en 1994, en a reporté l'examen à trois ou quatre ans plus tard);

c) Régime de la haute mer (Convention de Genève de 1958 sur la haute mer) et régime des eaux territoriales (Convention de Genève de 1958 sur la mer territoriale et la zone contiguë). En fait, la Commission a également mis au point des projets d'articles sur la pêche et la conservation des ressources biologiques de la haute mer et sur le plateau continental (ces matières ont fait l'objet des deux autres Conventions de Genève adoptées en 1958);

d) Nationalité, y compris l'apatridie (projet de convention sur l'élimination de l'apatridie dans l'avenir et projet de convention sur la réduction du nombre des cas d'apatridie dans l'avenir, qui ont débouché sur l'adoption en 1961 de la Convention sur la réduction des cas d'apatridie);

e) Droit des traités (Convention de Vienne de 1968 sur le droit des traités; Convention de Vienne de 1986 sur le droit des traités entre États et organisations internationales ou entre organisations internationales);

f) Relations et immunités diplomatiques (Convention de Vienne de 1961 sur les relations diplomatiques);

g) Relations et immunités consulaires (Convention de Vienne de 1963 sur les relations consulaires);

h) Procédure arbitrale (Modèle de règles sur la procédure arbitrale, 1958).

[302]Traitement des étrangers. Voir les rapports de M. Garcia Amador, *Annuaire de la Commission du droit international, 1958*, vol. II, p. 49 à 76; ibid., *1959*, vol. II, p. 1 à 36; ibid., *1960*, vol. II, p. 38 à 63; et ibid., *1961*, vol. II, p. 1 à 56.

[303]La Commission a décidé en 1963 d'étudier les règles générales ou « secondaires » de la responsabilité, voir ibid., *1963*, vol. II, p. 234. Les travaux, abordés dans le détail en 1969 seulement, se sont poursuivis avec différents Rapporteurs spéciaux (Ago, Riphagen, Arangio-Ruiz), jusqu'à la présente session, au cours de laquelle la Commission compte achever l'examen en première lecture de l'ensemble du projet d'articles.

[304]Reconnaissance des États et des gouvernements; Juridiction pénale en matière d'infractions commises en dehors du territoire national; et Droit d'asile. À propos du deuxième de ces sujets, le sujet connexe de la juridiction civile à l'égard des affaires survenant en dehors de l'Etat du for n'était pas inscrit sur la liste de 1949—et il était en fait difficilement discernable dans la liste plus longue qui a servi à établir celle qui a été retenue. Voir ibid., *1949*, p. 281.

le secrétariat[305]. Les conclusions auxquelles elle est parvenue étaient modestes : elle poursuivrait les travaux sur les principaux sujets alors en cours d'examen, et, à la demande de l'Assemblée générale, elle a ajouté à ces sujets le droit relatif aux utilisations des voies d'eau internationales à des fins autres que la navigation[306].

165. En 1992, la Commission a inauguré une procédure plus rigoureuse pour le choix des sujets[307]. Un groupe de travail a retenu à titre provisoire 12 sujets susceptibles d'être ultérieurement étudiés, et des membres de la Commission ont été appelés à rédiger un bref schéma donnant un aperçu de la nature du sujet, de son objet et de ce qui en avait déjà été traité dans des conventions ou dans des projets de codification émanant d'organismes privés comme l'Association de droit international ou l'Institut de droit international. Ces schémas ont été diffusés[308], et c'est sur la base de ces schémas que la Commission a recommandé en 1993 — et que l'Assemblée générale a approuvé — la mise en route de travaux sur la question des réserves aux traités et celle de la succession d'États et de la nationalité des personnes physiques et morales[309].

166. La Commission estime que cette méthode de sélection est meilleure que la précédente. Aborder un nouveau sujet, quel qu'il soit, comporte toujours quelque incertitude et suppose quelque discernement : l'incertitude est réduite et le discernement facilité si la sélection ne s'opère qu'après mûr examen, à partir de travaux qui n'engagent la Commission ni en ce qui concerne le sujet ni en ce qui concerne le choix de la manière dont il sera traité. En même temps, l'Assemblée générale et, à travers elle, les autres organismes des Nations Unies devraient être encouragés à soumettre à la Commission des sujets susceptibles de donner matière à une codification et un développement progressif du droit international. Il serait souhaitable d'inscrire à l'ordre du jour de la Commission à la fois des sujets qui lui sont renvoyés et des sujets qu'elle propose, et que l'Assemblée générale a approuvés, selon la procédure exposée plus haut.

167. Un groupe de travail sur le programme de travail à long terme, institué par la Commission, a établi un plan général de sujets de droit international parmi lesquels figuraient des sujets déjà abordés par la Commission, des sujets à l'examen à la Commission et des sujets qu'elle pourrait étudier dans l'avenir (voir annexe II).

---

[305]Voir ibid., *1969*, vol. II, p. 244 et 245; ibid., *1970*, vol. II, p. 265 à 288; et ibid., *1971*, vol. II (deuxième partie), p. 1 à 103. Pour l'examen de ces matières par la Commission et les conclusions auxquelles celle-ci est parvenue, voir ibid., *1971*, vol. II (première partie), p. 370 et 371; ibid., *1972*, vol. II, p. 221 à 230; et ibid., *1973*, vol. II, p. 229 à 235. La Commission avait procédé en 1962 à un examen de ce genre (ibid., *1962*, vol. II, p. 95 et 210) et avait refusé d'ajouter de nouvelles matières à une liste déjà longue.
[306]Voir ibid., *1973*, vol. II, p. 235; et résolution 2780 (XXVI) de l'Assemblée générale, en date du 3 décembre 1971. La Commission a achevé l'examen en deuxième lecture du projet d'articles sur le droit relatif aux utilisations des cours d'eau internationaux à des fins autres que la navigation en 1994. Voir *Annuaire de la Commission du droit international, 1994*, vol. II (deuxième partie), p. 93 à 143.
[307]Ibid., *1992*, vol. II (deuxième partie), p. 57.
[308]Document A/CN.4/454.
[309]*Annuaire de la Commission du droit international, 1993*, vol. II (deuxième partie), p. 99 à 101. En 1995, la question de la protection diplomatique a été retenue pour faire l'objet d'une étude de faisabilité sans établissement préalable d'un schéma. Voir Rapport de la Commission du droit international sur les travaux de sa quarante-septième session, *Documents officiels de l'Assemblée générale, cinquantième session, Supplément n° 10* (A/50/10), p. 280. Au paragraphe 8 de sa résolution 50/45, en date du 11 décembre 1995, l'Assemblée générale a pris note de cette « suggestion » et a invité les gouvernements à présenter des observations à ce propos.

c) *La codification et le développement progressif 50 ans après*

168. Il a été généralement admis après 1945 que le droit international était à bien des égards incertain et peu développé et qu'il demandait à la fois une codification et un développement progressif. L'idée simple qu'il serait possible, voire souhaitable, de faire tenir tout le droit international dans un « code » unique a vite été abandonnée[310]. Toutes autres considérations mises à part, l'élaboration d'un code de ce genre aurait été une tâche « napoléonienne ». Mais il est possible de discerner les fruits de la codification et du développement progressif à long terme dans des domaines tels que, par exemple, le droit des traités, les relations diplomatiques et consulaires et le droit de la mer[311]. Les règles de droit international applicables dans chacun de ces domaines sont énoncées dans des textes qui servent de point de départ à tout examen juridique qui pourrait être entrepris. C'est là un progrès indiscutable dans les relations entre États. C'est là également la preuve de la permanence de la valeur d'un processus ordonné de « codification et développement progressif ».

169. D'un autre côté, les relations entre États et les institutions internationales ont, au cours des 50 dernières années, subi de nombreux changements, susceptibles d'avoir des répercussions sur les travaux que la Commission pourrait utilement entreprendre. Parmi ces changements, il convient de citer :

i) Le caractère technique et administratif de nombreux problèmes de droit nouveaux;

ii) Une tendance à traiter de certaines questions juridiques dans un cadre régional (certains problèmes d'environnement, par exemple), voire bilatéral (la protection des investissements, par exemple);

iii) La prolifération d'organes dotés de mandats normatifs particuliers (qu'il s'agisse d'organes permanents comme la CNUDCI ou le Sous-Comité juridique du Comité des utilisations pacifiques de l'espace extra-atmosphérique, ou d'organes ad hoc comme la Troisième Conférence des Nations Unies sur le droit de la mer) ou d'une compétence institutionnelle principale dans un domaine donné (la Commission des droits de l'homme de l'ONU, le Comité des droits de l'homme, le Programme des Nations Unies pour l'environnement, l'Organisation mondiale du commerce, etc.);

iv) Les activités des institutions spécialisées des Nations Unies en général (Organisation maritime internationale, Organisation de l'aviation civile internationale, etc.).

170. Ces facteurs ne jouent pas tous dans le même sens. La prolifération d'organismes dotés d'attributions précises dans des domaines donnés du droit ou de la pratique limite le champ d'action dans lequel la Commission peut évoluer sans risque d'empiéter sur leurs travaux. En revanche, il existe une marge de collaboration avec ces organismes en ce qui concerne le développement de domaines du droit international revêtant un intérêt général aussi bien que spécialisé. La tendance à traiter de problèmes donnés sur une base bilatérale est peut-être une réponse aux déficiences du droit général qui sont constatées, déficiences qu'il faut malgré tout aborder. Il existe d'une façon générale un

---

[310]Voir *Annuaire de la Commission du droit international, 1973*, vol. II, p. 231 et 232 (par. 152 à 158).

[311]L'instrument qui régit la matière s'intitule désormais Convention des Nations Unies sur le droit de la mer de 1982, laquelle, sur certains points essentiels — la mer territoriale et la haute mer en particulier — reprend les dispositions des Conventions de 1958.

risque de fragmentation du droit international et de la pratique, que la Commission, avec le mandat général et la mission qui sont les siens, peut aider à contrecarrer.

171. Ainsi, s'il est vrai que les travaux sur nombre des grands sujets réputés mûrs pour être codifiés — par exemple le droit de la mer, le droit des traités, les relations diplomatiques et consulaires — ont été menés à bien, il n'en demeure pas moins que l'idée que la codification n'est plus nécessaire est erronée. Même en ce qui concerne des domaines désormais régis par un traité, la pratique peut se développer et soulever de nouvelles difficultés, appelant un nouvel examen, ce qui est le cas, par exemple, des réserves aux traités. Au niveau international, la codification et le développement progressif sont un processus continu. Qui plus est, le rythme de développement du droit international est désormais rapide, et le fait est que des organismes privés qui, comme l'Association de droit international et l'Institut de droit international, étudient les problèmes actuels semblent n'avoir aucun mal à recenser les domaines du droit qui doivent faire l'objet, sinon d'une codification, du moins d'une clarification, d'un développement et d'une formulation explicite. Or les organismes privés n'ont pas la faculté que la Commission, en sa qualité d'organe des Nations Unies, possède d'obtenir des informations des gouvernements et d'engager un dialogue avec eux. La Commission peut exercer cette faculté par l'intermédiaire de la Sixième Commission, à travers des demandes d'informations et d'observations adressées aux gouvernements et grâce aux liens directs qui existent entre elle et les comités consultatifs régionaux. Aussi longtemps que le processus de relations et de dialogue sera efficace, un organe comme la Commission conservera probablement son utilité.

172. D'un autre côté, les travaux de la Commission ont été ponctués de difficultés, même en ce qui concerne la *première* génération de projets. Pour diverses raisons, il a fallu beaucoup de temps pour mener à bien les travaux sur certains sujets majeurs inscrits à l'ordre du jour de la Commission, en raison notamment de leur importance, de leur ampleur et de leur difficulté. Cela a eu pour effet de ralentir les travaux sur d'autres sujets inscrits à l'ordre du jour de la Commission et de semer le doute quant à l'opportunité de lui confier de nouvelles tâches avant qu'elle n'achève celles qu'elle avait entreprises.

173. La Commission est d'avis qu'il est souhaitable d'apporter un certain nombre de modifications à ses méthodes de travail pour pouvoir faire face à la situation présente. Les sections du présent rapport qui suivent sont consacrées à la question des changements à opérer, sous les rubriques suivantes :

    i)   Les relations entre la Commission et l'Assemblée générale (Sixième Commission) [sect. 3];

    ii)   Le rôle du Rapporteur spécial (sect. 4);

    iii)   Les relations entre la Commission, le Comité de rédaction et les groupes de travail (sect. 5);

    iv)   La durée et la structure des sessions (sect. 6);

    v)   Les relations de la Commission avec d'autres organismes (sect. 7);

    vi)   La révision éventuelle du Statut de la Commission (sect. 8).

3. Les relations entre la Commission
et l'Assemblée générale (Sixième Commission)

174. Cette question est expressément mentionnée par l'Assemblée générale à l'alinéa 7 du préambule de sa résolution 50/45, où il est fait état de la nécessité. . .

« de renforcer encore les relations entre la Sixième Commission, en sa qualité d'organe constitué de représentants des gouvernements, et la Commission du droit international, en sa qualité d'organe constitué d'experts juridiques indépendants, en vue d'améliorer le dialogue entre l'une et l'autre ».

Tout en réaffirmant succinctement le caractère des deux organes, cet alinéa donne clairement à entendre que le dialogue entre eux pourrait être amélioré.

175. Aux termes de l'article 3 du Statut de la Commission du droit international, ses membres sont élus par l'Assemblée générale sur une liste de candidats présentés par les gouvernements des États Membres de l'Organisation des Nations Unies. Les électeurs, est-il précisé, « auront en vue que les personnes appelées à faire partie de la Commission réunissent individuellement les conditions requises et que, dans l'ensemble, la représentation des grandes formes de civilisation et des principaux systèmes juridiques du monde soit assurée » (article 8 du Statut). L'existence de groupes régionaux aux fins de l'élection des membres est expressément reconnue dans le Statut par suite de l'amendement de 1981 (article 9), ce qui contribue à assurer la représentativité de la Commission dans son ensemble. En revanche, il existe une saine tradition au sein de la Commission, qui est pleinement conforme au statut d'indépendance des membres, selon laquelle tous les membres participent à titre personnel aux travaux de la Commission et ne sont en aucune manière des «représentants »[312].

176. S'agissant des qualités individuelles requises, le paragraphe 1 de l'article 2 stipule que les membres « possèd[ent] une compétence reconnue en matière de droit international ». Les membres de la Commission sont rééligibles sans restriction (article 10 du Statut); il n'existe aucune limite d'âge. On peut noter qu'il n'y a jamais eu de femme membre de la Commission.

177. Ce rappel étant fait, la Commission aborde les questions de fond que soulèvent les « relations entre la Sixième Commission, en sa qualité d'organe constitué de représentants des gouvernements, et la Commission du droit international, en sa qualité d'organe constitué d'experts juridiques indépendants ».

a) Initiative de travaux sur des sujets spécifiés

178. Une source importante de nouvelles tâches éventuelles pour la Commission réside dans les demandes que lui adressent l'Assemblée générale ou d'autres organes des Nations Unies. Cette procédure est expressément prévue à l'article 16 et au paragraphe 3 de l'article 18 du Statut mais, au cours des années récentes, ces dispositions ont été peu employées. Le débat lié à la « Décennie du droit international » n'a pas non plus vu le développement de nouvelles idées susceptibles d'être portées à l'ordre du jour de la Commission par la Sixième Commission. Comme la Commission l'a montré lors de ses travaux sur le sujet de la protection et de l'inviolabilité des agents diplomatiques

---

[312]Le Statut lui-même est muet sur ce point.

et autres personnes ayant droit à une protection spéciale en vertu du droit international[313] et, plus récemment, sur le projet de statut d'une cour criminelle internationale[314], elle est capable de donner suite sans délai à de telles demandes. Elle peut ainsi produire un commentaire ou un avis ou, comme dans les deux cas cités, élaborer des projets d'articles sous une forme appropriée aux fins d'adoption lors d'une conférence diplomatique.

179. De l'avis de la Commission, il serait souhaitable que le programme de travail de la Commission comporte, d'une part, des sujets proposés au sein de la Commission et approuvés par l'Assemblée générale et, d'autre part, des sujets ayant leur origine dans d'autres organes du système des Nations Unies et expressément renvoyés à la Commission par l'Assemblée générale en application du Statut. Ce type de renvoi permet d'éviter des chevauchements et favoriser la coordination dans l'effort d'élaboration du droit international. Naturellement, les sujets renvoyés doivent être pertinents pour la Commission, « organe constitué d'experts juridiques indépendants » dans le domaine du droit international général.

b) *Aperçu des travaux en cours et commentaire*

180. L'examen des travaux de la Commission et la fourniture d'informations en retour par les États prennent de multiples formes. En particulier, dès le début des travaux sur un sujet, les États sont invités à donner des renseignements sur leur pratique et leur législation et à répondre à un questionnaire. Les représentants des États Membres à la Sixième Commission formulent oralement leurs observations sur le rapport annuel de la Commission, l'examen du rapport à la Sixième Commission étant désormais utilement divisé en fonction des différentes composantes du rapport. De plus, les États sont invités à fournir officiellement des observations écrites en réponse à des demandes particulières faites par la Commission dans son rapport ainsi que sur les projets d'articles adoptés sur tout sujet en première lecture.

181. Il existe toutefois des différences considérables quant à l'ampleur des renseignements et des observations fournis par les gouvernements sur les rapports et les projets de la Commission. Les gouvernements peuvent se contenter de laisser progresser les travaux sur un sujet ou, étant de manière générale à même d'accepter les orientations des travaux, ils peuvent ne pas ressentir le besoin de faire des observations. D'autres peuvent souhaiter infléchir le cours de travaux particuliers et, dès lors, s'exprimer davantage. De nombreux gouvernements, notamment ceux de pays en développement, ont très peu de ressources à consacrer à cette tâche. Il n'en est pas moins vrai que dans de nombreux cas, les demandes d'observations ou même de renseignements de la Commission restent sans réponse[315]. L'interaction entre la Commission et les

---

[313]Cette demande est venue du Conseil de sécurité via l'Assemblée générale. Voir document A/9407 et résolution 3166 (XXVIII) de l'Assemblée générale, en date du 14 décembre 1973. Voir aussi *Annuaire de la Commission du droit international, 1972*, vol. II, p. 339.

[314]Voir résolution 45/41 de l'Assemblée générale, en date du 28 novembre 1990, par. 3.

[315]S'agissant des réponses écrites fournies par les gouvernements à des questionnaires de la Commission sur quelques sujets récents, les chiffres sont les suivants :

Responsabilité des États : 15   [*Annuaire de la Commission du droit international, 1980*, vol. II (première partie), p. 85;

ibid., *1981*, vol. II (première partie), p. 73]

(Suite de la note page suivante.)

417

gouvernements est capitale pour le rôle de la Commission, et les choses pourraient être améliorées de part et d'autre.

182.   Pour sa part, la Commission estime qu'elle devrait s'efforcer d'étendre sa pratique consistant à identifier des questions sur lesquelles elle tient expressément à obtenir des observations, si possible préalablement à l'adoption des projets d'articles sur le point. Ces questions devraient revêtir un caractère général, « stratégique », et non se rapporter à des aspects de la technique rédactionnelle. La Commission devrait s'efforcer de faire en sorte que le rapport ainsi que tout questionnaire adressé aux gouvernements soient d'utilisation plus facile et qu'ils comportent des indications claires quant à l'objet et aux raisons d'une éventuelle demande. En particulier, le rapport de la Commission devrait être plus court, plus thématique, et viser autant que possible à mettre en relief et à expliquer les questions clefs. Le rôle du Rapporteur général dans l'élaboration du rapport devrait être renforcé[316]. La Commission devrait revenir sur ces questions au cours du nouveau quinquennat.

c)   *Rôle de la Sixième Commission à l'égard du texte final des projets de la Commission*

183.   La Commission a rempli sa tâche sur un sujet donné lorsqu'elle présente à la Sixième Commission une série complète de projets d'articles sur ce sujet. L'objet assigné à la Commission est — peut-on penser — pleinement accompli si les projets d'articles et les commentaires dont ils sont assortis énoncent les principes pertinents d'une manière propre, de façon générale, à permettre leur adoption par les États. En revanche, la question de savoir si telle ou telle série de projets d'articles est acceptable ou susceptible d'adoption à un moment donné relève essentiellement d'une décision de principe de la Sixième Commission et des États Membres.

184.   La réponse à un ensemble de projets d'articles ou à d'autres travaux de la Commission peut prendre diverses formes. En soumettant ses travaux, la Commission elle-même fait une recommandation initiale à cet égard[317] mais le choix des moyens relève de la Sixième Commission. Dans le cas d'un texte qui ne donne pas lieu à une recommandation d'adoption sous forme de convention, une simple décision de prendre acte ou une incorporation dans une résolution de l'Assemblée générale peut être suffisante. Dans le cas de projets d'articles susceptibles de constituer la base d'une convention, la Sixième Commission peut simplement prendre acte du résultat, elle peut le traiter à titre préliminaire

---

(Suite de la note 315.)

Cours d'eau :	21	(document A/CN.4/447 et Add.1 à 3)
Projet de code des crimes :	13	[*Annuaire de la Commission du droit international, 1985*, vol. II (première partie), p. 84;
		ibid., *1987*, vol. II (première partie), p. 11;
		ibid., *1990*, vol. II (première partie), p. 23]
Immunité des États :	28	[ibid., *1988*, vol. II (première partie), p. 45]
Valise diplomatique :	30	[ibid., *1988*, vol. II (première partie), p. 127;
		ibid., *1989*, vol. II (première partie), p. 81]
Réserves aux traités :	13	(au 5 juin 1996).

[316]Voir document A/CN.4/L.473, p. 8.
[317]Statut, article 23.

dans le cadre d'un groupe de travail ou convoquer une conférence préparatoire à une fin analogue, elle peut convoquer immédiatement une conférence diplomatique, ou (comme cela est le cas pour le projet d'articles sur les utilisations des cours d'eau internationaux à des fins autres que la navigation actuellement à l'examen) elle peut choisir de traiter elle-même les projets d'articles. Le paragraphe 2 de l'article 23 du Statut prévoit aussi que l'Assemblée peut « renvo[yer] à la Commission les projets aux fins de réexamen ou de nouvelle rédaction ». Cette possibilité pourrait être employée plus efficacement.

185.   La Commission fait simplement observer que, s'il existe des doutes sérieux quant à l'acceptabilité d'un texte quelconque concernant un sujet donné, il serait utile que l'Assemblée générale et les gouvernements les expriment fermement à un stade plus précoce, sans laisser les difficultés en suspens et attendre que la Commission ait achevé ses travaux et les ait présentés à la Sixième Commission.

4.   *Le rôle du Rapporteur spécial*

a)   *Désignation*

186.   Le Rapporteur spécial a joué un rôle central dans l'activité de la Commission. En fait, le Statut ne prévoit expressément la désignation d'un Rapporteur que dans le cas de projets concernant le développement progressif (alinéa *a* de l'article 16)[318]. Mais d'emblée, la Commission a pris l'habitude de désigner un Rapporteur spécial au tout début de l'étude d'un sujet, indépendamment de la question de savoir si celui-ci relevait de la codification ou du développement progressif[319].

187.   En pratique, les mandats des Rapporteurs sont généralement répartis entre des membres de régions différentes. Ce système, à condition d'être appliqué avec une certaine souplesse, présente de nombreux avantages, notamment en ce qu'il contribue à garantir que la formulation de rapports et de propositions s'inspire de conceptions différentes et de cultures juridiques différentes.

188.   Il faut souligner que les difficultés qu'a rencontrées la Commission au cours de ses travaux ont été largement imputables, non à la désignation d'un rapporteur spécial pour un sujet, mais au fait que les Rapporteurs spéciaux ont eu tendance, voire ont été incités, à travailler à l'écart de la Commission, pratiquement sans directives durant l'élaboration des rapports quant à l'orientation des travaux futurs. C'est à cette question essentielle, telle que la perçoit la Commission, que les paragraphes suivants sont en grande partie consacrés.

b)   *Élaboration des rapports*

189.   C'est en établissant des rapports (généralement annuels) que les Rapporteurs spéciaux délimitent et développent leur sujet, expliquent l'état du droit et font des propositions en vue de projets d'articles. L'élaboration des rapports pose un certain nombre de questions.

---

[318]L'article 16 du Statut ne fixe la procédure que « dans les grandes lignes », mais il est clair que le Rapporteur est censé en être une pièce maîtresse (voir, par exemple, les alinéas *d*, *f* et *i*).

[319]Voir, par exemple, *Annuaire de la Commission du droit international, 1949*, p. 281 (désignation initiale de rapporteurs pour les sujets des traités, de la procédure arbitrale et du régime de la haute mer). En même temps, la Commission a demandé aux gouvernements de lui fournir des renseignements en application du paragraphe 2 de l'article 19 du Statut, lequel n'est formellement applicable qu'aux projets intéressant la codification, ibid.

i) *Nécessité de l'approbation préalable par la Commission de la nature et de la portée des travaux prévus pour la session suivante*

190. La pratique actuelle de la Commission n'est pas uniforme. Certains Rapporteurs exposent de façon détaillée le type de rapport qu'ils envisagent de présenter à la session suivante; d'autres ne le font pas. Au bout du compte, même si l'on admet la nécessité de laisser aux Rapporteurs une certaine indépendance, la transparence devrait être la règle. Il est essentiel que les rapports futurs répondent aux besoins de la Commission dans son ensemble. L'information ouvre la possibilité d'un dialogue, tant sur des questions d'orientation générale que sur des points de fond précis. À l'inverse, si un rapport traite une question que la Commission considère comme périphérique, ou s'abstient de traiter une question que la Commission considère comme capitale, la session aura en fait été inutile.

ii) *Communication des rapports avant le début de la session*

191. Là non plus, la pratique n'est pas uniforme. Certains rapports sont diffusés à l'avance en vue de la session, d'autres ne le sont pas. Un Rapporteur spécial n'est bien sûr pas responsable des retards dans la traduction et dans la diffusion imputables aux restrictions financières à l'ONU ou aux règles de l'Organisation concernant la documentation[320]. Mais il est éminemment souhaitable que tous les rapports soient à la disposition des membres de la Commission quelques semaines avant le début de la session, pour permettre une étude et une réflexion. Ce le serait encore plus en cas de raccourcissement de la session.

c) *Nécessité d'un groupe consultatif permanent*

192. Il est prévu à l'alinéa *d* de l'article 16 du Statut que, « [l]orsque l'Assemblée générale renvoie à la Commission une proposition concernant le développement progressif du droit international », la Commission « désigne, s'il y a lieu, dans son sein les membres chargés de travailler avec le Rapporteur à la préparation d'avant-projets, en attendant les réponses » au questionnaire adressé aux gouvernements. Cela peut signifier qu'une fois muni des réponses le Rapporteur spécial travaille de manière indépendante. Mais dans la plupart des cas, il est devenu d'usage que le Rapporteur spécial travaille en grande partie seul à l'élaboration de ses rapports. Autrement dit, entre les sessions, un Rapporteur spécial n'a aucun contact officiel avec les autres membres de la Commission.

193. D'autres organismes, tels l'Association de droit international et l'Institut de droit international, travaillent différemment. Plusieurs membres sont désignés pour former un groupe consultatif de sorte que, entre les sessions, le Rapporteur peut obtenir leur avis sur la démarche qu'ils jugent la meilleure et la plus acceptable et sur les éléments essentiels du rapport suivant. Par des questionnaires, par la diffusion de rapports ou, à titre exceptionnel, par la convocation de réunions intérimaires, le groupe peut faire connaître son avis. Bien que le rapport reste celui du Rapporteur, il est probable que les contributions obtenues le rendront effectivement acceptable pour les membres du comité et, par extension, pour les membres de l'organisme dans son ensemble.

---

[320]On peut noter que la date limite pour répondre à des questionnaires communiqués au mois de septembre est souvent fixée très tard — en mars ou avril de l'année suivante, par exemple —, si bien qu'il est très difficile aux Rapporteurs spéciaux de prendre pleinement en considération les réponses dans leur rapport de cette année-là.

194. La Commission relève que cette méthode a été employée avec profit pour le récent sujet « Succession d'États et nationalité ». Il estime qu'elle devrait être généralisée, notamment en ce qui concerne les nouveaux projets, et être adoptée en particulier dès les premiers stades des travaux, y compris celui de l'orientation stratégique, sur un sujet. Le groupe consultatif devrait être nommé par la Commission elle-même, et il devrait être largement représentatif[321].

195. Il faut certainement se garder de tout formalisme excessif, et souligner que le rapport continuera de relever de la responsabilité du Rapporteur spécial, et non de celle du groupe dans son ensemble. Le groupe a pour fonction, non pas d'approuver le rapport du Rapporteur spécial, mais d'apporter une contribution à son orientation générale ainsi que sur tout point particulier que le Rapporteur spécial tient à soulever. La question de savoir si le groupe est nommé pour la durée du quinquennat ou pour une durée plus brève peut être déterminée dans chaque cas, en consultation avec le Rapporteur spécial.

196. Bien que ces modifications puissent être mises en œuvre sans révision du Statut, la Commission recommande aussi qu'à l'occasion de toute révision éventuelle du Statut le principe d'un tel groupe soit consacré. Contrairement à ce que prévoit le Statut en l'état actuel (voir plus haut, par. 186), il devrait l'être sans aucune distinction entre codification et développement progressif.

d) *Élaboration des commentaires relatifs aux projets d'articles*

197. Il faut faire le départ entre un rapport qui présente une analyse du domaine du droit et de la pratique à l'étude et un commentaire nettement circonscrit des projets d'articles. L'élaboration du premier correspond naturellement à une fonction essentielle du Rapporteur spécial, mais il en va de même de la rédaction du second. Or il n'est pas rare actuellement que des projets d'articles soient présentés sans commentaire au Comité de rédaction, contrairement à la pratique antérieure de la Commission. Il arrive même que des projets d'articles soient présentés à la Commission pour examen final sans leurs commentaires, qu'elle n'adopte, en ayant peu de temps pour les examiner, qu'au cours des dernières séances d'une session.

198. On peut faire valoir que, puisque les projets d'articles sont susceptibles d'être substantiellement modifiés au Comité de rédaction, la présentation à l'avance de commentaires par un Rapporteur spécial est prématurée. En revanche, le Comité de rédaction est en bien meilleure position s'il dispose en même temps des projets d'articles et des commentaires (ou au moins d'un schéma général de la teneur des commentaires). Les commentaires aident à expliquer l'objet des articles et à préciser leur portée et leur effet. Il arrive souvent qu'un désaccord sur un aspect d'un projet puisse être résolu par l'adjonction d'un commentaire ou par le transfert d'une disposition du texte dans le commentaire ou *vice versa*. La présentation du seul texte des articles interdit une telle souplesse et peut conduire à surestimer l'importance de l'insertion d'une disposition dans le texte. Un travail simultané sur le texte et le commentaire peut améliorer l'acceptabilité de l'un et l'autre. Il permettrait sans doute d'éviter la pratique inopportune consistant à insérer des exemples dans le texte d'un article — comme c'est actuellement le cas au paragraphe 3 du projet d'article 19 de la première partie du texte sur la responsabilité des États. Ce sera

---

[321] Cette méthode pourrait aussi être adoptée pour la seconde lecture du projet sur la responsabilité des États, qu'il serait hautement souhaitable d'achever avant la fin du prochain quinquennat.

aussi une précieuse composante des *travaux préparatoires* de toute clause conventionnelle susceptible d'être adoptée sur la base du texte proposé.

199. Il convient de souligner que les commentaires, sous leur forme définitive, sont destinés au premier chef à expliquer le texte finalement adopté. Bien qu'un rappel de l'évolution de ce texte soit opportun, un commentaire a pour principale fonction d'expliquer le texte lui-même, par des références pertinentes à l'essentiel des décisions, de la doctrine et de la pratique des États, afin que le lecteur puisse voir dans quelle mesure le texte de la Commission consacre ou, le cas échéant, développe ou élargit le droit. En règle générale, de tels commentaires n'ont pas pour fonction de faire état des désaccords concernant le texte tel qu'il a été adopté en seconde lecture; cela peut être fait en plénière au moment de l'adoption définitive et trouver sa place dans le rapport[322].

200. Vu sa charge de travail, on ne saurait attendre du Comité de rédaction qu'il révise lui-même les commentaires, mais, dès qu'il a approuvé un article déterminé, il faudrait que le Rapporteur spécial élabore ou révise, selon le cas, le commentaire de cet article, avec l'aide du Secrétariat. Le commentaire devrait alors être communiqué soit aux membres du Comité de rédaction, soit (le cas échéant) à ceux du groupe consultatif pour le sujet, afin de leur permettre de faire part individuellement de leurs observations. Comme il est clairement précisé dans le Statut[323], les projets d'articles ne peuvent pas être considérés comme définitivement adoptés si la Commission n'a pas approuvé les commentaires qui lui ont été soumis.

e) *Rôle du Rapporteur spécial au sein du Comité de rédaction*

201. Concrètement, c'est au sein du Comité de rédaction que les divergences de vues sur un sujet s'expriment le plus clairement et qu'il faut les aplanir; de même, c'est dans ce cadre que le rôle indépendant du Rapporteur spécial doit s'adapter à l'éventail des opinions des membres de la Commission. Les exigences de certains sujets et la démarche de tel ou tel Rapporteur spécial produiront toujours une certaine diversité des pratiques. Mais en règle générale, le Groupe de planification propose que le rôle du Rapporteur spécial comprenne les éléments suivants :

    i)   Production d'une série d'articles clairs et complets, assortis autant que possible soit de commentaires, soit de notes pouvant servir de base à des commentaires;

    ii)   Exposé succinct de la raison d'être des projets d'articles soumis au Comité de rédaction, y compris toutes modifications qui seraient indiquées;

    iii)   En dernière analyse, acceptation du point de vue du Comité de rédaction dans son ensemble, même s'il est contraire aux idées avancées par le Rapporteur spécial et, le cas échéant, traduction du

---

[322] Il en va assez différemment en première lecture. Selon l'alinéa ii du paragraphe *b* de l'article 20 du Statut (qui, au demeurant, concerne la codification par opposition au développement progressif), les commentaires afférents à des textes adoptés en première lecture doivent indiquer les « divergences et désaccords qui subsistent, ainsi que les arguments invoqués en faveur de chacune des thèses ». Mais le Statut ne contient aucune indication du même genre pour le texte final des projets d'articles, voir l'article 22.

[323] L'alinéa *i* de l'article 16 du Statut prévoit que « [l]e Rapporteur et les membres désignés à cet effet. . . élaborent le texte final de ce projet avec rapport explicatif, qu'ils soumettent pour adoption à l'examen de la Commission ». Une disposition analogue figure à l'article 22.

point de vue du Comité de rédaction dans des articles et/ou des commentaires révisés. Dans l'exercice de cette fonction, le Rapporteur spécial devrait être au service de la Commission, et non se faire le zélateur de quelconques vues personnelles avant la lettre.

202.   Il va de soi qu'un Rapporteur spécial qui désapprouve les vues exprimées en définitive par le Comité de rédaction a parfaitement le droit d'expliquer ce désaccord en séance plénière, au moment de la présentation du rapport du Comité de rédaction. Dans ce cas, il est loisible à la Commission plénière de préférer les vues du Rapporteur spécial à celles du Comité de rédaction. Toutefois, eu égard au nombre des membres du Comité de rédaction et au rôle de celui-ci vis-à-vis de la Commission plénière, une telle situation ne risque guère de se produire. De plus, il vaut mieux, dans le cas de désaccords importants qui ne peuvent être réglés au sein du Comité de rédaction, que la plénière en soit saisie à un stade plus précoce et qu'elle ait la possibilité de régler la question par un vote indicatif (voir ci-après, par. 209 à 211).

5.   Le rôle et les relations de la Commission plénière vis-à-vis du Comité de rédaction et des groupes de travail

a)   Les débats généraux en plénière

203.   La fonction principale du débat général en plénière est d'arrêter dans ses grandes lignes la manière dont la Commission abordera un sujet. C'est indispensable pour que le Comité de rédaction, ou un groupe de travail, entreprenne sa mission avec confiance. Ces organes subsidiaires doivent être certains qu'ils suivent une ligne de conduite acceptable en gros pour la Commission dans son ensemble.

204.   Actuellement, les débats en plénière ne remplissent pas très bien cette fonction, ce qui s'explique par deux raisons principales. La première est que le débat en plénière a souvent un caractère trop général, les interventions couvrant l'ensemble d'un rapport parfois très long sans faire de distinction entre différents problèmes et s'attachant quelquefois à des points précis de forme qui seraient mieux traités au sein du Comité de rédaction.

205.   Le second facteur qui joue est la tendance à faire de longs exposés, comme si la Commission constituait un public de conférence qu'il s'agirait d'instruire plutôt que de convaincre. De longs discours ne sont pas la forme idéale du débat, lequel devient diffus et cesse de servir son objectif premier qui est de guider la Commission, ses comités et les Rapporteurs spéciaux quant aux orientations à prendre.

206.   Dans les premiers temps de la Commission, les exposés étaient presque toujours courts et axés sur des problèmes particuliers qui risquaient de donner lieu à des difficultés ou des désaccords. De l'avis de la Commission, cette pratique est bien préférable, et la Commission devrait prendre des dispositions pour la rétablir comme norme.

207.   Les remèdes possibles sont notamment les suivants :

i)   Premièrement, il faudrait s'efforcer de structurer le débat pour que la Commission aborde successivement chaque point, les observations étant limitées au point à l'examen[324].

---

[324]Cette méthode a été utilement adoptée pour l'examen du neuvième rapport de M. Thiam sur le code des crimes, *Annuaire de la Commission du droit international, 1991*, vol. I, p. 5 à 52.

ii) Deuxièmement, les membres devraient s'astreindre à une discipline. Aux yeux du Groupe de planification, le meilleur moyen d'y parvenir est de bien structurer le débat. En outre, un « code de conduite » officieux, préconisant des interventions plus brèves, pourrait être adopté : le président pourrait s'y référer de temps à autre, si besoin est.

iii) Troisièmement, à l'issue du débat, le Président devrait tâcher de récapituler les conclusions générales de la Commission sur le point à l'examen, tout en relevant tout désaccord qui aurait été exprimé[325]. Cet exercice sera sans nul doute parfois difficile, mais, s'il est exécuté avec rigueur et, si les membres l'acceptent de façon générale comme un résumé fidèle, il aidera ensuite effectivement le Comité de rédaction ou le groupe de travail dans leur examen des questions. Pour l'examen du texte final des projets d'articles, cette fonction devrait revenir au Président du Comité de rédaction, en collaboration avec le Rapporteur spécial.

208. Cela conduit à examiner la question des modalités de vote. Actuellement, la Commission et ses organes subsidiaires s'efforcent de parvenir à un consensus, ce qui est incontestablement une bonne chose en règle générale.

209. Il y a cependant une différence entre l'adoption de décisions qui sont effectivement définitives et le type de conclusions que, selon nous, le Président devrait formuler à l'issue d'un débat en plénière. Ces dernières seraient provisoires et sujettes à révision; elles n'auraient qu'une valeur indicative, puisqu'il resterait beaucoup à faire avant que des décisions définitives puissent être prises. Sur des points particuliers pouvant prêter à controverse, il serait bon que le Président s'assure de l'acceptabilité de ses conclusions en invitant la Commission à procéder à un vote indicatif. Cela aurait encore plus d'intérêt pour les questions de détail, qu'il vaut mieux régler, dans un sens ou un autre, afin d'avancer. Les points de vue minoritaires pourraient naturellement être consignés dans les comptes rendus analytiques et dans le rapport de la Commission.

210. Des situations analogues se présenteront au sein d'organes subsidiaires comme le Comité de rédaction. À mesure que les travaux progressent, il faut prendre des « décisions » qui sont loin d'être définitives, et l'exigence d'un consensus sur toutes ces questions implique une procédure lourde et qui prend beaucoup de temps. Il serait loisible aux membres qui ne se trouvent pas dans la majorité à l'issue d'un vote indicatif de défendre leurs vues ultérieurement. Néanmoins, en cas de désaccord important sur un point de principe, il pourra être utile d'en saisir la plénière aux fins de décision par un vote indicatif ou tout autre moyen.

211. Lorsque finalement des décisions doivent être prises, il faut, là encore, ne ménager aucun effort pour parvenir à un consensus. Néanmoins, si ce n'est pas possible dans le temps disponible, il peut être nécessaire de procéder à un vote, peut-être après s'être accordé une pause, un délai de discussion et de réflexion. Un tel vote donnera sans doute une meilleure indication de l'opinion de la Commission qu'un « faux consensus » adopté simplement dans le but de gagner du temps.

212. Une modification mineure qui pourrait être utilement introduite consisterait à instituer une convention selon laquelle l'expression des remerciements, félicitations ou hommages que la Commission aurait à adresser serait

---

[325] Actuellement, cette tâche est accomplie, si tant est qu'elle le soit, par le Rapporteur spécial. Le Président s'en acquitterait peut-être mieux en laissant au Rapporteur spécial auteur du rapport examiné le soin de fournir des éclaircissements et des arguments en réponse aux observations.

réservée au seul Président, au nom de l'ensemble de ses membres. Le temps de la Commission devrait être consacré à ses travaux de fond.

b) *Le Comité de rédaction*

213. En 1958, la Commission avait officiellement reconnu au Comité de rédaction le caractère d'« un comité auquel pourront être renvoyés non seulement des points purement rédactionnels mais aussi des points de fond que la Commission plénière n'aura pu résoudre ou qui sembleront devoir susciter des débats trop prolongés »[326]. La nécessité de charger le Comité de rédaction de ce rôle s'est trouvée accentuée par la nouvelle augmentation du nombre des membres de la Commission en 1981, et il ne fait aucun doute qu'un tel rôle reste capital.

214. Cela ne veut pas dire que le Comité de rédaction devrait être le seul organe à remplir ce rôle. Il conviendra souvent de renvoyer à l'examen d'un groupe de travail plus restreint des questions sur lesquelles il existe un désaccord de principe très précis. Même si la question ne peut être réglée par ce groupe, les principaux points de désaccord pourront généralement être énoncés et présentés en plénière sous une forme qui permette à la Commission de prendre une décision, ou de procéder à un vote indicatif. Mais dans de nombreux autres cas, des problèmes moins caractérisés se poseront, ou des questions de principe imprévues surgiront au cours de la rédaction, ce qui obligera inévitablement le Comité de rédaction à tenter de trouver une solution.

215. Être membre du Comité de rédaction représente une lourde charge : le Comité se réunit presque quotidiennement, et parfois le matin et l'après-midi. C'est pourquoi il faut se féliciter de la pratique récemment instaurée consistant à donner au Comité de rédaction une composition largement différente selon les sujets; cela permet en effet de répartir la charge entre davantage de membres[327].

216. Pour un sujet donné, le Comité de rédaction est habituellement composé de 12 à 14 membres (les autres membres étant présents en tant qu'observateurs et n'intervenant que de temps à autre). L'avantage est qu'un consensus au Comité de rédaction a ainsi toutes chances de recueillir un appui substantiel en plénière.

217. Les longues déclarations sont rares (et doivent être découragées). Il y a souvent un véritable débat. Les discussions ont lieu essentiellement en anglais et en français, qui sont les langues de travail dans lesquelles sont rédigés les textes examinés, mais les membres sont libres d'employer d'autres langues officielles. En général, le Comité de rédaction fonctionne bien.

c) *Groupes de travail*

218. La Commission ou le Groupe de planification créent des groupes de travail dont l'objet et le mandat varient. Dans le cas d'un sujet nouveau, par exemple, il est habituel, avant de nommer un Rapporteur spécial, de constituer un groupe de travail qui aidera à définir le champ de l'étude du sujet et l'orientation à lui donner. Un autre genre de groupe a pour fonction d'examiner tel ou tel point précis pour sortir si possible la Commission d'une impasse[328]. En outre, des groupes de travail sont parfois formés pour s'occuper de l'ensemble d'un sujet, lorsqu'il y a urgence par exemple, et le groupe est alors assez

---

[326]Voir *Annuaire de la Commission du droit international, 1958*, vol. II, p. 112.

[327]La pratique a été adoptée en 1992, voir ibid., *1992*, vol. II (deuxième partie), p. 57.

[328]Voir, par exemple, le groupe de travail créé en 1995 sur les « droits et obligations des États en matière de protection de l'environnement », Rapport de la Commission du droit international sur les travaux de sa quarante-septième session, loc. cit. *supra*, note n° 309, p. 280 et 281.

nombreux. Ce qui distingue ce second type de groupe de travail du Comité de rédaction tient au fait que, si le Comité de rédaction travaille sur le texte des projets d'articles (et, en principe, aussi sur les commentaires) établis par un Rapporteur spécial, le groupe de travail intervient quant à lui plus en amont dans le processus, lorsque les idées sont encore en train de se décanter[329]; il peut très bien étaler ses travaux sur plusieurs sessions, avec une réelle continuité dans sa composition, alors que la composition du Comité de rédaction change d'une année sur l'autre. Ce groupe de travail participe donc de plus près à la formulation d'une approche et à la formulation des projets. Un bon exemple à cet égard est le groupe de travail qui a élaboré le statut d'une cour criminelle internationale permanente et qui, avant de se lancer dans le moindre travail de rédaction d'articles, s'est concentré sur un certain nombre de propositions de base sur lesquelles un accord pouvait être réalisé[330]. La fonction qu'il a assurée n'aurait certainement pas pu l'être par le Comité de rédaction.

219. Dans ce type de groupe de travail, il se peut qu'il n'y ait pas de Rapporteur spécial, ou que le Rapporteur spécial n'ait qu'un rôle limité. Dans la plupart des cas, si le groupe de travail a fait un travail de rédaction minutieux, rien ne sert de le faire refaire par le Comité de rédaction avant de présenter un texte en séance plénière, et cela risque d'entraîner des doubles emplois, voire des erreurs si des membres du Comité de rédaction n'ont pas participé à la discussion approfondie dont ce texte est issu. Il peut arriver que le Comité de rédaction ait un rôle à jouer, celui de l'examen final (la « toilette ») d'un texte pour s'assurer de la justesse et de la cohérence des termes employés, mais, en pareils cas, la discussion en groupe de travail constitue une formule de rechange, et non un simple prélude, à l'examen par le Comité de rédaction.

220. Un groupe de travail, quel que soit son mandat, est toujours subordonné à la Commission plénière, au Groupe de planification ou à l'autre organe qui l'a créé. C'est à l'organe compétent qu'il revient d'établir le mandat voulu, de fixer les paramètres de toute étude, d'examiner et, si nécessaire, modifier les propositions et de se prononcer sur le résultat des travaux.

6. La structure des sessions

221. À la lumière de cette analyse, nous passons à présent aux problèmes de structure des réunions de la Commission, y compris la planification des travaux sur un quinquennat, ainsi que de durée et d'organisation des sessions.

a) Planification des travaux sur un quinquennat

222. À la première session du présent quinquennat, en 1992, la Commission s'est fixé des buts pour les cinq années de son mandat, buts qu'elle a atteints et, dans un cas, dépassés[331]. Le Groupe de planification compte qu'elle procédera

---

[329]Dans le cas du Groupe de travail sur la cour criminelle internationale, le Groupe s'est, à un moment donné, scindé en sous-groupes pour la rédaction.

[330]*Annuaire de la Commission du droit international, 1992*, vol. II (deuxième partie), p. 61.

[331]Pour les objectifs fixés en 1992, voir document A/CN.4/L.473, par. 15. Conformément à ces objectifs, la Commission a terminé l'examen en seconde lecture du projet relatif aux cours d'eau en 1994 et du projet de code des crimes en 1996. Elle a achevé l'examen en première lecture du projet sur la responsabilité des États en 1996. Par l'intermédiaire d'un groupe de travail, elle a progressé dans l'examen de certains aspects du sujet de la responsabilité internationale pour les conséquences préjudiciables d'activités qui ne sont pas interdites par le droit international (plus précisément en ce qui concerne la prévention) et a commencé à travailler sur deux nouveaux sujets. L'élaboration du début jusqu'à la fin du projet de statut d'une cour criminelle internationale, qui n'était pas envisagée dans le rapport de 1992, est également à mettre à son actif.

à un exercice similaire en 1997, première année du quinquennat suivant. Il est aussi souhaitable qu'elle se livre à une évaluation à l'issue des cinq années du mandat pour apprécier les résultats obtenus et examiner les préparatifs à faire pour arrêter, sans perdre de temps au début de la première année, la planification de ses travaux pour le quinquennat suivant.

b) *Durée des sessions*

223. Le Statut ne précise pas quelle doit être la durée des sessions, encore qu'il indique que celles-ci se tiennent normalement à Genève (article 12, modifié en 1955). Effectivement, toutes les sessions se sont tenues à Genève, à l'exception de la session de 1954, qui s'est tenue à Paris, et de celle de 1965, qui s'est tenue en partie à Genève et en partie à Monaco. Il était certainement tenu pour acquis qu'il s'agirait de sessions annuelles, et tel a en effet été le cas depuis 1949. La durée des sessions était normalement de 10 semaines; les 12 semaines sont devenues la règle après l'adoption par l'Assemblée générale de sa résolution 3315 (XXIX) du 14 décembre 1974. Sauf en 1965, la Commission a toujours tenu une unique session continue par an.

224. En 1986, la durée normale de 12 semaines a été ramenée à 10 semaines pour des raisons budgétaires, mais la Commission s'étant exprimée en termes assez énergiques sur le sujet, la durée de 12 semaines a été rétablie l'année suivante et conservée depuis lors. L'Assemblée générale a réaffirmé qu'il était nécessaire que la Commission siège pour la durée habituelle de 12 semaines[332]. La Commission compte aujourd'hui presque deux fois plus de membres que lors de sa création. Ses débats sont forcément plus longs, facteur qu'il faut ne pas perdre de vue lorsqu'on procède à des comparaisons.

225. En principe, la Commission devrait pouvoir décider chaque année quelle serait la durée requise pour la session suivante (c'est-à-dire 12 semaines ou moins), compte dûment tenu de l'état d'avancement des travaux et des priorités que l'Assemblée aurait éventuellement fixées quant à l'achèvement de tel ou tel sujet.

226. Certaines années, une session de moins de 12 semaines suffira. D'autres années, surtout la dernière d'un mandat, il faudra bien 12 semaines à la Commission pour mettre la dernière main à un projet en première ou en seconde lecture avant que sa composition ne soit renouvelée. Pour diverses raisons, le Groupe de planification pense qu'il suffira d'une session de 10 semaines en 1997 pour les travaux en cours.

227. À plus long terme, la question de la durée des sessions est liée à celle de leur organisation, et en particulier à la possibilité de scinder les sessions, qui fait l'objet de la section suivante. Surtout si le principe d'une session en deux temps est adopté, la Commission estime qu'elle pourra normalement s'acquitter avec efficacité de ses tâches dans un délai inférieur à 12 semaines par an. Il lui semble qu'il y aurait de bonnes raisons pour que la Commission revienne à l'ancien système, où les travaux étaient étalés sur 10 semaines au total, tout en se ménageant la possibilité de prolonger sa session de deux semaines certaines années si nécessaire, et tout spécialement la dernière année du mandat.

---

[332]Voir, par exemple, les résolutions de l'Assemblée générale 41/81, en date du 3 décembre 1986, 42/156, en date du 7 décembre 1987 et, la dernière en date, 50/45, en date du 11 décembre 1995 (par. 11).

c) *Possibilité d'une session en deux temps*

228.   L'article 12 du Statut (modifié en 1995) dispose que la Commission se réunit à l'Office des Nations Unies à Genève, en ajoutant toutefois que, « après consultation avec le Secrétaire général », la Commission a « le droit de se réunir en d'autres endroits ». Il n'y a donc rien dans le Statut qui s'oppose à ce que la Commission scinde sa session annuelle en deux parties, ni même à ce que l'une des deux parties de la session se tienne au Siège de l'ONU, à New York. En 1991/92, une formule de session en deux temps a été proposée, mais il a été décidé de l'écarter pour le moment[333].

229.   Les partisans d'une session unique font valoir que seul un travail continu permet d'examiner avec toute la minutie nécessaire les projets d'articles proposés, tant en séance plénière que dans le cadre du Comité de rédaction. Quelle que soit la session considérée, la Commission s'occupe en général activement de quatre ou cinq sujets, dont deux peuvent être prioritaires. Si la session est plus courte et qu'elle se déroule en deux temps, l'examen des sujets qui ne sont pas jugés prioritaires à la session considérée risque d'être plutôt superficiel, moyennant quoi les progrès sur ces sujets seraient irréguliers et les orientations fournies au Rapporteur spécial insuffisantes. Il convient de souligner par ailleurs que la recherche d'un véritable consensus sur les projets d'articles peut se révéler difficile et qu'en tout état de cause elle prend beaucoup de temps. La Commission ne se contente pas de donner son aval aux propositions des Rapporteurs spéciaux, elle doit les examiner d'un œil attentif et critique. Si l'on considère qu'il fait intervenir 34 membres, venus d'horizons juridiques, culturels et linguistiques différents, ce processus ne saurait être hâté plus que de raison. Il se pose aussi un problème de « masse critique », à savoir que seul un examen minutieux collectif en séance plénière, au sein du Comité de rédaction et de groupes de travail peut permettre de dégager des conclusions réellement satisfaisantes, et le fait de scinder la session en deux risquerait d'interrompre et de fragmenter ce processus. De l'avis de ces membres, une session continue s'impose si l'on veut obtenir les meilleurs résultats sur les sujets prioritaires tout en maintenant le rythme et le cap pour les autres sujets.

230.   Les partisans de la session en deux temps font valoir quant à eux que cette formule faciliterait le travail de réflexion et d'étude des membres de la Commission et, en particulier, qu'elle permettrait un travail préparatoire entre les sessions qui ne pourrait que rendre la seconde partie beaucoup plus productive. Ainsi, les rapports ou propositions débattus en séance plénière pendant la première partie de la session pourraient être traités par le Comité de rédaction pendant la seconde. À l'inverse, lorsque le Comité de rédaction aurait achevé l'examen de certains projets d'articles au cours de la première partie de la session, les articles modifiés et assortis de commentaires pourraient être prêts pour l'examen en séance plénière pendant la seconde partie de la session, et les membres de la Commission auraient eu la possibilité d'en prendre connaissance et de les étudier à l'avance. Une session en deux temps encouragerait aussi le travail informel entre les sessions et donnerait du temps aux Rapporteurs spéciaux pour réexaminer les propositions débattues au cours de la première partie d'une session. Elle permettrait au Comité de rédaction ou à un groupe de travail de se réunir pendant une semaine, par exemple, à la fin de la première partie ou au début de la seconde, sans exiger la présence des membres de la Commission qui n'y siègent pas. Elle offre aux personnes qui, pour des raisons

---

[333]*Annuaire de la Commission du droit international, 1992*, vol. II, deuxième partie, p. 58.

professionnelles ou autres, ne peuvent pas s'engager à être présents 12 semaines durant à Genève, la possibilité de présenter leur candidature. Il y a tout lieu de penser qu'il serait plus facile pour les membres de la Commission qui ont d'autres engagements (qu'ils soient conseillers juridiques d'un gouvernement, juristes dans le secteur privé ou professeurs de droit à l'université) de passer une période continue de quatre à cinq semaines en session plutôt qu'une période de 12 semaines. À l'heure actuelle, certains membres de la Commission sont contraints de s'absenter de Genève pendant des périodes très longues. Le problème du choix entre des engagements contradictoires ne disparaîtra certes jamais totalement, mais la formule de la session plus courte et scindée en deux parties est probablement de nature à susciter une participation plus nombreuse et plus continue. Bref, elle assurerait davantage de souplesse.

231. Le choix est en l'occurrence tributaire de considérations financières qui échappent à l'emprise de la Commission. D'après des calculs provisoires, une session de 10 semaines, divisée à parts égales entre New York et Genève, coûterait très sensiblement moins cher qu'une session ininterrompue de 12 semaines. Et même pour une durée totale identique, il semble qu'une session en deux temps ne soit pas sensiblement plus coûteuse, parce que le surcroît de frais de voyage des membres de la Commission serait largement compensé par la réduction des dépenses liées à l'envoi à Genève de fonctionnaires du Secrétariat en poste à New York.

232. De l'avis de la Commission, il faudrait tenter l'expérience d'une session scindée en deux parties. Pour diverses raisons, y compris du fait des contraintes budgétaires et parce que 1997 se trouve être la première année d'un nouveau mandat quinquennal, il semble toutefois préférable d'entreprendre l'expérience en 1998, ce qui permettra de bien planifier cette session en deux temps, dont il sera possible de mesurer les avantages et les inconvénients dans la pratique.

233. La planification de la répartition des travaux entre les deux parties de la session, dans le cas d'une session ainsi scindée, est essentielle. Cette planification se fera nécessairement d'année en année, avec une certaine souplesse. Mais on pourra, par exemple, prévoir pour la première partie de la session l'examen de rapports de Rapporteurs spéciaux et de projets d'articles par le Comité de rédaction et, pour la seconde partie de la session, l'examen en Commission plénière des rapports du Comité de rédaction ou d'autres groupes et du rapport de la Commission elle-même. Il faudra que la seconde partie de la session s'achève au plus tard fin juillet pour que le rapport de la Commission à l'Assemblée générale soit prêt début septembre.

d) *Le caractère essentiel de la contribution du Secrétariat*

234. L'article 14 du Statut de la Commission dispose simplement que le Secrétaire général mettra, « autant qu'il lui est possible, à la disposition de la Commission le personnel et les facilités dont la Commission aura besoin pour accomplir sa tâche ».

235. Concrètement, la contribution du Secrétariat est essentielle. Outre les services fonctionnels fournis à la Commission et à ses organes subsidiaires, le Secrétariat effectue un travail considérable de recherche, souvent dans les plus brefs délais. Les fonctionnaires du Secrétariat prêtent leur concours aux membres du Bureau de la Commission pour l'ordre du jour, la tenue des dossiers, l'établissement des projets de rapports à la plénière, et ainsi de suite. Ils aident à la préparation des commentaires des projets d'articles, le Groupe de travail demeurant néanmoins convaincu que cette fonction incombe au premier chef

aux Rapporteurs spéciaux. Dans les groupes de travail, où il arrive qu'il n'y ait pas de Rapporteur spécial, ce concours est très précieux. Il conviendrait d'encourager les fonctionnaires du Secrétariat à apporter une contribution encore plus grande aux travaux de la Commission.

e) Le Séminaire de droit international

236. Le Séminaire est depuis de nombreuses années un élément caractéristique des sessions de la Commission, et plusieurs centaines de jeunes spécialistes ont pu se faire une idée de l'œuvre de l'ONU et de la CDI par ce biais. Il faut espérer que le Séminaire pourra se poursuivre en dépit des difficultés financières actuelles.

f) Publication des travaux de la Commission

237. Le rapport annuel de la Commission à la Sixième Commission sort quelques semaines après la fin de la session, et est ultérieurement reproduit dans l'*Annuaire*, qui est la publication essentielle qui rend compte des travaux de la Commission. L'*Annuaire* contient les comptes rendus analytiques des débats en plénière, le texte intégral des projets d'articles et des commentaires tels qu'ils ont été définitivement adoptés, les rapports des Rapporteurs spéciaux et un choix d'autres documents. La charge de travail en retard sur l'*Annuaire* a été quelque peu réduite. De plus, les Nations Unies publient périodiquement sous le titre *La Commission du droit international et son œuvre*, qui donne un aperçu général de ses activités, récapitule ses travaux et reproduit les projets d'articles qu'elle a adoptés ou, le cas échéant, les conventions ou autres textes adoptés sur la base de ces projets d'articles. La cinquième édition de cet ouvrage est parue en 1996.

238. Des comptes rendus non officiels des travaux de la Commission paraissent dans les revues de droit international. Chaque année, par exemple, une étude de ses travaux est publiée dans l'*American Journal of International Law* et l'*Annuaire français de droit international*. La publication d'analyses similaires dans les autres langues de la Commission doit être encouragée.

7. Les relations de la Commission avec d'autres organes ou organismes (au sein ou en dehors du système des Nations Unies)

239. S'il est une relation importante pour la Commission, c'est celle qui la lie à l'Assemblée générale par l'intermédiaire du rapport qu'elle présente à la Sixième Commission. Mais le Statut de la Commission prévoit la possibilité de toute une série de relations avec d'autres organes ou organismes :

a) En vertu des articles 16, *c*, 17, 2, *b* et 21, 2, la Commission doit adresser des questionnaires aux gouvernements ou solliciter leurs observations à propos de tout projet en cours d'examen.

b) En vertu de l'article 17, la Commission peut examiner « les plans et projets de conventions multilatérales émanant de Membres de l'Organisation des Nations Unies, d'organes principaux des Nations Unies autres que l'Assemblée générale, d'institutions spécialisées ou d'organisations officielles établies par accords intergouvernementaux en vue d'encourager le développement progressif du droit international et sa codification, que lui transmet à cet effet le Secrétaire général ».

c) En vertu du chapitre III de son Statut, la Commission est, de manière très générale, habilitée à consulter tout organe des Nations Unies sur tout sujet entrant dans la compétence de celui-ci, et toute organisation, nationale ou internationale, officielle ou non, sur tout sujet qui lui a été confié (voir para-graphe 1 de l'article 25 et paragraphe 1 de l'article 26).

d) Dans un certain nombre de cas, la Commission a eu des consultations systématiques avec certaines institutions (avec la FAO, par exemple, sur la question des pêcheries situées au-delà des limites des eaux territoriales). Elle a aussi sollicité des avis d'experts (par exemple, sur les questions de la délimitation des zones maritimes et du tracé des lignes de base).

240. La Commission a pour habitude à chaque session d'accueillir les représentants du Comité consultatif juridique afro-asiatique, du Comité européen de coopération juridique du Conseil de l'Europe et du Comité juridique interaméricain, qui font oralement rapport sur les activités desdits organismes. Ces visites sont certes utiles, mais elles prennent généralement la forme d'échanges formels et congratulatoires. La Commission se félicite de ces échanges, mais pense qu'ils gagneraient à ce qu'un bref rapport écrit sur les travaux des organismes respectifs, accompagné des documents pertinents, soit distribué à l'avance. Il pourrait y avoir un court échange de vues formel à consigner dans le compte rendu de séance, suivi d'une discussion moins formelle avec les membres de la Commission sur telle ou telle question intéressant les deux parties. Il faudrait aussi encourager ces organismes à renforcer leur coopération avec les Rapporteurs spéciaux de la Commission, selon les sujets traités, et stimuler la coopération entre le secrétariat de la Commission et les secrétariats de ces organismes et les échanges de documentation.

241. Il est en revanche une série de relations potentiellement importantes qui sont pour l'instant négligées, à savoir celles qui pourraient s'instaurer avec les organes spécialisés de l'ONU et autres qui ont des attributions juridiques ou dont les activités ont des incidences juridiques. Du moins est-il approprié d'inviter des organes ayant des responsabilités spécifiques dans un domaine donné à échanger des informations avec la Commission et à faire, le cas échéant, des observations sur ses travaux, mais, à l'heure actuelle, les différentes com-posantes du système des Nations Unies opèrent dans une large mesure chacune de son côté. Une autre possibilité serait en fait d'envisager l'étude conjointe, sous la direction de la Commission, d'un sujet juridique donné avec l'organisme compétent dans le domaine considéré. Les commissions juridiques nationales mènent des études conjointes de ce type dans des domaines techniques comme le droit douanier ou l'insolvabilité. Il n'y a à priori aucune raison pour que cela soit impossible au niveau international.

8. *La possibilité d'une révision du Statut*

242. Le Statut de la Commission a été rédigé peu après la fin de la seconde guerre mondiale, et bien qu'il ait été modifié à plusieurs reprises, jamais il n'a fait l'objet d'un examen et d'une révision approfondis. Dans l'ensemble, il s'est révélé suffisamment souple pour se prêter à quelques modifications dans la pratique. Ainsi, il contient plus ou moins suffisamment de dispositions sur des questions telles que l'approbation d'un plan de travail sur un sujet[334] et la nomination d'un groupe de membres chargés de collaborer avec le Rapporteur spécial[335].

---

[334]Statut de la Commission, article 16, *b*, article 17, 2, *a*, et article 19, 1.

[335]Statut de la Commission, article 16, *d* (encore que cette disposition ne vise que la période qui suit l'envoi d'un questionnaire aux gouvernements et qu'elle se termine par « en attendant les réponses à son questionnaire »). On pourrait reformuler cette disposition en termes plus généraux, afin de la rendre applicable à l'ensemble du processus d'examen d'un sujet, qu'il y ait ou non désignation d'un Rapporteur spécial.

S'agissant d'autres questions examinées ici (par exemple les sessions qui se dérouleraient en deux temps), il n'empêche pas de modifier les modalités de fonctionnement de la Commission. Pour la plupart, les modifications évoquées dans le présent rapport peuvent être mises en œuvre sans qu'il soit besoin d'aucun amendement au Statut.

243.   Il n'en demeure pas moins que certains aspects du Statut méritent d'être examinés et révisés alors que la Commission approche de son cinquantième anniversaire. Quelques dispositions du Statut sont anachroniques et pourraient être supprimées, par exemple l'article 26, 3, où il est question des « relations avec l'Espagne franquiste » et « les organisations qui ont collaboré avec les nazis et les fascistes ». On pourrait également, dans l'article 26, 4, ajouter à l'Union panaméricaine, parmi les organes intergouvernementaux dont la tâche est la codification du droit international, des organismes tels que le Comité consultatif juridique afro-asiatique, la Conférence de La Haye de droit international privé et UNIDROIT. Plus fondamentalement, la distinction établie, dans les articles premier et 15 notamment, entre la codification et le développement progressif du droit international, s'est révélée intenable, aussi pourrait-on explicitement fusionner les deux procédures. On pourrait en particulier étendre expressément à tous les travaux de la Commission la faculté « d'adopter pour chaque cas le plan de travail qui lui paraît approprié », qui lui est expressément reconnue dans le cas de la « codification » (paragraphe 1 de l'article 19 du Statut). Un certain nombre d'autres problèmes de fond demanderont à être examinés.

244.   La Commission devra réfléchir, à sa prochaine session, à la possibilité de recommander à l'Assemblée générale de réexaminer le Statut de façon à ce que cet exercice coïncide avec le cinquantième anniversaire de la Commission en 1999.

2.   PROGRAMME DE TRAVAIL À LONG TERME

245.   Considérant les progrès accomplis et les travaux qui ont été achevés au cours de la session, la Commission a à nouveau constitué un groupe de travail pour l'aider dans le choix des sujets à étudier dans l'avenir.

246.   La Commission a adopté le rapport du Groupe de travail et décidé de le faire figurer en annexe à son rapport[336].

247.   La Commission a relevé que si, en ses 50 ans ou presque d'existence, elle avait entrepris et mené à bien l'étude de très nombreux sujets dans diverses matières du droit international public, il restait cependant encore beaucoup à faire. C'est ce qui ressortait aussi bien de la liste générale des matières du droit international que des diverses questions de droit évoquées à un moment ou un autre au sein de la Commission comme sujets possibles de codification ou de développement progressif du droit international.

248.   Pour donner un aperçu d'ensemble des principales matières du droit international public général, la Commission a établi un plan général des sujets en les classant en 13 grandes matières du droit international public (par exemple, sources, compétences de l'État, droit international pénal, organisations internationales, espaces internationaux, et ainsi de suite)[337]. Cette liste, qui ne se voulait pas exhaustive, comprenait des sujets dont la Commission avait déjà achevé l'étude, des sujets qu'elle avait commencé à étudier mais, pour diverses raisons,

---

[336]Voir l'annexe II.
[337]Ibid.

432

« abandonnés », des sujets actuellement à l'étude et des sujets qu'elle pourrait étudier dans l'avenir.

249. Pour le programme en cours, trois sujets ont été jugés se prêter à la codification et au développement progressif : la protection diplomatique, la propriété et la protection des épaves au-delà des limites de la juridiction maritime nationale, et les actes unilatéraux des États. Un schéma préliminaire exposant les principaux problèmes juridiques que soulevait chacun de ces trois sujets était en outre joint à la liste. Dans chaque additif, des notes expliquaient pourquoi la question est d'actualité*.

---

*Ces additifs n'y sont pas inclus.

Annexe II

Rapport sur le programme de travail à long terme

1. Au cours des 50 années ou presque de son existence, la Commission a entrepris et mené à bien l'étude de nombreux sujets dans divers domaines du droit international public[1]. Mais si l'on considère l'œuvre accomplie par rapport à l'ensemble du droit international, et même par rapport à la liste des matières proposées à un moment ou un autre comme pouvant éventuellement se prêter à la codification et au développement progressif du droit international par la Commission[2], on se rend compte que beaucoup reste à faire.

2. Le présent document ne prétend pas donner un aperçu complet des sujets possibles (en particulier, les suggestions pour « les sujets que la Commission pourrait étudier dans l'avenir » reflètent des propositions faites à différents moments par certains de ses membres). En fait, certains sujets proposés dans le document font déjà l'objet d'études de la part d'autres organismes. Le rapport, dans son ensemble, vise :

a) À sérier quelques domaines très généraux du droit international public principalement régis par les règles du droit international coutumier;

b) À énumérer, sous chacun de ces titres très généraux, diverses matières qui ont déjà, à un moment ou un autre, été proposées par la Commission ou par tels ou tels de ses membres comme sujets possibles pour la CDI (les dates auxquelles les propositions initiales ont été formulées sont indiquées plus loin entre crochets);

c) À ajouter quelques autres sujets possibles dont la Commission n'entend pas affirmer catégoriquement qu'ils se prêteraient à des travaux dans l'avenir;

d) À indiquer les sujets dont l'étude a déjà été menée à bien en tout ou en partie; et

e) À exposer dans leurs grandes lignes les principaux problèmes juridiques soulevés par trois des sujets que la Commission pourrait étudier dans l'avenir et qui, de l'avis de [la Commission], se prêtent à la codification et au développement progressif. Ces sujets sont les suivants*:

   i) Protection diplomatique (Additif 1);

   ii) Propriété et protection des épaves au-delà des limites de la juridiction maritime nationale (Additif 2); et

   iii) Actes unilatéraux des États (Additif 3).

Ces trois sujets ont été indiqués en caractères gras dans le plan général ci-après.

3. Le plan général exposé ci-après illustre une approche générale qui, de l'avis de la Commission, permettrait de réserver, dans un examen global des principaux domaines du droit international public général, une place à un certain nombre de sujets que la Commission pourrait étudier dans l'avenir. La Commission se rend parfaitement compte que certains sujets mentionnés relèvent du

---

[1]Pour plus de détails, voir, ci-après, « Plan général ».
[2]Ibid.
*Les additifs mentionnés ci-dessus n'y sont pas inclus.

champ d'action d'autres organismes; s'ils ont été mentionnés c'est pour donner une idée de l'étendue du droit international. La Commission n'entend pas empiéter sur la compétence des institutions concernées.

4. Si cette approche paraît intéressante à la Commission et à la Sixième Commission, la Commission pourrait peut-être, à sa prochaine session, étudier plus avant la possibilité d'ajouter d'autres sujets à ceux proposés dans les additifs 1 à 3.

PLAN GÉNÉRAL[3]

I. LES SOURCES DU DROIT INTERNATIONAL

1. *Sujets dont l'étude a déjà été menée à bien :*
   a) Droit des traités
      i) Convention de Vienne sur le droit des traités, 1969;
      ii) Convention de Vienne sur le droit des traités entre États et organisations internationales ou entre organisations internationales, 1986;
      iii) Projet d'articles sur la clause de la nation la plus favorisée, 1978.

2. *Sujets à l'étude à la Commission :*
   Réserves aux traités.

3. *Sujets que la Commission pourrait étudier dans l'avenir :*
   a) Droit des traités :
      Processus d'établissement des traités multilatéraux [1979];
   b) Droit des actes unilatéraux [1971] :
      i) **Actes unilatéraux des États**;
      ii) Droit applicable aux résolutions des organisations internationales;
      iii) Contrôle de la validité des résolutions des organisations internationales.
   c) Droit coutumier international :
      i) Formation des règles coutumières;
      ii) Effets juridiques des règles coutumières;
   d) *Jus cogens* (et notions connexes) [1992];
   e) Instruments non obligatoires.

II. LES SUJETS DU DROIT INTERNATIONAL

1. *Sujets abordés mais abandonnés :*
   i) Droits et devoirs fondamentaux des États [1949];
   ii) « Succession » de gouvernements [1949].

---

[3]Cette liste est purement indicative; ni les formulations ni la teneur n'engageront la Commission dans ses entreprises futures.

2. *Sujets que la Commission pourrait étudier dans l'avenir :*
   a) Sujets du droit international [1949];
   b) La qualité d'État :
      i) Situation des États en droit international [1971];
      ii) Critères de reconnaissance [1949];
      iii) Indépendance et souveraineté des États [1962];
   c) Gouvernement :
      i) Reconnaissance des gouvernements [1949];
      ii) Gouvernements représentatifs.

III. SUCCESSION D'ÉTATS ET AUTRES PERSONNES MORALES

1. *Sujets dont l'étude a déjà été menée à bien :*
   a) Convention de Vienne sur la succession d'États en matière de traités, 1978;
   b) Convention de Vienne sur la succession d'États en matière de biens, archives et dettes d'État, 1986.

2. *Sujets à l'étude à la Commission :*
   Succession d'États en matière de nationalité.

3. *Sujets que la Commission pourrait étudier dans l'avenir :*
   a) Succession d'États en ce qui concerne la qualité de membre des organisations internationales et les obligations envers elles;
   b) « Droits acquis » au regard de la succession d'États;
   c) Succession d'organisations internationales.

IV. JURIDICTION/IMMUNITÉ DE JURIDICTION DES ÉTATS

1. *Sujets dont l'étude a déjà été menée à bien :*
   Immunités juridictionnelles des États et de leurs biens, 1991.

2. *Sujets que la Commission pourrait étudier dans l'avenir :*
   a) Immunités d'exécution;
   b) Compétence extraterritoriale :
      i) Reconnaissance des actes des États étrangers [1949];
      ii) Juridiction à l'égard des États étrangers [1949];
      iii) Juridiction pénale en matière d'infractions commises en dehors du territoire national [1949];
      iv) Application extraterritoriale de la législation nationale [1992];
   c) Compétence territoriale :
      Domaine territorial des États [1949];
   d) Compétences relatives aux services publics.

V. DROIT DES ORGANISATIONS INTERNATIONALES

1. *Sujets dont l'étude a déjà été menée à bien :*

   Convention de Vienne sur la représentation des États dans leurs relations avec les organisations internationales de caractère universel, 1975.

2. *Sujets abordés mais dont l'étude n'a pas été poursuivie :*

   Statut, privilèges et immunités des organisations internationales, de leurs fonctionnaires, experts, etc.

3. *Sujets que la Commission pourrait étudier dans l'avenir :*
   a) Principes généraux du droit de la fonction publique internationale;
   b) Personnalité morale internationale des organisations internationales;
   c) Compétences des organisations internationales :
      i) Pouvoirs implicites;
      ii) Compétence personnelle;
      iii) Compétence territoriale.

VI. SITUATION DE L'INDIVIDU DANS LE DROIT INTERNATIONAL

1. *Sujets dont l'étude a déjà été menée à bien :*
   Convention sur la réduction des cas d'apatridie, 1961.

2. *Sujets que la Commission pourrait étudier dans l'avenir :*
   a) Droit international relatif aux individus [1971] :
      L'individu dans le droit international;
   b) Traitement des étrangers [1949] :
      i) Droit de refuge politique [1949];
      ii) Extradition [1949];
   c) Droit relatif aux migrations internationales [1992];
   d) Droits de l'homme et défense de la démocratie [1962].

VII. DROIT INTERNATIONAL PÉNAL

1. *Sujets dont l'étude a déjà été menée à bien :*
   a) Projet de statut d'une cour criminelle internationale, 1994;
   b) Code des crimes contre la paix et la sécurité de l'humanité, 1996.

2. *Sujets que la Commission pourrait étudier dans l'avenir :*
   a) Le principe *Aut dedere aut judicare*;

b) Les crimes internationaux autres que ceux mentionnés dans le Code des crimes contre la paix et la sécurité de l'humanité.

VIII. DROIT DES ESPACES INTERNATIONAUX

1. *Sujets dont l'étude a déjà été menée à bien :*

    a) Droit de la mer :

    Les quatre Conventions de Genève de 1958;

    b) Régime juridique des cours d'eau internationaux :

    Projet d'articles sur le droit relatif aux utilisations des cours d'eau internationaux à des fins autres que la navigation, 1994.

2. *Sujets abordés et abandonnés :*

    Régime juridique des eaux historiques, 1962.

3. *Sujets que la Commission pourrait étudier dans l'avenir :*

    a) Droit de la mer :

    Propriété et protection des épaves au-delà des limites de la juridiction maritime nationale;

    b) Régime juridique des fleuves internationaux et questions connexes :
    Navigation sur les cours d'eau internationaux;

    c) Droit aérien [1971];

    d) Droit de l'espace [1962];

    e) Ressources naturelles partagées :

    i)   L'indivis mondial [1992];

    ii)   Le patrimoine commun de l'humanité;

    iii) Les ressources transfrontières;

    iv)   Le droit des eaux souterraines captives internationales;

    v)   L'intérêt commun de l'humanité.

IX. DROIT DES RELATIONS/DE LA RESPONSABILITÉ INTERNATIONALES

1. *Sujets dont l'étude a déjà été menée à bien :*

    a) Relations diplomatiques et consulaires :

    i)   Convention de Vienne sur les relations diplomatiques, 1961;

    ii)   Convention de Vienne sur les relations consulaires, 1963;

    iii) Convention de Vienne sur les missions spéciales, 1969;

    iv)   Convention sur la prévention et la répression des infractions contre les personnes jouissant d'une protection internationale, y compris les agents diplomatiques, 1973;

    v)   Statut du courrier diplomatique et de la valise diplomatique non accompagnée par un courrier diplomatique, 1989.

2. *Sujets à l'étude à la Commission :*

    a) Responsabilité des États;

b) Responsabilité internationale pour les conséquences préjudiciables découlant d'activités qui ne sont pas interdites par le droit international.

3. *Sujet que la Commission pourrait étudier dans l'avenir :*

   a) Responsabilité internationale :
      i) **Protection diplomatique**;
      ii) Responsabilité internationale des organisations internationales;
      iii) Protection fonctionnelle;
   b) Représentation internationale des organisations internationales.

X. DROIT DE L'ENVIRONNEMENT

Sujets que la Commission pourrait étudier dans l'avenir :

Droit de l'environnement :
Droits et devoirs des États en matière de protection de l'environnement [1992].

XI. DROIT DES RELATIONS ÉCONOMIQUES

   i) Relations économiques et commerciales [1971];
   ii) La condition juridique des investissements en capital et les accords y relatifs [1993];
   iii) Problèmes juridiques internationaux liés à la privatisation de biens d'État;
   iv) Principes juridiques généraux applicables à l'aide au développement.

XII. DROIT DES CONFLITS ARMÉS/DU DÉSARMEMENT

Sujets que la Commission pourrait étudier dans l'avenir :

   a) Mécanismes juridiques nécessaires à l'enregistrement des ventes ou autres transferts d'armements, armes et matériels militaires entre États [1992];
   b) Principes juridiques généraux applicables aux zones démilitarisées et/ou neutres;
   c) Principes juridiques généraux applicables aux sanctions armées en vertu du Chapitre VII de la Charte des Nations Unies.

XIII. RÈGLEMENT DES DIFFÉRENDS

1. *Sujets dont l'étude a déjà été menée à bien :*
   Modèle de règles sur la procédure arbitrale, 1958.

2. *Sujets que la Commission pourrait étudier dans l'avenir :*
   a) Règlement pacifique des différends internationaux [1949];
   b) Clauses types pour le règlement des différends relatifs à l'application ou l'interprétation de futures conventions de codification;
   c) Procédures de médiation et de conciliation par les organes des Nations Unies.

STATUTE OF THE INTERNATIONAL LAW COMMISSION

Article 1

1. The International Law Commission shall have for its object the promotion of the progressive development of international law and its codification.

2. The Commission shall concern itself primarily with public international law, but is not precluded from entering the field of private international law.

Chapter I. Organization of the International Law Commission

Article 2[a]

1. The Commission shall consist of thirty-four members who shall be persons of recognized competence in international law.

2. No two members of the Commission shall be nationals of the same State.

3. In case of dual nationality a candidate shall be deemed to be a national of the State in which he ordinarily exercises civil and political rights.

Article 3

The members of the Commission shall be elected by the General Assembly from a list of candidates nominated by the Governments of States Members of the United Nations.

Article 4

Each Member may nominate for election not more than four candidates, of whom two may be nationals of the nominating State and two nationals of other States.

Article 5

The names of the candidates shall be submitted in writing by the Governments to the Secretary-General by the first of June of the year in which an election is held, provided that a Government may in exceptional circumstances substitute for a candidate whom it has nominated before the first of June another candidate whom it shall name not later than thirty days before the opening of the General Assembly.

Article 6

The Secretary-General shall as soon as possible communicate to the Governments of States Members the names submitted, as well as any statements of qualifications of candidates that may have been submitted by the nominating Governments.

---

[a]Text amended by General Assembly resolution 36/39 of 18 November 1981.

Article 7

The Secretary-General shall prepare the list referred to in article 3 above, comprising in alphabetical order the names of all the candidates duly nominated, and shall submit this list to the General Assembly for the purposes of the election.

Article 8

At the election the electors shall bear in mind that the persons to be elected to the Commission should individually possess the qualifications required and that in the Commission as a whole representation of the main forms of civilization and of the principal legal systems of the world should be assured.

Article 9^b

1. Those candidates, up to the maximum number prescribed for each regional group, who obtain the greatest number of votes and not less than a majority of the votes of the Members present and voting shall be elected.

2. In the event of more than one national of the same State obtaining a sufficient number of votes for election the one who obtains the greatest number of votes shall be elected and if the votes are equally divided the elder or eldest candidate shall be elected.

Article 10^c

The members of the Commission shall be elected for five years. They shall be eligible for re-election.

Article 11

In the case of a casual vacancy, the Commission itself shall fill the vacancy having due regard to the provisions contained in articles 2 and 8 of this Statute.

Article 12^d

The Commission shall sit at the European Office of the United Nations at Geneva. The Commission shall, however, have the right to hold meetings at other places after consultation with the Secretary-General.

Article 13^e

Members of the Commission shall be paid travel expenses, and shall also receive a special allowance, the amount of which shall be determined by the General Assembly.

Article 14

The Secretary-General shall, so far as he is able, make available staff and facilities required by the Commission to fulfil its task.

---

[b]Text amended by the General Assembly resolution 36/39 of 18 November 1981.
[c]Text amended by the General Assembly resolution 985 (X) of 3 December 1955.
[d]Text amended by General Assembly resolution 984 (X) of 3 December 1955.
[e]Text amended by General Assembly resolution 485 (V) of 12 December 1950.

Chapter II. Functions of the International Law Commission

Article 15

In the following articles the expression "progressive development of international law" is used for convenience as meaning the preparation of draft conventions on subjects which have not yet been regulated by international law or in regard to which the law has not yet been sufficiently developed in the practice of States. Similarly, the expression "codification of international law" is used for convenience as meaning the more precise formulation and systematization of rules of international law in fields where there already has been extensive State practice, precedent and doctrine.

A. PROGRESSIVE DEVELOPMENT OF INTERNATIONAL LAW

Article 16

When the General Assembly refers to the Commission a proposal for the progressive development of international law, the Commission shall follow in general a procedure on the following lines:

(a) It shall appoint one of its members to be Rapporteur;

(b) It shall formulate a plan of work;

(c) It shall circulate a questionnaire to the Governments, and shall invite them to supply within a fixed period of time data and information relevant to items included in the plan of work;

(d) It may appoint some of its members to work with the Rapporteur on the preparation of drafts pending receipt of replies to this questionnaire;

(e) It may consult with scientific institutions and individual experts; these experts need not necessarily be nationals of Members of the United Nations. The Secretary-General will provide, when necessary and within the limits of the budget, for the expenses of these consultations of experts;

(f) It shall consider the drafts proposed by the Rapporteur;

(g) When the Commission considers a draft to be satisfactory, it shall request the Secretary-General to issue it as a Commission document. The Secretariat shall give all necessary publicity to this document which shall be accompanied by such explanations and supporting material as the Commission considers appropriate. The publication shall include any information supplied to the Commission in reply to the questionnaire referred to in subparagraph *(c)* above;

(h) The Commission shall invite the Governments to submit their comments on this document within a reasonable time;

(i) The Rapporteur and the members appointed for that purpose shall reconsider the draft taking into consideration these comments and shall prepare a final draft and explanatory report which they shall submit for consideration and adoption by the Commission;

(j) The Commission shall submit the draft so adopted with its recommendations through the Secretary-General to the General Assembly.

Article 17

1. The Commission shall also consider proposals and draft multilateral conventions submitted by Members of the United Nations, the principal organs

of the United Nations other than the General Assembly, specialized agencies, or official bodies established by intergovernmental agreement to encourage the progressive development of international law and its codification, and transmitted to it for that purpose by the Secretary-General.

2. If in such cases the Commission deems it appropriate to proceed with the study of such proposals or drafts, it shall follow in general a procedure on the following lines:

(a) The Commission shall formulate a plan of work, and study such proposals or drafts, and compare them with any other proposals and drafts on the same subjects;

(b) The Commission shall circulate a questionnaire to all Members of the United Nations and to the organs, specialized agencies and official bodies mentioned above which are concerned with the question, and shall invite them to transmit their comments within a reasonable time;

(c) The Commission shall submit a report and its recommendations to the General Assembly. Before doing so, it may also, if it deems it desirable, make an interim report to the organ or agency which has submitted the proposal or draft;

(d) If the General Assembly should invite the Commission to proceed with its work in accordance with a suggested plan, the procedure outlined in article 16 above shall apply. The questionnaire referred to in paragraph (e) that article may not, however, be necessary.

B. CODIFICATION OF INTERNATIONAL LAW

Article 18

1. The Commission shall survey the whole field of international law with a view to selecting topics for codification, having in mind existing drafts whether governmental or not.

2. When the Commission considers that the codification of a particular topic is necessary or desirable, it shall submit its recommendations to the General Assembly.

3. The Commission shall give priority to requests of the General Assembly to deal with any question.

Article 19

1. The Commission shall adopt a plan of work appropriate to each case.

2. The Commission shall, through the Secretary-General, address to Governments a detailed request to furnish the texts of laws, decrees, judicial decisions, treaties, diplomatic correspondence and other documents relevant to the topic being studied and which the Commission deems necessary.

Article 20

The Commission shall prepare its drafts in the form of articles and shall submit them to the General Assembly together with a commentary containing:

(a) Adequate presentation of precedents and other relevant data, including treaties, judicial decisions and doctrine;

(b) Conclusions relevant to:

(i)   The extent of agreement on each point in the practice of States and in doctrine;

(ii)   Divergences and disagreements which exist, as well as arguments invoked in favour of one or another solution.

Article 21

1.   When the Commission considers a draft to be satisfactory, it shall request the Secretary-General to issue it as a Commission document. The Secretariat shall give all necessary publicity to the document including such explanations and supporting material as the Commission may consider appropriate. The publication shall include any information supplied to the Commission by Governments in accordance with article 19. The Commission shall decide whether the opinions of any scientific institution or individual experts consulted by the Commission shall be included in the publication.

2.   The Commission shall request Governments to submit comments on this document within a reasonable time.

Article 22

Taking such comments into consideration, the Commission shall prepare a final draft and explanatory report which it shall submit with its recommendations through the Secretary-General to the General Assembly.

Article 23

1.   The Commission may recommend to the General Assembly:

(a)   To take no action, the report having already been published;

(b)   To take note of or adopt the report by resolution;

(c)   To recommend the draft to Members with a view to the conclusion of a convention;

(d)   To convoke a conference to conclude a convention.

2.   Whenever it deems it desirable, the General Assembly may refer drafts back to the Commission for reconsideration or redrafting.

Article 24

The Commission shall consider ways and means for making the evidence of customary international law more readily available, such as the collection and publication of documents concerning State practice and of the decisions of national and international courts on questions of international law and shall make a report to the General Assembly on this matter.

Chapter III.   Co-operation with other bodies

Article 25

1.   The Commission may consult, if it considers it necessary, with any of the organs of the United Nations on any subject which is within the competence of that organ.

2.   All documents of the Commission which are circulated to Governments by the Secretary-General shall also be circulated to such organs of the United Nations as are concerned. Such organs may furnish any information or make any suggestions to the Commission.

Article 26

1.   The Commission may consult with any international or national organizations, official or non-official, on any subject entrusted to it if it believes that such a procedure might aid it in the performance of its functions.

2.   For the purpose of distribution of documents of the Commission, the Secretary-General, after consultation, with the Commission, shall draw up a list of national and international organizations concerned with questions of international law. The Secretary-General shall endeavour to include on this list at least one national organization of each Member of the United Nations.

3.   In the application of the provisions of this article, the Commission and the Secretary-General shall comply with the resolutions of the General Assembly and the other principal organs of the United Nations concerning relations with Franco Spain and shall exclude both from consultations and from the list, organizations which have collaborated with the nazis and fascists.

4.   The advisability of consultation by the Commission with intergovernmental organizations whose task is the codification of international law such as those of the Pan American Union, is recognized.

STATUT DE LA COMMISSION DU DROIT INTERNATIONAL

Article premier

1. La Commission du droit international a pour but de promouvoir le développement progressif du droit international et sa codification.

2. Elle s'occupera au premier chef du droit international public, sans qu'il lui soit interdit de pénétrer dans le domaine du droit international privé.

Chapitre premier. — Organisation de la Commission du droit international

Article 2[a]

1. La Commission se compose de trente-quatre membres, possédant une compétence reconnue en matière de droit international.

2. Elle ne peut comprendre plus d'un ressortissant d'un même État.

3. En cas de double nationalité, un candidat sera considéré comme ayant la nationalité du pays dans lequel il exerce ordinairement ses droits civils et politiques.

Article 3

Les membres de la Commission sont élus par l'Assemblée générale sur une liste de candidats présentés par les gouvernements des États Membres de l'Organisation des Nations Unies.

Article 4

Chaque Membre peut présenter quatre candidats au plus, dont deux peuvent être ressortissants de l'État qui les présente et deux peuvent être des ressortissants d'autres États.

Article 5

Les noms des candidats doivent être communiqués par écrit par les gouvernements au Secrétaire général avant le 1er juin de l'année au cours de laquelle l'élection a lieu; toutefois, un gouvernement peut, dans des cas exceptionnels, substituer à un candidat qu'il avait présenté avant le 1er juin un autre candidat désigné au plus tard trente jours avant l'ouverture de l'Assemblée générale.

Article 6

Le Secrétaire général transmet aussitôt que possible aux gouvernements des États Membres les noms qui lui sont ainsi communiqués, de même que les *curriculum vitae* des candidats envoyés par le gouvernement qui les présente.

---

[a]Texte amendé par la résolution 36/39 de l'Assemblée générale en date du 18 novembre 1981.

Article 7

Le Secrétaire général dresse, par ordre alphabétique, la liste, prévue à l'article 3 ci-dessus, de tous les candidats dûment présentés et la soumet à l'Assemblée générale aux fins de l'élection.

Article 8

À l'élection, les électeurs auront en vue que les personnes appelées à faire partie de la Commission réunissent individuellement les conditions requises, et que, dans l'ensemble, la représentation des grandes formes de civilisation et des principaux systèmes juridiques du monde soit assurée.

Article 9[b]

1. Sont élus, à concurrence du nombre maximal de membres prescrit pour chaque groupe régional, les candidats qui obtiennent le plus grand nombre de voix et au moins la majorité des voix des Membres présents et votants.

2. Au cas où plus d'un ressortissant d'un même État obtiendrait suffisamment de voix pour être élu, celui qui aura obtenu le plus de voix sera élu, et, au cas où il y aurait partage égal des voix, le candidat le plus âgé sera élu.

Article 10[c]

Les membres de la Commission sont élus pour cinq ans; ils sont rééligibles.

Article 11

En cas de vacance survenant après élection, la Commission pourvoit elle-même au siège vacant, en tenant compte des dispositions contenues dans les articles 2 et 8 ci-dessus.

Article 12[d]

La Commission se réunit à l'Office européen des Nations Unies à Genève. Elle a toutefois le droit de se réunir en d'autres endroits, après consultation avec le Secrétaire général.

Article 13[e]

Les membres de la Commission reçoivent leurs frais de voyage et, de plus, une indemnité spéciale dont le montant est fixé par l'Assemblée générale.

Article 14

Le Secrétaire général mettra, autant qu'il lui est possible, à la disposition de la Commission le personnel et les facilités dont la Commission aura besoin pour accomplir sa tâche.

---

[b]Texte amendé par la résolution 36/39 de l'Assemblée générale en date du 18 novembre 1981.
[c]Texte amendé par la résolution 985 (X) de l'Assemblée générale en date du 3 décembre 1955.
[d]Texte amendé par la résolution 984 (X) de l'Assemblée générale en date du 3 décembre 1955.
[e]Texte amendé par la résolution 485 (V) de l'Assemblée générale en date du 12 décembre 1950.

Chapitre II. — Tâche de la Commission du droit international

Article 15

Dans les articles qui suivent, l'expression « développement progressif du droit international » est employée, pour la commodité, pour viser les cas où il s'agit de rédiger des conventions sur des sujets qui ne sont pas encore réglés par le droit international ou relativement auxquels le droit n'est pas encore suffisamment développé dans la pratique des États. De même, l'expression « codification du droit international » est employée, pour la commodité, pour viser les cas où il s'agit de formuler avec plus de précision et de systématiser les règles du droit international dans des domaines dans lesquels il existe déjà une pratique étatique considérable, des précédents et des opinions doctrinales.

A. DÉVELOPPEMENT PROGRESSIF DU DROIT INTERNATIONAL

Article 16

Lorsque l'Assemblée générale renvoie à la Commission une proposition concernant le développement progressif du droit international, la Commission suit, dans les grandes lignes, la procédure suivante :

a) Elle désigne un rapporteur parmi ses membres;

b) Elle établit un plan de travail;

c) Elle adresse un questionnaire aux gouvernements et invite ces derniers à lui fournir, dans un délai déterminé, des informations et des renseignements se rapportant aux sujets figurant dans le plan de travail;

d) Elle désigne, s'il y a lieu, dans son sein les membres chargés de travailler avec le Rapporteur à la préparation d'avant-projets, en attendant les réponses à son questionnaire;

e) Elle peut consulter des institutions scientifiques et des experts individuels; ces experts ne devront pas nécessairement être des ressortissants de Membres de l'Organisation des Nations Unies. Le Secrétaire général pourvoit, lorsque c'est nécessaire et dans les limites du budget, aux frais de consultations d'experts;

f) Elle étudie les avant-projets du Rapporteur;

g) Lorsqu'elle estime qu'un projet est satisfaisant, elle prie le Secrétaire général de le publier en tant que document de la Commission. Le Secrétariat donnera à ce document la publicité nécessaire et y joindra telles explications et pièces à l'appui que la Commission jugera appropriées. La publication doit comprendre les informations fournies à la Commission en réponse au questionnaire mentionné à l'alinéa *c* ci-dessus;

h) Elle invite les gouvernements à présenter, dans un délai raisonnable, leurs observations sur ce document;

i) Le Rapporteur et les membres désignés à cet effet réexaminent le projet à la lumière de ces observations et élaborent le texte final de ce projet avec rapport explicatif, qu'ils soumettent pour adoption à l'examen de la Commission;

j) Elle soumet, par l'entremise du Secrétaire général, le texte adopté ainsi que ses recommandations à l'Assemblée générale.

Article 17

1. La Commission examine également les plans et projets de conventions multilatérales émanant de Membres de l'Organisation des Nations Unies, d'organes principaux des Nations Unies autres que l'Assemblée générale, d'institutions spécialisées ou d'organisations officielles établies par accords intergouvernementaux en vue d'encourager le développement progressif du droit international et sa codification, que lui transmet à cet effet le Secrétaire général.

2. Si, en de tels cas, elle juge utile de poursuivre l'étude desdits plans ou projets, elle suit, dans les grandes lignes, la procédure ci-dessous :

a) Elle établit un plan de travail, étudie lesdits plans ou projets et les compare avec d'autres plans ou projets se rapportant aux mêmes sujets;

b) Elle adresse un questionnaire à tous les Membres de l'Organisation des Nations Unies et aux organes, institutions spécialisées et organisations officielles spécifiés ci-dessus qui sont intéressés à la question et les invite à faire connaître leurs observations dans un délai raisonnable;

c) Elle soumet un rapport et des recommandations à l'Assemblée générale. Elle peut aussi, si elle le juge désirable, faire, avant cela, un rapport intérimaire à l'organe ou institution dont émane le plan ou le projet;

d) Si l'Assemblée générale invite la Commission à poursuivre ses travaux selon un plan proposé, la procédure décrite à l'article 16 est applicable. Il se peut toutefois que le questionnaire mentionné à l'alinéa *c* dudit article soit inutile.

B. CODIFICATION DU DROIT INTERNATIONAL

Article 18

1. La Commission recherche, dans l'ensemble du droit international, les sujets appropriés de codification, en tenant compte des projets existants, qu'ils soient d'origine gouvernementale ou non.

2. Lorsqu'elle juge la codification d'un sujet nécessaire ou désirable, elle soumet ses recommandations à l'Assemblée générale.

3. Elle donne priorité à toute demande de l'Assemblée générale de traiter une question.

Article 19

1. La Commission adopte, pour chaque cas, le plan de travail qui lui paraît approprié.

2. Elle s'adresse, par l'entremise du Secrétaire général, aux gouvernements pour leur demander, avec toute la précision nécessaire, de lui fournir les textes de lois, décrets, décisions judiciaires, traités, correspondance diplomatique et autres documents relatifs aux sujets à l'étude et dont elle croit avoir besoin.

Article 20

La Commission rédige ses projets en articles et les soumet à l'Assemblée générale avec un commentaire comprenant :

a) Une présentation adéquate des précédents et autres données pertinentes, y compris les traités, les décisions judiciaires et la doctrine;

b) Des conclusions précisant :

i) L'étendue de l'accord réalisé sur chaque point dans la pratique des États et dans la doctrine;

ii) Les divergences et désaccords qui subsistent, ainsi que les arguments invoqués en faveur de chacune des thèses.

Article 21

1. Lorsque la Commission estime qu'un projet est satisfaisant, elle prie le Secrétaire général de le publier en tant que document de la Commission. Le Secrétariat donnera à ce document la publicité nécessaire et y joindra telles explications et pièces à l'appui que la Commission jugera appropriées. La publication doit comprendre les informations fournies à la Commission par les gouvernements en vertu de l'article 19. La Commission décide si des opinions émises par des institutions scientifiques ou des experts individuels consultés par la Commission doivent être comprises dans la publication.

2. La Commission demande aux gouvernements de lui faire connaître, dans un délai raisonnable, leurs observations sur ce document.

Article 22

La Commission prépare, à la lumière de ces observations, le texte final du projet et un rapport explicatif qu'elle soumet avec ses recommandations à l'Assemblée générale par l'entremise du Secrétaire général.

Article 23

1. La Commission peut recommander à l'Assemblée générale :

a) De n'entreprendre aucune action, le rapport ayant été publié;

b) De prendre acte du rapport, ou de l'adopter dans une résolution;

c) De recommander le projet aux Membres en vue de la conclusion d'une convention;

d) De convoquer une conférence pour conclure une convention.

2. Chaque fois qu'elle le juge utile, l'Assemblée générale renvoie à la Commission les projets aux fins de réexamen ou de nouvelle rédaction.

Article 24

La Commission examine les moyens susceptibles de rendre plus accessible la documentation relative au droit international coutumier, par exemple la compilation et la publication de documents établissant la pratique des États et des décisions de juridictions nationales et internationales sur des questions de droit international, et elle fait rapport à l'Assemblée générale sur ce sujet.

Chapitre III. — Coopération avec d'autres organismes

Article 25

1. La Commission peut consulter, lorsqu'elle le juge utile, tout organe des Nations Unies sur tout sujet entrant dans la compétence de cet organe.

2. Tous les documents de la Commission transmis aux gouvernements par le Secrétaire général seront également transmis aux organes de l'Organisation des Nations Unies qui y sont intéressés. Ces organes peuvent fournir des renseignements et présenter des suggestions à la Commission.

Article 26

1. La Commission peut consulter toute organisation, nationale ou internationale, officielle ou non, sur tout sujet qui lui a été confié, si elle le juge utile à l'accomplissement de sa tâche.

2. Aux fins de la distribution des documents de la Commission, le Secrétaire général établira, après avoir consulté la Commission, une liste d'organisations nationales ou internationales s'occupant du droit international. Il s'efforcera d'inclure dans cette liste au moins une organisation nationale de chaque Membre de l'Organisation des Nations Unies.

3. En appliquant les dispositions du présent article, la Commission et le Secrétaire général se conformeront aux résolutions de l'Assemblée générale et des autres organes principaux de l'Organisation des Nations Unies concernant les relations avec l'Espagne franquiste et excluront des consultations et de la liste les organisations qui ont collaboré avec les nazis et les fascistes.

4. L'utilité de consultations entre la Commission et les organes intergouvernementaux, tels que ceux de l'Union panaméricaine, dont la tâche est la codification du droit international, est reconnue.